A Test of Time
The Bible – From Myth to History

Little conclusive evidence for an historical Old Testament has come to light in two centuries of archaeological endeavour. Ever since excavations in the Lands of the Bible began at the beginning of the last century, biblical scholars have been systematically stripping out elements of the narratives – the stories of Joseph, Moses, Joshua, Saul, David and Solomon – and consigning them to the realms of myth and folklore.

Egyptologist and ancient historian David Rohl has made a discovery which challenges the modern sceptical view of Old Testament history. His revolutionary theory demonstrates that archaeologists have been looking in the right places for evidence of the Israelites – but in completely the wrong time.

The New Chronology developed in *A Test of Time* reveals the true historical setting of the biblical epics, providing astonishing archaeological evidence for the existence of the Old Testament's most charismatic personalities. For the first time the lives of Joseph, Moses, Joshua, Saul, David and Solomon are examined from an historical perspective, as David Rohl explores their cities, palaces and tombs. *A Test of Time* unveils such archaeological wonders as the desecrated statue of Joseph in his 'coat of many colours', the Israelite city of bondage in Egypt (including graphic evidence of the plagues), and letters from King Saul.

A Test of Time presents the most remarkable understanding of the Bible since archaeologists first began to recover the wonders of ancient times.

Aged forty-eight, David holds a University College London degree in Egyptology and Ancient History, and has excavated at Kadesh-on-the Orontes with the expedition of the Institute of Archaeology. He is currently the Archaeology Correspondent for the *Express* newspaper, Chairman of the Institute for the Study of Interdisciplinary Sciences and President of the Sussex Egyptology Society.

A Test of Time

Volume One

The Bible – From Myth to History

by

David M. Rohl

ARROW

Published by Century in 1995

1 3 5 7 9 10 8 6 4 2

Century Ltd
Random House, 20 Vauxhall Bridge Road, London, SW1V 2SA

Random House Australia (Pty) Limited
20 Alfred Street, Milsons Point, Sydney,
New South Wales 2061, Australia

Random House New Zealand Limited
18 Portland Road, Glenfield
Auckland 10, New Zealand

Random House South Africa (Pty) Limited
PO Box 337, Bergvlei, South Africa

Random House UK Limited Reg. No. 954009

A CIP catalogue record for this book
is available from the British Library

Papers used by Random House UK Ltd are natural, recyclable
products made from wood grown in sustainable forests. The
manufacturing processes conform to the environmental regulations
of the country of origin.

ISBN 0 09 941656 5

Subject classification: 1. Egyptology – Chronology. 2. Biblical
Archaeology – Bible Studies

Typeset by Ditas Rohl

Printed and bound in Great Britain by
Bookmarque Ltd, Croydon, Surrey

**For
Ditas**

Contents

Part One
Conundrums of the Pharaohs

Part Two
Unravelling the Gordian Knot

Part Four
Discovering the Israelites

Foreword

by
Professor Robert S. Bianchi

When one surveys the development of Egyptology as a discipline during the course of the nineteenth century, one is struck by the single-mindedness of purpose to which many of the great names of the day adhered. That sole purpose sought to discover in the ancient Egyptian cultural record evidence which would document, and thereby confirm, the events recorded in the Old Testament narratives.

Jean François CHAMPOLLION – the decipherer of the ancient Egyptian hieroglyphs – identified Shoshenk I, who inscribed a great military campaign relief at Karnak, with the biblical Shishak – the Egyptian pharaoh responsible for plundering the Temple of Solomon in Jerusalem, according to I Kings 14:25 26 and II Chronicles 12:2-9. In 1837, Pope GREGORY XVI, aware of the advances of Champollion, founded the MUSEO GREGORIANO EGIZIO in Vatican City, because he deemed that the faithful's awareness of things Egyptian would enhance their understanding of the Bible. And one of the compelling reasons the British formed the Egyptian Exploration Fund (now Society) in 1882 was to find archaeological confirmation of the Bible in Egypt. The discipline of Egyptology has, therefore, been traditionally regarded as the window opening up onto the biblical landscape. As a result, today's received wisdom attempts to site the Sojourn of the Israelites and the patriarch Joseph in the 18th Dynasty (1539-1295 BC) whilst Moses and the Exodus are placed in the time of the 19th Dynasty (1295-1186 BC). This neat chronological scheme has many supporters amongst members of the academic and religious communities alike, as well as amongst the general public.

In recent years, however, a certain degree of scepticism has developed regarding the historicity of the Genesis, Exodus and Joshua narratives, and doubt is now even being expressed about the later books of the Old Testament, such as Judges, Samuel, and the early sections of Kings and Chronicles. Some contemporary scholars – even the occasional theologian – would today prefer to treat the early books of the Bible as, for the most part, works of fiction. This is primarily because, in their view, these narratives are later compilations, prepared by post-exilic editors who had only an imperfect understanding of the more remote times about which they were attempting to narrate.

Clearly a wide philosophical schism has opened up between those who would accept the biblical narratives at face value and those who would entirely dismiss the historical accuracy of those accounts. This polarisation is rapidly becoming an issue of 'blind faith' versus 'scientific scepticism' with little room for compromise. How can an academic then reconcile the two opposing sides?

One attempt at such a reconciliation is the subject of this book by David Rohl, along with its three-part international television series. David demands a critical re-examination of the evidence – the archaeological and textual evidence. That re-examination produces some startling results. He notes the problems which have come to light over the last two centuries of archaeological endeavour in Egypt and the Holy Land where little corroborative evidence for the biblical traditions has been unearthed and, indeed, where contradictions abound. David's solution is simple: archaeologists have been looking in the right places for evidence to confirm the biblical stories but in entirely the wrong time. He thus relocates the events described at the end of Genesis and the beginning of Exodus to a quite different era than the received wisdom demands. Accordingly, the Sojourn in the land of Goshen and the Exodus from Egypt can be reasonably placed in the early second millennium BC – in Egyptian terms the time known as the SECOND INTERMEDIATE PERIOD – when a large population of Asiatics resided in the eastern Nile delta.

Many Egyptologists whose spheres of competence reside with texts and historical interpretation are in accord that the Asiatic/Canaanite entry into Egypt and subsequent occupation of the delta are the only historical events which can satisfactorily accommodate the Joseph/Moses episodes; these episodes cannot be easily understood within an Egyptian NEW KINGDOM context where they are currently placed.

Biblical archaeologists have some difficulties explaining why the material culture of UNITED MONARCHY Israel, presently datable to Iron Age IIA (c. 1000-900 BC), does not reflect the grandeur of the kingdoms of David and Solomon as described in the Bible, whereas, as David Rohl notes, certain Late Bronze Age levels appear to do just that.

If the era of Israel's heroic rulers could possibly be redated to the last phases of the Late Bronze Age, then the earlier events, recorded in the final chapter of the book of Genesis and in the book of Exodus, might be reasonably accommodated in the late 12th Dynasty (the Joseph story) and in the 13th Dynasty (the Sojourn and Bondage periods). This was the epoch which produced, at the city of Avaris, the most extensive traces of an Asiatic/Canaanite presence ever found in the land of the pharaohs.

I fully realise that this redating proposed by David Rohl in *A Test of Time* is provocative and may be dismissed out of hand by many traditionalists. I myself, as the television production's 'counterfoil' to the New Chronology theory, have raised a number of methodological objections – the type of objections which might be levelled by other scholars who would question the validity of some of David's conclusions. Yet the economy of his hypothesis, the support he gains from those well versed in the texts, and the aggressive suggestions to redate the United Monarchy period of Israel's history into the Late Bronze Age do make good sense. All of this then leads to Avaris and to the patriarch Joseph.

David's New Chronology theory has evolved out of his Egyptological research. This has suggested to him that the Egyptian Third Intermediate Period, usually dated between 1069 and 664 BC, is shorter in time than the traditional historical framework would allow. Much of his evidence is compelling. The architecture of the royal tombs at Tanis, for example, appears to demand that the 21st and 22nd Dynasties were contemporary rather than sequential. This single observation speaks volumes for compressing the time span of the Third Intermediate Period – a chronological compression which I support for several reasons which lie outside the purview of this book.

Because the chronology of Egypt has become, over the years, the principal dating tool for many other ancient world civilisations, David's revision of the Third Intermediate Period has dramatic implications for our historical interpretations of those civilisations. This book concentrates on one such civilisation – the nation of Israel – from its initial formulation in Egypt with Joseph and Moses to its cultural high point during the reign of King Solomon.

The results of David's re-exploration of the archaeological evidence in the light of his new chronological revision are often surprising. They provide us with a completely new cultural and historical setting for the Old Testament narratives dealing with the lives of Joseph, Moses, Joshua, Saul, David and Solomon.

Provocative? Yes. But then David himself would be the first to admit that his proposals will turn the academic disciplines of Egyptology, Near Eastern archaeology and biblical research on their heads, as well as many other related fields of study for that matter. He has not simply deconstructionalised Egyptian chronology and left the pieces for others to put back together, as is the current fashion in scholarship. He has been courageous enough to set up a new, revolutionary historical model for critical examination by his colleagues. I trust that they will be prepared to take up his challenge in the true spirit of vigorous and open-minded debate.

Robert Steven Bianchi
New York

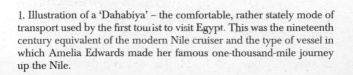

1. Illustration of a 'Dahabiya' – the comfortable, rather stately mode of transport used by the first tourist to visit Egypt. This was the nineteenth century equivalent of the modern Nile cruiser and the type of vessel in which Amelia Edwards made her famous one-thousand-mile journey up the Nile.

PREFACE

It was a searingly hot afternoon in the City of the Dead. The sensible FELLAHEEN of SHEIKH ABD EL-GURNA were inside their cool mudbrick houses taking a siesta before the evening meal. The tarmac roads which criss-cross the desert necropolis of Western Thebes bubbled like black soup under the crushing heat of an unusually oppressive Egyptian summer. Only the occasional Peugeot taxi flitted to and fro in search of tourists who had found themselves stranded on the west bank of the River Nile after a gruelling morning's visit to the Valley of the Kings.

Here I was, at the tourist entrance-gate to the shattered edifice of the Ramesseum – the mortuary temple of Rameses II – with a pair of heavy cameras shackled around my neck, a bottle of warm BARAKA water in one hand and site entrance ticket in the other. The coach park was bereft of visitors, so it looked as if I had the place to myself. Should I disturb the slumbering pile of GALABEYA in the ticket booth to legitimise my entry or just slip quietly by into the maze of ruins beyond? I decided to leave the old Ramesseum gatekeeper to his dreams.

A short pathway led me to the Second Court. As I trudged past the colonnade of mighty OSIRID statues of King Ramesses the Great my thoughts were focused on a

1

very different destination within the compound. These decapitated giants, guarding the inner sanctum of the temple, stood in their lofty arrogance as yet another eccentric English Egyptologist flitted in and out of their welcoming shadows.

I worked my way past 'Ozymandias' (the fallen colossus which provided the inspiration for Shelley's poem) and on down into the First Court. This part of the temple is not on the well-trodden tourist path for, in truth, there is little here to interest the non-specialist visitor. At this lonely spot the fertile Nile valley merges into the desert plateau, swathing the crumbling edifice of the PYLON gateway in its camouflage of acacia trees and bedraggled clumps of elephant grass. My destination was the rear façade of the northern pylon tower where I was in search of one particular block of weathered sandstone. The challenge was to obtain a photograph of a scene inscribed in shallow relief on that block – a scene which was of special significance to the theory which I had been developing over the past decade. This unprepossessing slab was for me a vital piece of the jigsaw which would help bring the stories of the Bible back onto the stage of world history. I had come to the temple of Ramesses in search of Jerusalem.

Although within a hundred metres of the regularly visited parts of the Ramesseum, this is a quiet and shady hollow, silent but for the occasional rustle of leaves in the branches above and the whispers of twisting sand eddies whipped up by the summer winds.

Having reached my goal and divested body and soul of the trappings of the west-bank tourist, I sat down on a fallen slab to assess the situation. Before me was the ochre façade of the pylon sloping upwards towards its shattered summit. Some time in the past there had been an earthquake in the area of Thebes which had devastated this most beautiful of temples. The violent tremor had brought down 'Ozymandias' and caused the upper part of the pylon to topple over; only the lower courses remained intact.

I had stayed out along with the mad dogs in the midday sun because I knew it would only be after the turn of day that the sun's rays would touch the carved relief which was the focus of my interest. Before two o'clock the west-facing façade of the pylon is always enveloped in shadow. Only in the early afternoon does it begin to reveal its secrets. Within minutes of my arrival the scene depicting Ramesses II's military campaign into SYRO-PALESTINE was bathed in the warm light of the Egyptian sun, defining the delicately cut scene in sharp relief. Within a matter of an hour or so the finest of the detail would be lost, washed out for another day, as RE moved inexorably towards his western horizon I only had a limited opportunity to take my photographs and scrutinise the carvings.

On that sticky afternoon in May 1983, as I stared up at the edifice, it seemed as if the block had been waiting patiently for my visit throughout the intervening centuries. Ever since the earthquake, the stone had been perched precariously atop the still standing remains. One more convulsion of the earth on that fateful day and it would have been buried for all time in the pile of sandstone chaos which had once been the upper half of the gateway. But there it was, skew-whiff from its original setting but still with enough purchase to remain in place for me to get the photographic evidence I needed.

The block is actually a cornerstone of the north tower of the pylon with two exposed surfaces and a broad rolled border running vertically up the adjoining edge. The only decorated surface is that facing west. This forms part of a large well-cut scene relating to the campaign of Ramesses into Palestine and Syria in the spring of his eighth regnal year. RAMESSES II was one of the legendary pharaohs of the NEW KINGDOM, when Egypt possessed a northern 'empire' in Palestine. This campaign – perhaps the most significant and successful of the young king's military adventures – is also recorded on the walls of other temples in Egypt, but, in most cases, the names of the towns captured by Ramesses are damaged, worn away, or hidden behind later Islamic building work (as at Luxor Temple). Here at the Ramesseum, however, the condition of the reliefs is relatively good and the city names easily read.

In the angled light of the two o'clock sun the wall slowly began to reveal to me the horizontal rows of fortress-towns, with groups of captives from those towns being brought in shackles to Egypt by Ramesses II's soldiers (see illustration on p. 1).

I moved as close as I could to the subject block. Even though I was still fifteen feet below the relief, through my camera's telephoto lens I gradually began to discern the hieroglyphic text running down the centre of the fortress. Perspiration from a combination of the oppressive heat and the strains of holding a heavy telescopic lens at an awkward angle caused the camera viewfinder to steam up continuously as I tried to focus on the target. Fortunately, the reading of the text was facilitated by the fact that it began with a fairly standard formula: 'The town which the king plundered in Year 8'. Then followed the name of the city. At this point the inscription was a little more worn than the upper section, but I could still make out the four hieroglyphic signs: 'sh-a-l-m'.

Visiting the site for myself had confirmed the research I had already completed in the library of the Egypt Exploration Society in London. The town which Ramesses II had plundered, and which appeared to be one of the high points of his Year 8 campaign into Palestine, was called 'Shalem' – the earliest-known name for the holy city of Jerusalem (mentioned in Genesis 14:18, Psalm 76:2, and Hebrews 7:1 & 7:2). Indeed, the later and better known name of 'Yerushalim' (Hebrew for Jerusalem) is made up of the WEST SEMITIC word Yeru meaning 'foundation' or 'city' and the name of the early local deity – Shalem – giving us 'Foundation' or 'City (of the god) Shalem'. My quest for Jerusalem in the ruins of Ramesses' temple had been successful.

I took my photographs. Pleased with my afternoon's work, I departed the scorching west bank, crossing the River Nile for a refreshing FROWLA JUICE in the lounge-bar of my hotel in Luxor town.

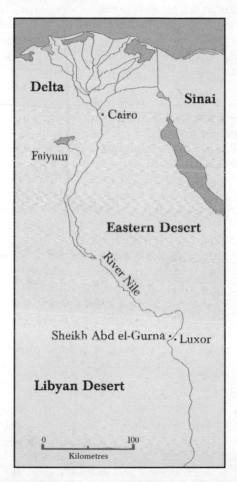

The Nile valley showing the main geographical features of Egypt and the location of Sheikh Abd el-Gurna village near Luxor.

INTRODUCTION

ere the great events of the earliest parts of the Bible real happenings or should we regard the biblical narratives purely as a collection of allegorical folktales? Simply put, is the early Old Testament real history or just legend?

> If we reflect on how easy it is to challenge the historicity not only of a David or Solomon but of events in the reigns of Hezekiah or Josiah, ... the very substance of any historical project that attempts to write a history of the late second- or early first-millennium B.C. in Palestine on the basis of a direct integration of biblical and extrabiblical sources, ... must appear not only dubious but wholly ludicrous.[1]

These are the words of Professor Thomas L. Thompson of Copenhagen University, one of the leading authorities on matters biblical. As I understand the overall conclusion of his thesis (exemplified in his book *Early History of the Israelite People from the Written and Archaeological Sources*) he is basically saying that the Old Testament stories are a fictional composition written in the second century BC and that, as a result, it would be a 'complete waste of time' (in his words) for anyone to attempt to confirm those stories through archaeology. Here then we have, in a nutshell, the approach that has become known as the 'Copenhagen school' of biblical exegesis: the Old Testament has no value as an historical source.

What lies behind this jaundiced opinion of the Bible as history? Peeling away all the layers of scholarly debate which have tended to camouflage the issue over the years, we are left with one fundamental problem for those who would advocate using the Bible as a source for history; archaeological excavations in Egypt and the LEVANT, ongoing for the best part of the last two centuries, have produced no tangible evidence to demonstrate the historical veracity of the early biblical narratives. Direct material support for the traditional history of the Israelite nation, as handed down in the books of Genesis, Exodus, Joshua, Judges, Samuel, Kings and Chronicles, is virtually non-existent. It is as if the Israelites had somehow failed to leave their archaeological footprint in the ancient lands of the Bible. Moses and the Israelites simply picked up their belongings, left Egypt in the reign of Ramesses II (thirteenth century BC) and walked into Sinai to miraculously disappear from history for around four hundred years before resurfacing in the campaign inscriptions of the ninth-century kings of Assyria. Where did they go? According to the Bible, they went to settle in Palestine where they were eventually to forge nationhood under the charismatic kings of the United Monarchy period – Saul, David and Solomon. But virtually nothing resembling this epic adventure is to be found in the archaeological record of Palestine. For that matter, their centuries-long Sojourn in the land of the pharaohs has also left absolutely no trace in the Nile valley or its delta. Small wonder then that specialists in biblical criticism and their colleagues, the Levantine archaeologists, prefer to see the stories of the Old Testament as 'traditions' rather than genuine 'history'.

Of course, if you are a devout Christian, Jew or Muslim you may have no doubts about the historical accuracy of the Old Testament or TANAAKH narratives and the parallel stories found in the Koran. Your weapon against negative biblical scholarship is your absolute faith. If, on the other hand, like me, you are primarily interested in the search for historical truth – without the sustaining support of particular religious beliefs – it is essential to find archaeological evidence which shows that the events recorded in the Old Testament actually happened and that characters such as Joseph, Moses, Saul, David and Solomon really walked this Earth some three to four thousand years ago. It is the lack of such evidence which, in essence, lies at the heart of the academic scepticism now prevalent in some areas of biblical scholarship.

So, perhaps I should explain how the writing of this book came about and what it was that origi nally triggered my quest to find a more promising synthesis between archaeology and the historical kernel which lies at the centre of the Bible stories.

As Edwin Thiele, recognised as one of the world's leading authorities on biblical dating, once wrote 'Chronology is the backbone of history'[2] and all historians agree that the flesh of

Early Dynastic Period
Dyn. 1-2

Old Kingdom
Dyn. 3-6

First Intermediate Period
Dyn. 7-10

Middle Kingdom
Dyn. 11-12

Second Intermediate Period
Dyn. 13-17

New Kingdom
Dyn. 18-20

Third Intermediate Period
Dyn. 21-25

Late Period
Dyn. 26-31

Ptolemaic Period

The basic structure of Egyptian history – divided into nine main eras and thirty-two dynasties.

history has to be applied to a solid and reliable chronological skeleton.

My research into Egyptian THIRD-INTERMEDIATE-PERIOD chronology began in 1973 with the publication of a remarkable book written by one of the most eminent Egyptologists of our time. Professor Kenneth KITCHEN's *The Third Intermediate Period in Egypt* [3] acted as the catalyst for more than twenty years' personal inquiry – an exercise which is still continuing today. By 1977, my study of the historical material published in that book had led me to a simple conclusion which has extraordinary implications for the chronology and history of the whole of the ancient world before the seventh century BC. For it appears that Egyptologists have constructed a dating framework for the Third Intermediate Period which is artificially over-extended – much longer than the available archaeological and textual evidence would seem to allow. This discovery has the potential, I believe, to affect the work of many scholars in many fields in some way or another. The reason for this is that Egyptian chronology lies at the very heart of our pre-Christian dating system. Let me explain.

The singular event of Christ's birth (conveniently dated to 'year zero') is the firm anchor point for our AD (*'Anno Domini'*) dating system. So, the year in which I write this book – AD 1994 – is one thousand nine hundred and ninety-four years since the established date for the birth of Christ. But what happens when we need to fix an event which occurred *before* Christ's birth in absolute time? Of course we give that event a date BC or BCE. That is all very well, but how do we actually establish that BC date? For instance, what methods do scholars employ to determine exactly how many years have elapsed since Pharaoh Ramesses II fought his heroic battle at KADESH or when Tutankhamun was buried in the Valley of the Kings? Clearly, the scribes and officials of those times were unable to look into the future in order to determine how many years were still to run before BC became AD. How then did the ancients date events? Well, they used what scholars call the 'regnal dating system'; that is, they dated events to the regnal years of the ruling monarchs. So we know from Egyptian inscriptions that the Battle of Kadesh took place in Year 5 of Ramesses II and Tutankhamun died in the boy-king's ninth regnal year or thereabouts (i.e. his last known year as pharaoh). In the same way we read in the Bible that the Temple of Solomon in Jerusalem was plundered of its treasures by an Egyptian king named Shishak in the fifth year of King Rehoboam of Judah [I Kings 14:25-26 & II Chronicles 12:2-9] – a subject to which we are going to return.

So far so good, but how then do scholars make the giant leap required to assign an absolute date of 1275 BC to the Battle of Kadesh, 1327 BC to the death of King Tut and 925 BC for the sacking of Solomon's Temple? The answer, in its crudest form, is that historians simply add up the sequence of regnal years (i.e. the number of years each king reigned) backwards from the birth of Christ to the event they wish to date. History is, however, never so simple, for there are many other factors which have to be taken into account – factors such as CO-REGENCIES, PARALLEL DYNASTIES and INTERREGNA. In essence, however, the methodology is to add up the intervening reign lengths between two events and apply certain other well-established historical cross-links (what we call 'synchronisms') between different ancient civilisations in order to construct a chronological framework upon which we can embroider the events of history. If mistakes have been made in the reconstruction of that framework then the great edifice of pre-Christian history would be something similar to a Hollywood film set – an artificial construct with a superficial integrity.

How, then, do we *know* if historians have built a reliable structure for us to place Ramesses II and Tutankhamun in time? The honest answer is we take it for granted that they know what they are doing. In the same way, today's academics themselves have relied on the framework supplied by their predecessors. But more recent research has led to the belief that fundamental mistakes in the currently accepted chronology were made in the formative years of ancient world studies.

This book will demonstrate that all is not well with the 'conventional' chronology and that the only real solution to the archaeological problems which have been created is to pull down the whole structure and start again, reconstructing from the foundations upwards.

When I began to delve into Professor Kitchen's book on Third Intermediate Period chronology, I discovered literally thousands of pieces of data resembling a giant jigsaw puzzle which, when assembled, represented the currently accepted historical picture of Egypt's First Millennium BC past. The Third Intermediate Period (from now on TIP) stretches back from 664 to 1070 BC – four centuries of time which link the well-established chronology of the Persian and Greco-Roman eras to the great Bronze Age civilisations of the ancient Near East. Between these two very different worlds lies a period of historical confusion. At its beginning, the powerful kingdoms of the LATE BRONZE AGE slump into deep decline and then oblivion.[4] It is hardly surprising that such an era of darkness and instability has the potential to confuse historians. The difficulties have been well recognised by scholars specialising in the period but, nevertheless, they have put together an historical picture which appears to make some sense of it all.

When I looked at Kitchen's assembled jigsaw in detail I began to find pieces which simply did not fit together. (Other researchers were coming to a similar conclusion.[5]) I also discovered a number of fundamental assumptions about the structure of the TIP which, in my view, were not based on sound historical methods. These assumptions were hardly the invention of Professor Kitchen himself but rather reflected the results of more than eight generations of Egyptological scholarship. What Kitchen had done was to bring all the material evidence and scholarly arguments together into a single volume for the very first time. Ironically, his remarkable work of synthesis has only served to reveal the underlying problems of TIP chronology, particularly the inclusion of one very basic assumption which had been handed down to him – that Shoshenk I, founder of the Egyptian 22nd Dynasty, was one and the same as Shishak, the Egyptian pharaoh who had plundered Solomon's Temple according to the Bible. This crucial assumption had not been seriously challenged within academic circles since the days of CHAMPOLLION, the 'father of Egyptology'.

It is impossible to ignore the fact that the two nations – Egypt and Israel – have been, and always will be, closely linked. It should be a relatively simple matter to construct a common, interrelated history for these neighbouring states. Unfortunately, the archaeology of early Israel is silent in the sense that the excavated monuments are virtually bereft of historical inscriptions, thus failing to provide confirmation of the chronological framework for the biblical narratives. It is inevitable, therefore, that scholars have looked to Egypt, embarrassingly rich in contemporary texts, to shed some much needed light on early-Israelite history. An apparent similarity of a name here, or a record of an Egyptian military campaign there, originally seized upon with enthusiasm in the Victorian era, continue to be the treasured possessions of some biblical historians, so that one or two crucial synchronisms between Egypt and Israel form the basis of the whole edifice of both Egyptian and biblical chronology. By linking Egypt's contemporary records with events recorded in the Bible scholars have constructed a chronology with fixed points which then determines the archaeological settings for the major biblical characters. The Shishak/Shoshenk equation is one of those key synchronisms.

I will be reviewing the bases of Kitchen's chronology during the first part of this book to demonstrate that his reconstruction of TIP chronology is wrong by several

centuries. A recognition that this fundamental misinter-
pretation of the archaeological evidence has occurred will
then lead on to some quite astonishing implications for
biblical research. My own efforts at unravelling the chronology of the TIP have led me out of Egypt in the footsteps of Moses and the Israelites to the world of Levantine
archaeology and Bible criticism. I have not exactly been
dragged out of my cosy Egyptological existence kicking
and screaming, but the reader should be aware that I did
not originally set out to change our current understanding
of the Old Testament narratives. This has come about
simply because of the need to explore the ramifications of
my TIP research. I have no religious axe to grind – I am
simply an historian in search of some historical truth.

This book is about that search. The journey of discovery
upon which you are about to venture is going to be intellec-
tually testing but, I hope, at the same time stimulating and
rewarding. As we travel together further and further back
in time, I will attempt to introduce you to the real historical
figures reflected in the personas of Solomon, David and
Saul – the Israelite kings of the United Monarchy period. I
will endeavour to guide you to a Promised Land ablaze
with the destructions of Joshua and the twelve tribes. We
can then take another step back into the distant past to try
and identify the cultural remains of the Israelites left behind
in Egypt after the Exodus. A tantalising prospect presents
itself. We will be given the opportunity to wander along
the dusty lanes between the houses of Jacob's descendants
and look into their courtyards to see bread-baking clay
ovens, grain silos and the mudbrick vaults of their tombs.
If the overall chronological framework proposed in this
book is anywhere near the historical reality, then the period
of the Israelite Sojourn will become readily apparent in
the archaeology of Egypt's eastern delta. The mass graves
of the victims of the final horrendous plague which fell
upon Egypt will lie at our feet. The archaeological remains
of the store-city built with the sweat of Israelite slaves during

the Bondage period will be identified. Finally, I intend to take you into the Egyptian tomb of the patriarch Joseph. There we will reach the end of our journey of discovery as we stand together before the cult statue of the great vizier of Egypt swathed in his coat of many colours.

But, before we begin, perhaps I ought to arm you briefly with some background material in preparation for our expedition. First, let me run through a general overview of Egyptian history – at this point employing the conventional chronology.

A Brief History of Pharaonic Egypt

In the case of pharaonic Egypt we are dealing with a civilisation which spanned a period of nearly three millennia – half as long again as the Christian era. Just think, when ALEXANDER the Great rested at the foot of the Great Pyramid in 332 BC that enigmatic monument, dedicated to the divine authority of one Egyptian ruler, had already cast its shadow over the Giza necropolis for more than two thousand years!

Throughout this great span of time a culture of extraordinary homogeneity existed in the Nile valley. Only rarely was the continuity in religious beliefs and political authority disrupted. The benevolent river, with its annual inundation of fertile water-borne silt, gave to the Egyptians a philosophy of cycle and rebirth which permeated all facets of existence. The mysteries of creation, of the death and resurrection of gods, of divine birth and royal destiny, all had their origins in the natural cycles of the Egyptian world order. Mummification, pyramids, the BOOK OF THE DEAD, the Valley of the Kings and Tutankhamun's golden hoard are all reflections of that Egyptian belief in the cycle of existence. The god-pharaohs built in imperishable stone to preserve this divine order for eternity. Generations of priests administered the great cult centres, the beginnings of which are now lost in legend. The interface between the gods of Heaven and Earth and the Egyptian people was the divine Pharaoh.

Tradition – principally in the form of a pharaonic history written by the third century BC Egyptian priest known as 'MANETHO' – informs us that the first king to wear the white and red crowns of Upper and Lower Egypt was MENES, founder of the 1st Dynasty and ancestor of all the pharaohs right down to Alexander. It is often suggested that Menes was a king of Upper Egypt (the Nile valley) who conquered the northern kingdom of Lower Egypt (the delta) to achieve, for the first time, the Unification of the TWO LANDS.

From the dim memory of the **Early Dynastic Period** of Menes and his immediate successors (Dynasties 1 and 2, *circa* 2920 to 2650 BC) grew the Pyramid Age when Pharaoh first attempted to commune with the sun god Re by erecting gleaming white limestone mountains which pierced the heavens along the 'horizon of eternity' – the western desert escarpment. These kings of the **Old Kingdom** (Dynasties 3 to 6, *circa* 2650 to 2150 BC) worked their divine magic long after their departure from this world through these mighty machines – controlling the perceived universe from within their granite SARCOPHAGI at the interface between the dual worlds of order (the black, fertile land of the Nile valley) and chaos (the desolate red land of the deserts) – the domains of the living and dead.

The Black Land (Egy. *Kemet*) – as the Egyptians themselves referred to their homeland – was the abode of Horus, the living king, and his divine mother, Isis. The Red Land (Egy. *Deshret*) – that is the great expanse of desert which surrounds the Nile valley – was the domain of danger and misfortune, ruled over by the all powerful god of chaos – Seth (Egy. *Set* or *Sutekh*). By its very nature, chaos is destined to push relentlessly at the vulnerable boundaries of world order. From earliest times, and right across the most ancient world, it became the sacred duty of the 'rain-maker' king to protect his subjects from life-threatening droughts, crop failures and famine. In Egypt the early rulers were not so much the guarantors of rain but rather celebrants of the Nile's life-giving annual inundation which, since time immemorial, had blessed Kemet with a regular supply of both irrigation water and rich black silt to cleanse the soil of natural salt build-up and replenish the fields with valuable nutrients. It was this spectacular annual miracle which made the Black Land a haven from the world of sterility and desolation which lay beyond its borders.

From PREDYNASTIC times it became the living pharaoh's supreme task to suppress Seth's ambitions, holding the two states of existence in near equilibrium. This concept of 'balance', personified in the majesty of the pharaoh, is encompassed by the Egyptian word *maat*, somewhat awkwardly translated into English as 'divine truth'.

When, at certain times, pharaonic authority waned through weak leadership or unwise rule, the world of chaos rapidly encroached upon the ordered existence of the Egyptian people and the universal balance tilted in favour of Seth. When the eras of chaos were severe and prolonged, the Egyptian state tended to fragment into smaller kingdoms ruled by rival local dynasts. Victorian scholars dubbed these chaotic times 'Intermediate Periods' – a term now well established in the literature. There are three of them in all – regarded, until recently, as the cultural troughs of Egyptian history which separated the great 'Kingdom' periods. Even though recent archaeological investigation has begun to change our perceptions of cultural decline during the intermediate periods, the regular break up of the unified state remains as an historical fact. If one stands back to get a broad perspective of ancient Egypt's progress through time it is easy to see the cyclical nature of Egyptian civilisation.

The historical events of the Old Kingdom are rather elusive simply because few inscriptions of an 'historical' nature have survived. What we do possess are great stone monuments which clearly attest to the vigour of certain outstanding reigns. In the 3rd Dynasty we remember

Dynasties 1 to 12 in the Conventional Chronology

Early Dynastic Period

1st Dynasty

Menes (= Aha)
Djer
Wadj
Den (Udimu)
Anedjib
Semerkhet
Kaa
[Dynasty dates – 2920-2770]

2nd Dynasty

Hetepsekhemwy
Reneb
Ninetjer
Peribsen
Khasekhemwy
[Dynasty dates – 2770-2650]

Old Kingdom

3rd Dynasty

Zanakht (= Nebka?)	2650-2630
Netjerykhet (Djoser)	2630-2611
Sekhemkhet	2611-2603
Khaba	2603-2599
Huni	2599-2575

4th Dynasty

Snefru	2575-2551
Khufu (Cheops)	2551-2528
Radjedef	2528-2520
Khafre (Chephren)	2520-2494
Menkaure (Mycerinus)	2490-2472
Shepseskaf	2472-2467

5th Dynasty

Userkaf	2465-2458
Sahure	2458-2446
Neferirkare Kakai	2446-2426
Shepseskare Ini	2426-2419
Raneferef	2419-2416
Niuserre Izi	2416-2392
Menkauhor	2396-2388
Djedkare Izezi	2388-2356
Wenis (Unas)	2356-2323

6th Dynasty

Teti	2323-2291
Pepy I (Meryre)	2289-2255
Merenre Nemtyemzaf	2255-2246
Pepy II (Neferkare)	2246-2152

First Intermediate Period

7th & 8th Dynasty
[Dynasties dates – 2150-2135]

9th & 10th Dynasty (Herakleopolitan)
[Dynasties dates – 2135-1986]

11th Dynasty

Montuhotep I	2080-2074
Inyotef I (Sehertawy)	2074-2064
Inyotef II (Wahankh)	2064-2015
Inyotef III	2015-2007
Montuhotep II	2007-1986

Middle Kingdom

11th Dynasty (cont.)

Montuhotep II (Nebhepetre) (cont.)	1986-1956
Montuhotep III (Sankhkare)	1956-1944
Montuhotep IV (Nebtawyre)	1944-1937

12th Dynasty

Amenemhat I (Schetepibre)	1937-1908
Senuseret I (Kheperkare)	1917-1872
Amenemhat II (Nubkaure)	1875-1840
Senuseret II (Khakheperre)	1842-1836
Senuseret III (Khakaure)	1836-1817
Amenemhat III (Nimaatre)	1817-1772
Amenemhat IV (Maakherure)	1772-1763
Neferusobek (Sobekkare) (female)	1763-1759

Djoser and his revered architect, Imhotep, builder of the Sakkara Step Pyramid – the first monumental stone building in the history of the world. Then in the 4th Dynasty comes Khufu, Khafre and Menkaure, the three pharaohs associated with the mighty pyramids of Giza – the only one of the seven wonders of the ancient world still surviving today. Another notable milestone of the Old Kingdom is the astonishing ninety-four year reign of the 6th Dynasty pharaoh Pepy II.

Following the 'high' of the Old Kingdom we have our first 'low' – the **First Intermediate Period** (c. 2150 to 1986 BC[6]). The demise of the great pyramid age seems to have been connected with a dramatic change of climate in the ancient Near East. The resultant droughts (apparently accompanied by a series of major earthquakes[7]) led to the collapse of the powerful Early Bronze Age city-states in the Levant and an incursion of Asiatic refugees into Egypt. The Black Land, under the strains of such incursions, fragments into petty kingdoms just as had existed prior to Egypt's unification under Menes. At this time there are at least two contemporary lines of kings – one based in the FAIYUM (the 9th and 10th Dynasties, c. 2135 to 1986 BC) and the other in Thebes (the 11th Dynasty, *c.* 2080 to 1937 BC). These two powerful ruling families eventually begin a series of military clashes for dominance of the Nile valley. After over a century of struggle, the Thebans are victorious under the charismatic leadership of Montuhotep II. Once again, just as with the traditional birth of pharaonic history, it is the Upper Egyptians who succeed in conquering the northerners.

With Montuhotep's victory comes the second great unification of the Two Lands, heralding a renaissance of pharaonic culture known as the **Middle Kingdom** (mid Dynasty 11 to the end of Dynasty 12, 1986 to 1759 BC). The monuments of this second 'kingdom' era are not quite as spectacular as those made for the pharaohs of the Old Kingdom. By around the middle of the 12th Dynasty royal pyramids begin to be constructed of mudbrick and only sheathed in limestone. The iconography of Pharaoh's semi-divine presence is generally represented on a more modest scale. However, artistically speaking, Egypt rises to a new peak with exquisite jewellery, reliefs and statuary, as well as wonderfully evocative literature written very much on the level of human experience. Towards the end of the 12th Dynasty, the kings themselves are portrayed in a less stylised form, their faces showing furrowed brows, age-lines and unsmiling lips turned down as if to show a stern authority. Egyptologists have interpreted this remarkable change as a reflection of worldly concern on the part of Pharaoh for his subjects. There is certainly evidence to suggest that, near to the end of the 12th Dynasty, Egypt begins to suffer from a prolonged famine which must have caused the king great anxiety for the well being of the Egyptian population.[8] The greatest ruler of the Middle Kingdom is Pharaoh Amenemhat III, who ruled for forty-five years. He is the mythical King Moeris of HERODOTUS – constructor of a Nile flood catchment hydraulic system within the Faiyum region and builder of the legendary Egyptian Labyrinth beside his pyramid at Hawara.

With the advent of the 13th Dynasty, Egypt slides into another era of chaos (perhaps partly as a result of the famine) known today as the **Second Intermediate Period** (Dynasties 13 to 17, 1759 to 1539 BC). At first the façade of pharaonic rule appears to be maintained, but, for some as yet unexplained reason, the majority of the rulers only manage to hold onto their crowns for an average of just five years apiece. Many are unrelated to their predecessors and some bear distinctly foreign names. This rapid turnaround reflects instability within the institutions of government at this time. Only after a score of short reigns does *maat* reassert herself with the rise to power of a mini-dynasty of rulers (c. 1696 to 1641 BC) consisting of Neferhotep I, Sobekhotep IV, Sobekhotep V, Iaib and Ay. Soon after, however, the kingship continues to decline. Within decades the pharaohs lose control of Nubia (conquered by the 12th Dynasty) and Lower Egypt.

From around the middle of the 13th Dynasty there appears to have been a number of kingdoms in the delta. One such line of kings may be represented by Manetho's 14th Dynasty which, according to scanty archaeological evidence, seems to have ruled from the eastern-delta city of Avaris (or Auaris).[9]

Archaeological evidence to flesh out the Second Intermediate Period has been, until fairly recently, somewhat elusive. Scholars, armed with due caution, have once more, therefore, to rely to a great extent on the traditions of Manetho.[10] He tells of an unexpected invasion of 'peoples of obscure race' who descended upon the Egyptian delta during the reign of King 'Tutimaos' (the 13th Dynasty pharaoh Dudimose), going on to capture Memphis and occupy much of Egypt. They appear to have met very little resistance from the Egyptians themselves, having 'overpowered the *rulers* of the land'. Temples were razed to the ground and cities ruthlessly burned as the foreigners marauded through the Black Land. This time the agents of Seth well and truly overcame the forces of order.

The leaders of this barbaric invading force eventually establish themselves as a new dynasty of pharaohs, ruling from their stronghold at Avaris. One of their number builds a temple to Seth at the city (according to an early 18th Dynasty tradition[11]). Manetho calls this 15th Dynasty 'Hyksos' which he translates as 'shepherd-kings'.

In the meantime, the native pharaohs – the last remnants of the failed 13th Dynasty – have retreated southwards to Thebes. From there they are at last able to resist the encroachment of the foreign invaders, thus preserving a true, though much reduced, native Egyptian kingdom.

After more than a century of foreign occupation of the lower Nile valley and delta, the Theban 17th Dynasty eventually succeeds in driving out the northern enemy from the Nile valley, trapping their leaders in the fortified stronghold of Avaris. The teenage king, AHMOSE, then succeeds in pushing the Hyksos out of the delta into Palestine and along the coastal plain. After a three-year siege of their last great bastion of Sharuhen near Gaza, the Hyksos are finally overrun, their refuge of last resort sacked and burned to the ground by vengeful Egyptian forces.

Ahmose's victory over the Hyksos heralds the second great renaissance of Egyptian civilisation – the **New Kingdom** (Dynasties 18, 19 and 20, 1539 to 1069 BC). The dynamic reaction to the trauma of foreign occupation is a rapid expansion of pharaonic military power. The rulers of the early 18th Dynasty soon succeed in creating a large northern empire in Palestine and Syria, primarily as a major source of economic wealth. But it is also partly intended to act as a buffer zone, giving them ample warning of any future invasion attempts against the Black Land by the military superpowers of Anatolia and Mesopotamia. This policy does indeed seem to work right down to the end of the New Kingdom when their Levantine hegemony disintegrates towards the end of the 20th Dynasty. The Egyptian failure to maintain the northern empire eventually leads to the catastrophic assault upon Egypt by the Assyrian king

Esarhaddon in 671 BC and the wholesale sacking of Thebes seven years later by his ruthless successor, Ashurbanipal.

Up until that fateful day in the mid seventh century, Egypt is to be ruled by pharaohs of widely differing origins. First we once again find a Theban family – the 18th Dynasty – wearing the Dual Crown of Upper and Lower Egypt. They are directly descended from the 17th Dynasty. Many of the rulers of the new dynasty are worthy of mention, but here, in this brief overview, I will just highlight three remarkable individuals.

A few generations after modern Egypt's favourite pharaoh, the liberator Ahmose, a new king named Thutmose III (the 'Napoleon of ancient Egypt') walks into the spotlight of history to begin his prolonged, vigorous military assault upon the city-states of the Levant. This military activity does not take place during the early years of his long reign but rather in the last twenty years when the king is in his thirties and forties. This is because Thutmose succeeds to the throne as a child and his ambitious aunt, Queen Hatshepsut, appoints herself senior co-regent, seizing effective power in Egypt from his seventh until twenty-first year. In this time the young Thutmose III is politically marginalised by the followers of the female pharaoh. After the death of Hatshepsut, however, her reliefs and inscriptions are systematically erased by her nephew in an act of frustration and revenge. Having long been deprived of the reins of power Thutmose III is finally sole ruler and able to pursue his own political agenda.

Pharaonic wealth and political power reach their apogee during the century which follows the reign of Thutmose III, but all of his international political achievements begin to slip from Egypt's grasp with the accession of perhaps the most controversial figure in pharaonic history.

Towards the end of the 18th Dynasty one of history's most astonishing individuals becomes the semi-divine ruler of the Black Land. At his coronation he bears the typical 18th Dynasty name, Amenhotep, but from his fourth year on he is known as Akhenaten ('Spirit of the Aten'). He is a philosopher, a revolutionary thinker who chooses to worship just one god – the sun-disk. He overthrows the traditional state religions in favour of his god Aten and is thus accredited as the world's first monotheist. His Atenist revolution fails after a brief, though at first glorious, flowering. The later Egyptians revile him as a heretic.

Tutankhamun, who ruled shortly after Akhenaten, died prematurely and without heir. With this withering of the royal bloodline the 18th Dynasty peters out as the kingship passes into the hands of two former officials – Ay and Haremheb. Then a military family, perhaps descendants of a Hyksos/Egyptian intermarriage, takes over the reins of power. This is Manetho's 19th Dynasty. They herald from the eastern delta – probably from Avaris itself. The new dynasty builds a capital and royal residence – Pi-Ramesse ('the estate of Ramesses') – at the same location as the old Hyksos city. The most famous pharaoh of the 19th Dynasty is the omnipotent Ramesses the Great – 'ruler of rulers'. He is later remembered, in Classical times, as the legendary King Sesostris (Herodotus [12]) or Sesoosis (DIODORUS SICULUS [13]), conqueror of the ancient world. He is also cast as the villain of the book of Exodus as it is during his long reign that historians have placed the Israelites' departure from Egypt. This last of the legendary hero kings of Egypt will play a major role in *A Test of Time*, as will a number of the other rulers mentioned in this brief summary of pharaonic civilisation. After the death of Ramesses II, there follows a brief period of political chaos which appears to have been sparked off, at least in part, by disputes over the succession within the extended royal family (Ramesses apparently had over two hundred offspring!).

The 20th Dynasty begins with the re-establishment of order under King Setnakht and his son, Ramesses III. In his eighth year, Ramesses repulses an attempted invasion of Egypt by the 'Sea Peoples' – a confederacy of Aegean and Anatolian groups who are migrating *en masse* from their homelands into the Levant, probably as a direct result of another devastating climate change which had already brought on decades of poor harvests and drought in the north. In spite of Ramesses III's boast at successfully keeping out the invaders, within a generation or so, the northern empire is lost along with all its valuable trading networks. The rich gold mining areas of upper Nubia, developed by the 18th and 19th Dynasty pharaohs, are also abandoned for lack of a credible military presence in the region. Egypt's wealth from these two sources rapidly begins to diminish. Towards the end of the 20th Dynasty a series of nondescript pharaohs, all calling themselves Ramesses, cling precariously onto the kingship. They rule from the old Ramesside capital of Pi-Ramesse, but they are mere shadows of their illustrious predecessor, Ramesses the Great. It is around this time that the Bronze Age comes to an end.

With the death of the last of these ineffectual 20th Dynasty rulers, Ramesses XI, the great empire period of the New Kingdom comes to a pitiful end, with even the Valley of the Kings suffering the indignity of tomb robbery and official 'quarrying' for precious metals, burial furniture and pharaonic jewellery. The kings of the succeeding two dynasties have no access to the natural resources of the empire period and so they simply resort to stealing what they need for their own burials from their illustrious ancestors. They order this sacrilege in the guise of pious restoration. The great hypogea of the Valley of the Kings are cleared of their royal occupants who are then stripped of their finery and dumped together in two secret caches for their own eternal protection!

The **Third Intermediate Period** (Dynasties 21 to 25, 1069 to 664 BC) brings us to my own area of specialism and to Professor Kitchen's book.

The period begins with the rise of two independent lines of rulers (both designated Dynasty 21) – the Tanites ruling from the new eastern delta capital of Tanis and the

Dynasties 13 to 20 in the Conventional Chronology

Second Intermediate Period

13th Dynasty

21 Kings for *circa* 63 years then

Neferhotep I	1696-1685
Sihathor	1685-1685
Sobekhotep IV	1685-1678
Sobekhotep V	1678-1674
Iaib	1674-1664
Ay	1664-1641

then 9 more kings for *circa* 20 years

15th Dynasty

6 'Hyksos' kings from the Levant

Salitis (Shalek?)
Bnon
Apachnan (Khyan)
Iannas (Ianassi son of Khyan)
Apophis (Auserre Apepi)
Assis (Khamudy?)
[Dynasty dates – 1633-1525]

14th Dynasty

76 (?) minor kings of the Delta who are contemporary with the rulers of the second half of the 13th Dynasty

16th Dynasty

32 minor 'Hyksos' (?) kings who are contemporary with the rulers of the 15th and 17th Dynasties

17th Dynasty

15 (?) Theban kings contemporary with the 15th Dynasty of which the final three were

[Tao I?] (Senakhtenre)
Tao II (Sekenenre)
Kamose (Wadjkheperre)
[Dynasty dates – 1606-1539]

New Kingdom

18th Dynasty

Ahmose (Nebpehtyre)	1539-1514
Amenhotep I (Djeserkare)	1514-1493
Thutmose I (Akheperkare)	1493-1481
Thutmose II (Akheperenre)	1481-1479
Thutmose III (Menkheperre)	1479-1425
Hatshepsut (Maatkare) (Female)	1473-1458
Amenhotep II (Akheperure)	1427-1392
Thutmose IV (Menkheperure)	1392-1382
Amenhotep III (Nebmaatre)	1382-1344
Amenhotep IV/Akhenaten (Neferkheperure-waenre)	1352-1336
Neferneferuaten (Ankhkheperure) (=Nefertiti) (Female)	1341-1337
Smenkhkare (Ankhkheperure)	1337-1336
Tutankhamun (Nebkheperure)	1336-1327
Ay (Kheperkheperure)	1327-1323
Haremheb (Djeserkheperure)	1323-1295

19th Dynasty	
Ramesses I (Menpehtyre)	1295-1294
Seti I (Menmaatre)	1294-1279
Ramesses II (Usermaatre-setepenre)	1279-1213
Merenptah (Baenre-hotephirmaat)	1213-1203
Amenmesse (Menmire)	1203-1200
Seti II (Userkheperure-setepenre)	1200-1194
Siptah (Akhenre-setepenre)	1194-1188
Tausert (Sitre-meritamun) (Female)	1188-1186

20th Dynasty	
Setnakht (Userkhaure-meryamun)	1186-1184
Ramesses III (Usermaatre-meryamun)	1184-1153
Ramesses IV (Hekamaatre-setepenamun)	1153-1147
Ramesses V (Usermaatre-sekheperenre)	1147-1143
Ramesses VI (Nebmaatre-meryamun)	1143-1136
Ramesses VII (Usermaatre-setepenre)	1136-1129
Ramesses VIII (Usermaatre akhenamun)	1129-1126
Ramesses IX (Neferkare-setepenre)	1126-1108
Ramesses X (Khepermaatre-setepenre)	1108-1099
Ramesses XI (Menmaatre-setepenptah)	1099-1069

Theban priest-kings. The two lines appear to exist in relative harmony, with the Thebans acknowledging the supremacy of their northern contemporaries.

At the end of this roughly century-long era there arises a powerful new line of kings who are of Libyan extraction. This 22nd Dynasty (945 to 715 BC) is founded by King Shoshenk I who records the first known military expedition into Palestine since the reign of Ramesses III in 1172 BC. Shoshenk's invasion of Palestine is equated by scholars with the campaign of 'Shishak king of Egypt', related in I Kings and II Chronicles. There it states that Shishak 'went up against Jerusalem' and took away the treasures of the Temple of Yahweh in the fifth year of Solomon's son, REHOBOAM. This event is dated to 925 BC according to the generally accepted chronology of the kings of Judah and Israel developed by Edwin Thiele.[14]

By the middle of the 22nd Dynasty a rival line of rulers appears on the scene – the 23rd Dynasty (818 to 720 BC). They seize power in southern Egypt and a long war breaks

Dynasties 21 to 26 in the Conventional Chronology

(Dates according to Kitchen)

Tanite 21st Dynasty

Smendes (Hedjkheperre-setepenre)	1069-1043
Amenemnisu (Neferkare-hekawaset)	1043-1039
Psusennes I (Akheperre-setepenamun)	1039-991
Amenemopet (Usermaatre-setepenamun)	993-984
Osorkon the Elder (Akheperre-setepenre)	984-978
Siamun (Netjerkheperre-setepenamun)	978-959
Har-Psusennes II (Tjetkheperre-setepenre)	959-945

Theban 21st Dynasty

Herihor (as HPA then king)	1080-1074
Piankh (as HPA)	1074-1070
Pinudjem I (as HPA)	1070-1055
Pinudjem I (as king)	1054-1032
Masaharta (as HPA)	1054-1046
Djedkhonsefankh (as HPA)	1046-1045
Menkheperre (as HPA then king)	1045-992
Smendes II (as HPA)	992-990
Pinudjem II (as HPA)	990-969
Psusennes III (as HPA)	969-945

22nd Dynasty

Shoshenk I (Hedjkheperre-setepenre)	945-924
Osorkon I (Sekhemkheperre-setepenre)	924-889
Shoshenk II (Hekakheperre-setepenre)	890-889
Takelot I (Hedjkheperre-setepenre)	889-874
Osorkon II (Usermaatre-setepenamun)	874-850
Harsiese (Hedjkheperre-setepenamun)	870-860
Takelot II (Hedjkheperre-setepenre)	850-825
Shoshenk III (Usermaatre-setepenre/amun)	825-773
Pimay (Usermaatre-setepenre/amun)	773-767
Shoshenk V (Akheperre)	767-730
Osorkon IV (Akheperre-setepenamun)	730-715

23rd Dynasty

Pedubast I (Usermaatre-setepenamun)	818-793
Iuput I (prenomen unknown)	804-803
Shoshenk IV (Usermaatre-meryamun)	793-787
Osorkon III (Usermaatre-setepenamun)	787-759
Takelot III (Usermaatre-setepenamun)	764-757
Rudamun (Usermaatre-setepenamun)	757-754
Iuput II (Usermaatre-setepenamun)	754-720
Shoshenk VI (Wasneterre-setepenre)	720-715

24th Dynasty	
Tefnakht (Shepsesre)	727-720
Bekenranef (Wahkare)	720-715
25th Dynasty	
Alara	780-760
Kashta (Maatre)	760-747
Piankhy (or Piye) (Usermaatre/Sneferre)	747-716
Shabaka (Neferkare)	716-702
Shabataka (Djedkaure)	702-690
Taharka (Nefertemkhure)	690-664
Tantamani (Bakare)	664-656
26th Dynasty	
Ameris (Nubian governor)	715-695
Tefnakht I	695-688
Nekauba	688-672
Necho I (Menkhcperre)	672-664
Psamtek I (Wahibre)	664-610
Necho II (Wehemibre)	610-595
Psamtek II (Neferibre)	595-589
Apries (Haaibre)	589-570
Amasis II (Khnemibre)	570-526
Psamtek III (Ankhkaenre)	526-525

out between the 22nd Dynasty delta monarchs and their
Theban-based rivals. We learn of this conflict through the
Chronicle of Prince Osorkon, son of King Takelot II. He is
commander of the Egyptian army and the high priest of
Amun at Thebes but, within a few years of assuming office,
the forces of rebellion in the south oust him from KARNAK,
establishing their own king and high priest. Osorkon
devotes the next twenty years of his life to the recapture of
Thebes and to a return of political control to the 22nd
Dynasty.

In the end, it is an invasion by a king of Kush (modern
Sudan) which brings a form of stability to Egypt under the
Kushite 25th Dynasty. When King Piankhy[15] journeys
northward from the upper reaches of the Nile to suppress
a revolt led by Prince Tefnakht of Sais (in the western delta),
the political situation in Egypt is confused. The Kushite
ruler already appears to hold sway at Thebes, but the rest
of the country is split up into several kingdoms. The great

basalt stela recording Piankhy's conquest of the Nile valley in Year 20 (728 BC) carries the names of four contemporary pharaohs and a gaggle of chieftains, each ruling in different areas of the land.

For sixty-odd years the 25th Dynasty dominates the political landscape in the Nile valley until the conquest of Egypt by ESARHADDON, king of Assyria, in 671 BC. So begins the short period of the Assyrian occupation of Egypt. The Kushite pharaoh, Taharka, based in Thebes, attempts on several occasions to throw off the Assyrian yoke by inciting rebellion in the north but eventually, in 664 BC, the new Assyrian king, ASHURBANIPAL, loses patience with him and his young co-regent TANTAMANI, despatching an army upstream to Thebes. The brutal Assyrian assault crushes all resistance. The Kushites flee south, never to be seen again in the Black Land. The Assyrians rampage through Thebes, stripping the temples of their treasures and slaughtering the population. This majestic sacred city never recovers from the trauma; the glories of its one-and-a-half-thousand-year history quietly decay as the 'city of a hundred gates' crumbles into legend.

During the latter years of the 25th Dynasty a new family of western delta rulers had begun to emerge, following the rebellion of Prince Tefnakht. These Saite kings (named after their capital at Sais), at first vassals of the Kushite pharaohs and then, later, of the Assyrians, are eventually in a strong position to seize control of Egypt following the demise of the last Kushite king. Within a few years of the sacking of Thebes, Ashurbanipal is forced to withdraw his troops from the southern Levant in order to protect the heartland of his Assyrian empire from the rising power of the Neo-Babylonians, ruled by NEBUCHADNEZZAR II. Psamtek I, fourth ruler of the Saite 26th Dynasty, had been subservient to his foreign master since succeeding to the Saite throne in 664 BC, but by 656 the Assyrians had withdrawn, leaving the king of Sais recognised throughout Egypt as the true sovereign of the whole land.

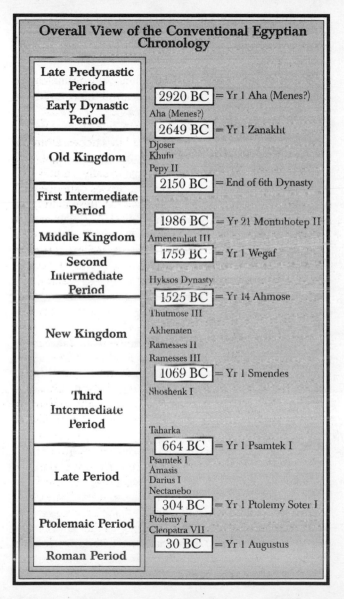

Overall View of the Conventional Egyptian Chronology

Late Predynastic Period	
	2920 BC = Yr 1 Aha (Menes?)
Early Dynastic Period	Aha (Menes?)
	2649 BC = Yr 1 Zanakht
	Djoser
Old Kingdom	Khufu
	Pepy II
	2150 BC = End of 6th Dynasty
First Intermediate Period	
	1986 BC = Yr 21 Montuhotep II
Middle Kingdom	Amenemhat III
	1759 BC = Yr 1 Wegaf
Second Intermediate Period	Hyksos Dynasty
	1525 BC = Yr 14 Ahmose
	Thutmose III
New Kingdom	Akhenaten
	Ramesses II
	Ramesses III
	1069 BC = Yr 1 Smendes
Third Intermediate Period	Shoshenk I
	Taharka
	664 BC = Yr 1 Psamtek I
	Psamtek I
Late Period	Amasis
	Darius I
	Nectanebo
	304 BC = Yr 1 Ptolemy Soter I
Ptolemaic Period	Ptolemy I
	Cleopatra VII
	30 BC = Yr 1 Augustus
Roman Period	

With the reign of Psamtek I we enter the **Late Period** in Egyptian history (Dynasties 26 to 30 – 664 to 332 BC). This is an era of alternating native and foreign rule with the 26th Dynasty (664 to 525 BC) 'renaissance' followed by the occupation of the Nile valley and delta by the Persians led by the 'mad' King CAMBYSES (Dynasty 27 – 525 to 404 BC). This first period of Persian dominance is brought to an end with a brief native revival lasting just over half a century (Dynasties 28 to 30 – 404 to 343 BC) when kings NECTANEBO I and II begin the restoration of a number of religious sites such as Karnak and Luxor Temples and the sacred Apis bull necropolis at Sakkara. The Persians then reinvade Egypt, occupying the Nile valley for a second time – but on this occasion for just eleven years.

The defeat of DARIUS III by ALEXANDER III of Macedon in the years 334 to 330 BC brings an end to the Persian domination of the Near East. Egypt is rescued from oppression by the young conqueror who is duly recognised as the son of Zeus-Ammon and crowned pharaoh. With the premature death of Alexander, the great empire which he had carved out for himself in the few short years between 334 and 323 is divided up into three main political areas with Pharaoh PTOLEMY SÔTER (I) (one of Alexander's generals) eventually taking the Egyptian throne following the death of Alexander's direct heirs PHILIP ARRHIDAEUS and ALEXANDER IV.

So begins the **Ptolemaic Period** (304 to 30 BC) which ends with the tragic suicide of Queen CLEOPATRA VII and the murder of Caesarion (PTOLEMY XV), her son by Julius Caesar. This young, half-Greek, half-Roman, Egyptian pharaoh is the last of his long and illustrious line to rule an independent pharaonic kingdom in the Nile valley.

Three thousand years of history comes to a close with the Black Land's involuntary incorporation into the Roman Empire – eventually no longer a sovereign state but merely a province of Rome. An astonishing royal culture had finally reached its sudden and dramatic end with the murder of a young and innocent boy who had been the heir to the thrones of both Egypt and the Roman Empire. The birth of Jesus Christ is now just three decades away.

***

Now that you have a general outline of the major events in Egyptian history it may be useful to do the same thing for the traditional history of the Old Testament.

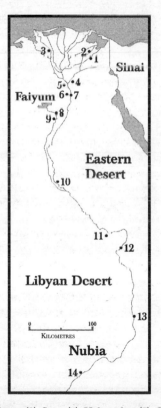

(1) Avaris; (2) Tanis; (3) Sais; (4) Heliopolis; (5) Giza; (6) Sakkara; (7) Memphis; (8) Hawara; (9) Heracleopolis; (10) Amarna; (11) Abydos; (12) Thebes; (13) Elephantine; (14) Abu Simbel.

A Brief History of Israel

Where does one begin Israelite 'history'? When can we say legend gives way to factual events? This is the issue I first addressed at the beginning of this *Introduction*, where I began to explain how the point when history takes over from myth has been dated later and later, until today, some influential scholars would argue that history only starts after the Solomonic Age when the kings of the Divided Monarchy of Israel and Judah first appear in the contemporary records of other civilisations. In essence, this book will serve to clarify the issue of the historicity of the early 'traditions' of Israel, so the events of the Old Testament narratives can re-emerge from the realms of myth and allegory.

I provide here a short overview of the chronological sequence of events as narrated in the books of Genesis through to II Chronicles, to refresh the memory. I will start with **Abraham**, the first patriarch [Genesis 11:28].

The youthful Abraham leaves MESOPOTAMIA with his father, Terah, and begins a long period of wandering which eventually sees him settle in the central hill country of Canaan (what we call today the West Bank). During his early travels he develops close ties with the city of Haran in north Syria. Over the years, many of the brides of Israelite men would originate from this region as a result of these ties. It was during Abraham's lifetime that a great cataclysm destroyed Sodom and Gomorrah [Genesis 19:23-26], an event preceded by a severe famine which decimated the population of the Levant – forcing Abraham to take refuge in Egypt [Genesis 12:10-20].

The Patriarchal line continued with **Isaac**, the son who had survived his own sacrifice at the hands of his father. The uncompromising god of Abraham (EL-ELYON/EL-SHADDAI) had demanded a human sacrifice to test out the loyalty of his protégé [Genesis 22:1-19]. Human first-born sacrifice was fairly common in those days and archaeological evidence for the practice has been found throughout the ancient world. Isaac was the father of **Jacob** who, in turn, had twelve sons, the second youngest of whom was Joseph.

The story of **Joseph**, as a piece of literature, is one of the highlights of the Old Testament. It begins with his brothers' jealousy and their attempt to do away with him [Genesis 37]. They sell Joseph to a group of MIDIANITE caravaneers on their way to Egypt and they, in turn, sell him into bonded slavery. Meanwhile the brothers spill goats' blood on Joseph's fine 'coat of many colours' and take it to Jacob saying that his son had been killed and eaten by a wild animal. The seventeen-year-old Joseph becomes a servant in the household of POTIPHAR, commander of the guard, where he makes himself a valuable asset to the estate until he suffers the amorous attentions of Potiphar's wife. His rejection of her advances results in the woman making accusations of sexual harassment and he is duly sent to prison for his crime.

In confinement, the young Joseph befriends two courtiers, the king's cup-bearer and the royal baker, who have been sent for punishment after some unexplained indiscretion. Joseph foretells their future by interpreting dreams and, sometime after his release and return to the palace, the cup-bearer informs Pharaoh of the young Hebrew's skills as a seer. Pharaoh has been troubled by a recurring dream in which he sees seven fat cows coming up out of the waters of the River Nile and then seven lean cows following behind them. The lean cows devour the fat cows [Genesis 41]. Joseph interprets the dream as a period of seven years of plenty for Egypt followed by seven years of famine. The king is impressed with this analysis and promotes Joseph to VIZIER of Egypt with specific instructions to prepare for the oncoming famine. The new Asiatic vizier (now thirty years old) sets about organising the storage of large quantities of grain during the years of plenty and, at the same time, brings Egypt's agricultural programme under central government control. When the famine strikes,

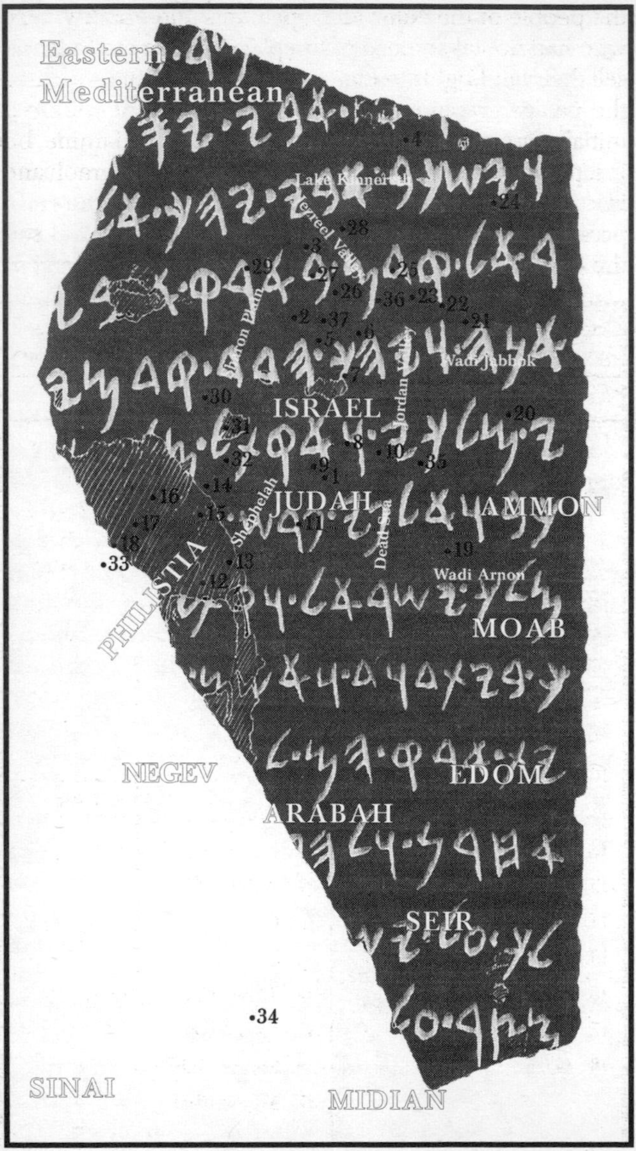
Eastern Mediterranean
Lake Kinnereth
Jezreel Valley
Sharon Plain
Wadi Jabbok
Jordan Valley
ISRAEL
JUDAH
AMMON
Shephelah
Dead Sea
PHILISTIA
Wadi Arnon
MOAB
NEGEV
EDOM
ARABAH
SEIR
SINAI
MIDIAN

the people of the Nile valley, peasants and nobility alike, who had not taken heed of Joseph's warning are forced to sell their land rights to Pharaoh in return for supplies from the palace granaries [Genesis 47:20]. Not only is Egypt initially protected from the worst effects of the famine, but Joseph has effectively increased the power of Pharaoh and, in doing so, his own influence as the second most powerful person in the land after the king, is greatly enhanced. Before the famine struck Joseph had married ASENATH, daughter

---

Opposite page: Relief map of Palestine showing the main geographical regions and their principal cities discussed in *A Test of Time*.

Key to Map

1. Jerusalem		19. Dibon		
2. Samaria		20. Rabath-Ammon		**Trans-Jordanian Cities**
3. Megiddo		21. Jabesh-Gilead		
4. Hazor		22. Mahanaim		
5. Shechem	**Israelite Cities/ Cult Centres**	23. Pella		
6. Tirzah		24. Ashtaroth		
7. Shiloh		25. Bethshan		
8. Geba		26. Ginae		
9. Gibeon		27. Taanach		
10. Jericho		28. Shunem		**Canaanite Cities**
11. Hebron		29. Dor		
12. Lachish		30. Joppa		
13. Bethshemesh		31. Aphek		
14. Ekron		32. Gezer		
15. Gath		33. Sharuhen		
16. Ashdod	**Philistine Cities**	34. Timna Copper Mines		
17. Ashkelon		35. Mount Nebo		
18. Gaza		36. Mount Gilboa		
		37. Mount Ebal		

of Potiphera (High Priest of HELIOPOLIS) and she had borne him two sons – Manasseh and Ephraim.

Joseph's reward for protecting Egypt is a royal decree which allows the vizier's brethren to settle in the eastern Nile delta where they can receive protection from the terrible famine currently also ravaging the Levant. After a series of encounters with his elder brothers, in which Joseph punishes them for their original misdeed against him, Jacob is finally reunited with his favourite son. The Israelites settle in the region of GOSHEN. At the beginning they number less than one hundred [Genesis 46:26-27],[16] but within a few generations the Israelites would multiply so that 'the whole land was full of them' [Exodus 1:7]. In the meantime, Joseph dies, is mummified and buried in an Egyptian tomb [Genesis 50:26]. He leaves instructions that, if and when the Israelites leave Egypt, they should take his coffin with them so that he may be buried in the Promised Land.

In the years following Joseph the rapid population increase of the Israelites begins to concern the pharaohs and eventually one of them takes action to counter the growing threat. He enslaves the Israelites and orders the culling of the male children. It is in this climate of oppression and fear that the baby **Moses** is born [Exodus 2:1-10]. His mother places Moses in a reed basket and sets him adrift on the Nile. The baby is discovered by Pharaoh's daughter who is unable to have children of her own. She adopts the boy and raises him in the palace of Pharaoh as a prince of Egypt.

When he matures, Prince Moses discovers his true identity and wishes to identify himself with his own people. He kills an Egyptian who is beating an Israelite slave and, in fear of his life, flees into exile beyond the reach of Pharaoh's wrath. His journey takes him to Sinai and the tent of Jethro, a Midianite priest, whose eldest daughter, Zipporah, he marries. This is the point in the story where we encounter for the first time the god of Moses – in some ways quite distinct from El, god of the patriarchs [Exodus

3]. This new metamorphosis reveals himself as 'I am who I am'. The God of Moses is Yahweh, the one god of the Israelites, and Jehovah of the Christian churches. Like the Egyptian Seth, he is a god of the desert wilderness. Moses receives his instructions to return to Egypt and lead Yahweh's chosen people out of bondage and into the Promised Land.

Moses, now of mature years, makes his way back to Egypt and confronts Pharaoh. The Egyptian king refuses to allow his slave population to leave and so the battle of wills between the leader of the Israelites and the stubborn Pharaoh commences. Ten plagues are inflicted upon the Egyptians, the final one of which – the death of the first-born – forces the king to capitulate [Exodus 12:29-34]. Moses leads his people into Sinai where they reach MOUNT HOREB to receive the Ten Commandments from Yahweh [Exodus 20]. Forty years of wandering ensue at the end of which Moses dies and is buried on MOUNT NEBO overlooking the Jordan valley and the Promised Land beyond [Deuteronomy 34].

So ends the story of Exodus and we enter the period known as the **Conquest**. Joshua's forces begin their assault on CANAAN with the sacking of JERICHO. They are aided in their endeavours by Yahweh who brings down the impregnable fortification walls of the city [Joshua 6]. The Israelite soldiers clamber into the midst of the enemy stronghold through the fallen walls and wreak havoc amongst the defenceless inhabitants of Jericho. Every last man, woman and child is slaughtered (excepting Rahab and her household – the prostitute who had earlier protected the Israelite spies). The city is burnt to the ground – remaining cursed and abandoned for several centuries.

The Israelites then go on to destroy Ai and a number of other cities in the hill country and SHEPHELAH before the climax of their conquest of the Promised Land – the assault on the mighty city of HAZOR. Jabin, king of Hazor, is killed and his city destroyed by fire [Joshua 11:10-11].

The Conventional Chronology of Israel

Patriarchal Period

Abraham	c. 1800
Isaac	c. 1770
Jacob	c. 1720
Joseph	c. 1650

Sojourn in Egypt

Israelites arrive in Goshen	c. 1640
Death of Joseph	c. 1580
Period of Bondage begins	c. 1295
Exodus	c. 1250
Conquest	c. 1210
Shechem Covenant	c. 1200

Judges Period

Othniel	c. 1180
Deborah	c. 1120
Gideon	c. 1100
Abimelech	c. 1080
Jephthah	c. 1060
Samuel	c. 1040

United Monarchy

Saul	1030-1010
David	1010-970
Solomon	970-930

Divided Monarchy

Israel		Judah	
Jeroboam	930-909	Rehoboam	930-913
Nadab	909-908	Abijah	913-910
Baasha	908-885	Asa	910-869
Elah	885-884	Jehoshaphat	869-848
Zimri	885-884	Jehoram	848-841
Tibni	884-880	Ahaziah	841-841
Omri	880-873	Athaliah	841-835
Ahab	873-853	Joash	835-796
Ahaziah	853-852	Amaziah	796-767
Joram	852-841	Azariah (Uzziah)	767-739
Jehu	841-813	Jotham	739-731
Jehoahaz	813-798	Ahaz	731-715
Jehoash	798-781	Hezekiah	715-686
Jeroboam II	781-753	Manasseh	686-642
Zechariah	753-752	Amon	642-640
Shallum	752-752	Josiah	640-609
Menahem	752-741	Jehoahaz	609-609
Pekahiah	741-739	Jehoiakim	609-598
Pekah	739-731	Jehoiachin	598-597
Hoshea	731-722	Zedekiah	597-586

Having completed their military campaign, the Israel-ites gather at SHECHEM, before the TEMPLE OF BAAL-BERITH ('Lord of the Covenant') where Joshua erects a standing stone. Before the great monolith the Israelite tribes pledge their eternal loyalty to Yahweh, the God of Moses and their redeemer from Egyptian bondage [Joshua 24].

We now enter the era of the **Judges** when the Israelite tribes struggle for independence and unity in their new homeland. Their principal enemy is the Philistine confederacy based in the five coastal-plain cities of Gath, Ashkelon, Gaza, Ashdod and Ekron. One incident in the long period of struggle is worthy of mention here as we will return to it in a later chapter. Several generations after the first covenant at Shechem, the citizens of the town elect themselves a king, Abimelech by name [Joshua 9]. His three-year reign is violent and oppressive, so much so that the Shechemites revolt against their evil king. Eventually Abimelech decides to rid himself of the citizens of Shechem and sends his troops to eliminate them. The panic-stricken Shechemites seek refuge in the great MIGDOL temple of the city before which the Israelite Covenant was made. Unable to break into the fortified CELLA of this holy place, Abimelech orders it to be set alight and all one thousand refugees perish in the flames. The king later meets his end during an assault on Thebez, when a woman casts a millstone upon him from the ramparts, crushing his skull [Judges 9:50-57].

After the judgeships of several charismatic Israelite leaders (Deborah, Gideon, Jephthah etc.) have passed and the Philistine yoke has been further tightened, we come to the time of **Saul** and **David**. The Israelites have become tired of their disunity and lack of hereditary leadership. They ask the last judge, Samuel, to choose a king to rule over them 'like other nations' and the prophet anoints the Benjaminite chieftain Saul as the first king over all of Israel [I Samuel 8-10]. One of his first acts as king is to initiate a revolt against Philistine hegemony in the region. His son, the brave warrior Jonathan, overthrows the Philistine pillar at GEBA and Saul's men sound the SHOFAR to let all the Israelites know that the rebellion has begun [I Samuel 13]. The war for control of the region culminates in the Battle of GILBOA, overlooking the JEZREEL VALLEY, where Saul and his three eldest sons are killed [I Samuel 28-31]. The remnants of the defeated Israelite army flee across the Jordan and the Philistine confederacy mark their victory by displaying the headless bodies of Saul and his slain sons on the city walls of Bethshan.

Over the years of Saul's brave but ill-fated reign the king had at first sponsored and then, later, outlawed a young warrior called David [I Samuel 16-27]. Through his marriage to Saul's daughter, Michal, David had become a potential claimant to the Israelite throne and Saul soon began to see his son-in-law's popularity amongst the Israelites as a direct threat to his own rule and authority. David fled with his followers into the wilderness of the southern hill country before offering his services to Saul's enemy, the king of Gath.

With the death of Saul on Mount Gilboa, David is now made vassal ruler of Hebron by the Philistines, but during the next seven years he gradually turns against his overlords and becomes an even greater threat to their control of Canaan than their old enemy, Saul. The second push for Israelite independence reaches its climax with David's seizure of Jerusalem, the Jebusite enclave which had remained outside the control of the twelve tribes ever since the Conquest [II Samuel 5]. At the dawn of the first millennium Jerusalem becomes the City of David and continues as the pre-eminent Israelite capital until its capture and subsequent destruction by the Babylonians in 587 BC.

David intensifies his wars against the enemies of Israel and raises his kingdom to become one of the more powerful states in the Levant of the tenth century BC. He is succeeded by his son, **Solomon**, who enjoys a long reign of peace and relative political stability. During the reign of this last king of the United Monarchy period Israel reaches its pinnacle of culture and prosperity. The kingdom of Solomon represents a flowering of art with the building of richly ornate palaces and the Temple of Yahweh in Jerusalem. Israel becomes a cosmopolitan nation, reflected in the large influx of foreign traders and artisans. Solomon marries an Egyptian princess and builds a palace for her in Jerusalem. His reputation as a wealthy merchant prince grows with every year as his people enjoy unrivalled stability and prosperity. The glories of his reign are such that even the queen of far-off Sheba pays a visit to the Israelite king.

As is often the case with long stable reigns, the years following Solomon's death see a disintegration of all that had been achieved. We now reach the **Schism**, when the unified state of Israel tears itself apart and divides into two rival kingdoms. In the south Rehoboam, the son of King Solomon, is left with the rump kingdom of Judah but retains the old capital of Jerusalem. To the north, the remaining Israelite tribes gather around a new leader – Jeroboam – who had made himself Solomon's enemy and sought refuge in Egypt until the old king's death. Now Jeroboam is established as ruler of the new state of Israel, based at Shechem.

In the fifth year of Rehoboam (925 BC) we hear of the successful campaign of Shishak, king of Egypt, against the cities of Judah. After taking many of Rehoboam's fortified towns, Shishak reaches the gates of Jerusalem and demands the Judahite king's capitulation. His price for not razing Jerusalem to the ground is to strip the palace and temple of Solomon of all its treasures which he takes back with him to Egypt. With this incident we reach our first 'confirmation' of an event in Israelite history from external sources. Scholars have identified the great campaign relief of Pharaoh Shoshenk I of the 22nd Dynasty with the attack upon Jerusalem by Shishak.

Then, from the middle of the ninth century onwards it is no longer necessary for us to rely on Egypt to date biblical events. Indeed Israelite chronology is verifiable through other, primarily Mesopotamian, sources. For it is in 853 BC that King SHALMANESER III of Assyria records the participation of King Ahab of Israel in the Battle of KARKAR. Later, in *circa* 825 BC, the same Assyrian ruler depicts the receipt of tribute from Jehu, king of Israel, on his 'Black Obelisk'. On the Moabite Stone (*c.* 840 BC) we have independent confirmation of the wars between the Transjordanian kingdom of Moab and the 'House of Omri' of Israel [II Kings 3:4-27].

I will finish this brief summary of Israelite 'history' with the capture of the two capitals of the Divided Monarchy period. Samaria, which had become the new capital of the Northern Kingdom of Israel in the reign of Omri, is seized in 722 BC by the Assyrians. The last king of Israel, Hoshea, is captured and imprisoned. The Southern Kingdom of Judah holds out against the Assyrians for a further century but finally succumbs to the new *force majeure* in the ancient Near East – the Babylonians of Nebuchadnezzar. Jerusalem falls in the summer of 587 BC and its king, Zedekiah, is forced to watch the execution of his sons before his own eyes are gouged out. A major part of the population of Judah is deported to Babylonia [II Kings 25:12] where they remain until the overthrow of Babylon in 539 BC by CYRUS of Persia. The exiles are then free to return to Jerusalem to rebuild their city and the Temple of Yahweh destroyed by Nebuchadnezzar's army.

***

We must always be aware that biblical research is an ongoing discipline. We are currently living in interesting times. From my visits to archaeological sites in the Near East, it seems to me that a wave of new discoveries is about to

2. In the 1930s, American archaeologists excavating the famous city of Megiddo unearthed a jasper seal which was inscribed 'belonging to Shema, servant of Jeroboam'. King Jeroboam II reigned in Israel between 781 and 753 BC. The original seal is lost but a copy is kept in the Israel Museum.

3. Fragment of the stela (tablet) found at Tel Dan. The text (below) mentions the 'House of David'. Archaeological Museum, Jerusalem.

'... my father went up ... and my father died, he went to [his fate ... Is]rael formerly in my father's land ... I [fought against Israel?] and Hadad went in front of me ... my king. And I slew of [them X footmen, Y cha]riots and 2000 horsemen ... the king of Israel. And [I] slew [... the kin]g of the House of David. And I put ... their land ... other ... [... ru]led over Is[rael ...] siege upon ...'

break. I anticipate that these discoveries will confirm the findings of my own research. Even whilst I have been writing this book fresh evidence has come to light concerning the early history of the Israelite monarchy. This comes from the land of Israel itself. The Israeli expedition working at Tel DAN has unearthed a stela fragment written in Aramaic which mentions 'the House of David'. This does not sit well with Professor Thompson's thesis that the Early Israelite Monarchy period is nothing more than myth and legend. His statement, quoted at the beginning of this *Introduction*, now appears to be premature. The inscription has been dated to the early eighth century BC – well before the time of the post-exilic writing of the Old Testament.[17] Even so, we have as yet no other material evidence for the reigns of David and Solomon, and the broken tablet from Dan was not discovered in a datable context, apparently being reused in a later pavement. We are unable, therefore,

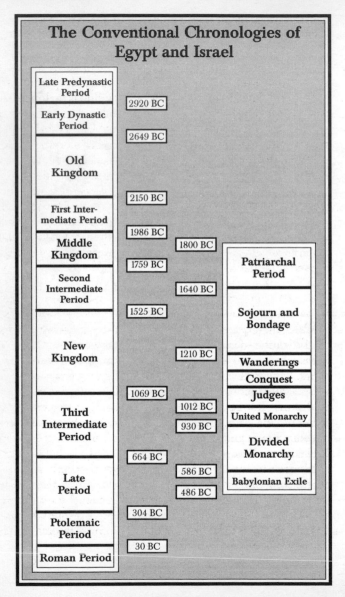

The Conventional Chronologies of Egypt and Israel

Late Predynastic Period

2920 BC

Early Dynastic Period

2649 BC

Old Kingdom

2150 BC

First Intermediate Period

1986 BC

Middle Kingdom

1800 BC

1759 BC

Second Intermediate Period

1640 BC

1525 BC

New Kingdom

1210 BC

1069 BC

Third Intermediate Period

1012 BC

930 BC

Late Period

664 BC

586 BC

486 BC

Ptolemaic Period

304 BC

30 BC

Roman Period

Patriarchal Period

Sojourn and Bondage

Wanderings

Conquest

Judges

United Monarchy

Divided Monarchy

Babylonian Exile

date the archaeological stratum (layer) in which the original stela was erected. Monumental structures once attributed to the building activities of Solomon in the cities of Megiddo, Gezer and Hazor have been shown over the years to date from various archaeological periods spanning centuries.[18] The 'Solomonic Gate' at Megiddo is no longer dated to the time of Solomon – yet the modern tourist sign erected in front of it continues to inform visitors that they are standing before a gate 'from the time of Solomon'.

In spite of these disappointments many people continue to hope that evidence will come to light confirming the existence of David, Solomon and even the earlier charismatic leaders of Israel such as Joseph and Moses. However, it is my belief that it is no longer necessary to wait for such evidence – all we need do is take a look at the archaeological material we already possess from the new perspective of a revised Egyptian chronology.

***

It is a sad reality that, in comparison to Egypt and Mesopotamia, there are very few artefacts and inscriptions which can be mustered in order to illustrate Israelite history. This in essence is what this reinvestigation in *A Test of Time* is all about. It is precisely this lack of archaeological confirmation – especially before the ninth century BC – which has led to the mythologising of biblical history. Again another rather disconcerting factor is the lack of archaeological links between Egypt and Israel – this in spite of the fact that the two countries were neighbours and the Bible is full of references to instances when their histories coincided. Surely something is not quite right with our present understanding of the relationship between ancient Egypt and ancient Israel. If you are intrigued to find a resolution to this puzzle, then follow me as I take you on a fascinating journey of archaeological discovery.

A Note on Methodology

At this point I need to raise one or two methodological issues. Up until now I have been using the term 'history' in the context of a series of real events occurring in a chronological sequence. In reality, though, the word has a more complex meaning, which needs to be clearly appreciated. The raw materials of historical research are not simply the available archaeological and textual evidence, but rather the *interpretations* which scholars deduce from that evidence. History itself is a rhetorical exercise whose success depends upon *reasonable argumentation*. The criterion of acceptance of any historical writing is whether it combines interpretations of evidence into a narrative consistent with our perceptions of the past.

In responding to the arguments of other scholars, I have often had recourse to using Ockham's Razor – the principle that history should not require the existence of people or events for which there is no direct evidence. For example, if an ancient royal tomb is found in modern times inscribed and decorated throughout for the burial of one king, we could not prove that no other king had been buried in the same tomb at an earlier date: but why should we suppose that this earlier burial had ever occurred? The answer, of course, is that, without direct evidence, we should not (see *Chapter Three*). Whilst what 'the Razor' yields is not absolute fact, it is a valuable tool for gauging the success of a particular historical explanation.

I take the view that it is certainly possible and reasonable to write a history of the Israelites based on the evidence provided by archaeology and the narrative texts. My point of departure from the stance of Thomas L. Thompson, for example, is my preparedness to accept that the Old Testament narratives are as valid a source for ancient history as any other ancient document. I am prepared to do so on the following grounds:

- *All* ancient documents are written by humans, and therefore embody the beliefs, aspirations and traditions of a particular culture. They are also, of course, susceptible to errors of fact, political bias, economy of truth and miscopying.

- The only way that an interpreter of a document (i.e. an historian) can judge the validity of any 'historical' statement contained in that document is by crosschecking the details of the statement against other independent documentation or, in a more general context, against archaeological evidence. If a particular interpretation of the statement is shown to be consistent with the overall pattern of evidence, then it becomes an 'historical fact' and may be utilised in an historical construction.

- The Old Testament is a compilation of ancient documents. It is at least in part the story of a nation. The only way to determine if it contains 'historical facts' is by employing the same criteria used for any other ancient document. If interpretations of independent texts and archaeological evidence are consistent with the non-miraculous and non-allegorical elements in the narratives then an historian is justified in employing them in his history.

- The objective of this book is to argue straightforwardly that the narratives contained in the Old Testament are consistent with the general cultural setting revealed through Egyptian and Levantine archaeology – once the correct chronology is applied.

I have little doubt that those who think like Professor Thompson will regard my approach as 'fundamentalist' – but this book is not written for them. They may wish to treat it as a work of pure fiction – a view to which I have no objection: this book is intended to be entertaining in the spirit of Herodotus' stories about the Greeks. But it is my firm belief that in this sense the story I have to tell is no different in character to the stories of more orthodox scholars. Even the standard reference work for students of the subjects which make up Old World Studies – *The Cambridge Ancient History* – only represents the conventions of scholars considered to be pre-eminent in their respective disciplines: but it is not the past itself. History is not a simple, single reality but a complex, living response to the evidence of our own past.

***

Before beginning our adventure, I finally need to explain one or two practical steps I have taken in *A Test of Time* to aid the reader through what may well be unfamiliar territory.

I have provided several forms of notes to supply information beyond that contained in the main body of the text. References to source material, books and papers are to be found in the *Notes and References* section at the end of this book. Please note that the embedded reference numbers are separately numbered for each chapter. In addition, you will have already observed that certain words are printed in small capitals. Explanations of these words and expressions, which may be unfamiliar to the reader, are provided in the *Glossary* also towards the back of the book.

Until we reach the section of the book which deals with the revision of Egyptian chronology – a task which is necessary to reveal the historical Bible – I have employed the dates calculated by Kenneth Kitchen for the pharaohs from Dynasties 11 to 25 (taken from *The Third Intermediate Period in Egypt*, 2nd ed., and his paper given at the *High, Middle or Low?* Colloquium held at the University of Gothenberg in 1987). For Dynasties 1 to 10 I have used dates supplied by John Baines and Járomír Malek in their *Atlas of Ancient Egypt*. The two dating systems are not altogether compatible (the Baines and Malek dates being based on a slightly higher chronology than that of Kitchen) but I am unable to use Kitchen throughout as, to my knowledge, he has not published dates prior to the 11th Dynasty. For biblical chronology I have made use of the now well-accepted dates published in Edwin Thiele's *The Mysterious Numbers of the Hebrew Kings* for the period from the Babylonian Exile back to the reign of Solomon.

Needless to say, when revised dates also begin to be introduced into the discussion, things could start to get a little complicated. To ensure that such potential for misunderstanding is kept to a minimum, when we come to the part of this book where New Chronology dates are also being used, I have distinguished the 'orthodox' or 'conventional' dating of Kitchen, Baines and Malek by appending 'OC' (for orthodox chronology) before the date and by adding 'NC' (for New Chronology) to the new revised dates being proposed here. I trust that this will avoid any confusion.

I suppose this would be an appropriate place to stress that *A Test of Time* is intended as a 'popular book' on the New Chronology theory which does not, therefore, cover *all* the arguments. For the same reason, I have left out much of the detail in respect of the issues which *are* covered here.

As I have said, one of the most difficult things about writing a book of this kind is knowing what to include and what to leave out. I trust that I have found the right balance and that the reader will make his final judgement on the research presented in *A Test of Time* on the basis of the cohesion of the entire theory rather than any single element which may or may not be dealt with fully here.

Part One

Conundrums of the Pharaohs

The Major Anomalies of Egyptian Chronology

Chapter One

THE SEARCH FOR APIS

The Discovery

n the 2nd of October 1850 a twenty-nine-year-old Frenchman, Auguste MARIETTE, attached to the Louvre Museum's Department of Egyptian Antiquities, found himself in Cairo with instructions to negotiate the purchase of COPTIC, Ethiopic and Syriac manuscripts.

Whilst whiling away his time in Egypt, waiting for the uncooperative Coptic Patriarchate to release the manuscripts, he observed that a number of small limestone sphinxes had recently come onto the antiquities market – very saleable artefacts which had soon been purchased for the private collections of the wealthy residents of Cairo and Alexandria. Mariette's enquiries led him to the conclusion that they had all come from the salerooms of an Italian dealer named Fernandez. Drawing upon all his powers of persuasion, Auguste Mariette eventually succeeded in getting Fernandez to divulge that the

4. AUGUSTE MARIETTE: (1821-1881).

55

sphinxes had recently been removed from the ancient Memphite necropolis of SAKKARA. This information appears to have remained in the forefront of Mariette's mind during those early days in Cairo and may have been the catalyst for the sudden change of plan which found him heading out of Cairo and into the history books as the first great Egyptologist-excavator.

As the warm October days of 1850 drifted slowly by and the negotiations for the Coptic manuscripts dragged on interminably, Mariette found himself with plenty of time on his hands. So it was that he ended up one evening visiting the Citadel of SALAH ED-DIN (Saladin), overlooking the city, to take in the magnificent view of the Giza Pyramids above and beyond the haze of Old Cairo. This appears to have been the crucial turning point in his life:

> ... the stillness was extraordinary. At my feet lay the city. Upon it a thick and heavy fog seemed to have settled covering all the houses to the rooftops. From this deep sea rose three hundred minarets like masts from some submerged fleet. Far away, towards the south, one could perceive the palm groves that rise from the fallen ruins of Memphis. To the west, bathed in the gold and flaming dust of the sunset, were the pyramids. The view was superb. It held me and absorbed me with a violence that was almost painful. The moment was decisive. Before my eyes lay Giza, Abusir, Sakkara, Dashur, Mit-Rahina. This life-long dream of mine was materialising. Over there, practically within my grasp, was a whole world of tombs, stelae, inscriptions, statues. What more can I say? The next day I hired two or three mules for my luggage, one or two donkeys for myself; I had bought a tent, a few cases of provisions, all the necessities for a trip to the desert and, on the 20th of October 1850, I pitched my tent at the foot of the Great Pyramid ...[1]

A week later Mariette had moved a few kilometres up the Nile valley to Sakkara – the dramatic desert necropolis situated to the west of the ancient pharaonic capital of Memphis.

Sakkara continues to hold its visitors in awe, not so much because of the size or magnificence of the monuments – the majority of which are relatively unspectacular by Egyptian standards – but because of the ageless desolation of its sandy terrain. In spite of the intensive excavation work which has gone on all over the necropolis since Mariette's arrival, there is still the feeling that beneath the sand and rubble much more is yet to be discovered. Over the years Egyptologists have unearthed tombs for all periods in Egyptian history from the low mudbrick 'royal' MASTABAS of the 1st Dynasty[2] to the great rock-cut shafts of the Saite and Persian periods. Of the four huge 3rd Dynasty enclosures which have been detected under the sands of the western desert at Sakkara only two (those of DJOSER and SEKHEMKHET) have been thoroughly investigated. The others still tenaciously guard their secrets and even the identities of the kings who built them remain unknown. Some nine pyramid tombs of the pharaohs have been discovered and entered, but there are also literally thousands of non-royal tombs which honeycomb the soft limestone rock lying beneath the sand. The concentration of burials is astonishing with older tombs regularly reused for later interments. As often as not, archaeologists uncover the shaft of a New Kingdom tomb to find it crammed full of coffins from the Late Period. The burial population of Sakkara is unmatched by any other site in Egypt. One should not forget that this was the necropolis which served ancient Memphis – the main administrative centre of Egypt for the best part of two thousand years.

Back in the early months of 1851 it was at Sakkara that Mariette made one of the most important discoveries of Egyptology. On a day spent wandering around the mounds and depressions of the Sakkara ruin-field, he came across the head of a sphinx protruding out of the sand to the north of the Djoser Step Pyramid complex. Mariette recognised that it was identical to those he had seen in Cairo and Alexandria, but this time he had been fortunate to locate one *in situ*. Immediately his Classical training, deeply impressed into a receptive mind during his school days at the Collège de Boulogne, was brought into play, for the words of the Augustan geographer and traveller, STRABO, came echoing back to him:

> One finds [at Memphis], a temple to SERAPIS in such a sandy place that the wind heaps up sand dunes beneath which we saw sphinxes, some half-buried, some buried up to the head, from which one can suppose that the way to this temple could not be without danger if one were caught in a sudden wind-storm.[3]

Mariette immediately set about hiring a team of thirty villagers to clear the desert sand and, on the 1st of November 1850, the workmen's shovels began to remove the wind-blown centuries which had concealed Strabo's trail to the sacred burial ground of the Apis bulls.

The Apis bull had been worshipped in Egypt from the earliest times because the bull was a potent symbol of fertility and strength – and therefore of kingship. Apis was the physical embodiment of PTAH, chief deity of Memphis. But he was also a manifestation of the River Nile and Hapi, god of the inundation. The Apis bull participated in the great HEB SED jubilee of the king when he performed the running ceremony beside the pharaoh. In this respect he is represented as one of the three living embodiments of the Egyptian king in the animal world (along with the falcon and the lion). When Apis died, just as was the case with the king, he became Osiris, god of the dead and, as such, received a magnificent burial at Sakkara. There could only be one living Apis at any one time. Upon his demise the

5. Mariette's map of the Serapeum showing the long avenue of sphinxes (1) leading from the Sakkara escarpment (2) to the Dromos (3) and Temple of Apis (4). Other features include the northern part of the Djoser Step Pyramid complex (5), the pyramids of Userkaf (6) and Teti (7), and the Anubeion enclosure (8).

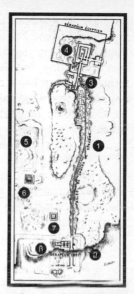

priests of Memphis would be despatched in search of the reincarnation of the recently deceased Apis. Their task was to find a new-born calf which had the special physical markings that distinguished it as the reborn god: an inverted white triangle on its forehead, white markings resembling a vulture over the shoulders and a falcon round the rump, a tufted tail, and the configuration of a scarab beetle on the tongue. Eventually the young calf would be brought in triumphant procession to his special 'Apis House', located within the enclosure of the great Ptah Temple at Memphis. There, during his eighteen-year (average) lifespan, the bull would regularly receive petitioners as he stood at his 'window of appearance', bedecked in the finery befitting a god of Egypt. When the bull died it received a 'royal' burial, the great funeral procession heading up to the Serapeum on the desert ridge overlooking Memphis. There the remains of Apis were interred in the underground vaults along with the dedicatory stelae of the officials and funerary offerings including USHABTI figurines. The cult of Apis continued right down into the HELLENISTIC PERIOD when it became transmuted into the popular cult of Serapis.

After days of effort, Mariette's small team had successfully exposed a long avenue of one hundred and thirty-four sphinxes, dating to the time of NECTANEBO I, which led westwards from the cultivation zone towards the Libyan desert. His conviction that this must be the ceremonial way leading to the Serapeum of the Classical writings inspired Mariette to press on, in spite of diminishing funds, in an attempt to reach his goal before being forced to explain his actions to his superiors back in Paris.

At one point the avenue of sphinxes came to an abrupt end – much to Mariette's initial disappointment. It was not long, however, before the discovery of another sphinx, at right-angles to the others, led the workmen to a hemicycle of Greek statues (the STIBADEION)[4] including those of the great philosophers and poets of the Hellenistic period. Here were assembled such honoured personages as Pindar, Plato, Protagoras and Homer, presiding over the way of pilgrimage to the great cult centre of the Serapeum itself. Soon his workmen had uncovered, immediately to the east, the remains of a temple built by NECTANEBO II with inscriptions showing that the building was indeed dedicated to the cult of Serapis. Now the young Frenchman knew for certain he was on the right track and so he pressed on with even greater vigour. Working westwards once more, another

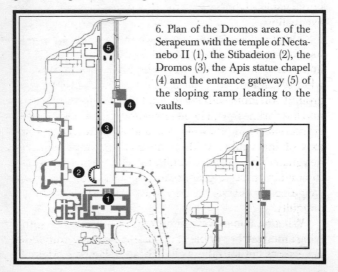

6. Plan of the Dromos area of the Serapeum with the temple of Nectanebo II (1), the Stibadeion (2), the Dromos (3), the Apis statue chapel (4) and the entrance gateway (5) of the sloping ramp leading to the vaults.

avenue revealed itself, but this time it was paved and lined with a low dressed wall on both north and south sides. Stone statues of animals, birds and humans had been placed on the walls on either side of this DROMOS and, beneath the paving stones (which Mariette removed in his search for the Serapeum entrance) he found hundreds of bronze statuettes of bulls. In a small chapel on the north side of the Dromos Mariette discovered an exquisite life-size statue of an Apis bull calf – a masterful sculpture from the LATE PERIOD of Egyptian history.

The Museum authorities back in Paris had now learnt of their employee's activities at Sakkara, but they were so delighted by the discoveries being made that all thoughts of a reprimand rapidly diminished and, indeed, a further sum of thirty thousand francs was despatched to support Mariette's excavations.

Finally, on the 12th of November 1851, following the exposure of the foundations of a pylon-gateway and enclosure wall within which the remains of the actual Late Period Apis temple were located, Auguste Mariette entered the burial vaults of the Serapeum, a full year after commencing excavations.[5]

The long descending entrance ramp of the Serapeum took the excavator down to a great doorway. Beyond that impressive portal of the sacred bulls Mariette discovered what seemed to be a maze built by giants. Long underground corridors with barrel-vaulted ceilings stretched off into the darkness with huge sepulchral chambers dispersed at intervals along their lengths and at right-angles to the axis of the vaults. Within the section which Mariette designated the 'Greater Vaults' the chambers were found to contain massive granite and basalt sarcophagi, some weighing as much as seventy tons.[6] All had been rifled in antiquity.

What remained were hundreds of votive STELAE, either lying amongst the rubble of the passageways or embedded in recesses cut into the walls. These stelae had originally

7. The grand gallery of the Greater Vaults of the Serapeum not long after the discovery in 1851. Engraving from *Le Sérapéum de Memphis*, published by Mariette.

been placed in the vaults by the priests of Ptah, the workmen who had excavated the tombs of Apis and the officials responsible for the funeral of the sacred bull. Occasionally a royal stela was also set up in the sealing wall of the Apis burial chamber. In placing their stelae within the tomb of Apis, the donors could expect their petitions and prayers to be favourably considered by OSIRIS-APIS in anticipation of their own journey into the netherworld. The stelae thus contained dedications to the god and were sometimes dated by the regnal years of the monarch in whose reign the sacred bull had been buried. This data would provide scholars with supportive evidence for the chronological sequence and reign lengths of the pharaohs from the Apis burial in Year 52 of PSAMTEK I (first king of the 26th Dynasty) through to the reign of Ptolemy (Euergetes) VII who ruled between 170 and 163 BC and again between 145 and 116 BC (following his earlier exile). The information thus obtained by Mariette from the Greater Vaults stelae corroborated the dates and order of kings, as given by Manetho (the Egyptian priest who served under PTOLEMY I), and helped to fix the history of Egypt from 610 BC (Year 52 of Psamtek) onwards to an accuracy of within one year.

But this was not all that Auguste Mariette unearthed in that momentous year of 1851. At the eastern end of the main gallery of the Greater Vaults, he discovered a further underground network of corridors and chambers belonging to an earlier period – dating from the middle of the 19th Dynasty to the end of the Third Intermediate Period. He gave this part of the Serapeum the designation 'Lesser Vaults', and began clearing the sepulchres of the Apis bulls on the 11th of February 1852.

Just as was the case in the Greater Vaults, Mariette discovered here numerous dedicatory funerary stelae – two hundred and thirty-eight in all – mounted in the walls of the main south to north corridor and in chaotic piles at either extremity of the main gallery; a crucial few were embedded in the partly sealed blocking walls of the sepulchres themselves. The information contained on the stelae in this section of the Vaults should have provided much needed help in unravelling the chronology of the 19th to 25th Dynasties – but alas this was not to be, as poor excavation techniques, historical misconceptions and sheer bad luck contributed to the establishment of what remains today an insecure chronology.

In fact, from an archaeological standpoint the excavation of the Lesser Vaults was little short of a calamity. Scant information has come down to modern scholarship to determine exactly how many Apis burials were discovered or, for that matter, what evidence Mariette found to attribute the different regnally-dated bull burials to each of the sepulchres. This information was never published and his excavation diary, which contained the vital material, has been missing now for over a century (see below). Researchers must therefore rely almost entirely on Mariette's simple plan of the Serapeum (the original of which is housed in the Bibliothèque Nationale in Paris[7]) to determine the sequence and locations of the Apis burials. We have little choice but to trust in his accuracy.

It is not really surprising that the exact locations of much of the Lesser Vaults material remain uncertain, for the chaos which greeted Mariette as he broke into these earlier Apis vaults is quite apparent from his own vivid description:

> The walls are covered with stelae, you walk on statuettes of all colours, on vases, on fragments of wooden sarcophagi. All this is in dreadful disorder, … I came upon … such a disorder that at first sight I despaired of ever recognising anything.[8]

The excavation of the Lesser Vaults continued throughout February, March and April. A further short season in late August and September 1852 resulted in the discovery, near-by, of a third group of isolated burial chambers for the Apis bulls which died between the time of AMENHOTEP III and Year 16 of RAMESSES II.

Having, in his own mind, completed the work at the Serapeum, Mariette moved on to other areas of the Sakkara necropolis in search of tombs, never to return to the vaults of the sacred bulls for further work. A huge collection of some eight hundred stelae was transported to the Louvre where it remains today, still, as yet, not fully studied, although this work is now in progress. The bulk of the remaining four hundred stelae were housed in the BULAK MUSEUM in Cairo where subsequently the majority were destroyed by flooding resulting from a severe inundation of the Nile in 1878. Only thirty survived to be transferred to the Cairo and Alexandria Museums where they remain today.[9]

Auguste Mariette himself went on to excavate more than twenty sites in Egypt over his long and distinguished career. The Egyptian government appointed him Director General of the newly established EGYPTIAN ANTIQUITIES SERVICE (EAS) set up to protect the pharaonic and Islamic

8. A massive granite sarcophagus abandoned in one of the main galleries of the Greater Vaults. Engraving from *Le Sérapéum de Memphis*, published by Mariette.

remains from plunderers and to conserve for posterity what was being uncovered by the excavators. Perhaps Mariette's greatest achievement, however, was the foundation of that enormous warehouse of treasures known as the Museum of Egyptian Antiquities or simply the Cairo Museum.

Little further research at the Serapeum has been undertaken in the intervening years. Although the Greater Vaults were opened to visitors soon after their discovery, the entrance-way to the Lesser Vaults was quickly covered by windblown sand and completely hidden. Thus the interior of this earlier burial complex remained very much in the state which Mariette had left it in 1852. Now, however, the Lesser Vaults are being re-excavated by Mohamed Ibrahim Aly and his team of archaeologists from the Supreme Council of Antiquities (formerly the Egyptian Antiquities Organisation). A number of significant finds have come to light during the first two seasons' work, including a further seventy-three stelae completely missed by Mariette's workmen.[10]

It is in this section of the tomb of Apis that our first major archaeological conundrum came to light back in 1852 – the first clue to suggest that something was amiss with the modern interpretation of Egyptian chronology.

The Puzzle

In April 1986 I flew to Cairo because news had reached me that the Egyptian Antiquities Organisation were in the process of re-excavating the Serapeum Lesser Vaults. On the 15th of April I found myself standing at the edge of the desert escarpment at Sakkara, waiting for the arrival of the Director of the Sakkara Inspectorate. The view eastwards across the Nile valley was spectacular with its verdant sea of tall date palms stretching over to the ancient limestone quarries of TURA in the far distance. The previous day I had spoken to Mohamed Ibrahim Aly on the phone and he had very kindly agreed to show me the work currently being undertaken by his Serapeum excavation team. As the minutes passed by, sitting on the steps which lead into the shady courtyard of the EAO offices, I contemplated what I might see in the coming hours. Over several years of research I had come to realise that the Lesser Vaults had retained many of their secrets – secrets which had, for over a century, patiently awaited the methods and technology of modern archaeology.

At about eight o'clock I glanced towards the southern

desert horizon to see what appeared to be a small sandstorm billowing up in the distance, then a brilliant flash as the sun's rays glanced off the windscreen of a four-wheel-drive jeep which suddenly emerged at breakneck speed from behind a sandy hollow. The white jeep shimmered in the heat haze as it hurtled along the desert track, throwing great clouds of dust and sand into the air. Finally it came to a slithering halt before the EAO inspectorate buildings and out stepped the Director of Sakkara with a broad smile upon his face. After the customary welcome drink of Egyptian tea, and in the wake of a flurry of signatures on documents and papers, Mohamed got up from behind his large desk and announced that it was time to go and inspect the morning's activities at the Serapeum. Because the excavations had only recently commenced and nothing had so far been published, I was politely asked to leave my cameras behind, so I have no visual record of that remarkable morning in April 1986 when I became the first westerner since Mariette to enter the Lesser Vaults of the sacred Apis bulls.

As we walked down the slope from the ruin of Mariette's dig house the Egyptian archaeologist and the English Egyptologist talked over the news which had just broken the previous night. American planes had bombed Libya and there was a sharp increase in tension throughout the Near East. We contemplated how this incident would affect Egypt and the possible implications for archaeological missions working in the Nile valley. We were soon at the edge of a deep vertical cutting in the mother rock of the Sakkara necropolis. As I looked down into that entrance to the netherworld a chaotic scene of epic proportions greeted my eyes.

The noise and dust was overwhelming as scores of men in white *galabeyas* scurried to and fro with ZAMBEELS full of sand and rubble wedged between neck and shoulder. At one end of the narrow defile was a dark rectangular hole – the ancient entrance to the long-lost Lesser Vaults of Apis.

Mohamed led the way down a rickety ladder which plunged towards the floor of the man-made canyon. The supervising EAO inspectors hurried out from the darkness of the vaults to greet their Director and his visitor.

The next two hours were spent looking at Mohamed's finds and the area of the vaults relieved of debris. Several new discoveries had already been made in the first thirty metres of the central corridor and the three chambers so far cleared. Evidence for the existence of a previously un-recorded bull burial from the 25th Dynasty had been found and numerous votive objects, including beautiful Apis-headed ushabtis, were coming to light. Most important, however, is the discovery of the hidden entrance to a burial chamber which Mariette had been searching for but could not find. It is hoped that further clearance of the catacomb will clarify Mariette's findings so that the problem I am about to outline can be solved once and for all.

Chaos and Confusion

When Mariette first undertook excavation work at Sakkara he was still in his late twenties and without previous ar-chaeological experience. In those days, tomb clearance and analysis of finds *in situ* were crude operations. It was not until the twentieth century that archaeology became a more exacting science. A modern Egyptologist, in research-ing the Serapeum excavations, might therefore expect inaccuracies to have crept into the Serapeum archaeological report which was finally published (posthumously) in the 1880s. But, unfortunately, the reality turns out to be consid-erably worse than that. Whilst Mariette had continued his work in other parts of Egypt his invaluable excavation diary, recording the finds and their provenance during the clearance of the Serapeum, was sent to the Louvre where it was later 'borrowed' by Eugène GRÉBAUT, future head of the Cairo Museum. (Grébaut was later to gain a reputation for his abrasive style and less than honest dealings with

other Egyptologists. He finally resigned from the Directorship of the Cairo Museum in 1892, returning to a teaching
post at the Sorbonne.) The loan of Mariette's 'Journal des
Fouilles' in 1882 to this notorious scholar resulted in a great
loss to archaeology, for it was never to be seen again.[11]

As I have mentioned, the main archaeological report
of the Serapeum excavations was not published until 1882
and had to be compiled by the new head of the Egyptian
Antiquities Service, Gaston MASPERO, following Mariette's
death. Maspero had to produce *Le Sérapéum de Memphis*
from an incomplete manuscript left by the discoverer – a
thankless task which could only compound the inaccuracies
already inherent in Mariette's archaeological methodology.

It was not until 1968 that the first volume of a comprehensive catalogue of the Serapeum stelae, containing the
monuments attributed to the late 18th to early 20th Dynas
ties, was finally published.[12] This first volume covers the
stelae of the isolated tombs and the Lesser Vaults whilst
those from the Greater Vaults await publication. The
authors of the new catalogue found it necessary to re-assign
a number of stelae to different dynasties, as Mariette or
Maspero had apparently incorrectly attributed them in the
original publication.[13]

The Stelae

The 1968 *Catalogue des Stèle du Sérapéum de Memphis* contains
descriptions of two hundred and fifty-one stelae of which
the first thirteen originate from the isolated tombs outside
the main vaults. From the remaining two hundred and
thirty-eight, about fifty percent can be attributed securely
to specific kings and a still smaller percentage contain actual
year dates from those rulers. The rest of the stelae must be
assigned on a more general basis using comparative analysis
techniques. (The contents of the inscriptions and style of
dedicatory text can give certain clues as to when a particular
donation stela was made.[14])

The majority of the stelae have rounded tops in which a scene of the worship of Apis is either carved or simply painted, depending on the importance and wealth of the donor. In the bottom half of the stela the dedication text is inscribed, naming the donor and sometimes a short genealogy. As already mentioned, a small proportion of the more important stelae also contain the name of the king, the year in which the bull was buried and, in some special cases, the date of INDUCTION of the bull and his age at death (see page 71).[15]

From the dedication stelae and other objects such as inscribed jars we can build up a list of pharaohs in whose reigns the Apis burials took place. Thus it would appear to be a relatively simple operation to formulate a chronology for the period of the Lesser Vaults from the compiled data; but archaeology and its interpretation (i.e. 'history') is never that simple!

One so far inexplicable aspect of the finds from the Serapeum is the complete lack of stelae for the whole of 21st Dynasty and for the first half of the 22nd Dynasty. Of the three hundred and eleven stelae found in the Lesser Vaults (including the seventy-three recently unearthed) not one single inscription can be attributed to the kings from SMENDES to TAKELOT I – a period assumed to have lasted around one hundred and ninety-five years. A time span of this length should have provided at least ten or eleven burials (the average age of the bulls being eighteen years[16]). We should therefore possess a number of stelae or other inscriptions with the names of the kings of this period on them – yet none were found.

Apart from the complete lack of stelae for the 21st Dynasty, there is a further argument which indicates that there is a clear problem with TIP chronology. This problem is perhaps best explained by listing six simple points:

1. The archaeology of the Lesser Vaults spans a time period beginning with the burial of an Apis in the

Typical Chronological Data
from the Lesser Vaults Stelae

The two documents recorded on Apis Stelae 21 and 22 provide the following historical information:

Stela No. 21

The stela was donated by the Great Chief (*wer aa*) of Ma (*Mau* – the shortened form of MESHWESH), Pediese, son of the Great Chief of Ma, Takelot, son of the HPM, Prince and Chief Noble of His Majesty (*iry-pat wer tepy en hemef*), Shoshenk, son of King Osorkon-meryamun.

The death of the Apis bull occurred in Year 28 of King Usermaatre-setepenamun Shoshenk meryamun Si-Bast.

(The installation (induction) date of the Apis bull not given.)

(The age at death of the bull also not given.)

Stela No. 22

This stela was donated by the Controller of Crafts (*wer kherep hemut*), Setem-priest in the Estate of Ptah (*setem em per Ptah*), Great Chief of the Meshwesh (*wer aa en-na Meshwesh*), Pediese, son of (same titles), Takelot.

(Egyptologists have concluded that this Pediese, son of Takelot, is the same Chief of Ma who dedicated Stela 21.)

This Apis was installed in Year 28 of King Usermaatre-setepenre Shoshenk-meryamun, following the death of his predecessor (recorded in Stela No. 21). (The epithets 'setepenamun' and 'setepenre' are interchangeable in this period, whilst the inclusion of the epithet 'Si-Bast' in Shoshenk's CARTOUCHE is also fairly arbitrary. There is no doubt that we are dealing here with the same king, otherwise identified as Shoshenk III.)

The Apis died in Year 2 of King Usermaatre-setepenamun Pimay at an age of 26 years.

From amongst all this valuable information we can be certain that Pimay ascended the throne 25 years after the 28th year of Shoshenk III, and that these monarchs reigned four and three generations, respectively, after a King Osorkon. This example illustrates the importance of the Apis stelae for fixing the reign-lengths and therefore chronology of the TIP.

Table of Apis Burials
Represented in the Lesser Vaults

Apis burials in the Lesser Vaults for which some archaeological evidence exists:

1. Ramesses II (Year 30) – Stela 5

2. Ramesses II (Year ??) – Mariette's attribution

3. Ramesses II (Year ??) – Mariette's attribution

4. Ramesses II (Year 55?) – Chamber K? graffito

5. Ramesses II (Year ??) – Mariette's attribution

6. Ramesses-Siptah (Year ??) – inscribed jar

7. Ramesses III (Year ??) – Mariette's attribution

8. Ramesses VI (Year ??) – inscribed jar

9. Ramesses IX (Year ??) – inscribed jar

10. Ramesses XI (Year ??) – Mariette's attribution

11. Ramesses XI (Year ??) – Mariette's attribution

12. Ramesses XI (Year ??) – Mariette's attribution

13. Takelot I (Year ??) – inscribed block (Stela 19)

14. Osorkon II (Year 23) – Stela 18

15. Shoshenk III (Year 28) – Stela 21

16. Pimay (Year 2) – Stela 22

17. Shoshenk V (Year 11) – Stela 27

18. Shoshenk V (Year 37) – Stela 31

19. Bakenranef (Year 6) – Stela 91

20. Taharka? (Year 4) – Stela 129[17]

21. Taharka (Year 14) – newly discovered stela[18]

22. Taharka (Year 24) – Stela 125

23. Psamtek I (Year 21) – Stela 192

Total of 23 burials spanning a period of 606 years in the orthodox chronology.

thirtieth year of Ramesses II, conventionally dated to 1250 BC.[19] The period ends with the interment of the Apis bull which died in the twentieth year of Psamtek I. This last burial is conventionally dated to 644 BC after which the Lesser Vaults are closed.[20]

2. The excavations of the Lesser Vaults produced evidence for a maximum of twenty-three Apis burials.

3. The average life-span of an Apis bull has been determined at eighteen years.

4. If we simply multiply the twenty-two periods of eighteen years which exist between the burial of the first Apis and that of the last, we get a figure of three hundred and ninety-six years for the duration of the Lesser Vaults burial activities – based on the archaeological data.

5. However, in the conventional chronology, a straightforward calculation (1250 minus 644) provides us with a duration for the period under discussion of six hundred and six years.

6. Clearly this is significantly longer than a straightforward interpretation of the archaeological data suggests. The discrepancy is two hundred and ten years!

How could the figures disagree so radically? For the answer we must focus on the kings of the 21st and early 22nd Dynasty, whose names, as mentioned earlier, are conspicuously absent from the archaeological data in the Lesser Vaults. There have been two recent suggestions offered to explain this conundrum. The first is that the burials of Apis bulls were dated to the reigns of these kings, but that they must have been interred elsewhere. To me this is an inherently implausible hypothesis due to the apparent continuity of burials in the Lesser Vaults. It is

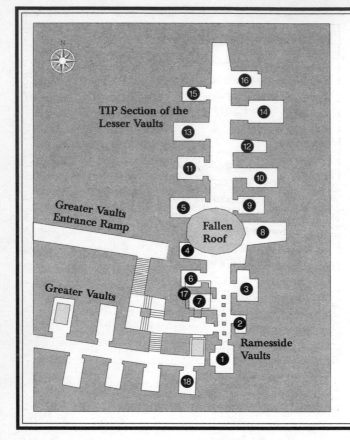

beholden upon the proponents of such an idea to produce tangible evidence of burials dated to any of these ten rulers, and they must also explain why kings, from Osorkon II onwards, then returned to the old vaults, which remained in use for at least another two centuries.[21] The second explanation is certainly more substantial: that the burial cult actually broke down for a time during a politically unstable period. A parallel might be drawn from the results of excavation work undertaken by Professor Harry Smith in

The Lesser Vaults of the Serapeum

1. Ramesses II (2 Apis? – after Yr 30)
2. Ramesside & then Late TIP
3. Ramesside (incl. Siptah?)
4. Ramesses II (around Yr 55)
5. Ramesses III
6. Ramesses IX (?)
7. Ramesses XI (3 or 5 Apis?)
8. An abandoned passage?
9. Takelot I (Yr 14) (?) & Osorkon II (Yr 23)
10. Shoshenk III (yr 28) & Pimay (Yr 2)
11. Shoshenk V (Yr 11)
12. Shoshenk V (Yr 37)
13. Bakenranef (Yr 6) & Shabaka (Yr 2?)
14. Taharka (Yr 4) & Taharka (Yr 14)
15. Taharka (Yr 24)
16. Psamtek I (Yr 21)
17. Lower chamber with 3 unidentified Apis
18. Psamtek I (Yr 52) – in the Greater Vaults

9. Plan of the Lesser Vaults with Mariette's location of the Apis burials dated to the reigns of the pharaohs from Ramesses II to Psamtek I.

the vaults of the MOTHER OF APIS, where no burials have been found for the years between 486 and 393 BC – an interval of ninety-three years, or five missing cows.

But can we arrive at a better solution derived only from the archaeology of the Serapeum itself without invoking events for which there is no direct evidence? Just such a potential solution revolves around a strange discovery made by Mariette during his final months at the Lesser Vaults.

A Hidden Chamber

As mentioned earlier, Mariette near the end of his work appears to have found an even deeper vault. It was located beneath Chamber 7 which housed the Apis burials of the late 20th Dynasty. The bad air and continuous infilling of sand forced Mariette to abandon his efforts to reach the floor of the lower vault and it remains uncleared to this day. I shall let Mariette himself describe the difficulties which he encountered in making this new discovery:

> During the clearing of the chamber in which the five previous Apis had been enclosed, certain indications gave rise to the suspicion that there was a second chamber underneath the first. A vertical shaft was sunk in the floor and, it turned out, there was an empty space beneath into which I descended. The new chamber was full up to the vault. A candle in each hand, I advanced, creeping my back against the ceiling and my belly on the sand. The heat was suffocating, and the air so rarefied that the candles were extinguished. I had to go back and give up the exploration of our new conquest for that day. The following day, I had the sand removed via the vertical shaft using our ordinary excavation equipment. But we soon realised that the walls, which had been intended to hold up the crumbling vaults, were built on the same sand and the enterprise had to be totally abandoned. The result of the operation, however, was that we were able to prove that the lower vault had been inhabited by three Apis; their graves, constructed with the same negligence as the upper chamber, provided the only data upon which I can rely in order to assign the construction of this chamber to a date close to that of the Apis of Ramesses XIV [Ramesses XI in modern terminology]. Otherwise, even the door of the lower chamber

remains unknown; with more expense and perseverance, perhaps we might have obtained results which would have made our effort worthwhile. However this may be, I conjecture that the three new Apis belong to the 21st Dynasty.[22]

Could this hidden chamber be the resting place of the 'missing' bulls of the early TIP – as Mariette himself concluded? Even if his three burials do represent part of the early TIP Apis cult, this still leaves us with nine 'missing' bulls. Do Mariette's three bulls belong to the 21st Dynasty, or are they perhaps the missing Apis of the early 22nd Dynasty? Clearly, the puzzle cannot be resolved in its entirety by this intriguing discovery, or potential discovery to be more precise, since the identification of the intact Apis burials is a prize still awaiting Mohamed and his team of EAO excavators. Whatever the case, a discrepancy remains of at least one hundred and sixty years between the conventional chronology and the historical conclusions which can be drawn from Mariette's remarkable discoveries in the Serapeum.

If this anomaly stood alone, then perhaps we might be able to dismiss it. But when I undertook my pilgrimage to the Serapeum in 1986, my other research had already led me to realise that an unexpected solution to the riddle of the 'missing' Apis was at hand.

Conclusion One

The archaeological evidence derived from the Lesser Vaults of the Serapeum suggests that the length of the Third Intermediate Period may have been artificially over-extended by historians.

Chapter Two

SECRET OF THE PHARAOHS

A detailed description of the initial discovery of the Royal Cache by the Abd er-Rassul brothers, recorded in their own words, has not survived. The story given here is therefore an account which has been assembled from various sources including the archaeological reports of Maspero,[1] contemporary writers' commentaries,[2] the summaries of later scholars,[3] and interviews with the living descendants of the Abd er-Rassul family still residing in Gurna village today.

The Discovery

hmed Abd er-Rassul regularly took the short cut to the Valley of the Kings from his father's large whitewashed mudbrick home in the village where his ancestors had lived for centuries. The strenuous climb, known today as 'AGATHA CHRISTIE'S PATH', is not recommended for those who suffer from vertigo, but it takes the nimble-footed rapidly to the top of the limestone ridge which overlooks the BIBAN EL-MULUK via a precipitous narrow track just to the south of DEIR EL-BAHRI. This quickest of routes to the tombs of the pharaohs begins its ascent of the great western mountain of MERETSEGER from behind the low hill of Sheikh Abd el-Gurna – a lump of white limestone, honeycombed with the tombs of the nobles who had administered on behalf of the Egyptian

10. The mummy of Ramesses II as it was found in the Royal Cache, re-wrapped by the 21st Dynasty priests.

crown in holy Thebes during the New Kingdom. Ahmed's village was spread out at the foot of this mound of the dead, the houses of the inhabitants having been built over the rock-cut sepulchres to provide cellars for the storage of food and 'valuables' (many of which had been purloined from the original owners of the tombs). Of all the villages in nineteenth-century Egypt, this meandering, ramshackle place was the abode of the tomb robbers *par excellence*.

A sinewy mountain-goat-of-a-man, Ahmed was the second eldest of the Rassul brothers, all five of whom were employed as sometime DRAGOMEN for the tourists visiting the great Theban necropolis. However, they had another 'side-line' which supplemented the meagre income derived from a burgeoning tourist industry.

Ahmed had often scrambled his way up the knife-edged spur leading to the top of the cliffs. For some reason on this spring morning in 1871, his attention was drawn to the shadowy recess of a natural rock chimney at the head of the desolate bay in the Libyan desert escarpment. From Ahmed's high vantage point on the ridge, he could see the slender cleft thrusting downwards to a narrow ledge at the base of the chimney. He quickly realised that here was a prime site for another of those remarkable Theban sepulchres of the dead – this one as yet awaiting discovery.

Ahmed hurried back down to the village to tell his brothers what he had seen. Gathering together shovels, reed baskets and a long length of knotted rope, three of the Rassul brothers – Mohamed, Ahmed and Hussein –

set off once again for the lonely valley at the foot of the cliffs. They soon reached the narrow rock cleft.

After a few minutes of shovelling away the windblown sand and debris which filled the bottom of the gully, the edge of a rock-cut shaft appeared. Several hours more digging took the brothers twelve metres down to the base of the roughly-made well. There in the north face they found a low sealed doorway. As they began to dismantle the wall of limestone blocks which prevented their entry into the tomb, the warm dry air — last breathed by the funerary priests nearly three millennia before — exhaled from the darkness beyond.

With the last block removed, the three brothers finally found themselves in a narrow one-metre-high corridor. It was crammed with wooden coffins. Tentatively they squeezed past four large mummy cases, accidentally kicking over and scattering smaller funerary objects lying unseen in the dim light as they shuffled towards the unknown. After about seven-and-a-half metres they reached a right-angled turn in the passage which led off in an easterly direction into the darkness. Hussein lit a torch and they penetrated deeper into the tomb — now able to stand erect. Past more coffins in this second longer corridor, they reached a stairway which plunged on downwards. To the left of this stairwell was a small chamber stacked to the ceiling with more than twenty mummiform coffers, many bearing the URAEUS serpent upon their brow. Hussein swept his flaming torch in a broad arc over the macabre scene. The brothers pressed on. Deeper and deeper they went – along a third even longer corridor beyond the stairs and finally into a large burial chamber. The Rassuls were now nearly eighty metres from the entrance of the tomb.

Here they found another ten mummy cases – replete with all the trappings of burial. In the centre of the room lay a beautifully painted anthropoid coffin. Ahmed gently levered open the lid to reveal a second inner coffin of a woman and inside that a small tightly-wrapped mummy bedecked in an ochre shroud. Lying beside the corpse was a large papyrus roll in a perfect state of preservation. Mohamed picked up this magnificent prize and slipped it inside the deep inner pocket of his black galabeya.

Perspiring heavily on account of the concerted efforts to reach their goal and gulping sharp breaths of desperately thin air, the three men set about prising open several of the other coffins in the chamber, relieving each of its sacred papyrus scroll. Although they knew full well that further untold treasures might be awaiting discovery just beneath the mummy wrappings, the brothers were reticent to disturb the long sleep of the dead. So, with the first profits of their momentous discovery stuffed inside his dusty garment, Ahmed led the escape from this dread place, scrambling and slipping in his haste to return to the world of the living.

Twenty-three years after Mariette's sensational discoveries at Sakkara, the second major clue in our investigation was beginning to reveal itself to scholarship. Early in 1874, Mrs. Amelia EDWARDS, a romantic novelist who would soon become the driving force behind the foundation of the British EGYPT EXPLORATION FUND (later Society), was undertaking her famous one-thousand-mile journey up the river Nile from Alexandria to the Second Cataract in NUBIA. Having reached her southerly destination, with only brief stops at the archaeological sites on the way upstream, she began her long return journey back north to the Mediterranean Sea – this time at a more leisurely pace, as was the custom in those early days for Nile exploration. She eventually reached the little town of Luxor (the site of ancient Thebes), for the second time, in March 1874 where she stayed for several weeks.

Within hours of her DAHABIYA mooring alongside the Temple of Luxor, Edwards began to sense the excitement and tension lurking just beneath the surface in this otherwise sleepy community of the east bank at Luxor:

There were whispers about this time of a tomb that had been discovered on the western side – a wonderful tomb, rich in all kinds of treasures. No one, of course, had seen these things. No one knew who had found them. No one knew where they were hidden. But there was a solemn secrecy about certain of the Arabs, and a conscious look about some of the visitors, and an air of awakened vigilance about the government officials, which savoured of mystery.[4]

During the three years immediately prior to Mrs. Amelia Edwards' trip up the Nile, a number of unusual and, more to the point, unprovenanced ancient Egyptian antiquities had been surfacing on the 'antika' markets of the Middle

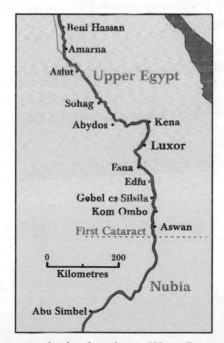

The major towns and archaeological sites of Upper Egypt and Nubia.

East. Two beautifully crafted papyrus scrolls, originally prepared for the funeral of a 21st Dynasty queen named HENTTAWY, had been sold to Mariette on a visit to Suez. During Mrs. Edwards' stay in Luxor, she was offered a papyrus roll replete with its own mummy! Days of protracted negotiations over the sum of BAKSHEESH appropriate for such a trophy ensued before two other English ladies, the Brocklehurst sisters (also doing a Nile cruise), intervened and, as Mrs. Edwards wryly notes, 'bought both mummy and papyrus at an enormous price'. Having purchased this gruesome hoard from certain undisclosed residents of Sheikh Abd el-Gurna, and having had their prize loaded on board the Brocklehurst dahabiya, the ladies set sail for Cairo. However, before the day was out, the mummy, obviously not long from its tomb, began to putrefy in the burning summer heat which hammered mercilessly down upon the deck of the slender sailing vessel. Needless to say, the pitiful corpse of 'the dear departed' met its sorry end in the thick black mud at the bottom of the river, somewhere on the great Kena Bend just to the north of Luxor. Mrs. Edwards and her party had to content themselves with a fine set of blue-glazed ushabti figurines plus a collection of statuettes and vases thrown in for good measure. According to the inscriptions on these artefacts, they had also belonged to the same 21st Dynasty royal family as the two papyri of Queen Henttawy.

In 1876, two years after Amelia Edwards had returned home to England, a funeral papyrus of another 21st Dynasty royal lady – this time Queen NUDJMET – found its way to Beirut. There, in this 'Paris of the Eastern Mediterranean', a dealer named Antoun Wardi was offering sections of the one-hundred-feet-long scroll to the agents of the richer museums of western Europe. (The pieces are now housed in the British Museum, the Louvre in Paris and the Egyptological Museum in Munich.) In the same year Wardi also sold a papyrus of the HIGH PRIEST OF AMUN, PINUDJEM II, to General Archibald Campbell, whilst at about this time ushabtis of the High Priest were turning up in the antique shops of the European capitals. Clearly an important discovery of a hitherto unknown royal tomb, or series of tombs, had been surreptitiously made in the mountains of the west bank at Luxor. The Egyptian Antiquities Service decided upon a determined policy to flush out the culprits.

Two new characters now enter the stage. With Mariette Pasha nearing the end of his life, the French diplomats in Cairo felt the urgent need to line up a 'prince-in-waiting' to take over the Directorship of the Antiquities Service – soon to be relinquished by its great founding father. Their choice – Professor Gaston Maspero of the Collège de France in Paris – arrived by packet steamer at the port of Alexandria in 1881 to take up his post as Director of the newly established French School of Archaeology in Cairo (known today as the Institut Française d'Archéologie Orientale). Within weeks he would become the second Director of the Egyptian Antiquities Service, but, in the meantime, with Mariette on his deathbed, Émil BRUGSCH – a German scholar whom the old Director had appointed as his right-hand man some years earlier – was left in charge of affairs in Bulak. In the weeks which followed Maspero's arrival in Cairo, Brugsch and his colleagues began to devise a plan intended to ascertain the whereabouts of the lost tomb. Their daring strategy involved sending a secret agent to Luxor. There he would let it be known that he was in the market for the acquisition of illicit finds from the Theban necropolis across the river. For this dangerous task Brugsch chose Charles WILBOUR – a retired American businessman, then aged forty-eight. The American arrived in Luxor on the 21st of January 1881.

The British Vice-Consular Agency in Upper Egypt had been in the hands of an Arab of Turkish extraction named Mustafa Aga Ayat for the past four decades. It did not take Wilbour long to discover that this well-liked figure, who had become locally renowned as a lavish entertainer of foreign guests (including royalty), was himself at the very centre of the illegal trade in antiquities. Rumour had it that the treasures of the secret tomb on the west bank were reaching the foreign antiquities' markets through his hands. Aga's consular status meant that he could not be prosecuted for his unlawful transactions, but it would be possible to apprehend and interrogate the Egyptians who had been supplying him with the artefacts – if only Wilbour could finger the culprits during his dealings with Mustafa Aga.

He did not have to wait very long for his quarry to reveal themselves. Whilst wandering through the great HYPOSTYLE HALL at Karnak Temple he was approached by a local dragoman and invited to visit a house on the west bank where 'he might see something to his advantage'. The next day he arrived in the early morning at the door of a large whitewashed house hugging the side of the hill of Sheikh Abd el-Gurna. He was greeted by a sinewy mountain-goat-of-a-man – one Ahmed Abd er-Rassul – who, in the tradition of Egyptian hospitality, politely offered the American several cups of Egyptian tea before producing from the back room a roll of papyrus for Wilbour's examination. The Antiquities Service spy soon knew that he was hot on the trail when he recognised the elder Rassul brother who now entered the room – he had observed Mohamed Abd er-Rassul in the employ of Mustafa Aga at the Vice-Consul's imposing villa, built inside the colonnaded ruins of the Temple of Luxor. The net was beginning to close in on the plunderers and their gang of associates.

A telegram was sent to Cairo. Maspero, now Director of the Service following Mariette's death on the 19th of January, immediately set sail for the south. On the 3rd of April he arrived in Luxor with the Bulak Museum's newly appointed assistant curator – Émil Brugsch. Following a more detailed personal report from Wilbour, the two men began the second phase of their plan. Ahmed Abd er-Rassul was brought to the Antiquities Service steamboat *Nimro Hadacher* on the very same day. The interrogation was long and searching but Ahmed was more than a match for

Maspero's delving. This 'upright citizen' of Gurna continued to deny all knowledge of the tomb, constantly professing his good name both in his home village and in Luxor itself. How could an Egyptian with such an exemplary reputation indulge in nefarious activities of this kind? The Antiquities Service men failed to extract any sort of confession from the wily Rassul and so had to release him from their clutches, allowing Ahmed to return across the river, back to the safety of Gurna village.

A couple of days later, though, Ahmed and his brother Hussein were formally arrested by the local police and sent to Kena to be 'interviewed' by the governor of the province, Daoud Pasha. This time the niceties of European scholarly interrogation were not observed. Daoud's men had different, less subtle, methods. The Rassuls were subjected to hours of brutal questioning which MUDIR Daoud set about 'with his habitual severity'. This included the use of the BASTINADO. Still the brothers refused to surrender their secret. Ahmed and Hussein (the latter now crippled as a result of the torture) were then thrown into prison for two months, finally being released after the constant petitioning of the elders of their village. (It was later revealed that the Rassuls had been supporting many families in Gurna with their earnings from the tomb – a generous act that had elevated them to hero status in the village.)

The weeks passed, but, in spite of their apparent success in avoiding prosecution, things were not going well in the Rassul family household. As is usually the way in close knit fellaheen communities, the need to 'save face' dominated village life, especially amongst the male elders of the tribe. On his triumphant return home to Gurna, Ahmed had decided that he and his younger brother should be rewarded for their suffering at the hands of the Kena authorities. Head of the family, Mohamed, on the other hand had got away scot-free, so it was only right, in Ahmed's view, that he and Hussein should get a greater share of the loot in recompense for their tribulations. A furious and long lasting row erupted amongst the five brothers, and the entire village was thrown into turmoil.

In early June Maspero returned to Paris leaving Brugsch behind in Cairo. While the Director was away, Mohamed Abd er-Rassul went secretly to Daoud Pasha in Kena and spilled the beans, making a clean breast of his family's involvement in the illicit trading with Mustafa Aga. To restore his authority at home, and as a face-saving measure, he secured a promise that no prosecutions would ensue if he agreed to lead the authorities to the hidden tomb. (Later the family was even given five hundred pounds sterling by the Antiquities Service as a reward for Mohamed's cooperation.) At last the truth, or at least part of the truth, about the discovery of the tomb was revealed – first to the authorities in Kena and then by telegram to Brugsch in Cairo. The latter immediately set out for Luxor with two of his colleagues – Madame Thadeos Matafian and Ahmed Effendi KAMAL – arriving on the 4th of June. Two days later, on Wednesday the 6th of June 1881, Mohamed took Brugsch and his party, together with the governor's WEKIL, to the lonely spot south of Deir el-Bahri where he revealed the location of the secret tomb to them. Brugsch was lowered by rope down to the bottom of the shaft to face his destiny.

> Finding Pharaoh was an exciting experience for me. It is true I was armed to the teeth and my faithful rifle, full of shells, hung over my shoulder; but my assistant from Cairo, Ahmed Effendi Kamal, was the only person with me whom I could trust. Any one of the natives would have killed me willingly, had we been alone, for everyone of them knew better than I did that I was about to deprive them of a great source of revenue. But I exposed no sign of fear, and proceeded with the work. The well cleared out, I descended, and began the exploration of the underground passage.[5]

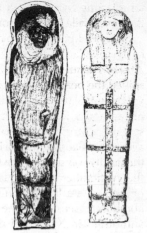

11. Mummy of an unknown man placed in the coffin of Nebseny. This was the last coffin to be interred in the Royal Cache. Cairo Museum.

The first person in nearly three thousand years able to identify the occupants of this gallery of the dead shuffled past the four coffins in the low entrance corridor, pausing in the dim light to read the cursive hieroglyphic script painted in black ink on the coffin lids. First, within a metre of the doorway, was the large whitewashed anthropoid coffer of a priest named Nebseny; then an even larger mummy case of a type 'recalling the style of the 17th Dynasty' (the female occupant later identified as Queen Inhapi). This was followed by the coffin of a Queen Henttawy. Then Brugsch's gaze fell upon the gently smiling countenance carved on the fourth coffin and he began to read the crudely painted cartouche on the chest just beneath the folded arms. In clear black hieroglyphs – within two ovals standing above the ancient Egyptian sign for gold – he read the name of the occupant of the fourth coffin: 'King Menmaatre Seti-merenptah'.

The import of the moment hit Brugsch like a hammer blow, as the unassuming German scholar began to realise his good fortune. It had fallen to him to be the first Egyptologist to be in the presence of the mortal remains of one of the greatest warrior pharaohs of the New Kingdom – King SETI I – builder of the splendid mortuary temple at Abydos, and father of 'Ramesses the Great' – the infamous Pharaoh of the Oppression and Exodus.

Brugsch and Ahmed Kamal pressed on into the depths of the tomb, where they were soon to be greeted by the extraordinary sight awaiting them in the small chamber next to the stairwell. You can sense the excitement as Brugsch recalls his remarkable day in this secret cache of ancient Egyptian royalty.

> Soon we came upon cases of porcelain funeral offerings, metal and alabaster vessels, draperies and trinkets, until, reaching the turn in the passage, a cluster of mummy-cases came to view in such number as to stagger me. Collecting my senses, I made the best examination of them I could by the light of my torch, and at once saw that they contained the mummies of royal personages of both sexes; and yet that was not all. Plunging on ahead of my guide, I came to the chamber, and there, standing against the walls, or lying on the floor, I

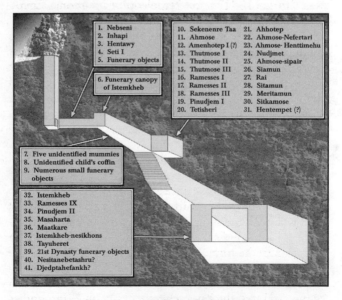

1. Nebseni
2. Inhapi
3. Hentawy
4. Seti I
5. Funerary objects

6. Funerary canopy of Istemkheb

7. Five unidentified mummies
8. Unidentified child's coffin
9. Numerous small funerary objects

10. Sekenenre Taa
11. Ahmose
12. Amenhotep I (?)
13. Thutmose I
14. Thutmose II
15. Thutmose III
16. Ramesses I
17. Ramesses II
18. Ramesses III
19. Pinudjem I
20. Tetisheri

21. Ahhotep
22. Ahmose-Nefertari
23. Ahmose- Henttimehu
24. Nudjmet
25. Ahmose-sipair
26. Siamun
27. Rai
28. Sitamun
29. Meritamun
30. Sitkamose
31. Hentempet (?)

32. Istemkheb
33. Ramesses IX
34. Pinudjem II
35. Masaharta
36. Maatkare
37. Istemkheb-nesikhons
38. Tayuheret
39. 21st Dynasty funerary objects
40. Nesitanebetashru?
41. Djedptahefankh?

12. Isonometric illustration of the Royal Cache produced from descriptions of TT 320. The locations of the mummies are speculative but based on contemporary reports.

found even a greater number of mummy-cases of stupendous size and weight. Their gold coverings and their polished surfaces so plainly reflected my own excited visage that it seemed as though I was looking into the faces of my own ancestors. The gilt face on the coffin of the amiable Queen Nefertari seemed to smile upon me like an old acquaintance.

The niche held in its protection some of the most powerful kings and queens in the ancient world. Here rested the mortal remains of Pharaoh Ahmose – expeller of the hated foreign Hyksos rulers of the 15th Dynasty and founder of the New Kingdom Empire of Egypt; alongside him was the sacred Amenhotep I – patron of the Royal Necropolis and deified by the local Egyptians after his death; here too was Thutmose III – the Napoleon of pharaonic Egypt; and, by no means least, Ramesses II himself – ruler of rulers, legendary king and conqueror. Brugsch shone his torch upon docket after docket, reading out the names for Ahmed Kamal to record in his notebook: King Sekenenre Taa-ken; the great early 18th Dynasty queens Ahhotep and Ahmose-Nefertari; Prince Siamun; Pharaohs Thutmose I, Thutmose II, Ramesses I, Ramesses III and Pinudjem I – all were here patiently awaiting their resurrection into the modern world.

Brugsch was suddenly overcome with an irrational sense of dread and made an undignified dash for the entrance shaft and fresh air. He was only able to return to the task in hand after a thirty-minute rest and quantities of cool water. Negotiating the obstacles in the entrance corridor for a second time, the two museum men dived on deeper into the tomb, past the niche and finally into the main burial chamber. There they found the havoc left by the Rassuls during their visits to the cache. They soon discovered that this large chamber contained the bodies and funeral equipment of the family of HPA Pinudjem II including the mummies of the noble ladies, Istemkheb,

Maatkare, and Istemkheb-Nesykhons; King Ramesses IX; and the High Priests Masaharta and Pinudjem II himself. Their cursory two-hour survey complete, the investigators finally returned to the surface.

Consideration now had to be given as to how exactly they were to execute a rapid clearance of the Royal Cache before the Gurna villagers could pluck up enough courage to mount some resistance to the removal of their inheritance. Brugsch remained at the entrance of the tomb overnight with his small force of policemen whilst a runner was sent to Luxor for further assistance. Early the next morning REIS Mohamed, the trusted Nubian pilot of the museum's steamer, arrived at the cache with Madame Matafian whilst Daoud's men began the forced conscription of three hundred disgruntled male citizens from Sheikh Abd el-Gurna.

Reis Mohamed was sent down the shaft into the tomb to organise the removal of the coffins. Brugsch and his assistants logged the finds as they were hauled up from the underworld, arranging them in an extended identity parade on the flat ground at the bottom of the valley. There they were covered in sailcloth before being raised onto the shoulders of the conscripts for transportation to the Nile. (Some of the coffins were so large and heavy that it required a dozen men to lift them.) The whole operation took forty-eight hours to complete, working day and night. The conveyance of the mummy cases, carried aloft in a great snaking procession through the arid desert landscape and on down into the lush valley, must have been an astonishing sight to behold.

By the 15th of June the museum's river-boat, fully laden with its royal cargo, set sail for Cairo. As the paddle-steamer made its steady progress northwards, the banks of the great river bristled with shadowy figures in black, the women wailing and tearing their hair, the men discharging their rifles into the air: the Egyptian fellaheen were saying a final farewell to the kings and queens who had ruled over their distant ancestors all those generations ago.

Some months later, upon his return to Egypt, Maspero went to Luxor and inspected the now virtually empty cache. There, in the cleft of rock above the shaft he posed with Ahmed Kamal and the three Rassul brothers for an official photo following their descent into the catacomb. The next day, Mohamed Abd er-Rassul was duly appointed foreman of the official Antiquities Service excavations in the Theban necropolis and soon obliged his superiors with the discovery (in 1891) of another huge cache of mummies (this time of the Theban priests) within the precincts of Queen Hatshepsut's Deir el-Bahri temple. Ahmed Abd er-Rassul continued to live on the west bank, earning a living from telling his remarkable story to visiting tourists, until his death in 1918. Mohamed survived his brother, passing away in venerable

13. The white-painted coffin of Seti I. Cairo Museum.

old age in 1926. His descendants still live in Gurna: the males, now honoured with the title Sheikh, owning various run-down hotels and 'Rest Houses' adjacent to the tourist sites. Sheikh Hussein Abd er-Rassul, proprietor of the Ramesseum Rest House, still recalls great-grandfather Mohamed getting him his job as a 'basket boy' for the Howard CARTER excavations in the Valley of the Kings. He proudly displays a framed photo of himself at the age of fourteen wearing one of Tutankhamun's exquisite royal pendants removed from the boy-king's mummy in 1923.

The Puzzle

The unwrapping of the royal mummies did not get under-way until May 1886 but, once begun, was completed within two months. The examination was supervised by Maspero and British anatomist Sir Grafton Elliot SMITH – the great mummy specialist of his day.

As we have already noted, Brugsch had observed that a number of the coffins of the deceased kings had ink dockets painted on their chests. In the more comfortable surroundings of the museum workshops, the curators and conservators now discovered more texts, including further coffin dockets and, as the corpses were being unwrapped, ink labels written on the bandages themselves.

These texts told the story of the removal of the royal mummies from their respective tombs in the Valley of the Kings and their transportation into temporary storage within the tomb of Queen Inhapi, located high above the royal wadi. The date of the transfer was Day 17, Month IV of the Winter Season, in the tenth year of King SIAMUN – the fifth ruler of the 21ST DYNASTY. The bodies remained in Inhapi's tomb for three days before their final transfer into the tomb of the High Priest of Amun, Pinudjem II, on the day of the latter's funeral. Pinudjem had acquired an old 18th Dynasty rock-cut cliff tomb which he had extended to provide a communal burial place for his family. When Pinudjem himself died in the reign of Siamun the tomb had already been used to bury several members of his large family.

The mortuary priest on the west bank and the officials at Karnak across the river decided on a bold strategy to preserve the mummies of the kings languishing in the royal necropolis, whose 'houses of eternity' were regularly being violated by tomb robbers. The plan matured during the seventy-day embalming period of their deceased master, the high priest. Their idea appears to have been to use the burial of Pinudjem as camouflage for the secret caching of the royal mummies. Ordinary Thebans (including any potential tomb plunderers) would have witnessed all the comings and goings in the western necropolis but would naturally have assumed that these activities were connected with the burial of the high priest of Amun. The bodies of the New Kingdom pharaohs were then lowered into the shaft of Pinudjem's family tomb, the last few probably in the dead of night, immediately following the public funeral. The deception worked well, as we now know that the Royal Cache remained hidden for nearly three thousand years, preserving the bodies of Egypt's royal ancestors for eternity.

For our story, the important points to note are that Pinudjem's burial in Year 10 of Siamun is dated to 969 BC in the conventional chronology and that the royal mummies were placed in Pinudjem's tomb towards the end of the 21st Dynasty.

The Mummy of the Second Prophet

So far so good. The wanderings of the royal mummies can be established from the various dockets associated with their reburial. But then, back in 1886, something happened to upset the applecart. During the anatomical examination of one of the less important mummies found in the Royal Cache – that of the Second Prophet of Amun, Djedptahef-ankh, son-in-law of Pinudjem II – the museum staff discovered ink-written labels on the bandages used to wrap the corpse. The main text gave the date of manufacture of the linen bandages:

> Noble linen which the Dual King, Lord of the Two Lands, **Hedjkheperre**, Son of Re, Lord of Appearances, **Shoshenk-meryamun** made for his father Amun (in) **Year 10**.

A second label mentioned a Year 11 – presumably of the same king.

14. The first corridor of the Royal Cache has maximum dimensions of 1.15m x 1.40m. The coffin of Seti I is the largest of the four coffins located in the first corridor, its maximum dimensions (at the feet) measuring 0.73m x 0.82m. Djedptahefankh's coffin has maximum dimensions of 0.65m x 0.76m. The diagram graphically demonstrates that it is quite impossible to transport this coffin through the first corridor and into the tomb whilst the coffin of Seti (and the other three coffins) are in place. Djedptahefankh must have been interred in the tomb (in Year 11 of Shoshenk I) before the four coffins found at the entrance and therefore before Year 10 of Siamun when Seti I was placed there.

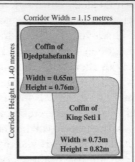

Corridor Width = 1.15 metres

Corridor Height = 1.40 metres

Coffin of Djedptahefankh

Width = 0.65m
Height = 0.76m

Coffin of King Seti I

Width = 0.73m
Height = 0.82m

Coffin	Max. Width	Max. Height	Length
Nebseni	0.52 m	0.63 m	1.97 m
Inhapi	0.74 m	0.70 m	2.39 m
Henttawy	0.71 m	0.53 m	2.15 m
Seti I	0.73 m	0.82 m	2.15 m
Djedptahefankh	0.65 m	0.76 m	1.99 m

The Libyan pharaoh Hedjkheperre SHOSHENK I was founder of the 22nd Dynasty and the date of his eleventh year has been established at 935 BC. Thus the body of Djedptahefankh had been wrapped in Year 11 of King Shoshenk – thirty-four years after the Royal Cache was sealed – yet the second prophet's mummy was found deep within the tomb. How could this be? Was the secret hiding place of the great pharaohs really reopened for the burial of an official from Karnak temple? This seemed inherently unlikely, but it was the only rational explanation scholars could come up with at that time. Ever since then (with little consideration given to any alternative interpretations) it has been acknowledged that the Royal Cache was not

finally sealed in the reign of Siamun but rather two generations later in the early years of the 22nd Dynasty.

However, in all this time one crucial factor appears to
have been overlooked. If Djedptahefankh was buried
decades after the Cache was filled with the royal mummies,
how did the priests manage to get his coffin past the blocked
entrance passage? Remember that Brugsch found this low
(1.40 metre-high) corridor crammed with four mummy
cases, the last of which (that of Seti I) bore a docket stating
that the king's body was placed there in Year 10 of Siamun.
Given the size of these coffins[6] and the restricted dimensions of the corridor, it is clear that no such operation would
have been possible, there being insufficient room for the
passage of Djedptahefankh's coffin and his pallbearers into
the deeper parts of the tomb.[7]

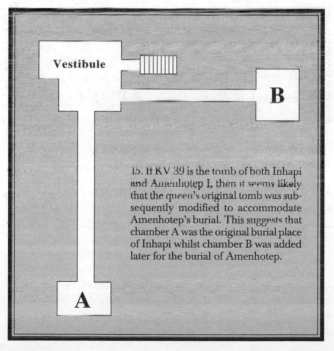

Vestibule

B

A

15. If KV 39 is the tomb of both Inhapi
and Amenhotep I, then it seems likely
that the queen's original tomb was subsequently modified to accommodate
Amenhotep's burial. This suggests that
chamber A was the original burial place
of Inhapi whilst chamber B was added
later for the burial of Amenhotep.

Djedptahefankh's burial in the Cache must therefore have taken place before the interment of Seti I in Year 10 of Siamun. We are thus left with only one real alternative. Straightforward logic requires that Year 11 of Shoshenk must have fallen before Year 10 of Siamun.

You will, of course, immediately see the implication of such an argument. If Siamun was the sixth king of the 21st Dynasty and Shoshenk I the first king of the 22nd Dynasty, then the two dynasties could not have been sequential as is the case with the chronological model of the TIP employed by today's Egyptologists. The historical imperative of the Royal Cache burials demands that the two dynasties were, at least in part, contemporary with each other.

Conclusion Two

The burial of Djedptahefankh in the Royal Cache indicates that the 21st and 22nd Dynasties were not chronologically sequential, as is currently believed, but partly contemporary.

***

To demonstrate that this was indeed the historical reality we need to journey down river into the eastern Nile delta where we will find the ruin-field of San el-Hagar – the site of the ancient city of Tanis – the Zoan of the Old Testament.

Chapter Three

THE ROYAL TOMBS OF SAN

The Discovery

San el-Hagar – 'San of the Stones' – is the most desolate place I have ever visited. The eastern delta road forks off the main highway to Ismaliya at the provincial capital of FAKUS and heads northwards towards the Mediterranean coast. After about half-an-hour's drive the rich green of the delta cultivation begins to fade imperceptibly into grey-brown salt flats and, almost without realising it, you find yourself approaching an immense range of hills on the horizon. These hills are no natural feature. Stretching as far as the eye can see to the east of the crumbling tarmac road are the remains of the once mighty city of San – the biblical ZOAN, called 'Tanis' by the Greek writer-travellers who visited Egypt in the Classical and Hellenistic periods.

This extraordinary place has always fascinated me. I have spent many a dusty hour wandering over its inhospitable terrain – something **akin** to a Martian landscape – trying to imagine what lies deep beneath my feet. Research has shown that Tanis had endured for nigh on a thousand years – from the beginning of the 21st Dynasty (1069 BC) down to the reign of AUGUSTUS CAESAR – when the city was finally relinquished to the depredations of time. Since then, through virtually the whole of the last two millennia, the open plain surrounding the sprawling mound has been populated only by roaming herds of wild boar and the occasional transient Bedouin encampment. Life in this part of Egypt has been very hard for the fellaheen of the little village of San, which has existed, just to the north-west of the mound, only since the middle of the last century.

San seems to represent a wholly other world. The visitor senses an age which has long since faded away in other parts of Egypt: the era of Napoleon and his great expedition of soldiers, scholars and artists; of early Nile exploration (Amelia Edwards); or of Flinders Petrie and his lonely excavation of Tanis during the winter of 1884. Even though archaeological work at the site has been underway (in fits and starts) for the best part of a century-and-a-half since Mariette first pitched his tent here in 1858, the place remains to this day an atmospheric reminder of the romantic days of Egyptology with its petrified forest of broken obelisks and colossal statues of Ramesses the Great lying scattered from horizon to horizon in chaotic splendour. There is little sign here of the manicuring of tourist sites now so typical in the Nile valley proper.

It was to 'San of the Stones' that yet another French archaeologist, Pierre MONTET, came in the late 1920s. He had previously been excavating the site of BYBLOS on the coast of modern Lebanon (ancient Phoenicia) just to the north of Beirut. There, between 1921 and 1924, his team of archaeologists had unearthed considerable evidence to suggest close political and cultural ties between Egypt and the rulers of Byblos during the late OLD KINGDOM (OK) and MIDDLE KINGDOM (MK).

Montet (then Professor at Strasbourg University) had become very interested in exploring the huge site of San el-Hagar/Tanis in the eastern Nile delta because he believed that it might provide him with further archaeological evidence for links between the Levant and Egypt which could corroborate and expand upon his findings in MIDDLE BRONZE AGE Byblos.[1] What his excavations actually turned up was an Egyptological sensation from an entirely different era.

Montet, accompanied by his wife and a small team of four colleagues, began work at Tanis in the winter of 1929. Over the next ten years the French archaeologists, armed with scores of workers from the village of San, were principally preoccupied with the uncovering of the main temple at Tanis dedicated to the god AMUN. It was not until early 1939, on the eve of the Second World War, that their astonishing discovery began to take shape in the south-west corner of the great enclosure which formed the sacred precinct of Amun. There, on the 25th of February, the workmen uncovered a 'pavement' of large limestone blocks which, when tapped with the Reis Hassanein's cane, produced a hollow sound indicating a cavity below. Two days of clearing later, Montet entered the tomb of King OSORKON II (Tomb I):

> At exactly 2 o'clock, I had the earth and stones blocking the entrance removed, and went down into a square chamber with walls covered with figures and hieroglyphics; this led into another chamber with a large sarcophagus emerging from the earth which filled three quarters of two rooms. The cartouche is that of Osorkon ... Everyone is overjoyed. I had Hassanein's team come with all the carts so that we could clear this remarkable structure as quickly as possible – its discovery rewards all our year's efforts.[2]

The complex of underground rooms entered by Montet on the 27th of February 1939 contained the remains of a number of royal interments. In the main granite-lined burial chamber (burial 3 – see p. 107) was the huge sarcophagus of Osorkon II containing the skeletal remains of a man and a woman – presumed to be the pharaoh and his queen. Their burial had been plundered at some unknown time in the past. Embedded in the rear wall of the king's chamber was the smaller mummiform quartzite sarcophagus of Osorkon's ten-year-old son – the High Priest of Amun, Harnakht, whose burial was virtually intact, the robbers failing to remove the lid of the coffin because it had been jammed in place within the recess during the original burial of the boy priest.

In the antechamber of the tomb (burial 12) was another large granite sarcophagus. This was empty, having been pillaged of its contents in antiquity.

There were two other side rooms in the complex, one of which contained the burial of a King Hedjkheperre Takelot (burial 1). During the half-century which followed Montet's discoveries at Tanis this pharaoh has always been identified as TAKELOT II, son and successor of Osorkon II; however, it has now been cogently argued that the burial in fact represents the mortal remains of Osorkon's father, TAKELOT I.[3] The remaining side chamber (Chamber C – the first to be entered by Montet) was empty but its walls were covered in finely cut scenes of King Osorkon II performing the rituals associated with the Book of the Dead.

All over the rest of the walls of the tomb complex were similar reliefs depicting King Osorkon II in the afterlife. The tomb was clearly primarily the 'House of Eternity' of the 22nd Dynasty pharaoh Usermaatre Osorkon (II) and the secondary burials were either of his direct family or represented a subsequent incursion into the vault to bury a later ruler from the same Dynasty (the empty sarcophagus of burial 12).

Further clearing of the sand and debris in the vicinity of Osorkon's tomb revealed a second major underground vault – this one with no signs of intrusion by tomb robbers. On the 17th of March Montet descended into the tomb of King Akheperre PSUSENNES (I) (Tomb III), via the entrance shaft, to herald 'a day of marvels worthy of *The Thousand and One Nights*'. Traversing a short low passage he was greeted by the extraordinary sight of a silver hawk-headed coffin lying on a stone pedestal occupying the right side of a small chamber. All around, scattered haphazardly, were hundreds of ushabti figurines decorated in blue FAIENCE. In another corner of the room were three sets of CANOPIC VESSELS and a large terracotta jar leaning against the wall. A closer inspection of the pedestal revealed two other shattered wooden coffins containing the rotting bones of their royal occupants. The silver coffin lying between these two anonymous corpses contained the mummy of King Hekakheperre SHOSHENK (II)– a previously unknown pharaoh of the LIBYAN PERIOD. The coffin of the newly discovered Shoshenk was opened in the presence of King Farouk on the 21st of March 1939. The other two sets of royal remains were not identified until recently when a detailed analysis of the ushabti figurine inscriptions found in the chamber produced the names of King Netjerkheperre SIAMUN and King Tjetkheperre HAR-PSUSENNES II.

In the left wall of the small chamber was an opening through which Montet scrambled to find an empty, unused sarcophagus intended for a son of Akheperre Psusennes – Prince Ankhefenmut. No one knows to this day why he was unable to occupy the place of burial prepared for him by his father (burial 6).

War was declared in Europe on the 1st of September 1939, but Montet continued to work in the recently discovered tomb in search of the hidden burial chamber of Psusennes I – the original tomb owner whose inscriptions adorned the walls of the small antechamber containing the three burials so far discovered. On the 16th of February 1940 part of the western wall of the antechamber was dismantled, revealing a pair of large granite plugs blocking the entrances to two burial chambers. The right plug was the first to be removed, surrendering to Montet the intact burial of King Psusennes (burial 5) replete with alabaster canopic jars, a full set of four hundred ushabtis, gold and silver vessels of all shapes and sizes and a magnificent pink granite sarcophagus which the 21st Dynasty ruler had usurped from the tomb of MERENPTAH in the Valley of the Kings. Inside this exquisite monument lay the mortal remains of the pharaoh, encased in a smaller black granite anthropoid coffin which itself protected a solid silver coffin. The mummy wore a magnificent solid gold funerary mask bearing a gently smiling countenance – an image of supreme confidence which belied the troubled times of his reign.

Following the clearance of the burial chamber of Psusennes, the second sealed passage was deprived of its granite plug (on the 16th of April) to reveal the intact burial of another 21st Dynasty pharaoh – the little known King AMENEMOPET (burial 4). His burial was poorer than that of Psusennes I but, even so, Montet's team recovered canopic vessels; gold and silver libation vases; an alabaster jar taken from the tomb of Seti I in the Valley of the Kings; a less elaborate sarcophagus usurped from a 19th Dynasty noble; and, within it, the badly decomposed mummy of the king wearing a crude gold funerary mask in his likeness. Montet was able to determine that the chamber and sarcophagus were originally intended for Queen Mutnodjmet, the wife of Psusennes I, but for some unknown reason it was King Amenemopet who had been interred in the Queen's burial vault.

Four other tombs were found in the Tanite royal necropolis in the same season: Tombs II and VI were uninscribed and empty but for a few fragments; Tomb IV was a small sepulchre containing a sarcophagus inscribed with the cartouches of King Amenemopet (this tomb probably represented his original place, or intended place, of burial); Tomb V was the two-chambered tomb of King SHOSHENK III.

All the treasures from the five burials found in the tomb complex of Psusennes were transported to the Cairo Museum by the beginning of May 1940 and have been on display near to the Tutankhamun collection ever since (apart from the brief interlude when some objects went on a tour of Europe in 1987 and 1988, exhibited in Paris and Edinburgh).

Montet returned to France on the 10th of May 1940 to wait out the rest of the war – the hostilities in North Africa preventing any further work at San. He was back in 1945 in order to witness the giving up of the final major secret of the royal necropolis at Tanis.

It was during this postwar return of the French expedition that a full survey of the tombs was finally undertaken by Alexandre Lézine. The new architect for the archaeological team soon determined that the known interior of the tomb complex of Psusennes did not appear to correspond with the exterior dimensions of the whole structure. The south-east corner had enough space for another room but no doorway was visible from inside the antechamber. Further excavations, involving the removal of one of the giant limestone roofing slabs, revealed a hidden chamber which contained the intact burial of General Wendjeba-endjed, Commander of the Egyptian Army – a close companion of King Psusennes who had been honoured with a burial close to the body of his lord and master. This supplementary interment provided another wealth of exquisite treasures.[4]

The Puzzle

When Alexandre Lézine undertook his survey of the royal burial ground at Tanis, just after the Second World War, he began to uncover some rather perplexing features relating to the architectural structures he was investigating. These features seemed to suggest to him that the tomb complex of Psusennes I was built after that of Osorkon II. Now this is entirely contrary to the chronology currently in use, according to which Akheperre Psusennes I died in 991 BC whilst the reign of Usermaatre Osorkon II came to an end one hundred and forty-one years later in 850 BC. The archaeology at Tanis and the chronology devised by the historians appeared to contradict each other.

The chronology of the royal tomb structures at Tanis is a fairly complex subject but absolutely essential to tackle here if we are to succeed in making our first step towards rediscovering the real history behind the Old Testament narratives.

The Cutaway

The first and most obvious curiosity which came to the attention of Montet and Lézine was the point of contact between the tombs of Osorkon (Tomb I) and Psusennes (Tomb III). The area we are dealing with here lies between the letters A and B on the plan. You will note that the south wall of Tomb III, where the two secondary burial chambers of Wendjebaendjed and Ankhefenmut (burials 7 and 6) are located, appears to cut into the north exterior wall of both the antechamber and Chamber C belonging to the Osorkon burial complex. If you set aside the requirements of the conventional chronology this looks fairly straightforward: if part of the structure of Tomb I was removed in order to accommodate a change of plan in respect of Tomb III then clearly Tomb III (of Psusennes) must have been constructed after Tomb I (of Osorkon). But, as we have noted, Psusennes built his tomb over a century before Osorkon was on the throne of Egypt – according to the conventional chronology.

Montet and Lézine had to find a solution to this enigma. Their best effort was to argue that Tomb I was indeed standing when Psusennes built Tomb III, but that Osorkon was not the original builder of Tomb I. Osorkon would then have usurped Tomb I from its original 21st Dynasty owner – perhaps SMENDES, the predecessor of Psusennes I. The problem is that evidence for this earlier builder of Tomb I is somewhat elusive. Indeed, Lézine himself was forced to admit that their 'solution' was inconsistent with the evidence of his own eyes:

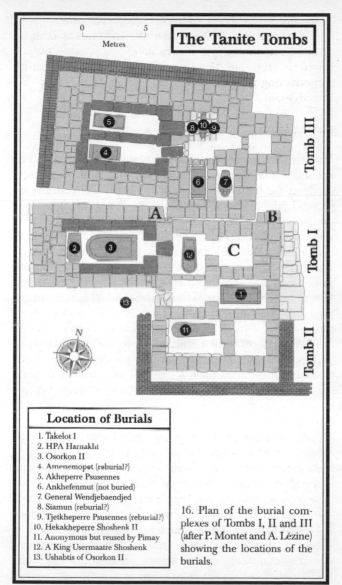

The Tanite Tombs

0   5
Metres

Tomb III

A   B

Tomb I

C

Tomb II

N

Location of Burials

1. Takelot I
2. HPA Harnakht
3. Osorkon II
4. Amenemopet (reburial?)
5. Akheperre Psusennes
6. Ankhefenmut (not buried)
7. General Wendjebaendjed
8. Siamun (reburial?)
9. Tjetkheperre Psusennes (reburial?)
10. Hekakheperre Shoshenk II
11. Anonymous but reused by Pimay
12. A King Usermaatre Shoshenk
13. Ushabtis of Osorkon II

16. Plan of the burial complexes of Tombs I, II and III (after P. Montet and A. Lézine) showing the locations of the burials.

> The interior decoration [of Tomb I] is of the period of Osorkon II. This king nowhere scratched out the cartouches of a predecessor in order to substitute his own. One could therefore conclude that Osorkon built this tomb.[5]

What is more, one inscription,[6] found in the antechamber, states that Tomb I was built on the instructions of Queen KAPES as a gift to her son, King Osorkon.[7] Montet and Lézine's 'original tomb' theory thus starts to look shaky even before we consider any additional arguments.

Because the archaeologists had found no textual evidence in the tomb for an earlier king, Montet and Lézine, insisting that Osorkon II *had* to be later than Psusennes I, were forced to argue[8] that the original version of Tomb I was dismantled to its foundations by Osorkon and then rebuilt on exactly those same foundations so that the interior walls could be decorated with fresh scenes depicting the 22nd Dynasty pharaoh. The questions which immediately come to mind are:

(a) Why go to all that effort? Osorkon could have simply removed the cartouches of the original owner of the tomb by cutting back the reliefs and having his own cartouches carved over the top. This technique of recutting PALIMPSEST inscriptions was regularly employed throughout the history of Egypt whenever one pharaoh wished to usurp the monuments of his predecessors.

(b) Another obvious point is why would Osorkon have built his tomb at exactly the same spot when he could have constructed it in open ground nearby – thus avoiding the difficulties created by the existing tomb of Psusennes? It is also much easier to dismantle a building at one location and use the materials from that structure to erect a new monument on a virgin site nearby. To erect a structure at exactly the same location as the original requires the moving of the stone blocks to a storage area until the whole of the first structure is removed. Then the workers have to transport the blocks back again to begin building the new monument – a doubling of the effort.

(c) In addition, if Montet and Lézine's theory is accepted, one would assume that Osorkon reused the original stone blocks of the earlier tomb, simply turning the inscribed surfaces to the outside in order to give himself nice clean interior walls for his own reliefs (again a technique often employed in the building of Egyptian monuments), but, in the case of Tomb I, there is absolutely no sign of any original 21st Dynasty inscriptions on the exterior surfaces of the stones.

(d) You can also see that at point B on the plan the east wall of Tomb I juts out northwards beyond the rest of the wall surface between A and B. Why would Osorkon rebuild the east wall of his tomb like this? It serves no obvious architectural or constructional purpose. The only logical interpretation of this jutting-out wall is that the north façade of Tomb I had to be cut away (not rebuilt) so as to accommodate the extension to Tomb III. This strange feature is thus explained: the north-east corner of Tomb I was left as it was simply because its removal was not required. Besides, by leaving the end of the east wall in place, the workmen cutting back the north wall of Tomb I were being very practical – the section intentionally left standing could act as a retainer wall to prevent the collapse of sand into the trench.

All the above points indicate that the cutting back of the north wall of Tomb I took place after Osorkon was buried in his tomb complex. Tomb I was never usurped by Osorkon from an earlier 21st Dynasty ruler and he did not rebuild the tomb one hundred and forty-one years after the construction of Tomb III. It was Osorkon II's wall all along which the workmen of Psusennes I attacked with their chisels and ADZES.

The published report on the construction of Tomb I by Lézine fails to provide a satisfactory solution to the cutaway problem and gives the impression that Montet's architect was never really convinced by his own 'usurped-tomb' theory. The passage of time and a fresh archaeological reinvestigation of the Tanite burial ground by Philippe Brissaud (the current Director of the French mission at Tanis) has done little so far to assuage that original doubt.[9]

A Change of Plan

Having reviewed the cutaway itself from the outside it is now time to visit the interior of Tomb III. First you will have to negotiate the rickety old ladder which takes us down to the bottom of the entrance shaft – watch your head as you shuffle through the short passage which leads to the antechamber of Psusennes' tomb – now, you can stand erect again. If you pan your torch across the wall immediately in front you will see the two open passages leading to the burial chambers of Amenemopet (left) and Psusennes (right). Further to your right is the recess where the silver coffin of Hekakheperre Shoshenk lay (with his two disintegrated companions), and, to the left side of the antechamber, the square hole in the wall which leads through to the chamber of Ankhefenmut. Take a peek inside and you will see the empty sarcophagus still occupying virtually the whole of the tiny room. Indeed, the interior of this part of the Psusennes complex gives an impression of everything being jammed into a restricted space.

First let us take a closer look at the passage leading to the sarcophagus chamber of King Psusennes (burial 5): you will observe that it forms an exact right angle to the north-south axis of the antechamber. Now examine the

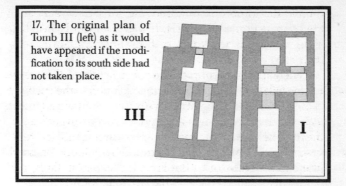

17. The original plan of Tomb III (left) as it would have appeared if the modification to its south side had not taken place.

III

I

passage which leads to King Amenemopet's burial chamber (burial 4): here it is quite obvious that the relative positions of antechamber and passage do not form a true right angle as might be expected – instead the passage veers slightly to the south creating an angle of approximately 80°. The question is why was this modification to the entrance passage of Amenemopet's burial chamber undertaken?

The answer lies in finding the correct interpretation of the sequence of building operations involved in constructing Tomb III. It looks as if the two subsidiary burial chambers (burials 6 and 7), located on the south side of the antechamber, were built only as an afterthought, following the completion of the two main burial chambers (burials 4 and 5). They were not part of the original design concept of the tomb. It was this subsequent addition of chambers for burials 6 and 7 which led to the cutting back of the north wall of Tomb I and which resulted in the internal modifications to the structure of Tomb III. These latter modifications involved a reduction in the floor area of the antechamber on the south side (in order to accommodate the additional chambers) which, in turn, required an adjustment to the angle of the passageway into Amenemopet's burial chamber – bringing its entrance northwards into the now smaller antechamber. Figures 17 & 18 visualise the original ground plan and the subsequent modification.

This later adjustment to Tomb III has thus brought us to another possible explanation for the strange chronological anomaly of the cutaway in the north wall of Tomb I. Is it feasible that the modification of Tomb III – which required this removal of part of the adjacent wall of Tomb I – was undertaken not at the time of Psusennes but rather after Osorkon had built his own tomb (one hundred and forty-one years later), thus solving the anomaly at a stroke? Unfortunately this is not a viable explanation either because of the evidence from the intact burial of General Wendjeba-endjed discovered by Montet in Tomb III (burial 7). A number of Wendjebaendjed's burial artefacts bear inscriptions which demonstrate that the General was a contemporary of King Psusennes. It is clear that he had been given the singular honour of burial near to his monarch. One of the treasures from the burial chamber is a silver dish bearing the following dedication:

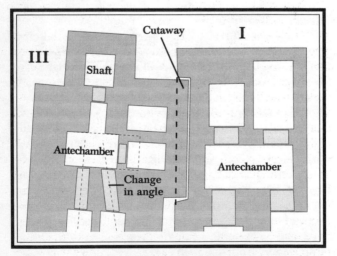

18. The eastern half of Tomb III showing the difference in angle between the two main burial chamber entrance passages. The dotted line indicates the original plan of the antechamber before the addition of the two extra burial chambers to the south.

The Dual King, Akheperre-setepenamun, the Son of Re, Pasbakhanniut-meryamun (i.e. Psusennes I). That which was given as a royal gift to the Overseer of the Estate of Khons in Thebes, Neferhotep; the *hem-netjer* priest of Khons; the Overseer of the Army; the Chief of the Archers of Pharaoh; the Overseer of the *hem-netjer* Priests of all the Gods; Wendjeba-enjed, true of voice, of the Estate of Osiris, Lord of Busiris.[10]

At best, this permits us to argue that the supplementary burial chambers in Tomb III might have been added to the structure within a generation of the burial of Psusennes himself – no later. This would still leave well over a century between the construction of the new Tomb III extension and the building of Tomb I by Osorkon II. Thus the chronological anomaly remains.

The Temple Pylon

There is another archaeological feature which puts the final nail into the coffin of Montet and Lézine's 'earlier tomb' theory. Let us, for the moment, try to imagine the sequence of events involved in the construction of King Psusennes' tomb. For the purpose of our discussion we will assume that a royal tomb (Tomb I) is already standing to the south of the building site. The workmen have already excavated a large deep building-trench adjacent to the north side of Tomb I, the latter acting as the south face of the trench (see Fig. 20). They then erect a mudbrick retainer wall along the north and west sides of the new cutting to prevent it from refilling with sand in a sudden collapse. Now they have three neat vertical sides to the trench with a sloping ramp leading from the open eastern side, down which the building blocks for the Tomb III construction can be easily conveyed. They begin to build the two main burial chambers (one for the king, the other for his queen). The first

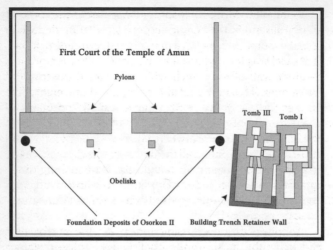

First Court of the Temple of Amun

Pylons

Tomb III   Tomb I

Obelisks

Foundation Deposits of Osorkon II   Building Trench Retainer Wall

19. Simplified plan of the proposed location of the First Pylon in relation to the royal necropolis.

task is to place the outer limestone blocks against the vertical inner faces of the mudbrick retainer walls; then they sheathe the burial chambers themselves with their granite lining. Now comes the sudden change of plan with the king's instructions to add two further burial chambers for his son, Prince Ankhefenmut, and for his devoted servant, General Wendjebaendjed.

We can imagine the discussion between the architect and his foreman as to where they should place the two new chambers. They finally decide to hack away a large chunk of Tomb I to squeeze the extension into the south side of Psusennes' tomb – but why? Would it not be so much easier, you ask yourself, to build the extension on the north side of the antechamber thus avoiding all that hard labour? Something must be preventing the Egyptian workmen from doing so. But what is this other structure which already exists on the north side during the building operations of Psusennes? To find out we need to return in time to the French excavations of 1940.

Soon after Montet's team had discovered the tomb of King Psusennes, they came across a foundation deposit in a shallow sandpit beneath a one-metre-thick mudbrick wall. The wall was located just a metre or so from the northern retainer wall of the trench which contained the tomb of Psusennes. This new wall and an identical one eighty-five metres further to the north represented the remnants of the north and south side walls of the great First Court of the Temple of Amun, between which the First Pylon would have once stood. Sadly, all the limestone blocks which once made up that imposing façade have been long since quarried away by the LIMESTONE BURNERS who thrived upon the ruins of Tanis during the Roman Empire and EARLY ISLAMIC periods.[11]

In spite of the now missing stone pylon, the lime burners did leave the hard granite obelisks and colossal statues (which were of no use to them) standing in front of the shattered remnants of the old façade – so we can be certain that the great gateway into the First Court stood exactly at the spot between the two mudbrick walls unearthed by Montet. Thus it was the south-west corner of the temple court which stood just a metre from the pit prepared for Psusennes' tomb – and this was the structure which prevented the construction of the two extra burial chambers on the north side of the antechamber of Tomb III. If we acknowledge that this was the actual situation facing Psusennes' workmen, we can begin to understand the true purpose of the mudbrick retainer walls which were erected on the north and west sides of the trench. Their main function must have been to prevent the compacted sand foundation beneath the temple from slipping into the building trench. Without the safety wall, any sand slippage would have undermined the south wall of the court and risked the collapse of the great façade. Psusennes' men knew this was too big a risk to take.

Now we can understand why the architects of Psusennes chose to dismantle part of the older Tomb I rather than expand the king's new tomb structure northwards. But who built the First Court of the Temple of Amun at Tanis?

When Montet discovered the foundation deposits beneath both the northern and southern court walls, the pits produced collections of small faience goblets and plaques bearing the cartouches of King Osorkon II – the pharaoh buried in Tomb I. So Osorkon was also the builder of the First Court of the great Temple of Amun at Tanis. For me, this clinches the case for Tomb III being built after Osorkon had constructed his Tomb I. This must be what happened:

- Psusennes decided to add two chambers to his own tomb complex after he had begun the construction of the main burial chambers of Tomb III;

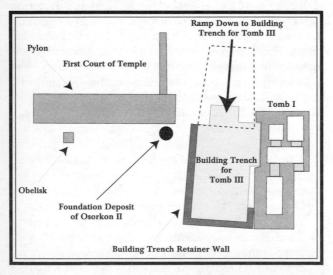

20. The construction technique for Tomb I, as suggested by Montet and Lézine, which involved the digging of an east-west trench in the sand bank. This trench was then lined with a mudbrick sleeve wall to prevent collapse whilst the limestone blocks, pre-cut for the tomb, were assembled within the contruction pit.

- But he could not build the additional chambers on the north side of his tomb because the First Court of the Temple of Amun, constructed by Osorkon II, was already standing there;

- Thus the building operations of King Psusennes of the 21st Dynasty were restricted on both north and south sides by structures of the 22nd Dynasty. Arguing that there was an earlier 21st Dynasty tomb to the south of Tomb III does not help resolve the conundrum when the additional factor of the temple wall is brought into play.

The evidence seems to be incontrovertible: Osorkon II of the 22nd Dynasty built his tomb and added to the Temple of Amun before Psusennes I of the 21st Dynasty began the construction of his own tomb within the sacred enclosure at Tanis. Therefore King Osorkon II could not have died one hundred and forty-one years after King Psusennes I as is currently believed. The implication of this is that the chronology of the Third Intermediate Period is in error by at least this number of years.

Conclusion Three

The burial of King Osorkon II at Tanis took place before the burial of King Psusennes I. Given that the former was a king of the 22nd Dynasty and the latter was a king of the 21st Dynasty, the archaeological evidence from Tanis tends to confirm that the two dynasties were contemporary for a considerable number of years. The order of burial of the two kings indicates that the number of years currently allocated to the TIP should be reduced by at least one hundred and forty-one years.

Part Two

Unravelling the Gordian Knot

Making Sense of Egyptian Chronology

Chapter Four

FOR GOD AND COUNTRY

By 1979, following several years' detailed scrutiny of Professor Kenneth Kitchen's book in combination with research into the anomalies just discussed, I had come to the conclusion that the whole premise upon which nineteenth and twentieth century scholarship had constructed Egyptian chronology was flawed. But how could it have been allowed to happen? And what was the root cause of this potentially catastrophic error? To answer these fundamental questions we must briefly return, once again, to the formative years of Ancient World studies – the days of Champollion, Mariette and Maspero and, following them, the generation of Heinrich SCHLIEMANN (discoverer of Troy and Mycenae), Flinders PETRIE (the 'father of Egyptian archaeology') and Arthur EVANS (founder of Minoan studies and excavator of Knossos).

Victorian Melodrama

The Victorian era was an extraordinary period in the Western world's development. The imperial powers were at their zeniths and European Man possessed the confidence to become master of all he surveyed. This was the age of adventure and discovery, of dashing (often reckless) heroes such as David LIVINGSTONE and General Charles

GORDON of Khartoum. Africa and the Middle East were the new frontiers of geographical and historical knowledge, and that new knowledge was deeply rooted in the distant pre-Classical past.

The nineteenth century was also the age of the great interdisciplinarian scholar – a man whose interests spanned from horizon to horizon and who could effortlessly wander through any number of scholarly disciplines in search of his intellectual goals. Old World researchers were often fluent in half a dozen ancient languages and scripts – some of which had only recently been deciphered.

The intelligentsia of nineteenth-century Europe were fortunate indeed: most were men of means, free to indulge their interests without the distraction of a modern 'nine to five' existence; nor were they weighed down by the heavy administrative burdens of late twentieth-century university academic life. These Victorian gentlemen could afford large libraries of leather-bound books to aid their research and they also had the time and inclination to indulge themselves in the company of like-minded intellectuals – members of the newly formed learned societies of the day.

The astonishing world of Ancient Egypt had been brought to Europe's attention by Napoleon's scholars in the early years of the nineteenth century, following the Emperor's invasion of North Africa and Palestine. Sensational discoveries followed thick and fast throughout the rest of the century as a result of the sustained efforts of archaeological missions despatched to the region from France, Britain, Germany, Austria and Italy. Diggers and adventurers swarmed all over the Middle East, unearthing ancient palaces, temples and tombs, from the Euphrates and Tigris valleys in the north right down to the Second Cataract of the Nile in southern Nubia. Treasures from the great pharaonic civilisation of the Nile valley were arriving in the capitals of Europe by the shipload, destined for national museums and the private collections of wealthy sponsors.

For a while, the 'cackling farmyard' of those weird and wonderful Egyptian hieroglyphs adorning the booty from the land of the pharaohs was taken over by mystics and occultists – the most extraordinary translations were offered up to the gods of esoteric wisdom in the name of Victorian melodrama. Then, in 1822, a young Frenchman named Jean François CHAMPOLLION claimed the decipherment of the Egyptian hieroglyphs by demonstrating, in his famous 'Lettre à M. Dacier' (Baron Bon Joseph DACIER), that the script of the ancient Egyptians was fundamentally a phonetic writing-form which was based on an alphabet of just twenty-six main signs.[1] From that moment those mysterious little icons of the pharaohs were removed from ignorance and placed firmly in the hands of scholarship. Literally thousands of ancient religious and historical texts were now readable and the first translations were circulating throughout the European academic institutions within a decade or so. This flood of information rapidly led to the first concerted efforts to produce a structured history of the ancient Egyptian civilisation.

It was at this crucial point – the very beginning of the process of compiling Egyptian chronology – that the first major slip-up occurred. It is not hard to understand how it

21. Engraving of the Giza Sphinx from Napoleon's *Description de L'Egypte*, published in 1809.

happened – one need only turn to the first page of the *Memorandum and Articles of Association* of the Egypt Exploration Fund, founded by Amelia Edwards in 1891, to observe one of the major influences pervading the new discipline of Egyptology. There it is expressly stated that the Fund's objectives should include the promotion of surveys, explorations and excavation work which would be 'for the purpose of elucidating or illustrating the Old Testament narrative'.

The educated Victorian gentleman was, above all, the product of a moralistic society. It was important to be seen as upstanding and charitable, with emphasis very much placed on the family, Sunday worship and a solid grounding in the narratives and teachings of the Christian Bible – what we today loosely call 'Victorian values'. The biblical stories lay at the heart of a European child's education and upbringing, and they were constantly being re-stated and re-read during adult life, through regular parlour Bible readings or in sermons during Sunday service. Likewise, every man, woman and child in the Jewish community was conversant with the Tanaakh and MIDRASHIC teachings. It was somewhat inevitable, therefore, that a search for archaeological proof of the biblical narratives should dominate the early years of excavation and exploration in Egypt – the mysterious land which played so dramatic and dominant a role in the early history of the Israelite nation according to the Old Testament narratives. This need to 'find' the Bible in Egypt was the principal reason why the earliest digs initiated by the Egypt Exploration Fund were concentrated in the Nile delta. Edwards' committee purposefully selected sites which were strong candidates for Raamses and Pithom – the store-cities of Exodus 1:11 built by the Israelites during their Bondage in Egypt.[2]

What were the British archaeologists searching for? Of course, they hoped to find direct evidence for the Israelites themselves, but just as important was to identify Raamses and Pithom by name in inscriptions at the sites and to confirm the identity of the Egyptian king in whose name these great building-works were constructed. That king was Ramesses II who was immediately identified as the Pharaoh of the Oppression.

Raamses and Ramesses

This then is the first important premise upon which the foundations of Ancient World chronology have been established:

- Ramesses II was the Pharaoh of the Oppression in whose time the Israelites were under the lash of slavery in Egypt.

Let us look in more detail at the reasoning behind this premise, first to see how it arose, and then how, when further analysed, it does not stand up to critical scrutiny. We may tabulate the points of the argument as follows:

1. Nineteenth-century scholars were the products of a Judaeo Christian world which was firmly rooted in the biblical tradition. When the Ancient World of the Near East opened up to the West, following Napoleon's military expedition into the region, it was inevitable that Victorian Judaeo-Christian society should be emotionally drawn towards the search for positive proof of the veracity of the Old Testament stories in the archaeology of Egypt and Palestine.

2. With Champollion's decipherment of hieroglyphics, the inscriptions on the monuments of Egypt brought one pharaoh to the fore above all others. The names, titles and deeds of Ramesses II were everywhere – on monuments bigger and more imposing than anything belonging to his predecessors or successors (excluding, of course, the mighty pyramids of Giza). The nineteenth-century world called him 'Ramesses the Great' in recognition of his spectacular accomplishments. This

powerful and long-lived 19th-Dynasty pharaoh built many cities and temples in the delta but, most significantly, he founded a new capital in the region which he named **Pi-Ramesse** – 'the estate of Ramesses'.

3. The first chapter of the book of Exodus states that, at some time following the death of the vizier Joseph, 'a new king who had never heard of Joseph' came to power in Egypt. The Egyptians then 'put taskmasters over the Israelites' who had settled in Egypt under Joseph's leadership 'so as to wear them down by forced labour' and 'in this way they built the store-cities of Pithom and **Raamses** for Pharaoh'. [Exodus 1:7-11]

4. Putting points one, two and three together, we are bound to conclude, along with the Victorian scholars, that it was Ramesses II who enslaved the Israelites and forced them to build his new eastern-delta capital – the biblical Raamses. The title of 'Pharaoh of the Oppression' has hung from the shoulders of poor Ramesses ever since, along with such epithets as 'megalomaniac' and 'autocratic despot'. Accused and convicted *in absentia*, it is hardly surprising that this pharaoh has suffered from such a 'bad press' for the best part of the two centuries since his monuments came to light. With Ramesses cast in his role, Victorian scholars moved a generation forward in time to identify the Pharaoh of the Exodus as Ramesses II's immediate successor – King Merenptah. In more recent times the start of the Israelite Bondage has been adjusted back by a few years into the time of Seti I (Ramesses II's father) so that the Exodus event falls within the long reign of Ramesses II himself.[3]

So far it is clear how scholars came to these conclusions. But there is other 'historical' material contained in the Old Testament which undermines this apparently straightforward biblical link with Egypt – material which was also readily available to academics of the time but which they preferred to dismiss in favour of the superficially attractive chronological synchronism outlined above. The following were thus labelled 'anachronisms'.

5. According to I Kings 6:1-2, the Exodus from Egypt took place four hundred and eighty years before the construction of the First Temple of Jerusalem. The building of the First Temple dedicated to Yahweh was begun in the fourth regnal year of King Solomon. In Victorian times, Solomon was believed to have reigned in the late eleventh century BC; today most biblical scholars would amend these dates, placing his first regnal year in around 971 BC and the foundation of the temple in circa 968.[4] Either way, this places the Exodus – according to the biblical data – securely in the fifteenth century BC (c. 1447 BC using modern calculations). Now Egyptologists had already worked out, by the middle of the last century, that Ramesses II's sixty-seven year reign had fallen within the thirteenth century BC (the modern preferred dates are 1279-1213 BC[5]). Clearly then there is a two-century discrepancy between the biblical date for the building of the store-city of Raamses and the Egyptological date for the building of Pi-Ramesse.

6. Furthermore, even if it could be argued that Ramesses II really was the Pharaoh of the Oppression (and the Exodus) and the Israelites did indeed build his new capital of Pi-Ramesse, we would then not expect to find earlier references in the Old Testament to a location called 'Raamses'; nor were there any pharaohs called Ramesses before Ramesses II's grandfather, Ramesses I (c. 1295 BC). The royal name Ramesses is a 19th Dynasty phenomenon. No such place-name existed before that time. Egyptian royal cities were named after their royal founders. So Raamses was built by Ramesses. But Genesis 47:11 clearly states that when Joseph had

become vizier of Egypt he 'settled his father (Jacob) and brothers, giving them land holdings in Egypt, in the best part of the country – **the region of Ramesses** – as Pharaoh had ordered'. So the Israelites settled in the 'region of Ramesses' centuries before the first king called Ramesses ascended the throne in Egypt! Scholars argued that in this case the name 'Ramesses' was anachronistic; in other words, the 'region of Ramesses' had been edited into the text in order to identify this area of the eastern delta to the contemporary readership of the biblical REDACTOR – they would know it best by the name which the site had held for the last half a millennium since the city of Pi-Ramesse had been founded. But, just a minute! If the 'region of Ramesses' in Genesis 47:11 was an anachronism, then why should the 'Raamses' of Exodus 1:11 not also be just such an anachronism – surely it too could have been 'edited' for a sixth-century BC Jewish audience? It is a bit like opening up a modern encyclopaedia and reading that the Romans crossed the English Channel to invade southern Britain in around AD 50 and that the Emperor Hadrian finally established a garrison of the Sixth Legion at York in AD 120. All perfectly clear to us, but we must not forget that in the second century AD the Latin name for the English Channel was *Litus Saxonicum* and the Roman town which occupied the site of modern York was called *Eboracum* (the city derived its modern name from 'Yorvic' – the Viking town established on the same site only in the ninth century AD).[6] Would we make the Sixth Legion contemporary with King Alfred the Great simply because a book we had read stated that the Romans had fortified York? Of course not. So why should we so readily accept that Ramesses II was the Pharaoh of the Oppression simply because, according to the book of Exodus, the Israelites built the store-city of Raamses? It is quite possible, taking our example of 'Roman York', that the Israelites built

Plate 1: A colossal Osirid statue in the Ramesseum (the mortuary temple of Ramesses II). The hill of Sheikh Abd el-Gurna rises in the background and beyond the mountain which separates the mortuary temples of the pharaohs from the Valley of the Kings.

Plate 2: The north tower of the pylon of the First Court at the Ramesseum, showing the sandstone block perched precariously on top of the ruin.

Plate 3: Detail of the 'Shalem block' with the outline of a fortress façade carved in shallow relief and, down the centre, the vertical column of text which reads: 'The town which the king plundered in Year 8 – Shalem'.

Plate 4: The fallen colossus of Ramesses II upon which Shelley based his poem 'Ozymandias'. To the left of Ramesses' shoulder is the famous scene of the Battle of Kadesh fought in the pharaoh's 5th regnal year.

Plate 5: The rediscovered entrance to the Lesser Vaults of the Serapeum, following the 1986 excavations by Mohamed Ibrahim Aly and his team.

Plate 6: The life-size statue of an Apis calf found by Mariette in a chapel along the dromos leading to the Serapeum. Louvre Museum.

Plate 7: The Grand Gallery of the Serapeum as it was in 1985.

Plate 8: Apis stela no. 31 ('Pasenhor Stela'). Louvre Museum.

Plate 9: Professor Mohamed Ibrahim Aly, excavator of the Serapeum.

Plate 10: The Lesser Vaults, looking north, following the 1986 excavations.

Plate 11: Aerial view of the village of Sheikh Abd el-Gurna with the White House of the Abd er-Rassuls located within the rectangle.

Plate 12: Restoration (by the author) of the original photograph taken at the Royal Cache in 1891. The negative of this famous scene has been long lost, but a computer-aided reconstruction is possible thanks to the survival of a copper plate etching made at the time of the discovery for newspaper reproduction. Maspero can be seen seated on the rock to the right with the dark-suited Ahmed Kamal standing at the edge of the shaft, looking down. The figure in white of the three Rassul brothers is Ahmed, with Mohamed to his left and Hussein to his right.

Plate 13: The valley of the Royal Cache. TT 320 is located at the base of the right-most gulley where the shadow is at its darkest.

Plate 15 (above): The face of Djedptahefankh from his inner coffin.

Plate 16 (right): The remarkable mummy of Djedptahefankh indicating that he died in his thirties or forties. Cairo Museum.

Plate 14: The outer coffin of the Second Prophet of Amun Djedptahefankh. Cairo Museum.

Plate 17: Area of the First Pylon of the Amun temple at Tanis with the royal necropolis in the foreground.

Plate 18: The gold funerary mask of Wendjebaendjed. Cairo Museum.

Plate 19: The golden funerary mask of King Shoshenk II. Cairo Museum.

Plate 20: The main area of the royal necropolis at Tanis, looking east.

Plate 21: Close-up of the cutaway looking east. Tomb I (Osorkon) is on the right and Tomb III (Psusennes) is on the left (darkened). The lines indicate the area which Tomb III occupies.

Plate 22: Detail of the north-east corner of Tomb I showing the cutting back of the tomb wall, leaving its blocks wrapped around the southern wall of Tomb III.

an earlier city at the same spot which, by the sixth century BC, was hidden deep under the ruins of Pi-Ramesse. The biblical redactor would naturally refer to the city by the name which was familiar to all his contemporaries – and that name was 'Ramesses' (this part of the delta was still referred to as Ramesses even as late as the fourth century AD[7]). We will return to the subject of this earlier city, lying buried under Pi-Ramesse, when we go in search of the archaeological evidence for the Israelite Sojourn later in our story.

A Conjuring Trick with Time

So, how were scholars able to dismiss these awkward problems? First, they proposed that the reference to four hundred and eighty years in I Kings 6:1-2 was an approximate time interval based on a counting of generations: given that a biblical generation (Heb. *dôr* meaning 'span of time'[8]) is generally considered as forty years and forty divides neatly into four hundred and eighty, it was suggested that the real interval was twelve generations ($12 \times 40 = 480$). However, the idea that the natural generation (from the birth of the father to the birth of his eldest surviving son) was considered by the Hebrews to be as long as forty years is based on a piece of very dubious reasoning: Joshua 5:6 states: 'the Israelites walked the desert for forty years, until the whole nation had died out, that is, the men who had come out of Egypt of age to bear arms'. Thus the generation which had departed from Egypt during the Exodus were not permitted by Yahweh to enter the Promised Land. Hence, the argument goes, the people of the Bible considered a generation to be equal to forty years. But the obvious connection between the Wandering Years and the Israelites who left Egypt is rather that it required forty years for the *adult* generation *to die out* – this is not the same as a natural generation (birth to birth) but rather the time span of manhood to death. Indeed, nowhere in the Bible does it state

Date BC	Biblical Chronology	Egyptians	Modern Revision	Date BC
1900	Jacob (?)	12th Dyn		1900
1850	Joseph (?)			1850
1800		Senuseret III Amenemhat III		1800
1750				1750
1700	Jacob (?)	13th Dyn		1700
1650	Joseph (?)			1650
1600		Hyksos Period	Jacob	1600
1550	Sojourn		Joseph	1550
1500		Ahmose		1500
1450	Moses	Thutmose III		1450
1400	Exodus Conquest	Amenhotep III	Sojourn	1400
1350		Akhenaten		1350
1300		Haremheb		1300
1250		Ramesses II	Moses	1250
1200	Judges	Merenptah	Exodus Conquest	1200
1150		Ramesses III		1150
1100			Judges	1100
1050		21st Dyn		1050
1000	Saul David		Saul David	1000
950	Solomon	Siamun 22nd Dyn	Solomon	950
900	Rehoboam	Shoshenk I	Rehoboam	900

Chart showing the chronology of the Old Testament – as given in the Bible (left) and as determined by the Pi-Ramesse/Raamses synchronism (right) – compared to the dates ascribed to the main Egyptian pharaohs as calculated in the orthodox chronology.

that a generation was considered to be forty years. The idea is an invention of biblical scholarship.

Of course, we all know that a generation is much less than forty years – in fact nearer to twenty-five years. So twelve generations would give a true time span of three hundred years (12 x 25 = 300). Now 968 BC (the founding of the Temple of Solomon) plus three hundred years gives an Exodus date of 1268 BC – near enough for nineteenth century scholarship to confirm the connection between Ramesses II and the last years of the Israelite Sojourn. In fact, as I have already stated, the modern dates for Ramesses II of 1279-1213 BC have led some scholars, including Kitchen himself, to assign the early period of the Oppression to Seti I whilst his son Ramesses II now takes on a new role as Pharaoh of the Exodus.[9]

At the end of the exercise, the four-hundred-and-eighty-year interval between the departure of the Israelites from Egypt and the fourth year of King Solomon has been miraculously reduced to three hundred years.

However, this clever sleight of hand may be all in vain because we have also to consider Judges 11:26 which appears to support the four-hundred-and-eighty-year time span. In this passage, the Israelite Judge, Jephthah, is negotiating with the king of the Ammonites; he refers back to the time when the Israelites first settled in Heshbon and Aroer, just prior to their invasion of the Promised Land – in other words approximately forty years after the Exodus from Egypt (following the years of Wandering in Sinai). Jephthah gives the interval from this settlement in Transjordan down to his own time as three hundred years. Now Jephthah – one of the last Judges to rule over the Israelite tribes prior to the anointing of their first king, Saul – is normally dated towards the end of the twelfth century BC (sometime between *circa* 1130 and 1110 BC).[10] If, for the purpose of our calculations, we place him in *circa* 1120, then add the three hundred years of Judges 11:26 plus the forty years of Wanderings, we arrive at an Exodus date of *circa* 1460 BC – generally supporting the date of 1447 BC derived from I Kings 6:1-2 and therefore confirming the four-hundred-and-eighty-year time span. Because three hundred years is not divisible by either forty or twelve and cannot, therefore, be manipulated in the same way as the number four hundred and eighty, biblical chronologists have chosen to ignore the Jephthah datum.

Conclusion Four

There is no compelling evidence to demonstrate that Ramesses II was either the biblical Pharaoh of the Oppression or the Pharaoh of the Exodus. The mention of the store-city of Raamses, upon which these identifications are based, may simply be anachronistic.

Chapter Five

THE FOUR GREAT PILLARS

y now it should be clear to you that Egyptian chronology exercises a major influence on the debate over the historicity of the biblical narratives. The civilisation of the pharaohs gives its dates to the archaeological levels in Palestine in which we search for confirmation of the Old Testament stories. For example, an artefact bearing the cartouche of Ramesses II found within a city mound dates the occupation level of the find to the thirteenth century in the conventional view; if, on the other hand, Egyptologists were to redate Ramesses to the tenth century, then that very same level would suddenly become Solomonic rather than pre-Exodus. As a corollary, this would move King Solomon from the somewhat impoverished period known as the Iron Age into the rich cultural milieu of the Late Bronze Age. It is obvious, therefore, that Egyptian chronology must be correctly worked out if we are to have any hope of locating the historical Israelites in the archaeological record of the Near East. So, let us see how strong the great edifice of Egyptian chronology really is.

The dating system for the pharaonic civilisation has been based on a number of key anchor points which appear at first sight to be interlocking and mutually supportive. There are four great pillars to the chronological edifice of

Egypt which we should now examine to find out if they are as sturdy as they look.

The Sacking of Thebes

The first of these is beyond reproach as a secure date in history – and is not in dispute in this thesis. In 664 BC ASHURBANIPAL, king of Assyria, brought an army to Egypt and sacked the sacred city of Thebes as the punishment for a revolt led by Pharaoh TAHARKA against the recent Assyrian occupation of Egypt. This date of 664 BC is supported by a whole network of interlocking data supplied by various independent sources, including BEROSUS, Manetho, Assyrian and Babylonian chronicles, Apis stelae and Egyptian regnal dates from the monuments. We can state without reservation that this crucial anchor point in Egyptian chronology is our first real 'fixed point' in history.

Pillar One

The sacking of Thebes by Ashurbanipal in 664 BC marks the last year of the rule of Pharaoh Taharka (his Year 26) and heralds the start of the Late Period of Egyptian history.

Having accepted unequivocally this first great pillar of the Egyptian chronological edifice, let us now take a more detailed look at the other pre-664 BC foundation pillars of the currently accepted chronology.

Shishak and Shoshenk

Following the identification of Pi-Ramesse with the biblical Raamses, the Victorian biblical scholars and their colleagues, the new breed of Egyptologists, bonded as they were by their commitment to the biblical texts, soon had another important chronological link between Egypt and the Bible – a link which appeared to confirm the chronology they had devised, based on their identification of Ramesses the Great as the Pharaoh of the Oppression.

In 1828, Champollion finally paid his first (and only[1]) visit to Egypt along with his travelling companion Professor Ippolito ROSELLINI of Pisa University. At last he was able to stand beneath the monumental inscriptions of the temples and tombs and record the utterances of Pharaoh and the gods directly from the very walls themselves.

So it was that Champollion found himself before the triumph scene of King Hedjkheperre Shoshenk I, cut into the south façade of the BUBASTITE PORTAL at Karnak. To his right he could recognise the faint outline of the pharaoh – wearing the tall white crown of Upper Egypt, with raised right arm and, in his fist, the royal mace poised to crash down upon the heads of bound captives at the centre of the smiting scene. To the left side of the wall stood the regal figure of Amun, the god of Karnak, and, below him, the goddess 'Victorious Thebes', both of whom were dragging towards the king tethered rows of oval name-rings surmounted with the heads of captive chieftains. Each name was enclosed within a crenulated border in the form of a fortress balustrade representing a city wall. The hieroglyphs inside the rings spelt out the names of cities and towns captured by King Shoshenk during his Year 20 military campaign into Palestine.[2]

Champollion began to read the city names: Aijalon, … Gibeon, Mahanaim, … Bethshan, Shunem, Tanaach, Megiddo – all familiar from the Old Testament stories. Then he came to name-ring 29 and read the signs: *y-w-d-h-m-l-k*. Could it be? He began to vocalise the consonantal letters (the ancient Egyptians did not write vowels): *Iouda-ha-malek* – 'Judah' (Heb. *Yehud*), followed by 'the Kingdom' (Heb. *ha-malcûth*).[3] Had Pharaoh Shoshenk conquered the Kingdom of Judah? Indeed he had! As I Kings 14:25-26 and II Chronicles 12:2-9 confirm, Shishak, king of Egypt, invaded Judah in the fifth year of King Rehoboam, son of Solomon, and took away the treasures of the Temple of Yahweh as his price for not ransacking Jerusalem. Champollion was delighted to have found another crucial chronological link between the events of the Bible and the history of the pharaohs. From that moment on, Shoshenk I, founder of the 22nd Dynasty, became identified with the biblical king Shishak who pillaged the Temple of Solomon in Year 5 of Rehoboam. This event – according to the biblical chronology – was datable to the first half of the tenth century BC.

The books of Kings and Chronicles detail chronological links between the reigns of the kings of Israel and Judah during the DIVIDED MONARCHY period and these (in combination with Assyrian annals mentioning Hebrew rulers) have enabled scholars to determine, with a fair degree of accuracy, the post-Solomonic biblical chronology. Again, as a direct result of some penetrating research undertaken by American biblical chronologist Edwin THIELE,[4] modern scholarship has reduced the Old Testament dates by fifty years, fixing Year 5 of Rehoboam at 925 BC. Shoshenk I's twentieth year was thus attached to the same anchor date and his first regnal year (the founding of the 22nd Dynasty) set at 945 BC. So came into being the second great pillar of Egyptian chronology.

Pillar Two

Shoshenk I, founder of the 22nd Dynasty is to be identified with the biblical 'Shishak, king of Egypt' who, according to I Kings 14:25-26 and II Chronicles 12:2-9, came to Jerusalem and despoiled the Temple of Solomon in Year 5 of Rehoboam. This event is datable to 925 BC using the widely accepted biblical chronology of Edwin Thiele.

Once more, the Egyptian monuments seemed to have confirmed the biblical narratives – but when we take a closer look at the Shoshenk campaign inscription, the whole edifice begins to collapse.

First, Champollion was entirely wrong in reading name-ring 29 as *Iouda-ha-malek* ('Judah the Kingdom'). As Wilhelm MAX-MÜLLER pointed out as early as 1888,[5] ring 29 should be read *Yad-ha-melek* which when translated literally means 'Hand of the King' and should be understood as 'Monument' or 'Stela of the King'. In other words it is a location in Palestine where some unnamed ruler had erected a commemorative stela.

More damaging still to Champollion's hasty reading is the geographical location of this Yadhamelek;[6] its position in the list locates it in northern Israel, well outside the boundaries of Judah, and so name-ring 29 cannot possibly be translated as 'Judah the Kingdom'.

Let us just remind ourselves of what we actually know about Shishak's campaign from the relevant biblical passages:

> Solomon tried to kill JEROBOAM but the latter made off and fled to Egypt, into the protection of Shishak, the king of Egypt. He remained in Egypt until Solomon's death. [I Kings 11:40]

In the last years of Solomon's reign Jeroboam, son of Nebat, became a threat to the throne. Following Solomon's attempt on his life, Jeroboam fled to Egypt where he received the protection of Pharaoh Shishak. He even married the Egyptian queen's sister. When Solomon died, Jeroboam returned to Israel and was

22. Name ring 29 containing the hieroglyphs which spell out the phrase 'Yadhamelek'.

proclaimed king of the ten northern tribes, whilst Solomon's eldest son and legitimate heir, REHOBOAM, was left with the rump kingdom of Judah – comprising the tribes of Judah and Benjamin. Jeroboam established his capital at Shechem and Rehoboam retained Jerusalem. This division of the Israelite kingdom (which lasted down to the fall of Samaria in 722 BC) is known in academic circles as 'the Schism' or 'Divided Monarchy'.

> Rehoboam, residing in Jerusalem, fortified a number of towns for the defence of Judah. He built Bethlehem, Etam, Tekoa, Bethzur, Soco, Adullam, Gath, Mareshah, Ziph, Adoraim, Lachish, Azekah, Zorah, Aijalon, Hebron, these being the fortified towns in Judah and Benjamin. He equipped these fortresses, stationing commanders in them, with supplies of food, oil and wine, and shields and spears in each of these towns, making them extremely strong and thus retaining control of Judah and Benjamin. [II Chronicles 11:5-12]

Why was Rehoboam so preoccupied with the fortification of these fifteen cities? What was the perceived danger to his small mountain kingdom? Certainly he may have felt threatened by his new northern neighbour, but the fortresses are located in an arc which sweeps around Judah's western and southern flanks. Was the perceived threat therefore from the south? The next crucial passage in II Chronicles gives us the answer.

> When Rehoboam had consolidated the kingdom and become strong, he and all Israel with him, abandoned the Law of Yahweh; and thus it happened that in the fifth year of King Rehoboam, Shishak king of Egypt marched on Jerusalem, because they had been unfaithful to Yahweh – with twelve hundred chariots and sixty thousand cavalry

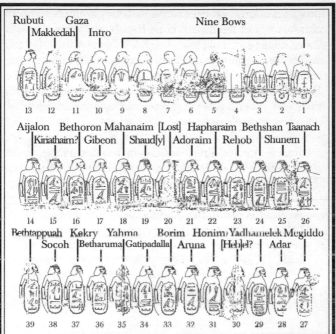

Rubuti Gaza Nine Bows
Makkedah Intro

13 12 11 10 9 8 7 6 5 4 3 2 1

Aijalon Bethoron Mahanaim [Lost] Hapharaim Bethshan Taanach
Kiriathaim? Gibeon Shaud[y] Adoraim Rehob Shunem

14 15 16 17 18 19 20 21 22 23 24 25 26

Bethtappuah Kekry Yahma Borim Honim Yadhamelek Megiddo
Socoh Betharuma Gatipadalla Aruna [Heb]el? Adar

39 38 37 36 35 34 33 32 31 30 29 28 27

23. Rows 1 to 3 of the Shoshenk I campaign city list. The boustrophedon principle is employed in this inscription for reading the order of march of the Egyptian army (i.e. right to left, then left to right, and right to left etc.). The campaign begins by listing the traditional enemies of Egypt known as the 'Nine Bows' (1 to 9), then a single name ring (10) carries the introductory phrase 'List of the towns [...]'. The campaign proper sets out from Gaza (11) and progresses through the Shephelah (12 to 14) before ascending the central ridge of Palestine via the Aijalon pass up to Bethhoron (16) and Gibeon (17). There is then a long geographical gap as the next city to be listed is Mahanaim in Transjordan (18). The main force of Shoshenk's army continues northwards up the Jordan Valley to Bethshan (24) turning westwards to enter the Jezreel valley. We then have the two major cities of Taanach (26) and Megiddo (27) listed at the end of Row II and the beginning of Row III respectively (thus demonstrating the boustrophedon principle). Next comes the submission of a series of towns in the western Jezreel before the army heads across the Carmel ridge via the Aruna pass (32) and on southwards through the Sharon plain back to Egypt. The other rows of the city list represent the itineraries of secondary strike forces sent to subdue the towns of the Jabbok valley (in Transjordan), the central hill country of Ephraim (Shechem and Tirzah), and a series of fortresses located in the Negev to the south of Judah. Only one of the towns designated as belonging to the kingdom of Judah (i.e. Aijalon) is mentioned in this list.

> and countless hordes of Libyans, Sukkiim and
> Kushites who came from Egypt with him. They
> captured the fortified towns of Judah and reached
> Jerusalem. [II Chronicles 12:1-4]

Shishak's army was enormous, consisting of foreign mercenaries as well as Egyptian troops. These 'countless hordes'
of foreigners included Kushites – soldiers from the warlike
kingdom of Kush located along the upper reaches of the
great Dongola Bend of the River Nile between the Third
and Fourth Cataracts (now in modern Sudan). This mighty
force easily overwhelmed Rehoboam's fortified strongholds
and soon stood outside the city gates of the Judahite king's
capital.

> So Shishak king of Egypt advanced on Jerusalem
> and carried off the treasures of the Temple and the
> treasures of the royal palace. He took everything
> away, including the golden shields which Solomon
> had made. [II Chronicles 12:9]

With no hope of redemption, Rehoboam had opened the
gates of Jerusalem and allowed the Egyptians to remove
all the treasures of the kingdom established by his predecessors, David and Solomon. In return for this gesture of
submission, Shishak went on his way and left Jerusalem
very much chastened but not destroyed.

These are the basic facts as derived from the biblical
narrative. Now let us see what we can learn from the Year
20 campaign city-list of Pharaoh Shoshenk I found on the
Bubastite Portal at Karnak.

The list itself would appear to be a genuine itinerary of
the campaign. Altogether there are ten rows of name-rings.
Rows VI to X involve a secondary campaign into the
NEGEV to the south of Judah which does not directly concern us here. Rows I to V, some sixty-five names in all, are
what we are really interested in.

We read the rows of name-rings in what is called 'BOUSTROPHEDON' order which means from right to left, then down a row and left to right, then down to the next row and right to left, etc. Row I begins on the right with the names of the 'Nine Bows' – the 'traditional enemies' of Egypt (occupying positions 1 to 9); then comes a single introductory phrase (no. 10) before we begin the campaign sequence proper with G[aza], Makkedah and Rubuti (nos. 11, 12 & 13). These last two towns are situated in the Shephelah – the foothills separating the coastal plain from the massif of the central hill country of Palestine. Clearly Shoshenk's forces had set out from Gaza on the coast and were heading inland and northwards.

Dropping down to the second row we find Aijalon at the left end of the line (no. 14). The Egyptians intended to strike into the uplands along the route which begins near Aijalon and leads up onto the central ridge. At position 17 is Gibeon. If Shoshenk is to be identified with the biblical Shishak, our next location should be Jerusalem itself, but instead we find Mahanaim (no. 18) – a city in Transjordan. Jerusalem simply is not there! Row II then lists a number of towns in the Jordan valley (nos. 19 to 23) before reaching Bethshan, Shunem and Taanach in the Jezreel valley (nos. 24, 25 & 26). Row III begins on the right with Megiddo (no. 27) and then goes on to list various other locations in the vicinity (including Yadhamelek). The row ends with Socoh and Bethtappuah in the Sharon Plain, back on the coastal strip to the south of the Carmel mountain range. Row IV is almost totally destroyed as a result of heavy erosion, but the names in Row V, most of which are located in the Jordan valley and the central ridge of the hills of Israel, suggest that both IV and V represent the itinerary of a second strike force which separated from the main army somewhere in the Jordan valley and then rejoined their colleagues at Megiddo.

Clearly, the main route of march of the Egyptian army was across the central hill country, down into the Jordan

Shoshenk Campaign List

1-9.	Nine Bows
10.	'List [of the towns …]'
11.	G[aza]
12.	Makkedah
13.	Rubuti
14.	**Aijalon**
15.	Kiriathaim?
16.	Bethhoron
17.	Gibeon
18.	Mahanaim
19.	Shaud[y]
20.	[Lost]
21.	Adoraim
22.	Hapharaim
23.	Rehob
24.	Bethshan
25.	Shunem
26.	Tanaach
27.	Megiddo
28.	Adar
29.	Yadhamelek
30.	[Heb]el?
31.	Honim
32.	Aruna
33.	Borim
34.	Gathpadalla
35.	Yahma
36.	Betharuma
37.	Kekry
38.	Socoh
39.	Bethtappuah
40-46.	[Lost]
47.	Bethsabu[ma]
48-51.	[Lost]

Fortified Cities of Rehoboam

A.	Bethlehem
B.	Etam
C.	Tekoa
D.	Bethzur
E.	Hebron
F.	Ziph
G.	Adoraim
H.	Lachish
I.	Mareshah
J.	Moresheth-Gath
K.	Adullam
L.	Socoh
M.	Azekah
N.	Zorah
14.	**Aijalon**

52.	Abel[meholah?]
53.	[P]enuel
54.	Hedeshet
55.	Succoth?
56.	Adam[ah]
57.	Zemaraim
58.	[M]igdol (Shechem?)
59.	[Ti]rzah
60.	[…]nar
61-63.	[Lost]
64.	H[…]pen
65.	Pa-Emek ('The Vale')

The campaign route of Shoshenk I superimposed upon a map of Palestine showing the fortified towns of Rehoboam which were purportedly captured by King Shishak of Egypt. Note that the thrust of Shoshenk's campaign is within the kingdom of Israel and the Negev whilst avoiding a penetration of the kingdom of Judah.

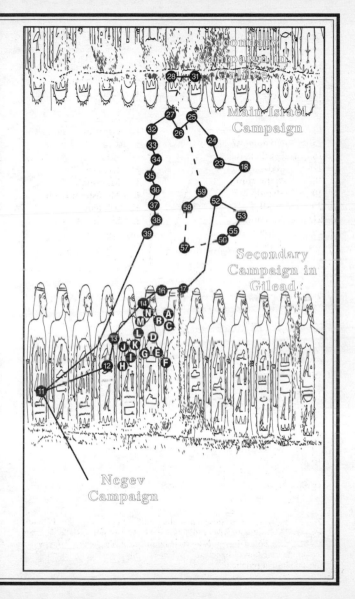

valley, up to the eastern entrance of the Jezreel valley and westwards along its floor before crossing the Mount Carmel ridge and heading south along the coastal plain for home. A secondary strike force also occupied themselves with the territory of the Northern Kingdom, whilst a third force campaigned in the Negev. The main campaign route did not enter the kingdom of Judah but rather skirted its northern border. Only one of the towns mentioned as being fortified by Rehoboam is listed as captured – the other fourteen are not mentioned at all. The real target of Shoshenk's campaign was the Jordan valley, the Jezreel valley and the Negev.

If Shoshenk I is to be equated with the biblical Shishak, why did he attack his ally Jeroboam in Israel whilst meticulously avoiding an incursion into the territory of his enemy, Rehoboam king of Judah? The whole situation is topsy-turvy: whilst Shishak attacks Judah and enters Jerusalem to plunder the Temple of Yahweh, Shoshenk attacks Israel and does not mention Jerusalem as one of the defeated cities in his campaign record; Shishak is allied to Israel and subjugates Judah whilst Shoshenk subjugates Israel and avoids confrontation with Judah. So can we honestly continue to contend that the Palestine campaign of Shoshenk I is identical with that of Shishak as mentioned in Kings and Chronicles?

There is a fundamental methodological problem here. Scholars are underpinning Egyptian chronology with a biblical synchronism. They readily accept the name-equation Shoshenk = Shishak and proclaim a correspondence between the Year 20 campaign of Shoshenk I and the Shishak assault upon Jerusalem. In doing so they dismiss the obvious discrepancies of fact between the two sources. If you are going to use biblical data to establish both the chronology of Egypt and the stratigraphical framework of Levantine archaeology, you cannot then go on to arbitrarily disregard selected sections of the historical material contained in the biblical source simply because they do

START OF THE TIP = 1069 BC

21ST DYNASTY

21st Dynasty dates are back-calculated from 945 BC (i.e. Year 1 Shoshenk I) using regnal data from contemporary texts and Manetho to reach 1069 BC for Year 1 of the dynasty founder – Smendes.

22ND DYNASTY

Yr 20 of Shoshenk I = 925 BC via the biblical synchronism of 1 Kings 14:25-26 and II Chronicles 12:2-9.

23RD DYNASTY

The 23rd Dynasty is synchronised to the 22nd by a double regnal date recorded in a Nile Level Text at Karnak making Shoshenk III (22nd Dyn.) contemporary with Pedubast I (23rd Dyn.)

24TH DYNASTY

25TH DYNASTY

The end of the 25th Dynasty is anchored to 664 BC – the sacking of Thebes by Ashurbanipal. The start of the dynasty is then established at c. 716 BC using regnal data from the monuments.

END OF THE TIP = 664 BC

Basic structure of the TIP in the conventional chronology of Kenneth Kitchen.

not fit your theory. Surely, if this were any sort of reliable historical synchronism, the facts from both sources, supposedly recording a single historical event, would agree in a substantial way. As it stands they do not agree at all. Confidence in this key synchronism and resulting chronological anchor point is misguided and dangerous.

To demonstrate how reliant we are upon this synchronism to determine the chronological length of the Third

Intermediate Period in Egypt we need only refer to a statement by one of the leading authorities on Egyptian
chronology – Professor Kenneth Kitchen himself. First he
establishes a date for the beginning of the 25th Dynasty
working back from our safe fixed point of 664 BC (death
of Taharka) using the highest regnal dates for the Kushite
pharaohs. He thus arrives at a date between 716 and 712
BC for the Year 1 of Shabaka, founder of the dynasty.[7]
Kitchen then reveals the conventional chronology's crucial
reliance on the Bible to establish the TIP chronology:

> Over two centuries earlier, the 21-year reign of the
> founder of the 22nd Dynasty, Shoshenk I, can be
> set at *ca.* 945-924 B.C., **thanks (i) to his synchro-
> nisms with the detailed chronology of Judah
> and Israel**, itself linked closely to a firm Assyrian
> chronology …, **and (ii) to the series of known
> regnal years of his successors, which fill up the
> interval 924-716/712 B.C. almost completely**, …[8]
> [my emphasis]

Note that the regnal years of Shoshenk I's successors are
made to 'fill up' a period of time which has been entirely
established in its length by the biblical synchronism
between Shoshenk I (= Shishak) and Rehoboam – which
in turn is dated by the biblical chronology of Edwin Thiele.
No wonder Kitchen regards the link between Shoshenk
and Rehoboam as 'the essential synchronism'![9]

The Ebers Calendar

The third great pillar of the currently accepted chronology
stems from a weird and wonderful thing called 'Sothic
Dating'. First let me explain exactly what this is and then I
will go on to demonstrate how it has been used to support
the orthodox dates for Ramesses II and Shoshenk I.

For countless centuries before the building of the High

The Names Shoshenk and Shishak

24. The cartouches of Pharaoh Shoshenk I found on a small stela fragment from the city of Megiddo. The hieroglyphic signs of the king's nomen (right oval) spell out *Sh-sh n k mry-imn* (Shoshenk, beloved of Amun).

In Egyptian hieroglyphs the name Shoshenk is usually written *Sh-sh-n-k* but occasionally as *Sh-sh-k* with the 'n' omitted. The latter form would thus appear to be an exact equivalent of the biblical name Shishak. However, the few monuments of Shoshenk I found in Palestine never display the missing 'n' form. Moreover, a contemporary text in east semitic (Akkadian) cuneiform transcribes the name Shoshenk as *Susink* – displaying both the 'n' and the common transposition of Egyptian 'sh' into semitic 's'. It is therefore apparent that the 'n' was part of the pronunciation of the king's name, even amongst the semitic-language speakers of the Near East. Hence the biblical name Shishak is not a straightforward equivalent of Shoshenk. It is, in fact, common for hieroglyphic writing not to indicate all the sounds which make up a particular word; the script itself is a monumental art form, and as such is governed by rules of aesthetic arrangement rather than simple 'phonetics' – in other words, the omission of the 'n' is a fact of the writing not of the pronunciation of the name Shoshenk.

Dam at Aswan in the 1960s the River Nile had overflowed its banks in the months of high summer, drowning the fertile Black Land which nestles between the desolate plateaux of the Sahara and Eastern Deserts.[10]

The phenomenon of the Nile inundation results from the annual rain storms which fall upon the Abyssinian and Ethiopian highlands far to the south where the Blue Nile and River Atbara have their sources. This event happens in early summer. The heavy downpours, combined with the melting of the winter snows on the highest peaks, result in an erosion of the rock and soil surfaces of those mountainous regions. The silt thus created is then washed down into the main stream of the Nile at Khartoum (Blue Nile) and ed-Damar (Atbara) where it flows northwards, reaching Egypt in mid July. Within weeks the high banks of the Nile are breached and the thick fertile soup of the waters of inundation covers the fields, washing the soil through to remove the damaging natural salts and replenishing the land with a deposit of rich black silt which provides valuable nutrients. By late September the flood has passed its peak and the waters begin to recede. The planting of crops takes place shortly after and a bountiful harvest can be expected in late spring/early summer, before the agricultural cycle begins all over again.

This was the basis of the ancient Egyptian year which was divided into three seasons – *Akhet* (Inundation), *Peret* (Emergence) and *Shemu* (Aridity). These main periods were, in turn, divided into four thirty-day months, each of three ten-day weeks. The total number of days in these twelve months was, of course, only three hundred and sixty, and so the Egyptians added five 'days upon the year', or EPAGO-MENAL days, to bring their civil calendar up to the required three-hundred-and-sixty-five-day year. The crucial factor for us here is the Egyptians' apparent failure to include a leap-year day every fourth year so as to allow for the extra quarter of a day which is needed to bring the Earth back to exactly the same location in its annual orbit of the Sun. The net result of this failure to measure the exact length of the astronomical year (365.25 days) is that the ancient Egyptian civil calendar slipped behind the Earth's natural clock by one day every fourth year. Let us take a look at how this works.

From earliest times, the Egyptian priest-astronomers had observed that the start of the inundation season was heralded by a celestial event. On the 21st of July (in the modern calendar) the Dog-star, otherwise known as SIRIUS, which is the brightest light in the Egyptian celestial sphere after Venus (Sun and Moon excluded), rises HELIACALLY at dawn. The ancient Egyptians identified the Dog-star with the goddess Sopdet – the Sothis of the Greeks (hence the term 'Sothic Chronology').

Now this event of the heliacal rising of Sopdet or Sothis does not happen every day of the year because the Earth's movement within its orbit alters the observation point on our planet relative to the fixed positions of the stars. Thus the stars of the universe appear not only to arc across the night sky as a result of the Earth's rotation but also their appearance and disappearance on the observer's horizon seems to move because of the change in the Earth's position in the Solar System. There is then a period of seventy days in the year when Sothis rises after the Sun has washed out the night sky and so the star's rising cannot be observed. The heliacal rising of Sopdet is therefore when the goddess is witnessed for the first time after the invisibility period, when sunrise is sufficiently late to permit Sothis to reappear for a brief moment before being masked again by the sunlight. It was noted by the Egyptian priests that this ephemeral event seemed to announce the beginning of the inundation and so Sothis became the herald of the Nile flood (represented by the god Hapy) and her first timid dawn appearance became recognised as the start of the civil calendar – the first day of the first month of Akhet. This official establishment of the Egyptian civil calendar, beginning with the rise of Sothis coinciding with the start of the inundation, is lost in the mists of time, but the system seems to have been in operation at least as early as the OLD KINGDOM.

When the civil calendar was first created, everything would have appeared to be fine for a couple of generations or so, but sooner or later the failure to accommodate the extra quarter of a day each year will have resulted in a slippage of the official dating system against the natural astronomical year. After four years, Sothis would have risen heliacally one day later – on the second day of the first month of Akhet. Four years on and its appearance would have occurred on day three, eight years later still on day five, and so on. By the end of forty years (approximately two generations) this Cinderella of the heavens would have been ten days late for the ball – still not a major problem but perhaps a little embarrassing for the priest-astronomers. However, some eight hundred years further down the road the Egyptians would have been in a total mess, with Akhet (normally the inundation season) falling in the time of the planting season! Only after a period of one thousand four hundred and sixty-one years would Sothis rise heliacally again on the first day of the first month of Akhet and the civil calendar would once again correspond to the natural year. This one thousand four hundred and sixty-one-year cycle has become known as the 'Great Sothic Year'.

How does this help us with establishing the dates for the New Kingdom and therefore the time of Ramesses II? Well, in around AD 238, the Roman grammarian, CENSORINUS, composed a work entitled *DE DIE NATALI* in honour of his patron, QUINTUS CAERELLIUS. In this book he relates that in AD 139 the Dog-star rose on the first day of Thoth (i.e. the first month of Akhet – named Tekhy by the Egyptians) which was equivalent to the twelfth day of the Kalends of August in the Roman calendar. From this information we can establish that Sothis rose heliacally on the first day of the Egyptian civil year precisely on the 21st of July – in other words at the beginning of one of the Great Sothic Year cycles when the civil calendar of Egypt briefly coincided with the natural solar year. If one Great Sothic Year began in AD 139, then the previous one must have commenced in 1321 BC (1461 years earlier[11]) and the one before that in 2781 BC. Now if a contemporary Egyptian text could be found with a calendar date for the heliacal rising of Sothis dated to a specific year in a pharaoh's reign, it would be a simple matter to place that year in absolute time by a straightforward calculation using the Sothic-dating framework.

That is precisely what happened in the 1870s when just such a calendar (acquired by Georg EBERS) was found at Thebes. This 'Ebers Calendar' was datable to the ninth year of AMENHOTEP I and it recorded the heliacal rising of Sothis on the ninth day of the third month of Shemu. The Sothic calculation made by the great calendrical scholar Richard PARKER in 1950 established the absolute date at 1542 BC (assuming an observation point at Memphis) which gave a date of 1575 for the start of the New Kingdom.[12]

The date of the heliacal rising observation has more recently been adjusted downwards by twenty-five years as a result of a scholarly consensus that the observation probably took place at Thebes (where the papyrus was found) rather than Memphis.[13] The difference in latitude between the two cities would require a lowering of the date because the heliacal rising of Sothis would have been one day earlier at the more southerly latitude on account of the Earth's curvature. Thus the currently accepted date for Year 9 of Amenhotep I is 1517 BC and the beginning of the 18th Dynasty set at 1550 BC with the accession of Ahmose I, Amenhotep's father. Here, then, we have reached our third main pillar of the orthodox chronology.

Pillar Three

The date for the beginning of the Egyptian New Kingdom can be set in the mid sixteenth century (1550 BC) – by means of the Sothic date of 1517 BC for Year 9 of Amenhotep I supplied in Papyrus Ebers.

The Lunar Date of Ramesses II

The fourth pillar is also based on astronomy. Using all the regnal data from the monuments of the 18th Dynasty kings (from the establishment of 1550 BC for the start of the dynasty), a date for the commencement of the 19th Dynasty can be set at the beginning of the thirteenth century BC (1295 BC).

- Papyrus Leiden I 350 (*verso* page III, line 6) is dated to Year 52 of Ramesses II. It records a series of month lengths according to the lunar cycle (the second form of calendar in use in Egypt). In contrast to the civil year of fixed thirty-day months, here we have a series of months whose durations vary between twenty-nine and thirty days – depending on the length of time between observations of the new moon. The sequence of short and long lunar months in any single year repeats itself in a cycle of twenty-five years when the same pattern can then be observed. As a result, using astronomical retrocalculations, we can place Year 52 of Ramesses only in years 1278, 1253, 1228 or 1203 BC – but only if we have already determined that the 19th Dynasty falls in the thirteenth century.

- Given that the regnal data from the monuments indicates the 18th Dynasty lasted around two hundred and fifty years, the 19th Dynasty must have started *circa* 1300 BC, the 18th Dynasty having begun in 1550 BC according to the evidence of Papyrus Ebers.

- With Ramesses I having ruled for just over one year and his son Seti I reigning for at least eleven years, Ramesses II could not have acceded to the throne before *circa* 1288 BC. His Year 52 could not therefore have fallen in either 1278 or 1253. Scholars also thought that the year 1203 seemed to be a little too low and, if entertained, would create a much longer reign for Seti

I than the inscriptional evidence requires (his highest regnal date being Year 11 [14]).

- This leaves candidate 1228 BC for Year 52 of Ramesses II – giving an accession date of 1279 BC for the Pharaoh of the Oppression.

Pillar Four

Ramesses II began to rule Egypt in 1279 BC because a lunar date supplied in Papyrus Leiden I 350 appears to confirm that his fifty-second year fell exactly in 1228 BC

This fine tuning of the 19th Dynasty dates has now become a major anchor in the chronology of Egypt around which much of the archaeology of the ancient world is structured

---

The Four Pillars

1. The sacking of Thebes by the Assyrians in 664 BC = Year 1 of Psamtek I.

2. The 925 BC campaign into Palestine in Year 20 of Shoshenk I = Shishak (based on I Kings 14:25-26 & II Chronicles 12:2-9).

3. The accession of Ahmose in 1550 BC (based on the heliacal rising of Sothis in 1517 BC = Year 9 Amenhotep I).

4. The accession of Ramesses II in 1279 BC (based on the Year 52 = 1228 BC lunar date).

The Papyrus Ebers Calendar

25

Figure 25 is a facsimile version of the Ebers calendar which is written from right to left in the original hieratic script. Altogether there are thirteen lines consisting of the regnal date 'Year 9' plus the prenomen and titles of the king, followed by twelve lines representing the individual twelve months of the year. The translation of the 'calendar' is provided on the right.

Line 1 has the year date and the coronation name of the king. Neither is in dispute as they are both clearly legible in the hieratic original. Line 2 gives us the following information:

The New Year's Festival (Egy. *heb wepet-renpet*) took place on the ninth day of Month III in the season of Shemu (of Year 9) when the star Sopdet (i.e. Sothis) went forth (understood to mean 'rose heliacally').

The remaining eleven lines start with the names of the months, followed by month number (I to IV), season and day (always 9) in that order. You will observe that lines 3, 5, 6, 7, 9, 10, 11 and 13 all have a dot in the place where lines 2, 4, and 12 have the name of the season written. These dots clearly represent ditto marks. Thus line 3 should be understood as Month IV of Shemu, lines 5, 6 and 7 as Months II, III and IV of Akhet respectively and lines 9, 10 and 11 as Months II, III and IV of Peret. Line 13's ditto represents Month II of

Year 9, under the person of the Dual King Djeserkare, living forever;
New Year's Festival, month III of Shemu, day 9, the going forth of Sopdet;
Tekhy, month IV of Shemu, day 9, the going forth of Sopdet;
Menkhet, month I of Akhet, day 9, the going forth of Sopdet;
Huther, month II of Akhet, day 9, the going forth of Sopdet;
Kaherka, month III of Akhet, day 9, the going forth of Sopdet;
Shefbedet, month IV of Akhet, day 9, the going forth of Sopdet;
Rekeh (1st), month I of Peret, day 9, the going forth of Sopdet;
Rekeh (2nd), month II of Peret, day 9, the going forth of Sopdet;
Renutet, month III of Peret, day 9, the going forth of Sopdet;
Khonsu, month IV of Peret, day 9, the going forth of Sopdet;
Khentykhet, month I of Shemu, day 9, the going forth of Sopdet;
Ipet, month II of Shemu, day 9, the going forth of Sopdet.

Shemu following on directly from the full writing 'Month I of Shemu' in line 12. This is all self-explanatory. But then how should one interpret the column of dots which runs vertically below the Line 2 phrase 'going forth of Sopdet' (Egy. *peret Sepdet*)? Surely these too are Egyptian ditto marks and must be an instruction to the reader to 'repeat the phrase above' – in other words, every line of the document from 2 down to 13 is completed by the phrase 'going forth of Sopdet'. Now we already know that the heliacal rising of Sothis only physically occurs once in a year, so how do we know which month actually contained the real heliacal rising event? Surely it could have fallen in any of the twelve civil months. But what about the phrase 'New Year's Festival' in Line 2? You should be aware that scholars have recently suggested that in the New Kingdom the pharaohs inaugurated a new type of year known as the 'Regnal Year' which began on the day of the king's coronation. As Professor Ulricht Luft has argued,[15] the Papyrus Ebers date 'Day 9, Month III of Shemu' is, in fact, the coronation day of Amenhotep I. Thus, the wepet-renpet day in ninth year of Amenhotep is an anniversary date of the coronation which marks the beginning of the Regnal Year calendar. Indeed, it does seem to be an 'auspicious', perhaps pre-arranged date given that it is the ninth day of the third month of the third season in the ninth year. Luft then argues that 'The Ebers calendar is an aborted experiment to substitute the Regnal Year for the Civil Year'.[16]

The Egyptian chronological edifice has thus been supported by four apparently mighty pillars upon which the otherwise floating chronologies of Mycenaean Greece, Minoan Crete, Hittite Anatolia, the Levantine city-states of the Late Bronze Age and above all pre-Solomonic Israel have all been constructed. However, as I will now attempt to demonstrate, they are not as strong as they look.

***

First, it should be noted that the date of pillar four is dependent on both pillars three and two, of which the former is directly derived from Sothic chronology whilst the latter has its date provided by the Bible. I have argued that the Shoshenk = Shishak equation is unsound and cannot safely be used to determine the chronology of Egypt for the First Millennium BC. Similarly the chronology of the latter half of the Second Millennium is held in place by the Papyrus Ebers Sothic calendar. So, let us now take a look at that document to see if it really does give a date of 1517 BC for the ninth year of Amenhotep I.

The caption accompanying the figure on page 154 describes in detail the types of questions which scholars have voiced concerning Papyrus Ebers. In essence there are two major problems: (a) the phrase 'going-forth of Sothis' (i.e. the heliacal rising) appears in every month of the calendar – but a heliacal rising can only take place once in a year; and (b) the New Year's Day festival occurs on the anniversary of Amenhotep's coronation day which further suggests that the date Year 9, Month III of the Third Season, Day 9 has nothing whatsoever to do with an actual observation of the heliacal rising of the Dog-star.

With such confusion and debate over this strange document, it is hardly surprising that respected Egyptologists such as Professors Jürgen von Beckerath,[17] Wolfgang Helck,[18] Erik Hornung,[19] Ulricht Luft,[20] Winfride Barta[21] and Jac. Janssen[22] are questioning the reliability of the Ebers 'Sothic date' as an anchor point for Egyptian chronology.

So, I cast off the tethering rope of Egyptian history from this long-used but now corroded and insecure anchor with a final statement on the matter from Professor Manfred Bietak, Director of the Austrian Institute for Egyptology in Vienna:

> The framework of regnal dates from the monuments together with the genealogical data has become so secure that it is possible from safe fixed points to calculate backwards with tolerable uncertainties. The chronology of the New Kingdom therefore no longer depends on the Sothis-date of the Year 9 of Amenhotep I, which is insecure and should not be used any more.[23]

Conclusion Five

Of the four chronological supports for Egyptian history, only Pillar One – the 664 BC sacking of Thebes by the Assyrians – is sound. Pillar Two – the Shishak/Shoshenk synchronism – is historically untenable; the value of Pillar Three – the Ebers Calendar Sothic Date – is disputed by many respected Egyptologists; and Pillar Four – the Year 52 lunar date of Ramesses II – is entirely dependant on Pillar Three. There are therefore no safe fixed points in the chronology of Egypt earlier than 664 BC.

Chapter Six

TOWARDS A NEW
CHRONOLOGY

t has taken quite a time to get to the point where we can begin our search for the historical Israelites. But before guiding you back into the pre-Classical period of Man's long history – to the great Bronze and Iron Ages – to the heroic age – the era of myth and legend – perhaps I should seize this opportunity to summarise quickly the arguments so far.

A Chance to Recap

In *Part One* I highlighted three chronological anomalies which led to the conclusion that something was drastically wrong with our chronological framework for the Third Intermediate Period in Egypt. The evidence from Mariette's excavation of the Serapeum had suggested that the time span of the orthodox chronology was far too long for the number of Apis bulls buried during the era.

When Brugsch cleared the Royal Cache near Deir el-Bahri, he found that it contained a mummy which was wrapped in Year 11 of Shoshenk I, founder of the 22nd Dynasty – thirty-four years after the final sealing of the cache in Year 10 of Siamun (a pharaoh who ruled in the mid 21st Dynasty). Here again the orthodox chronology had produced another puzzling chronological conundrum.

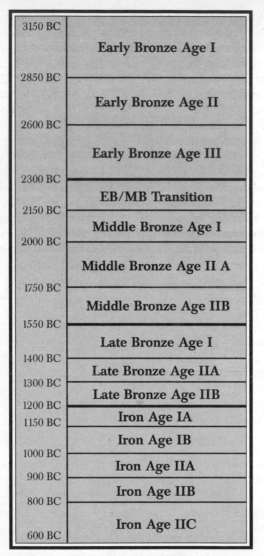

3150 BC	Early Bronze Age I
2850 BC	Early Bronze Age II
2600 BC	Early Bronze Age III
2300 BC	EB/MB Transition
2150 BC	Middle Bronze Age I
2000 BC	Middle Bronze Age II A
1750 BC	Middle Bronze Age IIB
1550 BC	Late Bronze Age I
1400 BC	Late Bronze Age IIA
1300 BC	Late Bronze Age IIB
1200 BC	Iron Age IA
1150 BC	Iron Age IB
1000 BC	Iron Age IIA
900 BC	Iron Age IIB
800 BC	Iron Age IIC
600 BC	

Chronological chart showing the archaeological ages and their dates as they have been established within the conventional chronology.

We decided that the best solution was to experiment with the idea that Shoshenk I somehow ruled before Siamun. This in turn required that the 21st and 22nd Dynasties were in part contemporary.

The archaeology of the royal burial ground at Tanis, excavated by Montet, seemed to confirm the dual-dynasty hypothesis. In this case the overlap between the two lines of pharaohs was in the order of at least one hundred and forty-one years. This was because the evidence from the Tanite necropolis indicated that Osorkon II, fifth ruler of the 22nd Dynasty, was buried before Psusennes I, second ruler of the 21st Dynasty.

In effect, what all three anomalies were trying to tell us was that the chronology of the TIP currently employed by historians had been overstretched or artificially expanded and that a radical and thorough re-examination of the era is now clearly required.

When in *Part Two* we then took a look at how this apparently overstretched chronology might have come about we discovered that the principal culprit had been a need, on the part of nineteenth-century scholars, to 'find' the Bible in Egypt. They had identified Ramesses II as the Pharaoh of the Oppression simply because they assumed an historical link between Pi-Ramesse (Ramesses' delta residence) and the store-city of Raamses (mentioned in the book of Exodus). Such a link was tenuous at best and was dependent on a subjective filtering of anachronisms in the Old Testament texts. The Israelites may have built a store-city *at the location* of Pi-Ramesse but they had not necessarily built the capital and residence of Ramesses II there in the 19th Dynasty. In fact, the biblical date for the Exodus (1447 BC) was entirely at odds with the dates for the 19th Dynasty (1295-1186 BC). The link between Ramesses II and the Israelite Bondage was an illusion without any real archaeological foundation.

Again Egyptologists of the last century bequeathed to us another fixed date in Egyptian chronology through their

adherence to the biblical narratives. Champollion's identification of the biblical Shishak with Shoshenk I had
resulted in the latter's twentieth year being tied to Year 5
of Rehoboam which biblical chronologists subsequently
dated to 925 BC. The beginning of the 22nd Dynasty had
thus been set at 945 BC (Year 1 of SHOSHENK I). Working
backwards, employing the regnal dates from the monuments and other texts, the date for the start of the 21st
Dynasty was duly established at 1069 BC. We saw how,
methodologically, the regnal dates of the Third Intermediate Period pharaohs were then made to 'fill up' the time
span between the start of the TIP in 1069 and the sacking
of Thebes by ASHURBANIPAL in 664 BC – our earliest
genuinely fixed date in Egyptian history. But the identification of Shoshenk I with Shishak was shown to be
untenable. The information derived from the two sources
– the Karnak campaign list and the books of I Kings and II
Chronicles – did not agree in any detail and a comparison
of the overall campaign strategies produced a total contradiction. How can it be methodologically sound to rely so
completely on such a dubious synchronism – especially
when the whole chronology of the Egyptian Third Intermediate Period hangs upon the resulting date?

We also saw how the Ebers Calendar Sothic date has
now been discarded by many Egyptologists. So the date
for the beginning of the New Kingdom (Year 1 of AHMOSE)
can only be established using highest regnal dates for the
pharaohs of the 18th, 19th and 20th Dynasties – working,
as Bietak states, backwards 'from safe fixed points' with
'tolerable uncertainties'. However, as the 'safe fixed point'
of 925 BC (Shoshenk = Shishak) is in reality unsafe, then
we must fall back on 664 BC for our next (now earliest)
secure date in Egyptian history – lying at the other side of
the chronological quagmire known as the Third Intermediate Period.

With so much doubt as to the real length of the TIP
the only option left is for scholars to dismantle the great

edifice of Egyptian chronology and begin the process of reconstruction all over again – basing the new model on archaeological and textual information available today which was not to hand during the last century when the foundations of the orthodox chronology were first being established. This benefit of hindsight will be very useful to that process as *Parts One* and *Two* of this book have made abundantly clear. One possible method for shortening the length of the TIP is to consider a greater degree of overlap between the five dynasties which make up the era. Scholars already accept the principle for the latter part of the TIP: the 25TH DYNASTY and early 26TH DYNASTY are recognised as being contemporary; the second half of the 22ND DYNASTY is known to have run concurrently with the so called 23RD DYNASTY; and even during the early TIP it is recognised that there was a 21ST DYNASTY line of kings ruling from Tanis whilst an offshoot 'royal' line ruled at Thebes. The concept of a contemporary 21st and 22nd Dynasties is not therefore such a radical departure from the political norm of the times.

A Genealogical Bridge to the Past

There is one further important class of material which enables us to assess the true historical duration of the TIP. During the Third Intermediate Period it was the practice for eldest sons and heirs to have monuments (usually statues) made in honour of their deceased fathers. These monuments were invariably inscribed with hieroglyphic texts recording a genealogy of the dedicator's ancestors, sometimes going back over ten generations and more. In most cases the genealogies prove to be of little chronological significance because those earlier generations are rarely identified with any specific contemporary reigning monarch. Thus counting the generations to estimate the time interval between the dedicator and his ancestor does not help us to determine the time span back to an ancestral king. There are, however, three (and to my knowledge only three) long genealogies which *do* give us a crucial connection with certain New Kingdom pharaohs. As such they provide an alternative means not only of assessing the length of the early TIP but also of establishing in which century Ramesses II ruled the Black Land. The three genealogies are:

1. The graffito genealogy of Khnemibre in the Wadi Hammamat;

2. The statue genealogy of Ankhefenkhons in the Cairo Museum; and

3. The Memphite Genealogy of the High Priests of Ptah, now in Berlin.

To demonstrate the potential of this dating tool I will discuss just the first of the three genealogies here whilst assigning the others to *Appendix B* for follow-up study. Before we tackle the Wadi Hammamat genealogy we have to determine the length of an average generation so that we can give some chronological meaning to these ancestral lists.

It is unfortunate – but the way of surviving historical evidence – that no data on the length of time between the birth of a father and the birth of his eldest surviving son has come down to us from the ancient world.[1] What we do have is a great deal of information about the lengths of the reigns of the rulers of the era. Now this, of course, is not the same as a natural generation, but it bears a reasonably close proximity – given that we are, in the majority of cases, dealing with a father to son succession. A detailed survey of the well-documented dynasties of the ancient world (see the table in *Appendix B*) produces an average reign length of seventeen years. If we round the figure up to twenty years (in order to allow for brother successions and usurpations[2]) and use this as our generation length, we will be sufficiently close to the truth to make some approximate dating calculations. (Kenneth Kitchen and Maurice Bierbrier – the two most prominent UK-based chronologists of the orthodox school – both use a twenty-year generation in their genealogical calculations.[3]) Given the various imponderables we have to put up with when using genealogical data, it would be circumspect to bear in mind that all dates in this section of the discussion will have a wide margin of error of up to ± twenty years.

Let me take you on an expedition into the great Eastern Desert along the route from the Nile at Koptos to the Red Sea near the port of Kuseir. An ancient road, linking the Nile valley with the sea trade routes to eastern Africa and Mesopotamia, follows the bed of a deep wadi which cuts its way through the limestone plateau. Roughly half way along the Wadi Hammamat the traveller reaches mountains of jet black stone. Here the Egyptians quarried the fine-grained SCHIST to make the magnificent royal statues of the pharaohs. To the south of the modern tarmac road a cliff of this pearl-like stone rises up almost vertically, cut and dissected by workmen into thousands of huge smooth facets. Here, all over the rock, the quarrymen and their supervisors inscribed graffiti. One particular inscription, high up on a very narrow sloping ledge, is what we have journeyed here to find. To the right of the main body of the inscription is a short 'label' text which dates the document to the twenty-sixth year of the Persian king, DARIUS I. The author of the inscription is the Royal Architect Khnemibre, son of Ahmose-saneit. Year 26 of Darius I can be securely dated to 496 BC (as it comes after – that is later than – our key anchor point of 664 BC). The text of Khnemibre's inscription extends backwards over an amazing twenty-two generations to the well-attested Rahotep – vizier of Egypt during the first half of the reign of Ramesses II.[4] Here, then, we have an opportunity to calculate an approximate date for Ramesses the Great by counting back through the twenty-two twenty-year generations.

The Genealogy of the Royal Architects

496 – Khnemibre = Year 26 Darius I
516 – Ahmose-saneit – born in reign of Amasis?
536 – Ankh-Psamtek – born in reign of Psamtek II?
556 – Wahibre-teni – born late in reign of Psamtek I?
576 – Nestefnut
596 – Tjaenhebyu
616 – Nestefnut
636 – Tja(en)hebyu
656 – Nestefnut
676 – Tja(en)hebyu
696 – Nestefnut
716 – Tja(en)hebyu
736 – Haremsaf
756 – Mermer (?)
776 – Haremsaf – temp. Shoshenk I (OC – *c.* 935 BC)
796 – Amunherpamesha
816 – Pepy
836 – [name lost]
856 – May
876 – Nefermenu
896 – Wedjakhons
916 – Bakenkhons
936 – Rahotep – early Ramesses II (OC – *c.* 1270 BC)

From this long genealogy we obtain a very rough date of *circa* 936 BC for the beginning of the reign of Ramesses II and this date is derived from a genealogy securely attached to 496 BC = Year 26 of Darius I – a date which is accepted by all scholars. Two conclusions can be drawn from this extraordinary genealogy.

1. It casts considerable doubt on the orthodox chronology with its thirteenth century dating of Ramesses II (start of reign 1279 BC). This would require an average generation of over thirty-five years (1279 BC – 495 BC = 784 years ÷ 22 generations = 35.64 years per generation). Can scholars justifiably argue for a generation of

such length given that the average age of death in the ancient world was probably around thirty-five years?[5]

2. We can surely identify the Royal Architect Haremsaf (dated in the genealogy to *circa* 776 BC) as the Royal Architect Haremsaf whose son inscribed the 'Stela 100' of Hedjkheperre Shoshenk I at the Gebel es-Silsila quarries. This inscription gives instructions for the cutting of sandstone blocks for the construction of the Bubastite Portal and Great Court at Karnak.[6] The New Chronology date for the cutting of Stela 100 is *circa* 795 BC whereas the conventional date is 925 BC. For a full discussion of the true dating of Shoshenk I the reader is referred to *Appendix A*.

26. Left: Khnemibre and the goddess Hathor, mistress of the desert.

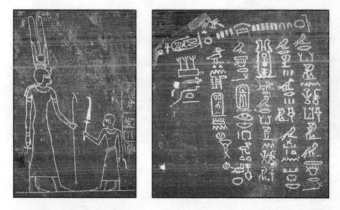

27. Right: The label text from the genealogy of the royal architects. The date 'Year 26, fourth month of Shemu under the Dual King Darius, living for all time' can clearly be seen in the horizontal line at the top. The name Khnemibre is carved at the top of the third column from the right standing inside a double-plumed cartouche; this is because the royal architect was born in the reign of Pharaoh Khnemibre Amasis and was given the same name chosen for that ruler's prenomen (complete with the royal cartouche!).

28. View of the whole Genealogy of the Royal Architects located in the Wadi Hammamat quarries. To the lower right is the 'label text' giving the date of the inscription as Year 26 of Darius I. Bottom left is the little scene of Khnemibre standing before Hathor. Above and between these two elements is the genealogy itself in two columns of text. The inscription begins at the top of the left column (reading right to left) and the generations progress backwards in time as you read down the column. As a result the two Haremsafs (highlighted) are located near the bottom of the first column. The genealogy then continues at the top of the right column, where about halfway down the early 19th Dynasty Royal Architect and Vizier Rahotep is located. The inscription is remarkably well preserved and there is therefore no reason to argue that any 'generations' are lost as a result of erosion.

If we take both observations together we find that the orthodox chronology produces a shortfall of up to ten generations between Ramesses II and Shoshenk I[7] and, at the same time, the interval between Shoshenk I and Darius I appears to be missing another eight generations.[8] Scholars usually explain this type of phenomenon by suggesting that the scribe omitted generations of ancestors through the process of HAPLOGRAPHY,[9] but is it really possible that Khnemibre made the same mistake twice?

It will not be surprising to learn that the other genealogies discussed in *Appendix B* appear to suffer from this same haplography. Applying the traditional chronology, the Nespaherenhat genealogy would be short of eight generations between MERENPTAH and OSORKON I,[10] whilst the Memphite Genealogy appears to have up to six generations missing for the period from the late 19th Dynasty to the early part of the 21st Dynasty.

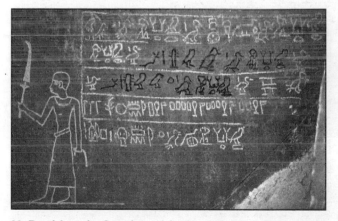

29. Detail from the Genealogy of the Royal Architects located in the Wadi Hammamat showing the hieroglyphs (in black) which spell out the name Haremsaf. Here there are two architects with the same name, the upper being the grandson of the lower. Haremsaf the elder would appear to be the best candidate for the royal architect of Shoshenk I as Haremsaf the younger would create even greater problems for TIP chronology, requiring another forty or so years to be removed.

The location of the Wadi Hammamat and Gebel es-Silsila quarries.

Can *all three* of the genealogies be in error to such a degree? Historians who are prepared to address this issue will either have to conclude that the three genealogies were all mis-recorded (bearing in mind that they are the *only* three genealogies which directly link the TIP back to the 19th Dynasty) or accept that we have here strong evidence that the conventional dates for the New Kingdom – in particular those of Ramesses II – are in error by a considerable number of years.

Conclusion Six

The Genealogy of the Royal Architects, discovered in the Wadi Hammamat, confirms that the era known as the TIP has been overstretched. Furthermore, all three key genealogies linking back to the New Kingdom indicate that over a century must be removed from the chronology of the transition period between the late-19th Dynasty and the early Third Intermediate Period.

This is perhaps a good place to summarise what we have achieved as we reach the end of Part Two of *A Test of Time*. The New Chronology has determined that Ramesses II should be dated to the tenth century BC – some three hundred and fifty years later than the date which had been assigned to him in the orthodox chronology. As a consequence, the archaeology of Palestine associated with the late-18th and early-19th Dynasties – Late Bronze II – now represents the historical period known as the Early Israelite Monarchy, the era of David and Solomon.

As I have argued, this shortening of the chronology can be achieved in part by overlapping the 21st Dynasty with the 22nd Dynasty. However, chronological adjustments within the sequence of reigns which make up Manetho's 20th Dynasty have also clearly to be made if the genealogies are to be regarded as accurate. Because of the complexities of 20th Dynasty chronology, my suggestions for a revision of that period have not been included in this book. An outline chronology has been developed, but further research is needed before the 20th Dynasty can be added to the New Chronology model. In effect, this chapter has been dedicated to the task of exploring ways to circumnavigate these 20th Dynasty difficulties. I trust that I have succeeded in demonstrating how, by using the genealogies as a bridge over troubled waters, we are able to step safely back into a 19th Dynasty which no longer belongs in the thirteenth century BC, as with the conventional dating, but rather in the tenth and ninth centuries.

***

The difficulty with complex arguments like these is knowing just what to include in the main text of the book and what to assign to the footnotes and appendices. I am further restrained by the university regulations regarding my PhD thesis which, as I write, is due for examination in a year's time. Publication of the research and detailed argumentation of a University of London thesis is not permitted prior to submission of the dissertation to the examiners. I am unable, therefore, to give you much more than a general outline of the model being developed for a revised Third Intermediate Period chronology – the basis of the overall historical construction being offered here. Some of the more difficult material which gives a clearer indication as to how the New Chronology of the TIP might work is contained in the *Appendices* in *Part Five* of this book. Those who are still thirsty for more sips from the TIP quagmire can, of course, refer to that material now before returning to begin *Part Three*.

Part Three

Legendary Kings and Chronicles

Egypt and the United Monarchy Period in Israel

𐤟𐤔𐤋𐤔

Chapter Seven

THE HISTORICAL SHISHAK

he preparation for our journey back into Old Testament times has been long and fairly meticulous. It was necessary for me to lay down a solid foundation of argument upon which to base our fresh search for the historical Bible before we started out on that journey – but now I think we are probably ready for the great adventure.

A New Chronology Date for Ramesses the Great

The genealogies have brought us to a situation in which we find Ramesses the Great on the throne of Egypt, towards the end of the tenth century – the time when Rehoboam becomes king of Judah and when the Temple of Yahweh in Jerusalem is plundered by the pharaoh known in the biblical tradition as Shishak. Is it remotely possible that Shishak is none other than Ramesses II, the ruler previously thought to have been the Pharaoh of the Oppression and Exodus?

Do we have a record of Ramesses II plundering Jerusalem? We may indeed have just such a reference. You will recall my 'expedition' to photograph the precariously situated block atop the north pylon of the Ramesseum at Thebes. Inscribed there is the following text:

The town which the king (Ramesses II) plundered (Egy. *khefa*[1]) in Year 8 – Shalem.

Shalem was the ancient name of the city of Jerusalem – indeed the 'City (or foundation) of Shalem' is precisely what 'Jerusalem' means.[2] We have come to the view, through the New Chronology, that it was Ramesses and not Shoshenk who campaigned against the capital of Rehoboam's mountain kingdom. This event took place in the pharaoh's eighth regnal year, according to the Ramesseum inscription – and we can further date that event to 925 BC through Thiele's biblical chronology. Professor Kitchen, having made a detailed study of the war reliefs of Ramesses II, confirms that Ramesses went up to Jerusalem.

… next spring for Years 7/8 … Ramesses took things in hand. In no time he reached Gaza … A flying-

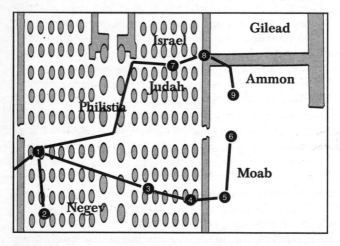

The Year 8 campaign of Ramesses II as described by Kenneth Kitchen, based on his study of the Ramesside war reliefs. The numbers correspond to *loci* in the routes of march of the different strike forces – according to the Kitchen quote above. The region names are those of the post-United Monarchy period.

column swept the Shosu (Beduin) back east, out of
Canaan entirely. Then Ramesses dealt with East
Palestine. Led by the senior prince Amen-hir-
khepeshef … the flying-column struck down
through the Negev hills, across the rift valley south
of the Dead Sea, and up into Edom-Seir, conquering
their settlements. Then the Prince's forces swung
north across the deep ravine of the Zered into the
heartland of Moab and along the traditional 'King's
Highway' to conquer Butartu (Raba Batora). **At the
same time, Ramesses himself swept round in a
clockwise arc to complete the pincer movement
– across the hilly central ridge of Canaan past
Jerusalem,** over the Jordan, past Jericho and the
north end of the Dead Sea, and south into Moab,
striking at Dibon. That settlement taken, he then
came on south across the Arnon valley stream, to
link up with Prince Amen-hir-khepeshef.[3] [my
emphasis]

Kitchen has determined, from the Year 8 campaign reliefs
that Ramesses entered the central hill country of Judah
and reached Jerusalem. Whereas Shoshenk I did not record
a victory over Jerusalem, Ramesses did go up into Judah
and did plunder the city of Shalem. Ramesses also had the
resources to muster a very large army on the scale of the
'twelve hundred chariots and sixty thousand cavalry and
countless hordes of Libyans, Sukkiim and Cushites' of II
Chronicles 12:3. There is considerable evidence to show
that Ramesses recruited foreign mercenaries in his army
and, during his reign, Egypt dominated the territories of
both the Libyans and Kushites. It is easy to imagine 'hordes'
of Kushites amongst the forces of Ramesses the Great, but
I have less confidence that this could have been the case in
the time of Shoshenk I – a delta king of Libyan origin who
had no political or military control over the lands of Kush
beyond Nubia.

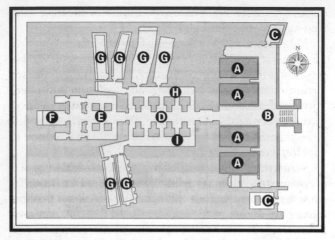

30. Plan of the great rock-cut temple of Abu Simbel: (A) Colossal seated statues of Ramesses II; (B) Terrace; (C) Chapel shrines; (D) Main hall with Osirid columns; (E) Inner hall; (F) Holy of Holies; (G) Storerooms; (H) Battle of Kadesh reliefs; (I) Scene of Ramesses II's assault upon a city in the hills (possibly Jerusalem).

Jerusalem at Abu Simbel?

Ramesses II's hegemony over Nubia and Kush is most impressively represented in the great rock-cut temple of Abu Simbel. Upon the precipitous face of a rocky crag overlooking the River Nile in southern Nubia the king ordered the hewing of an awe-inspiring monument to his power. Anyone travelling towards Egypt from the lands of Kush to the south could not have failed to be impressed by the four mighty twenty-one-metre-high seated colossi of the pharaoh, gazing out across the eastern desert. Here, carved in uncompromising hard sandstone, was the divine majesty of Pharaoh Ramesses in all his arrogant glory.

When I was just nine years old I ventured upon the first of my countless pilgrimages to Egypt. That earliest experience has remained in my memory ever since, but the passage of time has inevitably dimmed much of the detail. I do, however, vividly recall my first meeting with Ramesses at Abu Simbel.

My mother and I had sailed all the way from Cairo to Aswan on King Farouk's elegant Nile paddle-steamer the *KASED KHEIR*, recently confiscated by the new national government of Egypt following the revolution and over-throw of the monarchy in 1952. I had apparently insisted on being taken to the Land of the Pharaohs but, again, the motivation which lay behind that rather unusual request is now lost to me.

When the steamer reached the British-made dam south of Aswan (before the completion of the High Dam in 1970) we entered the great series of locks which took our pristine mahogany-decked vessel beyond the First Cataract and on southwards into desolate Nubia. After two long days of sailing past the whitewashed houses of Nubian villages, past the fortress-town of Kasr Ibrim on its high promontory, past Nile crocodiles sunbathing on desert shores, we finally reached the dark cliffs of Abu Simbel well after nightfall.

The next day, just before dawn, I walked down the gangplank of the *Kased Kheir* onto a sandy beach at the foot of the shadowy mountain. A halo of cool yellow light was beginning to crystallise across the river, above the eastern desert mountains. As I stood in silence before the final destination of my first Egyptian adventure, a thin black shadow began to reach towards the entrance to the great temple – pointing me towards its inner sanctum. The great colossi of the façade were beginning to glow ruby red as the first rays of the rising sun caressed the sandstone rock. Ramesses smiled contentedly from his lofty vantage point.

I entered the temple between and beneath the feet of the two inner colossi. The sun's rays now lit my path all the way to the holy of holies as I approached the four seated gods of the inner shrine, their faces aglow with the sun-god's breath of life. What a way for a young lad to complete his seven hundred-mile journey up the greatest river on Earth! For a brief moment I stared at the impassive countenances of Ptah, Amun-Re, Ramesses himself and RE-HARAKHTE before returning to the grand columned hall to begin my exploration of the rest of the temple.

Behind the towering OSIRID pillars on the north side of the main temple axis was the great battle scene of Ramesses' fifth year – the famous 'Battle of KADESH' – in which the youthful pharaoh had single-handedly (or rather with the support of Amun-Re) wrenched victory from the jaws of defeat by dint of his personal courage and strength. His 'defeat' of the northern confederacy, led by the Hittite emperor, Muwatalis, was a remarkable turnaround following the initial decimation of the vanguard battalions of the Egyptian army. Ramesses had triumphed on the day, but, with all the northern city-states having gone over to the Hittite side, there was no way for the pharaoh to retain his hold on the northern part of the old Egyptian empire. The battle may have been won but the war to save Amurru (ancient Syria) from falling into the Hittite sphere was lost. Ramesses would spend much of the next five years of his reign shoring up the southern part of the northern empire with a number of victorious campaigns to put down revolts following the Year 5 calamity.

The chaotic jumble of bodies which make up the Kadesh battle scene at Abu Simbel did not impress me greatly at the tender age of nine. For a historian there is much to study and analyse, but, somehow, the complex storytelling, in a muddle of vignettes, falls short of reflecting the heroism of the hour. I turned away to cross the main axis of the temple to the wall on the opposite (southern) side of the hall. Here was a scene in direct contrast to the mêlée of Kadesh – a scene of heroic simplicity to thrill any young Egyptophile.

In the centre of the high, wide wall stands Pharaoh Ramesses, resplendent in his golden chariot drawn by a team of proud young stallions. The king has the reins of his charging steeds wrapped tightly around his waist to allow him to fire his bow whilst at the gallop. Behind

Pharaoh's chariot come three young princes, driven into battle by their personal charioteers. Ahead of the king is a large citadel or fortified town standing upon a steep-sided hill. The citizens of the town, dressed in typical 'Canaanite' robes, are pleading with Ramesses to spare them and their families. A siege banner flies above the highest ramparts. Below, in the valley, a herdsman flees, driving his cattle ahead of him. Outside the gate of the fortress a man of high rank is on bended knee – pleading for the king's mercy. No one in the fortress-town is resisting the king's advance; no weapons are in evidence. High on the rampart a ruler with a long 'Canaanite' beard proffers an incense burner as a peace offering to Ramesses. Behind him stands his wife carrying their child. This is a city in abject defeat whose citizens are begging the Egyptian king to spare it from destruction. Unfortunately, the city is not identified by name and the year of the campaign is also not recorded.

I have always been deeply impressed by this graphic scene. On that first visit to Abu Simbel I was taken with the simple dramatic dynamic of the image. The pharaoh, surrounded by a plain background, stands majestic and brave as his chariot advances towards the city – his team of horses in full flight; the victims of the king's campaign are cowed and pitiful. The text inscribed between the advancing chariot and the besieged city reads:

> The perfect god, the son of Amun. Taking action, holding the scimitar which protects his army; (he) who knows his place when he controls the chariot, like the Lord of Thebes; the Lord of Might who fights hundreds of thousands; the Strong Bull with many tails, **who unites by might, and who crushes the rebels on top of the hills; they enter into their valleys like sons of cowards**, but you make slaughter in their place so that your enemies pour forth; O king, mighty of the scimitar, User-maatre-setepenre Ramesses-meryamun.

This is a campaign into a mountainous or hilly part of Palestine. The city atop a hill is the culmination of that campaign. The city surrenders without a fight. Could this be a graphic representation of the subjugation and plundering of Jerusalem in the fifth year of King Rehoboam? After all, Jerusalem is *the* major city in the central hill country of Palestine. Is the precipitous slope below the ramparts one and the same as the eastern escarpment of the City of David falling away into the Kidron valley? Might the bearded man offering the incense burner be King Rehoboam himself? The Year 8 campaign of Ramesses into Palestine was initiated to put down a revolt which appears to have been inspired by the Egyptian losses in Syria three years earlier. Was Rehoboam's fortification of the fifteen Judaean towns in the south and west of his mountain kingdom part of that revolt movement in Palestine? Whilst you ponder these possibilities, let me summarise the main points of the campaign in Year 8.

- Ramesses records the plundering of a city called Shalem in the Year 8 campaign reliefs from the Ramesseum.

- Kenneth Kitchen's study of the Year 8 Palestine campaign led him to the conclusion that Ramesses went up into the Judaean hill country and reached Jerusalem (which means 'City' or 'Foundation of Shalem').

- The New Chronology for Egypt (so far arrived at independently of biblical dating) places the reign of Ramesses II in the late-tenth and early-ninth centuries BC whilst the sacking of the Temple of Jerusalem is dated to the late-tenth century on the basis of Edwin Thiele's chronology for the kings of Israel and Judah.

We now have to deal with the name 'Shishak' to see if it can be linked in any way to Ramesses II.

Washmuaria Riamashesha

This extraordinary mouthful is how the ancient Hittites wrote 'Usermaatre Ramesses' – the prenomen and nomen of Ramesses II.

The fifteen years following the Battle of Kadesh were spent in a titanic political struggle between the Egyptian and Hittite empires for dominance of the Levantine city-states. Finally, having fought and cajoled themselves to a standstill, the two parties agreed to a lasting peace and a sharing of the vassal territories of AMURRU. That treaty, sealed by the marriage of Pharaoh to a daughter of the new Hittite emperor, Hattusilis III, was signed in Year 21 of Ramesses. Fortunately for historians, both the Egyptian copy of the treaty (recorded on a stela at Karnak) and the Hittite version (found at HATTUSAS) have been preserved. The Egyptian version is, of course, in monumental hieroglyphs, but the Hittite copy is written upon a clay tablet in CUNEIFORM. We are indeed fortunate to possess this relatively rare type of document which enables us to view an event recorded in Egyptian hieroglyphs from a foreign perspective and in a different language.

The peculiarities of the conservative hieroglyphic script are such that the full royal name Egyptologists express as 'USERMAATRE-SETEPENRE RAMESSU-MERYAMUN' (in the hybrid Egypto-speak of modern scholarship), would have sounded like double-Dutch to Ramesses' contemporaries and the foreign officials who had dealings with the pharaoh's court. In the Hittite copy of the peace treaty, the emperor's scribes, faced with a difficult foreign name, wrote down the titulary of the Egyptian signatory to the treaty as 'Washmuaria-shatepnaria Riamashesha-maiamana'. It is interesting to note that the Hittite scribes transcribed the Egyptian hieroglyphic 's' with the cuneiform 'sh' (for example writing 'wash' and 'shatep' for 'user' and 'setep').[4] Confusing as it at first seems, it is readily apparent that the semitic scripts of Western Asia often substituted Egyptian 's' with 'sh' and *vice versa.* One clear example of this phenomenon is the Egyptian royal name Shoshenk which is written in cuneiform as Susink(u),[5] indicating that the 'obvious similarity' between the names Shoshenk and Shishak may be more apparent than real.

Now, in Egypt, as in the rest of the ancient world, it was common practice to abbreviate names – just as we do today. This was not only the case for ordinary folk but also for the great rulers themselves. Thus we have 'nicknames' such as 'Ameny' for Pharaoh Amenemhat I ('The Prophecies of Neferti'[6]), 'Pul' for King Tiglath-pileser III of Assyria (II Kings 15:19 & I Chronicles 5:26) and 'Ululaya' for another Assyrian king whose official name was Shalmaneser (Babylonian King List A[7]). Could it be, then, that 'Shishak', rather than being the Egyptian name 'Shoshenk' (Akk. *Susinku*) as argued in the conventional chronology, is in fact a hypocoristicon (accepted shortening) of the full nomen of Ramesses II?

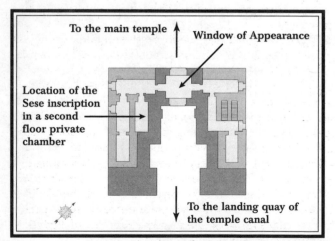

31. Plan of the sandstone migdol gateway (dark grey) with the mudbrick harem of Ramesses III (in light grey) built onto both the north-west and south-east sides. The harem construction is now destroyed – quarried away by the *sebakhin.*

To begin the process of revealing the secrets of the biblical name 'Shishak' come with me on the short walk southwards from the Shalem inscription at the Ramesseum to the fortified gate which leads into the mortuary temple of RAMESSES III at Medinet Habu. Having passed between the two imposing towers of the migdol gateway and under the 'WINDOW OF APPEARANCES' from which Ramesses III used to receive the acclaim of his subjects, we make a sharp turn to the left – as if heading for the 'TEMPLE OF RELIEF' located in the south-east corner of the spacious Medinet Habu compound. After a few paces south we stop and turn around. Stretching up towards the sky in front of us is the southern outer façade of the gate-tower.

At this point I should explain to you that this massive stone structure once had a multi-storeyed royal harem quarters attached to its northern and southern faces. Unfortunately, very little of this structure remains today because, having been constructed of mudbrick, the walls suffered systematic removal over the centuries by the 'SEBAKHIN'.

For a moment, we need to pause and think about just what we are actually looking up at. If Ramesses III's harem once stood up against the Migdol, then the fragmentary reliefs carved on the latter's sandstone walls would have originally decorated the inner walls of very private rooms in the royal apartments. So, although other harem scenes, painted on the plastered surfaces of the mudbrick walls, have been irretrievably lost with the depredations of the *sebakhin*, some of the very intimate images decorating the chambers of the ladies of the court remain preserved in stone. To find such scenes is very rare – in fact, the Medinet Habu reliefs, one of which we are about to discuss in detail, are, to my knowledge, the only examples of Egyptian harem scenes which have come down to us.

The relief we are particularly interested in is extremely badly eroded. Given its exposed position, high up on the south face of the migdol, this is hardly surprising. However,

32. Line drawing of the south-west wall of the migdol gateway at Medinet Habu showing the badly eroded scene containing the Sese cartouche and also indicating the positions of the king and his daughters.

the crucial brief hieroglyphic inscription is still very clear. The figures of the seated Ramesses III and three princesses, approaching him from the left, can be discerned only at close range, but they have been accurately recorded in the magnificent folio volumes of the Chicago Oriental Institute's epigraphic survey of the Medinet Habu temples.[8] The text located between the king and his daughters is in two parts. The cartouches on the right, in front of the king's head, give the official 'monumental' names and titles of Ramesses – both the prenomen (Usermaatre-meryamun) and nomen (Ramesse-NETJERHEKAIUN) – with the hieroglyphic signs facing to the left. The four columns of hieroglyphs on the left side face to the right – and therefore represent the spoken words of the princesses. They read:

> [For] your KA, **Ss**, the king, the divine one […], the sun for all the earth. May you repeat jubilees like ATUM, your might being like that of KHEPRI – vigorous for many years[9] during the lifetime of RE in heaven.

The name **Ss** (for the moment we can use the pronunciation 'Sese') is written inside a cartouche and clearly refers to the seated figure of Ramesses on the right of the scene. So the daughters of Ramesses III called their father 'Sese' – a hypocoristic form of the full name Ramesses. The name Sese had been around for a long time prior to the 19th Dynasty. From as far back as the Old Kingdom, there had been private individuals with this name, and it remained in regular (if not common) use through the Middle and New Kingdoms.[10] Most often the name was a personal nickname, but it also became one of the recognised abbreviations of the full-form name, Ramessu/Ramesse, for both kings and commoners. (The other hypocoristicon for Ramesses was 'Mose' or 'Mes'.)

So far I have vocalised the name as 'Sese' but we would be wrong to presume that this was how it was pronounced by the ancients. It is easy to be misled by the formulaic translations of the Egyptologists who have adopted the convention of slipping in the letter 'e' when vocalising ancient Egyptian. This is simply intended to facilitate the pronunciation of the consonantal skeletons as they are written in the hieroglyphic script. Thus we read 'Amenhotep' or 'Amenhotep' for the hieroglyphic consonantal group *Imnhtp*, which, on the other hand, in cuneiform was rendered 'Amanhatpi'. Of several examples revealed by the AMARNA LETTERS, the PRENOMINA of Amenhotep III and Akhenaten serve to demonstrate the problem. In the cuneiform syllabic script of the Amarna correspondence they appear as 'Nibmuaria' and 'Naphurria' but Egyptologists prefer to pronounce the hieroglyphic versions in their adopted Egypto-speak as 'Nebmaatre' and 'Neferkheperure'.

To discover more about the intriguing hypocoristicon of Ramesses we must now turn to another document – Papyrus Anastasi I – a satirical letter, written from one scribe to another. Here we see Hori, knowledgeable about Palestine, poking fun at his inexperienced colleague,

Amenemopet, for knowing little about the northern territories of the Egyptian empire.[11] The papyrus is dated to the late 19th Dynasty and reflects the political situation during the long reign of Ramesses II. The following excerpts are of considerable interest in respect to our 'Sese' research:

> What is it like, this **Simyra of *Sysw*?**
>
> Come, let [me] tell you many things as far as the Fortress of the Ways [of Horus]. I begin for you with the **Dwelling of *Sysw*!**
>
> Come now to the region of **Uto of *Sysw*!** – in his stronghold of Usermaatre, life, prosperity, health!

'Simyra of *Sysw*' was the Egyptian port of Sumer in northern Syria (identified with Tell Kazel[12]) named after Ramesses II but employing his hypocoristicon rather than full formal nomen. Similarly, the 'Dwelling of *Sysw*' was a residence of Ramesses II on the main route across northern Sinai to the Levant; and 'Uto of *Sysw*' was an oasis in Sinai. Here, then, we have three examples of the use of Ramesses II's hypocoristicon, demonstrating that it was in common use throughout the Egyptian northern empire – at least amongst the Egyptians.

From early on in my research, it seemed likely that the Papyrus Anastasi I name *Sysw* (for Ramesses II) was a second version of the hieroglyphic hypocoristicon 'Sese' used at Medinet Habu (for Ramesses III). Indeed, this had been suggested as long ago as 1904 by the great German scholar Professor Kurt SETHE of Berlin University,[13] but for many years I had no tangible evidence to show conclusively that the two names were one and the same. Then in November 1993, fellow UCL postgraduate researcher, Bob Porter, came up with the missing link – a faience chalice from the temple of Hathor at SERABIT EL-KHADIM in Sinai. Its few shattered fragments were found by Petrie in 1906[14] but were only pieced together in 1992.[15] Around the outer rim of the vessel is a band of black ink hieroglyphs (incised into the faience) giving the titulary of King Usermaatre-setepenre *Ssw*, providing the intermediate writing between *Sysw* and the hieroglyphic *Ss*.

Finally, in 1994 I came across the PYRAMIDION of a courtier named Meryamun Ramessu which is on display in the Kaiserliches Kunsthistorisches Hofmuseum in Vienna.[16] On two sides the hieroglyphic inscription gives the deceased's name as 'Meryamun Ramessu'. On the east face it appears as 'Usermaatre-setepenre Meryamun Ramessu'. But on the west face we read simply *Ssy*. Clearly this man was named after the reigning pharaoh, Usermaat-re-setepenre Ramesses-meryamun (i.e. Ramesses II), so in *Ssy* we have yet another version of the hypocoristicon of Ramesses.

So why should the same name be written in a number of different ways? The simplest explanation is as follows:

- *Ss* – the form of the name at Medinet Habu – is the stark hieroglyphic version of the word skeleton.

- *Ssw*, *Ssy* and *Sysw* – the fuller forms of the name – are trying to indicate the position of the vowels in the Egyptian word. It was common practice for Egyptian scribes to use the consonants *y* and *w* as 'vowel markers' for this purpose.

Unfortunately, the Egyptian scripts are rarely so helpful as to establish exactly how a name was vocalised by the ancients, but the fuller forms of the name *Ss* suggest that each 's' was followed by a vowel of indeterminate quality. To summarise what we have learned so far about the shortened name forms of Ramesses II and Ramesses III:

- Egyptian texts over several centuries demonstrate that there was a name written *Ss*, *Sysw* or *Ssy* which, in the

New Kingdom, was clearly adopted as a hypocoristicon for the royal name Ramesses. This familiar name, written in several ways, applied to both Ramesses II and Ramesses III.

- We cannot be sure how the abbreviated name was vocalised, but it must have been something like 'Sese', 'Sesy', 'Sesa', 'Sysu' or 'Sysa'.

However, we have not finished yet! Earlier I noted that the Akkadian writing of Ramesses in the Hittite treaty is Riamashesha, and that the hieroglyphic 's' was consistently represented by the cuneiform 'sh'. The problems faced by the Hittite scribes writing the Egyptian name in their own script would not have been far removed from those faced by the biblical redactor who gave us the name Shishak. There are several biblical examples where we see the Egyptian 's' (Heb. *sin*) rendered as 'sh' (Heb. *shin*).[17] Just as Egyptian '**A**skelan' is biblical '**A**shkelon' (and Arabic '**s**alam' is Hebrew '**sh**alom'), so with the biblical name 'Shishak'. We should expect it to represent an Egyptian original something like 'Sisak'.

Think about the implications of all this. At one time, we had an apparently convincing identification of the

33. The Hebrew forms of the names (a) Yzebel, (b) Ayzebel, (c) Shyshak, and (d) Shashak as they would have appeared in the pre-exilic script. The Hebrew text is read from right to left.

biblical Shishak with the Egyptian king Shoshenk I. But then we saw how the historical scenario created by this identification collapsed under the weight of a whole series of contradictions so that we were left with nothing more substantial than the superficial similarity between the names Shishak and Shoshenk. Even then we learnt that the name Shoshenk was transcribed in cuneiform as Susink(u) – just as you would expect with the common transformation of Egyptian 'sh' into semitic 's'. The same logic must apply to the biblical name Shishak which should therefore represent the Egyptian name Sysa. The historical record (and the chronological imperative) strongly suggests that Pharaoh Shishak of I Kings and II Chronicles was Ramesses II. The hypocoristic form of his name – *Sysw* (perhaps vocalised Sysa – and thus Shisha[k] in Hebrew) – was the original basis of the name which many centuries later became enshrined in a foreign text as Shishak.

The last round of the 'name game' is to explain the final 'k' (Heb. *qoph*) in the name Shishak which is not present in the original Egyptian. The best explanation is to be found in the way that the biblical redactor often makes a play on words, particularly when dealing with foreign names. This is usually done to pour scorn on those who do not follow in the path of Yahweh. For instance, the original writing of the famous name Jezebel (borne by the Phoenician wife of King Ahab) is attested on a contemporary ninth century scarab as Yzebel, meaning '[Baal] is prince'. However, the redactor turns this into Ayzebel which means 'Where is the piece of dung (i.e. Baal)'. Did the redactor do the same with the Egyptian name Sysa? If so, then he chose a very appropriate pun because the name Shishak may be derived from the Hebrew name Shashak, meaning 'assaulter' or 'the one who crushes [under foot or under wheel]' – a most descriptive synonym for Ramesses the Great who 'crushes the rebels on top of the hills'.[18]

It should be stressed here that the arguments for identifying Ramesses II with Shishak are not based on the similarity between the king's hypocoristicon and the biblical name (as has been the case with the Shoshenk = Shishak equation of the conventional chronology – which may be a red herring) but rather because there is evidence that Ramesses *did* undertake a military campaign into the hill country of Judah and *did*, according to Kitchen, reach Jerusalem. It is based on the campaign relief at the Ramesseum stating that Ramesses defeated a city called Shalem in his eighth year which, I argue, refers to the defeat of Rehoboam in that king's fifth year and the capture of the treasures of Solomon's Temple in Jerusalem. My identification of Ramesses II as the biblical Shishak is predominantly based on archaeological and historical arguments.

Conclusion Seven

The apparent equivalence between the biblical name Shishak and the pharaonic name Shoshenk is misleading. The Palestine campaign of Shoshenk I was very different from that described for the biblical Shishak. On the other hand, the name may have its origins in the hypocoristicon of Ramesses II ('Sysa' – equivalent to Hebrew 'Shisha[k]') – the only pharaoh known to have recorded a defeat of Jerusalem (= Shalem).

Ramesses II and Israel

For our final piece of the Shishak jigsaw we need to return to Karnak. Just fifty metres from the Bubastite Portal and the campaign list of Shoshenk I there is another key historical inscription known as the 'Ashkelon Wall'. For donkey's years it had been regarded as a campaign relief of Ramesses II whose works are all around this part of Karnak. However, in the 1970s a young American Egyptologist, working for the Chicago Oriental Institute's Theban Epigraphic Survey project, made a brilliant new discovery. Frank Yurco was re-examining the badly eroded 'Ashkelon Wall' reliefs when, in a moment of inspiration, he realised a vital connection between these Karnak scenes and the famous 'ISRAEL STELA' of Merenptah housed in the Cairo Museum.[19]

This link is based on a number of observations which are, once again, best presented in tabulated form.

- The Israel Stela is dated to the fifth year of Merenptah, successor of Ramesses II.

- Although most of the long text is dedicated to a defensive campaign against marauding Libyans, the most important historical section is the final strophe or 'poem' which summarises the Egyptian political world view in Merenptah's reign.

- The strophe mentions eight foreign elements with whom Egypt has been at war. They are: (1) Tjehenu (Libya); (2) Hatti (the Hittites); (3) Pa-Canaan (Palestine); (4) Ashkelon; (5) Gezer; (6) Yanoam; (7) Israel; and (8) Hurru (Syria).

- Yurco guessed that the mention of Ashkelon in the strophe might have a connection with the battle scene against the city of Ashkelon at Karnak. He then compared the whole wall of which the Ashkelon campaign is a part with the central stanza of the strophe and found a convincing match.

- The 'Ashkelon Wall' comprises four battle scenes depicted in two registers on either side of the Hittite Treaty inscription of Ramesses II. (1) The lower right register shows a pharaoh, astride his chariot, attacking a fortified city. This city is named as Ashkelon in the accompanying text. (2) In the lower left register another assault

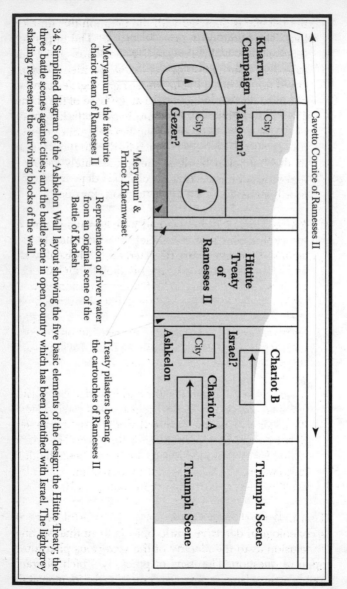

34. Simplified diagram of the 'Ashkelon Wall' layout showing the five basic elements of the design: the Hittite Treaty; the three battle scenes against cities; and the battle scene in open country which has been identified with Israel. The light-grey shading represents the surviving blocks of the wall.

'Meryamun' – the favourite chariot team of Ramesses II

'Meryamun' & Prince Khaemwaset

Representation of river water from an original scene of the Battle of Kadesh

Treaty pilasters bearing the cartouches of Ramesses II

Kharru Campaign

Gezer?

City
Yanoam?

City

Hittite Treaty of Ramesses II

Ashkelon

City
Israel!?

Chariot B

Chariot A

Triumph Scene

Triumph Scene

Cavetto Cornice of Ramesses II

upon a city is depicted with the pharaoh this time on foot. The name of the city is lost. (3) The upper left register shows a third city under attack and again, due to its very poor state of preservation, the identity of the city is not known. (4) The upper right register consists of only a few surviving blocks at the base of the scene. They show a battle in which the pharaoh attacks a group of Asiatics. The position of the king's team of chariot horses within the scene – much further to the left than in the Ashkelon battle scene immediately below – makes it quite clear that no city was depicted in this fourth scene: there simply is no room for one.

- Yurco concluded that we had here a visual record of the central stanza of the 'Israel Stela' strophe. Battles against three cities were depicted on the Karnak walls and a fourth scene showed the pharaoh fighting in open country. With the city of Ashkelon common to both strophe and campaign relief the other two anonymous cities must therefore be Gezer and Yanoam, and the fourth scene had to be the only representation in Egyptian art of Israelites in battle against an Egyptian pharaoh.

- Yurco closely re-examined the badly eroded cartouches associated with the 'Gezer' register and decided that the original name (overwritten by both AMENMESSE and SETI II) was Merenptah and not Ramesses II. Armed with his well-reasoned link to the 'Israel Stela' he duly announced, in 1977, the re-attribution of the 'Ashkelon Wall' to Merenptah rather than Ramesses II.

This in a nutshell is Frank Yurco's masterful piece of archaeological detective work, but I believe that his final conclusion as to the identity of the victorious pharaoh is open to question. The issue of precisely which pharaoh fought against Israel is obviously crucial to the identification of Shishak within the New Chronology model. I need, therefore, to demonstrate that the previous widely-held view that Ramesses II originally carved these scenes is indeed correct and that Yurco has gone too far in attributing the battle scenes to Merenptah. The evidence in favour of Ramesses II is as follows:[20]

- The central section of the 'Ashkelon Wall' contains the Hittite Treaty dated to Year 21 of Ramesses II and the BANDEAU inscription below the CAVETTO CORNICE bears the cartouches of Ramesses II. This shows that Ramesses built the wall and decorated at least part of it. Furthermore the treaty was carved into the wall after the latter's construction as the pilasters framing the treaty text are flush with the surface of the wall itself which has been carefully trimmed back on either side of the treaty in order to create the illusion that the pilasters stood proud of the wall. This suggests that the wall was built before the twenty-first year of Ramesses II but that the final decoration of the scenes on either side postdates that year in the king's reign (there being no loss of carving depth on the cambered sections of the wall).

- The two registers to the right of the Hittite Treaty (lower – Ashkelon and upper – 'Israel') are the original carvings on the wall surface. There is no evidence that there ever was another set of reliefs beneath those visible today.

- On the other hand, beneath the surface of the 'Gezer' register (to the lower left of the treaty) the faint outlines of rows of horses and a zigzag water pattern can still be discerned. We know from the adjacent outer south wall of the HYPOSTYLE HALL that an Asiatic campaign by Ramesses II (possibly that in Year 8), carved there, covers an original relief depicting the Battle of Kadesh in which rows of chariot horses and the River Orontes play a major part. It is evident, therefore, that the original Kadesh relief once extended around and onto the 'Ashkelon Wall' as far as the left edge of the Hittite Treaty. The faded carvings of horses and water ripples observable in the 'Gezer' register form part of that Battle of Kadesh scene. Thus Ramesses II had originally decorated at least a third of the total length of the 'Ashkelon Wall'.

- Yurco, recognising that the right side of the wall beyond the treaty had only ever contained one set of reliefs, argues that they belong to Merenptah on the basis of the connection with the Israel Stela. Yet, if this was the case, then Ramesses, having built the edifice and decorated the left section, would have allowed the rest of the wall to remain undecorated. How can one conceivably suggest – knowing what we know about Ramesses the Great – that he actually left a blank wall for his successor to fill in? There is no possibility that Ramesses ran out of time to complete the planned inscriptions as he reigned for over sixty-six years (even though the wall must have been finally decorated after Year 21 – the date of the Hittite Treaty).

- Two other telling points in favour of Ramesses as the author of the inscriptions are to be found in the 'Gezer' register. There we see that the pharaoh has dismounted from his chariot in order to lead the assault upon the city. His chariot horses are being tended by one of the king's sons. The inscription above the head of the prince reads: 'The royal son of his body, Khaemwaset, true of voice'. Khaemwaset was the fourth son of Ramesses II and the most famous of all his offspring. We currently have no evidence to show that Merenptah had a son called Khaemwaset. Furthermore, the team of horses attended by Khaemwaset is called 'The first great chariot

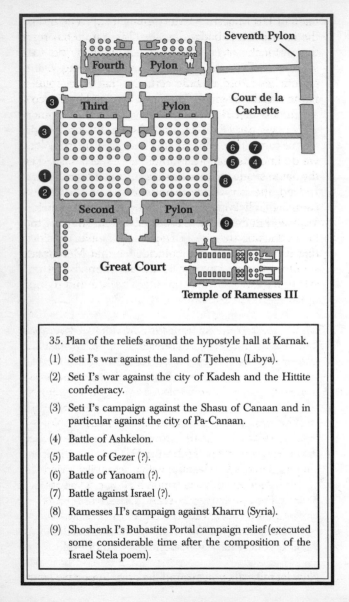

35. Plan of the reliefs around the hypostyle hall at Karnak.

(1) Seti I's war against the land of Tjehenu (Libya).

(2) Seti I's war against the city of Kadesh and the Hittite confederacy.

(3) Seti I's campaign against the Shasu of Canaan and in particular against the city of Pa-Canaan.

(4) Battle of Ashkelon.

(5) Battle of Gezer (?).

(6) Battle of Yanoam (?).

(7) Battle against Israel (?).

(8) Ramesses II's campaign against Kharru (Syria).

(9) Shoshenk I's Bubastite Portal campaign relief (executed some considerable time after the composition of the Israel Stela poem).

team of His Majesty – "Meryamun" [.....]'. The rest of the inscription is badly damaged but Yurco has read the cartouche of Merenptah overwritten by his two successors. The multiple erasures and recuttings of the cartouches afford us little certainty that Merenptah's name was the original. I am not convinced by Yurco's arguments that Ramesses II's nomen and prenomen were never carved on this wall – especially considering it once carried a scene from the Battle of Kadesh. What we do know is that 'Meryamun' is well established as the name of one of Ramesses II's favourite chariot pairs. Indeed, the very same team is shown in the Asiatic campaign reliefs immediately adjacent to the 'Ashkelon Wall' and in the scene at the Ramesseum showing the king attacking the city of Dapur. I personally believe that it is too much of a coincidence that Merenptah should not only have an identically-named (but un attested) son but also an identically-named (but unattested) chariot team.

- Finally there is the matter of the broader perspective. Yurco only employs the four elements of the central stanza of the strophe in his argument. If we take the strophe as a whole we can observe something even more interesting. The complete strophe reads as follows:

> The princes are prostrate, saying 'Peace!'. Not one raises his head among the Nine Bows. Desolation is for **Tjehenu**; **Hatti** is pacified; plundered is **Pa-Canaan** with every evil; carried off is **Ashkelon**; seized upon is **Gezer**, **Yanoam** is made non-existent; **Israel** is laid waste – his seed is no more; **Kharru** has become a widow because of Egypt. All lands together are pacified. Everyone who was restless has been bound.

Now let me walk you around the great hypostyle court

at Karnak to view the campaign reliefs of Seti I and Ramesses II. We begin at the north-west corner where in the upper register we see Seti I's campaign against the Libyans ('desolation is for **Tjehenu**'). Below that is the register depicting Seti's campaign against the Hittites in Syria ('**Hatti** is pacified'). As we walk eastwards along the northern outer wall we find Seti's campaigns against the Shasu of southern Palestine and an attack upon the city of Pa-Canaan ('plundered is **Pa-Canaan** with every evil'). Crossing over to the southern side of the hypostyle hall we reach the Hittite Treaty wall (an additional source for the expression 'Hatti is pacified'?). To the right of the treaty we have the register depicting the taking of Ashkelon ('carried off is **Ashkelon**'), followed to the left of the treaty by another city under siege ('seized upon is **Gezer**') and above that a third city ('**Yanoam** is made non-existent'). Above the Ashkelon scene we have the register containing a battle in open countryside ('**Israel** is laid waste – his seed is no more'). Finally, along the whole length of the southern outer wall of the hypostyle hall we have Ramesses II's Asiatic (Year 8?) war which included a prolonged campaign in Syria ('**Kharru** has become a widow because of Egypt'). The overall picture is complete and exact. The final strophe on the 'Israel Stela' is not a record of Merenptah's personal military activities but rather a view of the international scene as it appeared in his reign. What the king saw as he looked out into the northern theatre of Egyptian military operations was a world subjugated by his dynasty. The achievements listed in the final section of the 'Israel Stela' are not Merenptah's personal successes as such but rather the dynamic work of his father and grandfather.

There we have it. The aged Merenptah, incapable of doing very much more than defend Egypt from attack by Libyan tribes and perhaps undertake the suppression of a revolt at

Gezer (hence the carving of his cartouches over those of Ramesses II on the Gezer register),[21] was bathing in the reflected glory of his more powerful predecessors. His was the dynasty which provided Egyptologists with most of the surviving king-lists which we might perceive as 'a sense of history' on the part of the Ramessides. His was the dynasty which prided itself on the achievement of recovering the northern empire following the Amarna fiasco. Merenptah was not inventing a pack of lies when he commissioned the text containing the final strophe of his 'Israel Stela'. As he looked out northwards from his throne dais in the palace at Pi-Ramesse, colourfully decorated with the glazed tiles of captive chieftains from the Egyptian empire, Merenptah was in reality surveying the political accomplishments of the 19th Dynasty.

The 'Israel Stela' and the 'Ashkelon Wall' are consistent with the historical reconstruction we have been developing. It was Ramesses II who ordered the carving of the scene depicting a battlefield assault against Israelite forces. The military action represented here was the prelude to the siege of Jerusalem. The Bible informs us that Shishak defeated the princes of Israel and captured the fortified towns of Judah on his way up to Rehoboam's Jerusalem [II Chronicles 12:1-11].

Conclusion Eight

The evidence from the Egyptian monumental reliefs, artefacts and documents points to the identification of Ramesses II as the historical counterpart of the biblical Shishak, conqueror of Jerusalem.

Israelite Chariots on the Ashkelon Wall

I have a final point to add to the 'Ashkelon Wall' discussion which hammers one more nail into the coffin of the conventional chronology. The campaign scene which Yurco has identified as a battle against Israel (whether it belongs to Ramesses or Merenptah) presents a major problem for the orthodox dating of the Exodus. Beneath the horses of the pharaoh's chariot you can just make out a much smaller chariot belonging to a fleeing enemy chieftain. This is a typical iconographic formula which is illustrated time and again in Egyptian battle scenes – the mighty king crushing his enemies under the hooves of his advancing chariot team. But just a minute! Is this not the time when Moses is leading the Israelites out of Egypt in the orthodox scheme? Even if we assume that Ramesses II was not only the Pharaoh of the Oppression but also the Pharaoh of the Exodus and the 'Israel' scene belongs to Merenptah rather than his father, we could at best be in the time of the Conquest of the Promised Land and no later. So how come the Israelites are gadding about in chariots? There is no evidence whatsoever that the Israelites had chariots before the time of Solomon.[22] Indeed, their military tactics during the Conquest and Judges period demonstrate that they had no access to this form of military technology.[23] The appearance of a chariot in the 'Israel' register at Karnak is a complete historical contradiction within the conventional dating scheme. In contrast to this clear problem for the conventional dating of the Exodus, within the New Chronology we are in the period of Israelite history which immediately follows the establishment of a large chariotry force by King Solomon.

> Solomon then built up a force of chariots and cavalry; he had one thousand four hundred chariots and twelve thousand horses, these he stationed in the chariot towns and near the king in Jerusalem. [I Kings 10:26]

36. Side panel from the chariot of Thutmose IV found in his tomb in the Valley of the Kings. The king is depicted attacking Asiatic enemies in his chariot. Beneath the hooves of his horses an enemy chariot is fleeing towards its own lines; the horses of that chariot are thus facing in the same direction as the king's chariot team.

37. Detail from the 'Israel blocks' of the Ashkelon Wall. Beneath the hooves of the pharaoh's chariot team, there is a representation of a fleeing enemy chariot – just as with the Thutmose IV battle scene (and many others). If these blocks do represent a battle against Israel, as Yurco proposes, then these Israelites had chariots within their armed forces and were thus familiar with their use in warfare.

Chapter Eight

THE AGE OF SOLOMON

he reign of SOLOMON was the cultural apogee of the Israelite nation according to the biblical narratives. During his rule Israel was at peace with the world. The name of Solomon, by which we refer to the third ruler of Israel, actually means 'peaceful' (Heb. *Shelomoh* derived from *shalom* – 'peace')[1] and was probably attributed to the king long after his reign to reflect the political character of this period in Israelite history [I Kings 5:18].

In Solomon's time, great trading networks were established between the produce suppliers, Egypt and OPHIR (by land and sea), on one side and the Levantine city states on the other, with Israel acting as middleman [I Kings 9:26-10:29]. As a result, Jerusalem and the other cities of Israel were renewed and invigorated by the influx of luxury materials, in addition to the artisans needed to turn the exotic produce into marketable goods. Solomon requested and received all kinds of craftsmen from Phoenicia courtesy of HIRAM, king of Tyre, including masons, bronze-smiths and woodworkers [I Kings 5:15-32]. They set about constructing palaces and state apartments for the king of Israel and his Egyptian queen, turning Jerusalem into a truly royal city. The Temple of Yahweh was built on the rocky crag above Jerusalem and the old Jebusite city itself was much expanded with the construction of huge platform terracing which increased the building area around the crest of the narrow 'Hill of Ophel'. This stone-fill terracing was known as the Millo ('filling') and its construction, according to I Kings 9:15, 24, and 11:27, was begun in the middle years of Solomon's reign.

With the biblical narratives, clearly painting the era of Solomon as the cultural high point in the early history of Israel, we should expect to find considerable evidence of Solomon's wealth and Israel's internationalism within the archaeology of the period if the narratives are to have a basis in historical fact. In the orthodox chronology Solomon is dated to what archaeologists call Iron Age IIA. This is how two of the leading authorities in Palestinian archaeology have described the period. In discussing the so-called

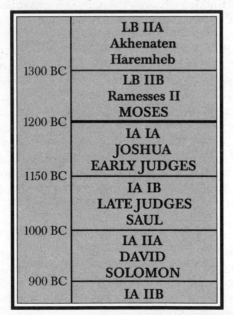

	LB IIA **Akhenaten** **Haremheb**
1300 BC	**LB IIB** **Ramesses II** **MOSES**
1200 BC	**IA IA** **JOSHUA** **EARLY JUDGES**
1150 BC	**IA IB** **LATE JUDGES** **SAUL**
1000 BC	**IA IIA** **DAVID** **SOLOMON**
900 BC	**IA IIB**

The approximate chronological position of the key biblical and pharaonic characters in relation to the archaeological eras according to the conventional chronology.

Solomonic cities of Iron Age IIA, Professor James Pritchard of Pennsylvania University writes:

> ... the so-called cities of Megiddo, Gezer and Hazor, and Jerusalem itself were in reality more like villages. ... Within were relatively small public buildings and poorly constructed dwellings with clay floors. The objects reveal a material culture which, even by the standards of the ancient Near East, could not be judged sophisticated or luxurious ... The 'magnificence' of the age of Solomon is parochial and decidedly lacklustre, but the first book of Kings implies exactly the opposite.[2]

Dame Kathleen KENYON was equally mystified by the general impoverishment of Iron Age IIA:

> Archaeology has provided us with little direct evidence of the glories of Solomon's court, and has shown that, away from the capital, the civilisation was not of a very high order, nor are there striking signs of economic prosperity ... The sites which have provided the best archaeological evidence, moreover, do little to illustrate another aspect of Solomon's innovations known to us from the Bible, his activities as a merchant prince. Almost no recognisably imported objects have been found in levels of this period in Palestine proper.[3]

There are no magnificent buildings, no fine artefacts adorned with semiprecious stones and inlays, no gold, silver or ivory, and no signs of a flourishing international trade. So once more the conventional chronology produces a negative result when comparing the archaeological remains with biblical history.

When we turn to Phoenicia in the Early Iron Age to seek evidence for the famed Phoenician craftsmanship in stonecutting, so prized by Solomon, we again find a complete absence of monumental ASHLAR building techniques – in fact we find no monumental stone buildings at all! As Israeli archaeologist Professor Yigael SHILOH of the Hebrew University of Jerusalem remarks:

> On those sites which have been examined over and over again – such as Sidon and Byblos – so far no relevant evidence from the Iron Age has come to light. There is no possibility today – in the light of the archaeological finds – of determining the existence of a clear connection between the ashlar masonry of Judah and Israel and Iron Age Phoenicia.[4]

Archaeological investigation undertaken in Lebanon and coastal Syria (ancient Phoenicia) has produced no evidence for monumental stone building between the end of the Bronze Age (OC – *c*. 1150 BC) and the start of the Hellenistic era (*c*. 332 BC). In the conventional chronological model the stories of Solomon – the builder king – and his ally Hiram of Tyre have to be complete exaggerations and pure fiction.[5]

Conclusion Nine

The cultural wealth of the era of Solomon, as described in I Kings and II Chronicles, is not reflected in the archaeology of Iron Age IIA Palestine which can only be described as a period of general impoverishment in the cultural history of the Levant.

But what happens if we apply our New Chronology placement for Solomon – now a contemporary of Haremheb and Seti I in Egypt?

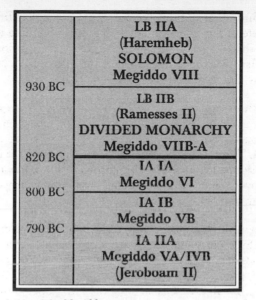

	LB IIA (Haremheb) **SOLOMON** Megiddo VIII
930 BC	LB IIB (Ramesses II) **DIVIDED MONARCHY** Megiddo VIIB-A
820 BC	IA IA Megiddo VI
800 BC	IA IB Megiddo VB
790 BC	IA IIA Megiddo VA/IVB (Jeroboam II)

A correlation of the Megiddo strata with the Israelite monarchy period in the New Chronology.

A Solomonic City – Megiddo VIII

When we come to dating an archaeological site by means of the pottery found in its different levels (or STRATA), we can determine with reasonable confidence which buildings belonged to Late Bronze IIA (LB IIA) and which were Late Bronze IIB (LB IIB).[6] Those containing LB IIA pottery were occupied when the pharaohs Amenhotep III to Haremheb ruled in Egypt. Equally, if LB IIB pots are associated with archaeological remains, it implies that this level (or stratum) of the site was contemporary with the 19th Dynasty in Egypt (possibly including the latter part of the reign of Haremheb at the end of the 18th Dynasty).

According to I Kings 9:15, Solomon built (at) the cities of Jerusalem, Hazor, Megiddo and Gezer. Let us now take a look at one of Solomon's most important cities – Megiddo in the Jezreel valley – to see what finds have been unearthed in association with late LB IIA and early LB IIB pottery (the archaeological phase contemporary with Solomon in the New Chronology). According to I Kings 9:15, Solomon built (at) the cities of Jerusalem, Hazor, Megiddo and Gezer. Stratum VII-B 'marks Megiddo's last great period of material wealth in the Bronze Age'[7] and was the city contemporary with Ramesses II and Merenptah in Egypt. The earlier stratum VIII represents a long phase of the city which included the Amarna period and the reign of Haremheb (possibly extending down into the time of Seti I).[8] Thus, we can place Solomon either in the last phase of Megiddo VIII or in the early phase of Megiddo VII-B. Stratum VII-A represents the first Iron Age city at Megiddo and would be contemporary with the reigns of OMRI and AHAB in Israel and Ramesses III in Egypt.

Having noted the relative impoverishment of Early Iron Age Megiddo, we can now, by contrast, demonstrate the great wealth and cosmopolitan character of the Late Bronze Age city by enumerating the noteworthy features of strata VIII and VII-B.

38. Left: The city gate and palace belonging to Megiddo stratum VIII.

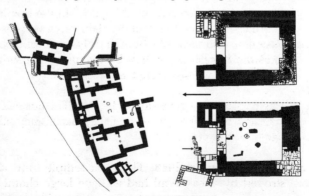

39. Right: Temple 2048, stratum VIII phase (above) and the later stratum VIIB phase (below).

1. **The Late Bronze Age Palace** (stratum VIII, continuing in use during stratum VII-B): The building is fifty metres in length with two-metre thick walls. An entrance gate leads the visitor into a large courtyard with plastered floor, surrounded on three sides by palace apartments. The largest hall (possibly the throne room) has an imposing portico flanked by two basalt pillars. One of the palace rooms is paved with seashells and has a square basin at its centre – obviously a bathing room.

2. **A royal treasure found in room 3100 of the palace**: This magnificent hoard included gold vessels; jewellery of different styles including gold and lapis-lazuli beads; and a collection of ivory plaques.

3. **The ivory hoard found in the palace treasury**: The collection of carved ivories numbered over two hundred items. The workmanship is described as 'Canaanite art at its best'.[9] The deposit has been dated to stratum VII-B. An even bigger collection, found in the treasury of the later stratum VII-A palace (a modification of the VII-B structure), has also been attributed to the historical period of stratum VII-B, recognised as 'leftovers' from Bronze Age Megiddo. In the opinion of Professor Yigael YADIN of the Hebrew University of Jerusalem 'the cache of ivories, mostly plaques, constitutes the largest and richest collection of Canaanite carved ivory yet discovered' in Palestine.[10]

4. **The triple-entry gateway to the city**: The fine ashlar gate, located just to the east of the palace, is usually dated to stratum VIII.

5. **Migdol Temple 2048**: The great temple (now destroyed by excavation) had a single large chamber measuring eleven metres by ten metres with exterior walls three metres thick. Two massive towers flanked

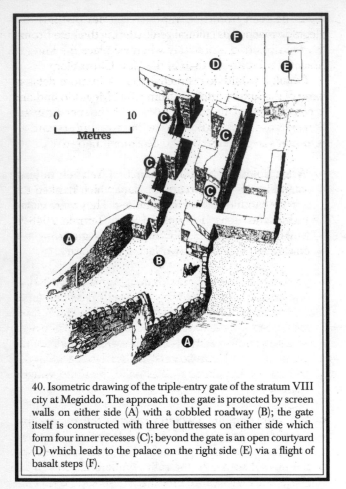

40. Isometric drawing of the triple-entry gate of the stratum VIII city at Megiddo. The approach to the gate is protected by screen walls on either side (A) with a cobbled roadway (B); the gate itself is constructed with three buttresses on either side which form four inner recesses (C); beyond the gate is an open courtyard (D) which leads to the palace on the right side (E) via a flight of basalt steps (F).

the entrance with a pair of columns erected in the entrance portico leading to the great CELLA. The date of construction of the temple is disputed – it may be earlier than stratum VIII[11] – but it certainly underwent a number of modifications during VII-B and VII-A, including the erection of the portico pillars.

It can be seen from this impressive series of finds that Megiddo reached its cultural zenith during the Late Bronze IIA to IIB period – precisely when we place the kings of Israel from David to Ahab in the New Chronology.

I think it would be instructive to look in more detail at some of the luxury artefacts from LB II Megiddo and one or two features of the architecture – with the specific intention of comparing them to what we understand of Solomon's reign from the Old Testament narratives.

- When Solomon built the Temple of Yahweh in Jerusalem, he erected two great pillars which flanked the entrance to the cella of the building. They were called Jachin and Boaz [I Kings 7:15-22]. Temple 2048 at Megiddo also has a pair of columns guarding the entrance – Megiddo's own Jachin and Boaz.

- Solomon married Pharaoh's daughter [I Kings 3:1] so one might expect a certain amount of Egyptian influence in the artistic tastes of the Solomonic court. If we look at some of the ivories from Megiddo's LB II palace we find a number of Egyptian motifs, including papyrus plants, lilies and lotus flowers (the floral motifs of Upper and Lower Egypt), as well as palm trees and winged sphinxes.

- The most famous Megiddo ivory is the remarkable panel depicting palace life in LBA Palestine. There are a number of intriguing elements, but first let me describe the overall scene. To the right, the king arrives in his chariot, driving before him two SHASU captives; in the centre is an intimate cameo of the same ruler, seated upon his throne with his queen and lyre player standing before him; to the left, behind the king, two courtiers attend to the royal couple's needs. Now let us pick out the Egyptian elements in the scene. First, above the chariot-horses is a winged sun-disk; second, the queen

41. Ivory panel, probably from the arm of a chair, showing a king and his queen attended by courtiers. From the ivory hoard of Late Bronze Age Megiddo. Rockefeller Museum.

offers a lotus flower to her husband; and third the king is seated upon a throne, the sides of which are guarded by winged sphinxes (i.e. human-headed lions). Surrounding the monarch we see four doves – a well-known motif of peace. Solomon married an Egyptian princess; he had 'a great ivory throne' made for him which was protected by 'lions' on either side [I Kings 10:18-20]; his name means 'peaceful'. Could we possibly have here a representation of King Solomon and his Egyptian queen?

Conclusion Ten

Solomon was not a ruler of the Iron Age IIA but instead reigned during the last century of the Late Bronze Age. The cultural zenith of the United Monarchy period in Israelite history (tenth century BC) is reflected in the archaeological remains of Megiddo VIII to VII-B.

42. Detail from the sarcophagus of Ahiram, ruler of Byblos, showing the Late Bronze Age king seated on a throne flanked by winged sphinxes or cherubim. Beirut Museum.

The Jerusalem Millo

Apart from the building of the Temple of Yahweh and the royal palace, Solomon's greatest building achievement was the Jerusalem Millo which took most of the second half of his reign to complete [I Kings 9:15 & 11:27]. The Hebrew word Millo translates as 'filling' and has been understood to mean a massive terrace system constructed with stone retainer walls back-filled with rubble. The terracing would have increased the building area within the City of David along the steep eastern slopes of the Hill of Ophel, affording an increase in population within the walls of the new Israelite capital city.

In 1961, Dame Kathleen Kenyon began her seven-year excavations of the eastern slopes of the ancient city of Jerusalem. Its southern spur, between the Kidron and Tyropoean valleys, is the oldest part of the site and the location of the JEBUSITE and Davidic city which the biblical writers call the 'City of David' or the 'Fortress of Zion'. The small, somewhat cramped hilltop city of early Jerusalem became the royal residence and capital of the rulers of United-Monarchy Israel and post-Schism Judah. Kenyon was in search of material evidence for this important period in Jerusalem's history and, in particular, for signs of Solomon's famous royal city.

Her strategy was to dig a great trench running down the eastern slope of the hill towards the floor of the Kidron valley. Excavations began beneath the HASMONEAN bastion, near the summit. As she removed the debris of centuries, Kenyon began to reveal a deeper, more massive structure which dated from a much earlier period. She had found a vast stone terracing system which stretched along the east scarp of the old city. It has been estimated that this 'extension' of the city summit added at least six thousand square metres to the occupational area of early Jerusalem.[12]

Dame Kathleen Kenyon believed that she had uncovered the Millo of Solomon and duly announced her discovery in the pages of the *Palestine Exploration Quarterly*.[13] However, once again, there was a problem. The associated pottery found in the filling material of the terraces proved to belong to the Late Bronze Age:

> There was not a great deal in the way of finds in the fill, but there was enough pottery, including a few sherds of Mycenaean ware and White Slip II milk-bowls, to show that the date is *c.* 14th century BC.[14]

The date-range of the LATE HELLADIC IIIA2 pottery found in the terrace fill has subsequently been refined to *circa* 1370-1310 BC – the time of AMENHOTEP III (late-reign) to Haremheb in the orthodox chronology.[15]

So, here was Kenyon's problem – the pottery suggested that the terraces which she had uncovered were constructed several centuries before Solomon was anointed king over all Israel (indeed, even before the Israelites had supposedly departed from Egypt for the Promised Land!). Her solution to this dilemma was to retain her identification of the great stone terraces with the biblical Millo, but then to 'doctor' or reinterpret the passage in I Kings 9:15, relating to the building-works of Solomon. She proposed that the Israelite king had not 'built' the Millo as the Old Testament text states, but rather 'rebuilt' or repaired it. There was no other possible explanation as her excavations had clearly demonstrated that the Millo was originally constructed some three hundred and sixty years before Solomon's reign.[16]

Kenyon's difficulties had come about, of course, as a direct result of her adherence to the orthodox dating of the Mycenaean (LH IIIA2) pottery – dated to the fourteenth century BC by finds of the same pottery at Tell el-Amarna. If we apply the New Chronology's dates for the Amarna period, as devised in the previous chapter, we get a date range of *circa* 1030 to 970 BC for LH IIIA2. According to the biblical chronology, Solomon succeeded David in 970

BC. It would hardly be surprising, therefore, to find pottery which was still in use at least as late as 970 BC associated with a Millo built by Solomon in *circa* 950 BC. Thus, the New Chronology can re-establish Solomon as the true builder of the Millo of Jerusalem and Kenyon's awkward 'repair' theory is no longer required.

Conclusion Eleven

The massive Late Bronze Age stone terracing system constructed along the eastern slopes of the City of David is to be identified with the Jerusalem Millo, constructed in the reign of Solomon, as stated in I Kings 9:15.

Pharaoh's Daughter

> Solomon moved Pharaoh's daughter **up from the City of David** to the palace which he had built for her. 'A woman', he said, 'must not live because of me in the palace of David, king of Israel, for these buildings to which the ark of Yahweh has come are sacred.' [II Chronicles 8:11]

This passage from the second book of Chronicles records the building of a residence by Solomon for his principal queen – the daughter of an anonymous Egyptian pharaoh. I have already proposed that the pharaoh who was reigning in Egypt during the early years of King Solomon was Haremheb.

When I began my research in the mid-1970s my expectations for confirmation of the New Chronology theory – through ongoing excavations in Egypt and Palestine – were not exactly high. For nearly two centuries archaeologists had been digging up the Holy Land with little real success in 'biblical' terms. They had been having a tough time in identifying buildings and artefacts connected with the Old Testament narratives. I could hardly, therefore, have expected evidence supporting the fledgling theory to surface immediately – but this is precisely what happened.

During the 1980s Professor Gabriel Barkay of Tel Aviv University began to piece together tantalising evidence from incompletely published excavations of the last century which, combined with his own archaeological investigations, confirmed that an Egyptian-style building had once existed to the north of the Damascus Gate, just outside the walled city of Herod's Jerusalem. He had already unearthed a collection of small artefacts from the 1882-3 excavations in the display cabinets of the École Biblique along with records of larger finds from the original excavation site now beneath the church of St. Etienne. The objects included a fragment of an Egyptian stela with hieroglyphic texts; a large *hotep*-class stone offering table; two Egyptian alabaster vessels; a headless statuette of a seated figure in typical Egyptian style; and a limestone column capital of the palmiform design relocated by Barkay in the grounds of the famous 'Garden Tomb' believed by some to be the place of Christ's interment following his crucifixion.

The original 1880s excavations were undertaken within the grounds of the École Biblique where the church of St.

43. The two alabaster vases found in the grounds of St. Etienne.

The Location of the Egyptian Residence or Tomb

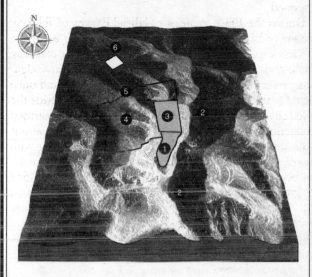

44. Relief model of ancient Jerusalem at the time of King Solomon. The City of David (1) is situated on a narrow spur to the east of which is the deep Kidron Valley (2). The Temple Mount northern extension to the city in Solomon's time (3) is on a higher ground. The later expansion of Jerusalem (4) is indicated by the Herodian wall extending west and north. Higher still a mountain ridge carries the Nablus Road out from the Damascus Gate (5) north along the central ridge of the hill country to ancient Shechem and beyond. It is to the east side of this ancient road that an Egyptian presence in Jerusalem has been uncovered within the grounds of the monastery of St. Etienne (6). The location of this Egyptian enclave clearly looks down upon the Temple Mount and the City of David.

> After Pharaoh's daughter had moved from the city of David **up to the palace which he had built for her,** he (Solomon) then built the Millo. [I Kings 9:24]

45. The serpentine statuette and stela found in the grounds of St. Etienne.

Etienne is situated, and so Professor Barkay has concluded that an Egyptian-style building once stood at this location, probably adjacent to the ancient road leading to Nablus (biblical Shechem). The Egyptian alabasters associated with this building are of 18th Dynasty type (i.e. LB IIA) and, as a result, Barkay has tentatively dated the structure to the time of the late 18th to early 19th Dynasties.[17]

The objects so far found do not tell us precisely what type of building we are dealing with – it could be a small temple within the residence of a native Egyptian of high rank or perhaps the tomb of that Egyptian (as the presence of the offering table suggests[18]). I must say I find all this extremely interesting. The simple facts are that (a) this is the only structure containing such Egyptian architectural elements (made of stone) ever found in Jerusalem (or anywhere in Palestine for that matter) and (b) the only building (that

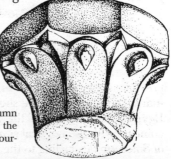

46. Sketch of the palmiform column capital found in the grounds of the Garden Tomb (reproduced by courtesy of Gabriel Barkay).

we know of) constructed for a native Egyptian in Israel was that built by Solomon for Pharaoh's Daughter (according to the Old Testament). In the orthodox chronology Barkay's Late Bronze Age structure is much too early to be associated with Solomon, whereas it fits in rather well with the chronology outlined in this book. If I am right in identifying the remains uncovered by Gabriel Barkay as elements from the residence of Solomon's Egyptian queen, we may find a ready explanation for the puzzling statement found in II Chronicles 8:11. There it states that 'Solomon moved Pharaoh's daughter **up from the City of David** to the palace which he had built for her'. We now know that the biblical historian was being very precise in his location of the Egyptian queen's residence. Solomon built her palace on a hill overlooking the city of Jerusalem which really was 'up from' the old city and its new sacred precinct on the temple mount.

Conclusion Twelve

The only Egyptian architectural remains ever found in Jerusalem are to be identified with the palace of Pharaoh's Daughter, constructed by Solomon after the completion of the Temple of Yahweh in the king's 11th year [I Kings 6:37-38]. These remains date to Late Bronze IIB and are contemporary with the reigns of the Egyptian pharaohs Haremheb (late-reign) and Seti I.

Given that the chronology being developed here identifies Haremheb as the pharaoh who gave his daughter in marriage to Solomon, we should now take a look at this Egyptian king to see if the circumstances of his reign coincide with the political situation prevailing in the time of Solomon (according to the biblical tradition).

Haremheb himself was not directly descended from the royal bloodline of the 18th Dynasty. Here then was a practical man – a nobleman but not of royal descent – who had made his career in the military and who had risen to become Commander-in-Chief of the Egyptian army (Egy. *imyr mesha wer*) during the short reign of the boy-king Tutankhamun. We may reason, therefore, that he was not so overly burdened with the sense of dynastic purity to which his predecessors had succumbed and which had contributed to the withering of the 18th Dynasty royal bloodline. Amenhotep II (Tutankhamun's great-grand-father) had once been asked by the king of MITANNI to supply one of his daughters to seal an alliance. The pharaoh had haughtily refused, claiming that no Egyptian princess had ever suffered the indignity of being married off to a foreign ruler. Things had certainly changed by Haremheb's time. The lady 'Sharelli' of Pharaoh's court (almost certainly a princess) was married to one of the more powerful city-state rulers of Western Asia – as evidenced by a hieroglyphic inscription and marriage scene inscribed on an alabaster vase excavated from the palace of King Nikmaddu in the city of Ugarit during the 1952 excavation season.[19]

So, if ever there was a time in New Kingdom history when a Pharaoh's Daughter might be offered to a foreign ruler this is it. The kings of the late-18th Dynasty may have judged it expedient to tie powerful Levantine rulers to the Egyptian throne through marriage alliance simply because Egypt was no longer in any position to recover the region by force of arms. It was not until the highly militaristic 19th Dynasty rulers took over the throne that the Egyptian army became a power to be reckoned with once more.

From what we know of Haremheb's reign he spent most of his time reorganising the state administration and rebuilding temples following the destruction and depravations of the Amarna heresy. He drew up new laws and completed the restoration of the cult of Amun at Thebes, begun during the reign of Tutankhamun. Nothing very much is known of military activities during Haremheb's *reign*, but there is pictorial evidence of a campaign into Palestine during the years when he commanded the Egyptian army under Tutankhamun. Scenes from the private tomb of Haremheb at Sakkara (the construction of which began before he became pharaoh) show him bringing Canaanite captives before the boy-king. It has been suggested by one eminent Amarna period authority that this was a military campaign against the city of Gezer.[20]

We can see that the overall political situation which prevailed in Palestine when Haremheb came to the throne fits well with that described in the Old Testament after David had captured Jerusalem and bequeathed to his son, Solomon, a powerful kingdom centred on the hill country of Canaan. Haremheb, having conducted a brief campaign into the coastal plain when he was army commander under Tutankhamun, set about reorganising the internal affairs of Egypt when he gained the throne. Using diplomacy as his principal tool he may have tried to repair the damage to the northern empire resulting from Akhenaten's neglect. In this light, a marriage alliance with the dominant ruler in the southern Levant would have been a smart move on the part of the new pharaoh. His intention may have been to ensure that such an alliance would result in a mutually beneficial trading partnership – just like the successful trading agreement between Egypt (with its African resources) and Israel which the biblical editors ascribe to Solomon's reign.

Conclusion Thirteen

King Haremheb is to be identified with the pharaoh who gave his daughter in marriage to Solomon along with the dowry of the city of Gezer which he had recently attacked and burnt.

Plate 23: The first three rows of the Shoshenk I campaign city list with the Yadhamelek name located within the box at the bottom right and an arrow (centre left) indicating where the name Jerusalem should have appeared if Shoshenk is to be identified with Shishak.

Plate 24: The schist quarries of the Wadi Hammamat – site of the genealogy of the royal architects (located within the box).

Plate 25: The Gebel es-Silsila quarries.

Plate 26: Stela 100 on the west bank at Gebel es-Silsila.

Plate 27: Ramesses II's cartouche. *Plate 28: The mummy of Ramesses II.*

Plate 29. The arm of a colossal statue of Ramesses II which once stood in front of the great temple of Pi-Ramesse. It is now located in a farmer's wheat field near the village of Kantir in the eastern Delta.

Plate 30: The harem palace of Ramesses III at Medinet Habu (right).

Plate 31: The 'Ashkelon Wall' at Karnak which forms the outer face of the western wall of the 'Cour de la Cachette' located on the south side of the Karnak complex.

Plate 32: Ashkelon Wall. Prince Khaemwaset (son of Ramesses II) tending the king's chariot team whilst the king assaults the fortress of Gezer on foot.

Plate 33: A fallen Israelite from the upper register of the Ashkelon Wall at Karnak.

Plate 34: The great temple of Ramesses II at Abu Simbel in Nubia.

Plate 35: A herdsman flees in panic.

Plate 36. The city in the hill country.

Plate 37: The great hall of Abu Simbel looking towards the holy of holies.

Plate 38: An aerial view of the ruin mound of ancient Megiddo.

Plate 39 Detail of the stratum VIII gate at Megiddo showing three courses of ashlar blocks built on top of a basalt foundation at the front façade.

Plate 40: The Megiddo stratum VIII gate looking into the city.

Plate 41: The famouse École Biblique in Jerusalem and the basilica of St. Etienne.

Plate 42: The Egyptian palmiform capital in the grounds of the Garden Tomb.

Plate 43: Detail of the stone terrace (with field-stone filling), excavated by Kenyon, which runs along the eastern slope of ancient Jerusalem.

Chapter Nine

THE LION MAN

n our long journey back in time we now come to the period of kings Saul and David *circa* 1010 to 971 BC and the biblical books of I and II Samuel. In the New Chronology, the Egyptian contemporaries of the first two Israelite rulers are the Amarna pharaohs Amenhotep III (his last few years), Akhenaten, Neferneferuaten (Queen Nefertiti as co regent of Akhenaten), Smenkhkare, Tutankhamun, Ay and Haremheb (early years).

As we immerse ourselves in the extraordinary era known as the Amarna heresy, when the traditional gods were abandoned in favour of monotheistic sun-worship, we find ourselves with an exceptional opportunity to test out the New Chronology. Archaeology has provided a fascinating archive of correspondence between the Egyptian kings and the city-state rulers of Palestine. If the New Chronology is correct in placing Saul and David in the Amarna period, then the political situation in Palestine –

47. Statue of Amenhotep IV – the sun-king. Cairo Museum.

225

as reflected in the Amarna Letters – should closely correspond to the history of Israel at the beginning of the Israelite Monarchy period – as handed down to us in I and II Samuel. With a little luck we might even be able to identify some of the main players of the books of Samuel in the Amarna correspondence. If we fail to do any of these things, then the theoretical TIP chronological revision advocated in this book would begin to look rather shaky. Conversely, if we are successful in comparing the detailed histories from the two sources (archaeological and biblical), then we would have a solid indication that the New Chronology is reliable.[1]

The Discovery of the Amarna Letters

In 1887 a peasant woman from the *fellaheen* community of Tell el-Amarna came across a number of small clay tablets buried beneath the ruins of an ancient mudbrick building located in the desert just behind her village. She had stumbled upon the 'House of Correspondence of Pharaoh' and that pharaoh was the remarkable sun-worshipping Akhenaten.

Eventually, after the archaeologists had got to work and museum curators all over the world had secured the purchase of the initial clandestine finds, the Amarna archive produced over three hundred and eighty tablets.[2] These remarkable documents are mostly written in AKKADIAN using the little wedge-shaped sign-groups we call cuneiform. The Akkadian language was the *lingua franca* of the time and was used as the official language of correspondence between the city-state rulers of the Levant and Pharaoh. The majority of the tablets found at Amarna were letters sent to Egypt from these city-state rulers or file copies of replies from Pharaoh (EA 45 to EA 382[3]), but there was also correspondence from the 'Great Kings' of the powerful northern kingdoms of Mitanni, Hatti (Turkey), Alashiya (Cyprus), Karduniash (Babylonia) and Assyria (EA 1 to

EA 45). The letters received in Egypt would have been despatched to Amarna by courier and translated by the scribes (probably both Egyptians and Semites) into Egyptian for the attention of Pharaoh and his advisors. Once translated and transcribed into HIERATIC on papyrus rolls, the tablets must have been put into storage in the House of Correspondence of Pharaoh where they were to be found some three thousand years later, cached beneath the floor of the building – presumably when the city was abandoned in the second or third regnal year of the boy-king Tutankhamun.

The 'Amarna Letters' present us with a marvellous opportunity to examine the political world surrounding Akhenaten. In particular they tell us much about the king's foreign policy – or, to be more precise, the lack of any decisive foreign policy during the ill-starred latter half of his reign.

Before we take a detailed look at the events in Palestine which are so vividly portrayed in these Letters I should tell you a little more about the extraordinary figure of Akhenaten and briefly review the major events of his era.

A Sun-King and his God

Born the second son of Amenhotep III and Queen Tiye, Prince Amenhotep (as he was originally named) eventually wore the Double Crown of Upper and Lower Egypt as NEFERKHEPERURE-WAENRE Amenhotep (IV), following the death of his elder brother Crown Prince Thutmose. I belong to the school of Egyptologists who argue that he acceded to the throne whilst his father Amenhotep III was still alive. (The co-regency question has still to be resolved, but it seems to me that the choice is now between no co-regency at all or one of eleven to twelve years.[4])

Within a few years of becoming Pharaoh, Amenhotep IV had changed his name to Akhenaten ('Glorious Spirit of the Aten') and started out on the religious and cultural revolution which was to turn him into the legendary tragic figure of ancient world history.[5]

Akhenaten was a truly enigmatic individual – a king fated with Seth-like characteristics. He has been described as both a humanist and a divine despot; a loving family man and a desecrator of temples; an inspired visionary and a malicious iconoclast. He took the rather stiff formality of 18th Dynasty Egyptian art (which was beginning to develop a more abstract style in his father's reign) and transformed it into something startlingly new, introducing more naturalistic imagery (perhaps as a result of foreign influences). This new artistic philosophy produced some beautiful treasures, now labelled 'Amarna art', scattered throughout the great museums of the world. On the other hand the iconography of kingship took on a character

48. Miniature stela of Akhenaten and Nefertiti with three of their young daughters. This affectionate family scene is typical of the iconography of the Amarna period and marks out the reign of Akhenaten as something quite exceptional in the history of pharaonic Egypt. Berlin Museum.

almost beyond recognition. The young Akhenaten ordered the craftsmen of Egypt to portray their new pharaoh, his queen – the beautiful Nefertiti – and the royal princesses in reliefs of grotesque, unflattering caricature. Yet some of the smaller sculptures which have been unearthed at Amarna are exquisite, refined works of art. Akhenaten was clearly a man of contradictions!

At the same time as Akhenaten's cultural revolution was under way, he took the astonishing step of elevating the sun-disk, Aten, to the head of the Egyptian pantheon, relegating many of the most powerful deities, such as Amun of Thebes, to a much lower status. With this reduction in status came impoverishment for the existing priesthood. The great cult centres of Egypt were at first deprived of revenues and later stripped of their enormous wealth as the religious tumult reached its fanatical and destructive climax. Near the end of his reign, Akhenaten would order the ritual regicide of Amun 'King of Gods' – so that 'none may speak his name'. All over Egypt the masons were set the task of erasing the hieroglyphic signs which spelt out the eponym of the once great god of the 18th Dynasty.

What the core motivation was which lay behind this extraordinary move we will probably never discover. However, it is clear that Akhenaten's traumatic revolution burst forth from an Egyptian court of an intensely cosmopolitan character which may have led to clashes with the ultra conservative Egyptian priesthood.

In spite of the glories of its initial flowering, Akhenaten's experiment was, at its end, not far from bringing the Egyptian empire to its knees. The political price paid for his extraordinary reign was a Palestine out of Egypt's political control for nearly half a century and, within Egypt itself, an ignominious end to the wealthiest and most powerful dynasty of rulers that the Black Land had ever nurtured.

The Amarna revolution was brought to an end shortly after the accession of the boy-king Tutankhaten. For the first couple of years he ruled from the city of Akhetaten

49. A relief from an Amarna tomb showing Akhenaten's soldiers parading at the double. Included are Libyan and Asiatic mercenaries.

before the royal court was transferred back to the old capital of Memphis. The pharaoh then changed his name to Tutankhamun in recognition of the rehabilitation of the persecuted 'King of Gods'. The Amun cult at Thebes was restored and Egypt began the long climb back towards recovery following the catastrophic years of the Amarna period. The Atenist experiment was finally over – but at what a cost!

A Window of Opportunity for Israel

During the period of Akhenaten's reign and for decades afterwards Egypt became militarily impotent, due almost entirely to the politically naive rule of the heretic and his sycophantic court. The prosperous northern empire, established by Thutmose III and his 18th Dynasty prede-cessors, had rapidly disintegrated for lack of a strong foreign policy. This chaotic era, with rumbling discontent and finally internal revolt in the Black Land itself, would have provided the opportunity for a new state to come into being in Canaan – and this is precisely what happened.

In the New Chronology the Amarna period is contem-porary with the rise of the Israelite monarchy. As you will shortly discover, the Amarna Letters log the whole process, beginning with the Hebrew revolt in the central hill country of Palestine at the beginning of King Saul's reign and ending with the assault upon Jerusalem in the eighth year of King David.

Some time during the nine-year reign of Tutankhamun there was a half-hearted attempt to recover control of the Asiatic empire but the evidence from 19th Dynasty military campaigns suggests that the late 18th Dynasty pharaohs generally continued to be militarily ineffective. As a result Palestine and Syria remained independent of Egypt for two generations. Tutankhamun's military effort was led by General Haremheb whose Memphite tomb contains reliefs showing captive Asiatic chieftains being brought to Egypt. Unfortunately the narrative text which once accompanied the scenes is now lost and so we are unable to identify the target of Haremheb's campaign.

Following Tutankhamun's death in his ninth regnal year (NC 993 BC) the throne was seized by the aged vizier, Ay (who had held the title 'Master of Horse' in Akhenaten's reign). Four years or so later and he too was dead, leaving the Egyptian throne to the most powerful man in the land – General Haremheb – who went on to complete the internal stabilisation of the Black Land. The later 19th Dynasty pharaohs would see this last ruler of the 18th Dynasty as the first since Amenhotep III to be untainted by the Atenist heresy. With Haremheb's long reign of about twenty-nine years Egypt did not, as far as we know, undertake any military ventures in the Levant – that task was left to Seti I and his son Ramesses II, the last truly great pharaohs of the Late Bronze Age.

I have already identified Ramesses II as the biblical Shishak, sacker of Solomon's Temple, and Haremheb as the pharaoh who gave his daughter in marriage to Solomon. Now let us continue the process by seeking out Saul and David.

The Amarna Habiru

In the Amarna Letters from the city-state rulers of Palestine and Syria (including Phoenicia) we find copious references to a group of people called the HABIRU (or in Sumerian

LOGOGRAM-form 'SA.GAZ'). From the Amarna Letters we can see that the Habiru groups are comprised of stateless persons who are outside the normal protection of city-state law.[6] The adult males tend to be fighting men who hire themselves out to the local rulers as mercenaries. In the earliest letters a number of the city rulers have platoons of Habiru troops which they use to guard their petty kingdoms and sometimes to settle feuds over disputed territory.

Egyptologists have long recognised that the appellation Habiru is the equivalent of the term *Apiru* found in Egyptian texts dating from the Middle and New Kingdoms whilst a number of biblical authorities have concluded that the designation Habiru/Apiru is also one and the same as the biblical term *Ibrim* (the plural of *Ibri* = Hebrew which stems from the eponymous ancestor Eber).

These equations have always presented biblical historians with a rather awkward problem since it is difficult to explain what Hebrews are doing marauding all over Palestine a century before the Exodus. If the Hebrews were bonded slaves in Egypt during the New Kingdom, then how could they be roaming around the Promised Land at the same time? This was the issue addressed by the great biblical scholar Albrecht ALT who concluded that the Habiru of the Amarna period were indeed Hebrews – but not the Hebrews of Moses or Joshua. They were an earlier group which had left Egypt several generations prior to the final Exodus under Moses. The Conquest of Joshua and the Israelites was rather a secondary incursion into a region already populated by the Hebrew tribes. This, of course, dilutes the Conquest narratives into something of a minor skirmish, only later to be transformed into a single epic struggle for nationhood. Again, archaeology (in the form of the Amarna Letters) was demonstrating that the biblical narratives had little to do with historical reality.

But, are the early Israelites, as described in the books of Joshua or Judges, in any way like the Amarna Habiru? Well, they certainly could be described as migrating stateless people, but there are no biblical passages which hint at the Hebrews being employed as mercenaries prior to the time of David. It is only when the rebel David breaks away from King Saul and offers his services to the Philistine king of Gath that we see a situation similar to that which pertains in Palestine during the Amarna era. Indeed, it has been noted by a number of Old Testament scholars that the life-style of the Amarna Habiru closely parallels that of the mixed band of Hebrews led by the rebel Israelite commander, David.[7] To emphasise this point I have chosen to quote from three of those eminent biblical historians.

1. Moshe Greenberg in his seminal work on the Habiru:

> In biblical traditions there are repeated examples of the sort of phenomena associated with the Amarna GAZ (Habiru). **The clearest example is that of David**. He lost status in the Israelite community by flight caused by the enmity of the king. … There gathered around him other refugees motivated by economic as well as other concerns. All were similarly without legal protection, and had to maintain themselves by forming a band under the leadership of David.[8]

2. George Mendenhall on the Amarna Habiru:

> **The most striking parallels by far are found in the story of David's outlawry.** … [David's gang] roam the countryside seeking the favour and protection of cities (Keilah), wealthy individuals (Nabal), and kings (?Nahash of Ammon, cf. Samuel 10:2). Finally David offers the services of his band (600 men – a veritable army!) to Achish, king of Gath. Achish assigns them quarters ('gives them' in biblical and el-Amarna usage) Ziklag. The town becomes the base of their marauding operations.[9]

3. Kyle McCarter on the historical David:

> **In short, David became an 'apiru (Habiru) chief. Like the 'apiru known from the Amarna Age**, David and his men were soldiers of fortune, who lived by hiring themselves out as mercenaries or subsisted on plunder.[10]

Here, then, is a quite extraordinary situation. Biblical scholars have come to the conclusion that the Hebrews under David are an exact (but later) reflection of the historical Amarna Habiru. The problem is that in the conventional chronology David and his band of Hebrews were marauding across Palestine in the last decade of the eleventh century whilst the Habiru of the Amarna age were doing their marauding in the fourteenth century BC. Mendenhall, Greenberg and McCarter had only the conventional chronology as their frame of reference. If the New Chronology had been available to them, they may well have come to a quite different conclusion: the Amarna Habiru do not simply bear a striking resemblance to David's Hebrews – they *are* David's Hebrews!

Conclusion Fourteen

In the New Chronology, the Habiru of Palestine mentioned in the Amarna Letters are recognised as the Hebrews (Heb. *Ibrim*) of I and II Samuel. In particular, they are to be identified with the followers of David during the period of the latter's exile from the Israelite court in the reign of Saul and David's first seven years as king of Hebron prior to the capture of Jerusalem.

The Egyptian Vassals

If we now compare the political topography of Amarna Palestine and Syria with the same geographical region as described in the books of Samuel we find a number of direct parallels. I have listed them in the table overleaf and provide here a summary of the conclusions reached regarding each major political grouping.

1. The western city-state rulers of the coastal plain in Amarna age Palestine would appear to be identical with the Philistine *SERANIM* of I & II Samuel. The former bear Indo-European names and represent a ruling élite which was probably established in Canaan during the latter part of the Middle Bronze Age. The leading figure in the western city-state confederacy is Shuwardata, king of Gath.

2. Milkilu, ruler of Gezer, would be a contemporary of King Saul. His city-state seems to be independent of both the Philistines and the Israelites (it is Canaanite and its rulers all bear west-semitic names). In the new historical model which I am putting forward Gezer remains an independent enclave until its capture and destruction by General Haremheb during the reign of Tutankhamun. It is then given to Solomon as a dowry for his marriage to Pharaoh's Daughter.

3. Amarna correspondent Abdihcba, king of Jerusalem, becomes the last ruler of the Jebus prior to the capture of Jerusalem by David.

4. Research has shown that the political expansion of the states of Amurru (OC – 13th century) and Aram-Zobah (OC – 10th century) were very similar. In the New Chronology the two kingdoms are a single entity – their historical separation being brought about only as a result

The Political Topography of Palestine

1a. **Amarna period**: In the coastal plain and Jezreel valley the city-state rulers who correspond with Amenhotep III and Akhenaten bear names of Indo-European origin. They include Shuwardata, king of Gath, Widia of Ashkelon, Biridiya of Megiddo, Yashdata (town unknown but in the Jezreel), Indaruta of Achshaph and Shubandu (town unknown but near the coast).

1b. **Old Testament**: In the time of Saul, the coastal plain is dominated by the five Philistine seranim ('lords') based at the cities of Ashkelon, Gath, Gaza, Ashdod and Ekron. Their leader appears to be the king of Gath. The Philistines are of Indo-European stock. King Saul does not hold sway over the Jezreel valley and its four major cities (Megiddo, Taanach, Shunem and Bethshan) are not within his control.

2a. **Amarna period**: The city of Gezer is in the hands of Canaanite rulers bearing west-semitic names (Milkilu succeeded by Yapuhu and Addadanu).

2b. **Old Testament**: During the early Monarchy Period, Gezer is ruled by Canaanite kings who are not a part of the Philistine confederacy (the Bible does not give their names). Gezer only comes under Israelite control when the city is given as a dowry to Solomon following its defeat and destruction by Pharaoh [I Kings 9:16].

3a. **Amarna period**: During the reign of Akhenaten the ruler of the independent city-state of Jerusalem is Abdiheba whose name means 'servant of Heba' – Heba being a Hurrian goddess.

3b. **Old Testament**: Jerusalem is also an independent enclave during the time of Saul (and David for the first seven years of his reign). It is ruled by the Jebusites – an Indo-European or Hurrian élite.

4a. **Amarna period**: To the north, the region of Syria is dominated by kings of Amorite stock – Abdiashirta and, later, his son Aziru. These rulers continuously stir up trouble in the region and attack neighbouring city-states.

4b. **Old Testament**: The major opponent of David during his long reign was Hadadezer, 'the Rehobite king of Zobah' [II Samuel 8:3] whose sphere of influence encompassed the whole of Syria. It is interesting to note that Abraham Malamat considers the political boundaries of the thirteenth-century Amorite state of Aziru and the tenth-century Aramean kingdom of Hadadezer to be virtually identical.[11] In his view, the territories over which Aram-Zobah held sway 'correspond to the expansion of the kingdom of Amurru which still flourished in the thirteenth century'. But chronology once again raises problems of political continuity:

> The question is whether Hadadezer's kingdom, like that of David, was not based, in one way or another, on a previously existing political organisation. It has to be pointed out, however, that in the case of Aram-Zobah, there was apparently no continuity in the transmission of political rule as in the case of Israel, and the influence of the political tradition reaching back to the days of the kingdom of Amurru could only be indirect.[12]

Malamat's 'indirect' link is merely a mirage of the traditional chronology. If he were now to apply the New Chronology to his comparative research of 1958, he might well come to the same conclusion that I reached in 1984: the kingdom of Amurru is one and the same as the kingdom of Aram (with Zobah).

We can go further than this. The el-Amarna name Aziru (king of Amurru) is a hypocoristicon (accepted shortening) of a longer, more formal name. This is a very common phenomenon in the ancient world and several correspondents employ hypocoristic name-forms in the Amarna Letters. Professor William Moran, the recognised expert on the archive, suggests that the name of the king of Amurru should be translated as '[N is the] helper' where 'N' represents the name of a deity. If we substitute the pre-eminent Syrian weather god Hadad for '[N]' then we would get 'Hadad is the helper' – in other words the biblical name Hadadezer.

Pierre Bordreuil and Javier Texidor have demonstrated that at least one ruler named Hadadezer was known by the hypocoristicon 'Ezra' which is clearly the direct equivalent of the Amarna hypocoristicon 'Aziru' (given that vowels are not written in Aramaic). They have studied the Melkart Stela from Aleppo and produced a new reading of the crucial passage already much discussed in scholarly circles.[13]

> The statue which Barhadad, son of **Ezra, the king, the Rehobite, king of Aram,** set up for his lord Melkart, to whom he made a vow and who heard his voice.

Here Barhadad is the biblical name Benhadad and Ezra is clearly the hypocoristicon of the Syrian dynastic name Hadad-ezra. Thus we can justifiably conclude that our el-Amarna Aziru is a Syrian ruler whose full name was probably Hadadaziru. Within the New Chronology he must be one and the same as King Hadadezer, long-time enemy of King David.

of the conventional chronology. King Aziru of the Amarna Letters is one and the same as Hadadezer (Ezra), the king of Aram-Zobah in II Samuel.

Conclusion Fifteen

The general political topography of the Levant in the Amarna period closely corresponds to that described in the second book of Samuel which deals with the beginning of the United Monarchy period in Israelite history.

King of the Hill Country

So far I have described the four major political elements making up Amarna age Palestine: (1) the western city-states; (2) the Canaanite enclave of Gezer; (3) the enclave of Jerusalem; and (4) the vast northern state of Amurru, ruled at first by Abdiashirta and then later by his son Aziru. However, there is a fifth political power in the region which we must now consider.

The hill country to the north of Jerusalem is dominated by a king who shows scant respect towards Egyptian sovereignty in Palestine. His hypocoristic name is Labayu – his fuller name being unknown. Moran suggests the name should be understood as 'Great Lion [of N]' where 'N' represents the name of a deity.[14]

If the New Chronology's synchronism of the Amarna period with the early Monarchy period is correct, then this Labayu must be none other than the first Israelite king – Saul. Now, of course, the name Saul bears no recognisable similarity to Labayu, but this is hardly surprising. 'Saul' is almost certainly not the name carried by the Israelite ruler during his lifetime. It is rather a 'legendary' name bequeathed to the king by the later biblical editors. The people of Israel asked the prophet Samuel to anoint 'Saul' so that they could have a king 'like the other nations' [I Samuel 8:4-5]. Saul's destiny was not anticipated, for the twelve tribes had been ruled by 'judges' throughout the past four centuries. It is significant to note that the name Saul (Heb. *Shaul*) means 'asked for' to be understood as 'asked for [by the people]'.[15] Similarly, as we have noted, Solomon's name means 'peace' because his reign encompassed forty years of peace for the Israelite nation. Neither name was given to the two kings at birth, nor probably during their lifetimes. We should not, then, expect the Amarna Letters to give Saul's 'legendary' name but rather his contemporary name. If Saul is to be identified with Labayu (as I shall now attempt to demonstrate by comparing their careers), then we could translate the name of the ruler of the hill country as 'Great Lion [of Yahweh]' – a most appropriate title for the first Israelite monarch and a mighty warrior.

It is also intriguing to note that Psalm 57 describes King Saul's personal bodyguards as *lebaim* (a word unique to the Old Testament, meaning 'great lions'). A collection of bronze arrow/javelin heads was unearthed in 1953 at the village of el-Khadr, near Bethlehem, some of which bear the inscription *hiz 'abd leb'at* meaning 'arrow of the servant

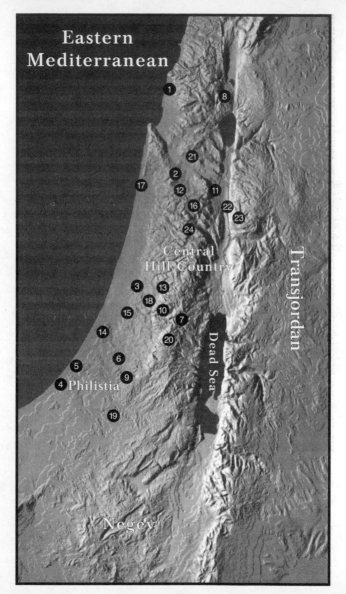

Opposite page: The cities and towns of Palestine which are mentioned in the books of I and II Samuel compared to the city-states and towns named in the Amarna Letters. The city-states are in bold type. This comparison demonstrates a close similarity in the political topography of Palestine as determined from the two sources.

I & II Samuel	Amarna Letters
1. **Acco**	1. **Acco**
2. **Megiddo**	2. **Megiddo**
3. **Gezer**	3. **Gezer**
4. **Gaza**	4. **Gaza**
5. **Ashkelon**	5. **Ashkelon**
6. **Gath**	6. **Gath**
7. **Jerusalem**	7. **Jerusalem**
8. **Hazor**	8. **Hazor**
9. **Lachish**	9. **Lachish**
10. Aijalon	10. Aijalon
11. Bethshan	11. Bethshan
12. Taanach	12. Taanach
13. Bethshemesh	13. [not attested]
14. **Ashdod**	14. (Shubandu's resident city?)
15. **Ekron**	15. [not attested]
16. [not attested]	16. Gina
17. Dor	17. [not attested]
18. [not attested]	18. Sarha (= biblical Zorah?)
19. Ziklag	19. [not attested]
20. Hebron	20. [not attested]
21. [not attested]	21. Shunem
22. [not attested]	22. Pella
23. Mahanaim	23. [not attested]
24. [not attested]	24. Shechem

of the great lioness'.[16] Professor Benjamin Mazar proposes that the men who once owned these arrows had formed a corps of professional archers in the service of King Saul. He goes on to suggest that their emblem was an obscure lioness goddess.[17] Could there be a connection between these initially disparate elements: (a) a king called 'Great Lion'; (b) a royal bodyguard named the 'Great Lions' and (c) a corps of Saul's archers who were 'servants of the great lioness'? If so, then David's vivid description of Saul's men as he hid from their presence in the cave of En-Gedi (described in I Samuel 24) takes on a whole new meaning.

> I lie surrounded by lions (Heb. *lebaim*), greedy for human prey, their teeth are spears and arrows, their tongue a sharp sword. [Psalm 57:4]

This may be the one surviving Old Testament clue to Saul's real name – a remnant of authentic political history surrounding the Lion Man and his bodyguard of Great Lions.

When we take a look at the Lion Man himself as revealed in the Amarna Letters we find a number of remarkable similarities with King Saul of I Samuel. The latter was a major political figure in eleventh century Palestine. He controlled most of the central hill country and parts of Transjordan. However, Jerusalem remained in the hands of the Jebusites until the reign of Saul's successor, David. King Saul fought against the Philistines but did not attempt to conquer their strongholds in the southern coastal plain. He appears to have been allied to the Canaanites of Gezer following Samuel's earlier victory against the Philistines at Mizpah when 'There was peace also between Israel and the Amorites' [I Samuel 7:14].[18]

Nearing the end of his reign, Saul is active in the Jezreel valley area, presumably his concern being to link the

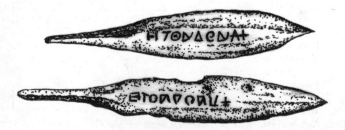

50. Two of the el-Khadr arrowheads. Israel National Museum, Jerusalem (reproduced by courtesy of Peter van der Veen).

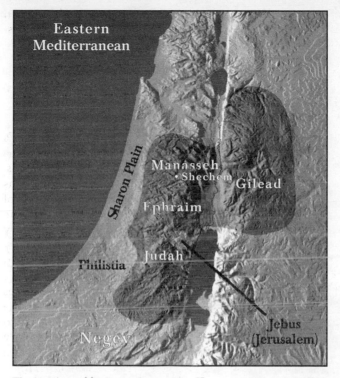

The kingdom of Saul according to John Hayes and Maxwell Miller is illustrated in the map.[19] According to Aharoni the geopolitical situation in the highlands during the Amarna period was as follows: 'In the hill country there were only a few political centres, and each of these ruled over a fairly extensive area. In all the hill country of Judah and Ephraim we hear only of Jerusalem and Shechem ... Apparently the kings of Jerusalem and Shechem dominated, to all practical purposes, the entire central hill country at that time. The territory of Labayu, king of Shechem, was especially large in contrast to the other small Canaanite principalities round about.'[20] But, as de Vaux notes: 'Labayu was not, however, given the title of king of Shechem and it is doubtful whether he ever was'.[21] It seems fairly clear that Labayu ruled over a kingdom which included Shechem but his capital or home town was elsewhere. It is clear from EA 255 that Labayu also supervised caravan traffic in large areas of northern Transjordan which indicates political control in that region as well.

Israelite tribes of Asher, Zebulun, Naphtali and Issachar (north of the Jezreel) with his newly forged Israelite kingdom in the central hill country. This struggle finally leads to his death at the Battle of Mount Gilboa, looking down on the Jezreel valley, when the Israelite forces are roundly defeated by the Philistine confederacy.

The general political situation in Palestine at the time of Labayu is much the same. Labayu's status is described as follows:

> Labayu was a serious contender with the kings of Jerusalem and Gezer. EA 250 indicates that for some time he even dominated the entire SHARON, having conquered Gath-padalla (Jett in the central Sharon) and Gath-rimmon (apparently the biblical town of this name, perhaps to be identified with Tell-Jerisheh on the Yarkon). Even in the north Labayu was not content to possess only the hill country; he tried to penetrate into the Jezreel valley, laying siege to Megiddo [EA 244] and destroying Shunem and some other towns [EA 250].[22]

There is no doubt that Labayu is seen by the Egyptian vassals as a major threat to the stability of the region and even Pharaoh gets a taste of his rebellious, uncompromising spirit early on. In letter EA 252, sent by Labayu to the Egyptian king (probably Amenhotep III) he uses what can only be described as a biblical proverb to warn off the pharaoh and his other vassals from interfering in his affairs.

> If an ant is struck, does it not fight back and bite the hand of the man that struck it?

Could it be that we actually have in our possession a letter from the earliest Israelite king? If so, then this, thus far, little-regarded tablet may become one of the world's most treasured relics.

An Untutored Monarch

In 1943, the great American biblical scholar and archaeologist, William ALBRIGHT, noted that in EA 252 Labayu
had employed the Hebrew word *nemalah* for 'ant' whereas
one would have expected Akkadian *zirbabu*.[23] In fact,
Albright goes much further than this. Having analysed the
letters of Labayu, he concludes that the scribes of Labayu's
court were unfamiliar with the Akkadian language used
by the rest of the Amarna correspondents.

> That ... [Labayu's] beginnings were insignificant also
> appears in one of the earliest letters from him to the
> pharaoh, which was written by a scribe so untutored
> that he wrote the second half of the letter in almost
> pure Canaanite, obviously not knowing enough
> Akkadian to translate it even into the strange jargon
> taught in the schools.[24]

What does Albright mean by 'almost pure Canaanite'? The
answer comes in another article on the Amarna Letters
published by him in the same year.

> ... phonetically, morphologically and syntactically
> the people then living in the district later occupied
> by Manasseh (i.e. Labayu's kingdom) spoke a dialect
> of Hebrew (Canaanite) which was very closely akin
> to that of Ugarit. The differences which some scholars
> have listed between biblical Hebrew and Ugaritic are,
> in fact, nearly all chronological distinctions.[25]

In other words, the reason why Albright and other scholars
use the term Canaanite in relation to Labayu's letters is
because in the conventional chronology the Hebrew language does not yet exist in Palestine. The Israelites are still
more than a century away from entering the Promised
Land. In reality, however, Labayu's 'Canaanite' is simply

early Hebrew. There is no doubt about it. In dealing with the 'proverb' of EA 252, Albright is unequivocal: 'As already recognised by the interpreters, this idiom is pure Hebrew'.[26]

We have to ask ourselves why Labayu's scribes are so poorly versed in the *lingua franca* employed by the rest of the Amarna correspondents. Albright thinks it is because Labayu was new to the game of international politics: he was a king whose 'beginnings were insignificant'. This comment could equally apply to King Saul who was never groomed for kingship. When Samuel selects him to be the first king of Israel Saul's reaction is surprise and humility.

> Saul then replied, 'Am I not a Benjaminite, from the smallest of Israel's tribes? And is not my family the least of all the families of the tribe of Benjamin? Why do you say such words to me?' [I Samuel 9:21]

Saul was indeed a warrior (Heb. *bahur*) and the son of a nobleman (Heb. *gibbor hayil*), but his was a rustic nobility void of any courtly tradition. One would hardly expect his scribes (if he had more than one) to be conversant with Akkadian.

The Rebellious Vassal

Saul was the first king of Israel and his rise to the kingship was closely linked to an Israelite revolt against the oppressive dominance of the Philistine city-states to the west. The Philistines, in turn, owed their allegiance to Egypt. So do we have any evidence that Labayu was a rebel?

There are a number of Amarna letters which attest to the disruptive activities of this king of the hill country. We hear of Labayu's close connection with the Habiru:

> Are we to act like Labayu, when he was giving the land of Shechem (Akk. *Sakhmu*) to the Habiru?

Here in EA 289, Abdiheba, ruler of Jerusalem, is informing Pharaoh that Labayu had at one time established a power base in the region of Shechem for his Habiru mercenary forces.[27] If Labayu was the historical Saul, then he had assigned a part of his domain to Hebrew troops. What then do we understand by the biblical term Hebrew? Most non-specialist readers of the Old Testament fail to distinguish between Hebrews and Israelites. However, this equation of Hebrews and Israelites is an oversimplification because the narratives suggest that they were distinct groups. The best way to understand their relationship is to follow a simple rule: all Israelites were once Hebrews but not all Hebrews in the Old Testament are Israelites. The Hebrews who entered Egypt in the time of Jacob and Joseph became Israelites through their common heritage as they endured their prolonged slavery under the pharaohs. When they finally settled in the Promised Land, other groups with similar ethnic origins and status to the Israelites were already populating the more barren parts of the Levant. These stateless peoples had remained 'wanderers' and were therefore true Habiru/Hebrews, whereas their ancestral kin, the Israelites, regarded themselves as a distinctive entity – 'the chosen people'. This distinction, made by the Israelite tribes themselves, was probably lost on the Philistines and Egyptians. To them the Israelite tribal groups were still Habiru.

It is interesting to note that in the Old Testament, nine times out of ten, it is non-Israelites who use the term 'Hebrew' to describe the people of Israel and not the Israelites themselves. It becomes a pejorative term.[28] When 'Hebrews' is used to describe 'Israelites' in the Old Testament it is in the spoken words of Egyptians or Philistines (in other words an insult from the mouths of Israel's enemies). If, on the other hand, the term appears in the books of Samuel as part of the historical narrative, then 'Hebrews' does not refer to Israelites but rather to the mercenary forces hired by Saul and the Philistine kings or those disenfranchised followers of the rebel chieftain, David. For example:

(a) Following the capture of the Philistine outpost at Michmash.

> Those **Hebrews** who had earlier **taken service with the Philistines** and had accompanied them into camp, now **defected to the Israelites** who were with Saul and Jonathan. Similarly, all those Israelites who had been hiding in the highlands of Ephraim, hearing that the Philistines were on the run, chased after them and joined in the fight. [I Samuel 14:21-22]

(b) Following the massive Philistine counter attack.

> When **the men of Israel** saw that they were in a strait (for the people were hard pressed), then the people hid themselves in caves, in thickets, in cliffs, in cellars, and in pits. Also **some of the Hebrews** crossed the Jordan into the land of Gad and Gilead. [I Samuel 13:6-7]

It is quite obvious from these two passages that the writer is making a clear distinction between the Hebrews and the Israelites. As Joyce Baldwin confirms:

> If, as we have argued, these 'Hebrews' are the un-committed recruits whom Saul had attracted to himself, it is understandable that they should be singled out for separate action. The text needs no emendation. The hirelings fled.[29]

There is thus a clear parallel here between Labayu and his Habiru mercenary forces garrisoned at Shechem and Saul with his Hebrew mercenaries. It is hardly surprising, therefore, to find Labayu himself being named by Shuwardata of Gath as 'the Habiru who was raised up against the lands' [EA 366] just as Saul was the figurehead of the Israelite and Hebrew revolt movement against the Philistines.

The Israelite uprising began with the defeat of the Philistines at Michmash followed by the immediate capture of Gibeah. There, Saul's eldest son, Jonathan, cast down the standing stone (Heb. *netsib* [30]) which had been set up by the Philistines sometime earlier to establish their hegemony over the central hill country of Benjamin.

> Jonathan smashed the Philistine pillar which was at Gibeah and the Philistines learnt that the Hebrews had risen in revolt. Saul had the trumpet sounded throughout the country, and the whole of Israel heard the news: Saul has smashed the Philistine pillar, and now Israel has incurred the enmity of the Philistines. [I Samuel 13:3 5]

It is interesting that the SEPTUAGINT (or LXX) records that the Philistine pillar had been erected at Gibeah – Saul's home town – whereas the Masoretic version of I Samuel gives 'Geba'. Scholars have long been aware of the confusion in the biblical text between these two names. Both Gibeah and Geba mean 'hill' and it has recently been suggested by Maxwell Miller that they are, in fact, one and the same location [31] Saul's dynastic seat would then have been at Geba of Benjamin, on the south side of the Wadi Suweinit opposite Michmash. Miller's arguments thus cast doubt on Tell el-Ful as the site of ancient Gibeah. This would be consistent with the New Chronology because the small fortified residence there was not built until the Iron Age – long after the Amarna period when we have determined that Saul became king of Israel.

If Geba of Benjamin is identical to Gibeah of Saul (or at least the two places are closely related geographically – perhaps both a town and citadel at the same hilltop location[32]), then Saul is recapturing his home town in I Samuel 13:3-5. So, when his son, Jonathan, topples over the Philistine pillar erected there he is overthrowing the symbol of the Philistine yoke which had stood before his father's dynastic residence.

How does this incident compare with what we know of Labayu from the Amarna correspondence? In EA 252 Labayu himself writes to the Egyptian court complaining that his enemies have been maligning him in their letters to Pharaoh. He protests that his crime was simply to retake his home town after its illegal seizure by an unnamed enemy.

> It was in war that the city was seized. When I had sworn my peace – and when I swore the (Egyptian regional) governor swore with me – the city, along with my god, was seized. I am slandered before the king, my lord. Moreover, if an ant is struck, does it not fight back and bite the hand of the man that struck it? How at this time can I show deference and then another city of mine will be seized? … I will guard the men that seized the city [and] my god. They are the despoilers of my father, but I will guard them.

This is a difficult text to interpret, and translations vary in many details, but I think we can recover from it the following four basic elements.

1. Labayu loses his home town to a sudden attack (presumably when he is not there to defend it) – in spite of the fact that an agreement had been sworn on both sides to keep the peace.

2. Connected with Labayu's residence is a sacred site which has something to do with his god who was seized along with the town.

3. He recovers the town by force of arms – but this had been an act of retaliation against the initial aggression.

4. The original aggressors, having been defeated, have complained to Pharaoh that Labayu is holding some of their men captive. Labayu is forced to write one of his rare letters to Egypt to defend his actions, arguing that he is entitled to imprison those who had seized his town and god. However, in spite of this, he will protect them from the anger of his own people.

When we compare what little we know about Saul's home town with the details gleaned from EA 252 we find a set of close parallels.

1. In I Samuel 11 Saul is away fighting against the Ammonites of Transjordan. It is presumably at this time that the Philistines seize the opportunity to capture Michmash and Geba/Gibeah.

2. Very close to Saul's house is a 'high place' attended by priests. We learn this from an earlier passage [I Samuel 10:2-6]. Following Saul's anointment, the prophet Samuel predicts what will happen to Saul upon his return journey to his home town.

> ... after leaving me today ... you will come to **Gibeah of God (where the Philistine pillar is)** and, when you are just outside the town, you will meet a group of prophets coming down from the high place, headed by lyre, tambourine, pipe and harp; they will be in a state of ecstasy. The spirit of Yahweh will then seize on you, and you will go into ecstasy with them, and be changed into another man. When these signs have occurred, act as occasion serves, for God is with you.

'Gibeah of God' (Heb. *Gebeath-elohim*) is another name for Saul's home town[33] and it is here that the Philistines had erected a pillar. The high place there is also sacred to the Israelites and is dedicated to Yahweh. Saul's home town is thus a holy site connected with his god. When he takes Gibeah/Geba back from the Philistines and Jonathan smites the pillar of the Philistines erected there, Saul is acting as Labayu did in EA 252. The fact that the Philistine pillar is located at Gibeah of God [I Samuel 10:5] and Geba [I Samuel 13:3] confirms that we are dealing with a single location.

3. One further parallel can be drawn from the two texts (EA 252 and I Samuel). In the translation on page 250 of EA 252 by Moran, we read: 'How at this time can I show deference and then another city of mine will be seized?' However, Albright had earlier given a quite different translation of the same passage: 'How could I hold back this day when two of my towns have been taken?'. In the case of Saul, he recaptured two towns – Geba/Gibeah and Michmash.

The King's Son

In Labayu's third letter to Pharaoh (EA 254) we learn that the king's son (unnamed) has been implicated in the activities of the Habiru. This is without the knowledge of his father. Labayu writes:

> Moreover, the king wrote for my son. I did not know that my son was consorting with the Habiru. I herewith hand him over to Addaya (the Egyptian commissioner in Gaza).

Here, again there is a clear parallel with the story of King Saul's reign. In I Samuel 20:30-31 Saul accuses his son, Jonathan, of a secret association with the rebel chieftain,

David. The close friendship between David and Jonathan is legendary, and David, as Mendenhall and Greenberg observe, is the 'clearest example'[34] of a Habiru leader one could find. In a rage of displeasure Saul lashes out at his eldest son:

> 'Son of a rebellious slut! Do I not know that you side with the son of Jesse (i.e. David) to your own shame and your mother's dishonour? As long as the son of Jesse lives on earth, neither you nor your royal rights are secure.'

The Great Lion Falls

It is now time to turn to perhaps the most dramatic incident in the story of King Saul – his last great battle on the slopes of Mount Gilboa. The series of events leading up to the final clash between Saul and the Philistines begins to come into focus around I Samuel 27 where the rebel chieftain, David, fleeing from Saul's pursuit, takes up with Achish, King of Gath. David offers the services of his men as mercenary troops to supplement the army of the Philistine king. Achish assigns the town of Ziklag to the Hebrew chieftain and his soldiers to use as their military headquarters. In return, when the crunch comes a year and four months later, David is ready to fight on the side of the Philistine confederacy as they prepare for battle in the Jezreel valley against his own kin, the Israelites. However, the other Philistine *seranim* ('lords') do not trust Achish's Hebrew mercenaries and their leader:

> 'What are these Hebrews doing? ... Send the man back,' they said, 'make him go back to the place which you assigned to him. He cannot go into battle with us, in case he turns on us once battle is joined.' [I Samuel 29:3-4]

The forces of the Philistine confederacy move into the Jezreel valley and muster at Shunem [I Samuel 28:4]. Meanwhile the fighting men of the Israelite tribes had already been gathering around Saul and his sons at the Fountain of Jezreel [I Samuel 29:1]. Saul then makes a strategic withdrawal onto the heights of Gilboa to make it difficult for the Philistines to use their chariots and cavalry.[35] In spite of this apparent disadvantage, the Philistines pursue the Israelite army up the mountain and press home their superiority in numbers. Thousands of Israelites are slaughtered and Saul's sons, Jonathan, Abinadab and Malchishua are slain [I Samuel 31:2]. Saul himself is mortally wounded by a Philistine arrow and takes his own life rather than risking capture by the enemy [I Samuel 31:3-4]. When David, left behind in southern Palestine, hears the news of Saul's death on Gilboa he rents his clothes and sings a lament for Saul and Jonathan [II Samuel 1:19-27].

> Does the splendour of Israel lie dead on your heights? How are the mighty fallen!

> Do not speak of it in Gath, nor broadcast it in the streets of Ashkelon, for fear the daughters of the Philistines rejoice, for fear the daughters of the uncircumcised gloat.

> You mountains of Gilboa, no dew, no rain fall upon you, O treacherous fields where the heros' shield lies dishonoured!

In the rest of the lament David continues to ask the same question. How did the heroes fall? In the third stanza he hints at treachery (Heb. *sede tarmit* = 'treacherous fields'). Were Saul and the Israelites betrayed in some way by their allies? How were the Philistines successful in pursuing Saul up Gilboa in their chariots? The Bible fails to give us any answers to these intriguing questions – but the Amarna

Letters do. Following Labayu's death in battle against a confederacy of western city-state rulers, his surviving sons send a message to one Balu-UR.SAG (city unknown) who immediately reports their rebellious activities to Pharaoh in his letter EA 250. There he states that the sons of Labayu have been urging him to 'wage war against the people of Gina for having killed our father'. So the townsfolk of Gina (biblical En-Ganim, modern Jenin) were in some way implicated in the death of Labayu. Letter EA 245 from Biridiya, ruler of Megiddo, relates that Labayu was killed in battle before he could be taken alive and sent to Egypt for public execution. Biridiya, making his excuses to Pharaoh writes:

> Moreover, I urged my brothers, 'If the god of the king, our lord, brings it about that we overcome Labayu, then we must bring him alive to the king, our lord.' My mare, however, having been put out of action, I took my place behind him and rode with Yashdata. But before my arrival they had struck him (i.e. Labayu) down.

The 'they' in 'they had (already) struck him down' suggests that some advanced forces had reached Labayu and dealt him a mortal blow before the main body of the army were able to surround the rebel king and take him alive. Or had Labayu taken his own life knowing what fate awaited him if he were to give himself up? Were 'they' the men of Gina whom the sons of Labayu accuse of killing their father? It would be a good idea to look at the location of Saul's last battle on Gilboa and see if we can combine the information from our two sources to come up with a clearer picture of the tragic events surrounding Saul's death.

Reference to the aerial photograph of the Jezreel valley with Gilboa at its centre shows that the town of Gina is situated close to the southern slopes of Gilboa. It is from this side of the mountain that the terrain slopes up to the summit in a gentle incline. This is in stark contrast to the steep, almost precipitous northern and western slopes. If the Philistines had been allowed access to the mountain top via the territory of Gina, then the strategic advantage of Saul's position would have been lost. The Israelite forces could then have been outmanoeuvred by a flanking assault. In this battle scenario it is envisaged that the men of Gina had been positioned to defend the Israelite rear but that they betrayed Saul by allowing the Philistine archers to ascend the mountain unopposed. The latter's surprise attack resulted in Philistine arrows raining down on Saul and the élite Israelite troops, leaving his son dead and the Isralite king himself mortally wounded. With this new information, gleaned from the Amarna Letters, it is finally possible to understand and appreciate the poetic reference to 'treacherous fields' in David's lament. Saul had been betrayed by his own people.

Aftermath

> When the Israelites who were on the other side of the (Jezreel) valley saw that the men of Israel had taken flight and that Saul and his sons were dead, they abandoned their towns and fled. The Philistines then came and occupied them. [I Samuel 31:7]

The disaster of Gilboa was to have serious implications for Israel and the house of Saul. Only the king's youngest son, Ishbaal[36] and his son-in-law, David, were still alive to succeed him. Ishbaal was taken over to Transjordan by Saul's military commander, Abner, where they remained for the next seven years. In the sixth year following the death of his father, Ishbaal was proclaimed king by Abner, but within two years the young ineffectual second king of Israel was murdered in his palace.[37] David, on the other hand, set himself up as ruler of Hebron before becoming king of all Israel upon the death of Ishbaal.

In the immediate aftermath of the Battle of Gilboa the Jezreel valley was occupied by the armies of the Philistine western allies. Bethshan was garrisoned to prevent the remnants of the Israelite army from regrouping. The fortress of Bethshan guards the eastern end of the Jezreel valley at the point where it joins the Jordan valley, enabling the men of the garrison to monitor any incursions from the isolated northern tribes in Ephraim and the tribes located across the Jordan to the east.

The Amarna Letters tell exactly the same story. In EA 289, Abdiheba of Jerusalem writes that the troops of Gath now garrison Bethshan. The Letters also begin to relate the activities of 'the two sons of Labayu'. The events of the next eight years are the subject of the following chapter where I shall deal with the rise of David to the kingship of all Israel and his capture of Jerusalem. All that is left for me to do in order to bring the extraordinary life of the 'Great Lion of Yahweh' to a close is to quote the terse report to Pharaoh of the death of the rebel king. The leader of the victorious confederacy, the ruler of Gath, writes in EA 366:

> Let the king, my lord, be informed that the Habiru (singular) who was raised up against the lands; the god of the king, my lord, delivered him to me, and I have smitten him.[38]

Conclusion Sixteen

Labayu, the 'Lion [of Yahweh]', ruler of the hill country in the Amarna period is the historical figure upon whom the writer of the books of Samuel based the life of Saul, first king of the Israelite nation.

ᐸᕝᑫᎳ፧·ᕝᐸᕲ
ᐃᖿᐊᕿᕧᕒ

Chapter Ten

THE BELOVED

ollowing the Battle of Gilboa a complex political picture is developed in the biblical narrative involving at least four major players. Ruling from Transjordan we have the legitimate heir to Saul's throne, Ishbaal/Mutbaal. However, in the view of Alberto Soggin and Kyle McCarter, the text of II Samuel 2:10 implies that he is not officially crowned until several years have elapsed following the death of his father.[1] This may have been as a result of the political chaos generated amongst the Israelite tribes stemming from the disastrous defeat at the hands of the Philistines. The ineffectual Ishbaal is very much controlled by his military commander, Abner, who had rescued him from the Philistines at Gilboa [II Samuel 2:8-9]. There can be little doubt that Abner is the effective policy-maker over the rump Israelite kingdom in Transjordan.

In the central hill country of Canaan we find David and his Habiru army. He had not participated in the Battle of Gilboa – on either side – and after the death of Saul his position becomes even more ambiguous. He is still in the pay of Achish, king of Gath, but the other Philistine rulers do not trust him. On the other hand, David is the son-in-law of the first Israelite king and thus a direct claimant to the Israelite throne. He holds the loyalty of the tribe of

Judah in which his father, Jesse, is a leading figure, but the other eleven tribes remain loyal to Saul's natural son, Ishbaal. David also has a powerful military commander in Joab. The Israelites and Habiru under David's influence settle in Hebron (just to the south of Jerusalem) and proclaim their leader king of that city [II Samuel 2:1-4].

The relationship between the two Israelite factions is difficult to clarify. They appear at times to be allies but their co-operation is certainly strained to breaking-point on numerous occasions (cf. the battle at the Pool of Gibeon narrated in II Samuel 2:12-28). For a few years they may have acted together in an attempt to regain political control of the lands lost to the Philistines – hence the letter from the 'two sons of Labayu' sent to Balu-UR.SAG, the contents of which the latter reports to Pharaoh in EA 250. In their letter to Balu-UR.SAG Labayu's sons encourage the former ally of their father to rise up against the Egyptian/Philistine hegemony.

> Why have you handed Gath-padalla to the king, your lord, a city which Labayu, our father, had taken? … Wage war against the people of Gina for having killed our father. … Wage war against the king, your lord, as our father did, when he attacked Shunem, Burkuna and Harabu, and deported the evil ones, lifting the loyal. [EA 250]

This Israelite tribal co-operation, born out of adversity, appears to break down as David becomes stronger and Ishbaal is marginalised. Seeing his power-base threatened, Abner secretly dumps his royal protégé and begins negotiations with David.

> Abner sent a message on his own behalf to say to David, 'and furthermore, come to an agreement with me and I will give you my support to win all Israel over to you.' [II Samuel 3:12]

The 'double-monarchy' in the land of Israel finally collapses in a series of murders. First Abner is stabbed to death by Joab at the gates of Hebron [II Samuel 3:22-39] and then, shortly after, King Ishbaal is assassinated by two of his own chieftains, Baanah and Rechab [II Samuel 4:1-12]. With no son of Israel's first king left alive to rival David's claim to the succession, the son-in-law and enemy of Saul is proclaimed king over all Israel [II Samuel 5:1-5].

This is the biblical version of events following the Battle of Gilboa. What can the el-Amarna Letters add to this complex picture?

As with Labayu (Saul) we find MUTBAAL (Ishbaal) corresponding with Egypt. He writes to Yanhamu the Egyptian commissioner based at Gaza. Mutbaal has been accused of harbouring Ayab whom the Egyptian authorities wish to arrest. In EA 256, despatched from the city of Pella in Transjordan, he professes his innocence to Akhenaten's representative.

> How can it be said in your presence: 'Mutbaal has fled. He has hidden Ayab'? … As the king, my lord, lives, as the king, my lord, lives, I swear Ayab is not in Pella.

Who is Ayab? Now that we have the biblical source to complement the Amarna correspondence it becomes obvious. Ayab is Joab, commander of David's Habiru forces. The name Joab (Heb. *Youb*) means 'Yo is the father' (Yo or Ya(h) is a common abbreviation for Yahweh). As Peter van der Veen has cogently demonstrated,[2] the el-Amarna name Ayab is in reality the name Ya-ab prefixed by what is called the 'PROSTHETIC aleph'. He cites several examples from the Amarna Letters ONOMASTICA to make his point, but a couple will suffice here.[3]

1. Artamanya king of Ziribashani [EA 201] is an Indo-European ruler whose name, according to Manfred

Mayrhofer, means 'in memory of (the god) Rta'. Thus a prosthetic aleph has been added to the god's name to give **A**-Rta-manya.

2. Aaddumi is the ruler of a town in the Bekaa valley (in modern Lebanon). Moran translates his name as 'it is (the god) Haddu' (often written Addu). Again the prosthetic aleph has been added to give **A**-Addu-umi.

Just like these two examples from the Amarna onomastica, the name Ayab should be interpreted as **A**-Ya-ab. With the prosthetic aleph removed we are left with 'Ya-ab' which means 'Ya is the father' (Akk. *Ya* = Heb. *Yo*). The man sought by Pharaoh's agents in Mutbaal's kingdom is none other than Joab, commander of the rebel Habiru forces under King David.[4]

Revolution in Judah

Our next task is to identify David himself in the Amarna Letters. This is not so easy because the correspondents in communication with Akhenaten after the death of Labayu do not mention the Habiru chieftain by name. Instead we begin to hear constant reference to an ever increasing military threat from the mountains.

At first, immediately following the overthrow of Labayu, we see an alliance formed between the kings of Gath (Shuwardata) and Gezer (Milkilu) who use their Habiru mercenaries to take the towns and villages of the central hill country. Abdiheba, the ruler of Jerusalem, sees this as a threat to his own security and writes several complaining letters to Pharaoh.

> Here is the deed against the land which Milkilu and Shuwardata did: against the land of the king, my lord, they ordered troops from Gezer, troops from Gath and troops from Keilah. They seized Rubute.

The land of the king has deserted to the Habiru. [EA 290]

And again in a follow-up letter he directly links the challenge to Egyptian authority with an alliance between the king of Gezer and the two surviving sons of Labayu.

This is the deed of Milkilu and the deed of the sons of Labayu, who have given the land of the king to the Habiru. [EA 287]

Remembering that David is the hireling of Achish, king of Gath, Abdiheba's letters appear to be referring to David's move to Hebron from his original base at Ziklag which had previously been assigned to him by Achish. Small wonder that the king of Jerusalem was becoming nervous: the Habiru were moving into settlements immediately adjacent to his own territorial boundaries.

So David went up, with his two wives Ahinoam of Jezreel and Abigail widow of Nabal of Carmel. In addition David brought up the men who were with him, each with his family, and they settled in the towns of Hebron. [II Samuel 2:2-3]

Before we go further I should deal with the apparent conflict between the two names (Amarna and biblical) for the ruler of Gath. This can be done fairly succinctly.

- The Bible gives the name of the Philistine king of Gath as Achish (Heb. *Akish*). R. Corney argues that this name is a Hurrian hypocoristicon of an original Aki-[deity N], meaning '[deity N] has given'. Peter van der Veen has suggested Aki-Shimige ('Shimige has given') – Shimige being the Hurrian sun-god.[5] The name of Akish, king of Gath in II Samuel, might thus be translated as 'the sun has given'.

- The name Shuwardata, carried by the king of Gath in the Amarna period, is Indo-European, according to Manfred Mayrhofer.[6] Annelies Kammenhuber offers the translation 'the sun has given'.[7]

- The two names potentially have the same meaning. It is not unusual for people of the ancient world to carry more than one name – especially with the common usage of hypocoristicons. Egyptians had their birth names and their 'good names' (what we would call nick-names) – for example Amenhoteps were often called Huy. We may reasonably propose, therefore, that Shuwardata of Gath was an Indo-European ruler (perhaps with mixed Hurrian blood) who was known by the writer of the books of Samuel by his Hurrian name of Akish[imige].

Meanwhile, back in Jerusalem, Abdiheba's letters are sounding more panic-stricken as the days go by. His position is becoming quite isolated.

> May the king give thought to his land; the land of the king is lost. All of it has attacked me. I am at war as far as the land of Seru [Seir] and as far as Gath-carmel. All the rulers are at peace, but I am at war. I (myself) am treated like a Habiru, and I do not visit the king, my lord, since I am at war. I am situated like a ship in the midst of the sea. The strong arm of the king took the land of Naharim (Mitanni) and the land of Kasi (Cush), but now the Habiru have taken the very cities of the king. Not a single ruler remains to the king, my lord, – all are lost. … Behold, Turbazu was slain in the city-gate of Sile (on the border of Egypt). The king did nothing! Behold, servants who were connected with the Habiru smote Zimredda of Lachish, and Yaptihadda was slain in the city-gate of Sile. (Again) the king

> did nothing! … may the king send a commissioner
> to fetch me, along with my brothers, and then we
> will die near the king our lord. [EA 288]

The pitiful plea for rescue appears to have gone unanswered. This is the last we hear of Abdiheba. The New Chronology provides an explanation of his fate. In *circa* 1003 BC David and his Habiru seized Jerusalem and established it as the capital of the Kingdom of Israel.

A New Enemy from the Mountains

With the capture of Jerusalem the plans of the Philistines in Gath and their allies at Gezer begin to come unstuck. They had used their Habiru mercenaries to settle an old score with the Jebusites of Jerusalem but now they realise they have made a fatal error of judgement. David, protégé of Achish/Shuwardata, has suddenly become more powerful than his former adversary, Abdiheba. The new Israelite king forgets his loyalty oath to the ruler of Gath and turns his well-trained guerrilla force onto his former master. Other Habiru still serving in the armies of the city-state rulers are suddenly perceived as a potential source of revolution from within. Milkilu of Gezer is greatly concerned by this turn of events and pleads for military assistance from Egypt.

> May the king, my lord, know that the war against
> me and against Shuwardata is severe. So may the
> king, my lord, save his land from the power of the
> Habiru. Otherwise, may the king, my lord, send
> chariots to fetch us lest our servants (i.e. the Habiru)
> kill us. [EA 271]

This unhappy state of affairs could not be allowed to continue or degenerate further. The turncoat David and his followers had to be dealt with if Philistine hegemony of the coastal plain was not to haemorrhage.

When the Philistines heard that David had been anointed king over all Israel, they all marched up to seek him out. On hearing this, David went down to the stronghold (i.e. Adullam). When the Philistines arrived they deployed in the Valley of Rephaim. [II Samuel 5:17-18]

The Amarna Letters also refer to these preparations for a war against the new power in the mountains. Milkilu has recently died (perhaps he really was assassinated by his servants?) and his son Addadanu now rules at Gezer. In EA 292 the new king writes:

There being war against me from the mountains, I built a house (i.e. a fortress) – its name is **Manhatu** – to make preparations before the arrival of the archers of the king, my lord, …

Manhatu is biblical Manahath in the vale of Rephaim.[8] Baal-perazim, the site of David's first victorious battle against the Philistines and their allies, is a stone's throw from the modern village of Manahath.

This first battle is followed by another in the same valley which is even more decisive. II Samuel 5:22-25 describes David's forces pursuing the enemy right down into their own lands.

Again the Philistines invaded and deployed in the Valley of Rephaim. … David did as Yahweh had ordered and beat the Philistines from Gibeon to the **Pass of Gezer**. [II Samuel 5:22-25]

The Habiru are virtually at the gates of Gezer. Urgent messages fly between Egypt and Addadanu's beleaguered city. The Canaanite ruler assures Pharaoh that he will prevent his city from falling into the hands of the enemy from the mountains:

> I have heard the order that the king, my lord, wrote to his servant, 'Guard the place of the king where you are.' I am indeed guarding day and night! [EA 293]

Gezer does not fall to the Israelites. As we later learn from the first book of Kings, Gezer becomes an Israelite city only when it is burnt to the ground by the Egyptians and handed to Solomon as a dowry for his marriage to Pharaoh's Daughter. Ernest Wright notes the restraint of the Israelite forces in their pursuit of the enemy and suggests that political expediency lies behind David's actions in not taking the lowland cities.

> From this it may be inferred that David purposely refrained from taking Gezer, but left it completely isolated and surrounded. ... He did not take over these cities (i.e. Gaza, Ashkelon and Ashdod), and the situation with Gezer may provide the clue to his reason. David refrained from taking over their original city-state grant for the same reason he refrained from taking Gezer, namely his respect for Egyptian claims, and his desire not to become involved with Egypt if he could help it.[9]

Again, the Letters and II Samuel provide close agreement at another vital moment in the political struggle between the established city-states and the Habiru rebels (and Israelites) from the hill country.

Do the Amarna Letters specifically identify the rebel city located in the mountains which is at war with the city-states of the coastal plain? The answer is to be found in EA 298 from Yapahu, presumably the next ruler of Gezer.

> May the king, my lord, be informed that my younger brother, having become my enemy, entered Muhhazu and pledged himself to the Habiru. As

Tianna is at war with me, take thought for your land.

Among the many rulers who complain to Pharaoh that their Habiru foe is too powerful for them, Shuwardata of Gath [EA 284] and Shubandu (city unknown) [EA 306] also mention the city of Tianna as their enemy. What can we make of the name Tianna? If this is the capital of the Habiru kingdom then it must be identified with Jerusalem, following its capture by David. II Samuel designates David's base of operations not only as Jerusalem and/or the 'City of David' but also by another name.

And David conquered the stronghold of **Zion** [Heb. *Tsiyon*], which is the City of David. [II Samuel 5:7]

Zellig Harris[10] and Wilhelm Gesenius,[11] in their detailed studies of Canaanite dialects, have demonstrated that the Hebrew *ts* (*tsade*) is often interchanged with a hard *t* (*tet*) in other west-semitic languages such as Ugaritic, Phoenician and Aramaic, and also in Indo-European Greek. The following table gives a few examples of this phenomenon.

Hebrew	Ugaritic	Phoenician	Aramaic	Greek	Meaning
hatser	hater	hater			'courtyard'
natsar		natar			'to guard'
qats	qat				'summer'
tsabiy			tabaya		'gazelle'
tsahar			tahara		'to step forward'
Tsor				Turos	the city of Tyre

With this linguistic trait in mind you will clearly be able to recognise the Amarna period city of **T**ian (with its Akkadian termination '-na') as the equivalent of Hebrew **Ts**iyon which the English Bibles translate as Zion. We thus have a linguistic path of Zion = Tsiyon = (Tsian[-na]) = Tian[-na].

Conclusion Seventeen

The situation described in several Amarna Letters from Palestine reflects the activities of David during his seven years as king of Hebron prior to the capture of Jerusalem. The stronghold of the Habiru enemy from the mountains mentioned in the late Amarna letters EA 298, 284 and 306 – there named Tian-na – is to be identified with the 'fortress of Zion' (Heb. *Tsiyon*) captured by David in his eighth regnal year – in other words Jerusalem.

Dadua – Beloved of Yahweh

Earlier in this chapter I said it was unlikely that we would be able specifically to identify David in the Amarna onomastica because, in the letters to Pharaoh, the enemy leader from the hills is never mentioned by name. This, however, is not quite the case. There is one letter which does supply the Amarna period (and therefore original) name of David. It is a letter to which I have often referred and from which I shall now provide a more substantial quote. That letter is EA 256 written by Mutbaal (Ishbaal) son of King Labayu (Saul) from Pella, one of his strongholds in Transjordan following the Battle of Gilboa. It is the same letter in which Mutbaal claims ignorance as to the whereabouts of Ayab (Joab), David's army commander. This is what Mutbaal has to say to the Egyptian commissioner in Gaza.

> Say to Yanhamu, my lord: Message of **Mutbaal**, your servant. I fall at the feet of my lord. How can it be said in your presence: 'Mutbaal has fled. He has hidden **Ayab**'? How can the king of Pella flee from the commissioner, agent of the king, his lord? As the king, my lord, lives, as the king, my lord, lives,

> I swear Ayab is not in Pella. In fact, he has [been in the] field (i.e. on campaign) for two months. Just ask **Benenima**. Just ask **Dadua**. Just ask **Yishuya**.

Here we are introduced to three new personalities connected with both Mutbaal and Ayab. They are Benenima, Dadua and Yishuya. I will deal with them in the order of their appearance.

The biblical equivalent of the Amarna name Benenima[12] is a little tricky to decode because it involves several stages of argument. I think it might be best to work backwards from our New Chronology identification of this individual in EA 256 – that way the logic is a little easier to follow. My fellow researchers and I have determined that the first witness upon whom Mutbaal calls to prove his innocence is none other than Baanah, one of Israel's tribal chieftains and the very man who would later act, along with his brother Rechab, to assassinate Ishbaal in his own royal apartments [II Samuel 4]. The argument goes as follows:

- Israeli scholar Benjamin Mazar has proposed that the biblical name Baanah (Heb. *Ba-anah*) should be interpreted as Ba[n]-Ana with the meaning 'son of (the god) Ana' (Heb. *Bin-Anah*).[13]

- Biblical Hebrew occasionally employs something scholars call the 'majestic plural'. In effect it is a plural ending added to a deity's name to confer status or majesty. In the Old Testament the best example is *Elohim* which does not mean 'the gods' but is rather the god El with the majestic plural *im* appended.

- The Amarna name Benenima may be divided into three elements: (a) *Ben* or *Bin*, meaning 'son', (b) *En[a]* or *An[a]*, the Canaanite god's name, and (c) *ima*, the majestic plural ending.

The meaning of Bin-Ana-ima is therefore 'son of Ana' – exactly the same reading as that proposed by Mazar for the biblical Ba[n]-Anah. In EA 256 we thus far have three personalities from the books of Samuel – Mutbaal/Ishbaal, Ayab/Joab and Benenima/Baanah.

We now come to the most crucial of all the identifications. Next of the three witnesses is Dadua. I believe it is possible to demonstrate that this Amarna eponym is the authentic name of Israel's dynastic founder – David.

In its earliest Hebrew form the name David (late Heb. *Dawid*) is written *Dwd* [cf. I Samuel 16:13] and perhaps vocalised as Dud or Dad. The Septuagint renders the name as Dad [cf. 1 Kings 2.33 (ALEXANDRINUS COPY) and Ecclesiasticus 47:1]. As Kenneth Kitchen notes, this name appears in the Middle Kingdom in Egypt as *Twtw* (probably pronounced Dadu).[14] Like many other ancient names, Dadu is a hypocoristicon with the meaning 'beloved [of deity N]' or 'favourite [of deity N]'. The great biblical scholar Martin Noth has suggested that in King David's case we should understand the full name as 'beloved of Yahweh'[15] – that is Dudiyah or Dadiyah or Daduyah. Other scholars have recognised that the Hebrew name Dad/Dud is the exact equivalent of Akkadian Dadu as found in names such as Dadiya, Daduilu, Dadusha and Dadanu.[16]

I am sure you have already got the drift. Dadua of EA 256 is none other than Dad/Dadu – the biblical David. The letter was probably written during the period when David was ruler of Hebron and sometime ally of his brother-in-law, Ishbaal (Mutbaal), king of Israel.

This astonishing missive from the least known king of Israel has just one more secret to give up. The third witness to his claim of innocence – Yishuya – is to be identified with David's father Jesse (Heb. *Yishay*) whose name means '[deity N] exists'. It is well established that the Hebrew phonetic ending *ay* is equivalent to the Akkadian and west-semitic hypocoristic ending *uya*.[17] Thus the Canaanite name Yish-uya and the Hebrew name Yish-ay are identical.

Conclusion Eighteen

El-Amarna letter EA 256 contains the names of five of the leading players from the books of Samuel. The letter itself is written by Ishbaal, son of Saul, who in turn refers to Joab (David's military commander), Baanah (one of Israel's chieftains), David (ruler of Hebron and son-in-law of Saul), and finally Jesse (father of David).

A Convincing Synthesis?

The crucial test of the New Chronology was to compare the events and characters of the Early Monarchy period with the detailed political history provided in the Amarna Letters, and I think it is fair to say that, so far, this has been a success. But I am not quite finished yet. There are still a number of players in the Amarna correspondence who can be linked with personalities from the Early Monarchy period in Israelite history.

We have already identified Aziru king of Amurru with Hadadezer, king of Aram-Zobah, proposing that Aziru is the hypocoristic form of the name Hadad-azru ('Hadad is the helper'). As Malamat notes, the military and political expansions of the two kingdoms were identical.

To the west of Hadadezer's domain we find a king Tou, ruler of Hamath [II Samuel 8:10]. Tou is an ally of David in his protracted wars against Hadadezer. The king of Hamath is called Toi in the Masoretic text of the Old Testament but the Septuagint, Vulgate (Latin) and Samaritan versions all give Tou, suggesting again that the Hebrew version is perhaps less reliable. Kyle McCarter proposes that Tou/Toi is the biblical variant of the Hurrian name Tehu or Tehi – yet another hypocoristicon where the deity's name has been omitted.[18] However, this time it is the Amarna correspondence which provides us with the full name of David's Syrian ally. He is Tehuteshub, the sender of letter EA 58 from northern Syria.

Another northerner is Lupakku, commander of 'the troops of Hatti' [EA 170] and, according to Hittite documents, leader of a major military campaign in the land of Amku (the Bekaa valley).[19] The 'troops of Hatti' would, of course, include the armies of all the vassal states of the Hittite emperor, Suppiluliumas I. Lupakku is to be identified with the biblical Shopak (Heb. *Shupak*), commander of Hadadezer's army who, according to I Chronicles 19:16, returns from Aram-Naharaim (otherwise known as Mitanni) so as to defend Syria from David's army. We learn from Hittite documents that Aziru (Hadadezer) signed a treaty with Suppiluliumas. So it should not be a surprise to find his general serving as a commander in the Hittite army campaigning against Mitanni. Not only do the political circumstances surrounding the two generals match but their names bear a close similarity. The best understanding of the name Lupakku would be 'man of Pakku' whereas Shupak means 'he of Pak[ku]'.

There are other identifications which could be made between the bit-part players of the Early Monarchy era and the el-Amarna period – we even see the name Goliath in its Amarna form of Gulatu [EAs 292 & 294].[20] However, I would like to remind you that these name identifications were not used to *establish* the synchronism between Akhenaten and David. That came about as a result of the Third Intermediate Period chronological revision and the historical identification of Ramesses II (Shisha) with the biblical Shishak. That said, the very striking parallelism between the personalities of the Amarna Letters and the principal figures of the books of Samuel offers strong support for our thesis. Let me quickly recap the various levels of comparison we have been able to make between the two historical sources.

First there is the ethnic level. We have the Amarna Habiru and the Hebrews of David's time whose activities, according to influential scholars such as Mendenhall and Greenberg, are indistinguishable from one another. We have Indo-European rulers in the Amarna period cities of the coastal plain just as we have Indo-European Philistine *seranim* ('lords') in those same cities in the Early Monarchy period. There are ethnic enclaves centred around the cities of Jerusalem (Jebusite) and Gezer (Canaanite) in both episodes. Then there is the political situation which is similar in both instances. In particular, we have picked out incidents from the reign of King Labayu which are closely paralleled in the biblical stories surrounding the life of King Saul. It is remarkable that this has not been noticed before – but then I suppose that any comparison was quite out of the question before the New Chronology came along.

---

1. Labayu = Saul (= Shaul) = 'the lion [of Yahweh]'/'asked for'.
2. Mutbaal = Ishbaal (= Eshbaal/Ishbosheth) = 'man of Baal'.
3. Dadua = David (= Dadu) = 'the beloved [of Yahweh]'.
4. Ayab = Joab (= A-Ya-ab) = 'Ya[weh] is the father'.
5. Yishuya = Jesse (= Yishay) = '[Yahweh] exists'.
6. Benenima = Baanah (= Bin-Ana-ima) = 'son of Ana'.
7. Shuwardata = Achish (= Aki-Shimige) = 'the sun has given'.
8. Aziru = Hadadezer (= [Hadad]-ezra) = 'Hadad is the helper'.
9. Tehuteshub = Tou/Toi = '?? of Teshub'.
10. Lupakku = Shopak (= Shupak[ku]) 'man of Shupakku'/'he of Shupakku'.

The el-Amarna/Early Monarchy parallels have convinced me, above all else, that the chronological revision I have been developing with my fellow researchers over the last twenty years has to be somewhere very close to the historical reality. Surely the odds against so many direct equivalencies being nothing more than a fluke – a strange quirk of history – must be so enormous as to make our hypothesis virtually certain. A late eleventh century BC date for Akhenaten simply has to be correct!

Conclusion Nineteen

King David, the dynastic founder of Israelite Jerusalem, was a contemporary of Akhenaten, Tutankhamun, Ay and Haremheb (early reign) in Egypt and the great Hittite Emperor, Suppiluliumas I. He forged his kingdom in the historical period when Egypt was politically and militarily weak and when the latter's northern ally, the kingdom of Mitanni, was disintegrating under the combined pressure of the Hittites to the west and the Assyrians to the north-east.

Part Four

Discovering the Israelites

The Sojourn in Egypt and the Conquest of the Promised Land

A Change of Evidence

At this point I need to make a statement concerning the character of this fourth section of the book. Until now the arguments for the structure of the New Chronology and its resulting biblical synchronisms have been based on established methods and sound historical sources. Indeed, I have employed precisely the same logic which scholars of the past used in constructing the orthodox chronology. The difference is that I did not adopt certain preconditions in the construction of the new Egyptian chronology – such as the Shoshenk/Shishak equation and the identification of Ramesses II as Pharaoh of the Oppression and Exodus. Otherwise I used the same types of material evidence: archaeological stratigraphy, pottery seriation, genealogical material, royal inscriptions, archives and, of course, certain 'historical' passages from the Old Testament.

With the era about to be discussed in *Part Four* you will find yourself in a very different kind of world. This is a world where the surviving material – especially the contemporary written sources – is very much thinner on the ground. After I conclude our New Kingdom discussion with a brief section on the dating of the 18th Dynasty, we enter a realm of darkness in Egypt which lasts several centuries before our journey backwards in time reaches the Middle Kingdom. There we can re-emerge into the light of the 12th Dynasty. Because of the scarcity of source material in this dark period, we are compelled to rely more heavily on the traditions. As a result, the emphasis will shift towards the biblical narratives and Manetho's history of Egypt, supplemented by other snippets of information derived from various traditional histories. It is important, therefore, to stress that the nature of the evidence is about to change. The reader should bear this in mind and regard what follows as quite distinct from, although perfectly complementary to, the reconstructed history which has preceded it.

In spite of this methodological caveat, I am confident that you will be surprised with what we will uncover together as we go in search of the ancient Israelites and their charismatic leaders Moses, Joshua and Joseph.

Chapter Eleven

NAVIGATING BY THE STARS

n *Chapter Nine* I proposed that the el-Amarna period began near the end of the eleventh century and continued into the second decade of the tenth century. However, we can actually do much better than that!

The Ugarit Solar Eclipse

I will now quote a passage from an Amarna letter which I have held back until this point because it plays a crucial role in establishing an accurate date for the death of Amenhotep III. From this new anchor point we will then be able to calculate backwards, using highest regnal dates from the monuments, so as to establish the New Chronology date for the beginning of the New Kingdom (i.e. Year 1 of Ahmose, founder of the 18th Dynasty). The letter we are now interested in – EA 151 – was written to Akhenaten by Abimilku, ruler of Tyre.[1]

> To the king, my Sun, my god, my gods. Message of Abimilku, your servant. ... Fire destroyed the palace at Ugarit; (rather) it destroyed half of it and so half of it has disappeared.[2]

Related correspondence indicates that this letter from Abimilku was written soon after the death of Amenhotep III when Nikmaddu was ruler of Ugarit.[3]

As a result of one of those amazing pieces of fortune which so rarely occur in archaeology, we have the opportunity to date the burning down of the palace of King Nikmaddu II by means of an astronomical retrocalculation. In a small room adjacent to the palace entrance archaeologists discovered a clay tablet baked hard and blackened by the disastrous fire which struck the 'Western Archive'. This little tablet – KTU-1.78 – bears the following inscription on the OBVERSE:

> The day of the new moon of Hiyyaru was put to shame (as) the sun (goddess) set, with Rashap as her gate-keeper.[4]

The REVERSE gives the astronomer-priest's warning of a disaster about to strike the kingdom of Ugarit, following the sacrifice of a sheep and inspection of the liver to interpret the heavenly portent:

> Two livers examined: danger!

The following details can be extracted from the short text:

1. 'The day of the new moon' means that the observation took place on the first day of a lunar month. Solar eclipses can only occur with a new moon as the crescents of invisibility and visibility are created by the moon moving in its orbit to a position between earth and sun.

2. 'The day (i.e. daylight) … was put to shame' is understood to mean that a total eclipse of the sun occurred, turning day into night.[5]

3. The observation took place in the month of Hiyyaru (Heb. *Iyyar*, Baby. *Aiaru*) which is the equivalent in the Julian calendar of mid-April to mid-May.

4. The eclipse took place at sunset[6] – a very rare event indeed!

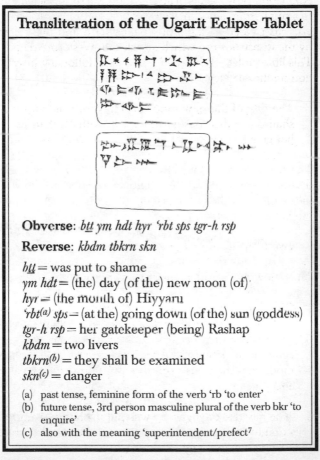

Transliteration of the Ugarit Eclipse Tablet

Obverse: *bṯṯ ym hdt ḥyr 'rbt šps tgr-h ršp*

Reverse: *kbdm tbkrn skn*

bṯṯ = was put to shame
ym hdt = (the) day (of the) new moon (of)
ḥyr = (the month of) Hiyyaru
'rbt[(a)] *šps* = (at the) going down (of the) sun (goddess)
tgr-h ršp = her gatekeeper (being) Rashap
kbdm = two livers
tbkrn[(b)] = they shall be examined
skn[(c)] = danger

(a) past tense, feminine form of the verb 'rb 'to enter'
(b) future tense, 3rd person masculine plural of the verb bkr 'to enquire'
(c) also with the meaning 'superintendent/prefect'[7]

51. Obverse and reverse of tablet KTU-1.78. Damascus Museum.

5. The eclipse of the setting sun (a goddess in the Ugaritan pantheon) was accompanied by another celestial phenomenon which the Ugaritans called 'Rashap'. We may be dealing here with a planet (or a conjunction of planets) or star, or some other bright celestial phenomenon in the darkened sky. The priest-astronomers viewed Rashap as the gatekeeper or guardian of the entrance to the underworld towards which the solar disc was descending and this 'god' was then seen to attend the sun as she descended into the night.

6. This was such an unusual occurrence that a divination was required which produced an ominous portent of disaster – an evil omen.

Indeed, a solar eclipse at sunset is such an unusual phenomenon that it is unlikely that anyone reading this book will have witnessed one without having especially travelled a considerable distance to make the observation. It has been calculated that a total solar eclipse occurs only once every three hundred and sixty years (on average) at any point on Earth.[8] A total eclipse which took place in April/May and specifically during the last hour of daylight at Ugarit must therefore have been quite exceptional and probably unique within historical time. So we have an excellent opportunity to pinpoint exactly (by astronomical retrocalculation) the event described in tablet KTU–1.78. As the burning of the palace following the omen occurred very soon after the death of Amenhotep III, we can then produce an absolute date for the last year of the old king's reign and therefore also the twelfth year of Akhenaten who, having recently become senior monarch, received news of the palace's destruction from Abimilku of Tyre.

In 1988, using powerful university mainframe computers[9] and the most advanced software for astronomical retrocalculation,[10] American New Chronology researcher, Wayne Mitchell, began to investigate the solar eclipse data

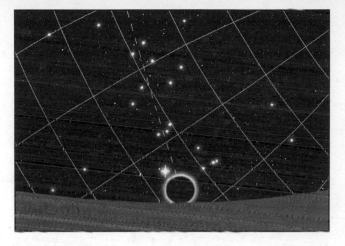

52. The sky at Ugarit on the 9th of May in 1012 BC, at 6.09pm – as reproduced by the computer program *Redshift.*

for periods outside the conventional dating in order to test out the chronology which I had been developing. His de tailed work, re running the retrocalculation programs of Professor Peter Huber, then of the Massachusetts Institute of Technology, demonstrated that there is only one candidate for a near-sunset total eclipse at Ugarit in April/May during the second millennium BC.[11] Mitchell's research led him to a startling conclusion: King Nikmaddu II and the priests of Ugarit watched with foreboding from the roof of the temple of Baal as the day was 'put to shame' at sunset at precisely 6.09 pm on the 9th of May 1012 BC – just thirty minutes before the sun set! The gatekeeper, Rashap, is believed to be the planet Mars which would only have been visible in the daylight sky, near to the sun, if the solar disc was eclipsed at the time.

This new astronomical date was the independent scientific confirmation of the New Chronology which I had been waiting for. I could now anchor the twelfth year of Akhenaten (his first as sole monarch following the death of Amenhotep III in the latter's 37th year) securely to within a year of the astronomically derived absolute date of 1012 BC. Astronomical research has not only supported the New Chronology's dates for the late 18th Dynasty but has refined the absolute dating to within a single year.

Conclusion Twenty

Astronomical retrocalculation produces the only possible date for the near-sunset solar eclipse observed at Ugarit and recorded on Tablet KTU-1.78. The eclipse occurred on the 9th of May in 1012 BC – just months after the death of Amenhotep III according to the internal chronology of the Amarna Letters. This entirely independent chronological determination confirms that the el-Amarna period fell in the late eleventh century BC and not in the mid fourteenth century BC as previously believed.

In the New Chronology Pharaoh Amenhotep III dies late in the eleventh regnal year of his son Akhenaten. The solar eclipse at Ugarit would have taken place towards the end of Year 11 and the letter informing Akhenaten of the burning down of the palace would then have been received early in Year 12. This is the same year as the great DURBAR held at the new capital – Akhetaten – which was organised to celebrate the rise of the heretic king to the status of senior monarch, and thus to the overlordship of the Egyptian empire. Akhenaten would therefore have become junior co-regent eleven years earlier in 1022 BC.

Using our starting point of 1022 BC for the coronation of Akhenaten we can assign the following regnal dates to the kings of the Amarna period.

Amenhotep III	– 1050-1012 (dying in Akhenaten's 11th year)
Akhenaten	– 1022-1006 (co-regent with Amenhotep III for 11 yrs)
Nefertiti	– 1011-1007 (co-regent with Akhenaten for 5 yrs)
Smenkhkare	– 1006-1003 (co-regent with Akhenaten for 1 yr)
Tutankhamun	– 1003- 995 (sole reign of 9 years)
Ay	– 995-990? (exact reign length unknown)

If we now continue our journey backwards in time we can reach an approximate date for the beginning of the New Kingdom. With Amenhotep III coming to the throne in 1050 BC we arrive at the following dates for his 18th Dynasty predecessors (as determined by using the reign lengths for these rulers which are currently employed by Egyptologists).

Ahmose (24 years)	– 1194-1170 BC
Amenhotep I (21 years)	– 1170-1150 BC
Thutmose I (12 years)	– 1150-1139 BC
Thutmose II (2 years)	– 1139-1138 BC
Thutmose III (54 years)	– 1138-1085 BC
Hatshepsut (15 years)	– 1131-1116 BC (co-regent)
Amenhotep II (27 years)	– 1085-1059 BC
Thutmose IV (10 years)	– 1059-1050 BC
Amenhotep III (37 years)	– 1050-1012 BC

> ## Conclusion Twenty-One
>
> The 18th Dynasty did not begin in circa 1570 BC, as the conventional chronology proposes, but rather some three hundred and seventy-seven years later in 1194 BC.

Still relying only on the Egyptian archaeological and textual evidence, it is possible to take just one more step back in our search for the origins of the Israelite nation. Prior to the beginning of the New Kingdom, northern Egypt was occupied by foreign rulers for a period of at least a century. We are now entering the Second Intermediate Period (SIP) – otherwise referred to, somewhat misleadingly, as the 'Hyksos period'. This was the chaotic time when 'people of obscure race' (as Manetho calls them) established foreign rule in the Egyptian Delta, eventually forcing the native pharaohs southwards into Upper Egypt. For generations the Egyptian kings, then based at Thebes, did little to redress the situation. There must have been some military skirmishes but no direct evidence of conflict has come down to us. Perhaps it took several generations for the 'Hyksos trauma' to manifest itself in a determined effort to re-establish native rule in Lower Egypt. But then, towards the end of the Theban 17th Dynasty, the momentum to cast off those foreign shackles became unstoppable.

First of the pharaohs believed to have attempted a repulsion of the Hyksos was Sekenenre Taa-ken ('Taa-the-brave') whose body, found in the Royal Cache, bears the horrendous scars of violent death in battle. It is generally assumed that he fathered two kings, the elder of which – Kamose – continued the assault upon the Hyksos rulers of Avaris. He was more successful than his father, reaching the very walls of the Hyksos capital. However, he failed to take the city and the war continued. Kamose's fate is unknown but we can speculate that he too died in the conflict as his reign lasted a brief three years. Kamose in turn was succeeded by his younger brother, Ahmose.

It has long been recognised that Ahmose came to the throne as a boy and that he was not old enough to lead an Egyptian army into battle against the northerners. In the first decade of his reign the King's Mother, Ahhotep, also appeared on the monuments in her role as Great Queen. Previously scholars considered that she may have acted as regent whilst her surviving son grew to maturity – although there is actually no direct evidence for this.[12] Eventually, by around his eleventh year as king, Ahmose was physically strong enough to lead his troops into battle against Avaris – this time to victory and the final dramatic expulsion of the hated occupiers of Lower Egypt. Thus the 15th Dynasty of Avaris came to a sudden end some eleven years or so after the date which we have established for the inception of the 18th Dynasty (NC – 1194 BC). We can therefore assign an approximate date of 1183 BC for the end of Hyksos rule at Avaris.

We now come to a very important piece of our giant historical jigsaw. The 'Royal Canon of Turin' is a badly damaged papyrus which contains a detailed list of Egyptian rulers dating from earliest times down to the beginning of the New Kingdom. It was composed in the 19th Dynasty, presumably from palace or temple records, and is the most accurate and therefore valuable king-list currently available. Not only does it catalogue the sequence of kings but it also gives their reign lengths to an accuracy of days and occasionally provides the total number of years for historical eras. Sadly, as I have said, it is in a very fragmentary condition, and so that which remains (housed in the Egyptian Museum in Turin) can give only a hint of what might have been if the papyrus had survived entirely intact.

One small fragment (as yet not correctly mounted in its original place in the papyrus roll) does however mention the foreign rulers of the SIP. The fragment reads '[Rulers of] Foreign Lands – 6: they made 100 + [...] years'. The hieratic signs making up the total were once read as '108' years but this can no longer be confirmed as the papyrus has further deteriorated since its discovery. However, if we assume that the total figure was indeed one hundred and eight years and that the six foreign kings are to be identified with Manetho's six rulers of the 15th Dynasty (as most scholars accept), then we have a means of dating the beginning of the 15th Dynasty in the revised chronology. The 15th Dynasty began its rule in Avaris one hundred and eight years before their expulsion by Ahmose in 1183 BC. Thus Salitis, first ruler of that dynasty, came to power in *circa* 1290 BC in the New Chronology.

Beyond this point we cannot proceed with any accuracy without recourse to astronomical dating simply because the contemporary inscriptional sources almost completely dry up. However, Wayne Mitchell's research has supplied a further lifeline which will enable us to date an important pharaoh of the 13th Dynasty, thus providing the stepping-stone which will link us to Moses, Joshua and Joseph.

Ammisaduga and the Venus Solutions

For many years there has been a debate going on between ancient historians and astronomers over the value of a set of astronomical observations dating from the OLD BABYLONIAN PERIOD. The 'Venus Tablets of Ammisaduga' were found in 1850 by Sir Austin Henry LAYARD within the NINEVEH palace archives of the Assyrian king ASHUR-BANIPAL (7th century BC). The main Ammisaduga text (K.160) was the sixty-third tablet in a series of astronomical observations compiled by the Assyrians under the title 'Enuma Anu Enlil', meaning 'when ANU and ENLIL'. It has been demonstrated that the late Assyrian tablets are genuine copies of original records from the reign of King Ammisaduga of the 1st Dynasty of Babylon.[13] The dating of this Babylonian ruler has thus been determined using astronomical retrocalculation based on information contained in the tablets. But, as you might expect, having been introduced to the vagaries of chronology, no less than three schools of thought have emerged as to what his absolute dates should be. They have been dubbed the 'High', 'Middle' and 'Low' chronologies with dates for the accession of Ammisaduga of 1702, 1646 and 1582 BC respectively. How can that be? After all, astronomical dating is, by its very nature, supposed to be an exact science. In order to understand the 'High, Middle or Low' debate I will need to familiarise you with the material contained in the Ammisaduga tablets and throw in one or two basic astronomical concepts for good measure.

The Ammisaduga Texts

- The dating of the Venus observations, recorded on British Museum Tablet K.160 (and its complementary tablets K.2321 and K.3032), to the reign of Ammisaduga can be ascertained by the appearance of the phrase 'Year of the Golden Throne' before the astronomical observations which it records for 'Year 8'. Other tablets from the Old Babylonian period have demonstrated that the phrase 'Year of the Golden Throne' was the date formula for the eighth regnal year of King Ammisaduga of Babylon I.[14]

- Combining the information given in the three tablets results in an almost complete record of observations for the rising and setting of Venus over a period of twenty-one years and, coincidentaly, King Ammisaduga reigned for twenty-one years according to Babylonian King-List B. As John Weir notes[15] '... there is every reason to believe that the observations were made during his reign' and that the years of the observations coincided exactly with the years of Ammisaduga's kingship. Thus 'Year 1' of the observations is identical with Year 1 of King Ammisaduga of Babylon.

- The Venus cycle – that is the period of time between exact repetitions in the observations of the rising and setting of Venus – is either fifty-six years or sixty-four years. (The reason why there are two intervals is complex but in essence has to do with the synodic period of the planet in relation to the solar year and lunar months.[16]) So the starting point for the twenty-one-year period of observations falls once every half-century – not a lot of help in our attempt to date Ammisaduga! As a result of this leeway, various 'Venus Solutions' have been proposed within the expected date-range for Ammisaduga in the conventional chronology, with the 1702 BC, 1646 BC (– 56 years) and 1582 BC (– 64 years) candidates given most attention in recent years.

- It is however possible to determine which is the most *probable* Venus Solution. What makes all the difference is that we also possess ancient documents (usually business contracts) containing information concerning the lengths of lunar months during the same king's reign. These extra data, recording the number of days between new moons, should provide very clear confirmation as to which Venus Solution is the true accession year of Ammisaduga. What one has to do is test each of the Venus Solutions by comparing the astronomical retrocalculation determinations for the periodicity of the lunar months to the actual month lengths recorded in the Babylonian texts. If the astronomically determined month lengths closely match the observations recorded by the ancients, then we have excellent reasons to believe that the Venus Solution under test is historically correct. Needless to say, the results may not be one hundred percent accurate as cloud cover may have obscured the first crescent of visibility on certain nights. This could result in the occasional late observation which would then have been out by one day compared to the modern retrocalculation determination. However, one would not expect more than a couple of such observation errors in a set of around twenty or so.

- The Old Babylonians dated their documents to the days of the lunar month (which began with the first crescent of the moon). Certain texts have been discovered which are dated to the thirtieth day of particular named months. Now we know that the actual length of a natural lunar month is 29.5545 days and so some months will have been observed as thirty-day months and others as twenty-nine-day months. When the computer determination of the month length agrees with the observed month-length of thirty days in a particular named month in the texts we can regard this as a good match. When the two are one day out (i.e. the computer gives twenty-nine days for a recorded thirty-day month) then we have a mismatch. There are twenty-two thirty-day months recorded in the ancient contracts which can be used for astronomical retrocalculation as they provide both month name and regnal year. The table below gives the results of this comparison test for our three orthodox candidates for the Venus Solutions.

Date BC	Month Length Matches	Month Length Mismatches
1702	20 months of 30 days	5 months of 29 days
1646	14 months of 30 days	11 months of 29 days
1582	18 months of 30 days	7 months of 29 days

It will be clear to you that the three main candidates for Year 1 of Ammisaduga are not particularly convincing when it comes to the astronomical retrocalculation test. The best result (1702 BC) still has five mismatches out of twenty-five. However, the two most popular date-choices for Ammisaduga as far as the archaeologists and historians are concerned (1646 and 1582 BC) have eleven and seven mismatches – the month lengths simply do not agree!

30-day Months	VS = 1702 BC	VS = 1582 BC	VS = 1419 BC
Year 1 Month I	30 days	•• 29 days ••	29+ days
Year 1 Month VIII	30 days	30 days	30 days
Year 1 Month XII	30 days	30 days	30 days
Year 2 Month XII	•• 29 days ••	30 days	29+ days
Year 3 Month IV	30 days	30 days	30 days
Year 3 Month VI	30 days	29+ days	30 days
Year 4 Month XIIb	30 days	•• 29 days ••	30 days
Year 5 Month XII	30 days	•• 29 days ••	30 days
Year 6 Month VI	29+ days	29+ days	30 days
Year 7 Month XII	30 days	30 days	30 days
Year 11 Month II	29+ days	30 days	30 days
Year 12 Month IV	30 days	30 days	29+ days
Year 12 Month VIII	30 days	29+ days	30 days
Year 13 Month II	•• 29 days ••	30 days	•• 29 days ••
Year 13 Month XII	30 days	•• 29 days ••	30 days
Year 14 Month IV	•• 29 days ••	29+ days	30 days
Year 14 Month VI	30 days	30 days	30 days
Year 14 Month VIII	30 days	29+ days	29+ days
Year 15 Month II	30 days	29+ days	30 days
Year 15 Month X	29+ days	•• 29 days ••	30 days
Year 15 Month XII	30 days	•• 29 days ••	30 days
Year 16 Month I	•• 29 days ••	•• 29 days ••	29+ days
Year 16 Month V	30 days	30 days	30 days
Year 16 Month XI	•• 29 days ••	30 days	•• 29 days ••
Year 16 Month XII	30 days	29+ days	30 days

When, in 1988, Mitchell re-ran Huber's retrocalculation programs in search of a lower dated Venus Solution compatible with the New Chronology he came across 1419 BC – a date for Ammisaduga which gives the following result.

Date BC	Month Length Matches	Month Length Mismatches
1419	23 months of 30 days	2 months of 29 days

This amazing result – a ninety percent agreement – is considerably better than any Venus Solution previously proposed. Furthermore, Mitchell went on to undertake a re-examination of all the other recorded eclipses from ancient times using the 1419 BC (Ammisaduga) and 1012 BC (Ugarit) eclipse dates as his anchor points. He was astonished to find that thirty out of a total of thirty-one eclipse observations fitted exactly with the New Chronology, whilst Huber's 1702 BC date for Ammisaduga could only muster twenty matches. The Levantine archaeologists' preferred date of 1582 BC did even worse with only nineteen out of thirty-one fits. Thus Mitchell has provided an independent confirmation that the chronology outlined in this book is very close to the historical reality. Astronomical dating techniques have clearly demonstrated that the New Chronology is soundly based.

Conclusion Twenty-Two

According to astronomical retrocalculation the clear date for Year 1 of Ammisaduga of the 1st Dynasty of Babylon is 1419 BC. This is one hundred and sixty-three years lower than the 'Low Chronology' date of 1582 BC, currently advocated by some Levantine archaeologists, and two hundred and twenty-seven years lower than the 'Middle Chronology' date of 1646 BC.

The Link to Egypt

Why have I taken you through all this complex astronomical material just to date Ammisaduga? After all, how can this help us with our dating of Egypt and the Israelite Sojourn? The answer is that we have another neat little series of synchronisms which will get us to Egypt and to the pharaoh who raised Moses in his palace.

With our new accession date of 1419 BC for Ammisaduga we can now utilise Babylonian King-List B to provide regnal dates for the whole of the 1st Dynasty of Babylon.

Sumuabum	c. 1667-1653
Sumulael	c. 1653-1617
Sabium	c. 1617-1603
Apilsin	c. 1603-1585
Sinmuballit	c. 1585-1565
Hammurabi	**c. 1565-1522**
Samsuiluna	c. 1522-1484
Abiesha	c. 1484-1456
Ammiditana	c. 1456-1419
Ammisaduga	**1419-1398**
Samsuditana	1398-1362

The most famous of all the kings of Babylon I is, of course, Hammurabi, the great conqueror and lawgiver of ancient Mesopotamia. His reign now begins in *circa* 1565 BC.

In Hammurabi's thirty-fifth year he attacked the city of MARI in north-east Syria, destroying the beautiful palace of King Zimrilim.[17] When the remains of that palace were unearthed by French archaeologist André Parrot in 1933 he found an archive of cuneiform tablets (25,000 in all). Many of these documents were administrative records rather than letters. One tablet in particular was an inventory of presents received by Zimrilim of Mari and amongst that list was the gift of a gold cup which had been received from Yantin-Ammu, king of Byblos.[18]

From this we can conclude that Yantin-Ammu of Byblos was a contemporary of Zimrilim of Mari and that both ruled their city-states at the time when Hammurabi sat upon the throne in Babylon. Zimrilim's reign came to an end with the destruction of his palace by Hammurabi – an event which we can now date to 1531 BC. If we assume our average reign length of twenty years for the last ruler of Mari we get an accession date of *circa* 1550 BC for Zimrilim. We might then also assign rough dates of 1550 to 1530 BC to his contemporary, Yantin-Ammu of Byblos.

Now we come to the Egypt connection. From Old Kingdom times Byblos had maintained close political and trading ties with the land of the pharaohs. With its location on the coast of the eastern Mediterranean, at the foot of the Lebanese cedar mountains, Byblos was ideally placed to act as a supply *entrepôt* for the Egyptian trading fleet. Good quality wood was, of course, much in demand in Egypt and they in turn had the produce of Africa for supply to the Levant.

The site of Byblos was first systematically excavated by Pierre MONTET in 1921-4 and then later by Maurice DUNAND from 1925 onwards. Both archaeologists

53. Left: Plan of the huge royal palace of Zimrilim at Mari.

54. Right: Fresco of Zimrilim (2nd left, upper register) discovered in the main court of Mari's palace. Louvre Museum.

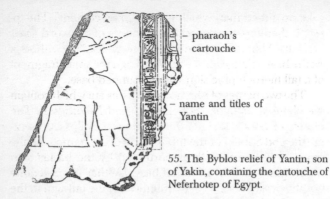

– pharaoh's cartouche

– name and titles of Yantin

55. The Byblos relief of Yantin, son of Yakin, containing the cartouche of Neferhotep of Egypt.

unearthed Egyptian and Egyptianised artefacts and statuary within the walls of the city. One particular find made by Dunand, currently housed in the basement of the shell-damaged Beirut Museum, is a large slab of limestone carved in shallow relief. The block is broken at the left edge and so only part of the scene is preserved. What remains is the torso and legs of a seated dignitary – in all probability a ruler of Byblos. To the right is a hieroglyphic text in two columns. The right column reads:

> [An offering which the king gives to[19]] Re-Harakhte, that he may cause Horus and Re to be adored each day. The Governor of Byblos, Yantin, living again, son of the Governor [Yakin(?)], true of voice.

The text thus indicates that the figure to the left is that of the deceased king, Yantin, son of the previous ruler of Byblos, Yakin. Albright was the first to recognise that this Yantin on the Dunand block was one and the same as the king of Byblos named Yantin-Ammu on the Mari tablet.[20]

The right-hand column of hieroglyphs on the Byblos relief is very broken but the cartouche of a pharaoh can be seen followed by the epithet 'enduring like Re [forever]'. The last sign in the cartouche is clearly the letter 'p' (a rectangular mat). Above it is the left half of the *hotep* sign (a cake on a reed mat) which means 'to be content'. The 'p' sign is therefore the consonantal ending of the word *hotep*. So far, our pharaoh's name is then to be read as […]hotep. At the broken edge above the *hotep* sign is a small fragment of a tall hieroglyphic sign with a rounded base.

The two names of pharaohs from this era which contain the element *hotep* are Sobekhotep and Neferhotep. The writing of 'Sobek' is either the sign for crocodile (representing the god Sobek) or the full spelling of the name with the signs *s-b-k*. The final 'k' is portrayed by the basket sign which has a shallow rounded base. Neither the crocodile nor the basket resemble the fragment of the tall sign in the cartouche we are currently studying. So let us look at the alternative candidate name – Neferhotep. Here we have the match we are searching for as the sign for *nefer* (meaning 'beautiful') is the lungs and windpipe of an ox. This sign is tall (the windpipe) and has a steeply rounded base (the lungs) – exactly as our broken sign in the cartouche. The name of the pharaoh on the Yantin block is therefore Neferhotep and this is the nomen of the twenty-first ruler of the 13th Dynasty in Egypt – Khasekhemre Neferhotep I. On the basis of this inscription it is reasonable to assume that Neferhotep was the reigning pharaoh at the time when Yantin(-Ammu) was ruling in Byblos, and so he must also have been a contemporary of Zimrilim and Hammurabi. We may therefore assign Neferhotep an approximate accession date of 1540 BC for the purpose of our chronological calculations.

Conclusion Twenty-Three

Pharaoh Neferhotep I of the 13th Dynasty reigned during the second half of the sixteenth century BC, rather than at the beginning of the seventeenth century as in the conventional chronology.

Chapter Twelve

MOSES AND KHENEPHRÊS

ccording to I Kings 6:1 the Exodus from Egypt occurred four hundred and eighty years before the founding of the Temple of Jerusalem in the fourth year of Solomon. Thiele's chronology of the Israelite kings, which I have been employing throughout *A Test of Time*, places Solomon's coronation in *circa* 931 BC. Thus the temple was founded in 928 and Moses brought the Israelites out of Egypt four hundred and eighty years earlier in *circa* 1447 BC. This date for Exodus is supported by Judges 11:26 where it states that around three hundred years had elapsed from the Conquest of the Promised Land to the judgeship of Jephthah (*c.* 1110 BC). Exodus 7:7 informs us that Moses was eighty years old when he returned from exile in Sinai to demand of Pharaoh the release of his people from bondage.[1] The exaggerated ages given in the early books of the Old Testament should, of course, always be treated with caution when employed in chronological calculations. If such a person as Moses ever lived and was acknowledged as the man who would lead the Israelites out of Egypt (if they were ever in Egypt), then it is not unreasonable to assume that he was of mature years at the time. He may not have been exactly eighty years old (a good biblical number) but he could easily have been in his seventies and still reasonably agile. (Nelson Mandela was 75 years old when he became President of South Africa after twenty-six years of 'exile' from his people.) Whether Moses lived on for a further forty years during the wilderness wanderings is another matter. For now let us accept this venerable age for the Israelite leader at the Exodus and consider his birth to have been, according to the biblical tradition, in *circa* 1527 BC.

We have determined that the New Chronology accession date for Neferhotep I of the 13th Dynasty was *circa* 1540 BC. The Royal Canon of Turin (column VI, line 25) records an eleven-year (and one-month) reign for Neferhotep and so his last year fell in 1530 BC. If we combine the biblical date for Moses and our New Chronology date for Neferhotep, we discover that this most charismatic of Israelite leaders was born a few years after the end of the reign of one of the great pharaohs of the 13th Dynasty. Do we have any specific historical or traditional support for this theoretical synchronism? The answer is to be found in fragmentary excerpts from a little known historical work of the Hellenistic era.

Artapanus

The early Christian historian Eusebius, in his work *Evangelicae Preparationis* ('Preparation for the Gospel'), refers to the writings of a Jewish historian named Artapanus.[2] The latter compiled a history of the Israelite nation entitled *Peri Ioudaion* ('Concerning the Jews'). The original work has not survived but we have certain extracts paraphrased by Eusebius[3] and a second partial summary in Clement's *Stromata*.[4] The name Artapanus suggests that he was a Jew of mixed descent whose family originated from Persia. However, he researched and compiled the material for *Peri Ioudaion* in Egypt during the late third century BC[5] and probably had access to ancient records which were housed in the great Egyptian temples and perhaps in the famous library at Alexandria founded by Ptolemy I.

The story of Moses' early life as an Egyptian prince and his subsequent exile to Sinai is related in some detail by Artapanus, but is very difficult to interpret. One scholar notes that 'Artapanus has his closest literary parallels in the historical romances; and he freely mixes fantasy with traditional lore'.[6] Separating fact from fancy is therefore a tricky business. The basic elements of the story which might possibly turn out to be of some historical value are as follows:

1. A pharaoh named 'Palmanothês' was persecuting the Israelites living in Egypt. He built the city of Kessan[7] and founded a temple there. He also established a temple (or shrine) at Heliopolis.

2. Palmanothês had a daughter called 'Merris'. She adopted a Hebrew child who grew up to become Prince Mousos.

3. Merris married a Pharaoh Khenephrês 'who was king over the regions beyond Memphis, for at that time there were many kings of Egypt'.

4. Having grown to manhood, Prince Mousos administered to the land on behalf of Khenephrês and became very popular with the people of Egypt. 'Formerly the masses were disorganised and would at one time expel kings, at others appoint them, often the same people but sometimes others'.

5. Prince Mousos led a military campaign against the Ethiopians who had invaded Egypt. He besieged the city of Hermopolis. According to Artapanus, the war lasted ten years.

6. Upon Mousos' return, Khenephrês tried to have the prince killed because he was jealous of him, but 'Mousos

fled to Arabia and lived with Raguel, the ruler of the region, whose daughter he married'.

7. Raguel ordered the Arabs to plunder Egypt but withheld them from a full campaign because Mousos restrained him for fear of the safety of his own Hebrew brethren still living in the Black Land.

8. Khenephrês died and Mousos eventually returned to Egypt to face a new pharaoh.

9. The plagues struck Egypt, the last of which was of hail and earthquakes. Mousos then led the Israelites out of Egypt.

A number of the above points are consistent with the Exodus narratives, but others need special comment.

1. Palmanothês, the Greek name of the pharaoh whose daughter raised Moses, is difficult to equate with any Egyptian king's name. Kessan appears to be the Egyptian 'Kes' which reveals itself in the Septuagint as 'Kessan' and in the MASORETIC text as 'Goshen' – the area of the eastern delta in which the Israelites were settled by Pharaoh. Heliopolis is the Egyptian city of On (Egy. *Iunu*) where the sun cult of Egypt had its principal temple. The building works undertaken by the Israelite slaves in these two locations correspond with the *locations* of the cities Raamses (Pi-Ramesse, the Estate of Ramesses, situated in Goshen) and Pithom (Pi-Atum, the Estate of the sun-god Atum, sometimes identified with On/Heliopolis).

2. It is possible that the name Merris, given by Artapanus, may be associated with Lake Moeris in the Faiyum basin. Josephus, on the other hand, gives the name of Pharaoh's daughter as Thermuthis – the Greek version

of Tawaret, the hippopotamus goddess of wet-nursing who was a manifestation of Isis. There may be an attempt on the part of both authors to link the mother goddess Isis, who protects her child Horus by hiding him in the delta marshes, with the Egyptian princess who nurtures and protects Moses having discovered him in the bulrushes. Thus they make Prince Moses synonymous with Horus, the legitimate heir to the Egyptian throne.

3. We shall return to the name 'Khenephrês' shortly. For now I will deal with the question of his kingdom. Artapanus states that Khenephrês ruled Egypt beyond Memphis. This can be interpreted in two ways: either he ruled the delta (north of Memphis) or he ruled the Nile valley (south of Memphis). It seems more likely, given the Hellenistic viewpoint (based at Alexandria), that 'beyond Memphis' refers to Upper Egypt (i.e. upstream from Memphis) and that, Khenephrês had his capital somewhere in the Nile valley. His father in law, Palmanothês, would then have been a ruler based in the delta. The reference to 'many kings of Egypt' at this time suggests that we are dealing here with one of Egypt's Intermediate Periods. The TIP is much too late for the Moses tradition (although it may have influenced the final writing down of the Exodus narrative in the sixth century BC) and the FIP (First Intermediate Period) would appear to be too early.[8] The obvious candidate is the SIP, that is Dynasties 13 to 17 when there was indeed a political break-up following the powerful Middle Kingdom.

4. Artapanus' statement that the previous rulers had regularly been overthrown by the people appears to presage the division of Egypt into petty states and this may well reflect the political uncertainty which is readily observable in the first half of the 13th Dynasty when

the average reign length of the kings is a mere five years (see *Chapter Fifteen*).

5. The Ethiopian campaign led by Moses is also discussed by Josephus, the Jewish historian of the first century AD, and taken up in the rabbinic writings.[9] Artapanus' location of the conflict in Middle Egypt (around Hermopolis) seems to be erroneous simply because, as far as we know, the Ethiopians invaded Egypt for the first time in the eighth century BC. Artapanus may have interpolated the 25th Dynasty invasion (in particular Piankhy's siege of Hermopolis) into his Moses story in error or simply as a fanciful elaboration. Josephus, on the other hand, after an initial incursion by the Ethiopians into Egypt, has Moses campaigning securely towards the upper reaches of the Nile where the 'Ethiopians' (i.e. Kushites) were based. Apart from the 25th Dynasty, the only other era when a powerful Kushite kingdom existed was during the period of the 13th to 15th Dynasties. This kingdom was centred at its capital of Kerma, located near the Third Cataract. A ten-year campaign also seems a little far-fetched. Normally Egyptian military expeditions took place annually and the actual campaign season would only have lasted a few months. If Moses did indeed lead an expedition to Kush/Ethiopia, then it would probably have taken place in a single year following a defensive war in Egypt lasting for an indeterminate period.

6. The Arabian chieftain Raguel is referred to in the Bible as the Midianite priest Reuel [Exodus 2:18] – clearly the same name – but also as Jethro [Exodus 3:1, 4:18, 18:1] and Hobab, son of Reuel [Numbers 10:29], as well as Hobab the Kenite [Judges 1:16, 4:11]. It therefore appears that the words 'Hobab, son of' may have dropped out of the original Exodus document immediately before the name Reuel/Raguel and that Artapanus

himself had access to a copy of this early text which already contained the omission. I would suggest that Moses married Zipporah, the daughter of Hobab (also called Jethro), son of the Midianite priest and tribal chieftain, Raguel.

7. Raguel was also, it appears, a warlord capable of raising a large military force with which to invade Egypt. Artapanus' Arabic hordes will indeed soon make their epic onslaught upon the delta – but not until the Israelites have left Egypt under the guidance of Moses. We will meet these 'King-Shepherds' again when we deal with the matter of the 'Hyksos' invasion in the next chapter.

8. Following the death of Khenephrês a new Egyptian ruler confronts Moses. It is this pharaoh who refuses to let the Israelites go and so brings down the terrible plagues upon Egypt. His identity will also be revealed shortly through the words of Manetho as quoted by Josephus.

9. The aftermath of the devastating plague – the mass burial pits of its victims – will become obvious to you once we have located the capital city within which the majority of the Israelites lived. Artapanus tells us that the final blow meted out by Yahweh, the god of Moses, involved the casting down of hail which was accompanied by a violent earth tremor during the hours of darkness. The last phenomenon is not mentioned in the Old Testament narrative, but is consistent with its interpretation.

Pharaoh Khenephrês

I said that we would take a look at the name Khenephrês to see if we could find an Egyptian equivalent to this Greek vocalisation. Let us begin the exercise by extracting elements of ancient Egyptian names/words from Manetho's king-list which was also vocalised in Greek. Manetho gives the name of the third ruler of the 5th Dynasty as 'Nepher-kherês' and the monuments identify him as Neferirkare. We can immediately see the three elements of the name (1) Nepher = Nefer[ir]; (2) khe = ka; and (3) rês = re. There are literally dozens of examples of the ending 'rês' for 're' and a number of 'nepher's for Egyptian 'nefer'. The element 'khe' also represents 'kau' (the plural of 'ka' as in Menkherês = Menkaure = Mykerinus) and also, as a number of scholars have suggested, 'kha'.[10] Armed with these basic facts we can now tackle our name 'Khenephrês'. I will divide the elements thus – Khe-neph[er]-rês – and then substitute the Egyptian counterparts – Kha-nefer-re. So Artapanus' Greek name 'Khenephrês' represents the Egyptian royal name 'Khaneferre' meaning 'the perfection of Re shines in the horizon'.

I think you will be surprised to hear that only one pharaoh in the whole of Egyptian history is known to have taken this name. Following the death of Neferhotep I and his short-reigned son, Sihathor, a younger brother of the former took the throne as the twenty-third ruler of the 13th Dynasty. At birth he was given the name Sobekhotep ('Sobek is content') but he took at his coronation the pre-nomen 'Khaneferre'. The great American Egyptologist, James Henry Breasted, assessing the political situation during the SIP, was of the opinion that this Sobekhotep was the greatest king of the era.[11] So the birth of Moses coincided with the coming to the throne of a new, powerful pharaoh named Khaneferre Sobekhotep IV and it was in his reign that Moses was raised as a prince of Egypt.

Why had Artapanus chosen such an obscure name as Khenephrês for the stepfather of Moses? He could have picked 'Ramesses' or 'Sesostris' or some other such famous name, but no, he instead produced a name that does not survive in any other Hellenistic or Classical source. Surely his unusual choice indicates that he had access to a document of considerable antiquity which linked the Israelite leader, Moses, with the 13th Dynasty pharaoh, Khaneferre Sobekhotep IV.

What do we know about the reign of Sobekhotep IV? Well, as Breasted observed, he seems to have been one of the most powerful and successful rulers of his dynasty. Two colossal statues of the king were found at Tanis (and were therefore probably originally from Pi-Ramesse/Avaris), another smaller schist seated statue at Moalla, and a further headless life-size statue was unearthed on the Island of Argo, just upstream from Kerma, the capital of the old Kushite kingdom (now in modern Sudan). Unfortunately, we have little idea how long Sobekhotep's reign lasted. Manetho gives no names or reign-lengths for the 13th Dynasty and the Royal Canon is damaged just at the point where Khaneferre Sobekhotep's years, months and days of rule were recorded. The highest regnal date on the monuments is Year 8,[12] but the inscriptional evidence for this obscure period is so sparse that this relatively low date cannot confidently be used as an indicator for the length of the king's reign. For example, Merneferre Ay, a later successor of Sobekhotep IV, reigned for twenty-three years according to the Royal Canon but only a stela and a lintel have been found which bear his name. Therefore, the twenty-year reign I have assigned to him is not unreasonable – assuming our average reign length. With Neferhotep beginning his rule in *circa* 1540 BC we then get the following dates for this vigorous sub-dynasty of kings who come to power halfway through the 13th Dynasty.

Khasekhemre Neferhotep I (11 yrs 1 m)	c.1540-1530
Sihathor (3 m)	c.1530-1529
Khaneferre Sobekhotep IV (20 yrs?)	c.1529-1510
Khahotepre Sobekhotep V (4 yrs 9 m)	c.1510-1506
Wahibre Iayib (10 yrs 9 m)	c.1506-1496
Merneferre Ay (23 yrs 8 m)	c.1496-1473

Moses, having been born in around the third regnal year of Khaneferre, grows up in the principal royal palace at Itj-tawy ('seizer of the Two Lands'), forty kilometres north of the entrance to the Faiyum basin. This was the capital of Egypt from the beginning of the 12th Dynasty (when it was founded by Amenemhat I) down to the Hyksos invasion and subsequent retreat of the native pharaohs upstream to Thebes. In Khaneferre's marriage to the daughter of the delta ruler Palmanothês we might see a clever political marriage alliance which brought the minor delta kingdom back under the control of the main 13th Dynasty line. The discovery of colossal statues of Khaneferre in the eastern delta at Tanis attests to this king's influence in that region. Along with most of the obelisks and statuary found at Tanis, these huge pink granite statues were probably removed from the city of Ramesses at Kantir when the new TIP capital was established on the Tanitic branch of the Nile some twenty kilometres to the north. Of course, Khaneferre reigned long before Pi-Ramesse was itself founded in the early 19th Dynasty, but texts from that dynasty refer to the southern quarter of the Ramesside city as Avaris, confirming that the much older SIP city was later incorporated into the new city of Ramesses. The statues of Khaneferre would then have originally stood within Avaris, perhaps in the temple precinct and palace known to have been built there in the 12th Dynasty and presumably still in use during the 13th Dynasty.

The Land of Goshen

Can we pinpoint the town in which Moses and his people resided in the eastern delta? In recent years, excavations in the eastern delta have confirmed that the region of Khatana/Kantir, just to the north of the town of Fakus, is the site of Pi-Ramesse, capital of the 19th and 20th Dynasties. What is more, the intensive archaeological work undertaken by the Austrians in the area since the 1960s has demonstrated that the southern sector of the excavation zone contains the even more ancient site of Avaris. The latter is centred at the little village of Tell ed-Daba – a place which will be very familiar to you by the time you reach the end of this book.

The Hellenistic geographer, Ptolemy, states that between the Bubastite and Sethroite delta nomes lay the NOME of Arabia with its metropolis of Phacusa.[13] Champollion, Ebers and Brugsch all recognised that the name of the capital of the Arabian nome was identical to the modern regional capital of Fakus in Sharkiya province.[14] It seems certain that Fakus is the ancient Egyptian city which the Greeks called Phacusa and modern Fakus is located just seven kilometres south of Khatana/Kantir – ancient Avaris/Pi-Ramesse.

We should now take a closer look at the name Phacusa to see if we can determine its original Egyptian form. Let me start by taking the example of 'Faiyum' – the name of the large oasis to the west of the Nile, some eighty kilometres south of Cairo. In this case it is easy to work out the derivation of the modern Arabic name. 'Faiyum' is ancient Egyptian 'Pa-Yam' – which means 'the sea'. The Faiyum basin surrounds an inland sea known to Herodotus as Lake Moeris (modern Birket Karun). The word 'Yam' is also found in the story of Exodus where the Israelites cross the Sea of Reeds (Heb. *Yam suf*). The element 'Pa' in Pa-Yam is simply the Egyptian definite article. It follows that the 'Fa' or 'Pha' in Fakus/Phacusa is also 'Pa' and that the definite article precedes a place called 'Kus' or Cusa'. This is the Egyptian eastern delta city of Pa-Kes. The Septuagint calls the region where the Israelites settled 'Kessan'. Here then we have the link we need. The Goshen of the Masoretic (Hebrew) scriptures is the Septuagint's Kessan which is related in some way to the ancient Egyptian city of Pa-Kes – and Pa-Kes (Fakus) was a stone's throw from the ancient site of Avaris (Tell ed-Daba). Avaris appears therefore to have been located within the region of Kessan/Goshen.

An interesting manuscript found at Arezzo in Italy confirms much of what I have been proposing. It contains the diary of Abbess Etheria who went on a pilgrimage to the lands of the Bible in the fourth century AD. During her stay in Egypt she travelled through the land of Goshen, passing by the ruins of 'Ramesses', which she states was just four Roman miles from the capital of the Arabian nome.

> Our desire was to go from Clusma to the land of Goshen, that is to the city of Arabia (i.e. Phacusa/Pa-Kes). This city is in the land of Goshen, and the territory itself derives its name from it (i.e. Kessan).[15]

Prince Moses and the Kingdom of Kush

As we have seen, there is a tradition, first discussed by Artapanus then taken up by Josephus, of a military campaign by Prince Moses against the Ethiopians. I have already dealt with Artapanus' version of events and now we are going to take a look in more detail at what Josephus has to say on the subject.

The Jewish historian we call Josephus was born in the year Caligula became Emperor of Rome (AD 37) and named 'Joseph ben Matthias'. The son of a priestly family connected through his mother to the Hasmonean Dynasty of Palestine, he later became a Roman citizen and took the name Flavius Josephus after the family name of his patron, Emperor Vespasian. Having sailed to Italy in AD 64, Josephus wrote his *Antiquities of the Jews* whilst residing in Rome in around AD 93. He had previously accompanied Vespasian's son, Titus, to Jerusalem and was witness to the destruction of the holy city by the Roman legions in AD 67. For his 'assistance' in securing the submission of the Jewish state Josephus was offered a number of rewards by Titus. Needless to say, the Romanised Jew was despised by his Palestinian contemporaries for aiding and abetting the plunder of his home country. The crucial 'reward' from our point of view comes at the end of Josephus' own statement on the subject.[16]

> Titus Caesar, when the city of Jerusalem was taken by force, persuaded me frequently to take whatever I pleased out of the ruins of my country; for he told me that he gave me leave to do so. But there being nothing that I much valued, now my country was destroyed, I only asked of Titus liberty for myself and my family, as the only comfort now remaining in my calamities; **I also had the holy books by his concession**.

Scholars have focused on the last remark and understood it to mean that Josephus was permitted to remove those sacred scrolls of the Second Jerusalem Temple which had not been destroyed in the temple's demolition. The Jewish historian would then have been writing his *Antiquities of the Jews* armed with the most authentic and probably oldest copies of the books of the Old Testament. It has also been suggested that he actually possessed the scrolls held in the library of NEHEMIAH (5th century BC) whose collection of biblical documents was probably stored in the Herodian temple.[17] Thus, when Josephus tells us an Old Testament story which cannot now be found in the canonical scriptures, it may be that that story was contained in the original collection of temple texts but was subsequently left out of the approved version of the Tanaakh (Judaic scriptures). It is equally possible that Josephus obtained the story of Moses' Ethiopian campaign directly from the Jewish history written by his predecessor, Artapanus, but this seems less likely given that the Josephus version is much more detailed than that of Artapanus. It looks as if Josephus did indeed have another source. I will quote selected passages from Moses' Ethiopian campaign as narrated by Josephus so that you can get the gist of the tale.

Moses, … when he … came to the age of maturity, made his virtue manifest to the Egyptians …

The Ethiopians, who are adjacent neighbours to the Egyptians, made an incursion into their country, which they seized upon, carrying off the effects of the Egyptians …

They proceeded as far as Memphis and the sea itself, whilst not one of the cities was able to oppose them. The Egyptians, under this sad oppression, took themselves to their oracles and prophecies and when God had given them this counsel – to make use of Moses the Hebrew and take his assistance – the king commanded his daughter to produce him, that he might be the general of their army. …

So Moses, at the persuasion both of Thermuthis and the king himself, cheerfully undertook the task.

… he came upon the Ethiopians before they expected him and, joining battle with them, he defeated them, depriving them of the hopes they had of success against the Egyptians and went on in overthrowing their cities and indeed made a great slaughter of these Ethiopians. …

… at length they retreated to Saba, a royal city of Ethiopia, which Cambyses later named Meroë, after the name of his own sister. The place was to be besieged with very great difficulty, since it was both encompassed by the Nile all around, and the other rivers, Astapus and Astaboras, … being encompassed with a strong wall … and having great ramparts between the wall and the rivers …

However, while Moses was uneasy at the lying idle of the army (for the enemy dared not come to battle) this incident happened: THARBIS was the daughter of the king of the Ethiopians and she happened to

> see Moses as he led the army near the walls, fighting
> with great courage … she fell deeply in love with
> him and … sent him the most faithful of all her
> servants to talk with him about their marriage. He
> thereupon accepted the offer, on condition that she
> would procure the delivering up of the city …
>
> No sooner was the agreement made than it took
> effect immediately and, when Moses had suppressed
> the Ethiopians, he gave thanks to God and consum-
> mated his marriage, leading the Egyptians back to
> their own land. [Book II, Ch. X]

What do we make of all this? An invasion of Egypt by
Ethiopians is not attested in the Second Intermediate
Period. As I have already said, it is very possible that this
story derives from a tradition conflating the historical
invasion of Egypt by the Ethiopian 25th Dynasty (in the
late 8th century BC) *and* the tradition of a Moses campaign
beyond the Second Cataract. On the other hand, the SIP
is a confused and dark period and, by its very nature, a
short-lived invasion is always extremely difficult to pin
down archaeologically. I suppose that it is possible that
there was a Kushite (= Ethiopian) assault against Egypt
during the 13th Dynasty – perhaps even, as the New
Chronology would require, in the time of Sobekhotep IV,
within the second decade of his reign. It is intriguing to
note that the only reference to a military campaign on the
part of the Egyptians into Upper Nubia during this era is
recorded on a stela fragment held in the British Museum.[18]
The king whose cartouche dates the stela is none other
than Sobekhotep IV.

Clearly the royal city of Ethiopia in the Josephus story,
located near the confluence of the Nile and Atbara
(Astaboras) rivers, is the Late Period Meroitic capital of
Meroë which has nothing whatsoever to do with the time
of a fifteenth-century Moses or the 13th Dynasty. However,
there clearly was a powerful Kushite state contemporary

313

56. A modern hand copy of the stela fragment of Sobekhotep IV in the British Museum mentioning a military campaign into Kush.

with the SIP Egyptian dynasties. It was located along the Dongola Reach with its capital at Kerma, some two hundred and fifty kilometres south of the Egyptian border at Semna. If the historical Moses was really the commander of a 13th Dynasty Egyptian army and fought against the 'Ethiopians' then his enemy would have been the Kushite kingdom of Kerma. Let us journey up river to the Third Cataract to see if we can find any archaeological evidence which might suggest an Egyptian military occupation of the Kushite kingdom in this era.

The city of Kerma is located on the east bank of the Nile at the extreme northern end of the Dongola Reach, easily the most fertile district in Upper Nubia. George REISNER excavated the site in the years between 1913 and 1916 for the Universities of Harvard and Boston. Apart from the astonishing royal TUMULI with their mass burials of servants, the most interesting and unusual feature of the site is the great mudbrick platform known locally as the Western DEFFUFA. This enormous solid mound of bricks, rising to over twenty metres, once supported a building now completely disappeared through erosion or quarrying. Access to this 'stronghold' was via a broad staircase which rose through the solid brick platform to the summit. At the foot of the Deffufa's western face Reisner discovered a complex of buildings containing numerous Egyptian artefacts, including alabaster vessels.[19] There seems also to have been a sanctuary or shrine.

Egyptologists recognise that 'The character of the Deffufa brickwork is unmistakably Egyptian'. Furthermore, Nubiologist William Adams argues that the Deffufa 'was

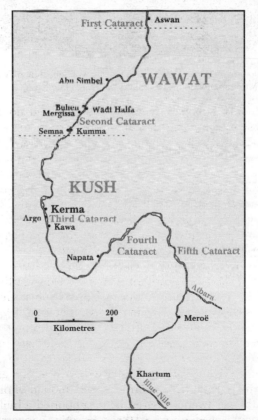

The principal sites of the Upper Nile showing the Egyptian territory of Wawat (Nubia) and the land of Kush.

designed and constructed under Egyptian supervision'. He concludes that it 'seems beyond dispute' that there were Egyptians resident at Kerma. But which Egyptians built this 'embassy' or 'governor's residence'? The exact date of the structure cannot be determined because royal texts have not been unearthed, but it was certainly built during the SIP. Could it have been the work of Moses' military governor/agent following the Egyptian capture of the city of Kerma?

A short distance from the Western Deffufa the French have uncovered the brick foundations of a large circular building which has been interpreted as a ceremonial meeting hut of unmistakably African design.[20] Such huts are still to be seen today in tribal villages. Could this building have been the royal hall of the prince of Kush, erected next to the residence of his overlord – the Egyptian governor established there by Moses?

One clue which might point to Sobekhotep's successful young general as the builders of the Deffufa is the discovery in the last century of a life-size statue of Khaneferre Sobekhotep IV on the Island of Argo, near Kerma. Nobody can understand what this Egyptian royal statue is doing here, deep in the land of Kush. It has been suggested that it was taken as plunder from one of the Second Cataract Egyptian fortresses following their abandonment at the end of the 13th Dynasty.[21] But why should the Kushites go to such lengths to transport such a heavy statue? What would it have been used for? And, even if they did expend all this effort on Sobekhotep's statue, why then transport only one such royal trophy? Sir Alan Gardiner's words sum up the problem and his last thoughts on the matter are rather intriguing:

> ... it is difficult to know what to make of a headless statue of him (Sobekhotep) found at the Island of Argo just south of Kerma, more especially since a damaged inscription in the British Museum alludes

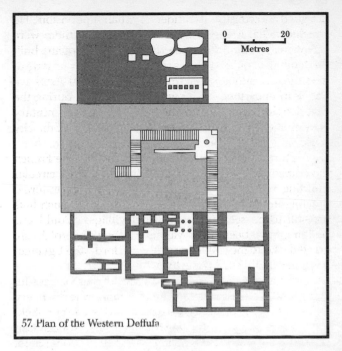

57. Plan of the Western Deffufa

to hostilities in that direction. Can the enterprise of this Dyn. XIII king have dispatched his agents or soldiers beyond the Third Cataract?[22]

With Moses as the agent of Sobekhotep's conquest of Kush we have a ready explanation. The commander-in-chief of the Egyptian forces had the sovereign's statue erected to honour his stepfather. It was probably set up in a small temple and, indeed, was discovered within a temple of later date which may have been erected over an earlier, more modest shrine. However, an earlier king – Senuseret III of the 12th Dynasty – had erected a statue of himself on his own southern border staring defiantly out at the people of Kush, and nearby his stela exhorted the Egyptian garrison to fight on his behalf with the words:

317

Now, I have caused a statue of myself to be made upon this boundary, which I myself made, in order that you would be inspired by it and that you would fight for its sake.

The 12th Dynasty border was at the head of the Second Cataract, whereas the Island of Argo is over two hundred kilometres further south beyond the Third Cataract. Perhaps the statue of Sobekhotep IV was erected for the same purpose as the statue of his predecessor, representing a dramatic southward extension of Egyptian authority in the mid-13th Dynasty?

The Mound of the Hyena

I first visited Tell ed-Daba in 1989 when I called in to the Austrian mission's dig house whilst on my way to Tanis. I had been following the work of Professor Manfred Bietak and his team for some years and had corresponded with the field director on a couple of occasions. As my journey into the eastern delta coincided with the autumn excavation season I felt it was about time I introduced myself to Bietak in person.

On the 1989 trip to Egypt I was accompanied by my wife, Ditas, and a longtime friend and fellow chronologist, Val Pearce. We had set out early from our Cairo hotel so as to get to Tell ed-Daba by mid morning. The three-hour journey was hot and sticky, as Ditas and I sat in the back of a Cairo taxi with only the open windows for our air-conditioning.

By the time we turned off the main Ismaliya road just before Fakus and began to strain our eyes for signs of an ancient TELL somewhere on the verdant horizon we were well and truly in need of liquid refreshment and some welcoming shade. Five minutes down the road which hugs the west bank of the Didamun Canal I spotted the gleaming white walls of the Austrian dig house and, behind it, the low sprawling profile of the main tell. But how were we to get there? That was the immediate problem. There was no bridge across the canal at this spot, so we kept going. A further half-kilometre was clocked up before we found a little bridge linking the village of Ezbet Rushdi, on the east bank of the canal, to the tarmac road.

The arrival of our Cairo taxi brought forth an eruption of activity as our driver carefully plied his way through the crowd of boisterous, smiling faces. Amongst the clouds of dust flung into the air and the mêlée of water-buffalo, camels and scuttling chickens, the colourful galabeyas of the Ezbet Rushdi kids weaved and twirled around the car as we inched our way down the narrow lane. Eventually, breaking free from the hubbub, we found ourselves in a wilderness of sandy mud-flats dotted with tired-looking scrub. The deafening silence of this vast open expanse was in stark contrast to what we had just experienced.

The narrow village lane had by now virtually disappeared. Instead of following a clear pathway our driver was forced to manoeuvre his way around mounds of grey sand banks crowned with bedraggled clumps of gorse. He achieved this with great skill and, it has to be said, with a certain degree of good-humoured resignation. He knew that his precious Mercedes would need a really good wash and brush up by the end of the day. Up hill and down dale we went for what seemed like an age before finally arriving at the centre of a dusty football pitch full of potholes and discarded cans. Not a blade of grass was to be seen between the rusting sets of goal posts. Beyond the far touchline stood the small village of Tell ed-Daba.

It still seems remarkable to me that such an unpretentious little place should be synonymous with the greatest excavation project of modern times in Egypt. Tell ed-Daba means 'Mound of the Hyena'. It does not take much imagination to picture this still isolated settlement as it would have been a century or so ago, nestled within the ruins of a great ancient city – the nightly hunting ground of many a wild beast. The ancient spirits of Avaris still haunt the site – as archaeologists who have worked there will gingerly attest. It is just something which you feel in your bones. The momentous goings-on which took place between the end of the 12th Dynasty and the beginning of the 18th Dynasty within the confines of Avaris seem to hang in the air as the occupational history of the epoch is gradually released from the earth at every forage of the excavator's trowel.

With taxi and driver parked up in the centre of the football pitch we headed off on foot over the tell towards a clump of trees which camouflaged Bietak's centre of operations. A small door led us through into a pleasant courtyard bedecked with mimosa in full bloom. In the corner of the yard the Austrians had re-erected a small limestone chapel dated to the reign of Ramesses II which had been recovered from the city of Pi-Ramesse. Scattered amongst shady nooks and crannies were trestled tables covered in piles of pottery sherds. Archaeologists – students and academics alike – sat examining the collections, cleaning and drawing the important diagnostic pieces. The atmosphere was relaxed but studious.

A young Austrian student led us around the corner to the main door of the workshop area where we were then escorted in to meet the great professor. All about us, on the floor and around the walls were cardboard boxes and wooden trays crammed with artefacts of different shapes and sizes: giant Canaanite storage jars, small buff-coloured pots, numerous examples of the famous black TELL EL-YAHUDIYA WARE. It was a nightmare simply negotiating the tiny area of floor left clear to afford a means of passage. At the end of our yellow brick road we came to a room wallpapered in gigantic maps and plans, and there we spent a happy and instructive hour with the mudir learning all about the excavation work and the topography of the vast site. Avaris/Pi-Ramesse once covered an area of more than ten square kilometres, making it one of the biggest cities in the ancient world. It amazes me to think that so little of this great city remains today.

Manfred Bietak is an extraordinary man. He has been excavating in Egypt for more than thirty years. The Bietak beard creates an aura of stern authority befitting his great experience, but the glint in his eye betrays the excitement and fascination he still has for his life's work. Bietak has had more than his fair share of remarkable discoveries. Season by season his archaeological revelations continue to amaze and thrill audiences the world over. A good part of his year, outside the two main excavation seasons, is spent lecturing in Europe and America or attending conferences, yet he still finds time to teach several Egyptological courses to his students at the Austrian Institute of Egyptology in Vienna. The man is a whirlwind.

Much of what I am going to suggest to you in this last part of our journey through time has been based on the excavation results of Manfred Bietak and his colleagues, principally Joseph Dorner, Diethelm Eigner, Peter Jánosi, Gilbert Wiplinger, Irmgard Hein, conservator Lyla Pinch-Brock, and anthropologists Eike-Meinrad Winkler and Harald Wilfing. Without their friendship and unselfish co-operation, I would not be in a position to complete my tale and lead you to the historical Joseph. So let me start by giving you a brief history of the Austrian excavations.

Bietak and his team first arrived at Tell ed-Daba in 1966. The surrounding area, defined by the villages of Kantir in the north and Khatana in the south, had been cursively explored in 1883 by Ahmed Effendi Kamal, the Egyptian inspector who had accompanied Brugsch to the Royal Cache in the previous year. Then came Eduoard NAVILLE in 1885. He uncovered a large temple compound containing columns and a sphinx inscribed with the cartouches of Queen Sobekneferu, last ruler of the 12th Dynasty.[23]

In 1929 Mahmud HAMZA excavated a large Ramesside palace located just to the south of the village of Kantir.[24] Hundreds of beautifully coloured faience tiles were collected, some inlaid with alabaster and glass, which, when reconstructed, formed the decoration for doorways, windows and several throne daises (one now in the Metropolitan Museum). Many of these tiles depict vassals and prisoners-of-war from the northern and southern empires of Egypt. This great palace of Seti I and Ramesses II must have been spectacularly colourful and exquisitely exotic. Hamza correctly concluded that this was the royal residence of the Ramesside capital, Pi-Ramesse, but it took a further forty years for his identification to be fully accepted. Until fairly recently, most scholars had stubbornly continued to identify Tanis with the city of Ramesses, but now we know that Tanis was only established during the early years of the TIP and so there is a consensus that the archaeological site of the city of Pi-Ramesse (biblical Raamses) is centred on the modern village of Kantir.

In 1937 Zaki Sous of the Egyptian Antiquities Service cleared the granite blocks belonging to a gateway of the *djadja* ('court') of Amenemhat I ('restored' by Senuseret III) previously examined by Naville within the small village of Ezbet Helmy.[25]

The next Egyptologist to explore the Kantir/Khatana region was the great Egyptian archaeologist Labib HABACHI who, in the early 1940s, retrieved more statues of Queen Sobekneferu and others belonging to an obscure 13th

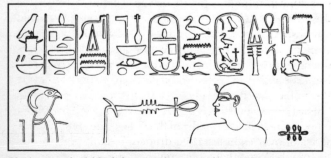

58. An inscribed block bearing the cartouches of Hetepibre Amusaharnedjheryotef from Avaris.

Dynasty pharaoh, Amu-Saharnedjheryotef ('The Asiatic, son of Harnedjheryotef').[26]

Finally, in 1955, at the little village of Ezbet Rushdi, another Egyptian excavator, Shehata ADAM, discovered a settlement of Middle Kingdom date surrounding a large temple built by Amenemhat I and extended by Senuseret III.[27] Moving north to Kantir he then unearthed a limestone statue base of Ramesses II, broken off at the feet. Nearby Adam cleared the foundations of a large mudbrick structure probably representing the remains of a temple pylon in front of which the colossus had once stood.

Clearly the scattered monuments of the 12th, 13th and 19th Dynasties, spread over a wide area, pointed to the existence of a huge city which had endured here for over half a millennium. This was what the Austrian expedition set out to uncover and define in 1966.[28] Little did they know then that they would not only find the city of Pi-Ramesse, but also the much older city of Avaris and, with it, archaeological evidence of the Israelite Sojourn in Egypt.

Avaris and the Israelites

Early in the Austrian expedition's time at Tell ed-Daba Bietak explored some of the outlying areas in order to determine what exactly he had taken on. Soon though he was concentrating his efforts on the low tell just north of the village of Tell ed-Daba where his dig house had been established. The rambling mound turned out to be the last vestiges of the ancient city of Avaris which New Kingdom documents identified as the southern quarter/district of Pi-Ramesse. Bietak quickly realised that many centuries before Pi-Ramesse had been built by the first pharaohs of the 19th Dynasty the city of Avaris had been founded on the east bank of the Pelusiac branch of the Nile in the same area. A series of over eight hundred drill cores sunk into the soil by Joseph Dorner have since revealed the ancient topography of the area.[29]

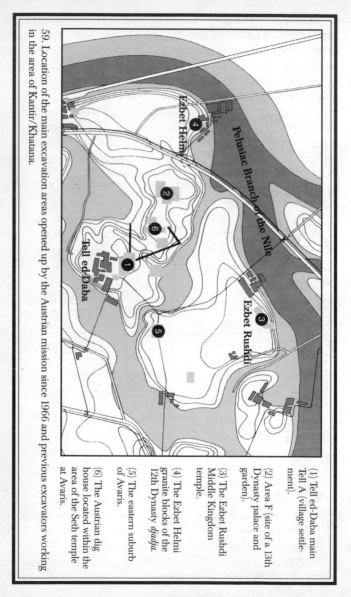

59. Location of the main excavation areas opened up by the Austrian mission since 1966 and previous excavators working in the area of Kantir/Khatana.

(1) Tell ed-Daba main Tell A (village settlement).

(2) Area F (site of a 13th Dynasty palace and garden).

(3) The Ezbet Rushdi Middle Kingdom temple.

(4) The Ezbet Helmi granite blocks of the 12th Dynasty *djadja*.

(5) The eastern suburb of Avaris.

(6) The Austrian dig house located within the area of the Seth temple at Avaris.

Avaris was built on a series of sandy hillocks (turtlebacks) surrounded by swamplands to the east and south and the river to the west and north. The higher dry land was densely populated with modest domestic residences tightly packed together around narrow alleyways and streets. All the buildings were constructed of mudbrick.

Associated with the houses were the burials of the occupants, usually interred in vaulted mudbrick tombs within the compound of the family home. Bietak made the startling discovery that the grave goods associated with

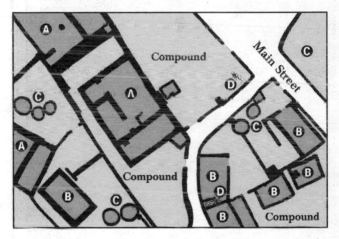

60. A part of the town plan of Avaris during the 13th Dynasty (i.e. the Israelite occupation of the site in the New Chronology) as determined from the Austrian excavations of the main tell (stratum G/1-2), comprising:

(A) Large mudbrick houses with several rooms and a spacious compound for keeping the domesticated animals. The compounds are delineated by a low mudbrick wall of just one brick thickness.

(B) Smaller single-roomed houses, probably for the married offspring of the principal householder.

(C) Separate grain silos for each of the family units.

(D) Graves, either sunk into the floor of the compound or attached to (sometimes within) the houses themselves.

BC	Palace Area F
1193	Expulsion of the 15th Dynasty elite by King Ahmose of the 18th Dynasty.
1300	An elite group of Indo-European origin establish a fortified palace at Avaris as the Egyptian *entrepot* for their large Eastern Mediterranean trading network. The Asiatic town of Avaris continues to develop to the east of the citadel over the earlier Israelite village of Rowarty/Avaris.
	A new settlement is established at Avaris of Asiatic warriors with no cultural ties to Egypt. The MB II B town is built on a new plan and orientation to the earlier Israelite town.
	Invasion of Shasu tribes from the Negeb and southern Palestine.
1447	Exodus of Israelites – site abandoned.
	At the end of the village's life there is a calamity which necessitates the rapid burial of the victims in shallow pit graves.
	The abandoned palace is eventually built over as the main town expands westwards. In Area F new houses are constructed with similar layouts to the main tell.
1583	Palace abandoned.
	Joseph builds an Egyptian-style palace for his retirement over the original mansion of his father.
1646	Jacob dies and is buried in Hebron.
1662	Jacob settles in Rowarty where he builds a Syrian style mansion.
	Hiatus
1783	Village abandoned.
1812	Workmen's village for the construction of monumental buildings of Amenemhat I in the area.

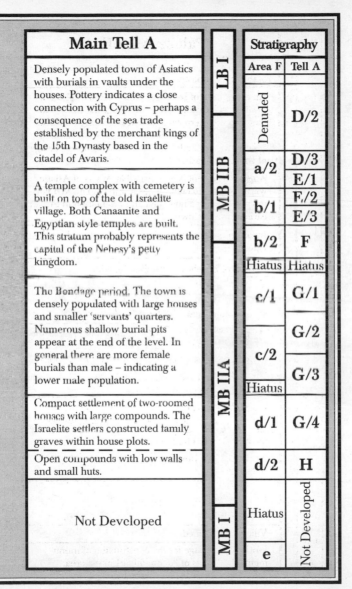

Main Tell A		Stratigraphy	
		Area F	Tell A
Densely populated town of Asiatics with burials in vaults under the houses. Pottery indicates a close connection with Cyprus – perhaps a consequence of the sea trade established by the merchant kings of the 15th Dynasty based in the citadel of Avaris.	LB I	Denuded	D/2
A temple complex with cemetery is built on top of the old Israelite village. Both Canaanite and Egyptian style temples are built. This stratum probably represents the capital of the Nehesy's petty kingdom.	MB IIB	a/2	D/3
			E/1
		b/1	E/2
			E/3
		b/2	F
		Hiatus	Hiatus
The Bondage period. The town is densely populated with large houses and smaller 'servants' quarters. Numerous shallow burial pits appear at the end of the level. In general there are more female burials than male – indicating a lower male population.	MB IIA	c/1	G/1
			G/2
		c/2	G/3
		Hiatus	
Compact settlement of two-roomed houses with large compounds. The Israelite settlers constructed family graves within house plots.		d/1	G/4
Open compounds with low walls and small huts.		d/2	H
Not Developed	MB I	Hiatus	Not Developed
		e	

327

the majority of these tombs were of Asiatic origin. The people who had populated the sprawling city of Avaris originated from Palestine and Syria! Archaeologists call the material culture of these Levantine folk 'Middle Bronze II' (or MB II).

The initial influx of Asiatics into the region of Kantir/ Khatana appears to have been during the late 12th Dynasty (MB IIA) with the first settlement concentrated at the site of Tell ed-Daba – later to become the central core of the city of Avaris. The Asiatic occupation ended with the expulsion of the 15th Dynasty 'Hyksos' rulers of Avaris by Ahmose at the beginning of the New Kingdom (MB IIB[30] overlapping with LB I). Bietak has identified eleven main levels of occupation during that period indicating a considerable time interval between the arrival and departure of the foreigners.

In the New Chronology these Asiatics have to be the proto-Israelites. Our Israelite population – that is to say the Asiatic peoples whose historical existence formed the basis of the traditional history of late Genesis and Exodus – occupied strata H and G/4 to G/1, the first levels of the Asiatic town. The later strata F to D/2 also represent an Asiatic settlement but these people, although culturally similar, were distinct from the earlier group of H to G/1. Bietak notes that the early Asiatics were highly 'Egyptianised'.[31] The later Asiatics, whom I shall subsequently identify with the Hyksos invaders who entered Egypt during the late 13th Dynasty, were very different. According to Bietak the tombs of this group were 'purely Canaanite … and showed little Egyptian influence' – in other words newcomers from the Levant. Why were the early Asiatics so much more Egyptianised than their later cousins? Now that we can identify the former with Joseph's brethren the answer is obvious. It is clear from the Bible that Joseph himself was highly Egyptianised and readily accepted the influences of Egyptian culture for his people. However, adopting a partly Egyptian way of life did not mean sacrificing the most important Hebrew cultural traits which were of religious significance – in other words their burial practices.

It is readily apparent that there was a clearly defined settlement break between Stratum G/1 and F. For the historical model being developed here, it is important to note that this break marks the biblical Exodus in the archaeology of Tell ed-Daba as will become clear in the next chapter.

Let us look in a little more detail at the inhabitants of the earlier strata H to G/1. There are several interesting aspects to this settlement group which merit discussion. First, an anthropological analysis of the skeletal remains by Eike-Meinrad Winkler and Harald Wilfing shows that more adult women were buried in the settlement than adult men.[32] This could simply indicate that there was a disproportionately high female population at Avaris. In the context of the Sojourn tradition this can be explained by the culling of the Israelite male children – an act of the 'pharaoh who did not know Joseph' in fear of the perceived political threat resulting from a strong Asiatic population in Egypt.

In the context of this same story it was discovered that there was a higher percentage of infant burials at Tell ed-Daba than is normally found at archaeological sites of the ancient world.[33] Sixty five percent of all the burials were those of children under the age of eighteen months. Based on modern statistical evidence obtained from pre modern societies we would expect the infant mortality rate to be around twenty to thirty per cent.[34] Could this also be explained by the slaughter of the Israelite infant males by the Egyptians?

In the graves of Stratum G the Austrians found broadbladed ceremonial daggers made of bronze, copper ornamented belts, various types of pottery and dismembered sheep, the latter undoubtedly funeral offerings. Analysis of the sheep remains has shown that they were of the long-haired variety. The Asiatic folk of early Avaris introduced the Levantine long-haired sheep into Egypt clearly indicating their pastoralist origins.

> Taking their livestock and all that they had acquired in Canaan, they (the Israelites) arrived in Egypt – Jacob and all his offspring. [Genesis 46:6]

The pottery included the type of small oil or perfume vessel known as Tell el-Yahudiya Ware. This black or dark grey ceramic, decorated with incised patterns which were then highlighted with white pigment, comes in three basic forms: ZOOMORPHIC (usually fish-shaped), PIRIFORM and CYLINDRICAL. The latter appears to be generally later than the piriform type. This chronological trend will play a part in the story of the conquest and destruction of Jericho when I deal with the Joshua narratives.

The adult male graves found in strata H to G/1 were found to contain a number of weapons (mainly daggers and socketed spears). These men were not just shepherds but also clan warriors. The Bible tells us little about the military character of the early Hebrews, though it is interesting to note that the extra-biblical rabbinic writings, fanciful as they may be, do contain traditions in which the Israelites fight to protect Egypt's eastern border from the marauding nomads listed as 'the sons of Esau', the Ishmaelites and the Edomites – one battle event takes place at Raamses.[35]

What the Austrian archaeological mission has unearthed at Tell ed-Daba is a fascinating Western Asiatic culture which, in virtually every respect, mirrors the Western Asiatic settlers known to us from the Old Testament as the early Israelites. Archaeological evidence of the Israelite Sojourn in Egypt has been sought in Egypt for the best part of two centuries but the archaeologists have searched in vain. No Israelite settlement has ever been found in the 19th Dynasty occupational levels where the orthodox chronology predicted its stratigraphical locus. Within the strata of New Kingdom Pi-Ramesse (biblical Raamses) so far no evidence has been unearthed to support the conventional hypothesis that a large Asiatic population resided there. On the other hand, dig down below the 19th Dynasty capital and you reach the city of Avaris, the vast majority of the population of which was Asiatic.

The only period in Egyptian history with incontrovertible archaeological evidence for a large Asiatic population in the eastern delta (i.e. Goshen/Kessan) is the Second Intermediate Period – the era into which the New Chronology places the historical events believed to lie at the heart of the traditional stories of the Israelite Sojourn, Bondage and Exodus.

Conclusion Twenty-Four

The Israelite Sojourn in Egypt began in the late 12th Dynasty and continued throughout most of the 13th Dynasty. It is represented in Egypt's archaeological record by the Asiatic culture known as Middle Bronze IIA. The main settlement of the Israelites in Egypt was located at the city of Avaris in the region of Goshen. Their archaeological remains are represented by the dwellings and tombs of Tell ed-Daba strata H to G/1.

Chapter Thirteen

EXODUS

In *Chapter Four* I explained how the Exodus 1:11 reference to the city of Raamses was simply an anachronism. We subsequently discovered that the real Israelite city of the Bondage was Avaris, buried beneath the 19th Dynasty capital, Pi-Ramesse. This was the setting-off point for the Israelites' epic journey to the Promised Land. Before we deal with traditions surrounding the events immediately leading up to Exodus and then, following the departure from Egypt, the Wilderness Years in Sinai, I want briefly to deal with the issue of bonded Asiatic servants in Egypt. In doing so I will demonstrate that there was indeed a large western-Asiatic slave population sojourning in the delta and Nile valley during the 13th Dynasty.

Israelite Slaves

Then there came to power in Egypt a new king who did not know Joseph. 'Look', he said to his people, 'the Israelites are now more numerous and stronger than we are. We must take precautions to stop them from increasing any further or, if war should break out, they might join the ranks of our enemies. They might take up arms against us and then escape from the country.' Accordingly they put task masters over the Israelites to wear them down by forced labour. ... So the Egyptians gave them no mercy in the demands they made, making their lives miserable with hard labour: with digging clay, making bricks, doing various kinds of field-work – all sorts of labour that they imposed on them without mercy. [Exodus 1:8-14]

The Brooklyn Museum possesses a tattered papyrus roll, whose uninspiring catalogue number is Brooklyn 35.1446.[1] The papyrus was originally purchased by Charles Wilbour, the intrepid 'secret agent' of Émil Brugsch sent to Thebes in 1881 on a mission to ferret out the tomb robbers believed to have found an intact royal tomb. (As you now know that tomb turned out to be the famous Royal Cache.) Wilbour's papyrus roll is dated to the reign of Sobekhotep III, the predecessor of Neferhotep I, and therefore the king who reigned in Egypt a generation before the birth of Moses in the New Chronology. The biblical narrative tells us that, prior to the birth of Moses, the Israelite population was subjugated by the native Egyptians and forced into slavery.

The RECTO of the Brooklyn Papyrus contains a copy of a royal decree by Sobekhotep III which authorises the transfer of ownership of a group of domestic slaves/servants (Egy. *khenmu*) to an estate in the Theban area. The VERSO then contains a list of household servants which can probably be identified with the slave group mentioned on the recto. Analysis of the list of servants reveals that over fifty percent of the ninety-five names are Semitic in origin. These foreign servants are each clearly designated as *aamu* – the Egyptian term for 'Asiatic'. Their Egyptian names are also separately listed – the names given to them by their owners. For example we read: 'The Asiatic Dodihuatu, who is called Ankhuemhesut'.

So, half of the domestic slaves of this Egyptian estate were Asiatics who had been given Egyptian names. What is more, when we study the actual appellations themselves we find that several are biblical names.

61. A section of the Brooklyn Papyrus listing the domestic servants of an Upper Egyptian household. The two boxes encompass two of the biblical names – Shiphrah (upper) and Asher (lower).

(a) Thus we see at position 11 the name 'Menahem' later recorded for the sixteenth king of Israel (743-738 BC);

(b) At 13, 14, 16, 22 and 67 we have variants of the tribal eponym 'Issachar' the name of the fifth son of Leah by Jacob;

(c) At 23 the name of the clan 'Asher' occurs, named after its eponymous ancestor, the second son of Zilpah by Jacob;

(d) And finally at position 21 we read 'Shiphrah', the name carried by one of the two Hebrew midwives instructed to kill the Israelite newborn males in Exodus 1:15-21.

The Egyptian term Apiru, which as we have noted in the Amarna period has clear historical affinities with the biblical term 'Hebrew' (Heb. sing. *ibri* pl. *ibrim*), also appears in the Brooklyn Papyrus. Thus we read 'Apiru-Rishpu' at position 9.

If the verso of the Brooklyn Papyrus is representative of a typical Egyptian estate in the mid-13th Dynasty then at least half the total servant population in Egypt at this time was of Syro-Palestinian origin. The great American philologist William Foxwell Albright long ago recognised that the names of these Asiatic people belong to the north-west-semitic language group which includes biblical Hebrew. Bearing in mind that the Brooklyn Papyrus lists the domestic slaves of an Upper Egyptian estate we may logically conclude that the Asiatic slave population in the north (Lower Egypt), and especially the delta nearest to the Levant, would have been much larger and may have constituted the vast majority of the bonded work force. Other documents confirm that the size of the Asiatic community in Egypt at this time was significant. This state of affairs accords well with the biblical tradition.

> But the Israelites were fruitful and prolific; they became so numerous and powerful that eventually the whole land was full of them. [Exodus 1:7]

In the previous chapter I noted that an analysis of the graves at Tell ed-Daba has shown that there were more females than males in the burial population of Avaris. I suggested this could conceivably reflect the story of the culling of the Israelite males described in Exodus 1:15-22. A similar picture emerges from the Brooklyn Papyrus. In his commentary on the text William Hayes (the editor of the document) remarks on the problem of determining the origins of this large Asiatic slave population and then goes on to ponder the high proportion of female slaves listed in the papyrus.

Perhaps the most surprising circumstance associated with these Asiatic servants is that an Upper Egyptian official of the mid-Thirteenth Dynasty should have had well over forty of them in his personal possession. If a comparable number of similar servants was to be found in every large Egyptian household **one wonders by what means such quantities of Asiatic serving people found their way into Egypt at this time and how they chanced to be available as domestic servants for private citizens. ... The ratio of women to men, which is here about three to one**, might further suggest that they were the spoils of war taken during military campaigns or raids in which most of the local male population went down fighting. We know, however, of no large-scale Egyptian military operations in Western Asia at any time during the Middle Kingdom and certainly of none during the Thirteenth Dynasty.[2]

By applying the New Chronology model for the SIP it is now possible to explain the quandaries highlighted by Hayes. The reduction in the male Asiatic population is not due to a series of (unattested) wars in the north but rather as a result of a deliberate policy on the part of the Egyptian state to reduce the perceived Israelite threat by means of male infanticide (as described in Exodus 1:15-22). The origin of these foreigners is also explained: they entered Egypt in the years following the arrival of Jacob and his immediate brethren into the land of Goshen. During their long sojourn these disparate Asiatic groups (which we could give the overall classification of 'Hebrews/Habiru/Apiru' – including the Israelites themselves) would gradually forge nationhood through the common burden of slavery under the late 13th Dynasty pharaohs.

> ## Conclusion Twenty-Five
>
> The bonded Asiatic servants recorded in documents of the 13th Dynasty (especially Papyrus Brooklyn 35.1446) are to be identified with the 'mixed multitude' of Asiatics who eventually departed from Egypt under the leadership of Moses [Exodus 12:38]. The Israelite population, descended from Jacob, formed the major part of this group and a number of Hebrew/Israelite names can be recognised within the documents of the period.

The Tenth Plague

> And at midnight Yahweh struck down all the first-born in Egypt from the first-born of Pharaoh, heir to his throne, to the first-born of the prisoner in the dungeon, and the first-born of all the livestock. Pharaoh and all his officials and all the Egyptians got up in the night, and there was great wailing in Egypt, for there was not a house without its dead. [Exodus 12:29-30]

Whatever it was that struck Egypt in a single night it was a devastating blow to the king and his subjects. Whether we are really dealing with a sudden catastrophe, as the Exodus tale relates, or an event which took place over a longer time-scale – a disease or plague does not take its toll literally overnight – the aftereffects of the disaster (that is to say the burials of the victims) should survive in the archaeological record. So in our new chronological model we must look for that evidence at the only major late 13th-Dynasty site so far investigated. Do we have any evidence of a sudden catastrophe at Avaris which might in some way mirror the events of the Exodus tradition? The answer is a qualified yes – but with a salutary reminder that, without contemporary texts to describe the cause and effect, I am only offering an *interpretation* of the archaeological evidence. However that interpretation is consistent with the biblical narrative.

At the end of stratum G/1 at Tell ed-Daba, which is roughly dated to the middle of the 13th Dynasty, Bietak and his archaeological team began to uncover a gruesome scene. All over the city of Avaris they found shallow burial pits into which the victims of some terrible disaster had been hurriedly cast. These were no careful interments of the deceased. The bodies were not arranged in the proper burial fashion but rather thrown into the mass graves, one on top of the other. There were no grave-goods placed with the corpses as was usually the custom. Bietak is convinced that we have here direct evidence of plague or sudden catastrophe at Avaris [3]

What is more, analysis of the site archaeology suggests that the remaining population of the town abandoned their homes and departed from Avaris *en masse*.[4] The site was then reoccupied after an interval of unknown duration by Asiatics who were not 'Egyptianised' like the previous population of stratum G.

> Stratum F marks a new beginning in the settlement of purely Asiatic (Canaanite) people, who had strong cultural ties with the previous settlers of stratum G. The inhabitants of the site were now fewer, but richer, than in the time of stratum G. The housing installations on the other hand looked rather rudimentary, so that the conclusion may be drawn that the inhabitants were complete newcomers. The inhabitants of stratum G seem to have left the site before the arrival of another wave of Asiatic immigrants, who settled and remained there until the beginning of the New Kingdom.[5]

13th Dynasty	
1632	Sobekhotep I
1627	Sekhemkara
1622	6 years of no king
1616	Amenemhat V
1612	Sehetepibre
1607	Iufni
1602	Sankhibre
1597	Smenkhkare
1592	Sehetepibre
1587	Sewadjkare
1582	Nedjemib[...]re
1577	Sobekhotep II
1575	Renseneb
1575	Awibre Hor
1570	Sedjef[...]kare
1565	Wegaf
1563	Khendjer
1558	Mermesha
1553	Inyotef
1548	[...]set
1543	Sobekhotep III
1540	Neferhotep I
1530	Sihathor
1529	Sobekhotep IV
1508	Sobekhotep V
1503	Iayib
1493	Ay
1470	Sobekhotep VI
1469	Sankhrenesewadjtu
1467	Ined
1464	Hori
1459	Sobekhotep VII
1457	[...] – [lost]
1455	[...] – [lost]
1452	[...] – [lost]
1450	[...] – [lost]
1448	Dudimose
1447	EXODUS

New Chronology dates for the 13th Dynasty down to Dudimose. The dates are based on data supplied in the Royal Canon and an average reign length at this period of five years.

The Asiatic folk who established themselves at Avaris in stratum F 'used as living quarters ... the ruins of stratum G' yet their graves were richly endowed with precious metals and jewellery.[6] This strange combination of poor housing conditions and rich treasure will be explained shortly when we identify the new group of Asiatics whose arrival is associated with stratum F.

Is it possible to date the catastrophe then abandonment of Avaris, and finally the city's subsequent reoccupation, historically?

As I have already mentioned, we have one pseudo-historical source from Ptolemaic Egypt which covers this earlier period. That source is Manetho – more specifically, the quotations from Manetho by Josephus. This is what Manetho has to say on the fall of the 13th Dynasty and the occupation of Egypt by foreign elements.

> **Tutimaos**. In his reign, for what cause I know not, a blast of **God** smote us; **and** unexpectedly, from the regions of the East, invaders of obscure race marched in confidence of victory against our land. By main force they easily seized it **without striking a blow**; and having overpowered the rulers of the land, they then burned our cities ruthlessly, razed to the ground the temples of the gods, and treated all the natives with a cruel hostility, massacring some and leading into slavery the wives and children of others. **Finally**, they appointed as king one of their number whose name was **Salitis**. He had his seat at Memphis, levying tribute from Upper Egypt, and always leaving garrisons behind in the most advantageous positions. Above all, he fortified the district to the east, foreseeing that the **Assyrians**, as they grew stronger, would one day covet and attack his kingdom. ... In the Saite [Sethroite] nome he found a city very favourably situated on the east of the Bubastite branch of the Nile, and called **Auaris** after

an ancient religious tradition. This place he rebuilt and fortified with massive walls, planting there a garrison of as many as two hundred and forty thousand heavily-armed men to guard his frontier. Here he would come in summertime, partly to serve out rations and pay his troops, partly to train them carefully in manoeuvres and so strike terror into foreign tribes.

There are interesting points to note here.

- It has long been recognised that the Egyptian king Tutimaos (the Greek form of his name) is to be equated with Pharaoh Dudimose, one of the later rulers of the 13th Dynasty.[7]

- The smiting of Egypt by 'God' is a distinct event from the arrival of the 'invaders of obscure race' – the 'and' (Gk. *kai*) linking the two statements is preceded in the published Greek text by a punctuation mark which serves to distinguish them. The smiting of God is not the invasion – the latter only followed on from the original 'blast of God'/catastrophe. This is clearly implied by the fact that the foreigners were able to overwhelm Egypt 'without striking a blow' – the Egyptians were unable to defend themselves precisely because of the earlier disaster which had befallen them.

- The word 'Finally' suggests that the interval of time between the initial invasion and the establishment of a fortress by Salitis at Avaris may have been of some duration. This could mean anything from a few months to several generations.

- Salitis is otherwise stated as being the first ruler of the 15th Dynasty in the Manethonian redactions of Africanus and Eusebius. Thus the invasion occurred some (perhaps considerable) time before the establishment of Manetho's 15th Dynasty.

- The term 'Assyrians' is another example of an anachronism. The domination of the ancient world by the Assyrian empire did not occur until the ninth century BC.

- Auaris, the fortified summer residence of Salitis, is, of course, Avaris (Egy. *Hatwaret*).

The New Chronology date for Dudimose, in whose time disaster befell Egypt, can be approximated by reference once again to the Royal Canon of Turin. Following on from the bottom of column VI, where the cartouche of Khaneferre Sobekhotep IV is located, we begin reading downwards from the top of column VII. The list of rulers of the 13th Dynasty continues as follows:

24. Khahotepre Sobekhotep V	– 4 yrs 9 m
25. Wahibre Iaib	– 10 yrs 9 m
26. Merneferre Ay	– 23 yrs 8 m
27. Merhotepre Sobekhotep VI	– 2 yrs 2 m
28. Sankhreneswadjtu	– 3 yrs 2 m
29. Mersekhemre Ined	– 3 yrs 1 m
30. Sewadjkare Hori	– 5 yrs 8 m
31. Merkaure Sobekhotep VII	– 2 yrs 4 m
32. [lost]	– x yrs 11 m (?)
33. [lost]	– x yrs 3 m (?)
34. [lost]	– x yrs y m
35. [lost]	– x yrs y m
36. [Dudi]mose	– x yrs y m

Thus we have twelve kings reigning between Khaneferre Sobekhotep IV and Dudimose. In the last chapter we gave Sobekhotep IV regnal dates of *circa* 1529-1510 BC. The first year of Sobekhotep VII (31st ruler of the dynasty),

COLUMN VII

Sobekhotep V – 4 yrs 8 ms 9 days —
Iayib – 10 yrs 8 ms 28 days —
Ay – 23 yrs 8 ms 18 days —
Sobekhotep VI – 2 yrs 2 ms 9 days —
Sankhrenesewadjtu – 3 yrs 2 ms —
Ined – 3 yrs 1 m 1 day —
Hori – 5 yrs 8 ms —
Sobekhotep VII – 2 yrs 4 ms —
[...] – [lost]
[...] – [lost]
[...] – [lost]
[...] – [lost]
EXODUS = 1447 BC   [Dudi]mose – [lost] — -
[...] Ibi – [lost] — -
[...]weben[re] Hor – [lost] — -
[...]ka – [lost] — -
[...]n – [lost] — -
[...] – [lost]
[...] – [lost]
[...] – [lost]
Merkeperre – [lost] — -
Merka[...] – [lost] — -

COLUMN VI

Neferhotep I – 11 yrs 1 m — -
Sihathor – 3 ms — -
Sobekhotep – [lost] — -

62. Column VI and VII of the Royal Canon of Turin showing the
position in the 13th Dynasty of Dudimose, the thirteenth successor
of Khaneferre Sobekhotep IV.

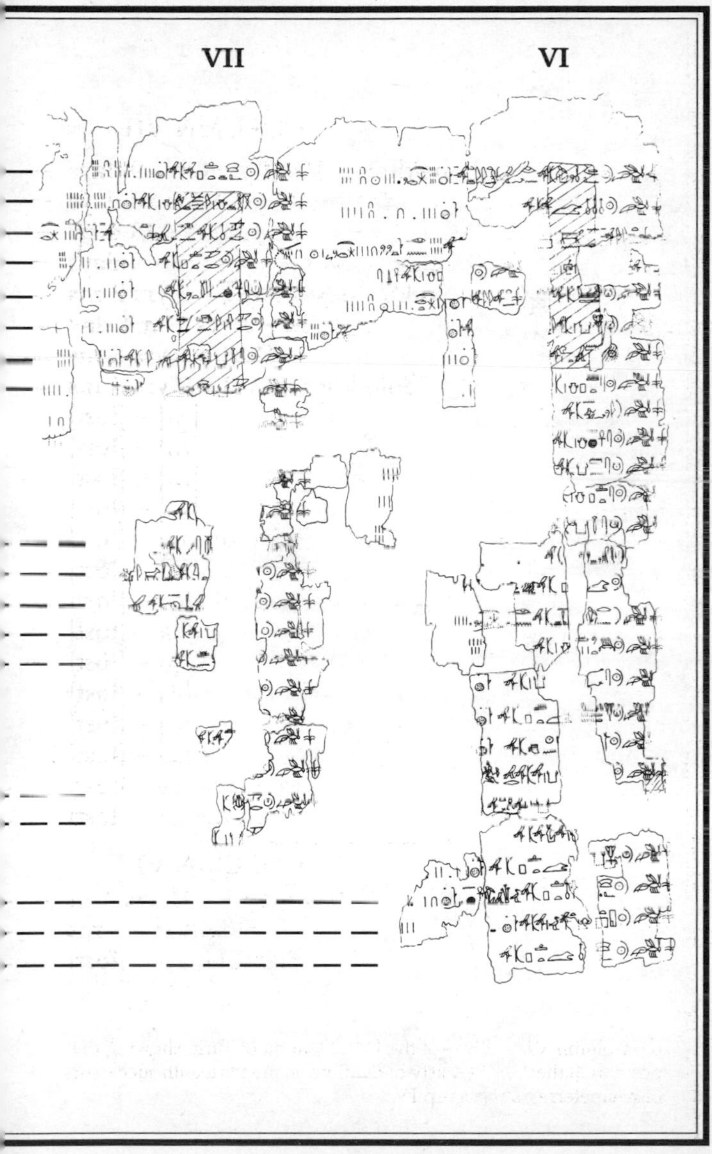
VII
VI

would then have fallen in *circa* 1461 BC. The names and regnal years of the four kings following Sobekhotep VII are lost through damage to the papyrus. We could assign each a minimum reign of one year and a maximum of five years to reach an approximate date range for the accession of Dudimose of 1457 to 1444 BC. The biblical date for the Exodus is 1447 BC (Thiele's foundation date of the temple in 968 BC plus 479 years) and so Dudimose was in all likelihood the Pharaoh of the Exodus.

We also determined in the last chapter that the biblical tradition gives a birth-date for Moses of 1527 BC. He would then have been between seventy-two and eighty-five years old at the accession of Dudimose.

It might be useful to reiterate the coincidences that appear to stem from these identifications and calculations.

- Moses, according to Artapanus, was born in the reign of a pharaoh called Khaneferre (Khenephrês).

- Khaneferre Sobekhotep IV began his reign in *circa* 1529 BC, according to the 'best fit' astronomical retrocalculations for the Ammisaduga Venus observations. The Bible gives a date of 1527 BC for the birth of Moses (using Thiele's widely accepted chronology for the kings of the Divided Monarchy period and the chronological data provided by the Bible for the eras of the United Monarchy and Judges). This date for Moses' birth, should, however, be regarded as an approximation due to the employment of 'round figures' of forty years for the second and third Israelite kings of the Early Monarchy period and a similar 'round figure' for the age of Moses at Exodus (80 years = 2 x 40). However, the simple fact is that the New Chronology *does* place a ruler called Khaneferre Sobekhotep IV at the time of Moses' birth as determined from the biblical tradition. Furthermore, this is the only king named Khaneferre throughout the whole of pharaonic civilisation.

- The Old Testament informs us that Moses was eighty years old at the time of Exodus which, in the New Chronology, would place the momentous events of that epic tale contemporary with the 13th Dynasty pharaoh, Dudimose, his dates having been determined by utilising the data provided in the Turin Canon.

- According to Manetho, in the reign of Dudimose 'a blast of God smote us (i.e. the Egyptians)' and the archaeology of Avaris shows that, approximately at this time, there was a terrible catastrophe. The book of Exodus relates that the departure of the Israelites for the Promised Land was preceded by a series of 'plagues' which devastated Egypt. The final Tenth Plague was sudden and dramatic.

All this material appears to be telling one story. The sources are quite unconnected, yet there is an intriguing consistency in the details. In terms of the overall historical picture developed in this book the biblical episode detailing the life of Moses and the Exodus of the Israelites from Egypt once again appears to slot neatly into place within the new chronological framework.

I am not the first to suggest an Exodus date in the late 13th Dynasty. In the 1950s Immanuel Velikovsky, in his book *Ages in Chaos*, proposed just such a scheme.[8] There he raised a telling point in his discussion of the Exodus story by questioning the causes which lay behind the event of the Tenth Plague and its supernatural ability to select only the 'first-born' victims amongst the native Egyptian population. I too have difficulty with this. If we are looking for a cause for the Exodus/stratum G catastrophe then it should be readily explainable within the context of an event such as plague or earthquake or some other such natural calamity. Indeed, it is Artapanus who tells us that on the night before Exodus Egypt was struck by a terrible hailstorm and a violent earthquake.

> But as the king still persisted in his folly, Moses caused hail and earthquakes by night, so that those who fled from the earthquakes were killed by the hail, and those who sought shelter from the hail were destroyed by the earthquakes. And at that time all the houses fell in and most of the temples.[9]

This natural disaster, of course, could not have been so selective as to choose only the Egyptian first-born.

If we are dealing here with an earthquake then the mass graves at the end of stratum G at Avaris have a ready explanation, as does the subsequent abandonment of the site. In both ancient and modern times serious earthquakes have required drastic measures on the part of the inhabitants of devastated areas. These include mass burials of the victims and major population movements away from the destroyed settlements. When the Asiatics of stratum F reached Avaris they found a town fallen into ruin. I am suggesting that this was a destruction by violent earth tremor. They chose to utilise some of the collapsed walls of the stratum G settlement as temporary shelter following their arrival in the eastern delta. Only later did they construct new houses and temples upon the ruins of the 13th Dynasty town.

But what about the issue of the selecting-out of the 'first-born'? Velikovsky provides an explanation.[10] The Hebrew word for 'first-born' is *bekore* whilst the Hebrew for 'chosen' is *bakhur* (with the meaning of 'choice youth'). Both words appear to stem from *bakhar* meaning 'prime root'. There is a clear connection in the Bible between these two words. When God refers to 'Israel, my chosen' the phrase in Hebrew is either *Israel bechiri* or *Israel bechori*; when God refers to 'Israel, my first-born' the Hebrew is *Israel bekhori*. We may therefore understand the passage concerning the death of the Egyptian first-born as a literary device which should better be understood as 'the chosen of Egypt' or, in modern parlance, 'the flower of Egypt'. Egypt's future was cut short by Yahweh's punishment, personified in the death of the crown prince, first-born son of Pharaoh Dudimose.

Conclusion Twenty-Six

The Pharaoh of the Exodus is to be identified with King Dudimose, thirty-sixth ruler of the 13th Dynasty, in whose reign, according to Manetho, 'God' smote the Egyptians. The death-pits found at the end of Tell ed-Daba stratum G/1 may provide some archaeological evidence for the disasters associated with the Tenth Plague tradition of the Exodus.

Pharaoh's Chariots

In the midst of the calamity afflicting Egypt, Moses led the Israelites out of Goshen via Succoth (Egy. *Tjeku*) in the Wadi Tumilat to the Sea of Reeds (Heb. *Yam-suf*). But Pharaoh had resolved to pursue the runaway slaves.

> So Pharaoh had his chariot harnessed and set out with his troops, taking **six hundred of the best chariots** and all the other chariots in Egypt, with officers in each. [Exodus 14:6-7]

> Then Moses stretched out his hand over the sea and Yahweh drove the sea back with a strong easterly wind all night and made the sea into dry land. The waters were divided and the Israelites went on dry ground right through the sea, with walls of water to right and left of them. The Egyptians gave chase and all Pharaoh's horses, chariots and horsemen went into the sea after them. [Exodus 14:21-23]

> … and Yahweh overthrew the Egyptians in the midst

of the sea. The returning waters washed right over the chariots and horsemen of Pharaoh's entire army, which had followed the Israelites into the sea; not a single one of them remained. [Exodus 14:28]

One of the arguments which might be raised against placing the Israelite Exodus in the 13th Dynasty is the fact that scholars have always believed it was the Hyksos who introduced the chariot into the Levant and Egypt. Therefore, the Egyptians could not have assembled a chariot force to pursue the Israelites until they had acquired the technology from their foreign Hyksos oppressors. This understanding has recently been brought into question by the discovery of horse skeletons in archaeological contexts datable to the 13th Dynasty.[11] If horses were introduced into Egypt prior to the Hyksos occupation, then they must have been employed to pull chariots – simply because horseback riding was not introduced until much later. One further important clue has to do with gloves!

63. Left: Part of a limestone relief from the tomb of Ay at Amarna showing the heavily decorated 'Master of Horse' wearing his leather chariot gloves.

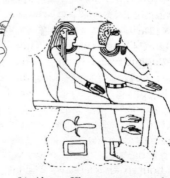

64. Above: Khonsuemwaset and wife seated on a couch with symbols of their activities in daily life under the seat (including a pair of his chariot gloves).

Egypt possesses a hot climate and it will be obvious to you that the ancient Egyptians did not wear gloves in order to keep their hands warm. When you see leather gloves amongst Tutankhamun's treasures in the Cairo Museum you immediately recognise that these are 'chariot gloves' which the boy-king wore to protect his hands from the chafing of leather reins. When we look at a wall relief from the el-Amarna tomb of Ay, 'Master of Horse', showing the tomb owner wearing gloves at a royal investiture in his honour, we again know that these gloves are part of the trappings of a charioteer – in this case the commander of the chariot forces of Egypt.[12] These chariot gloves were clearly a status symbol to be displayed as a mark of rank, singling out the wearer as a member of his majesty's élite troops.

Thus, when I show you a fragment of a stela showing the King's Son and Army Commander of Edfu, Khonsu-emwaset, seated with his wife on a chair with a pair of gloves depicted under his seat,[13] then you will come to the same conclusion as the great German scholar Wolfgang HELCK: Prince Khonsuemwaset was the commander of a force of Pharaoh's chariots.[14] The mirror and jewellery box beneath the wife's chair 'labels' her as the lady of the household. Likewise, the gloves 'label' Khonsuemwaset as a charioteer by profession. Who was this prince's royal father? The answer is rather extraordinary given the arguments I have been putting before you in this chapter. The king whose son was a commander of the chariot forces of Egypt was none other than Dudimose – the pharaoh who pursued the Israelites to the Sea of Reeds where, according to tradition, the pride of Egypt's army was decimated. It is hardly surprising that the Hyksos hordes were able subsequently to overcome the Egyptian state 'without striking a blow'. The latter's mobile defence force had recently been annihilated in a freak accident which had taken place during the pursuit of absconding Asiatic slaves somewhere in the area of the Bitter Lakes.

The King-Shepherds

Following the Israelite Exodus in the reign of Dudimose we are told by Manetho that the Black Land was invaded by people of obscure race, coming from the east. Who were these barbarous hordes that burned the cities and temples of Egypt and massacred the native population? The answer is to be found in the traditions of Islam.[15]

During their Sinai wanderings, the Israelite warriors, under the command of Joshua, had clashed in battle with the Amalekite forces and defeated them. Amongst the medieval authors of Arabia there is a tradition of the time when 'the Amalekites reached Syria and Egypt and took possession of these lands, and the tyrants of Syria and the pharaohs of Egypt were of their origin'. These authors, including EL-SAMHUDI (quoted above), MASUDI and ABU EL-FEDA, all identify the occupiers of Egypt with Amalekite tribesmen who came from Arabia (to the east of Egypt). Masudi tells us that the arrival of the Amalekites in the Nile valley bore all the hallmarks of a brutal invasion:

> The Amalekites invaded Egypt, the frontier of which they had already crossed, and started to ravage the

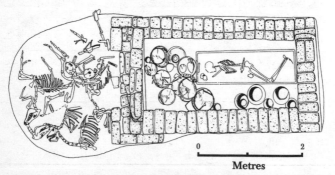

0   2

Metres

65. Plan of a typical Hyksos tomb at Tell ed-Daba with pottery in the mudbrick vaulted chamber and equid burials at the front of the tomb (reproduced by kind permission of M. Bietak).

Plate 44: The head and shoulders of a colossal statue of Akhenaten. Cairo Museum.

Plate 45: The ruins of the House of Correspondence of Pharaoh at Tell el-Amarna.

Plate 46: EA 252 from Labayu.

Plate 47: EA 256 from Mutbaal.

Plate 48 : Akhenaten. Luxor Museum.

Plate 49: EA 245 from Biridiya.

Plate 50: The village of Michmash viewed from Saul's high place at Gibeah.

Plate 51: The 'fields of treachery' atop Mount Gilboa.

Plate 52: The long, desolate mound of ancient Jericho.

Plate 53: Kenyon's Jericho trench showing the glacis (diagonal white line).

Plate 54: The MB II revetment wall of Jericho exposed by John Garstang in the 1930s (courtesy of the Palestine Exploration Fund).

Plate 55: David Rohl inspecting the archaeological section of the balk of Kenyon's Trench One at Jericho.

Plate 56: An aerial photograph of Area A at Hazor, showing (1) the six-chambered gate of stratum X; (2) the casemate wall of the same Iron Age stratum; (3) the entrance portico to the newly discovered Late Bronze Age palace; and (4) the north-eastern corner of the Middle Bronze Age palace.

Plate 57: Remains of the north-east corner of the MB palace already excavated by the archaeologists of the Hebrew University in Jerusalem. This is the palace from which the Ibni-Addu (Jabin) tablet originated, although the tablet was actually found in the excavators' spoil heap.

Plate 58: Amnon Ben Tor (right) and his site guardian, Alheib Hussein.

Plate 59: The Jabin tablet.

Plate 60: A panorama of the inner city of Shechem.

Plate 61: Part of the cyclopean fortress wall surrounding Shechem.

Plate 62: Joshua's covenant stone at Shechem.

country … to smash the objects of art, to ruin the monuments.

This story closely parallels that of Manetho's 'invaders of obscure race'. In his version the tribal origins of the invaders are not stated, but he does inform us that they hailed from the east. When Moses and the Israelites were journeying eastwards through Sinai they were confronted by an Amalekite army. Was this Arabian horde on its way into Egypt? If so, then Manetho's Hyksos invaders were one and the same as the Amalekites who clashed with the Israelites during the first year of the Wilderness Wanderings and, at the same time, can be recognised as the Amalekite invaders of Arabian tradition who became pharaohs of Egypt. These barbaric tribesmen cannot, however, be closely identified with the rulers of Avaris designated by Manetho as the 15th Dynasty and whom he states originated in Phoenicia. Remember that Salitis, the first pharaoh of that dynasty, fortified Avaris some considerable time after the initial invasion – the word 'finally' being used by Manetho to separate out the two events in time. Sir Alan GARDINER thought that an interval of half a century may have been involved.[16]

I am going to hold over my views on the quite different origins of the rulers of the 15th Dynasty for another time. The story of the 'Lords of Avaris' is an epic tale in its own right and merits a separate discussion of some length. For now I will designate them simply as the 'Greater Hyksos' whilst assigning the title 'Early Hyksos' to the warrior clans of the initial invasion whose rulers I equate with Manetho's 16th Dynasty of lesser 'King-Shepherds'.

There is one possible biblical reference to Egypt's Hyksos oppressors and this occurs in the Psalms.

He (i.e. God) loosed the full heat of his anger, fury, rage and destruction by sending **evil angels** against them (i.e. the Egyptians). [Psalm 78:49-50]

The context of this verse is that of God's final punishment following the calamitous events of Exodus. Who then are the 'evil angels' sent by God to destroy the Egyptians? Velikovsky again comes up with an interesting observation.[17] He notes that the phrase usually translated 'evil angels' is *malakhei-roim*, but the literal translation would then be 'angel of evils'. The correct Hebrew for 'evil angels' is *malakhim-roim*. Could it be that we have another textual corruption resulting from a misunderstanding on the part of the redactor? If the Psalmist, who originally composed this verse probably sometime in the tenth century BC, was aware of the agents of God's punishment of the Egyptians then he would have written the verse as follows:

> He loosed the full heat of his anger, fury, rage and destruction by sending an invasion of **king-shepherds** against them.

The phrase 'king-shepherds' in biblical Hebrew is *malakhei-roim*!

The warrior clansmen of the early Hyksos/Amalekite chieftains brought their families with them into Egypt because, according to the Arabian traditions, the disaster which had smitten Egypt had also desolated their own homeland, forcing the population to migrate to the relative safety and abundance of the Nile valley and delta.[18] These would be the Asiatic folk of Bietak's stratum F at Avaris who 'showed little Egyptian influence' and whose rich grave deposits included damning evidence of their plundering of the native Egyptian Middle Kingdom tombs. The mud-brick vaulted tombs of the stratum F males vividly reveal their Amalekite warriorlike character:

> Male burials with weapons show a warrior strain in the newcomers. Especially at the beginning, they possess very original features; some of them, indeed, look rather barbarous.[19]

Manetho informs us that the Hyksos 'treated all the natives with a cruel hostility, massacring some and leading into slavery the wives and children of others'. Archaeology has revealed that the stratum F warriors were accompanied by their servants into the next world. The graves at Tell ed-Daba, containing sacrificial burials of young females, provide us with further indications of the brutality of the early Hyksos invaders. It is, of course, difficult to identify unambiguously the unfortunate victims as Egyptian girls, but how chillingly these graves reflect Manetho's story of the Hyksos barbarians 'leading into slavery the wives and children' of the Egyptians massacred in the initial onslaught.

The abandoned suburbs of stratum G at Avaris were reoccupied by these Hyksos/Amalekite immigrants as temporary accommodation, prior to the building of their own new settlement (stratum E/3) over the ruins of the old Israelite town. The Amalekite population, along with other disparate Asiatic folk from southern Palestine and the Negev, remained at Avaris throughout the Hyksos period and were only removed from Egyptian soil as a consequence of the war of liberation led at first by the Theban pharaohs of the late 17th Dynasty and then finally by the victorious King Ahmose, founder of the New Kingdom.

Conclusion Twenty-Seven

The 'Early Hyksos' invaders of Egypt were Amalekite tribesmen who migrated through Sinai from northern Arabia. There they met the Israelites in battle. They then settled in the eastern delta and drove the Egyptian pharaohs back to their capital at Itj-Tawy in Upper Egypt. The Amalekites can be identified with the non-Egyptianised Asiatic newcomers who occupied Avaris at the beginning of stratum F.

Chapter Fourteen

THE WALLS CAME TUMBLIN' DOWN

he book of Exodus comes to an end with the death of Moses on Mount Nebo. The story of the Israelites is then picked up in the book of Joshua which narrates the Conquest of the Promised Land. The interval of forty years between the Exodus from Egypt and the crossing of the River Jordan into Palestine is another of those biblical round numbers and should be treated with caution. We may rightly be dealing with several decades for the Sinai wanderings but a figure of exactly forty years seems too neat. Using a date-range, and with the Exodus set at around 1447 BC, we might place the start of the Conquest between say 1420 and 1400. For simple convenience I will select 1410 BC. In archaeological terms we are still within the Middle Bronze Age – MB IIB to be precise. In Egyptian history, the Second Intermediate Period still has a full two centuries to run its course and the Greater Hyksos 15th Dynasty is more than a century from its foundation by Salitis. We are thus in the Early Hyksos period.

The first major act of the invading Israelites is the siege and destruction of Jericho at the southern end of the Jordan valley. This city is strategically located on the west bank of the Jordan by a lush oasis of palms. It protects the route up into the hill country of Palestine which Joshua and his forces must take to gain access to the heights of Canaan.[1]

Every child knows the story of the walls of Jericho which collapsed, affording the Israelites entry into the city to exact their bloody reprisal upon the population of the Promised Land. Many thousands of Jericho's citizens – men, women and children – were mercilessly slaughtered in the name of Yahweh on that terrible day.

Following the collapse of the city wall and the subsequent slaughter of the innocent, Jericho's houses were burnt to the ground and the site cursed with a long period of abandonment.

> Accursed before Yahweh be the man who rises up and rebuilds this city! On his first-born will he lay its foundations, on his youngest son set up its gates! [Joshua 6:26]

The curse was later fulfilled when, in the time of King Ahab, Hiel of Bethel built a residence on the ruin mound. By doing so Yahweh required two of Hiel's sons as his price for breaching the curse.

> It was in his (Ahab's) time that Hiel of Bethel rebuilt Jericho. Laying its foundations cost him his eldest son Abiram and erecting its gates cost him his youngest son Segub, just as had been foretold through Joshua son of Nun. [I Kings 16:34]

The Problem of Jericho

We now come to one of the principal reasons why biblical scholars and Levantine archaeologists have tended to abandon the view that the Old Testament, prior to the Monarchy period, is historically accurate. Back at the turn of the century archaeology in the Holy Land was beginning to get under way and much effort was concentrated on finding evidence for the biblical stories. Thus was born the now somewhat unfashionable enterprise known as 'Biblical Archaeology'. We have seen how and why it has become unfashionable: the last ninety years have provided embarrassingly little archaeological evidence which can be directly connected to the biblical traditions of a Conquest or wealthy United Monarchy period. Nowadays archaeologists working in the Holy Land prefer to call themselves Levantine archaeologists to avoid any direct association with what is, to all intents and purposes, a failed discipline. The failings of Biblical Archaeology were most clearly highlighted in the saga of the Jericho excavations. Here at Tell es-Sultan was a clear archaeological test of the veracity of the Conquest narrative. The mound had long been identified with the site of ancient Jericho; it could therefore be excavated and the city burnt by Joshua identified.

Serious excavations first began in 1907 with three seasons by an Austro-German expedition under the direction of the respected German biblical scholar Ernst Sellin. Professor John Garstang of Liverpool University was the next archaeologist to tackle the site between the years 1930 to 1936 and it was not very long before he was proclaiming the discovery of the fallen walls of Joshua's Jericho. He found a thick, reddish mudbrick city wall encircling the upper slopes of Tell es-Sultan and in places it appeared as if this wall had indeed collapsed.[2] At last one of the biblical stories seemed to be confirmed: Jericho's wall had come tumblin' down!

Over the years further work was undertaken at other sites thought to be the cities conquered and destroyed by the Israelites. Gradually a picture was emerging which appeared to conform to the understanding scholars had of the Joshua campaign. Of course, by this time, archaeologists were looking for a series of destructions which post dated the time of Ramesses II, because it was this Egyptian king who had already been cast as the Pharaoh of the Oppression and hapless Pharaoh of the Exodus. In archaeological terms this meant that Joshua's wholesale destruction of the cities of Canaan had to be sought in the strata marking the end of the Late Bronze Age (contemporary with the late 19th and early 20th Dynasties). The early Israelite settlement of Palestine was thus placed in the Early Iron Age (or Iron Age I). There are indeed widespread city destructions at around this time but gradually it has become clear that these destructions span a period of more than a century and so cannot all have been the work of Joshua and his men.

At the time of Garstang's Jericho dig the archaeological phases had not yet been so well defined. It took the follow-up excavation by Dame Kathleen Kenyon of the Institute of Archaeology, London, to put the record straight. It was her discoveries at Jericho which would have such a crucial influence on the late twentieth century's rejection of the 'historical' Bible.

Kenyon began work at Tell es-Sultan in 1952. She excavated a series of deep trenches which cut through the outer slope of the mound. By using this technique Kenyon was able to study the side balks of the trenches to record what was effectively a chronological and stratigraphical chart of the city's life. The lowest level or stratum in a mound is the earliest and the uppermost the latest. Ancient Near Eastern city mounds or tells are generally formed by the gradual deposition of occupation levels, one on top of the other, giving an inner structure somewhat like a layer cake. If an archaeologist then comes along and cuts himself a slice of that cake the various layers can easily be seen. With an occupational mound this method gives you a good idea of the chronological development of the site but fails to provide much indication as to the cultural content of any specific stratum. For that one needs to open out a larger area and peel off each level as the excavation team slowly works down into the mound. This technique employs a grid of five- or ten-metre squares, each with its own set of balk walls in which the chronological profile of the city can be plotted. Kenyon used this technique for a small area on the eastern side of the tell where the mound profile suggested Late Bronze Age occupation might be found.

Kenyon's detailed stratigraphical analysis of Jericho's occupational history demonstrated that Garstang's walls in reality belonged to the Early Bronze Age, a thousand years before the time of Joshua. The problem for Kenyon was that her work produced no walls belonging to the Late Bronze Age or Early Iron Age. In fact, her analysis seemed to show that there was no Late Bronze Age city of Jericho at all which the Israelites could have destroyed during their entry into the Promised Land. There was evidence for a small Late Bronze Age village but this certainly had no defensive fortifications that could conceivably represent the walls which came 'tumblin' down'. In the orthodox chronology most of the mound of Jericho had already been a desolate ruin (with occasional meagre settlement) for several centuries by the time the Israelite tribes crossed the Jordan. In the late 1950s there was only one conclusion which could be drawn from Kenyon's discovery: the story of Joshua's conquest of Jericho had to be a myth.

Conclusion Twenty-Eight

There was no walled city of Jericho during the Late Bronze Age when, in the conventional chronology, the Israelites were supposed to have massacred the population and burnt the city to the ground.

You may now be ahead of me. If Jericho was at best an unfortified village at the end of the Late Bronze Age, then when was it a thriving city with impressive defensive fortifications? The answer, of course, is some three hundred and fifty years earlier in the Middle Bronze Age when the New Chronology places the Israelite Conquest. So, let us now take a look at what Kenyon found for Middle Bronze Age Jericho.

In her deep cuttings through the outer slopes of the mound Kenyon was able to trace a thin plaster surface sloping down from the top of the trench. Archaeologists call this feature a 'glacis'. The idea of the builders was to create a slippery gradient beneath the main city wall which was constructed at the top of the outer slope of the mound. This had many functions including preventing the access of chariots and battering rams to the base of the main wall; making the undermining of the city wall by sappers much more difficult; exposing an enemy assault to the scaling of a treacherous 'killing field' immediately beneath the defenders' archery positions atop the main city wall; and, most practically, retaining the loose debris of the city mound behind a ten-centimetre sheath of plaster to prevent land slippage and thus a natural undermining of the heavy mud-brick wall at the crest of the slope.

Near to the bottom of her cuttings Kenyon observed that the glacis came to a sudden end and that beneath it the builders had constructed a wall of FIELD STONES. Beyond this 'REVETMENT wall' was a deep trench, no doubt intended to slow down any assault upon the lower slopes of the mound. The very top of the Jericho tell has been badly eroded by centuries of weathering. As a result remains of the Middle Bronze Age city wall no longer exist to any great extent. However, remember that the walls of Joshua's Jericho came tumblin' down. Where would they have tumbled down to? The bottom of the glacis slope is the obvious answer! In the trench at the foot of the mound Kenyon found a thick deposit of red-brown earth which she interpreted as the remains of the great MB city wall which had collapsed outwards and fallen down into the defensive ditch. The walls of MBA Jericho had indeed tumbled down, thus affording any attacker easy access into the city by filling up the ditch which protected the base of Jericho's elaborate defensive system.

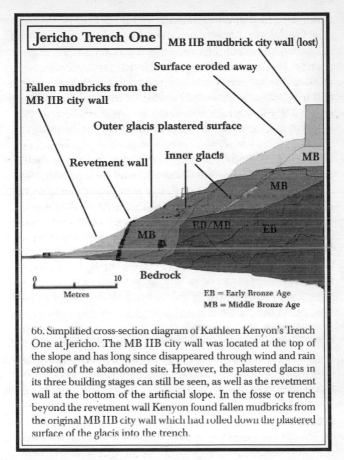

66. Simplified cross-section diagram of Kathleen Kenyon's Trench One at Jericho. The MB IIB city wall was located at the top of the slope and has long since disappeared through wind and rain erosion of the abandoned site. However, the plastered glacis in its three building stages can still be seen, as well as the revetment wall at the bottom of the artificial slope. In the fosse or trench beyond the revetment wall Kenyon found fallen mudbricks from the original MB IIB city wall which had rolled down the plastered surface of the glacis into the trench.

Within the MBA city itself all the houses and civic buildings had been blackened by a severe conflagration. In some places the ash and debris was a metre in depth.[3]

> They (the Israelites) burned the city and everything inside it, except the silver, the gold and the things of bronze and iron; these they put in the treasury of Yahweh's house. [Joshua 6:24]

According to Joshua 3:15 the assault upon Jericho took place during the harvest season in the Jordan valley. When Garstang uncovered the floors of the houses of the MBA city he found large storage jars filled to the brim with carbonised grain.[4]

Evidence of mass burials in the rock-cut tombs of MBA Jericho, contemporary with the very last phase of the city's existence, suggested to Kenyon that a plague had struck in the period immediately prior to its destruction.[5] The abundance of food in the city ruled out famine and there were no visible signs on the skeletal remains of war wounds. Her archaeological interpretation of a Jericho plague provides another striking parallel with the biblical narratives. We learn from the book of Numbers, verse 25, that the Israelites themselves were devastated by a plague, whilst they were encamped at Shittim in Transjordan, immediately prior to their assault upon Jericho. Twenty-four thousand Israelites were struck down. It is just possible that the plague may have been brought into Jericho by Joshua's spies – sent to reconnoitre the city's defences – where they were protected by the prostitute, Rahab, in her 'house of ill-repute'. Indeed the Shittim plague was associated with widespread sexual intercourse which had been going on between Israelite men and Moabite prostitutes prior to the invasion.[6]

I will let archaeologist Piotr Bienkowski sum up Kenyon's analysis of the fate of MBA Jericho.

> Jericho was destroyed at the end of the MBA, probably by enemy action and possibly through a failure of the fortification system. Perhaps there was a fatal flaw in the design of the fortifications, … The reason for the destruction of Jericho is unknown.[7]

Bienkowski's last sentence no longer applies thanks to the work of Dr. John Bimson, which I will now come on to, and the revised archaeological date for the destruction of

MBA Jericho provided by the New Chronology. Both have determined that Middle Bronze Age Jericho was attacked and destroyed by invading Israelites.

Conclusion Twenty-Nine

Biblical Jericho, destroyed by Joshua's forces, is to be identified with the Middle Bronze Age city at Tell es-Sultan which was devastated by fire and remained a desolate ruin for several centuries thereafter.

Relocating the Archaeology of the Conquest

During the 1970s, in preparation for his doctoral thesis (which was subsequently reworked into a book entitled *Redating the Exodus and Conquest*[8]), John Bimson undertook a detailed analysis of the archaeological evidence for a Middle Bronze Age Conquest of the Promised Land. Much of the material we are now going to touch upon stems from that research. I have known John for well over a decade and have followed his pioneering work with much interest. In essence, he proposes to date the Israelite entry into Canaan to the time of the widespread city destructions usually assigned to the end of the MBA. Needless to say, I find his arguments compelling. He has clearly shown that the cities which the biblical narrative records as being destroyed by Joshua were indeed burnt at this time. Equally, those cities which the Israelites left untouched were not burnt according to the archaeological evidence. The Bible and archaeology thus appear to be consistent. This is in marked contrast to the situation at the end of the Late Bronze Age when there is a clear conflict between the biblical narrative of the Conquest and the archaeological record. If one studies the table on page 368 we see that the

Shoshenk I's Campaign List		
11. Gilead	26. Tanaach	47. Bethdabu[ma]
12. M[akkedah]	27. Megiddo	48-51. [Lost]
13. Rubuti	28. Adar	52. Abel[meholah?]
14. Aijalon	29. Yadhamelek	53. {P]enuel
15. Kiriathaim?	30. [Heb]el?	54. Hedeshet
16. Bethhoron	31. Honim?	55. Succoth?
17. Gibeon	32. Aruna	56. Adam[ah]
18. Mahanaim	33. Borim	57. Zemaraim
19. Shaud[y]?	34. Gathpadalla	58. [M]igdol (Shechem?)
20. [Lost]	35. Yahma	59. [Ti]rzah
21. Adoraim?	36. Betharuma	60. [...]nar
22. Hapharaim	37. Kekry?	61-63. [Lost]
23. Rehob	38. Socoh	64. H[...]pen
24. Bethshan	39. Bethtappuah?	65. Pa-Emek ('The Vale')
25. Shunem	40-46. [Lost]	

Opposite page: a map of Palestine showing the campaign route of Shoshenk I in its new context – a retaliatory strike against Aramaean raids into Transjordan, the Jezreel valley and the coastal plain in *circa* 800 BC.

key sites of Jericho, Debir (Tell Beit Mirsim), Lachish, Bethel, Gibeon, and Hazor all suffer destruction by fire during the MBA but only Hazor suffers the same fate in the LBA. Moreover, recent archaeological work at Hazor has shown that the LBA destruction occurred a century before the time of the Conquest in the orthodox chronology, leaving us without a burnt layer to proclaim as the work of the Israelites![9]

A comprehensive survey of the central hill country of Palestine has revealed that the new Early Iron Age settlements which are attributed to the incoming Israelite tribes are heavily concentrated in the territory of Ephraim and Manasseh – that is north of Jerusalem but south of the Jezreel valley.[10] The influx of settlers appears to originate from the north and north-east whereas the Israelite entry into the Promised Land was from the south-east (at Jericho) according to the biblical narrative. Here is yet another contradiction between the archaeological findings and the

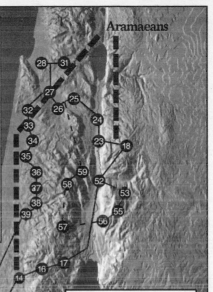

At that time Hazael king of Aram went to war against Gath, and captured it; he then prepared to attack Jerusalem. Jehoash king of Judah took all the sacred offerings dedicated by his ancestors, the kings of Judah, … he sent it all to Hazael king of Aram, who retired from Jerusalem. [II Kings 12:18 19]

Aramaeans

Judah

At that time Yahweh began to whittle Israel down, and Hazael defeated the Israelites throughout the territory east of the Jordan: the whole territory of Gilead – of the Gadites, the Reubenites and the Manassehites – from Aroer on the River Arnon: Gilead and Bashan. [II Kings 10-32-33]

Negev Campaign

Jehoahaz, however, tried to placate Yahweh, and Yahweh heard him, for he had seen the oppression which the king of Aram was inflicting on Israel. Yahweh gave Israel a saviour who freed them from the grip of Aram, and the Israelites lived in their tents as in the past. [II Kings 13:4-5]

367

Biblical City	Extant in LB II B	Extant in MB IIB	Destroyed in MB IIB
Jericho (T. es-Sultan)	No	Yes	Yes
Ai (et-Tell?)	No	No	No
Ai (Khirbet Nisya?)	No	Yes	Abandoned
Gibeon (el-Jib)	No	Yes	Abandoned
Hebron (el-Khalil)	No	Yes	Yes
Hebron (T. el-Rumeideh)	?	?	?
Hormah (T. el-Meshash)	No	Yes	Uncertain
Arad (T. Arad)	No	Yes	Yes
Debir (T. Beit Mirsim)	Yes	Yes	Yes
Lachish (T. ed-Duweir)	Yes	Yes	Yes
Hazor (T. el-Kedah)	Yes	Yes	Yes
Bethel (Beitin?)	Yes	Yes	Yes
Bethel (el-Bireh?)	?	?	?

A comparison between the end of the MB IIB and LB II in Palestine showing that the MB IIB destructions fit the Conquest narratives far better than those of the LB II. At the end of the MB II only the city of Ai does not fit the pattern of destructions described in the book of Joshua; however, et-Tell does not fit the LB II scenario either and may not therefore be the site of the historical Ai. Otherwise there is an 80% agreement between the MB II archaeological results and the Joshua Conquest narratives. On the other hand, with the LB II archaeological results there is a huge discrepancy with over 60% of the sites not matching the pattern of destructions described in the book of Joshua.

Bible. However, in the New Chronology there is a ready explanation for the impoverished Iron Age settlements discovered by the survey.

In the Divided Monarchy period the kingdom of Israel was invaded by marauding Aramaeans who set about attacking and burning the towns of Galilee, the Jezreel and Gilead (in Transjordan). This era in Israelite history, often referred to as the 'Aramaean Supremacy', is dated to *circa* 841 to 798 BC – the very time of Iron Age I in the New Chronology. The Aramaeans are then repelled when Israel is sent a 'saviour' [II Kings 13:5] in the guise of Pharaoh Shoshenk I and his Egyptian army. As we have seen, Shoshenk's campaign was mainly directed east of the River Jordan and in the Jezreel valley. Now we know why. His objective was to protect Egypt's allies within its old sphere of influence and to repulse the northern invader – Hazael of Damascus. The sudden increase in new settlements in Iron Age IA are a direct result of Aramaean military sorties into the territory of Israel during the reigns of JEHU and JEHOAHAZ. The population increase in the central hill country is thus the result of a refugee movement from the outlying areas of the kingdom into the heartland of Israel where protection was at hand. The reason for the concentration of settlements in Ephraim and Manasseh is obvious: this area was the nearest bolt-hole from Gilead and was immediately south of the Jezreel lowlands where the Aramaeans were rampaging. A synthesis between archaeology and biblical history is once more attainable by application of the New Chronology.

Conclusion Thirty

The Early Iron Age settlements of the central hill country of Palestine are not evidence of early Israelite settlement in the Promised Land but rather represent the refugee settlements from the Aramaean Supremacy which brought the Kingdom of Israel to crisis point towards the end of the ninth century BC. Israel's 'saviour' was Shoshenk I who campaigned in Transjordan and the Jezreel valley in order to put an end to the Aramaean incursions into the Egyptian sphere of influence.

The arguments of relative stratigraphy are complex and open to much disagreement. However, it is certainly reasonable to argue, as John Bimson has done, that the orthodox archaeological date for the Conquest/settlement does not produce anything like a consistent picture, whereas the Middle Bronze Age date finds a close match between the archaeological evidence and the biblical tradition.

Of course, John was working within the conventional dating scheme but employing the 'high' Exodus date of 1447 BC rather than the most popular 'low' date of *circa* 1250 BC. In doing so he was obliged to place the Exodus event in the mid 18th Dynasty when most scholars would assert the LBA was well under way. This meant that he was forced to argue for a relocation of the MBA destruction horizon from the very beginning of the New Kingdom (*c.* 1550 BC) down to the reign of Thutmose III or thereabouts (*c.* 1447 BC). This in turn required either a century-long overlap of the late MBA with the early LBA or a radical reduction in the length of the LB I phase. Neither proposal has been widely accepted although Bietak has also recently argued for an overlap of MB II and LB I based on the Tell ed-Daba evidence. My feelings are that there may well be some mileage in this second hypothesis. It does appear likely that the population of the hill country of Canaan in the period of the early 18th Dynasty (LB I) continued to use pottery which was indistinguishable from that used in the latter part of the Middle Bronze Age.

The New Chronology postulates that the Exodus took place during the 13th Dynasty (that is at the end of the archaeological phase known as MB IIA). The Conquest would then have taken place during the MB IIB. Moreover, our new dating for the Hyksos period places that Conquest well before the foundation of the Greater Hyksos 15th Dynasty. I should now demonstrate how this might be possible using evidence from the Middle Bronze Age tombs at Jericho.

A Hyksos Named Sheshi

In addition to excavating the mound of Tell es-Sultan, Kenyon cleared a number of rock-cut tombs belonging to Jericho's MBA cemetery. In these rock-cut sepulchres she found an astonishing array of funeral equipment, including wooden beds and tables, reed baskets, quantities of pottery and some fine jewellery. The scene which greeted her each time she entered one of the chambers was always the same – complete chaos! These family tombs had been in constant use for over a century, reopened upon the death of a family member for internment with his/her ancestors. The practice was to push the remains of the previous burial (including the skeleton) to the sides of the chamber so as to create a clear space at the centre for the new burial. From an archaeological standpoint this made a precise dating of the finds rather difficult. However Kenyon was a good archaeologist and designed a method of dating objects by contextual association with a particular pottery SERIATION.

As we have seen from the Tell ed-Daba excavations, a very distinctive type of juglet was manufactured during the Middle Bronze Age which has been labelled 'Tell el-Yahudiya Ware'. These small black pots show a general pattern of development from the piriform shape to the cylindrical. By analysing the proportion of piriform to cylindrical juglets in each tomb Kenyon was able to place the burials into five chronological categories which she numbered Group I (earliest) to Group V (latest). Since Kenyon's pioneering work at Jericho the scheme has been slightly modified by scholars such as Israeli archaeologist Aharon Kempinski so that her Groups II and III have been made roughly contemporary whilst the same applies to Groups IV and V.[11] In spite of the general shortcomings of Kenyon's Jericho tomb assignments, archaeologists continue to use her five-phase grouping as a framework for dating the historical life of MBA Jericho and so I shall retain the practice here. The following key finds from the tombs enable us to date the burial groups to Egyptian history.

1. Babylonian cylinder seals stylistically typical of the period of Hammurabi, or slightly earlier, appear in tombs classified as Group II. As Hammurabi was a contemporary of Neferhotep I, the twenty-first pharaoh

of the 13th Dynasty, we may assign Group II to the first half of the 13th Dynasty.

2. In a Group III tomb Kenyon recovered a scarab bearing the name of Kahotepre Sobekhotep V, twenty-fourth pharaoh of the 13th Dynasty and the immediate successor of Sobekhotep IV. Sobekhotep V ruled for less than five years and so it is unlikely that the scarab was the treasured heirloom of a great ancestral king. Its presence in a collection of funeral goods would tend to date the burial to his reign or not significantly later. Thus the appearance of the Sobekhotep V scarab in a Group III tomb roughly dates this phase of the cemetery to the time of Moses' exile in Sinai, following his flight from Egypt in the reign of Khaneferre Sobekhotep IV.

3. In Tomb H13, belonging to the last phase of burials (Group V), we have the very important discovery of a scarab bearing the name of the Hyksos king, Sheshi. From the archaeological contexts of other scarabs of this ruler, found in both Palestine and Egypt, and the development of scarab design, Aharon Kempinski[12] and William Ward[13] have placed the reign of Sheshi near the beginning of the 15th Dynasty. Numerous Sheshi scarabs were found by Petrie at Tell el-Ajjul in the earliest phase of City II. As we have seen, City II is now identified with the Hyksos citadel of Sharuhen, its destruction level being contemporary with the fall of the 15th Dynasty. Sheshi cannot therefore be dated to the end of the 15th Dynasty but rather to a much earlier period at the beginning of the life of Hyksos Sharuhen. It is important to remember that Kempinski and Ward were both working under the premise that the 15th Dynasty followed soon after the reign of Pharaoh Dudimose. They did not have an 'Early Hyksos' dynasty in which to place Sheshi because the conventional chronology was forced to allocate a much shorter time

span to the SIP than is now possible in the New Chronology. (Bietak and other Middle Bronze Age specialists have all commented that the archaeology of the MBA appears to require a longer chronology than is currently permissible within the orthodox scheme.) It seems clear to me that Sheshi was a ruler of the Early Hyksos period and that Jericho Group V must be dated to that era rather than the Greater Hyksos period which followed. I will return to Sheshi and his dating shortly.

4. Although it is an argument *ex silentio*, I think it is also crucial to note that no Bichrome Ware was found in the tombs of the MBA cemetery at Jericho — it is 'completely missing' from the pottery corpus.[14] This suggests that the burials ceased before this type of pottery was introduced into Palestine. I am by no means the first to make this point. As John Bartlett notes:

> … the important point for our purpose is that Jericho, along with other sites of southern and central Palestine (Tell Beit Mirsim, Tell Gezer, Shiloh, Bethel and Gibeon), does not show any sign of having used the bichrome ware and imported Cypriot pottery. The explanation is not simply that Jericho was a backwater in the Jordan valley which bichrome ware, spreading inland from the coast, failed to reach, for that leaves its failure to reach places like Tell Beit Mirsim unexplained, and in any case it is not just bichrome ware but a whole range of pottery of the period that is missing from Jericho. The obvious explanation is that there was a break in the occupation of the tell after the destruction of the MB II city.[15]

As I have already stated, Bichrome Ware has been found both at Tell ed-Daba and throughout the Levant in strata datable to the late 15th Dynasty in Egypt. All the Group V burials at Jericho must therefore be dated prior to the end of the Hyksos period.

The relative dating of Kenyon's tomb-groups against Egyptian history may thus be tabulated as follows:

Group I – Late 12th Dynasty (NC – 1650-1600 BC)
Group II – Early 13th Dynasty (NC – 1600-1530 BC)
Group III – Mid 13th Dynasty (NC – 1530-1490 BC)
Group IV – Late 13th Dynasty (NC – 1490-1450 BC)
Group V – Late 13th Dynasty/Early Hyksos (NC – 1450-1410 BC)

In archaeological terms Group I is MB IIA; Groups II & III (remembering Kempinski's observation that III is indistinguishable from II) are effectively the transition phase between MB IIA and MB IIB; whilst IV and V cover the early part of MB IIB.

67. A large Late Bronze Age Bichrome Ware crater found in the early 18th Dynasty level at Tell ed-Daba i.e. Avaris (reproduced by courtesy of M. Bietak).

It is clear from Kenyon's work that the last phase of Group V in the cemetery was contemporary with the massive destruction of MBA Jericho. Indeed, Tomb H13 containing the scarab of Sheshi is, in the archaeologists' view, one of the very last interments made by the citizens of Jericho. We have noted the occurrence of multiple burials just prior to the city's demise and Tomb H13 was one of the sepulchres utilised for this purpose. Kempinski has thus argued that Jericho fell soon after, or during, the reign of King Sheshi, some considerable time before the end of the Middle Bronze Age.[16] He also made one other very interesting observation regarding this shadowy Hyksos ruler which now has direct relevance to our MBA Conquest date. Kempinski noted that the name Sheshi actually occurs in the narratives dealing with the distribution of land to the victorious Israelite tribes – in particular the story of the expulsion of the three Anakite rulers from the kingdom of Hebron.

> Caleb son of Jephunneh was given a share within that of the sons of Judah, in accordance with Yahweh's order to Joshua: Kiriath-Arba, the town of the father of Anak – that is, Hebron. Caleb drove out the three sons of Anak: **Sheshai**, Ahiman and Talmai, descended from Anak. From there he marched on the inhabitants of Debir; Debir in olden days was called Kiriath-Sepher. [Joshua 15:13-15]

These same chieftains had been ruling the Hebron region at the time Moses was bringing his people out of Sinai.

> Yahweh spoke to Moses and said, 'Send out men, one from each tribe, to reconnoitre the land of Canaan which I am giving the Israelites. Each of them is to be a leading man of the tribe.' At Yahweh's order, Moses sent them from the desert of Paran. … They went up by way of the Negeb as far as

Hebron, where Ahiman, **Sheshai** and Talmai, the
Anakim, lived. [Numbers 13:1-3 & 22]

The biblical name of one of the Anakim of Kiriath-Arba/
Hebron – Sheshai – is identical to the nomen Sheshi
inscribed on numerous MBA scarabs found in southern
Palestine. Could it be that the Jericho Tomb H13 scarab of
Sheshi is connected with this Sheshai of Hebron? It is
commonly assumed that the Hyksos rulers of Palestine
copied their Egyptian delta kin in the use of the scarab
design for their ring-seals. In doing so, they employed crude
hieroglyphs to spell out their names on the underside or
base of the scarabs. This inscribed surface could then be
pressed into a pottery jar. Not all scarabs were therefore of
Egyptian manufacture.

It is quite possible then that Sheshi, whose scarabs certainly predominate in southern Palestine, may not have
(initially) ruled directly from Egypt but rather from the
Hyksos domains to the north of Sinai. The attack of Caleb
and his army may have driven the Hyksos chieftain to the
safety of Sharuhen or even into Egypt itself. One of the
best attested Early Hyksos rulers may thus have been a
refugee from the Israelite assault on the Promised Land.

Kempinski recognised the possibility that Sheshai of
Hebron may be one and the same as Sheshi the Hyksos
chieftain – but only in the sense that somehow a piece of
Hebronite Hyksos history had been transferred into the
biblical tradition of Caleb's expulsion of the Anakim from
Hebron 'about 500 years after he actually ruled':

In both Joshua 15:14 and Judges 1:10, we are told
that Caleb defeated and destroyed 'Sheshai, Ahiman
and Talmai,' the three Anakites from Hebron, as if
the three had lived in Caleb's time rather than in
the Hyksos period. We have here an excellent illustration of the way the Biblical writer uses traditional
materials.[17]

Once again it is the conventional chronology which gets in the way of a straightforward historical synchronism. In the New Chronology there is no such problem: the biblical Sheshai of Hebron and the historical Sheshi are indeed identical – precisely because the events of the Conquest and the stratigraphical horizon containing the so-called Hyksos scarabs are contemporary.

Conclusion Thirty-One

The Hyksos ruler Maibre Sheshi, whose nomen appears on numerous MBA scarabs from southern Palestine (and in Tomb H13 at Jericho), is to be identified with the biblical king Sheshai of Hebron who was forced to flee from his homeland because of the recent invasion of the Israelite tribes from the east in *circa* 1410 BC. The archaeological concentration of Sheshi scarabs at Tell el-Ajjul in southern coastal Palestine indicates that he fled to Sharuhen. There he probably built 'City II' and a new royal residence ('Palace II') for the Early Hyksos dynasty of southern Palestine of which he was the founder.

Jericho Resettled

Before we leave Jericho I would like to add a couple of further potential points of consistency between the New Chronology and the archaeological record. During Garstang's excavations at Tell es-Sultan he uncovered a substantial building near the summit of the mound. The archaeological date of this structure has been notoriously difficult to pin down but the general feeling is that Late Bronze IIA is most likely.[18]

In the New Chronology the end of LB IIA is the time of David and Solomon in Israel (*c.* 1010-931 BC). It is interesting to note therefore that the next time we hear mention of Jericho after Joshua's destruction of the town is during the reign of David. In II Samuel 10 the king sends his ambassadors to Hanun son of Nahash, ruler of the Ammonites. But, Hanun insults David by cutting off the beards of the Israelite representatives before sending them home. The embarrassment to the Davidic court was too great to allow their return to Jerusalem so David told his delegation to 'Stay in Jericho … until your beards have grown again and come back then' [II Samuel 10:5].

We may envisage in this strange folktale some temporary occupation of the ruin-mound at Jericho, lasting a few years, for a limited group of David's courtiers. This fits nicely with Garstang's 'Middle Building' which was abandoned within a short period of its construction.

The next phase of occupation at Jericho is during the Late Bronze IIB when there is limited evidence of some construction work on the mound, including what may have been a small palace. The village – for that is all it could have been – remained unfortified, although it may have had a perimeter ring of houses as was the case with some Late Bronze Age settlements. Now let me remind you of the passage in I Kings 16:34 where we hear of the rebuilding of Jericho during the reign of King Ahab.

It was in his time that Hiel of Bethel rebuilt Jericho. Laying its foundations cost him his eldest son Abiram and erecting its gates cost him his youngest son Segub, just as Yahweh had foretold through Joshua son of Nun.

Ahab's reign is dated in the New Chronology to the time of the late 19th Dynasty in Egypt – in other words the very end of the Late Bronze Age.

> ### Conclusion Thirty-Two
>
> Garstang's 'Middle Building' at Jericho is to be identified as the residence of David's ambassadors, following their unsuccessful embassy to Ammon in Transjordan. The later LB IIB village represents the rebuilding of Jericho by Hiel (*c.* 850 BC) during the reign of Ahab.

Jabin, King of Hazor

In 1992 the joint Israeli/Spanish archaeological mission at Hazor (Tell el-Kedah) discovered a fragment of clay tablet which further supports our chronological placement of the Conquest during the Middle Bronze Age. Field Director Professor Amnon Ben Tor of the Hebrew University of Jerusalem has been concentrating his team's efforts on the 'Upper City' where the royal residences of the kings of Hazor were located throughout the site's history. A combination of the Upper (royal) City with the huge rectangular compound of the 'Lower City' makes Hazor unequivocally one of the largest population centres in the Levant during the MBA. Correspondence (over twenty letters) from the royal archives at Zimrilim's Mari indicate that Hazor was a major trading partner with Mesopotamia (in particular Babylon), demonstrating its influence in the northern Levant. The Middle Bronze Age kings of Hazor were without doubt the most powerful city-state rulers in Canaan.

In spite of the fact that it receives less coverage in the book of Joshua than the conquests of Jericho and Ai, there can be little doubt that the Israelite defeat of the northern city-state coalition was a very significant event in the settlement of the Promised Land. The focus of this major military action is an assault upon Hazor. Unlike most of the other campaigns where the city-rulers remain anonymous (except for the three rulers of Hebron and Horam of Gezer), here we are given the name of the king of Hazor – Jabin – and his ally, the ruler of Merom – Jobab.

When news of the success of the Israelite assault on southern Canaan reaches Jabin he calls upon all the city-state rulers of the north to assemble their forces so that they can confront the Israelites and destroy them. The armies of Hazor, Merom, Shimron, Achshaph and the lesser towns are gathered together at the Waters of Merom. This formidable force is 'as numerous as the sands of the sea, with a huge number of horses and chariots'. According to Joshua 11:10 'Hazor in olden days was the capital of all these kingdoms' and it is this great city which pays the high price of defeat at the hands of Joshua's warriors. With the surprise attack of the Israelites at Merom the Canaanite coalition is routed and Joshua moves to take Hazor. There he puts King Jabin to the sword and once again Yahweh demands his blood sacrifice for guaranteeing the Israelite victory.

> In compliance with the curse of destruction, they put every living creature there to the sword. Not a living soul was left, and Hazor was burnt to the ground. [Joshua 11:11]

But how does the story of the destruction of Hazor as told in the book of Joshua compare with what Professor Ben-Tor is currently unearthing in the Upper City? Ever since excavations began in the 1920s with Garstang's tentative soundings it has been known that there are several layers of conflagration at Tell el-Kedah. The major destruction observed at the end of stratum XVI included a severe conflagration which produced a metre of ash and debris – also found in the equivalent stratigraphic horizon of the Lower City. This stratum XVI marks the end of the MBA city and, in the New Chronology, would be the city destroyed by Joshua.

In 1955 Israel's most famous archaeologist, Yigael Yadin began his epic series of digs at Hazor. The site became the training ground for modern Israeli archaeology. Over five seasons of work his team included Aharoni, Amiran, M. Dothan, T. Dothan, Dunayevsky, Epstein, Perrot, Shiloh, Mazar and Ben-Tor himself. These are some of the most famous names in recent biblical archaeology. Many great discoveries were made by Yadin's team but one in particular interested the director above all in the last decade of his life. Unfortunately ill health prevented him from personally investigating the object of his interest and so it was left to Ben-Tor to fulfil Yadin's great ambition – to uncover the huge Middle Bronze Age palace of the kings of Hazor.

The resources of the current expedition have been concentrated in Area A on the upper tell. It was here that Yadin uncovered the gate to the royal compound of the Iron Age and the famous pillared building so often used to illustrate the archaeology of Hazor in popular guide books of Israel. What is not widely known is that Yadin made a limited sounding on the northern side of the pillared building to determine what lay beneath it. There the Israelis found the corner of a major structure with massive walls made of mudbrick laid over stone foundations.[19] Years after the excavations at Hazor were completed a young boy came across a fragment of clay tablet lying in the excavation rubbish removed from Yadin's sounding. The tablet appeared to come from an archive which subsequent analysis of the cuneiform text showed must have belonged to the Middle Bronze Age administrative complex of Hazor. Yadin quickly realised that the thick walls, which lie almost entirely beneath the later pillared building and surrounding Iron Age structures, must belong to the palace of the MBA kings of Hazor and that fresh excavations would almost certainly reveal one of the most important archives in the ancient world.

Yadin died in 1984 before getting the chance to prove his theory, but three seasons of work in the Upper City by

68. Tablet A2/3423/92/17-23086, discovered at Hazor, mentioning a King Ibni (biblical Jabin). The writing indicates that the tablet originated from an archive of the Middle Bronze Age palace.

the Israeli/Spanish mission has brought them to the archaeological horizon just above the MBA palace. In doing so they had to remove the pillared building from its original location and re-erect it on another part of the site – a difficult and time-consuming task. The reward for their effort is that in the 1992 season objects from the MBA were just beginning to surface. This is where a new tablet fragment discovered in that year comes into the story. It would appear to belong to the stratum XVI palace whose city was destroyed by fire during the Middle Bronze Age. The broken text reads as follows:

> To **Ibni-[Addu]** … Thus Irpa [says] … Regarding bringing the young woman in the care of … A certain woman, Aba … Raised objections [against] … Thus she (said): 'Until …[20]

Ben-Tor realised that the name of the addressee, Ibni-Addu, was the ruler of Hazor at the time the letter was written. The name 'Ibni' is the equivalent of Hebrew 'Yabin' – the biblical name 'Jabin'. So, the name of the ruler of Hazor found on a tablet datable to the palace and the city destroyed by fire during the MBA is the same as that of the king of Hazor killed by Joshua who then burnt the city to the ground.[21]

Conclusion Thirty-Three

The city destroyed by Joshua's army was MB IIB Hazor, burnt at the end of stratum XVI. The Middle Bronze Age ruler of Hazor, Ibni, whose name appears on Tablet A2/3423/92/ 17-23086, may therefore be identified with King Jabin of Hazor who was put to the sword by the Israelites in Joshua 11:10.

Shiloh and the Ark of the Covenant

One excellent way to test out the New Chronology date for the Israelite settlement during MB IIB is to analyse the excavations on the sacred hill of Shiloh, thirty kilometres north of Jerusalem. Shiloh was the site chosen by the Israelite tribes as the home of the Ark of the Covenant immediately after the Conquest. There they established the great tented shrine which contained the casket of the Laws of Moses.

The site of Shiloh (KHIRBET Seilun) was first excavated by the Danes in 1922 and again from 1926 to 1932.[22] A third series of campaigns was initiated in 1981 by the Israelis under the directorship of Professor Israel Finkelstein of Tel Aviv University.[23] Let us now compare the excavation results with what we know of the history of the site from the Bible. I will use archaeologist Finkelstein's own words to describe what he unearthed.[24]

- **(a)** 'Shiloh was first occupied in the period archaeologists call the Middle Bronze Age IIB.' **(b)** In the New Chronology the Israelites entered the Promised Land during MB IIB.

- **(a)** 'Perhaps the most intriguing aspect of the Middle

Bronze Age finds is that, already in this period, there appears to have been a shrine at the site.' (**b**) Of course there was, because this is precisely the time when the Israelites erected the sacred TEMENOS of the Ark at Shiloh.

- (**a**) 'Shiloh thus joins several other sacred Israelite places where a cultic tradition had existed continuously ever since the Middle Bronze Age – long before the Israelite settlement in the 12th-11th centuries BC.' (**b**) These 'sacred ... places' do not predate the Israelite settlement at all – they are the Israelite sacred sites. The early Israelites were the carriers of the Middle Bronze Age culture of the central hill country.

- (**a**) '... people from all over the region must have participated in the building activities at Shiloh – a possibility that casts an interesting light on the city's importance, perhaps as a cult site, already in the Middle Bronze Age.' (**b**) The Israelite tribes came together from all over Israel to gather around the shrine of the Ark and would have worked together as a combined labour force in order to construct the temenos with its great enclosure wall.

- (**a**) 'Shiloh was destroyed at the end of the Middle Bronze Age ... inside and on top of the Middle Bronze fortification wall, there was an accumulation of earth, ashes and stones, nearly five feet thick.' (**b**) Finkelstein's date for the destruction of Shiloh is a *TERMINUS POST QUEM* for the abandonment of the site: a sherd of 'chocolate-on-white' ware – associated with LB I – was found in a storeroom, suggesting that the site was not destroyed until sometime after the Late Bronze Age had begun. Given, as I have suggested, that the MB II (tribal) culture in the hill country was contemporary with the LB I (urban) culture of the surrounding territories, it is possible that the destruction of Shiloh could be dated as late as the LB IIA. I Samuel 4 tells us of the seizing of the Ark of the Covenant by the Philistines at the Battle of Ebenezer about a dozen years before the reign of Saul, which falls in LB IIA according to the New Chronology. Professor Finkelstein's post-MB destruction level would correspond to destruction meted out by the Philistines after the Battle of Ebenezer.

- **(a)** 'The Israelite settlement at Shiloh began in the twelfth century BC, at the beginning of Iron Age I, after the tell had been abandoned for some time. We found remains from Iron Age I virtually everywhere we dug.' **(b)** This is not the Israelite settlement but rather the redevelopment of the site which begins in the reign of Jeroboam I [I Kings 14:2-4], continuing throughout the Divided Monarchy period.

Conclusion Thirty-Four

Excavations at the sanctuary of Shiloh demonstrate that the Israelites developed the site to house the Ark of the Covenant during the Middle Bronze Age and not the Early Iron Age. The MB IIB culture of the central hill country of Palestine therefore represents the true archaeological remains of the Judges period in the history of Israel.

Migdol Shechem

Joshua gathered all the tribes of Israel together at Shechem; he then summoned all the elders of Israel, its leaders, judges and officials, and they presented themselves in God's presence. [Joshua 24:1]

> That day Joshua made a covenant for the people;
> he laid down a statute and ordinance for them at
> Shechem. Joshua wrote these words in the Book of
> the Law of God. He then took a large stone and set
> it up there, under the oak tree in Yahweh's sanctuary.
> [Joshua 24:25-26]

This was Joshua's final act before his death. The story of
the Israelite Covenant takes us to Shechem (modern Nablus) and the ruin-mound of Tell Balatah. Do the archaeological investigations of that site shed any light upon our
efforts to demonstrate the historicity of the early Israelite
presence in Canaan? You will find that the architectural
history of Middle Bronze Age Shechem fits exactly with
the biblical narrative now that the Old Testament and the
archaeological record have been re-synchronised.

Biblical scholar Ernst Sellin began work at Tell Balatah
in 1913, completing two seasons before the outbreak of
war. He picked up where he had left off with four further
seasons (winter and spring) in 1926 and 1927. A great
CYCLOPEAN fortification wall (Wall A) was unearthed along
with its gateway and, inside this formidable rampart, Sellin
revealed an extensive platform filling upon which a great
temple had been erected. It had walls five metres thick
and a large open cella (13.5 metres long by 11 metres wide),
the roof of which was originally supported by six columns.
The entrance portico of the temple had been flanked by
two tall towers, giving the whole structure the appearance
of a fortress-tower. Sellin immediately identified the building as the Temple of Baal-Berith ('Lord of the Covenant')
or El-Berith and dated its construction to the early Late
Bronze Age. This impressive temple of Shechem was also
known as Migdol Shechem ('Tower of Shechem') [Judges
9:46] and Beth-Millo ('House of the Millo' – remember
millo means filling or terrace) [Judges 9:6 & 20]. The biblical
names seemed to fit perfectly with the fortress-temple of
Tell Balatah, built on its terrace-filling. However, many

scholars disagreed with Sellin because the structure appeared to have been built in LB I – far too early to be associated with the incidents in the book of Judges which in the orthodox chronology would have fallen in the Iron Age I period. Sellin was dismissed by the dig's sponsors.

In 1956 the Americans took over the Tell Balatah excavations under the directorship of George Ernest Wright who worked the site for five further seasons. His excavations clarified the complex stratigraphy of Shechem and contributed to the religious history of the city with the discovery of a 'courtyard temple' in a level beneath, and in front of, Sellin's fortress-temple. This smaller structure lay outside the original inner city wall (wall D) and appeared to be dated to the MB IIA. Wright also determined that the later migdol temple had been constructed in the MB IIB era but that it probably continued in use into the LB I when it was destroyed by a violent conflagration. With the archaeological evidence in mind let me now summarise the role of Shechem in the Israelite story.

When Abraham entered Canaan he sojourned within 'the holy place at Shechem – the Oak of Moreh' [Genesis 12:6]. His grandson Jacob buried the confiscated foreign idols worshipped by his family beneath the same oak – but this time the Bible tells us that the tree was located 'near' or 'by' Shechem [Genesis 35:4]. Furthermore:

> Jacob arrived at the town of Shechem in Canaanite territory, on his return from Paddan-Aram. He encamped opposite the town and for one hundred pieces of silver he bought from the sons of Hamor, father of Shechem, the piece of land on which he had pitched his tent. There he erected an altar which he called 'El – God of Israel'. [Genesis 33:18-20]

It is my conviction that the courtyard temple complex found by Wright is the site of Jacob's altar dedicated to El, erected alongside the venerable Oak of Moreh under which

The Temple of Baal-berith

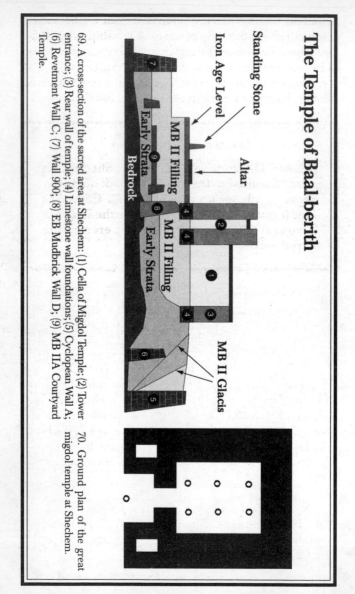

69. A cross-section of the sacred area at Shechem: (1) Cella of Migdol Temple; (2) Tower entrance; (3) Rear wall of temple; (4) Limestone wall foundations; (5) Cyclopean Wall A; (6) Revetment Wall C; (7) Wall 900; (8) EB Mudbrick Wall D; (9) MB IIA Courtyard Temple.

70. Ground plan of the great migdol temple at Shechem.

Abraham had rested. The courtyard plan of the sacred precinct reflects the style of open-air worship implied by the Genesis narrative. The buildings of the complex appear to have been built around the courtyard area in the MB IIA which is when, as you will learn in the next and final chapter, Jacob was resident at the city of Shechem.

Conclusion Thirty-Five

The MB IIA courtyard temple at Shechem is to be identified as the site of the Oak of Moreh where Jacob set up an altar to El. Centuries later it was the gathering place for the Israelite Covenant ceremony where Joshua erected the sacred *massebah*.

In the interval of time which corresponds to the Israelite Sojourn in Egypt (NC – 1662-1447 BC) the courtyard temple remained in use, but in MB IIB it was partially covered over with the filling upon which the great temple was erected. In the open court which was constructed in front of the massive new fortress-temple (and above the old courtyard temple) a great white stone measuring one and a half metres wide by around two metres high had been erected. Sellin identified it as a *massebah* or sacred stone pillar. Let me remind you of the passage in the book of Joshua concerning the Israelite Covenant, the events of which we are now dating within the MB IIB archaeological phase.

> That day Joshua made a covenant for the people. … He then took a large stone and set it up there, under the oak tree in Yahweh's sanctuary. [Joshua 24:25-26]

Sellin re-erected the great monolith believing it to have been the Covenant stone of Joshua. He was later criticised for his hasty conclusions because his temple and standing stone were far too early to be identified with Joshua. But we now know that Sellin was right all along. Still on the spot where he set it up, the Joshua stone – a tangible piece of early Israelite history – stands today in its neglect, covered in the yellow and green paint of Palestinian political grafitti. This is surely the saddest testimony to the lost history of the Conquest – all brought about by a simple mistake in chronology.

Conclusion Thirty-Six

The standing stone which was discovered in front of the great MB fortress-temple at Shechem is to be identified with the cultic stone of the Covenant erected by Joshua. During the era of the early Judges the stone was established in front of the Temple of Baal-Berith which is now recognised as the MB IIB temple.

The next time we hear of Shechem is in the tale of Abimelech, son of the judge Gideon and his Shechemite concubine.

After Gideon's death, the people of Israel again began to prostitute themselves to the Baals … All the leading men of Shechem and all Bethmillo then met and proclaimed Abimelech king at the oak of the cultic stone at Shechem. [Judges 8:33 & 9:6]

With the election of Abimelech as king of Shechem we reach another bloody passage in the story of the Israelite settlement in Canaan. We are now in a time more than two centuries after the death of Joshua. In the New Chronology the date is *circa* 1170 BC – the last year in the reign of Ahmose, founder of the New Kingdom in Egypt. It is the Late Bronze I period in the coastal and lowland cities but still the Middle Bronze IIB in the central hill country. The great Temple of Baal-Berith has been erected at the site of the Israelite Covenant and the cyclopean wall surrounding the town has also risen up to protect one of the Israelites' most sacred sites.

Abimelech's three-year rule was exceptionally brutal and eventually the Shechemites revolted against their king. The culmination of the rebellion was yet another slaughter. The vast majority of the citizens of Shechem were slain by Abimelech's warriors. The surviving remnant of one thousand Shechemites sought refuge in the great migdol temple with its thick walls, believing it to be not only secure but also sacrosanct. But Abimelech had no such religious foibles.

> As soon as Abimelech heard that the leading men inside Migdol Shechem had all gathered there, he went up Mount Zalmon with all his men. Then, taking an axe in his hands, he cut off the branch of a tree, picked it up and put it on his shoulder, and said to the men with him, 'Hurry and do what you have seen me do'. Each of his men similarly cut off a branch; then, following Abimelech, they piled the branches over the crypt and set it on fire over those who were inside; so that all the people in Migdol Shechem died too, about a thousand men and women. [Judges 9:46-49]

Here again we have a remarkable parallel between the early biblical narratives and archaeology. The Middle Bronze Age fortress-temple discovered by Sellin was destroyed by fire and, as Kenyon notes, 'the succeeding occupation was slight, and there was possibly even a complete gap'.[25] The only biblical passage which records an abandonment of Shechem is Judges 9:45 where we read that Abimelech 'stormed it and slaughtered the people inside, razed the town and sowed it with salt'.

Conclusion Thirty-Seven

The destroyed second stage of the massive MB fortress-temple at Shechem is to be identified with Migdol Shechem burnt to the ground by Abimelech with one thousand Shechemites inside. The subsequent abandonment of the site is consistent with the Abimelech story in which he razed the town and sowed it with salt.

Chapter Fifteen

JOSEPH THE VIZIER

e have now reached the final chapter in our epic journey through time and I guess this is an appropriate moment to look back down that road to remind ourselves of the various milestones we have passed along the way.

First we witnessed how scholars of the last century had taken the wrong path at the very beginning of their own journey of discovery. That false trail, signposted to 'Raamses' and 'Shishak', led modern scholarship into a quagmire of confusing anomalies in the chronology and archaeology of the ancient world. Although we began our journey at the same junction and with the same map (i.e. the available evidence), we decided to take the alternative road signposted 'archaeology of the TIP'. It was not very long before we arrived at an entirely different ancient world – one with a much greater potential for biblical and archaeological synthesis. The irony was that although the conventional chronology had been based on two key biblical synchronisms it produced an unhappy marriage between excavation results and the Old Testament narratives, whereas we chose to refer directly to the archaeological evidence and now had a framework which produced clear links between the Bible and archaeology.

By constructing our 'New Chronology' from the foundations of Egyptian TIP archaeology, in combination with a group of ancient genealogies handed down to us by the officials of the period, we were able to uncover the true historical figure hidden behind the biblical name 'Shishak'. He was none other than Ramesses the Great – the Ozymandias of Shelley's famous poem; the king whom Egyptologists refer to as Usermaatre-setepenre Ramessesmeriamun. Ramesses II was thus the despoiler of Solomon's temple in 925 BC, and not the Pharaoh of the Oppression and Exodus as is conventionally believed.

Having reached this conclusion, we looked for evidence of Solomon's activities in Palestine during the time of the late 18th Dynasty and early 19th Dynasty in Egypt. We came across the remains of an Egyptian-style shrine in Jerusalem which could have belonged to the palace of Pharaoh's Daughter – the principal wife of King Solomon. We were also able to compare the mysterious Millo built by Solomon with the massive terrace structure on the eastern slopes of the City of David. The Late Bronze Age, into which 'merchant prince' Solomon is now securely placed, provided us with the appropriate cultural setting for Israel's wealthiest ruler and his wide-reaching trading empire. The cities and royal residences of LB IIA-B in Palestine were built of fine ashlar masonry befitting the 'Phoenician tradition' as described in Kings and Chronicles. The literary tradition of Psalms has now been set in an era of great hymns and epic poetry, vividly represented in the literature of LBA Ugarit. Akhenaten's 'Hymn to the Aten', so often closely compared to Psalm 104,[1] would have been composed in Egypt when King David, the author of Psalm 104, ruled in Israel. Without question, both culturally and historically, the Late Bronze Age best reflects the era of the rise and then artistic culmination of Israel's United Monarchy.

We searched for a new signpost to guide us on our way. We found it pointing to 'Tell el-Amarna'. Here was a very exacting test of our sense of direction, for the contemporary written documents found at that site are open far less to speculative interpretation than dumb building stones. When we read the correspondence from the city-state rulers of Palestine, we discovered a political situation which matched in detail the period of the Early Monarchy in Israel. The Habiru of the Amarna Letters were the Hebrews under Saul and David and we had in our possession the actual tablets written by the first king of Israel. Many of the characters whose exploits fill the pages of the books of Samuel then began to appear in the Letters. Their names were camouflaged in the language of ancient Canaan, but when translated into their 'meaning' became exact equivalents of their Old Testament Hebrew counterparts. So, from out of the mists of time we listened to the very words of Saul and Ishbaal as their letters were read out to Pharaoh in his royal palace. We heard too about the deeds of King David as he pushed for control of the central hill country and relentlessly pressured the Philistine rulers of the coastal plain. Other players in the dramatic story of David's rise to power wrote to Akhenaten, including Hadadezer of Aram-Zobah and Achish of Gath. Several other bit-part actors turned up in the Letters, including Jesse (David's father), Joab (David's general), King Toi of Hamath and the Syrian army commander Shopak. We were able to read reports of Saul's death in the Jezreel region and then, later, about the isolation of the Jebusite Jerusalem and the subsequent political rise of the city of Zion – the capital of David's Israelite kingdom.

We took out our trusty sextant and made sure of our chronological navigation by plotting the heavenly bodies, discovering that the near-sunset solar eclipse observed at Ugarit could only have taken place in 1012 BC. In that same year the palace of Ugarit had been burnt to the ground and a report of its demise sent to Akhenaten. The Amarna period must then have fallen in the last years of the eleventh century BC and not in the mid-fourteenth century as in the traditional chronology. The biblical date for the first year of King David is around 1010 BC, so the New Chronology's placement of Akhenaten and Tutankhamun as contemporaries of the ancestral king of Israel was confirmed by astronomical retrocalculation.

Setting off once more upon our journey back in time, we reached the period of the Israelite Conquest of the Promised Land. Here we witnessed Joshua's destruction of Jericho in the Middle Bronze Age (NC – c. 1410 BC). We unearthed letters bearing the name of King Jabin of Hazor who died at the hands of the Israelites as they destroyed his mighty city. The sacred temenos of the Ark of the Covenant at Shiloh was revealed with its cult objects and furniture. We stood before the huge monolith erected by Joshua in front of the Temple of Baal-berith at Shechem. Here it was that the Israelite tribes had pledged their allegiance to Yahweh and here, just a century later, one thousand terrified refugees were burnt to death as King Abimelech put the great migdol temple to the torch.

We then reached the time of Moses and the pharaoh who raised him up as a prince of Egypt. This was achieved by locating the 13th Dynasty ruler Neferhotep I in the mid-sixteenth century BC – again by employing astronomical retrocalculations – this time using the Venus observations and month-length data found in the *Enuma Anu Enlil* texts of Mesopotamia. We came across Artapanus who told us the story of Prince Moses and Pharaoh Khenephrês whom we identified as Khaneferre Sobekhotep IV, the brother and successor of Neferhotep. He was ruling Egypt when Moses fled into Sinai. Decades later the now aged Moses was to return to Egypt during the reign of Pharaoh Dudimose (Manetho's Tutimaos) having been instructed by his god Yahweh to lead his people out of Egypt.

We were able to identify the store-city which the Israelites built as the sprawling MB IIA metropolis of Avaris, upon the ruins of which the later Ramesside capital of Pi-Ramesse was constructed. We saw death pits with multiple, hasty burials. We wondered if these could have any connection with the plague traditions of Exodus – especially when, immediately afterwards, the Asiatic population then residing at Avaris appears to have left *en masse*. We further speculated that the new influx of barbaric non-Egyptianised Asiatics who subsequently settled in the abandoned ruins of Avaris were Manetho's 'people of obscure race' who came from the East and seized Egypt 'without striking a blow'. Could these invaders have been the biblical Amalekites who fought with the Israelites as the latter entered Sinai?[2]

Having come all this way we have just one more section of our journey to complete. By tonight we should be encamped within the beautiful gardens of the vizier Joseph's palace situated close to the banks of the Nile, with the prospect of an early morning's stroll through the village of the first Israelite settlers to enter the Land of Goshen. But first we need to work out how far down the road we have yet to travel.

The Length of the Israelite Sojourn

In most commentaries or popular books on the Old Testament you will read that the Israelite Sojourn in the land of Egypt lasted four hundred and thirty years. However, this figure is by no means certain. In fact, there is clear evidence that the true period of the Sojourn was no more than two hundred and fifteen years.

In the Masoretic version of the Old Testament the passage in Exodus 12:40 reads as follows:

> The time that the Israelites spent in Egypt was four hundred and thirty years.

If we turn to the history of Israel recorded by Josephus in his *Antiquities of the Jews* [Chapter XV:2] we get an entirely different version of events:

A Summary of the New Chronology

An overall view of the new relationship between Egyptian history and the Bible. The left column gives the New Chronology of Egypt whilst the right column has the biblical chronology which has been calculated using the chronological data provided in the books of 1 Kings, Judges and Exodus.

	19th Dynasty
c. 950 BC	HAREMHEB — —
	AKHENATEN — —
	18th Dynasty
	AHMOSE
c. 1193 BC	APOPHIS
	15th Dynasty
c. 1290 BC	SALITIS
	Early Hyksos
	SHESHI
	NEHESI
c. 1450 BC	DUDIMOSE — —
	SOBEKHOTEP IV
c. 1540 BC	NEFERHOTEP I
	13th Dynasty
c. 1632 BC	**12th Dynasty**
	AMENEMHAT III — —

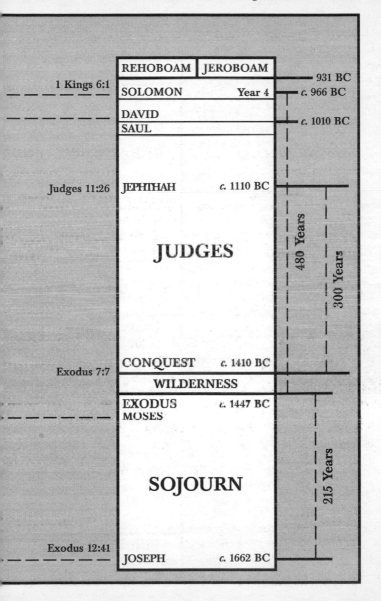

REHOBOAM	JEROBOAM	— 931 BC
SOLOMON	Year 4	— c. 966 BC
DAVID		— c. 1010 BC
SAUL		

1 Kings 6:1

Judges 11:26 — JEPHTHAH — c. 1110 BC

JUDGES

480 Years

300 Years

CONQUEST — c. 1410 BC

Exodus 7:7

WILDERNESS

EXODUS — c. 1447 BC
MOSES

SOJOURN

215 Years

Exodus 12:41 — JOSEPH — c. 1662 BC

> They (the Israelites) left Egypt in the month of Xanthicus, on the fifteenth day of the lunar month; four hundred and thirty years after our forefather Abraham came into Canaan, but two hundred and fifteen years only after Jacob removed into Egypt.

Now, according to the statements of Josephus himself, he had access to very old documents formerly housed in the Temple of Jerusalem from which to draw his account of early Israelite history. Josephus lived in the first century AD and so his writings are dated hundreds of years before the Masoretic text of the Tanaakh (Hebrew Old Testament) was compiled in the fourth century AD. If his source documents were genuine, then the information he gives for the duration of the Sojourn derives from a much earlier period than that employed by the Masoretes when they made their version of the history of Israel and a further several centuries before the earliest extant copy of the Masoretic text.

It is fairly easy to see what happened in the interval of time between Josephus' day and that of the Masoretes. During the process of copying down the original scrolls over the intervening centuries, a section of text something on the lines of 'and in the land of Canaan' had fallen out (or had been edited out). This is confirmed by the Greek rendition of the Old Testament (the Septuagint or LXX) which retains the original full version of the passage:

> And the sojourning of the children of Israel, which they sojourned in the land of Egypt **and in the land of Canaan**, was four hundred and thirty years. [Exodus 12:40]

The Septuagint was first written down in the time of Ptolemy I during the third century BC and the earliest surviving manuscript is again much older than the earliest surviving Masoretic copy. The Samaritan version of the first five books of the Old Testament (the Pentateuch) is also considerably more ancient than the Masoretic scriptures and it too retains the longer rendition of the passage on the length of the Sojourn. Thus, three out of four sources for the book of Exodus state that the four-hundred-and-thirty-year interval represents the whole period from Abraham's descent into Canaan all the way down to the Exodus of Moses and the Israelites from Egypt. Various passages in the book of Genesis have led scholars to determine that the period from Abraham's descent to Jacob's arrival in the Land of Goshen was two hundred and fifteen years and so the Sojourn in Egypt (from Jacob's arrival to the Exodus) lasted around the same length of time – in other words *circa* two hundred and fifteen years.

We can find support for this duration in the long genealogy of Joshua found in I Chronicles 7:20-27. There ten generations are recorded from Joshua (a man of fighting age at the time of Exodus) back to Joseph's son, Ephraim (who would have been something like five years old when Jacob arrived in Egypt[3]). Using our twenty-year generation, we can arrive at an approximate duration of two hundred and twenty years for the eleven generations – pretty close to the two hundred and fifteen years of Exodus 12:40 (LXX).[4]

With the biblical date of the Exodus set at *circa* 1447 BC (Year 4 of Solomon = *c.* 967 + 480 years

Joseph – 1667 BC
Ephraim – 1647 BC
Beriah – 1627 BC
Rephah – 1607 BC
Resheph – 1587 BC
Telah – 1567 BC
Tahan – 1547 BC
Laadan – 1527 BC
Ammihud – 1507 BC
Elishama – 1487 BC
Nun – 1467 BC
Joshua – 1447 BC

The genealogy of Joshua from I Chronicles 7:23-27 which confirms an approximate duration of 215 years for the Sojourn in Egypt (*c.* 1667-*c.* 1447 = 220 years).

of I Kings 6:1-2 = 1447) we can now add the two hundred and fifteen years of the Sojourn period to arrive at the date of *circa* 1662 BC for the arrival of Jacob and the Israelites in Egypt.

In the Beginning

So we have established that the Sojourn of the Israelites in Egypt began in *circa* 1662 BC – according to Genesis 45:6 during the second year of the great famine. Eight years earlier, in 1670, Joseph was appointed vizier of Egypt at the age of thirty [Genesis 41:46]. Thirteen years before his sudden elevation to the highest office in the Black Land, the seventeen-year-old Hebrew had been brought into Egypt to be sold into slavery by Midianite caravaneers [Genesis 37:2]. Joseph's arrival in Egypt can then be dated to around 1683 BC. Who was ruling Egypt in the years from 1683 to 1662 in the New Chronology? To answer that question we must return to our astronomically derived date for Neferhotep I of the 13th Dynasty and then work our way back through the king-list of the Royal Canon.

71. Detail from the famous scene of a trading caravan of thirty-seven 'Midianites' depicted in the tomb of Khnumhotep at Beni Hassan. Some of the men wear multi-coloured coats.

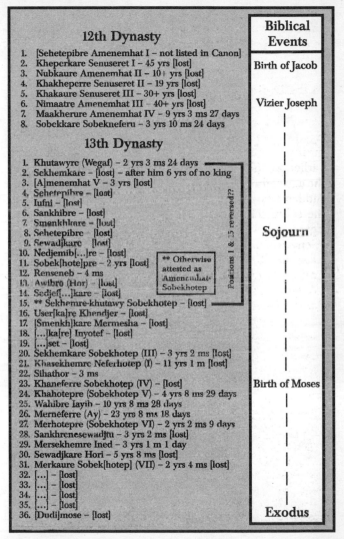

12th Dynasty

1. [Sehetepibre Amenemhat I – not listed in Canon]
2. Kheperkare Senuseret I – 45 yrs [lost]
3. Nubkaure Amenemhat II – 10+ yrs [lost]
4. Khakheperre Senuseret II – 19 yrs [lost]
5. Khakaure Senuseret III – 30+ yrs [lost]
6. Nimaatre Amenemhat III – 40+ yrs [lost]
7. Maakherure Amenemhat IV – 9 yrs 3 ms 27 days
8. Sobekkare Sobekneferu – 3 yrs 10 ms 24 days

13th Dynasty

1. Khutawyre (Wegaf) – 2 yrs 3 ms 24 days
2. Sekhemkare – [lost] – after him 6 yrs of no king
3. [A]menemhat V – 3 yrs [lost]
4. Sehetepibre – [lost]
5. Iufni – [lost]
6. Sankhibre – [lost]
7. Smenkhkhare – [lost]
8. Sehetepibre – [lost]
9. Sewadjkare – [lost]
10. Nedjemib[...]re – [lost]
11. Sobek[hote]pre – 2 yrs [lost]
12. Renseneb – 4 ms
13. Awibre (Hor) – [lost]
14. Sedjef[...]kare – [lost]
15. ** Sekhemre-khutawy Sobekhotep – [lost]
16. User[ka]re Khendjer – [lost]
17. [Smenkh]kare Mermesha – [lost]
18. [...]ka[re] Inyotef – [lost]
19. [...]set – [lost]
20. Sekhemkare Sobekhotep (III) – 3 yrs 2 ms [lost]
21. Khasekhemre Neferhotep (I) – 11 yrs 1 m [lost]
22. Sihathor – 3 ms
23. Khaneferre Sobekhotep (IV) – [lost]
24. Khahotepre (Sobekhotep V) – 4 yrs 8 ms 29 days
25. Wahibre Iayib – 10 yrs 8 ms 28 days
26. Merneferre (Ay) – 23 yrs 8 ms 18 days
27. Merhotepre (Sobekhotep VI) – 2 yrs 2 ms 9 days
28. Sankhrenesewadjtu – 3 yrs 2 ms [lost]
29. Mersekhemre Ined – 3 yrs 1 m 1 day
30. Sewadjkare Hori – 5 yrs 8 ms [lost]
31. Merkaure Sobek[hotep] (VII) – 2 yrs 4 ms [lost]
32. [...] – [lost]
33. [...] – [lost]
34. [...] – [lost]
35. [...] – [lost]
36. [Dudi]mose – [lost]

Positions 1 & 15 reversed??

** Otherwise attested as Amenemhat Sobekhotep

Biblical Events

Birth of Jacob

Vizier Joseph

Sojourn

Birth of Moses

Exodus

The data provided by the Royal Canon of Turin for the kings of the 12th and 13th Dynasties. In the right column is a general outline of biblical history for the period as it now appears in the New Chronology.

Although column VI of the Royal Canon is extremely fragmentary, it is possible to determine that Neferhotep was the twenty-first ruler in the list following the last pharaoh of the 12th Dynasty – Queen Sobekneferu. Only about half of the reign lengths for the early 13th Dynasty survive in the damaged papyrus, but, from the fifteen (of the first thirty-six) that do, we can calculate an average reign duration of five years in this particular period. So, if we assign five years each to the fifteen missing reign lengths prior to Neferhotep in the Canon, then add the five extant reign lengths and the six years recorded at column VI:4, when there was no king ruling Egypt, we arrive at a total

72. Columns VI and VII of the Royal Canon which contain the 12th and 13th Dynasties.

— — **Amenemhat IV** – 9 yrs 3 ms 27 days
Sobekneferu – 3 yrs 10 ms 24 days
Total kings of the Residence [Itj-tawy] = 8, making 213 yrs 1 m 16 days
— — **Khutawyre (Wegaf)** – 2 yrs 3ms 24 days
Sekhemkare – [lost] after him 6 years of no king
[A]menemhat V – 3 yrs [lost]
Sehetepibre – [lost]
Iufni – [lost]
Sankhibre – [lost]
Smenkhare – [lost]
Sehetepibre – [lost]
Sewadjkare – [lost]
Nedjemib[...]re – [lost]
— — **Sobek[hote]pre** – 2 yrs [lost]
Renseneb – 4 ms
Hor – [lost]
Sedjef[...]kare – [lost]
Sobekhotep – [lost]
— — **Khendjer** – [lost]
— — **Mermesha** – [lost]
Inyotef – [lost]
[...]set – [lost]
— — **Sobekhotep III** – 3 yrs 2 ms [lost]
— — **Neferhotep I** – 11 yrs 1 m [lost]
Sihathor – 3 ms
— — **Sobekhotep IV** – [lost]

of approximately ninety-two years between the end of the 12th Dynasty and the first regnal year of Neferhotep (15 x 5 = 75 + 3 + 0.3 + 2 + 3 + 2.3 = 85.6 + 6 = 91.6). As in the New Chronology Year 1 of Neferhotep fell in *circa* 1540 BC, then the 13th Dynasty must have begun in around 1632 BC. Joseph, appointed to office in 1670, was therefore a 12th Dynasty vizier. But under which king precisely? Finding an answer to this question is a little tricky because we need to consider the chronological effects of the practice of co-regency which appears to have been in use during the Middle Kingdom.

There is some convincing evidence to suggest that most of the years of the reigns of the last two rulers of the 12th Dynasty should be subsumed into the long reign of Amenemhat III.[5] In other words, King Amenemhat IV and Queen Sobekneferu – both offspring of Amenemhat III – were junior co-regents of their father, Queen Neferusobek perhaps only surviving as sole pharaoh for two to three years beyond her father's death. Amenemhat III probably reigned for a grand total of forty-seven years and so we can estimate that his reign would have begun around fifty years before the end of the dynasty. His accession year can then be assigned to *circa* 1682 BC. With Joseph becoming vizier in *circa* 1670 BC, it must have been King Amenemhat III who raised the Hebrew slave up to the highest political office in the land.

Conclusion Thirty-Eight

Joseph, son of Jacob, was vizier of Egypt during the reign of Amenemhat III – the most powerful pharaoh of the Middle Kingdom – and continued in office through the reigns of the first rulers of the 13th Dynasty.

According to the traditional history of Genesis, Joseph's appointment was marked by a seven-year period of abundance and prosperity in the Nile valley (1670-1664) when Egypt enjoyed bumper harvests. This was then followed by seven years of disastrous famine which must have begun in around 1663 BC – that is Year 20 of Amenemhat III in the New Chronology. The Israelites then arrived in Egypt a year later in 1662 BC. So, can we find any evidence for famine at this period in the reign of King Amenemhat?

Floods and Famine

During the Middle Kingdom the pharaohs constructed a series of forts along the length of the Second Cataract in southern Nubia. The purpose of these military strongholds was to protect Egypt's new African frontier and to act as launching stations for military campaigns and trading expeditions into the southern continent. Upstream from

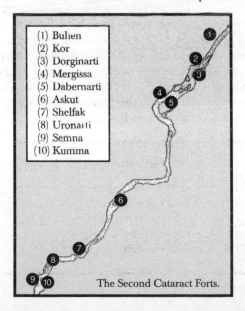

(1) Buhen
(2) Kor
(3) Dorginarti
(4) Mergissa
(5) Dabernarti
(6) Askut
(7) Shelfak
(8) Uronarti
(9) Semna
(10) Kumma

The Second Cataract Forts.

the Second Cataract was the kingdom of Kush. The Egyptians were constantly at war with their southern neighbours and many of the 12th Dynasty rulers undertook military campaigns beyond the Second Cataract fortresses.

The southernmost Egyptian bastions were located either side of the Nile, at the start of the cataract, where the desert escarpment encroaches into the valley on both sides leaving a narrow rocky defile. On the western ridge stood the citadel of Semna and on the east side the twin stronghold of Kumma. Between them, in the narrow gorge (now submerged under Lake Nasser), the white waters of the Nile used to dance northwards along their rocky course towards Egypt. In summer the annual Nile flood raised the river into a fast-flowing torrent many metres higher than that of the regular low Nile. This was an ideal spot to monitor the level of the Nile inundation, and for a brief period the Egyptians did precisely that. For about sixty years, starting in the reign of Amenemhat III and lasting down into the early 13th Dynasty, the highest point to which the Nile flood reached in a given year was marked by a short hieroglyphic inscription on the rock face. Each text gave the name of the king and the regnal year of the high Nile. These inundation records were discovered by the great German Egyptologist, Karl Richard LEPSIUS, in 1844 and began a controversy which still continues today. Archaeologists have not been able to find an inscription for every single year of the period, either because not every inundation level was originally recorded or because some have fallen away from their setting and then been washed away. A number of texts were indeed found on rocks at the bottom of the cliffs, having toppled from their original positions (and so are no longer measurable) but around fifteen were recorded *in situ* to give Egyptologists an idea of the height of the high Nile levels in this area during the late Middle Kingdom.

The first question scholars asked was why these inscriptions were made in the first place? What was different about

73. Karl Richard Lepsius.

the inundations of the late Middle Kingdom to require that they should be so closely monitored? Why were only about a third of the inundations of the period recorded? Even allowing for lost or destroyed texts, it did not seem as though the Egyptians made a record for every year. Why were there no inscriptions at all on the rocks from the years immediately following Year 8 of Senuseret III when the fortresses were first garrisoned? To find out what prompted scholars to believe that these inscriptions were abnormal we must determine what was regarded as a 'good inundation' level during the Middle Kingdom and then compare that level to the records of high Niles in the Semna Gorge.

In the reign of Senuseret I (near the beginning of the 12th Dynasty) we are told that a 'good flood' reached a level of twenty-one and a half cubits (11.3 metres) at the island of Elephantine (Egy. *Abu*, at modern Aswan). This compares well with inundations of modern times (prior to the construction of the ASWAN DAMS). Lepsius noted that

1685		16 –	Senuseret III
1684		17	
1683		18	Joseph arrives in Egypt
1682	1–	Amenemhat III = = 19	
1681	2	20	
1680	3	Good floods begin 21	
1679	4	22	
1678	5	23	
1677	6	24	
1676	7	25	
1675	8	26	
1674	9	27	
1673	10	28	
1672	11	29	
1671	12	30	
1670	13	31	Joseph appointed vizier
1669	14	32	Years of plenty begin
1668	15	33	
1667	16	34	
1666	17	35	
1665	18	36	
1664	19	37	
1663	20	High floods begin 38	Start of famine
1662	21	39	Israelites arrive in Egypt
1661	22		
1660	23		
1659	24		
1658	25		
1657	26		
1656	27		
1655	28		
1654	29		
1653	30	= =1–	Amenemhat IV crowned at Amenemhat III jubilee
1652	32	2	
1651	33	3	
1650	34	4	
1649	35	5	
1648	36	6	
1647	37	7	
1646	38	8	
1645	39	9	
1644	40		
1643	41		
1642	42		
1641	43		
1640	44		
1639	45		
1638	46		
1637	47	= =1–	Sobekneferu
1636		2	
1635		3	
1634		4	End of 12th Dynasty

**Late 12th Dynasty
in the
New Chronology**

Lamarês for 8 years ...
(Manetho – Africanus version)

New Chronology dates for the end of the
12th Dynasty showing how the regnal dates
of the kings relate to incidents in the life of
Joseph as recorded in Genesis.

13th Dynasty	
1632	Wegaf
1630	Sekhemkare
1625	6 years of no king
1619	Amenemhat V
1616	Sehetepibre
1611	Iufni
1606	Sankhibre
1601	Smenkhkare
1596	Sehetepibre
1591	Sewadjkare
1586	Nedjemib[...]re
1581	Sobekhotep I
1579	Renseneb
1578	Awibre Hor
1573	Sedjef[...]kare
1568	Sobekhotep II
1563	Khendjer
1558	Mermesha
1553	Inyotef
1548	[...]set
1543	Sobekhotep III
1540	Neferhotep I
1530	Sihathor
1529	Sobekhotep IV
1508	Sobekhotep V
1503	Iayib
1493	Ay
1470	Sobekhotep VI
1469	Sankhre
1467	Ined
1464	Hori
1459	Sobekhotep VII
1457	[...] – [lost]
1455	[...] – [lost]
1452	[...] – [lost]
1450	[...] – [lost]
1448	Dudimose
1447	EXODUS

the high water level at Semna in the 1840s was twelve metres above the low water level. In other words the river surface rose by twelve metres in the peak month of inundation (August) as it passed through Semna gorge. When we compare this to the late Middle Kingdom levels recorded on the rock face we get a bit of a shock. The average high Nile level in this period was *nineteen* metres above the low water mark! So, there appears to have been a dramatic rise in the Nile flood levels in the reign of Amenemhat III compared to those recorded in the early Middle Kingdom and in modern times.[6]

The evidence from Semna indicates that, during the first two decades of Amenemhat's reign, the Egyptians observed a rise in the flood levels to about the seventeen-metre mark (probably beginning in Year 3[7]) – an increase of about five metres above the norm for the previous period. This may not have been problematical for the agriculture of the Nile valley and, indeed, may have been a 'very good flood' bringing extra silt and expanding the area of cultivation to its

New Chronology dates for the 13th Dynasty down to Dudimose. The dates are based on data supplied in the Royal Canon and an average reign length at this period.

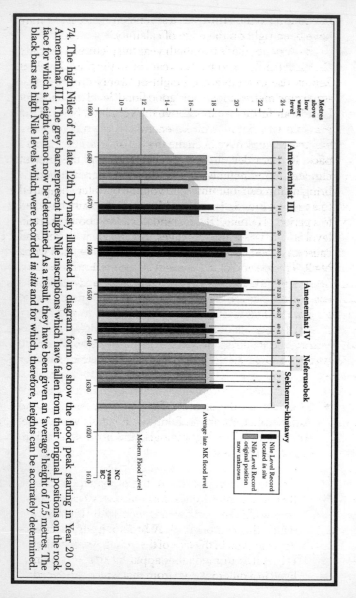

74. The high Niles of the late 12th Dynasty illustrated in diagram form to show the flood peak starting in Year 20 of Amenemhat III. The grey bars represent high Nile inscriptions which have fallen from their original positions on the rock face for which a height cannot now be determined. As a result, they have been given an 'average' height of 17.5 metres. The black bars are high Nile levels which were recorded *in situ* and for which, therefore, heights can be accurately determined.

412

maximum extent. However, a seventeen-metre flood may have been right on the edge of calamity.[8]

By Amenemhat's twentieth year the picture drastically changes. For the next twelve years or so the flood levels at Semna rise to an average height of twenty-one metres – some nine metres above the 'good flood' level of Senuseret I, and four further metres above the very high Niles of the previous two decades of Amenemhat's reign. This extra four metres may have been the straw that broke the camel's back. Barbara Bell, an American specialist in the ancient climates, convincingly argues that these great floods – bringing three to four times the volume of water compared to a normal inundation – would almost certainly have led to a period of famine.[9] If the inundation rises above a certain level it can wash away villages, break down dykes and causeways, and flood temples, tombs and palaces; but worst of all, if the period of the rise is sustained as is the case in a normal inundation, then the waters take much longer to subside and, as a result, the fields cannot be made ready for the planting season.

Bell highlights various aspects of late Middle Kingdom history and culture which indicate that Egypt was indeed suffering great trials and tribulations in this era. For example:

- The faces of the statues of Kings Senuseret III and Amenemhat III are well known for their stern, care-worn demeanour. Egyptologist and art historian William SMITH writes:

> The dominating quality of these (statue) heads is that of an intelligent consciousness of a ruler's responsibilities and an awareness of the bitterness which this can bring … A brooding seriousness appears even in the face of the young Amenemhet III … it is immediately apparent that this man lived in a different time from that which produced

the serene confidence of the people of the Old Kingdom.[10]

In one of his more speculative moments, Pierre Montet pondered whether these sad heads portrayed some kind of premonition of impending collapse in pharaonic authority and presaged an end to their magnificent dynasty.

Perhaps Amenemhet III had sensed that his family and all Egypt were to fall on evil days and the sculptors of Karnak caught these forebodings.[11]

Bell, however, suggests that the 'erratic behaviour of the Nile, evidenced by the Semna inscriptions' may have been the real cause of the anxiety etched on the faces of these pharaohs.[12] In the New Chronology, the second decade of Amenemhat III's reign (contemporary with the fourth decade of Senuseret III[13]) was the time of Joseph's prophecy relating to the oncoming famine – ample reason, I believe, for concern on the part of the co-regent pharaohs.

- During the time of the high Nile floods (extending down into the early 13th Dynasty) we begin to see, for the first time, the appearance of the crocodile god, Sobek, in the names of the pharaohs. So Amenemhat III's daughter and future co-regent is called Sobekkare Sobekneferure ('Sobek is the spirit of Re' and 'Sobek is the perfect form of Re') and in the next dynasty we find that the most common nomen is Sobekhotep ('Sobek is satisfied'), carried by at least six rulers. The great crocodile god was intimately associated with the River Nile and this royal emphasis upon his cult does suggest some tangible concern over the water levels of the great river and perhaps reflects, in Barbara Bell's words, 'a desire (on the part of Pharaoh) to propitiate this water god'.[14]

- Bell also invokes the political history of the early 13th Dynasty, arguing that the remarkable series of very short reigns which follow that of Amenemhat III reflect the unstable situation brought about by erratic inundations.

If we now put all this into the historical context revealed by the New Chronology, a very attractive picture begins to emerge.

The book of Genesis tells us that Joseph arrived in Egypt as a prisoner of Midianite caravaneers and was sold into slavery. According to the New Chronology this happened during the reign of Senuseret III. Whilst Joseph served in the household of Potiphar (a commander in the armed forces) Senuseret's son, Amenemhat III, was crowned co-regent. The young Hebrew slave was then thrown into prison for several years (accused of molesting the wife of his Egyptian master). In Amenemhat's thirteenth year Joseph was released from prison and elevated to the position of vizier as a reward for his interpretation of Pharaoh's dreams.

Joseph, the seer, had predicted first a period of plenty for Egypt lasting seven years. The number seven, of course, is again one of those biblical numbers (like the number 40) which has a traditional significance. This period of plenty (which according to the Nile records seems to have commenced before Joseph's elevation to the vizierate and then continued for a *further* seven years) represents symbolically the years of the seventeen-metre floods at Semna which, once adjusted to, would have produced very generous crop yields in the Nile valley proper.

At the end of the second decade in Amenemhat's reign the annual floods suddenly rose to twenty-one metres at Semna and the inundation of the Nile valley continued to drown the land for weeks beyond its due time of recession (assuming the period of rising of the waters to have followed the usual pattern). Seed could not be planted and so the harvest was badly affected. A severe famine would have rapidly ensued if Joseph had not persuaded the king to store vast quantities of grain harvested during the period of plenty. The local chieftains of the NOMES (the 'NOMARCHS'), having failed to take Joseph's warning seriously soon found their own grain silos exhausted. As Genesis 47:20 informs us, these local bigwigs were then forced to sell their land holdings to Pharaoh. The power of the nomarchs was broken and the palace administration became the sole authority in the Black Land.

This fundamental political transformation is readily apparent in the late Middle Kingdom. Some time in the reign of Senuseret III the grand tombs of the nomarchs ceased to be built in Middle Egypt. Egyptologists have, in the past, generally recognised this as signalling the diminution of the authority of a semi-independent nobility and the return of political control to the kingship. In accordance with the scenario being developed here, I would continue to see this as a period of momentous political change in which Joseph's agrarian policy had a direct and lasting impact. By monopolising the Egyptian grain supply, the Asiatic vizier had brought the nobility cap in hand to the palace and had provided the 12th Dynasty co-regents, Senuseret and Amenemhat, with the means to control the powerful baronies.

Conclusion Thirty-Nine

The extremely high Niles, recorded at Semna Gorge from the twentieth year of Amenemhat III, were the root cause of the severe famine in Egypt which played a major part in the Joseph story [Genesis 40-41].

The era of King Amenemhat III is recognised as a floruit in pharaonic power, his long reign and spectacular building projects attesting to the success of his policies. We now know why. The man behind the throne – Pharaoh's ring-bearer and special advisor – was none other than the biblical patriarch Joseph, son of Jacob.

King Moeris and the Labyrinth

> … it happened that Pharaoh had a dream: there he was, standing by the Nile, and there, coming up from the Nile, were seven cows, sleek and fat, and they began to feed among the rushes. And then seven other cows, wretched and lean, came up from the Nile, behind them; and these went over and stood beside the other cows on the bank of the Nile. The wretched and lean cows ate the seven sleek and fat cows. Then Pharaoh woke up. [Genesis 41:1-4]

In the context of what I have already said about the relationship between Joseph's famine and the inundation, we can see a new allusion in Pharaoh's dream. Joseph sees in the seven fat cows seven 'very good inundations' *rising up from the river* and, in the wretched cows, seven 'disastrous inundations' which bring starvation. The clue that the Nile would be the cause of both plenty and famine had been there all along but the link between the rising of the cows from the water and the rising of the inundation has only been realised because of the new chronological setting of the tale. We can now pinpoint these good and bad inundations to the time from Amenemhat III's thirteenth regnal year down to his thirty-second regnal year when the twenty-one-metre floods finally cease. After that the flood records return to their seventeen-metre average until they come to an end in the reign of Sekhemkare Amenemhat-senbuef (second ruler of the 13th Dynasty).

Armed with Joseph's warning of what was to come,

did Amenemhat make any preparations for the very high inundations? Again the archaeological evidence and the traditional histories of Manetho, Herodotus and Diodorus Siculus (along with the geographer STRABO) come together to show that this was the case. It is clear from the archaeological record that Amenemhat III was the most active pharaoh in the Faiyum basin. He constructed his pyramid at Hawara overlooking the waterway which leads from the Nile into the lake, today called Birket Karun, and, beside the pyramid, he built a rambling structure known to Hellenistic writers as the Egyptian Labyrinth. This strange building consisted of scores of rooms centred around a dozen open courts, each unit of which, according to the priests of Herodotus' day, represented one of the Egyptian nomes. The Greek traveller recounts his visit to the Labyrinth with great admiration and a certain amount of awe.

> I myself have seen it, and indeed no words can tell its wonders; ... Though the pyramids were greater than words can tell, and each one of them a match for many great monuments built by Greeks, this maze surpasses even the pyramids. It has twelve roofed courts, with doors over against each other: six face the north and six the south, in two continuous lines, all within one outer wall. There are also double sets of chambers, three thousand altogether, fifteen hundred above and the same number underground. ... The outlets of the chambers and the mazy passages hither and thither through the courts were an unending marvel to us as we passed from court to apartment and from apartment to colonnade, from colonnade again to more chambers and then into yet more courts. [Book II, 148]

The building of the Labyrinth is attributed by Manetho to King Moeris, who also gave his name to the great lake of the Faiyum which, according to tradition, he also created.[15]

I asked myself the question: was the Labyrinth in some way connected to Joseph's administration of the country and the distribution of grain supplies? Did Joseph order the building of this 'miniature Egypt' as one of his administration headquarters? At first the answer to both questions seemed to be 'no' as the Labyrinth of Amenemhat appeared to have a clear connection with the mortuary cult of the pharaoh. However, it was possible – just as was the case with the great funerary complex of Zoser's Step Pyramid at Sakkara – that the mortuary buildings may have mimicked or reflected an existing complex of buildings used during the lifetime of the king. In the case of Zoser, his architect Imhotep recreated, in eternal stone, the shrines and courts of the king's *Heb Sed* or jubilee festival. Enormous effort went into the construction of this 'dummy' complex so that the deceased pharaoh could forever continue to perform the ceremonies of his divine rejuvenation in the afterlife. In the case of Amenemhat's Labyrinth we may see in its design an eternal representation of the Black Land's reorganised administrative structure undertaken during the king's lifetime. Perhaps the idea was that this 'dummy' complex would enable the deceased monarch to continue his divine administration of the Black Land throughout eternity.

The concept of the 'caring monarch' is a most remarkable feature of both the reigns of Senuseret III and his son Amenemhat III (also manifest in the literature of Senuseret III's father, Senuseret II). Amenemhat's funerary monument might well have reflected this concern for the welfare of the Egyptian people and there is a possibility that its design was based on an existing, but now lost, administrative building (made of mudbrick) located in the capital, ITJ-TAWY, a few kilometres to the north. Just such a building is mentioned in records of the time. It is called the *khenret* and is closely connected with the organisation of agricultural labour and the 'Department of Redistribution' (Egy. *kha en ded remetj*).[16]

That was my view in summer 1994 as I began to write this chapter, but a recent trip to Egypt in November of the same year has led me to consider new possibilities. On that visit I went to see Dieter Arnold and his Metropolitan Museum mission at Lisht – site of the pyramids of Amenemhat I and Senuseret I. I was accompanied by Tell ed-Daba archaeologist, Peter Jánosi, and his wife Lisa, a talented illustrative artist working for Arnold's team. The museum mission has for the last few seasons been working at Dashur, several kilometres to the north of Lisht, where the team are clearing the areas around the pyramids of Senuseret III and Amenemhat III. I have already mentioned that the pyramid of Amenemhat was located beside the Labyrinth at Hawara, but he, in fact, had two pyramids. The first to be built – at Dashur – appears to have shown signs of instability and potential collapse during the later stages of construction. As a result, it looks as though Amenemhat III decided to build a replacement pyramid at Hawara in which he was probably buried. The building work on the Hawara pyramid would not therefore have begun until quite late in the long reign of the king.

An interesting discussion between Peter, Dieter and myself revealed that the director of the Dashur excavations is now thinking along the lines that the Labyrinth was constructed before the pyramid at Hawara – in other words whilst Amenemhat still intended to be buried at Dashur. Thus it would appear that the Labyrinth was not originally planned as a mortuary complex for the Hawara pyramid but rather as an independent structure of unknown function. This raised the tantalising possibility that the great stone complex of courts and halls may have been a real – rather than dummy – administrative building specifically intended to administer to the needs of the Nile valley – and intended, moreover, to last for many centuries.

I had often wondered if the Arabic name of the site of the Labyrinth – Hawara – could have an Egyptian origin. I had mused over the possibility with my Egyptological colleagues that we had here the name Avaris (or Auaris) and that this building complex was the southern counterpart to the 'Avaris of the Delta' mentioned in the SPEOS ARTEMIDOS inscription of Queen Hatshepsut – in other words the later Hyksos capital which Egyptologists in their Egypto-speak call Hut-waret but which was probably originally pronounced *Haware* in Egyptian (the feminine ending 't's were not pronounced). The name means 'Estate' or 'House of the Department' and, as you will shortly learn, this 'Department' has an important role in the historical story of Joseph the vizier.

It was also in Amenemhat's reign that massive hydraulic projects were initiated in the Faiyum. A wide natural waterway was exploited in order to channel the excess waters of the inundation into LAKE MOERIS (a) to protect Lower Egypt from excessive flooding and (b) to store water for times of low inundation. Diodorus Siculus explains the purpose of King Moeris' activities in the Faiyum.

> For since the Nile did not rise to a fixed height each year and yet the fruitfulness of the country depended on the constancy of the flood-level, he (Moeris) excavated the lake to receive the excess water, in order that the river might not, by an excessive volume of flow, immoderately flood the land and form marshes and pools, nor, by failing to rise to the proper height, ruin the harvests by the lack of water. He also dug a canal, eighty stades (14km) long and three plethra (90m) wide, from the river to the lake, and by this canal, sometimes turning the river into the lake and sometimes shutting it off again, he furnished the farmers with an opportune supply of water, opening and closing the entrance by a skilful device and yet at considerable expense; ... [Book I, 52]

The canal referred to by Diodorus ran through a natural cutting in the low desert ridge which separates the Faiyum

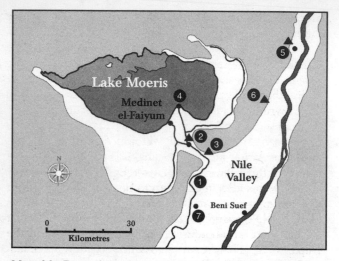

Map of the Faiyum basin showing the Bahr Yussef (1); the pyramid and labyrinth of Amenemhat III at Hawara (2); the pyramid and pyramid town of Senuseret II at el-Lahun (3); the statue bases of Amenemhat III at Biahmu (4); the pyramid of Amenemhat I at Lisht and the site of the Middle Kingdom capital of Itj-tawy (5); the Old Kingdom pyramid of Maidum (6); and the important ancient city of Heracleopolis (modern Ihnasya el-Medina) (7). The approximate extent of Lake Moeris in ancient times (dark grey) covered three to four times the area of the modern Birket Karun (light grey).

basin from the Nile valley and it was overlooking this canal that Amenemhat located his Labyrinth (and later pyramid). The canal did not, however, link Lake Moeris directly to the Nile. Instead it formed the last nine kilometres of a natural waterway which leaves the river just to the south of Tell el-Amarna. It seems likely that this was the original feeder system which created the great lake and that the cutting of Diodorus' 'canal' was in reality more of a dredging and widening operation to assist the flow of water in and out of the lake. Today, this important water channel still runs parallel to the great river for over two hundred kilometres before flowing past the Labyrinth of Amenemhat and disgorging into Birket Karun. What is the traditional name of this 'second river Nile'? Why, the *Bahr Yussef* ('waterway of Joseph') of course!

I have shown you that the location of the Labyrinth is intimately connected, geographically, with the hydraulic system devised by Pharaoh's administration. I began to realise that it may not be too far fetched to imagine that the Labyrinth of Hawara was once a fully functioning building (not a spiritual dummy) housing the administrative quarters of the Nile valley (Upper Egypt) whilst the 'northern Avaris' (at Tell ed-Daba) was the administrative centre of the delta region (Lower Egypt). But, however attractive this idea might seem to be, I still had no proof that the name Hawara was the ancient Egyptian name Haware (Ha(t)-ware(t)) which would confirm absolutely that we had here an administration centre or 'House of the Department'. Then I came across the very proof I needed.

In the late 1880s Petrie had been digging at Hawara in the Hellenistic and Roman cemetery to the north of Amenemhat's pyramid. There he found fragments of papyri bearing Greek documents from an embalmer's archive. The material was not published until 1973 when the Ashmolean Museum in Oxford (who now hold these papyri) published the texts.[17] In this specialist catalogue I found the ancient name of the Hawara Labyrinth site. One of the documents reads:

> Year 10, 29th (day of the month of) Mesore: registered through the registry of PTOLEMY EUERGETES (III): a sale and cession of the six-fifteenth part of a house and courtyard and appurtenances, common and undivided, in **Aueris** of the outer localities of the division of Herakleides; vendor Marres, son of Paios ...[18]

As Eve Reymond, the translator, points out:

> There can be no doubt about the identity of *Aueris* of the Greek records and the Egyptian name *Hwt-*

wrt, Hawara, first recognized by F. Ll. Griffith, but later denied by Greek papyrologists. The contents of the Embalmers' Archives put this question beyond doubt.

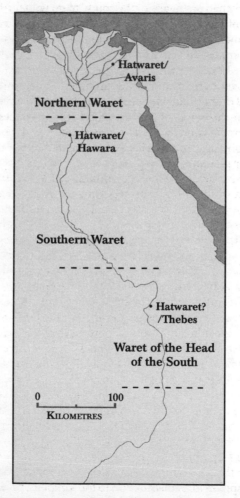

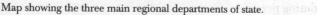

Map showing the three main regional departments of state.

I had not been aware of Griffith's identification of Avaris with Hawara,[19] but I had the satisfaction of now knowing that my hunch had proved to be right: the ancient name for the site of the Labyrinth was indeed Avaris and so we definitely had an 'Avaris of the south' to go with the known 'Avaris of the north' at Tell ed-Daba. Each 'House of the Department' was established in the reign of Amenemhat III according to the archaeological evidence which, in turn, suggested that it was in his reign that a major reorganisation of the state government was initiated. This important political change had previously been thought to have taken place in the reign of Senuseret III, the predecessor of Amenemhat, but the *buildings* associated with this new development can now clearly be assigned to the time of the later pharaoh.

The reorganisation of the administration involved the creation of three regional departments of state. Perhaps the most important was called the 'Department of the Head of the South' (Egy. *waret tep-resy*), responsible for the Nile valley from the First Cataract (at Aswan) up to Akhmim (north of Thebes). This regional department was therefore the supplier of the exotic produce from Nubia and Punt. The rest of Egypt was divided into the 'Department of the South' (from Akhmim north to Itj-tawy) and the 'Northern Department' (which was responsible for the lands north of Itj-tawy, including the delta). There were two other offices which covered the whole of Egypt. These were called the 'Department of the People's Giving' (Egy. *kha en ded remetj*) and the 'Department of the Treasury' (Egy. *per hedj*).

Given that we have determined the time of Joseph to be contemporary with the reign of Amenemhat III, I would suggest that this fundamental reorganisation of the Egyptian administration was also the work of the vizier Joseph and that the Department of the People's Giving was set up to oversee the agricultural labour CORVÉE and the storage of grain supplies for redistribution to the Egyptian population during periods of famine. Thus its function was to organise the giving of the people's labour to the state and, in return, the giving of the state grain back to the people when needed. The establishment of this department, put into the context of Joseph's reforms and the eradication of the nomarchs, fits neatly into the historical picture which we have been building up for the reign of Amenemhat III and with the Egyptian government's preparations for the predicted high Nile floods. What is more, we can say that the establishment of two departmental headquarters at the two locations identified with the name Avaris (the Northern and Southern Departments) are also the work of the vizier Joseph and that he was responsible for the great hydraulic scheme undertaken in the time of his monarch Amenemhat III.

That the Labyrinth was the central office of the Department of the South finds further support from the observations of Herodotus. If you remember, he states that on his visit to Hawara he discovered that the Labyrinth had twelve main courts, each surrounded by numerous rooms. The simple fact is that there are twelve nomes in the region controlled by the Department of the South between Nome 10 (the first north of Akhmim) and Nome 21 (the first south of Itj-Tawy).

The Egyptian Name of Joseph

Pharaoh named Joseph Zaphenat-Pa'aneah, and gave him Asenat daughter of Potiphera, priest of On, to be his wife. [Genesis 41:45]

If we are to succeed in identifying Joseph amongst the viziers of the late 12th and early 13th Dynasties, we will have to make some sort of sense of the garbled Old Testament vocalisation of the name given to the Asiatic vizier by Pharaoh. What on earth might 'Zaphenat-Pa'aneah' have been in its original form? The most convincing solution has come from none other than Kenneth Kitchen who tackled the issue in 1993.[20] His solution is as follows:

(a) In respect of the first element, 'Zaphenat', we have here an example of METATHESIS where the letters 't' and 'p' have been reversed. This is a regular (though unintentional) practice which occurs when difficult words and names are transferred from one language into another. The Hebrew scribe must have slipped into the use of the common Semitic root 'zaphan' when writing 'zaphenat' for the unfamiliar vocalisation of Joseph's Egyptian name. Kitchen concludes that the original was probably 'zat-en-aph', that is *Djed(u)-en-ef* (in Egyptospeak) meaning 'he who is called' – a phrase familiar to all Egyptologists. The expression was probably vocalised as 'zatenaf'. So far, then, we can take Genesis 41:45 one stage further in our translation of the first sentence: 'Pharaoh named Joseph "He who is called Pa'aneah"'.

(b) The second element in Joseph's Egyptian name – Pa'aneah – is fairly straightforward. It has long been recognised that 'aneah' represents the Egyptian word *ankh* (meaning 'life') or *ankhu* (meaning 'is alive'). Kitchen proposes that the initial 'Pa' or 'Pi' element stands for Egyptian *Ipi* or *Ipu*. Thus we discover that the Asiatic vizier of Egypt was given the name 'Joseph who is called Ipiankh(u)'. The practice of giving foreigners Egyptian names is very common in this period and is especially notable in Papyrus Brooklyn 35.1446 where, as we have already noted, we find a number of Asiatic slaves whose Egyptian names are preceded by the phrase 'he/she who is called'.

The name Ipiankhu (and its variants) is common in the Middle Kingdom but, as Kitchen emphasises, 'not any later' – a further argument to suggest that the historical Joseph should be sought in this era. Asenat too, according to Kitchen, would be a good Middle Kingdom type name which he gives as *Ius-en-at* ('she belongs to you').[21] It is interesting to note also that the hypocoristicon Ankhu is very common at this time, and may be another disguise in which the historical Joseph could be hidden. So perhaps we should be looking more widely for a vizier called Ankhu rather than the fuller form Ipiankhu.

Unfortunately, as yet, we have no names which we can directly associate with the vizierate in the reigns of Amenemhat III, Amenemhat IV, Sobekneferu, Amenemhat-Sobekhotep and Amenemhat-senbuef, but we can be certain that the office of the vizier continued to function. Indeed, Egypt's political organisation appears to have remained very much in the hands of this foremost official of the land. The headquarters of the vizier (who is always unfortunately unnamed) is regularly mentioned in the KAHUN PAPYRI – a valuable collection of administrative documents dated to the late 12th Dynasty. There was a renowned vizier called Ankhu in the early 13th Dynasty, but scholars presently find it very difficult to reconstruct his career or pinpoint him in time. It is also intriguing to note the mention of 'a storehouse of Ankhu' in a document of the period (Papyrus Bulak 18, lesser fragment) – perhaps one of the old grain-stores constructed by the vizier in preparation for an impending seven year famine? Nevertheless, if our 'Joseph, who is called Ipiankhu' is really to be found, he is at this stage no more than a phantom with no clear identity.

Conclusion Forty

The major administrative and agricultural reforms undertaken during the late 12th Dynasty were the work of the greatest vizier of Egypt during the Middle Kingdom who is now identified as the patriarch Joseph.

A Curse Upon the House of Joseph

> Then there came to power in Egypt a new king
> who did not know Joseph. 'Look,' he said to his
> people, 'the Israelites are now more numerous and
> stronger than we are. We must take precautions to
> stop them from increasing any further, or if war
> should break out, they might join the ranks of our
> enemies. They might take up arms against us and
> then escape from the country.' Accordingly they put
> taskmasters over the Israelites to wear them down
> by forced labour. [Exodus 1:8-10]

I have proposed that the new pharaoh who 'did not know
Joseph' was Neferhotep I or his immediate predecessor
Sobekhotep III. Neferhotep was the first of a new, more
powerful line of kings who succeeded the weak rulers of
the early 13th Dynasty. He came to the throne some seventy
years after the death of Joseph when the memory of the
Asiatic vizier would have been dimmed by the passage of
time. Perhaps the phrase 'who did not know Joseph' in this
instance simply means 'who had not known Joseph (when
he was alive)' rather than that the pharaoh was not aware
of the vizier's reputation. The growing threat posed by
Joseph's rapidly multiplying descendants would certainly
have failed to enhance his memory in the eyes of a new
line of pharaohs struggling with the 'Israelite problem'.

It was also around this time that collections of interesting
curse texts were recorded on clay figurines and pottery
which were then smashed to activate a spell of destruction
against Egypt's enemies. Two main series of EXECRATION
TEXTS, as they are called, have so far been found, the second
of which can be safely assigned to the 13th Dynasty. The
earlier texts (now housed in Berlin) were at first dated by
Kurt Sethe to the 11th Dynasty,[22] but Pierre Montet subsequently demonstrated that the orthography of the hieratic
writing could not be any earlier than the late 12th Dynasty

and so these curses may also belong to the 13th Dynasty along with the second corpus (housed in Brussels).[23]

If we read the names of the proscribed towns and peoples in the Execration Texts in the light of our New Chronology, we discover two entries with intriguing possibilities. The first is the appearance of the name Yakkub which is clearly the biblical name Jacob, father of Joseph and former head of the Hebrew tribe of Abraham. The second, amazingly enough, is the non-Egyptian name of Joseph himself.

Both names appear to be associated with towns in Palestine which presumably would have been named after the Patriarchs by their Levantine kin, either during their lifetimes or shortly after. The naming of settlements after eponymous ancestors is a common feature of ancient Near Eastern topography. Scholars immediately recognised that the 'Ishpi' featured in the Execration Texts was the name 'Yaseph' (Joseph/Yusef).[24] However, they were obviously prevented from identifying this name with *the* Joseph simply because of the chronological imperative which then existed. In the chronology we have established here, Joseph/Ishpi has already made his mark on western semitic civilisation and may well have been commemorated in the naming of a new Hebrew settlement in Canaan. It would then not be surprising to find that place listed amongst the proscribed towns in the Levant, given the new threat posed by the growing Israelite population upon the Egyptian state in the time of Neferhotep and his immediate predecessors.

Even if this name has no verifiable historical connection with the Patriarch, it is still one further indication (as with the Egyptian name of the Asiatic vizier) that the events surrounding the life of Joseph and the Israelite Sojourn belong to this historical period (archaeological era MB IIA) rather than the later Hyksos period (MB IIB) and New Kingdom (LB I) as in the orthodox chronology.

There is one further possibility which needs to be raised. If 'Ishpi' is the Egyptian writing of the western semitic name

'Joseph', then is it within the bounds of possibility that 'Pa'aneah' is not (I)piankhu but rather (Ish)piankhu – 'Joseph lives!' – an appropriate name for a favourite son who was believed by his father to have died and who had subsequently languished in Pharaoh's prison for many years?

The Origins of Avaris

With all the issues relating to Joseph's dating and identity in mind, I want now to take you north to the biblical land of Goshen and Joseph's personal estate.

In *Chapter Twelve* I introduced you to the city of Avaris and identified the Middle Bronze Age Asiatic settlement there as the main centre of the Israelite slaves during the Bondage period. We also learnt that Avaris was located within the land of Goshen. Is it possible, then, that the very first Israelite settlement was founded at this very spot? It would seem logical. So, what do we know about the early history of Avaris?[25]

The topography of the city (in the vicinity of the modern village of Tell ed-Daba) is quite unusual in that there were several centres separated and surrounded by swampy, low-lying ground which, during the inundation season, became flooded.[26] This left a series of islands upon which the city developed. The central island (or 'turtleback' as archaeologists refer to these sandy hillocks) has provided clear evidence of a Middle Kingdom occupation which surrounded a temple erected by Senuseret III. There is, however, both archaeological and inscriptional evidence which indicates that the foundation of this complex dates to the earlier reign of Amenemhat I (NC – c. 1812 BC).[27] The main southern island was used for the construction of a well-planned workers' town which Bietak dates to the very early 12th Dynasty, also suggesting that monumental buildings of the early Middle Kingdom era were located in the vicinity.[28] However, this workers' settlement was abandoned soon after the reign of Amenemhat I and the site left unoccupied for around one hundred and forty years.

Towards the end of the 12th Dynasty we see the beginnings of a new settlement – but this time of Asiatics. At first there were only a few simple houses surrounding a Syrian-style mansion erected over the abandoned workers' town. A little way to the east, an open area of animal compounds with simple stalls was also constructed. Before very long, though, the animal stalls were replaced by quite substantial houses with their own yards (presumably for the penning of animals) – about a dozen or so in all. Over the years, the small village rapidly expanded to become the central core of the town of Avaris.

Who were these Asiatics? I guess that you are already ahead of me. Let us see what the book of Genesis has to say concerning the settlement of the Israelites in the eastern delta.

- When Joseph became vizier, Pharaoh granted him permission to settle his father Jacob and the families of his eleven brothers in Egypt so that they might be protected from the worst of the famine which was becoming widespread throughout the Levant [Genesis 47:1-6]. We have determined that the famine struck Egypt in the twentieth year of Amenemhat III which in the New Chronology falls in *circa* 1663 BC.

- Jacob and his brethren arrived in Egypt in the second year of the famine (1662 BC). They settled in the 'region of Goshen' [Genesis 47:27] – also referred to as the 'region of Ramesses' [Genesis 47:11]. The later city of Pi-Ramesse was built over the ruins of ancient Avaris. The biblical editor was quite correct, therefore, in stating that the location of the first Israelite settlement was at Ramesses – but he was referring to the name of the place in his own day rather than its more ancient designations of Rowarty ('Mouth of the Two Ways', i.e. the place where the Pelusiac branch of the Nile divides into two channels – the earliest name of the site) and Avaris ('Estate' or 'House of the Department') by which it became known in the Second Intermediate Period.

- Joseph's brethren were shepherds who brought their flocks with them [Genesis 47:3-4]. Analysis of the skeletal remains of the livestock found in the compound area of Rowarty shows that the Asiatic settlers introduced the long-haired sheep into the delta at this time.

- Genesis 46 enumerates the men, women and children of Jacob's large family who entered Egypt with him in 1662 BC. They totalled seventy persons (including Joseph's two sons) made up of eleven or twelve households (including Jacob's own residence). The excavations on the main mound at Tell ed-Daba have revealed a small village in stratum G/4 (the earliest permanent settlement on the main tell). Slightly earlier, and built on top of the original workers' town to the west of the main tell, there was a community of houses surrounding a large Syrian villa.

- An analysis by Winkler and Wilfing of the human remains discovered at Tell ed-Daba has resulted in two very important findings: (a) that the male population derived from outside Egypt, most likely from Syria/ Palestine, and that (b) the females came from an anthropological group distinct from the males.[29] The sexual DIMORPHISM revealed in the population of Rowarty is consistent with the idea of an influx of foreign males into the eastern delta who are then partly assimilated, or we might say 'Egyptianised', through marriages to local Egyptian females.

- Following the death of Jacob, seventeen years after his arrival in Egypt (1662 – 17 = 1645 BC), 'Joseph stayed with his father's family' [Genesis 50:22]. This passage indicates that the vizier had an estate in Goshen (as is suggested by Genesis 45:10) and, in all likelihood, built a modest palace or residence there which formed the focal point of the Israelite settlement. When Joseph was actively pursuing his duties as vizier he was undoubtedly either touring the country or in residence at Amenem-hat's capital, Itj-tawy ('Seizer of the Two Lands', otherwise referred to simply as 'The Residence'). At that time he may have only occasionally visited Rowarty, staying at Jacob's house. Upon the death of his father and a lessening of his duties, he would probably have required his own residence at Rowarty where he had become head of the community. So, has the Austrian excavation revealed any sort of archaeological evidence which might confirm this part of the biblical tradition?

Let us now concentrate on the archaeological site at Tell ed-Daba designated by Bietak as Area F. There, lying on top of the century-old ruins of the workmen's town, the Austrians unearthed a large Egyptian-style palace, to which was attached a beautiful garden.[30] The pottery and stratigraphy indicated that the palace had been built during the early 13th Dynasty. This fine residence clearly either belonged to a local eastern delta ruler or was the home and private estate of a very important official.

Once this splendid structure had been removed by the archaeologists, a much smaller villa was revealed immediately below the heart of the 13th Dynasty palace. This earlier building was of Syrian design classified by the archaeologists as a 'Mittelsaal Haus' ('central hall house'). The modest villa represented the first 'residence' built at Rowarty on the southern turtleback. The tombs located in the garden of the Mittelsaal Haus contained Asiatic grave goods confirming that the occupants also originated in the Levant. The Syrian villa has been dated by Bietak to the late 12th Dynasty – in other words to the time of Jacob's

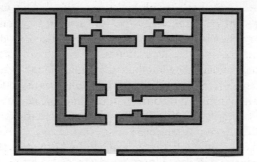

75. Plan of the 'mittelsaal' residence found at Tell ed-Daba, typical of the well-to-do residences of northern Syria in the Middle Bronze Age.

arrival in Egypt according to the New Chronology. Everything fits. This surely has to be the residence of Jacob, built and planned in the tradition of his original homeland.

The much grander palace, built over Jacob's dwelling, can be ascribed to the period following the death of Jacob when Joseph was of mature years (perhaps about fifty) and, no doubt, occupied with the administration of his own large estate bequeathed to him by the grateful pharaohs of the late 12th and early 13th Dynasties.

Here, then, we have an historical setting for this remarkable palace which, at the same time, sheds further light on the origins of the name Avaris which comes into use during the Second Intermediate Period. As we have seen, the Egyptian name which Manetho later recorded as Auaris or Avaris derives from *Ha(t)-ware(t)* or 'Hawara' meaning 'The House of the Department'. It is my contention that Joseph was the man who created the new administrative set up at the centre of which was the division of the Black Land into three geographical regions with their own departments of state. We have located the Department of the South at Hawara in the Faiyum and it is clear that Avaris (Tell ed-Daba) should be recognised as the site of the Department of the North. It is not unreasonable, therefore, to suggest that Joseph/Ankhu, as administrative head of

435

the departments of state, would have wished to locate his private estate near to one of these department centres. Indeed, one could argue that Joseph set up the administrative headquarters of the Department of the North at Avaris precisely because he wanted them to be in the region of Goshen allocated to him and his brethren by Pharaoh.

Following the successful reorganisation of the land and the completion of the hydraulic operations in the Faiyum, Joseph's duties would have been less pressing, allowing him more time with his people. He may have been permitted to settle near his people where he could still function as overseer of the 'Department of the North' – the Avaris of the Delta. There a new palace was constructed for him by the Egyptian craftsmen in his employ.

Joseph's Palace

Let us take a wander around the palace built for Joseph's retreat. We enter via an impressive portico of nine columns. Straight ahead are two entrances leading into a pair of identical suites of rooms. This may be an accommodation area for guests, or perhaps audience rooms (although this seems unlikely given the double configuration). It also occurred to me that, in the situation postulated here where the palace is identified as that belonging to Joseph, these twin suites of chambers may represent the quarters of Joseph's two sons, Manasseh and Ephraim. When they had reached marriageable age they would have needed accommodation for their families and these apartments might have been built precisely for that purpose. The double suite was probably an addition to the original building which we are now about to enter.

At the western and eastern ends of the entrance portico two passages lead around the twin suites and into an enclosed courtyard fronting the main residence. This charming private court is surrounded on three sides by slender columns which support the roof of a cloister. On

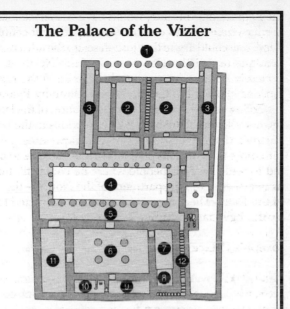

The Palace of the Vizier

76. The central and oldest section of the MB IIA palace complex at Tell ed-Daba (Area F).

(1) Entrance colonnade to the palace which was later blocked in to form a corridor; (2) A pair of identical apartments (perhaps for the two sons of Joseph and their families?) with a staircase leading up to the roof between them; (3) Side corridors leading around the twin apartments and through to the main central courtyard; (4) A large rectangular courtyard surrounded by a cloister, at the centre of which was a stone basin fed by a water conduit; (5) Entrance colonnade of twelve large pillars (representing the twelve sons of Jacob?); (6) The main columned hall where Joseph would have received guests and where his family would have spent much of their time; (7) Joseph's bedchamber; (8) The mudbrick platform which acted as a plinth for Joseph's bed – the largest surviving bed ever found in Egypt – including those which have been found in royal palaces; (9) The dressing room; (10) Joseph's wardrobe where he would have kept his coats of many colours and his Egyptian state costume; (11) Storeroom or second bedroom; (12) Staircase leading up to the roof of the palace.

the fourth and principal side of the court stands a second portico, this time supported by twelve stouter columns (representing the twelve sons of Jacob?) which fronts the great hall of the palace. Architect Dieter Eigner has determined that the court was erected after the twin suites but almost certainly also after the main palace building. I would suggest that the great hall was constructed first, followed by the twin suites and finally the courtyard which was built to integrate the two original elements of the complex.

As we enter the hall, the beautiful blues and greens of the painted brick floor reflect and diffuse the indirect sunlight coming from the court. The cool colours reach into the darker recesses of the chamber creating a relaxing ambience. Four large columns stretch up to support the roof at the centre of the hall. This is where Joseph and his family received visitors and where petitioners came to seek an audience with the great vizier.

Joseph's own bedchamber is located next to the main hall and can be visited on our tour. A doorway set in the north-east wall of the hall leads into the private sleeping quarters of the vizier and his wife Asenat. At the far end of a large narrow room the archaeologists unearthed the actual plinth upon which Joseph slept. It is an impressive size – a fitting resting place for the 'interpreter of dreams'. To the rear of the hall another doorway leads into two rooms, one of which was apparently the dressing-room of the vizier. Just think, it was in this little chamber that Joseph kept his wardrobe full of coats of many colours!

The palace is not grandiose or ostentatious either in size or layout, but it is a fine villa for a man who has done well for himself during his active lifetime. In the peaceful garden to the south – furnished with its ornamental pool, shady trees and flower beds – Joseph passed his remaining years in the company of his sons, their wives and his grandchildren and great-grandchildren. Eventually, after a prolonged and fruitful life, he was placed in the tomb long since prepared for him within the garden he had so much enjoyed during his retirement. Joseph was laid to rest amongst his brethren, at the very heart of the Israelite settlement. The garden tomb had already been surrounded by the graves of his elder brothers before the Patriarch was interred there. The entrance doors to the bedroom and dressing-room of the vizier were sealed and the hall was converted into a shrine to the great leader of the Israelites. The mortuary cult of Joseph was maintained throughout the ensuing difficult years of the Sojourn until, eventually, it was time for the Israelites to leave Egypt under the guidance of their next charismatic leader – Moses.

> ### Conclusion Forty-One
>
> **The elegant palace unearthed by the Austrian excavators at Tell ed-Daba, Area F, was originally erected as the residence for the vizier Joseph in the regional capital of Avaris – the headquarters of the delta administration known as the Department of the North.**

Midianite Caravaneers

Before we reach the climax of our search for Joseph, I would briefly like to deal with the historical context for Joseph's arrival in Egypt at the tender age of seventeen.

In Genesis 37 we learn that Joseph is the favourite son of Jacob and that his elder brothers are jealous of him. They decide to do away with their young brother by selling him to a caravanserai of Midianite/Ishmaelite tradesmen who are on their way to Egypt. Upon arrival in the Black Land, Joseph is then sold as a slave into the house of Potiphar, commander of Pharaoh's guard, where he becomes a trusted servant. Genesis 39 goes on to relate the tale of the amorous advances towards the young Hebrew slave

77. The 'ruler of the hill country, Abishai' – leader of a caravan of thirty-seven Asiatics whose arrival in Egypt is recorded in the tomb of the 12th Dynasty nomarch Khnumhotep III. Abishai is wearing his multi-coloured coat like the rest of the men in his tribe, only his is certainly more elaborate.

from the mistress of the house which result in false accusations and Joseph's despatch to prison for sexual harassment.

What interested me in this story was the method by which Joseph arrived in the Nile delta. We have placed Joseph's appointment as vizier in around the thirteenth year of King Amenemhat III which corresponds to the thirty-first year of his father, Senuseret III. The Bible provides an absolute date for this event of 1670 BC – a date which has been independently confirmed by the New Chronology. Joseph was thirty years old at his appointment and seventeen when he was first brought into Egypt by the Midianites [Genesis 37:2]. So he arrived in Egypt in the eighteenth year of Senuseret III (1683 BC). Just two decades earlier we find ourselves in the reign of Senuseret II when we are confronted with a remarkable parallel to the story of Joseph's arrival in Egypt.

In Middle Egypt there is a street of thirty-nine rock-cut tombs located high up in the cliffs near the village of Beni Hassan. The eight largest tombs were cut for the 'Great Overlords of the Oryx Nome' who held sway in the region during the Middle Kingdom. The size and superb decoration of these tombs attest to the power and wealth of the local baronies at this time. We have already noted that the series of almost 'royal' sepulchres of the nomarchs comes to a sudden end in the reign of Senuseret III (perhaps as late as the early years of his co-regency with Amenemhat III). We have connected this decline in the fortunes of the nobles of Middle Egypt to Joseph's land reforms which returned political authority to the central government based around Pharaoh's palace. This resulted in a dissolution of the local barony system and put an end to the construction of 'kingly' tombs for the nomarchs. So, the last of the great tombs at Beni Hassan was decorated in the time of Senuseret II, its owner perhaps being buried in the succeeding reign of Senuseret III.

The most famous of these rock-cut mausolea is also the very last to be constructed — that of Khnumhotep III. As I have said, he lived during the reign of Senuseret II – and therefore perhaps a decade or two before Joseph was brought into Egypt by the Midianite caravaneers. On the north interior wall of Khnumhotep's grand chapel is painted the well-known scene of Asiatics entering Egypt, carrying packs of eye paint (kohl) to sell to the Egyptians. The short text accompanying the scene informs us that there are thirty-seven persons in all (men, women and children) and that the leader of the group is named 'The chief of the hill country (heka-khaset), Abishai' – a good biblical name!

The remarkable thing about these people is that they wear colourful striped garments which numerous commentators have likened to Joseph's 'coat of many colours'. It is as if the Midianite traders of Genesis 37:28 had decided to have their picture taken to commemorate their successful journey into Egypt. Being Asiatic Habiru themselves, they wore the same type of garments as Jacob's Hebrew sons and so are depicted in Khnumhotep's tomb in their fashionable multicoloured woven coats. Although the Beni Hassan caravaneers are just a little too early to be *the* Midianite caravaneers who brought Joseph into Egypt, the setting of the story in Genesis 37 not only closely parallels the scene portrayed in Knumhotep's tomb but now originates from the same period.

The Tomb of Joseph

> So Joseph stayed in Egypt with his father's family; and Joseph lived a hundred and ten years. Joseph saw the third generation of Ephraim's line, as also the children of Machir son of Manasseh, who were born on Joseph's lap. At length Joseph said to his brothers, 'I am about to die; but God will be sure to remember you kindly and take you out of this country to the country which he promised on oath to Abraham, Isaac and Jacob.' And Joseph put Israel's sons on oath, saying 'When God remembers you with kindness, be sure to take my bones away from here.' … Joseph died at the age of a hundred and ten; he was embalmed and laid in a coffin in Egypt. [Genesis 50:22-26]

From this Old Testament 'historical' passage we learn the following:

• Joseph lived to the rather extraordinary age of one hundred and ten years. Whatever we may make of this, I suppose we might simply conclude that Joseph died at a ripe old age, having outlived his own sovereign, Amenemhat III, and witnessed the advent of the 13th Dynasty.

• Having requested that his embalmed body be taken out of Egypt when the Israelites eventually leave for the Promised Land, Joseph was buried in a coffin within his own tomb, presumably near to the palace where he spent the last forty years of his life.

We later learn in Exodus 13:19 that 'Moses took with him the bones of Joseph' when the Israelites departed from the Raamses (i.e. Avaris) fulfilling the Patriarch's last wish. So, if we are going to find Joseph's original place of burial it must possess the following characteristics:

1. If it is found in an intact archaeological context, there should be clear evidence of the body having been removed in ancient times, but without signs of the grave having been plundered.

2. It is likely to be characteristic of an Egyptian tomb given Joseph's Egyptianisation.

3. Although Joseph was highly Egyptianised, there may still be some indications of his Asiatic origins in the grave.

4. Because of his prestige and high status within the Egyptian hierarchy, it is likely that his tomb was an impressive edifice. We should therefore be looking for a large monument.

Bearing these four basic points in mind, let us see what has turned up at Avaris, in particular, within the cemetery located in the gardens of Joseph's palace.

In the spring of 1987, Bietak's excavation team began to uncover a very large tomb situated in the southern part of the stratum d/1 palace garden. The foundations of the superstructure measured twelve metres by seven metres – fulfilling our fourth requirement as far as size is concerned. This tomb (to which Bietak has assigned the number F/1-p/19:1) is the largest sepulchre so far found at Avaris and is certainly the most substantial tomb in the garden compound. Unfortunately, most of the superstructure of the monument had been stripped away in antiquity. Even so, the Austrian archaeologists determined from the foundations (and a comparison with other better preserved structures of similar type found elsewhere) that our tomb was once surmounted by an elegant steep-sided pyramid. This again is what we might expect for a much respected vizier of the Black Land. So far, I think we have here a good candidate for Joseph's tomb – at least on the grounds

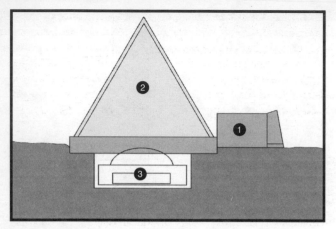

78. Cross-section through the pyramid tomb F/1–p/19:1, showing the chapel (1); the mudbrick pyramid (2) and the underground vaulted burial chamber (3).

of the last of our four points. Let us now take a look at the interior of Tomb F/1-p/19:1.

Unfortunately, the monument itself no longer exists as it has been removed by the archaeologists in order to expose the earlier stratum beneath the structure (i.e. the workmen's village). Archaeology by its very nature is a process of destruction and only becomes acceptable if detailed follow-up reports, plans and photographs are published by the excavators. Sadly, the publication intentions of some archaeologists are rarely completely fulfilled and, as a result, the information regarding their finds languishes in old shoe boxes and decaying notebooks. With Bietak's work,

79. An example of the type of tomb envisaged for the occupant of F/1–p/19:1 is to be found in Nubia where a Prince Amenemhat from the 18th Dynasty was buried in a very similar structure.

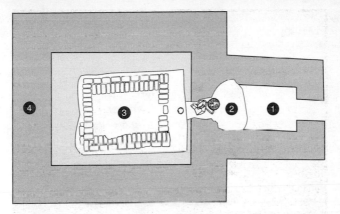

80. Simplified plan of tomb F/1-p/19:1 with the chapel (1), the robbers' tunnel (2); the empty burial chamber (3) and the pyramid plinth (4).

however, we are fortunate in this respect as the Director of the Austrian Mission at Tell ed-Daba has a well-organised publications programme which has already produced several volumes of detailed excavation reports. In the case of Tomb F/1-p/19:1 the full publication is still awaited but, in the interim, Bietak has written a number of articles which together provide an overview of the discoveries made in 1987. From these brief reports I have been able to put together the following main points.

There were two elements to the interior of the pyramid: a burial chamber and a mortuary chapel. I will deal with the latter first.

The mudbrick chapel was attached to the east side of the pyramid superstructure and measured approximately three and a half metres square. Tomb F/1-p/19:1 is the only grave in the palace complex to have a funerary chapel, marking it out for special attention. Clearly the owner of the tomb was very important to the community. Given the size of the tomb and its stratigraphic position, it appears to be one of the earliest major funerary monuments at the site. Its size and stratigraphic locus indicate that the tomb

445

belonged to the man who had founded the palace (and therefore the settlement). We will shortly return to what Bietak discovered in this chapel, but now we must take a look at the burial chamber itself.

As the excavators began to clear out the interior of the plinth foundation which supported the pyramid, they came upon a rectangular mudbrick chamber roofed over by a roughly circular dome also constructed of mudbricks. The chamber lay below the foundation level of the pyramid and the chapel. When the floor of the vault was reached, Bietak was surprised to find that the tomb was almost completely empty. There were some tiny fragments of bone (which may not have been human) and some small pieces of limestone. In every other grave in the cemetery, despite the depravations of tomb robbers, the broken remains of numerous grave goods were found surrounding the fossilised skeletons of the deceased. But here in Tomb F/1-p/19:1 there was no body and no grave goods. The burial chamber had been stripped clean (point 1 above).

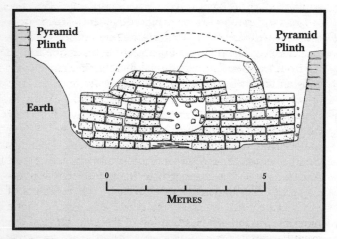

81. Profile view of the burial chamber of tomb F/1–p/19:1 with its mudbrick dome and the robbers' tunnel which breaks into the burial chamber from the chapel of the tomb.

It was soon discovered that a 'robber's tunnel' had been cut from the chapel down into the east wall of the burial chamber so that the body and grave goods could be removed. All the signs pointed to a careful clearance of the vault rather than the usual ransacking. This reopening of the tomb had taken place whilst the chapel was still in use and before the later occupation levels had covered the tomb. It looks as if somebody had removed the body either before or during the abandonment of Avaris at the end of stratum G (mid-13th Dynasty). The new settlers of stratum F built their houses over the stratum G cemetery and, in doing so, probably destroyed the pyramid and its chapel.

As soon as I heard about the large pyramid tomb which had been found in the palace garden at Tell ed-Daba I instinctively realised what Bietak and his team had uncovered. Without knowing it, they had unearthed the Egyptian tomb of the Patriarch Joseph from which Moses had subsequently extracted his ancestor in order to take his remains to the Promised Land. My early intuition was confirmed in my own mind when I first gazed upon the last of the strange discoveries made by the Austrians in that momentous spring excavation season of 1987.

As Bietak cleared the infill out of the access tunnel which led from the chapel into the burial chamber he came across substantial lumps of white limestone. It soon became apparent that these broken blocks represented the remains of a large seated statue. Most of the twice-size colossus had disappeared, no doubt carried off for use as building material, but the head and shoulders remained. The statue clearly belonged to the owner of Tomb F/1-p/19:1 and must have stood in the chapel, acting as the focus of offerings and prayers made by the deceased's descendants. If this was the tomb of Joseph, then these few rather pathetic blocks represented what was left of the cult statue of the great Patriarch.

The head was in a forlorn state. Some vengeful, anonymous individuals in antiquity had attempted to cleave it in

82. Full-frontal and profile view of the cult statue head from tomb F/1–p/19:1 giving a very clear idea of the unusual mushroom-shaped hair-do of the man who was buried and worshipped here.

two, the scar of their violent blows clearly visible on the crown of the head. The face was in a similar state of devastation. The nose had been smashed off and the inlaid eyes gouged out. Whoever was responsible for the destruction of the tomb owner's statue had clearly been wreaking vengeance on the memory of the deceased. We can guess who the perpetrators might have been. When Joseph's body was removed from his Egyptian tomb the Black Land had recently succumbed to the wrath of Yahweh – its pharaoh, the living god of the Egyptians, humiliated and bowed. Following the Exodus from the Land of Goshen the main Israelite settlements were substantially depopulated – as was the case at the end of stratum G at Avaris. Those who remained were the Egyptians living in the towns. Exodus 12:35-36 tells us that these unfortunate neighbours of the Israelites, their former taskmasters, were robbed of their

Plate 63: Tablet K.160 containing the reference to the 'Year of the Golden Throne'. British Museum.

Plate 64: The lunette of the Hammurabi Law Code stela showing the king (left) before Enlil. Louvre Museum.

Plate 65: Pink granite statue of Sobekhotep IV, stepfather of Moses.

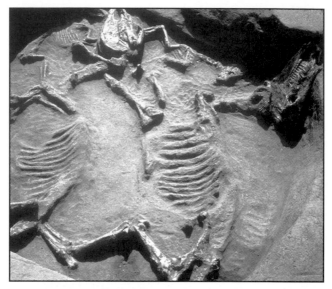

Plate 66: *Donkey burials in front of a Tell ed-Daba tomb with the skeletons of sheep to the left of the skulls of the equids.*

Plate 67: *One of the plague pits which mark the end of stratum G at Tell ed-Daba. Note that the bodies lie on top of each other*

Plate 68: The black granite statue of Amenemhat III in the Luxor Museum.

Plate 69: Aerial view of Semna Gorge at the start of the Second Cataract with the fortresses of Semna at the top and Kumma at the bottom.

Plate 70:Senuseret III.

Plate 71: Amenemhat III.

Plate 72: The Labyrinth viewed from the Hawara pyramid of Amenemhat III.

Plate 73: A reconstruction of Joseph's palace.

Plate 74: The Bahr Yussef ('Waterway of Joseph') at sunset.

Plate 75: Tomb F/1-p/19:1 as the excavation team reach the burial chamber.

Plate 76: Looking down onto the exposed burial chamber of F/1-p/19:1.

Plate 77: The desecrated head belonging to the cult statue from F/1-p/19:1.

Plate 78: Rear view of the cult statue head showing the deep gouge in the crown.

Plate 79: The restored cult statue now identified as that of the patriarch Joseph.

valuable possessions whilst they were still reeling from the devastating effects of the Exodus plagues. It is not hard to imagine the men of the town later descending upon the tomb of Joseph so as to vent their wrath upon the well-known cult statue of the Israelite progenitor.

At the beginning of our journey back in time I promised you that we would stand together before the cult statue of Joseph and look upon the likeness of this remarkable legendary figure from the past. With the advent of modern computer technology I am able to keep my promise. Using all the shattered remnants of the statue, we can restore Joseph to his original splendour and re-establish him in his darkened chapel. But, before we enter to pay our respects, pause for a minute to contemplate what we have been able to achieve by applying the New Chronology to the histories of Egypt and Israel.

From an Old Testament of myth and legend we have uncovered a living history. We have touched upon the lives of real people whose deeds were later to become the stuff of legend. In the Bible, the story of these Habiru folk goes back to a time before Joseph, but the true historical beginnings of the Israelite people are really to be found at Avaris where nationhood was forged in the adversity of bondage. In that sense Egypt is the original ancestral home of our Judaeo-Christian tradition and the birth place of the historical Bible. The seventeen-year-old boy who gave us our heritage was brought into the Black Land against his will but, through his remarkable abilities, was later to win the trust and respect of one of the great Middle Kingdom pharaohs. That simple Habiru pastoralist was made vizier of Egypt and from his powerful position was able to initiate a programme of radical agrarian and administrative reforms which transformed the physical and political structure of the Nile valley. For his services to Egypt, the former slave was honoured with a cult statue of 'kingly' proportions. What other man in Egyptian history (other than the pharaohs themselves[31]) was held in such high esteem by the people that a colossal statue was made for him in his own lifetime? Permission from Pharaoh for such a monument is even more astonishing when one considers that this man was not even a native Egyptian. The story of Joseph and the discovery of the colossal statue of a Middle Kingdom official come together in a palace garden at Avaris. Bietak has found it difficult to accept that a colossal statue could have been commissioned for a non-royal person and certainly believes such a thing to be 'unthinkable for the time of the 12th Dynasty' – but then, at the time of writing, he was not aware of the extraordinary possibilities provided by the New Chronology. He, of course, is quite right: it would be unthinkable for a commoner to receive such honours from an Egyptian state at the peak of its power – that is unless you happen to be Joseph the saviour of Egypt!

It is now time to visit the mortuary chapel of Tomb F/1-p/19:1 to pay homage to the great Asiatic vizier of Amenemhat III.

The Cult Statue of Joseph

As your eyes gradually adjust to the darkness the first thing you see are the gleaming white inlaid eyes of the statue staring serenely eastward towards the Promised Land. Soon the shadows become less penetrating and you can make out Joseph's gently smiling countenance. The sculptor has captured him in the prime of life, his upright seated posture full of dignity and assuredness, as befits the chief minister of the Black Land. The vizier's face is painted in pale ochre – the standard pigment used by the Egyptian artists to indicate the skin colour of a northerner heralding from the Levant. Although he is an Asiatic, Joseph does not carry the usual beard. He is clean shaven.

> Then Pharaoh had Joseph summoned, and they hurried him from the dungeon. He shaved and

changed his clothes, and presented himself before
Pharaoh. [Genesis 41:14]

One of the most unusual features of this remarkable
statue is the coiffure or wig. Joseph's hair is painted flame
red, fashioned into what can only be described as a
mushroom-shape. It has been carefully trimmed and is
neatly curled under at the back and sides.

Across his right breast the vizier holds his insignia of
office. Pharaoh holds the crook and flail, but Joseph holds
his 'throw-stick' – the Egyptian hieroglyphic symbol used
to denote a foreigner. The imagery of the cult statue is
telling us to recognise a man of foreign origins – but a man
who has become completely integrated in the highest
reaches of Egyptian culture.

There is one final feature of the statue, above all others,
which identifies the man himself. Wrapped around the
Asiatic official, enveloping all but his head, neck, arms and
feet, is a wondrous coat of many colours. The rich reds
and blues are trimmed with black and white to produce a
simple but effective geometric pattern of stripes and
rectangles, similar to the costumes worn by the Asiatics
represented in the tomb of Khnumhotep at Beni Hassan.
The effect is dazzling.

Joseph has been remembered throughout the last three
thousand years for his magnificent coat. It is quite extraordinary for me to be able to show you that amazing coat
of many colours in all its original glory. Legend and history
have fused together inside a darkened chapel, within a
palace garden, at a place called Avaris, situated on the banks
of the River Nile.

Just as the legends of golden Troy and the amazing
Labyrinth of King Minos have been revealed to us as real
places associated with real events – thanks to the archaeological discoveries made in the last century – so our search
through the archaeology of Egypt and the Levant has
brought its own series of new revelations.

Conclusion Forty-Two

The pyramid tomb, discovered by Manfred Bietak and his team in Area F at Tell ed-Daba, was the original burial place of the patriarch/vizier Joseph (before his body was removed by Moses for reburial in the Promised Land). The shattered limestone head and shoulders found in the tomb originally formed the upper part of a cult statue of Joseph, awarded to him by Amenemhat III for the Hebrew vizier's outstanding services to the Egyptian nation during a time of great trials and tribulations.

*****

With this book I have attempted to demonstrate how traditional history can make a significant contribution to the collective knowledge of our ancient past. Not everything in myth and tradition is true, but I believe this study has shown that it would be imprudent for scholars of ancient world history to underestimate the significance and tenacity of our legendary past. Without initially starting out to discover the historical Bible, I have come to the conclusion that much of the Old Testament contains real history. It has certainly been an interesting exercise for this Egyptologist who has found himself wandering into many unfamiliar areas of Old World research in his quest for history. Only time will tell if the New Chronology, tentatively proposed here, is correct in most of its details. In the meantime, I hope that I have at least been able to bring the issue of the historicity of the Old Testament back into the spotlight. I leave you to judge if I have succeeded in that aim.

*****

Part Five

Additional Research

Appendices Λ to E

Appendix A

DATING SHOSHENK I

In *Chapter Five* I demonstrated how Egyptologists came to rely upon the Shoshenk I/Shishak identification in order to synchronise Egyptian and Israelite history. Rather than establishing Egyptian chronology on the basis of the internal evidence from the Nile valley, scholars had taken a biblical date to set up one of the major pillars of Egyptian chronology – 925 BC for Year 20 of Shoshenk I. From this anchor point the surviving historical data from the TIP were then made to 'fill up' the interval between 925 and 664 BC when the era known as the Late Period begins.

John Bimson[1] and I[2] have been arguing for a number of years that the evidence for the identification of Shoshenk I with Shishak is contradictory. It seems clear that Shoshenk cannot be securely identified with Shishak and that, therefore, the 925 BC date for this king must be abandoned. So when did Shoshenk I reign?

The Evidence from Byblos

There is an interesting possibility for dating Shoshenk I – at least in an approximate fashion – which comes from an investigation of Phoenician inscriptions discovered at Byblos. The first object in the chain of argument is the famous statue of Pharaoh Osorkon I found in the 1890s and now in the Louvre Museum.[3] On the chest of the statue two inscriptions are carved: (a) the prenomen of Osorkon (Sekhemkheperre-setepenre), within a cartouche, and (b) a Phoenician dedication text which reads:

83. Upper part of the statue of Osorkon I from Byblos with the prenomen (Sekhemkheperre) of the pharaoh carved on the chest and the Phoenician dedication of Elibaal surrounding it. Louvre Museum.

Statue which **Elibaal**, king of Byblos, son of **Yehimilk**, [king of Byblos], made [for] Baalat-Gebel, his lady. May Baalat-[Gebel] prolong [the days of] Elibaal and his years over [Byblos].

Albright[4] maintains that King Elibaal of Byblos was 'obviously almost contemporary' with Osorkon I on the grounds that the dedication of an Egyptian royal statue to a foreign goddess – in this case the female patron deity of Byblos – would take place when the pharaoh ruled in Egypt rather than after his death. The statue would have been sent to Byblos from Egypt as a gift to the local king, just as a statue of Shoshenk I – the predecessor of Osorkon – was brought to Lebanon in the reign of Abibaal, the ruler of Byblos prior to Yehimilk, father of Elibaal. On the Shoshenk statue, found in 1894, the Phoenician text explicitly states that the gift from Egypt for the temple of Baalat Gebel was brought by king Abibaal himself. We would thus have a sequence of rulers presumably on the following lines:[5]

Abibaal --------------	temp. Shoshenk I
Yehimilk -------------	(temp. Shoshenk/Osorkon I)
Elibaal ----------------	temp. Osorkon I

The next item is a limestone slab found at Byblos in 1935 which bears a further dedication text in the Phoenician script.

> Wall built by **Shipitbaal**, king of Byblos, son of **Elibaal**, king of Byblos, for Baalat-Gebal, his lady. [May] Baalat-Gebel prolong the days of Shipitbaal and his years over Byblos.[6]

This brief text informs us that King Elibaal's son and successor was a King Shipitbaal. Crucially, a king bearing this name appears in an Assyrian inscription of the eighth century BC.[7] The text comes from the annals of Tiglath-pileser III and is securely dated by the Assyrian Eponym List to 738 BC.[8]

> [I (Tiglath-pileser) received] the tribute of Kushtashpi of Kummuh, Urik of Que, Sibittibael of Byblos, … Enil of Hammath, Panammu of Samaal, … Matan-bael of Arvad, Sanipu of Bit-Ammon, Salamanu of Moab, … Mitinti of Ashkelon, Jehoahaz of Judah, Kaushmalaku of Edom, …[9]

Tiglath-pileser's 'Sibittibael' is the Phoenician name 'Shipitbaal' and this Shipitbaal was a contemporary of 'Jehoahaz' (Akk. *Ia-u-ha-zi*) of Judah (Akk. *Ia-u-da-a-a*).

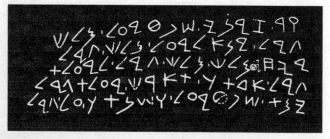

84. Text of the Shipitbaal inscription discovered in a supporting wall of the water reservoir belonging to the city of Byblos. Beirut Museum.

85. Side panel of a throne base which once formed the lower part of a statue of Shoshenk I, discovered at Byblos. The pharaoh's cartouches (including his nomen containing the hieroglyphic sign for 'n') are again surrounded by a Phoenician dedicatory text – this time written by King Abibaal of Byblos. Beirut Museum.

This Jehoahaz is not the Judahite king who reigned for three months in 609 BC. Neither can he be King Joash (834-794 BC) as that king reigned decades before Tiglath-pileser came to the throne in 744 BC. He must therefore be Ahaz (741-725 BC), demonstrating once more the use of hypocoristicons in the biblical text. The full name of Ahaz was 'Jeho-ahaz'. An earlier inscription of Tiglath-pileser III mentions tribute sent by 'Azriau from Iuda' which has to be Azariah of Judah (790-738 BC) and 'Menahem of Samaria' (i.e. Israel, 752-743 BC), thus confirming the general position of the Assyrian king in relation to the dynastic lines of Israel and Judah.

The *circa* 738 BC Shipitbaal of Byblos is normally assigned the numeral 'II' after his name because in the orthodox scheme he cannot possibly be the same king as Shipitbaal son of Elibaal, the contemporary of Osorkon I (OC – 924-889 BC). Shipitbaal 'I' would have ruled at Byblos in the first half of the ninth century. However, we now know that this date for Shipitbaal 'I' is based on the 925 BC anchor of Shoshenk I which is unsafe. If we were to identify Tiglath-pileser's Shipitbaal 'II' with Shipitbaal 'I' – making just one attested Shipitbaal of Byblos[10] – then we could establish guideline dates for both Osorkon I and his predecessor Shoshenk I using the genealogy assembled from the Byblite inscriptions.

Abibaal ------ temp. Shoshenk I	= c. 798 BC
Yehimilk ----- (temp. Shoshenk/Osorkon I)	= c. 778 BC
Elibaal --------temp. Osorkon I	= c. 758 BC
Shipitbaal --- temp. Tiglath-pileser III	= c. 738 BC

The dates thus derived for Osorkon I and Shoshenk I (based on a 20-year average reign-length) are of course only rough guides, but they would imply that the true era of the first two rulers of the 22nd Dynasty was the late-ninth and early-eighth centuries and not the late-tenth century as in the conventional chronology. It is therefore interesting to note that a study by Ronald Wallenfels of the Phoenician texts under discussion here concludes that they should be dated to the eighth century rather than the tenth century BC.[11] Let us now see if the general date of *circa* 798 BC for Shoshenk I is feasible within a revised TIP chronology.

The Temple of Osiris Hekadjet

There is another route which tends to bring us to the same dating period for Shoshenk I. In the north-east corner of the great temple enclosure at Karnak there is a small temple of the late TIP dedicated to Osiris Hekadjet ('Osiris Ruler of Eternity'). The inner sanctum is decorated with scenes depicting the gods and members of the family of Osorkon III. Here the cartouches of Osorkon III, his co-regent Takelot III, his son Rudamun and the God's Wife all appear. On the façade of the two inner rooms Shepenwepet is joined by a second ('adopted') God's Wife. She is Amenirdis, the daughter of King KASHTA of the proto-25th Dynasty and the sister of King Piankhy.

The walls of the small court which stands immediately before the sanctuary are decorated with more scenes of Amenirdis, but this time she is accompanied by King

Shabataka, third ruler of the 25th Dynasty, whilst the outer façade of the temple also has a large scene of the same Kushite ruler.

The important point is that this is a small temple which would not have taken more than a few years to build, yet the interval between the co-regency of Osorkon III and Takelot III (OC – c. 750 BC) and the reign of Shabataka (OC – c. 700 BC) is calculated as 50 years. This seems far too long for the construction work unless there was a long cessation in the building operations. This is of course possible, but equally likely is that the building was completed within five years and that Shabataka therefore soon followed Takelot as the recognised pharaoh in Thebes.

If we assume this second proposition then we can undertake an exercise of chronological retrocalculation through the kings of the 22nd Dynasty to reach an approximate date for the dynasty founder – Shoshenk I.

1. The reign of Shabataka immediately preceded that of Taharka and we know that the latter's reign came to an end in 664 BC. Taharka had 26 years as pharaoh, making his 1st year 690 BC. There is uncertainty as to whether Shabataka died in this year or whether there was a co-regency with his nephew for 6 years. It is my view that there was just such a 6-year co-regency and so I would establish a date of 698 BC for the 1st year of Shabataka's 14-year reign. Shabataka is first attested at Thebes in his 3rd regnal year (696 BC) when he appears to have been crowned as pharaoh of Egypt (he would have been king of Napata in Kush before that).[12] The completion of the temple of Osiris Hekadjet would then have taken place between 696 and 690 BC.

2. If the building operations under Osorkon III and Takelot III immediately preceded Shabataka's arrival in Thebes then we could date the 5-year co-regency period to *circa* 700-696 BC.

3. The co-regency began in Osorkon III's Year 24 which would now be dated to *circa* 700 BC. His reign would then have begun in *circa* 723.

We now have to deal with the problem of the identity of this King Osorkon III so as to tie him historically and chronologically to the 22nd-Dynasty line.

Prince Osorkon

On the inner west side wall of the Bubastite Portal at Karnak there is a long inscription known as the Chronicle of Prince Osorkon.[13] It details the career of the High Priest of Amun (HPA) and Crown Prince Osorkon, son of King Takelot II and great-grandson of Osorkon II. The big question has always been whether this Crown Prince became Pharaoh Osorkon III. Kitchen dismissed the connection on the grounds that Prince Osorkon would have been far too old at his coronation to have then reigned for 28 years as Osorkon III. I have never accepted this argument because it is based on a very peculiar interpretation of the Chronicle. My view of what the text is telling us was first aired in 1982[14] and since then David Aston has come to precisely the same conclusion on independent grounds.[15] The chronological data in the Chronicle of Prince Osorkon are as follows:

- Prince Osorkon is first attested as High Priest at Karnak in Year 11 of his father Takelot II. He travels upstream to Thebes from his headquarters at EL-HIBA – presumably for his induction. There appears to be political unrest in the Nile valley. A potential revolt is quickly suppressed. Osorkon is back at Karnak in Year 12 of Takelot to officiate at temple festivities.

- In Year 15 a violent civil war breaks out, the ignition for which is an uprising in Thebes. The conflict appears to last for a decade.

- By Year 24 exhaustion drives the warring parties to a political compromise. HPA Osorkon returns to Thebes laden with gifts for Amun.

- The peace is brief. In Year 26 the whole nasty business erupts all over again and Osorkon is once again driven from Thebes. (King Takelot II died in his 26th year and it may have been this event which brought on the second insurrection.)

- The offerings made by HPA Osorkon to the Karnak temples during his father's reign span a period of 14 years between Years 11 and 24.

- The final set of dates mentioned in the Chronicle consists of a list of offerings to Amun which HPA Osorkon made between Years 22 and 29 of King Shoshenk III.

- Finally, a Nile Level Text recorded on the West Quay at Karnak mentions Osorkon as High Priest in the 39th year of Shoshenk III.

Kitchen, because he is preoccupied with the task of 'filling up' the 405 years he has allocated to the TIP, envisages Shoshenk III crowned upon the death of Takelot II. Thus Prince Osorkon serves as high priest from Years 11 to 26 of Takelot II and then from Years 1 to 39 of Shoshenk III. Kitchen would have Prince Osorkon serving as high priest for 53 years before he could be crowned as King Osorkon III. Add say 20 years before Osorkon becomes high priest (remembering that he is commander of the army as well as HPA in Year 11 of Takelot) plus the reign of 28 years (as Osorkon III) and you get a total age for Osorkon of 101 years! It is not difficult to see why Kitchen rejected the identification of HPA Osorkon with King Osorkon III. But he made one important assumption which is almost a prerequisite of his long TIP chronology – he assumed that Shoshenk III began his reign in the year that Takelot II died. This is not what the Prince Osorkon Chronicle seems to be telling us. It states that the high priest made gifts to the temple of Amun at Karnak from Year 11 to Year 24 of Takelot II and then from Years 22 to 29 of Shoshenk III. There is no mention of offerings between Years 1 and 21 of Shoshenk. The implication is that Year 22 of Shoshenk III followed directly on from Year 24 of Takelot II (perhaps in the same calendar year). The two kings may thus have ruled contemporaneously for 21 years.

At the other end of Shoshenk's reign his highest attested date is the Year 39 of the Nile Level Text mentioning HPA Osorkon for the last time. We have no evidence that Shoshenk III reigned beyond his 39th year. If we assume that his reign came to an end in his 40th year and that Shoshenk's 1st year coincided with the 3rd year of Takelot II, then we get a completely different view as to the age at death of King Osorkon III (formerly HPA Osorkon). His pontificate now lasts for 31 years, and if we add the 20 years prior to his period in office plus his 28 years as king we get a grand total of 79 years – a reasonable age at death for the king who had formerly served as High Priest.

There are two other pieces of evidence which tend to confirm the identity of HPA Osorkon as the future Osorkon III.

The name of the mother of HPA Osorkon is known to have been Karomama Merytmut[16] whilst King Osorkon III's mother is attested as Kamama Merytmut. The two names are considered to be the same, the second being a hypocoristic form of the first.

A further, more conclusive, proof came in 1982 when a Japanese mission working at Tehna (ancient Akoris) discovered a donation stela which gives one of the titles of King Osorkon III as 'High Priest of Amun'.[17] There can now be little doubt that Pharaoh Osorkon III and HPA Crown Prince Osorkon, son of Takelot II, are the same individual.

Two Hedjkheperre Takelots

Earlier we established an accession date for Osorkon III at around 723 BC. If we now add to this date the 32 (inclusive) years of his pontificate we reach *circa* 754 BC for Year 11 of Takelot II (when Osorkon became high priest). Thus Takelot II was crowned in 764 BC. David Aston has cogently argued that Hedjkheperre Takelot II was not a Tanite ruler but rather a king of Upper Egypt probably based at both Heracleopolis and Thebes.[18] He is not to be identified with the Hedjkheperre Takelot I buried in the tomb complex of Osorkon II at Tanis who was the father of Osorkon II. However, Takelot II was a grandson of Osorkon II as the Chronicle of Prince Osorkon attests and thus belongs to a subsidiary line of the 22nd Dynasty. His father was Nimlot, commander of Heracleopolis, who was appointed high priest at Karnak in Osorkon II's reign. It has often been suggested that Takelot II was made a co-regent of his grandfather following the death of Nimlot. However, there is no direct evidence to support this hypothesis. Even so it remains a possibility. The interesting point is that the king who appears to succeed Osorkon II upon the old king's death is Shoshenk III (who was indeed buried at Tanis), yet we know from the Osorkon Chronicle that Takelot II preceded Shoshenk as pharaoh. Aston postulates that Takelot II became ruler of Upper Egypt just 3 years before his brother succeeded to Osorkon's throne in Tanis. Osorkon II would then have died in Year 3 of Takelot II (i.e. 762 BC) to be succeeded in that year by his son Shoshenk III. It is already well established that the High Priest of Amun Harsiese was recognised as king in Thebes towards the end of Osorkon II's reign. What I am suggesting is that Takelot II was enthroned in Thebes as Harsiese's successor, thus giving Osorkon greater control of Upper Egypt through his grandson. It was this move which would create the climate for rebellion some 15 years later when the descendants of Harsiese (in particular his son HPA

[Pe]du[bast], later Pedubast I) took up arms against their northern overlord Shoshenk III and his nephew Takelot II ruling from Tanis and Heracleopolis respectively.

In the context of all these political manoeuvrings we have the very interesting proclamation of Osorkon II contained in an inscription on a fine statue originally set up in the temple of Amun at Tanis.[19]

> [You will fashion] my issue, the seed that comes forth from my limbs, [to be] great [rulers] of Egypt, princes, high priests of Amenresonter, great chiefs of the Ma, [great chiefs of] foreigners, and prophets of Arsaphes ... You will turn their hearts towards the Son of Re, Osorkon II, you will cause them [to walk] on my path. You will establish my children in the [posts] [which] I have given them, so that brother is not jealous (?) of brother.[20]

Israel's Saviour

The highest attested date for Osorkon II is a Year 23 recorded on an Apis stela found in the Serapeum. However, some scholars believe that he may have reigned for up to 30 years. The best we can do without further evidence is to assign him a reign of 24 years with Takelot II becoming ruler of Thebes and Heracleopolis in his grandfather's 22nd year (764 BC). This would result in the chronological alignment for Takelot II and Shoshenk III suggested by the Prince Osorkon chronicle. Osorkon II's Year 1 would then have fallen in 785 BC. Manetho gives Takelot I a reign of 13 years but there is some confusion in the redactions of his 22nd Dynasty king-list. Eusebius offers the following:

Sesônchôsis	– 21 years
Osorthôn	– 15 years
Takelôthis	– 13 years
Total	= 49 years

Whilst Africanus lists the kings in the same order, he adds some extra information which completely changes our perceptions of the identifications and the reign lengths:

Sesônchis	– 21 years
Osorthôn	– 15 years
Three other kings	**– 25 or 29 years**
Takelôthis	– 13 years
Three other kings	**– 42 years**
Total	= 116 or 120 years

The best way to interpret Africanus' version is to assume that his Takelôthis is not Takelot I, son of Osorkon I, but rather Takelot II and that the 'three other kings for 25 or 29 years' represents the reigns of Takelot I, Osorkon II and Shoshenk II (the latter having been a son and earlier co-regent of Osorkon II in the New Chronology). We would thus arrive at the following dates and locations for the rulers of the mid-22nd Dynasty.

Takelot I (Bubastis)	– 789-781 BC
Osorkon II (Tanis and later Bubastis)	– 785-762 BC
Shoshenk II (Thebes & Heracleopolis)	– 772-769 BC
Harsiese (Thebes & Heracleopolis)	– 769-764 BC
Takelot II (Thebes & Heracleopolis)	– 764-739 BC
Shoshenk III (Bubastis and later Tanis)	– 762-723 BC

We have just two more rulers to place chronologically in this tentative model for the 22nd Dynasty. Before Takelôthis Manetho lists Osorthôn with 15 years of reign and Sesônch[ôs]is with 21 years. Scholars have concluded that these kings are Sekhemkheperre Osorkon I and Hedj-kheperre Shoshenk I respectively. Our calculations based on the Byblos statue of Osorkon I place this pharaoh in approximately 775 BC. Our second dating method – working backwards from the construction date of the temple of Osiris Hekadjet – produces an accession date for Osorkon I of 803 BC. His predecessor is dated to 798 BC via the Byblos connection whereas our second dating method results in a Year 1 for Shoshenk I in 823 BC. However, both methods have considerable error factors which have to be brought into the calculations. These include (a) the use of 20-year average reign lengths which are only accurate to within ± 20 years over several generations; (b) a number of reigns for which we have no certain reign lengths (e.g. Osorkon II); (c) uncertainty as to whether co-regencies were practised regularly in this dynasty (could Osorkon I have been a junior co-regent of Shoshenk I?); and no direct proof of the order of the earliest rulers of the dynasty (how does one explain the fact that the inner hall of the temple of Bubastis was built by Usermaatre Osorkon (II) whilst the first (outer) court was constructed by Sekhem-kheperre Osorkon (I)? – the building order is not consistent with the presumed order of the two kings). One might conclude, therefore, that the reign of Shoshenk I, founder of the 22nd Dynasty, began any time between the years 830 and 790 BC – a wide range of dates but the only fair way to assign a date for the beginning of the dynasty. However, we cannot work with such a cumbersome datum as we proceed with the rest of our calculations, so I will elect for a working accession date for Shoshenk I of 823 BC and a Year 1 for Osorkon I of 803 BC. This approximate date for Shoshenk raises the possibility of a new synchronism with the Old Testament narratives. In the reign of Jehoahaz of Israel (814-798 BC) the Northern Kingdom was being oppressed by the Aramaean kings Hazael and his successor Benhadad who were determined to take over parts of Transjordan and the Jezreel valley.

> In the twenty-third year of Joash son of Ahaziah, king of Judah, Jehoahaz son of Jehu became king of Israel in Samaria. He reigned for seventeen years. He did what is displeasing to Yahweh and copied the sin into which Jeroboam (I) son of Nebat had led Israel …

> This aroused Yahweh's anger against the Israelites, and he delivered them without respite into the power of Hazael king of Aram and of Benhadad son of Hazael. Jehoahaz, however, tried to placate Yahweh and Yahweh heard him, for he had seen the oppression which the king of Aram was inflicting on Israel. **Yahweh gave Israel a saviour who freed them from the grip of Aram** and the Israelites lived in their tents as in the past. ... Of Jehoahaz's army Yahweh left only fifty horsemen, ten chariots and ten thousand foot soldiers. The king of Aram had destroyed them, making them like dust trampled under foot. [II Kings 13:1-7]

Who was this 'saviour' who came onto the scene to rid Israel of the Aramaeans? This has been a perplexing mystery ever since the early days of biblical research. With a date of 823 BC for the accession of Shoshenk I, his campaign into the territory of Israel takes on a completely new significance. He now becomes the saviour of Israel mentioned in II Kings 13. The Egyptian military expedition, usually considered to have taken place late in Shoshenk I's reign, is therefore explained – the campaign is directed against the occupation of the vassal state of Israel by Syrian invaders who had penetrated the outlying territory of the Northern Kingdom during the reign of King Jehoahaz.

A Second Shoshenk I?

There is one further complication which has the potential to influence the above tentative dates for the early 22nd Dynasty. In 1986 I first hinted of some tantalising evidence which suggested that there were two Shoshenks bearing the prenomen Hedjkheperre.[21] The arguments were then more fully explored in a paper published in 1989.[22] If this was the historical reality then it would mean that some of the regnal data currently attributed to Hedjkheperre

Shoshenk (I) may date to his later namesake. Although it does not impinge directly on the date of the first Hedjkheperre Shoshenk, I think it is only proper at least to present the case for the second Hedjkheperre Shoshenk for others to consider the implications.

- In the tomb of Shoshenk III at Tanis (Tomb V) Montet discovered two sarcophagi – one large (for Shoshenk himself) and one considerably smaller. Also found in the chamber were fragments of two surviving canopic jars (virtually complete), one bearing the names and titles Hedjkheperre-setepenre Shoshenk-sibast-mery-amun-netjerhekaiunu I.[23]

- In the Staatliche Museum in Berlin there is a canopic chest of Hedjkheperre Shoshenk I.[24] Canopic chests ceased to be used as receptacles for the royal viscera near the end of the New Kingdom as far as we are aware.[25] This chest is the only example of a stone canopic chest from the TIP, which in the conventional chronology makes it an exceptional artefact. In the New Chronology Shoshenk I reigned in the era of political chaos towards the end of the 20th Dynasty when the use of a canopic chest would not have been out of place.

- More significant, however, is the straight-forward fact that the canopic vases found at Tanis are too large to fit into the compartments of the Berlin chest. They must consequently belong to a separate burial. If this is the case then there must have been two Hedjkheperre Shoshenks.

- In St. Petersburg Museum there is a stela of the Chieftain of the Libu Niumateped.[26] It is dated to Year 10 of Hedjkheperre Shoshenk I. However, Niumateped is otherwise attested in the 8th year of Shoshenk V. The office of Chieftain of the Libu is not attested before the reign of Shoshenk III (Year 14) – 113 years after the death of the well-known Shoshenk I. To overcome this problem Kitchen has to postulate an earlier Niumateped separated from his attested fellow office-holders by over a century. Niumateped is certainly a very rare name which makes Kitchen's hypothesis seem inherently implausible. Given the evidence for two burials of kings called Hedjkheperre Shoshenk, it would perhaps be better to consider the possibility that a second Hedjkheperre Shoshenk reigned soon after the death of Shoshenk III, thus explaining the second burial in Tomb V at Tanis. This raises the clear possibility that the actual successor of Shoshenk III was this Hedjkheperre Shoshenk – a new ruler of Tanis who now neatly fills the 12-year gap between Year 40 of Shoshenk III and the accession of Pimay.

In consideration of the problems and confusion it would cause to renumber the kings of the TIP named Shoshenk (making the new Hedjkheperre Shoshenk into Shoshenk IV, Shoshenk IV into Shoshenk V and Shoshenk V into Shoshenk VI), I have decided it would be better to refer to this newly identified king as Shoshenk I(b) thus requiring the earlier Hedjkheperre Shoshenk to bear the designation Shoshenk I(a).

Appendix B

TIP GENEALOGIES (CONTINUED)

I have included here, rather than in the main text, two further genealogies which support the findings of the Genealogy of the Royal Architects. I decided to do this so as to avoid adding further details to *Chapter Six* beyond what was necessary to make the chronological point. As you will see, both the Nespaherenhat and Memphite Genealogies confirm that the interval between the late 19th Dynasty and the early TIP must be radically reduced.

Calculating an Average Generation

In order to determine what would be a reasonable number of years to allocate to a generation in the ancient world I have averaged over three hundred reign lengths from ancient royal dynasties, the dates for which are well established. Although reign lengths are not the same as natural generations they are the only data we have available to us and they do represent, in the majority of cases, father to son successions.

The table on the following page gives an average reign length of 16.75 years for 329 kings in a total of 5,511 years. I have chosen to increase this figure to 20 years so as to allow for the occasional usurpations and brother successions, and also to conform to the average generation length used by other scholars such as Kitchen and Bierbrier. However, in my opinion this figure may be a little too high. The data suggests that an 18-year average reign length may be nearer the mark. As a result, the dates for the two genealogies discussed here (as well as that of the Khnemibre genealogy dealt with in *Chapter Six*) could be lowered by at least twenty years.

The Generations of Nespaherenhat

Statue 42189 in the Cairo Museum represents Nespaherenhat and was dedicated by his son, Ankhefenkhons. The genealogical text records nine generations back from Nespaherenhat to a Second Prophet of Amun, Roma, father of Ipuy. This Ipuy (of the 8th generation) bears the title 'Sem-priest of the Temple of Baenre' making him a contemporary, or near contemporary, of the 13th son and successor of Ramesses II – Baenre Merenptah.[1] Roma is, in all likelihood, the same individual as the Second Prophet of Amun, Rama, father of the High Priest of Amun, Bakenkhons. Bakenkhons is attested in Year 46 of Ramesses II, making his father, Rama/Roma, contemporary with the early years of King Ramesses.

The statue of Nespaherenhat is dated to the reign of Sekhemkheperre Osorkon I (NC – c. 803-789 BC – see *Appendix A*), successor to Shoshenk I(a) – founder of the 22nd Dynasty (NC – c. 823-803 BC). Ankhefenkhons, who dedicated the statue to his deceased father, would be datable to around 790 BC in the New Chronology. Nespaherenhat was also a contemporary of Osorkon I, having died in his reign. This would allow us to date the end of Nespaherenhat's career at 790 BC on the minimum possible figures.

Using this calculation as a fixed point, the following dates can be postulated for the nine generations of the family attested on statue 42189 based on a 20-year generation length. Note, however, that in this instance we are calculating from the career-end of Nespaherenhat to the career-end of his earliest-named ancestor, Roma, and that we can establish the floruits of Roma and his son Ipuy in the reigns of Ramesses II and Merenptah respectively.

Royal Dynasty	Number of Kings and Duration	Average
18th Dynasty (Egypt)	10 kings for 225 years (Ahmose to Haremheb)	22.5 years
19th Dynasty (Egypt)	6 kings for 104 years (Ramesses I to Septah)	17.3 years
20th Dynasty (Egypt)	8 kings for 106 years (Setnakht to Ramesses XI)	13.3 years
26th Dynasty (Egypt)	7 kings for 147 years (Neko I to Psamtek III)	21.0 years
Early Kings of Assyria	37 kings for 638 years (Ashur-nirari I to Ashur-dan II)	17.2 years
Later Kings of Assyria	19 kings for 305 years (Adad-nirari II to Ashuruballit)	16.0 years
Kings of Israel (Palestine)	20 kings for 209 years (Jeroboam I to Hoshea)	10.5 years
Kings of Judah (Palestine)	20 kings for 345 years (Rehoboam to Zedekiah)	17.3 years
Babylonians (Mesopotamia)	88 kings for 1,476 years (Sumuabi to Sennacherib)	16.8 years
Agiads (Sparta)	14 kings for 275 years (Leonidas I to Agesipolis III)	19.6 years
Eurypontids (Sparta)	14 kings for 279 years (Leotychidas II to Lycurgus)	19.9 years
King of Persia (Iran)	11 kings for 228 years (Cyrus to Darius III)	20.7 years
Macedonians (N. Greece)	9 kings for 90 years (Archelaus to Alexander III)	10.0 years
Ptolemies (Egypt)	13 kings for 274 years (Ptolemy I to Cleopatra VII)	21.1 years
Seleucids (Mesopotamia)	23 kings for 259 years (Philip Arrhidaeus to Philip II)	11.3 years
Antigonids (N. Greece)	6 kings for 138 years (Antigonus I to Perseus)	23.0 years
Attalids (Turkey)	7 kings for 154 years (Philetaerus to Eumenes III)	22.0 years
Kings of Parthia (Iran)	8 kings for 144 years (Vologeses II to Vologeses VI)	18.0 years
Hasmoneans (Judah)	9 kings for 115 years (Jonathan to Antigonus)	12.8 years
Total = 329 kings for 5,511 years Average Reign Length = 16.75 years		

The Genealogy of Nespaherenhat – NC

790 – Nespaherenhat – temp. Osorkon I (OC – *c.* 900 BC)
810 – Nespatytawy (b)
830 – Khonskhu
850 – Nespatytawy (a)
870 – Ankhef
890 – Nesamun
910 – Ipuy (b)
930 – Iufenamun – Ramesses II/Merenptah (?)
950 – Ipuy (a) – temp. Ramesses II (?)/Merenptah
970 – Roma – temp. early Ramesses II (OC – *c.* 1270 BC)

The date thus derived for Ipuy, mortuary priest of Merenptah, is *c.* 950 BC and his father, a contemporary of Ramesses II, is datable to *c.* 970 BC. This is some 38 years higher than our date for early Ramesses II (*c.* 932 BC). However, given that the genealogy is only nine generations in length, there is room for a wider margin of error. In addition, the strictly more accurate average generation of 18 years would reduce Roma's floruit to *circa* 970-952 BC. But, more importantly, Ipuy probably died soon after he attained his highest office — as suggested by the fact that his brother, Bakenkhons, succeeded Roma (presumably on the latter's death) as 2nd Prophet of Amun (2PA) before later becoming High Priest of Amun (HPA) by Year 46 of Ramesses II, – i.e. Ipuy was born absolutely no later than Year 46 and was probably in his mid life years by that date. This would certainly make him an old man on the accession of Merenptah some two decades later. In fact, we can reasonably suppose that Ipuy already had an adult son (Iufenamun) and perhaps even an adult grandson (Ipuy) by the end of Ramesses II's reign. For calculation purposes, therefore, a minimum of one generation (that of Ipuy himself) must be removed from the genealogy because his career as mortuary priest of Merenptah was wholly contemporary with the careers of his son and grandson. This

Opposite page: Table of average reign lengths for the dynasties of known duration during the pre-Christian era.

further reduces Roma's dates to 952-934 BC – just within the ± 20-year margin of error for genealogical calculations.

If we employ the same technique (using a 20-year generation) but from the starting point of Osorkon I's orthodox dating (924-889 BC) we get the following results.

The Genealogy of Nespaherenhat – OC
920 – Nespaherenhat – temp. Osorkon I
940 – Nespatytawy (b)
960 – Khonskhu
980 – Nespatytawy (a)
1000 – Ankhef
1020 – Nesamun
1040 – Ipuy (b)
1060 – Iufenamun – temp. Ramesses II/Merenptah (?)
1080 – Ipuy (a) – temp. Merenptah (OC – c. 1200 BC)
1100 – Roma – temp. early Ramesses II (OC – c. 1270 BC)

With Roma at *circa* 1100 BC rather than *circa* 1270 BC we have a shortfall of 170 years between the date calculated via the Nespaherenhat genealogy and the orthodox dating of Ramesses II. This strongly indicates that the time interval between the 19th and 22nd Dynasties must be radically reduced in line with what I have been arguing throughout *Part One* of this book.

The Memphite Genealogy

Now we need to take a look at the generations between the 19th Dynasty and the early TIP as given on the Memphite Genealogy. This genealogy was recorded in the form of four rows of figures representing a line of priestly officials from the temple of Ptah in Memphis. In many instances the cartouches of the rulers in whose reign they were appointed are also included. At the left edge of Row I we find the entry 'CONTROLLER OF CRAFTS Ashakhet' and the cartouche of Amenemnisu (Row I, 15). The title 'Controller of Crafts' was carried by the High Priest of Ptah in Memphis. Remembering that we are not here reading in boustrophedon order but instead starting each row from the right side, the next High Priest of Memphis is Ptahemakhet, located at Row II, position 1. The entry for Ptahemakhet does not include the cartouche of a pharaoh. At II:2 we read 'Controller of Crafts Neferrenpet' and the cartouche 'Usermaatre-setepenre' – i.e. Ramesses II. Positions II:3, II:4 and II:5 also contain the same cartouche covering the 67-year reign of Ramesses the Great. Thus the time span between the end of the reign of Ramesses II and the 4-year reign of Amenemnisu is represented by the generations of Memphite officials between Neferrenpet (II:2) (the last of four HPMs covering the reign of Ramesses) and Ashakhet (I:15) (inducted in the reign of Amenemnisu).[2]

It is not difficult to work out how many generations span the interval – just two! But we have to take into consideration the fact that the left side of the great slab of the Memphite Genealogy is broken away and so the names of some officials may have been lost at the end of Row I. It is, however, possible to determine the number of missing names by scrutinising the data in Rows II and III.

At position II:14 we have the cartouche of Thutmose III. Position II:15 is missing (but we know it once existed because Row I contains a minimum of 15 positions). Position III:1 does not contain a cartouche. The next entry, working backwards in time, is position III:2 in which we find the cartouche of Amenhotep I. Now we can be confident that the time interval between Amenhotep I and Thutmose III lies between 14 years and 89 years. The shorter number of years represents the interval from the death of Amenhotep I (OC – 1493 BC) to the coronation of Thutmose III (OC – 1479 BC), whilst the longer number of years represents the interval between the coronation of Amenhotep (OC – 1514 BC) and the death of Thutmose (OC – 1425 BC). The well-attested series of regnal dates during this era makes it very unlikely that the interval falls outside this fairly broad range. If we take the minimum

Key to Abbreviations

Sh – Hedjkheperre Shoshenk (Ib)	**H** – Haremheb	**Iby** – Iby
Ps – Psusennes (III?)	**A III** – Amenhotep III	**S III** – Senusret III
Akh – Akheperre (Psusennes II)	**T III** – Thutmose III	**Am II** – Amenemhat II
Amn – Amenemnisu	**A I** – Amenhotep I	**S I** – Senuseret I
R II – Ramesses II	**Ah** – Ahmose	**Am I** – Amenemhat I
St I – Seti I	**Ap** – Apophis	**M II** – Montuhotep II
	Srk – Sharek	
	Aken – Aken[emre]?	

86. Diagram of the whole Memphite Genealogy showing the 4 rows of 15 panels. Each panel contains the figure of a high priest (or some other temple official as not all are designated 'Controller of Crafts') with the man's name and titles. In about a third of the panels the cartouche of a king is also recorded, informing the reader in whose reign the high priest was inducted. At the bottom of each panel the hieroglyphic sign for 'son of' links each priest to his predecessor. The Egyptian term *sa* can also have the meaning 'successor'. The fact that the same priestly titles are not used for every individual tends to suggest that all 64 generations of officials belonging to the temple of Ptah in Memphis were descended from their predecessors or that they were at least married into the priestly family. The Memphite Genealogy is therefore a true genealogy – in the most straightforward sense – and should be considered as a reliable source for chronological calculations using a 20-year generation.

The shaded area on the left indicates the missing section of the block, but the permissible date-range between Row II:14 and III:2 may allow only for a 16th panel on the left edge.

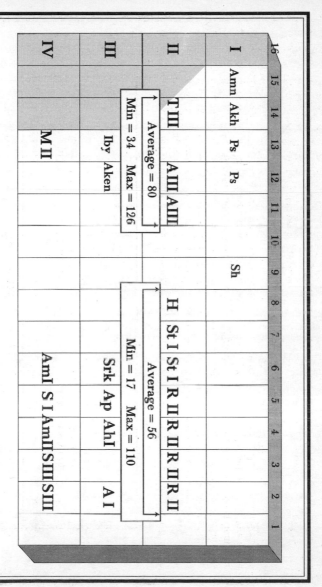

14-year span, then we need not consider the possibility that there was once an entry II:16. However, if the longer span of 89 years is correct, then we would have to introduce a position II:16. Each of the five positions between III:2 and II:14 (inclusive) would represent a 20-year (average) term of office and so the total interval between the high priest of Amenhotep and the high priest of Thutmose would be up to 100 years in length – agreeing with the maximum actual historical interval based on the monumental evidence. So we can say that the Memphite Genealogy might once have contained sixteen entries in each of the four rows – but probably no more than sixteen. However, the probability is that no entries are missing on the left edge of Row I – limiting the layout to fifteen generations per row.

Applying this to the interval between Row I, position 15 (Amenemnisu) and Row II, position 2 (Ramesses II) we can say that the time span is represented by two or three generations – that is from 40 to 60 years.[3] The figure of 60 years for the interval is based on the maximum number of generations allowable.

We now have a rough duration for the period from late Ramesses II to the early 21st Dynasty (assuming Amenemnisu to have been the co-regent of Psusennes I early in the latter's reign, or perhaps even his predecessor). This interval roughly corresponds to the length of the 20th Dynasty – give or take a couple of reigns either side which might reduce the duration of the dynasty to around 50 years. However, the conventional chronology allocates 117 years to the 20th Dynasty which is more than twice the number of years indicated by the Memphite Genealogy. Again the standard explanation of this difficult problem is that haplography has occurred, but the genealogy is entirely consistent with the New Chronology which argues for a radically reduced time span for the era between the late 19th Dynasty and the start of the TIP.

Appendix C

RADIOCARBON DATING

In recent years a new dating method has been developed which is based on scientific techniques and is therefore quite independent of archaeologically and historically based chronologies. This new technique is radiocarbon dating which works in conjunction with its associated dendrochronological calibration. As far as the lay public are concerned, the impression has been given that this scientific method of dating the past is supportive of the conventional chronology. However, this is not in fact the reality. Needless to say, in this book I have produced a chronology which is in direct conflict with modern calibrated high precision radiocarbon dates. As a result, I am obliged to give a short account of the reasons why I, and others, currently reject calibrated C-14 as a dating method.[1] (I assume here that the basic principles of radiocarbon dating are understood by the reader.)

It is not generally appreciated but a number of historians of a conventional persuasion are similarly troubled by the radiocarbon dates applied to archaeological samples. Some academics are more aware of the problems than others because these problems impinge directly on their personal field of study. They often resort to extreme measures to deal with the dating conflicts which arise, whilst others perceive only a small scale problem and think that they can live with the implications. In reality, the constraints imposed by a radiocarbon-based chronology are such that (a) few historians would willingly abandon a history-based scheme in favour of one based on C-14 and (b) consequently the historian tends to be selective in his use of C-14 dates. As noted by R. Hedges:

> … material is often submitted for dating in the spirit of adding a scientific precision to the archaeologists' pre-existing beliefs.[2]

The Problem for Radiocarbon Dating in Early Times

In the late 1970s, when C-14 dates were corrected by use of the bristlecone pine calibration curves, a 'problem' soon became apparent for the third millennium BC and earlier times. In 1976, R. D. Long looked at the published radiocarbon dates and found them generally older than the historical chronology. He suggested that the calibration of C-14 dates (based on American trees) was not applicable to Egypt – a conclusion which now seems less tenable in the face of the publication of the new European oak chronologies. The following year J. Callaway and J. Weinstein produced a chronology for Early Bronze Age Palestine based on the published C-14 dates.[3] This, however, was very unsatisfactory because they had to select out 25 of the 55 dates, a 45% rejection rate which they themselves describe as 'disappointing' – a splendid example of the arbitrary selection of dates by historians! In 1979, J. Mellaart suggested a stretched chronology to accommodate the new radiocarbon dates.[4] He was vociferously criticised by his fellow archaeologists and was forced to withdraw his proposal.[5] The problems created by radiocarbon dating remain to this day: for example, Israeli archaeologist A. Mazar refuses to use C-14 dating for Palestinian archaeological remains of the fourth and third millennia BC.[6]

The scale of the problem is best illustrated by reference to the chart reproduced opposite and that on page 484.

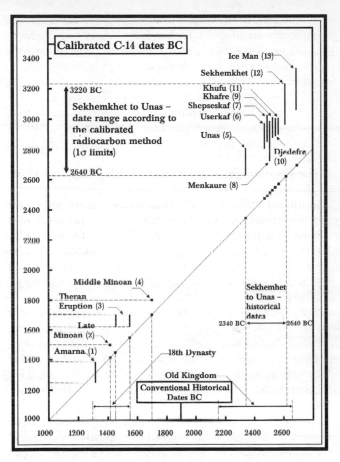

87. An illustration of the progressive divergence between historically derived dates and calibrated C-14 dates.

Sources of C-14 data: 1. B. Kemp: *Amarna Reports* I (EES, 1984), p. 185; 2 & 4. *Expedition* 32:3 (Crete Issue) (1990), p. 3; 3. Theran historical dates established at *c.* 1550 BC to *c.* 1480 BC versus Theran Conference C-14 dates ranging between 1680 BC and 1619 BC; 5 to 12. H. Haas *et al.*: 'Radiocarbon chronology and the historical calendar in Egypt' in O. Aurenche *et al.* (eds.): *Chronologies in the Near East*, Pt. II (1987), p. 606; 13. 'Horizon' (BBC 2).

In 1987, F. Hole summarised the problems for the period between 8000 and 6000 BP (Before the Present) bequeathed to Mesopotamian archaeology by the radio-carbon method:

> In view of the prevailing lack of sites ascribed to this phase, not to mention the lack of stratigraphic evidence for a substantial gap time, we can hardly be comfortable with the situation: a chronological 'fault-line' on either side of which exist abundant sites, but across which the evidence is scarce to non-existent. While calibration of dates has resolved some problems, it has created this giant enigma. The possibilities are as follows: 1) the calibration curve is wrong, 2) the date ascribed to written history is wrong, 3) archaeological stratification has been grossly misinterpreted, 4) the region was depopu-lated for a thousand years, or 5) the ceramics in use during this period are not diagnostic. Since none of these seems tenable, the enigma remains.[7]

In 1987, H. Haas *et al.,* using modern high-precision methods, discovered that Old Kingdom C-14 dates from Egypt were an average 374 years higher than the historical dates established for the associated archaeology given in the *Cambridge Ancient History.*[8] Clearly, the conventional historically-derived dating for the third and fourth millennium BC is at odds with the dates obtained from the calibrated radiocarbon method.

The Problem for Radiocarbon Dating in the 18th Dynasty

What is much less well known is that the C-14 problem also affects Egypt's 18th Dynasty. We have towards the end of this dynasty a set of calibrated radiocarbon dates from Tell el-Amarna which tie in acceptably well with the conventional chronology.[9] On the other hand, at the beginning of the dynasty we have the eruption of Thera, whose ash straddles the Late Minoan IA period (in Aegean archaeology terms). For many years archaeologists had tied LM IA into the early 18th Dynasty on the basis of their ceramic chronology.[10] This dated the eruption to the reign of Ahmose or later. The date for the eruption, established by the archaeologists, has recently received dramatic confirmation in M. Bietak's discovery of pumice within a stratified context at Tell ed-Daba (Ezbet Helmy) which spans the period from Ahmose to Thutmose III (OC – 1539-1425 BC).[11] However, C-14 dates for short-lived materials from the Theran eruption span the period 1760-1540 BC with the great majority falling earlier in that period. As a result, in 1989 the Third International Thera Congress favoured an eruption date between circa 1680 and 1670 BC. Of course, this was before the discovery of pumice in a datable Egyptian context. In the conventional chronology, the earliest Ahmose could have reigned according to Egyptian dating is circa 1550 BC which is at least 120 years later than the date of the eruption established by the radiocarbon method. If the eruption took place sometime later than the reign of Ahmose, the chronological chasm between Egyptian archaeology and radiocarbon dating would be even greater.

The problem for conventional historians is how to live with even a 120-year discrepancy. Can we expand the history of the 18th Dynasty by over a century in order to accommodate the C-14 dates established at either end of the period (the eruption of Thera to the Amarna period) – equivalent to the reigns of six pharaohs of whose monuments, inscriptions, officials, etc. we know absolutely nothing?

From the standpoint of the radiocarbon scientists their method is a considerable improvement on the various dating methods used by archaeologists and historians. As leading dendrochronologist, M. Baillie, writes:

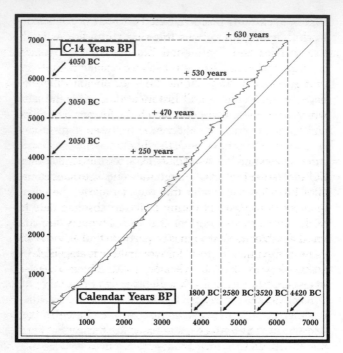

88. Graph showing the deviation of the C-14 (dendrochronology) calibration curve from the standard radiocarbon decay curve (uncalibrated).

After G. W. Pearson *et al.*: 'High Precision 14C Measurement of Irish Oaks to Show the Natural 14C Variation from AD 1840 to 5210 BC' in *Radiocarbon* 28:2B (1986), pp. 911-34 (with additions).

In terms of absolute chronology the science of dendrochronology *is* superior to the disciplines of archaeologists and historians. The method is based on a natural clock securely anchored to the present day. In comparison, archaeology and ancient history are relative dating schemes with no uncontested fixed points before the mid-1st millennium BC. Dendrochronology thus represents the ultimate chronological yardstick.[12]

This is an extreme position, based on years of painstaking work, building up various tree-ring chronologies in the British Isles and continental Europe which appear to replicate each other. Baillie's absolute certainty permits him to argue that if there should be a significant difference between radiocarbon and historical dates, it is the latter which need to be revised to match the former. This is not an argument which readily commends itself to historians.

Indeed, as we have seen, the difference between radiocarbon dates and historical dates from the third millennium BC and earlier is of such a magnitude that historians cannot afford to view the matter this way. Similarly, the consequences of using C-14 dating to fix an absolute date for both the start and end of the 18th Dynasty are also unacceptable: the historian is required to find an extra 120 years of Egyptian 'history' for which there is absolutely no archaeological evidence. Clearly, it would be inconsistent to use C-14 to fix an absolute date for just one end of this dynasty: it is therefore an 'all or nothing situation' in which radiocarbon dating has to be embraced (with all its consequences) or rejected – even where the dates it yields seem to agree with the chronology.

The Nature of the Problem

Reference to the radiocarbon calibration curve supplied by the science of dendrochronology shows that there is close agreement between the standard decay curve of C-14 and the dendro calibration for the last two and a half millennia, but at around 500 BC the two begin to diverge. As we work backwards, starting near the end-date for the TIP, we see the calibrated dates gradually getting older than the standard decay curve dates – so that by 4000 BP the gap is 250 years and by 7000 BP it has risen to 630 years. It has thus been recognised (ever since Long's work) that the problem for historians therefore derives from the calibration curve. Mazar's refusal to use calibrated dates

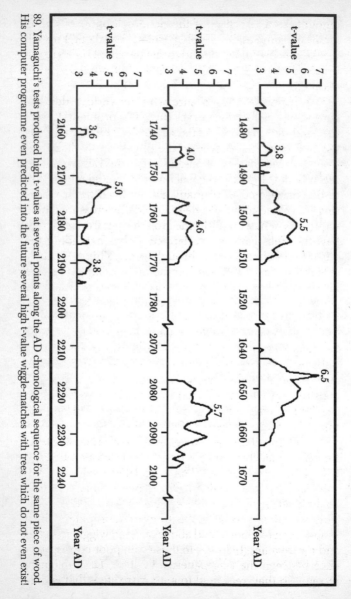

89. Yamaguchi's tests produced high t-values at several points along the AD chronological sequence for the same piece of wood. His computer programme even predicted into the future several high t-value wiggle-matches with trees which do not even exist!

amounts to a rejection of the dendrochronology curve. Until such time as this problem can be sorted out, I myself would only be prepared to advocate the adoption of *un*calibrated dates in support of a *relative*, but not an *absolute*, chronology.

We cannot know for sure why the various dendrochronology calibration curves cause this problem. Unlike the dendrochronologies of the sequoia and bristlecone pine where it was possible to read the rings of individual trees over a period of a few thousand years, the European and recently-developed Turkish dendrochronologies have had to be constructed from many shorter-lived trees, whose rings have had to be 'wiggle-matched'. By cross-matching sequences of narrow and wide growth rings from different logs the trees can be overlapped – thus extending the chronology backwards through time. This is a fairly straightforward technique and should be relatively easy to implement. However, a number of difficulties have recently come to light. Some published chronologies have had to be withdrawn from time to time: for example, the Sweet Track chronology from South-West England which had to be 'remeasured' after it did not conform to the already published dendrochronology of Northern Ireland (Belfast);[13] and the South German sequence whose detailed construction was abandoned in favour of one based on the Belfast chronology – even though its authors had originally been convinced of its accuracy.[14]

Another notable weakness in the construction of the European oak chronologies is the use of statistics. In 1991, J. Lasken raised the problem of inflated t-values.[15] A t-value is given to a wiggle-match on the basis of a statistical analysis of the correspondence between two wood samples. This statistical assessment is done by computer which assigns high t-values (3 and above) to good wiggle-matches and low t-values (below 3) to those with poor correspondence between the ring patterns. In 1986, D. Yamaguchi recognised that trees tend to auto correlate – that is they

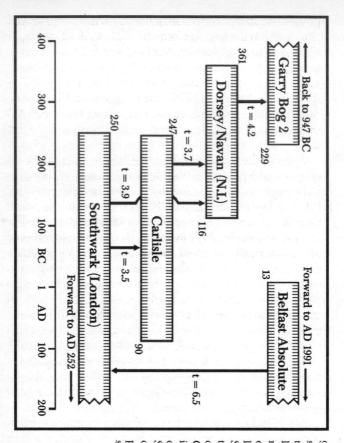

90. This diagram from Baillie shows how the Belfast absolute tree-ring chronology has been linked to the Belfast long chronology. The absolute chronology, extending back from the present, links to the tree-ring sequence of Southwark (t = 6.5), which links to Carlisle (t = 3.5), in turn linking on to Dorsey/Navan (t = 3.9) and Gary Bog 2 (t = 4.2). Gary Bog 2 is then linked to the Belfast long chronology (in the BC) via the Swan Car sequence (t = 6.3). This chain is dependent on the t-value probabilities which have been shown to be inflated.

possess the ability to cross-match with each other in several places within the tree-ring sequence. He took a Douglas fir log known to date between AD 1482 and 1668 and demonstrated that it could cross-match with other tree-ring sequences to give t-values of around 5 at AD 1504, 7 at AD 1647 and 4.5 at AD 1763. Indeed, he found 113 significant candidate wiggle-matches throughout the entire AD tree-ring sequence.[16] It is therefore interesting to note that a fair number of the crucial dendrochronology sequences – for example the Garry Bog 2 (GB2) to Southwark sequences which connect the Belfast Absolute chronology (AD sequence) to the 'floating' Belfast Long chronology (BC sequence), and ultimately used to redate the South German chronology, have t-values of around 4. These t-values are considerably lower than those obtained for some of the historically incorrect dates produced by Yamaguchi's experiment. Thus one would be justified in asking if the crucial cross-links which connect up the floating sequences of the Belfast and German chronologies are based on incorrect wiggle-matches which have resulted from the phenomenon of auto-correlation. This prompts a second very basic question: as noted by Lasken, should we really *expect* tree-ring-growth patterns to produce genuine correspondences at the same historical dates when the climates (and in particular the micro-climates) of Ireland, England and Germany are so different?

As a final example of the problems which radiocarbon dating and dendrochronology are currently going through I refer to a recent set of remarkable statistics published by P. Kuniholm – the man responsible for producing the new Turkish dendrochronology. He has been trying to date wood from a city gateway at Tille Hoyuk.[17] The problem he found was that the t-value wiggle-match computer test produced not one but three results – 1258, 1140 and 981 BC. Each had a t-value greater than 4 which, according to the dendrochronologists, makes all three 99.9% certain to be correct! As R. M. Porter noted in 1994, Kuniholm ended up rejecting the date with the highest t-value of 5 (981 BC) in favour of 1140 BC, presumably because the latter better fitted the historical expectations for the destruction of the gate.[18] Kuniholm's difficulties seem to be consistent with the problems resulting from the auto-correlation phenomenon described by Yamaguchi and raise the question of whether the phenomenon may significantly affect the construction of all the other dendrochronologies currently being used to date archaeological artefacts.

Appendix D

SOTHIC CHRONOLOGY

In *Chapter Five* I introduced you to Sothic dating techniques so that we could deal with the problems associated with the so-called Sothic date at the beginning of the 18th Dynasty (Year 9 of Amenhotep I). There we learnt that the interpretation of the Papyrus Ebers calendar is so fraught with difficulties that many Egyptologists reject its use as a method for dating the start of the New Kingdom.

However, there is another document purporting to contain a Sothic observation which scholars continue to employ in order to date the late 12th Dynasty. I believe this 'Sothic date' is also suspect and would argue that the Middle Kingdom document should likewise not be employed in calculations to establish an absolute chronology.

Papyrus Berlin 10012

The pyramid of Senuseret II is situated on the desert plateau near to the modern village of el-Lahun in the Faiyum. Just a kilometre to the south Petrie excavated the 'pyramid town' of the funeral complex which archaeology has demonstrated continued in use long after the burial of the 12th Dynasty pharaoh. Numerous papyrus fragments were found at the site which dealt with the administration of the town, the local temple activities and the arrangements for religious festivals. Amongst these was a document (now designated Papyrus Berlin 10012) which contained the following text:

> You should know that the going forth of Sopdet will
> happen on the fourth month of Peret, day 16.

At first sight this seems to be a clear reference to the heliacal rising of Sothis which, when retrocalculated, results in an absolute date of 1871 BC.[1] The regnal date of the papyrus is Year 7 – but the name of the king is not given. Scholars have determined that the Year 7 belongs to Senuseret III based on the orthography of the heiratic hand in relation to other documents from the town site. With the Year 7 attributed to Senuseret, his reign would then have begun in 1877 BC and the dynasty brought to a close in around 1800 BC. The New Chronology date for Year 1 of Senuseret III is *circa* 1700 BC and the end of the 12th Dynasty is dated to 1633 BC. Thus the 12th Dynasty 'Sothic date' would appear to rule out the chronology being proposed in this book. However, there are a number of reasons why I have my doubts about this second Sothic anchor point.

- First, the text is clearly *a prediction* and not a record of whatever event is under discussion.

- Second, there is some doubt as to whether we are dealing here with the heliacal rising of Sothis at all. We saw how in the Ebers Calendar the term *peret Sepdet* seemed to have nothing to do with the annual first dawn appearance of the star Sirius – on the fairly straight-forward grounds that the *peret Sepdet* phrase occurs in every month line of the calendar! Moreover, in the Canopus Decree of 239 BC, where we do have an indisputable record of the heliacal rising of the Dog-star, the phrase used is *kha Sepdet* – 'the appearance of Sothis'. *Peret* is regularly used to describe the procession of statues of deities on festival days. So, for example, the Osiris festivals at Abydos included *peret neferet* – 'The Beautiful Procession (of Wepwawet)' and *peret aat* – 'The Great Procession (of Osiris)'. Could the expression *peret Sepdet* not also refer to the bringing forth of a statue of the goddess for a festival? In this context it should be noted that Papyrus Berlin 10012 belongs to a group of texts concerned with religious festivals. We might therefore understand the crucial line as:

> (Instruction to the priests:) You should know that the bringing forth of the statue of Sopdet will happen on the fourth month of Peret, day 16 (that is the day arranged for her festival).

- The most convincing arguments against the 1871 BC Sothic date have come from Professor Lynn Rose of the State University of New York in Buffalo. As with the Venus Solutions of Ammisaduga in Babylon we possess a series of month-length records for the late Middle Kingdom in Egypt which can be used to check the proposed Sothic date. Rose has demonstrated that all attempts to reconcile the month-lengths with the 1871 BC date (or other alternative dates based on heliacal observation points other than Memphis) have failed because the month-length retrocalculations make a very poor match with the ancient records – nearly half, on average, missing the target by at least one day. He therefore concludes that: 'No one seems to have been able to establish an early second-millennium chronology for the Twelfth Dynasty by calculating exact placements both for the Sothic date and for the el-Lahun lunar documents.'[2] Given that we should be able to establish a high degree of compatibility between the retrocalculated month-lengths and the original month-length records, the indications are that Year 7 of Senuseret III could not have fallen in 1871 BC, and therefore the supposed Sothic date is not a true Sothic date at all.

Given the objections which have been raised, I think it is legitimate to question whether this so-called Sothic date is strong enough evidence on its own to date the late Middle Kingdom. What is more, there is also an internal inconsistency within the Sothic chronology which suggests that the conventional dating for the end of the 12th Dynasty – and consequently the orthodox dates for the kings of the following 13th Dynasty – is out by a considerable margin.

The Inundation Stela of Sobekhotep

In 1956 fragments of a royal stela were discovered in the fill of the Third Pylon at Karnak.[3] The stela belonged to an otherwise almost unknown king of the Second Intermediate Period – Sekhemre-seusertawy Sobekhotep. On one side the king is depicted before the god Hapy who personifies the Nile inundation. The hieroglyphic text below this scene is badly damaged but fortunately a second version of the inscription, in a slightly different wording, is preserved on the reverse of the stela:

> Living: The Son of Re, Sobekhotep, beloved of the great Hapy, given life forever. **Year 4, 4th month of Shemu, the five days upon the year**: before the said god who lives forever. The king's procession to the columned hall of this temple so that the great inundation could be witnessed. **He came just as**

91. Hand copy of part of the decorative scene surmounting the 'Inundation Stela' of Sobekhotep VIII. The caption reads: 'The Perfect God, Lord of the Twin Lands, Lord of Ritual, Sekhemre-seusertawy, beloved of Great Hapy for all time, given life, stability and authority like Re for all time'.

the columned hall of this temple was inundated with water. Then he waded in it together with [the court …].

The crucial observations which can be made from this short text are as follows:

- The specific date of the stela is Year 4, 4th month of the summer season (Shemu), during the five epagomenal days which bring the Egyptian year to an end – in other words just before the beginning of the New Year on Day 1 of the 1st month of Akhet (Inundation).

- It is possible to narrow down the period within the inundation sequence to which the stela is referring. It seems reasonable to assume that we are dealing with one of two moments during the Nile flood, either: (i) the point at which the Nile has risen so high that it has (unusually?)

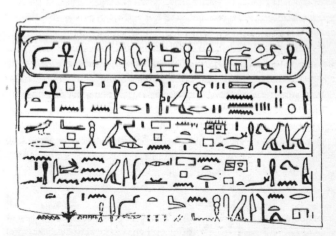

92. Hand copy of the upper part of the better preserved text on the reverse side of the 'Inundation Stela'. The first line is completely occupied by an elaborate cartouche of the king's name, and the second line begins on the right with the dating formula.

flooded a columned-hall at Karnak, or (ii) the Nile has reached its highest point in the cycle – hence the attendance of the king at some sort of celebratory ritual. Point (i) could be dated at any time throughout August or early September – once the Nile has flooded its banks. (The Nile usually begins its rise soon after the heliacal rising of Sothis on the 19th of July and overflows its banks in mid-August; it then begins to return to its normal course by mid-September.) Point (ii) could be dated as early as the first week in September (when the flood normally reaches its peak). However, it might be advisable to assume an 'observation' period during which the priests could satisfy themselves that the Nile was indeed no longer rising (this last assumption would at least ensure that the 'high' dating was the highest possible).

From these starting assumptions we can determine an absolute date range for Year 4 of Sobekhotep based on the Sothic cycle.

Minimum dating

This would assume: (a) that the stela is dated to the fifth and last epagomenal day (i.e. the day before the beginning of a new civil year), and (b) that the event referred to in the stela is an exceptionally early 'high' Nile which has flooded the temple in mid-August – for argument's sake the 15th of August. Thus the 5th Epagomenal day would be established at the 15th August on the basis of the event described in the stela. However, the 5th Epagomenal day would have been on the 18th of July if the Egyptian civil calendar had not been slipping by a quarter of a day each year against the natural calendar. (Remember that the New Year begins on the 19th of July.) The discrepancy amounts to 28 days (13 days remaining in July + the first 15 days of August). The civil year slips by one day every four years, therefore

Year 4 of Sobekhotep would fall 112 years before the beginning of the next great Sothic cycle. That began in 1320 BC, so Sobekhotep would have come to the throne in 1435 BC. According to the conventional chronology this would be in the middle of the 18th Dynasty – centuries after the date normally allocated to Sekhemre-seusertawy Sobekhotep (OC – *c.* 1650 BC).

Maximum dating

This would assume: (a) that the stela is dated to the first epagomenal day (i.e. five days before the beginning of a new civil year), and (b) that the event referred to in the stela is a visit of the king after the high point of the Nile had been reached and perhaps after this state of affairs had been observed for up to a week – for argument's sake the 15th of September. Thus the 1st Epagomenal day is established at the 15th of September on the basis of the event described in the stela. However, the 1st Epagomenal day would have been on the 14th of July if the Egyptian civil calendar had not been slipping by a quarter of a day each year against the natural calendar. The discrepancy amounts to 63 days (17 days remaining in July + the 31 days of August + the first 15 days of September). Therefore Year 4 of Sobekhotep would fall 252 years before the beginning of the next great Sothic cycle (i.e. 1320 BC), and Sobekhotep would have come to the throne in 1572 BC. According to the conventional chronology this would be towards the very end of the Hyksos 15th Dynasty and during the late-Theban 17th Dynasty, the rulers of which do not include a king named Sobekhotep. Again, even on the maximum permissible range for the inundation event, Sekhemre-seusertawi Sobekhotep falls a century after his usual dating in the mid-seventeenth century BC.

Assigning the event to some time in the middle of the dating range for the flood would give us an absolute date of *circa*

1500 BC. This would place him squarely in the late-13th Dynasty in the New Chronology – where a king bearing the names Sekhemre and Sobekhotep would naturally be expected. However, it is interesting to note that if we opt for a date tending towards the minimum dating for the flood event (which I believe is suggested by the text itself) then it would permit us to assign this King Sobekhotep to one of the four missing places in column VII of the Royal Canon between Sobekhotep VII (NC – *c.* 1459 BC) and Dudimose (NC – *c.* 1447 BC). This would be a very good chronological position for the king who could then legitimately be designated Sobekhotep VIII. It is important to note that Sobekhotep VIII is not dated in the New Chronology by Sothic calculations. However, if one was inclined to accept these calculations, then the dating would be based on a clearly described phenomenon within the observed agricultural year of Egypt, rather than a doubtful reference to a supposed astronomical observation.

Appendix E

ASSYRIAN CHRONOLOGY

The greatest challenge to the New Chronology of Egypt is undoubtedly the second pillar of Near Eastern history – the orthodox chronology of Mesopotamia as determined by the King-lists of Assyria and Babylon and the Eponym-lists from the city of Ashur. These would appear to be supportive of the conventional chronology of Egypt and clearly argue against the chronology put forward in this book. As you are now well aware, the complexities of Egyptian history are such that it is a daunting task simply to keep abreast of the issues which arise out of this area of research. My expertise lies in the chronology of Egypt and I readily admit that the subject of Mesopotamian chronology lies outside my competence. As a matter of policy, I have therefore decided, at this stage, to avoid opening up a 'second front' in the chronology debate. A revised Mesopotamian chronology will have to wait for a while, and then may require the attentions of other, more competent scholars to put together a new model. However, I did devote some time to the subject in the early 1980s and have a few thoughts on the matter which may suggest fruitful avenues of research which may lead to a revised Assyrian chronology.

Before I offer those ideas, I should briefly outline the basis of the current Mesopotamian dating scheme in order to demonstrate how this seems to support the conventional Egyptian chronology.

The Basis of the Current Chronology

As with the Egyptian chronology we start with the key anchor point of the sacking of Thebes in 664 BC by Ashurbanipal of Assyria. His father, Esarhaddon, had previously invaded Egypt in 671 BC. A few decades prior to that event King Sargon II, the grandfather of Esarhaddon, had ventured south as far as the northern border of Egypt in 716 BC. There he received tribute from a 'King Shilkanni of Egypt'.

Scholars have reasonably concluded that the Assyrian vocalisation 'Shilkanni' represents the Egyptian name [O]sorkon (with the 'O' dropped and with the interchangeable 'r'/'l') which may have been pronounced something like Osilkan.[1] However, there is little indication as to which pharaoh named Osorkon we are dealing with. Before this date there are no surviving contemporary documents which link Egypt with Assyria until we reach way back to the Amarna period (OC – c. 1350 BC). There is, therefore, a gap in our records of contact between the two states lasting some six hundred and fifty years in the orthodox chronological model.

However, the Amarna period synchronism is crucial in establishing a date for Akhenaten via Assyrian chronology. In the Amarna archive there are two letters (EA 15 & EA 16) addressed to Egypt from a King Ashuruballit of Assyria.[2] This Ashuruballit has been identified in the Assyrian King-List and dated to 1362-1327 BC on the basis of that king-list.[3] This date was achieved by assuming a continuous sequence of Assyrian rulers (without parallel dynasties) and by adding up their reign lengths as recorded in the king-list. So, there appears to be strong external confirmation that Akhenaten ruled in the mid-fourteenth century. However, I think there are a number of observations which might make questionable the basic assumption that the Assyrian monarchs formed a single continuous line of rulers.

APPENDIX E

Potential for a New Assyrian Chronology

I will deal briefly with five examples of the sorts of issues raised by the currently accepted Assyrian chronology and at the same time suggest some ideas as to how the arguments which have been raised against acceptance of the New Chronology might be alleviated.

1. Multiple kingship in Assyria

It is not true to say that the Assyrian king-list demonstrates a single continuous line of succession. There is unequivocal evidence that, in one period at least, there was more than one king ruling in Assyria at the same moment in time. Adad-shuma-usur, ruler of Karduniash (i.e. Babylonia), addressed one of his letters as follows:

> [To] Ashur-nirari and Ili-Had[da ...], **kings of Assyria**, speak! [The words of] Adad-shuma-usur, great king, strong king, [king of the universe], king of Karduniash, ... etc.[4]

Here, then, two kings of Assyria are being addressed by the ruler of Babylonia in a single letter. One assumes therefore that they both ruled by common consent of the great council based in the capital city of Ashur. It has been suggested by R. Borger that Ili-Hadda was king of Hanigalbat in northern Assyria.[5] Could it be that a dynasty of kings ruled the northern part of Assyria whilst another line ruled in the south with the administrative capital of the whole state remaining in Ashur where the governing institutions were based? If so, when did this arrangement start and when did it come to an end? The great Assyrian scholar A. Poebel believed that the assassination of the powerful king Tukulti-Ninurta I brought about a schism in Assyria shortly before the time of Ili-Hadda and Ashur-nirari III.[6] Perhaps the Ashuruballit of the Amarna correspondence is one of the non-canonical rulers of this post Tukulti-Ninurta era which scholars have dubbed the 'Assyrian Dark Age'.

2. Synchronisms with the Hittites

Several letters found in the archives of Boghazköy (the capital city of the Hittite empire) were from rulers of Assyria. Given that Hittite chronology is tied to Egypt via several synchronisms (such as the letters of Suppiluliumas I to Amenhotep III and the treaty between Hattusilis III and Ramesses II) it is important to identify the Assyrian correspondents in these Boghazköy letters.[7]

Letters KBo XVIII:25, KUB III:74 and KUB XXVI:70 are written to Tudhaliyas IV of Hatti and are from a King Tukulti-Ninurta of Assyria. In the conventional chronology he is Tukulti-Ninurta I (OC – 1242-1206 BC), but in the New Chronology the candidate ruler would be Tukulti-Ninurta II (OC & NC – 890-884 BC).

Letter KBo I:20 is dated to the reign of Hattusilis III (based on the events described in the letter) and is from Adad-nirari of Assyria. Again in the conventional scheme he is Adad-nirari I (OC – 1304-1273 BC) whereas the New Chronology would identify the sender as Adad-nirari II (OC & NC – 911-891 BC).

Finally, KUB XXIII:99 and KUB XXIII:88 are both addressed to Tudhaliyas IV from a King Shalmaneser of Assyria. In the orthodox chronology the latter would be identified with Shalmaneser I (OC – 1272-1243 BC), but as Shalmaneser III (OC & NC – 858-828 BC) in the revised scheme. It is interesting, therefore, to note A. Hagenbuchner's arguments that the form of the name Shalmaneser in both letters is never attested in the Middle Assyrian inscriptions of Shalmaneser I.[8]

3. An anomaly in Babylonian chronology

One intriguing Mesopotamian chronological anomaly comes from the Babylonian royal line. King Nebuchadnezzar I of the Second Isin Dynasty is dated to 1126-1105 BC because he is known to have been a contemporary of the Assyrian king Ashur-resh-ishi I (OC – 1133-1116 BC) – as attested in the Synchronistic History. Thus the Babylonian king is dated via Assyrian chronology. One hundred and forty years after the accession of Nebuchadnezzar we find, according to the conventional chronology, a king Shirikti-Shukamuna on the throne of Babylonia. He is the last ruler of the Bazi Dynasty, the dates of which are also determined through Assyrian chronology. The problem is that, according to a Babylonian chronicle text, Shirikti-Shukamuna was the brother of king Nebuchadnezzar![9] That is, of course, quite impossible if the two kings are to remain separated in time by over a century. The obvious solution would be to have the Bazi Dynasty following the Second Isin Dynasty shortly after the death of Nebuchadnezzar – thus allowing the three-month reign of Shirikti-Shukamuna to fall within say thirty years of the death of his elder brother. If this were to be accepted as the historical reality then, clearly, Assyrian chronology would also have to be modified in order to accommodate the change in Babylonian chronology. This example serves to demonstrate that there are good reasons to re-examine Mesopotamian chronology which are quite independent of the requirements of the New Chronology in Egypt and the Levant.

4. Gaps in the Synchronistic History

The Synchronistic History is an important tablet from Babylon recording contacts between the kings of Babylonia and their contemporary rulers in Assyria. Most of the passages in the document deal with conflicts between the two states but also included are diplomatic marriages and political alliances. According to this remarkable document, following the reign of Ashur-bel-kala (OC – 1073-1056 BC) there appears to have been a long gap in contact between the two neighbouring states – if one were to interpret the absence of nine Assyrian kings from the narrative as absence of political relations. Immediately after Ashur-bel-kala the Synchronistic History records Adad-nirari II (911-891 BC) as the next Assyrian king to have dealings with

Babylon. There is therefore a one-and-a-half-century gap which the document under discussion appears to ignore as if it had never happened. The question which might legitimately be asked is whether such a break really did occur or whether some or all of the missing nine kings of Assyria were not rulers of the northern kingdom of Hanigalbat which was not in direct contact with Babylonia – unlike their contemporary southern Assyrian kings who are attested in the Synchronistic History. This scenario would be consistent with Poebel's suggestion that there may have been more than one Assyrian kingdom after the assassination of Tukulti-Ninurta I and would support the proposed resolution of the Babylonian anomaly raised in point 3. At the same time, it would fit nicely into the hypothesis which I will now put forward in point 5.

5. *The Ashuruballit problem assessed*

There is one obvious difference between the Ashuruballit who wrote to Akhenaten and the Ashuruballit recorded in the Assyrian King-List – they have different fathers. In a letter to Egypt Ashuruballit writes:

> When Ashur-nadin-ahhe, my father, wrote to Egypt, twenty talents of gold were sent to him. When the king of Hanigalbat wrote to your father in Egypt he sent twenty talents of gold to him. [Now] I am [...] king of Hanigalbat, but you send me [...] of gold and it is not enough for the pay of my messengers on the journey to and fro. [EA 16]

Whether the third sentence should be restored as 'Now I am the reigning king of Hanigalbat' or 'Now I am the equal of the king of Hanigalbat' is difficult to say. If the former, then it would fit very nicely with Ashuruballit belonging to the Hanigalbat Assyrian dynasty following the overthrow of the rulers of Mitanni (the Egyptian name for Hanigalbat) at around the time of the death of Amenhotep III (which would be consistent with point 1 above).

When we look at the Assyrian King-List we see that the father of Ashuruballit is given as Eriba-Adad whereas the Amarna Ashuruballit has a father called Ashur-nadin-ahhe. Now, it is accepted that the term 'father' can have the meaning ancestor, but as D. D. Luckenbill notes 'even so our difficulties are not all cleared up. In the texts ... Ashur-uballit does not include Ashur-nadin-ahhe among his ancestors, although he carries his line back six generations.'[10]

Not only can we observe difficulties with the lineage of the King-List Ashuruballit and the Amarna period Ashuruballit, but there is one further tantalising piece of evidence which suggests we may have two distinct Assyrian rulers with the same name – one from the fourteenth century and the other from the eleventh century.

Draped around the neck of the mummy of King Psusennes found by Montet at Tanis was a large necklace of lapis-lazuli beads. A fascinating feature of this necklace is that one bead is quite different from the rest. Darker and considerably more pure than the others, it is the only decorated bead – bearing an inscription in cuneiform! R. Borger determined that this short Akkadian text was datable to the eleventh century BC on both palaeographic and historical grounds – in other words datable to the time of the United Monarchy in Israel. However, the official whose name is recorded in the inscription is otherwise only attested in the time of the Amarna pharaohs. The text reads as follows:

> (Property of) Ibashshi-ilu, the great vizier. For the preservation of the life of his eldest daughter whom he loves, he has had (made this object property of the) gods Ashur, Enlil and Ninlil of the town of Ashur. May no one steal it through covetousness or appropriate it for themselves (by swearing) oaths in the name of the god and king.[11]

How did this object end up in the burial goods of the 21st Dynasty pharaoh Psusennes? I have a speculative scenario to put to you.

- When the Valley of the Kings was being cleared of the royal mummies for their deposition in the Royal Cache and the second cache in the tomb of Amenhotep II it is clear that the then current rulers of Egypt 'quarried' the treasures of the New Kingdom tombs for their personal enrichment – particularly their own burials.

- The bodies of Amenhotep III and Queen Tiye were found in the tomb of Amenhotep II which acted as a secondary repository for some of the royal mummies. It seems likely that this smaller cache was the first to be utilised and that the operations surrounding the initial clearance of the royal tombs took place before those of the greater Royal Cache – perhaps immediately prior to the reign of Siamun. In other words the stripping of the treasures from Amenhotep III's tomb (WKV 22) and the entry into KV 55 to remove the mummy of Tiye took place at around the time of King Psusennes. In KV 55 the priests left behind a royal mummy whose identity they attempted to hide by erasing all the cartouches of the king. The latest research on this mysterious occupant of Tomb 55 tends to support the identification of the mummy as that of Akhenaten. So, in all likelihood, the lapis bead inscribed with the cuneiform text of Ibashshi-ilu came from one of two possible locations – WKV 22 or KV 55 – the two tombs in Thebes dated to the Amarna period. The bead therefore probably originally belonged to the burial regalia of an Amarna period pharaoh.

- Astonishing as it may seem, we may actually have a reference to this bead, despatched to Egypt as a gift from Ashuruballit. In EA 15 the Assyrian king states: '... today I write to you. I send you a beautiful chariot, two horses and **a date-stone of genuine lapis lazuli** as your greeting gift'.

- The first translation of the bead text was undertaken by J. Lewy in 1948. He proposed that the inscription was written at the time of the Amarna era, yet a date in the eleventh century is now preferred on the basis of the Akkadian language used in the inscription. Could both interpretations be right? In the New Chronology the Amarna period is contemporary with the early United Monarchy period – that is eleventh century Israel. The Amarna period Assyrian vizier, Ibashshi-ilu, would then naturally have been writing in eleventh century Akkadian.

- We know that the Assyrian king contemporary with the Amarna period was an Ashuruballit – so is it possible that there was a ruler bearing this name in the eleventh century BC – assuming, that is, that we are unable to adjust Assyrian chronology from that century onwards because of the extant annual Eponym or Limmu List?

- In the eponym of 1007 BC, at a point where the tablet is very fragmentary, we can, in fact, read the name 'Ashur[u]bal[lit]'. In several instances in the Eponym List – especially in this section – when the limmum year is named after the Assyrian ruler himself, he is not specifically given the title 'king' (e.g. Ashur-nirari IV, Ashur-rabi II, Tiglath-pileser II, Ashur-dan II). So, could this limmum of 1007 BC be a reference to a second king Ashuruballit otherwise not recorded in the King-List canon for some unexplainable reason? As I have already mentioned, we know of at least one other example of an Assyrian monarch – Ili-Hadda – who was recognised as king of Assur by the ruler of Babylonia even though he is not directly attested as king in the Assyrian King-Lists.

- If there was indeed a King Ashuruballit in the late eleventh century BC, then the Assyrian chronology would no longer be an obstacle to the New Chronology of Egypt and Palestine. The 1007 BC limmum of (King) Ashur[u]bal[lit] falls precisely in the time of Akhenaten's rule as senior monarch according to the New Chronology which, in turn, is so strongly supported by the Ugarit eclipse date of 1012 BC.

Part Six

Reference
Section

Acknowledgements
Abbreviations
Sources for Illustrations
Glossary
Bibliography
Notes & References
Index

ACKNOWLEDGEMENTS

It has always been my practice either to quote directly from, or refer to, the published works of other researchers in the various disciplines concerned. The reason for this is to emphasise that most of the arguments which I have employed have already been made by scholars more qualified than myself to comment on the specifics of any single argument. What is different about my approach is that I have brought all these individual arguments together for the first time into one complete and wide-ranging theory. I would argue that this multidisciplinary approach is what has been missing in the past. It should be obvious that such an approach is inherently weak because no one scholar can be an expert in all fields. To that extent, I have been reliant, to a considerable degree, on the published and unpublished work of others – some of which I do not have the competence to check thoroughly for myself. Their collective wisdom forms the major part of this book, coupled with the expertise and advice of my academic colleagues and fellow researchers who have been involved in what has become known as the 'New Chronology'. Without that past and present research the New Chronology could never have been devised and the historical Bible would probably never have been revealed.

As I have already mentioned, the greatest debt for setting me off on this exhilarating adventure must be paid to Professor Kenneth Kitchen of Liverpool University. Without his incredible energy and commitment in bringing all the data relating to the Third Intermediate Period together, the task of reworking the chronology of this complex period would have been nigh on impossible. Whatever his response turns out to be in regard to this book (and I would expect it to be critical), I wish him to know that I will continue to respect his undoubted expertise in the field of Egyptian chronology.

At this point I should also pay due acknowledgement to the work of those 'revisionists' who have gone before me.

The first intellectual to attempt a revision of the chronology of the ancient world was, believe it or not, Sir Isaac NEWTON – the world-renowned 'inventor' of gravity. Few people realise that he was also an alchemist and historian. Ironically enough, his book *The Chronology of Ancient Kingdoms Amended*[1] was published in 1728 – nearly a century prior to the decipherment of Egyptian hieroglyphs in 1822 and therefore long before scholars had access to translations of the contemporary historical documents from Egypt itself. All Newton had to work from were the 'histories' handed down in the Classical literature of Greece and Rome. One could almost argue, then, that revisionists were revising ancient history even before a comprehensive old world chronology had been devised! Newton identified the legendary Scsostris/Sesoosis as Pharaoh Shishak of the Bible who sacked the Temple of Solomon. Amazingly enough, as you now know, Newton was indeed correct in this assumption because Sesoosis is none other than Sysu/Sysu, i.e. Ramesses II.

In the 1880s the eminent Norwegian Egyptologist Professor Jens LIEBLEIN of the University of Christiana began his challenge to the chronology of pharaonic Egypt which had been developed over the previous fifty years. He argued that the genealogical material from the 21st to 23rd Dynasties indicated that the chronology of Egypt's Third Intermediate Period had been artificially extended and that the problems might be resolved by making Dynasties 21 and 22 contemporary rather than sequential. In the first part of this book, I reached precisely this conclusion myself during the late 1970s, well before I had come across Lieblein's work, published in 1873 and 1914.[2]

Next came the eccentric classical scholar, Cecil TORR, who spent the best part of the last decade of the nineteenth century arguing points of chronology with the recently formed British Egyptological fraternity. His first sally forth to contest the conventional viewpoint was against the 'father of Egyptian archaeology', Professor William Matthew Flinders PETRIE of University College London. Their often ill-tempered and very public debate was published at length in the pages of the *Academy*.[3] The contest lasted over twenty-one bloody rounds, occupying much of the latter half of 1892. Exhausted by the dogged and unremitting onslaught of his knowledgeable opponent, Petrie finally retired from the debating arena leaving Torr to have the last word in print on the subject. The fact that Petrie had been basically right from the outset is somewhat disturbing. Torr had been able to argue from entirely the opposite standpoint to Petrie with devastating effect, demonstrating that logical argumentation – based on the same archaeological and textual evidence – can produce a range of quite different chronological results. This made me wonder if something of that nature might have happened with the conventional chronology. Could it be that logical argumentation had built a structure which was simply not real?

Torr then went on to dish out similar treatment to another respected ancient historian of the time – John Myres – who had dared to challenge Torr's proposed alternative chronology for the ancient world. He should really have known better given what had already happened to his eminent Egyptologist colleague a few years earlier! This time the battle was fought out in the pages of the *Classical Review* and again Torr remained unbowed.[4]

In 1896 Torr had published his own revision of Egyptian chronology in a now rare little volume entitled *Memphis and Mycenae*, recently reprinted by the Institute for the Study of Interdisciplinary Sciences.[5] In that work he argued for a radical reduction of Egyptian chronology and a lowering of the dates for the Mycenaean period in the Aegean – effectively removing the Greek Dark Age which had been introduced by scholars following Petrie's discovery of Mycenaean pottery in datable Egyptian contexts. An 1896 *Guardian* review of *Memphis and Mycenae* neatly sums up the attitude of most academics to Cecil Torr's radical proposals for Bronze Age Greek chronology: 'Mr. Torr, if we say so, is a heretic in the region of early Greek archaeology'. Disillusioned by the less than favourable reception with which his revised chronology was greeted by the academic world, Torr retreated to his Devonshire home to write no more on matters of chronology and ancient history.

The next half-century was all quiet on the revisionist front. In those five decades the orthodox chronology became well established and few, if any, felt the urge openly to challenge the dates assigned to the pharaohs. Then, in the 1950s, the infamous Dr. Immanuel Velikovsky began his crusade against scientific and historical orthodoxy. This non-Egyptologist (he was trained as a psychologist under Jung in Vienna) was a true heretic – much in the mould of his hero, Akhenaten. With the publication of his first two books, *Worlds in Collision* and *Ages in Chaos*, he shook the scholarly world to its very foundations, stirring up a gaggle of scientists and historians to mount a savage and prolonged assault on his academic credibility. Even before the publication of those first controversial books, leading American academics were threatening the withdrawal of all support and co-operation from Velikovsky's original publishers, Macmillan, who had dared to contemplate making the wayward polymath's theories available to the public. The first publisher caved in and withdrew its contract but, fortunately, Doubleday stepped into the breach to ensure that free and independent scholarship could not be so easily suppressed.[6]

This disgraceful attempt at censure, subsequently followed by a vicious character assassination of Velikovsky with the publication of the two books, soon backfired on the would-be assassins. Their widely publicised efforts helped to push both *Worlds in Collision* and *Ages in Chaos* to the top of the best-seller lists in the USA and Europe. Those academics who had tried to silence the heretic had thus inadvertently elevated him to cult status.

In a nutshell, what Velikovsky proposed was that Egyptian chronology was too long by as much as 500 years! He argued that the Israelite Sojourn in Egypt had taken place during the 12th and 13th Dynasties and that, according to biblical chronology, this was in the 19th to 15th centuries BC (1877-1447). Now, the conventional chronology of Egypt placed 12th and 13th Dynasties in the twentieth to seventeenth centuries BC (1937-1606). His initial idea thus only resulted in a difference of around 200 years. But then he tried to equate the 18th Dynasty female pharaoh, Hatshepsut, with the Queen of Sheba (who visited Solomon in Jerusalem) and Pharaoh Thutmose III with the biblical King Shishak. Solomon is normally dated 970 to 930 BC whilst Hatshepsut is conventionally dated from 1479 to 1457 – a discrepancy of around 500 years. In effect, in order to arrive at his Egypto-biblical synchronisms, Velikovsky had stretched Egyptian chronology for the Second Intermediate Period by several centuries, but this had, in turn, the effect of creating tremendous tensions in the rest of Egyptian chronology following on from the 18th Dynasty. His solution (published in a series of follow-up books to *Ages in Chaos*[7]) was to create the notion of alter-ego rulers. This 'game' is all about identifying one historical ruler with another by comparing their reigns in the most general and uncritical way. So, Velikovsky turned Seti I of the 19th Dynasty into Psamtek I of the 26th Dynasty and likewise Ramesses II into Neko II. Even the most accommodating scholars found this methodology totally unacceptable and the archaeological evidence was wholly against any such equations. Getting himself deeper and deeper into trouble he then equated Ramesses III of the 20th

Dynasty with Nectanebo I of the 30th Dynasty. In the end his whole thesis degenerated into farce with dynasties leap-frogging over each other in their undignified clamour towards the Hellenistic Age.

During the three decades between 1950 and his death in 1979, Velikovsky found himself loyally supported by a large and enthusiastic non-academic following which avidly acquired and devoured each of the heretic's published offerings on revised chronology and catastrophism as soon as they appeared in the book stores. These followers were tagged 'Velikovskians' and Velikovskian societies soon began to sprout up in North America and Europe. At first there was uncritical support for the doctor's revised chronology amongst these groups, then, in the 1970s, the British *Society for Interdisciplinary Studies* began to undertake a serious review of the Velikovskian chronological thesis. This fair and unbiased attempt to evaluate his chronological revision culminated in an international conference held in Glasgow in 1978.[8] The majority of historians who gave papers at the Glasgow Conference concluded that, although Velikovsky had highlighted a number of problems prevalent in the orthodox chronology, his own chronology was itself untenable. The archaeological evidence was un-equivocally against him.

So, by the early 1970s, an awareness of the problems of the conventional chronology had been raised in the lay readership who were interested in ancient history and biblical research. Unfortunately, at the same time, a harden-ing of the arteries had occurred in academia towards any re-examination of ancient chronology. Now that Velikovsky had been proved wrong – even by some of those who had at first supported his revision – the spectre of further heretical challenges to the conventional wisdom was at last fading away. It was time to put Jack safely back in his chronological box – or so they thought!

This is where things stood when Kitchen produced his book on Third Intermediate Period chronology in 1973.

What he did not anticipate was that he was, in fact, reigniting the flame of chronological debate all over again. His *Third Intermediate Period in Egypt* was to light the path for a new generation of younger academics who would finally begin to unravel the Gordian Knot of ancient world chronology originally entwined by their eminent academic forebears.

Unfortunately, anyone attempting to re-examine old world chronology today continues to be stigmatised as a 'Velikovskian'. As recently as 1991, Professor Kitchen himself branded a group of young academics as 'sons of Velikovsky' in a national newspaper book review.[9] Their crime was to publish a work entitled *Centuries of Darkness* which questioned the existence of the great 300-year Dark Age which is supposed to have descended upon the ancient world in around 1150 BC. Their conclusion was that this Dark Age was an artificial construct which had developed out of a faulty Egyptian chronology – an invention of scholarship rather than a real historical event. Even though their arguments were based on archaeological evidence and, some would argue, grounded in sound academic methodology, Kitchen elected to play the Velikovskian card, clearly demonstrating to those who are familiar with the history of the 'Velikovsky affair' that academia continues to be irritated by the infamous bogeyman of old world chronology.

I began to publish my own research into TIP chronology in 1983,[10] by which time a number of researchers had been involved in developing the original theory. Peter James, the principal author of *Centuries of Darkness*, was introduced to the TIP revision in 1979 and added much to the initial chronological model over the following four years. In 1984, by the end of that period of joint research, many of the anomalies of TIP chronology had been noted and catalogued. James, an ancient historian rather than Egyptologist, then went off to develop his ideas on the Bronze to Iron Age Dark Age with other researchers, resulting in the publication of *Centuries of Darkness* in 1990. In the meantime, I went on to prepare my PhD thesis on the original chronological revision of the TIP at University College London.

During the twenty years it has taken to develop this New Chronology theory, there have been many scholars and researchers who have contributed to the work. They come from many different disciplines for which I have no special training. Without the input of their specialist skills, the New Chronology would certainly be in a less robust condition as I complete the writing of this book. The work, of course, does not stop with Volume One of *A Test of Time*, or my PhD thesis, and I look forward to continuing the development of the New Chronology with my fellow researchers and colleagues, as well as any new friends who might join the research team in future years.

Having briefly reviewed the history of the revisionist movement I will now turn to the present and to all those friends and colleagues who have offered their advice and encouragement during the course of writing *A Test of Time*. It is important to stress, however, that encouragement does not necessarily imply support for, or agreement with, the ideas proposed in this book for which I bear most, if not all, of the responsibility.

During the preparation and writing of *A Test of Time* I have relied heavily on the support and technical advice of Dr. Bill Manley and Dr. Bernard Newgrosh who have been my academic proofreaders. Bill has also contributed his expertise as an Egyptian language specialist in the preparation of new translations of the hieroglyphic texts. This input from Bill and Bernard has made a great difference to the clarity of argumentation at a number of points in the book and I am grateful to them both for their knowledge, care and attention.

At University College London, where I completed my degree and where I am currently completing my PhD research, I have to thank my supervisors Amélie Kuhrt in the History Department and Dr. Geoffrey Martin, former Edwards Professor of Egyptology (now retired). Interest and assistance was also gratefully received from Professor Harry Smith (Edwards Professor of Egyptology, retired), Professor Nicolas Coldstream (Department of Classical Archaeology, retired), Professor Jac. Janssen (Emeritus, Leiden University), Peter Parr (Institute of Archaeology, retired) and Vronwy Hankey (Honorary Research Fellow of the Egyptology Department).

There are a number of academics from other universities who should be thanked for their friendship and support. Professor Mohamed Ibrahim Aly of Alexandria University has contributed a great deal to my work on the Apis bulls, including sight of his as yet unpublished PhD thesis on the Serapeum. In Vienna the staff and students of the Austrian Institute of Egyptology have offered me considerable kindness whenever I have been to Vienna or Tell ed-Daba. Professor Manfred Bietak and his team are not only great archaeologists but also generous hosts. In particular I would wish to single out Dr. Peter Jánosi who has shown much interest in my theory. In Israel I have had many long and fascinating discussions with the teaching staff and archaeologists of Jerusalem and Tel Aviv Universities. Professors Amnon Ben-Tor, Israel Finkelstein, Gabriel Barkay, Amihai Mazar and David Ussishkin have all listened with interest and offered their constructive criticisms, as has the Deputy Director of the British School of Archaeology in Jerusalem, Dr. John Woodhead. It is good to see so many open-minded scholars in Levantine archaeology today.

It has been a delight to work on the TV production of *A Test of Time* with Professor Robert Bianchi from New York. Bob is a genuine enthusiast and his constructive criticisms and positive interest in the material evidence which I took him to see in Egypt greatly helped in the fine tuning of the arguments in this book. The day we spent high up on that craggy cliff of schist in the Wadi Hammamat with the rain spattering the shiny black rock will last long in my memory – friends, well met, on a great adventure together.

Three scholars who have made a major contribution to the New Chronology are: astronomer Wayne Mitchell for his astonishing eclipse computer retrocalculation research; Peter van der Veen who did so much to sharpen my insight into the el-Amarna/Early Monarchy synchronism (with a major input also from Bernard Newgrosh); and Dr. John Bimson who was always ready to help with a reference or query and who inspired me with his work on the archaeology of the Conquest. I would also like to thank Edward Rogers for helping with the cross-checking of Wayne's astronomical retrocalculations across this side of the pond. It was great to see the 1012 BC Ugarit eclipse appear in glorious technicolor on my own computer screen just as Wayne had predicted – right on time! Nice one Eddie. Undergraduate students in the Egyptology department at UCL also offered their help in finding references and bibliographical details during the final rush to complete the manuscript: thanks Jan, Jackie, Jo and Alison.

On a more personal note, it has been a blessing to have my elder brother, Professor John Röhl, around to lend an ear when I needed support or advice. That sentiment also applies to Lebanese archaeologist and film producer, Mouna Mounayer – a great friend over the last few years ever since we excavated together at Kadesh-on-the-Orontes with the Institute of Archaeology Tell Nebi Mend mission, led by Peter Parr. She and her family have been a great source of strength in times of self-doubt. Again, in a similar vein, close friends such as Peter Allingham, Nesta Caiger and Roy Spence, who have come to know me through my work, have always been very supportive. That also goes for the whole ISIS Board of Trustees, as well as Jim and Betty Dunn (thanks for the use of the pics Jim!) and all the other folks in Egyptological circles who support what I am trying to do.

Special mention must go to my literary agent, Jonathan Harris of Associated Publicity Holdings, for all his unstinting efforts on my behalf: thanks Jonathan – and here's to the next venture together!

Those people who work tirelessly behind the scenes in the production of a book are often neglected in authors' acknowledgements – an oversight which I intend to avoid. *Century* are a fine publisher and I must express my gratitude to Production Manager, Barry Featherstone, for helping me to realise the feel and quality of this book – something which was so very important to me. Copy Editor, Myra Jones, did a marvellous job checking continuity throughout a very complicated tome. Thanks must also go to Kate Parkin, Publisher and Managing Director, Simon King, and to my USA publisher, Jim Wade, for their unstinting belief in me. Above all, my Editor, Mark Booth, has to receive the greatest accolade of all for putting up with, it has to be said, a difficult author. I was inspired by your friendship and the genuine interest which you showed in what I was attempting to put across in volume one of *A Test of Time.* I look forward to starting the whole process all over again with volume two!

The final word must be for my wife, Ditas Rohl, who has had to endure a decade of ceaseless commitment to this project. She has been at my side through thick and thin and has always been a great pillar of strength. Her many talents are reflected in the typesetting of this book. It would have been quite unthinkable to have dedicated this work to any other person. Thank you Ditas.

ABBREVIATIONS

ÄF = Ägyptologische Forschungen
AJA = American Journal of Archeology
ANET = Ancient Near Eastern Texts
ASAE − Annales du Services des Antiquites de l'Égypte
BA = Biblical Archaeologist
BAR = Biblical Archaeology Review
BASOR = Bulletin of the American Schools of Oriental Research
BIFAO = Bulletin de l'Institute Francais d'Archéologie Orientale
BSFE = Bulletin de la Société Francais d'Égyptologie
BSOAS = Bulletin of the School of Oriental & African Studies
CAH = Cambridge Ancient History
C & C Review − Chronology and Catastrophism Review
GM = Göttinger Miszellen
HML? = High Middle or Low?
HUCA − Hebrew Union College Annual
JA − Journal Asiatique
JACF = Journal of the Ancient Chronology Forum
JANES = Journal of the Ancient Near Eastern Society
JAOS = Journal of the American Oriental Society
JARCE = Journal of the American Research Center in Egypt
JEA = Journal of Egyptian Archaeology
JHS = Journal of Hellenic Studies
JNES = Journal of Near Eastern Studies
IEJ = Israel Exploration Journal
ISIS − Institute for the Study of Interdisciplinary Sciences
MDAIK − Mitteilungen des Deutschen Archäologischen Instituts
        Abteilung Kairo
PEFQS = Palestine Exploration Fund Quarterly Statement
PEQ = Palestine Exploration Quarterly
PSBA = Proceedings of the Society of Biblical Archaeology
RT = Recueil de Travaux Relatifs à l'Archéologie Egyptiennes et
        Assyriennes
SAK = Studien zur Altägyptischen Kultur
SIS = Society for Interdisciplinary Studies
SSEA = Journal of the Society for the Study of Egyptian Antiquities
TIPE = The Third Intermediate Period in Egypt (1100-650 BC)
VT = Vetus Testamentum
ZÄS = Zeitschrift für Ägyptische Sprache und Altertumskunde
ZDPV = Zeitschrift des Deutschen Palaestina-Vereins

SOURCES FOR ILLUSTRATIONS

All photographs and illustrations are by the author except the following.

A number of images have been taken from works published before 1945 which are now out of copyright.

The author wishes to thank the following for permission to reproduce their photographs and illustrations:

A. Ben-Tor – 68; M. Bietak, Austrian Archaeological Institute Cairo – 59 (after J. Dorner), 60, 65, plate 66, plate 67, 75 (after D. Eigner), plate 75, 76 (after D. Eigner), plate 76, 81, 82, (page 299); C. Bonnet – 57; T. Copestake – plate 38; S. Crisp – plate 55; J. Dunn – plate 11, plate 24; I. Hein – 67; Palestine Exploration Fund Archive (Cat. JER/GAR/PN/552) – plate 54; D. Roth – plate 56; P. van der Veen – 2, 42, 50.

Thanks must go to the École Biblique in Jerusalem for permission to photograph and reproduce here the artefacts excavated from St. Etienne – 43, 45.

GLOSSARY

21ST DYNASTY: 1069-945 BC.

Overlap with previous dynasty = 0 yrs.

22ND DYNASTY: 945-715 BC.

Overlap with previous dyn. = 0 yrs.

23RD DYNASTY: 818-715 BC.

Overlap with previous dyn. = 103 yrs.

25TH DYNASTY: 780-656 BC.

Overlap with previous dyn. = 65 yrs.

26TH DYNASTY: 715-525 BC.

Overlap with previous dyn. = 59 yrs.

ABU EL-FEDA: ((1273-1331).

ADAM: (1917-1986).

ADZES: Hoe-like implements used for breaking up soil or planing back wood. Adzes come in all different sizes and are still in use today in the Middle East. The adze was also represented in the hieroglyphic sign *setep* which had the meaning 'choice' or 'chosen'.

AGATHA CHRISTIE'S PATH: So-called after the publication of her book *Death Comes at the End.*

AHAB: 873 853 BC.

AHMOSE: 18th Dynasty, reigned 1539-1514 BC.

AKKADIAN: Named after the ancient city of Akkad or Agade in Mesopotamia.

ALBRIGHT: (1891-1971).

ALEXANDER III: 332-323 BC.

ALEXANDER IV: 316-304 BC.

ALEXANDRINUS COPY: One of the earliest surviving manuscripts of the Greek translation of the Old Testament, from Alexandria.

ALT: (1883-1956).

AMARNA LETTERS: Correspondence between the Levantine rulers and the Egyptian pharaohs of the Amarna period. The letters, in the form of clay tablets, were found at Tell el-Amarna at the turn of the last century.

AMENEMOPET: 21st Dynasty, reigned 993-984 BC.

AMENHOTEP I: 18th Dynasty, reigned 1514-1493 BC.

AMENHOTEP III: 9th ruler of the 18th Dynasty, reigned 1382-1344 BC.

AMENMESSE: 19th Dynasty, reigned OC – 1203-1200 BC.

AMUN: 'The Hidden One'. State God of the New Kingdom whose principal centre of worship was at Thebes.

AMURRU: An Egyptian designation for a region of Syria where the biblical Amorites dwelt.

ANU: Assyrian sky god, formerly the Sumerian deity An or Anum whose main temple was at Uruk.

ASENATH: Possibly Egy. Iusenat.

ASHLAR: Cut and dressed stone.

ASHURBANIPAL: King of Assyria, reigned 669-627 BC.

ASWAN DAMS: The British dam was built in 1902 and raised and widened in 1912 and 1923, whilst the High Dam (built by the Soviet Union) was completed in 1971.

ATUM: The creator god (in human form) whose temple was at Heliopolis.

AUGUSTUS CAESAR: 30 BC-AD 14.

AVARIS: The ancient Egyptian city of Haware (*Hutwaret*), located at the modern village of Tell ed-Daba.

BAKSHEESH: Arabic for money or tips.

BANDEAU: A single row or column of hieroglyphs used to frame a scene.

BARAKA™: Egyptian bottled mineral water from the Delta.

BASTINADO: An instrument of torture made of wood and used to beat the soles of the feet.

BC: Before Christ.

BCE: Before the Common Era.

BEROSUS: A Babylonian priest who wrote three books on Babylonian history utilising the archives from the temple of Bel in Babylon. His books, written in Greek, were popular in Greece and Rome. Like Manetho only excerpts survive in the writings of Josephus, Eusebius and Syncellus. His floruit was around 260 BC.

BIBAN EL-MULUK: 'Gate of the Kings', i.e. the Valley of the Kings.

BOOK OF THE DEAD: The prayers and incantations which aid the deceased upon his journey through the netherworld.

BRUGSCH: (1827-1894).

BUBASTITE PORTAL: A gateway constructed and decorated by the kings of the 22nd Dynasty whose capital Manetho places at Bubastis.

BULAK MUSEUM: The first Egyptological museum in Cairo; precursor to the Cairo Museum.

BUSTROPHEDON: Greek for 'as the ox ploughs'.

BYBLOS: The Greek name for the port of Gubla (Akk.), Kepen (Egy.), Gebail (Arab.).

CAMBYSES: 525-522 BC.

CANAAN: The biblical (and Egyptian) name for the southern Levant (mostly identified in the Bible with the lowland regions).

CANOPIC VESSELS: Four large jars containing the viscera of the mummy.

CARTER: (1874-1939).

CARTOUCHE: The oval which contains a royal name.

CAVETTO CORNICE: Overhanging capping blocks running along the top of a wall.

CELLA: The main chamber of a temple.

CENSORINUS: A Roman grammarian whose works also include *De Accentibus*.

CHAMPOLLION: (1790-1832).

CLEOPATRA VII: 51-30 BC.

CO-REGENCY: When the ruling king appoints his son (or other relative) as co-regent king.

CONTROLLER OF CRAFTS: Egy. *wer kherep khemet* – one of the main titles carried by the High Priest of Ptah in the great Temple at Memphis.

COPTIC: The ancient Egyptian language as written in the early Christian era, using a combination of native and Greek letters. Also, the term used to describe the native Christian church of Egypt and Ethiopia.

CORVÉE: Conscript labour based on the farming cycle. Farm workers gave their time to state projects during the inundation season when they were unable to tend the fields because they were under water.

CUNEIFORM: A script of signs made by a wedge-shaped implement which is pressed into wet clay in different configurations to form syllables. The language of this script is usually Akkadian.

CYCLOPEAN: A term borrowed from the world of Greek archaeology to describe walls built of huge stones ('built by giants').

CYLINDRICAL: In the form of a cylinder.

CYRUS: The first king of Persia, reigned 559-529 BC.

DACIER: (1742-1833).

DAHABIYA: A sailing boat designed for navigating the Nile. The accommodation was usually well appointed with all the necessary comforts for the western traveller.

DAN: Formerly known as Laish. Located below the southern slopes of Mount Hermon in northern Israel.

DARIUS I: King of Persia, reigned 521-486 BC.

DARIUS III: 335-332 BC.

DE DIE NATALI: 'On the birthday'.

DEFFUFA: A local Dongalawi (Arabic) word meaning 'walled village' or 'fort' – probably originally from the ancient Nubian word *diffi*.

DEIR EL-BAHRI: The great bay of cliffs in which are located the terrace temples of Montuhotep II, Hatshepsut and Thutmose III. Its ancient Egyptian name was Djeser – 'Sacred'.

DIMORPHISM: Biological differences within a species of community.

DIODORUS SICULUS: Greek historian living in Sicily who wrote a partial history of Egypt in the 1st century BC.

DIVIDED MONARCHY: The period of Israelite history following the break up of the United Monarchy at the death of Solomon in 931 BC.

DJOSER: 3rd Dynasty, reigned *c.* 2630-2611 BC.

DRAGOMAN: The traditional name of a tourist guide.

DROMOS: Greek for 'paved road'.

DUATHATHOR-HENTTAWY: Great Royal Wife of Pinudjem I, the High Priest of Amun at Karnak who proclaimed himself king of Thebes during the first half of the 21st Dynasty.

DUNAND: (1898-1987).

DURBAR: From Hindi *darbar* meaning 'court'. A grand reception at which the king or governor receives ambassadors and vassal rulers.

EARLY ISLAM: From Caliph Omar to the rise of Ahmed Ibn Tulun, Umayyad and Abbasid periods, AD 639-868.

EAS: Later to become the 'Egyptian Antiquities Organisation' (EAO) and now renamed the 'Supreme Council of Antiquities'.

EBERS: (1837-1898). Professor of Egyptology at Leipzig.

EDWARDS: (1831-1892).

EGYPT EXPLORATION FUND: Jointly founded by Amelia Edwards, Reginald Poole and Sir Erasmus Wilson in 1882.

EL-ELYON/EL-SHADDAI: 'God (El) most high'/'God (El) of the mountain'.

EL-HIBA: A large tell situated on the east bank of the Nile opposite the town of el-Feshn in Middle Egypt. The occupation of the site dates from the 18th Dynasty right down to the Roman era. During the TIP it was a military stronghold and headquarters of the High Priest of Amun who was often also commander-in-chief of the armed forces.

EL-SAMHUDI: (844-911).

ENLIL: 'Lord of the Air', the chief god of Nippur.

EPAGOMENAL: 'Intercalary days' (Grk.).

ESARHADDON: 681-669 BC.

EVANS: (1851-1941).

EXECRATION TEXTS: Names of cities or rulers usually written on pottery or some other form of ceramic which can be smashed in order to destroy Egypt's enemies – somewhat akin to a voodoo wax doll.

EXEGESIS: The interpretation or exposition of Scripture.

FAIENCE: A general term for glazed earthenware.

FAIYUM: Fertile natural basin, west of the Nile, some 90 kms. south of Cairo.

FAKUS: Phacusa (Grk.), Pa-Kesan (Egy.) = 'The Goshen' of Genesis.

FELLAHEEN: Plural of fellah (Arab.) – an Egyptian peasant farmer.

FIELD STONES: Stones which have been gathered for building use but have not been cut by the saw or finished in any way.

FROWLA JUICE: An exotic concoction predominantly consisting of crushed strawberries.

GALABEYA: A long cotton robe.

GEBA: Meaning 'hill' – often confused in the Bible with Gibeah which also means 'hill'.

GILBOA: A mountain ridge overlooking the Jezreel valley between the cities of Taanach and Bethshan.

GORDON: (1833-1885).

GOSHEN: Biblical name for a region of the Eastern Delta (Egy. *Kesan*). The ancient name may be preserved in the name of the modern capital of Sharkiya province – Facus (i.e. Egy. *Pa-Kes*).

GRÉBAUT: (1846-1915).

GREGORY XVI: Previously the Camaldolese monk, Bartolomeo Alberto Cappellari.

Habachi: (1906-1984).

Habiru: Probably derived from the Akkadian verb *habaru* meaning 'to migrate'.

Hamza: (1890-1980).

Haplography: The accidental omission of a word, syllable or letter in writing.

Har-Psusennes II: 21st Dynasty, reigned 959-945 BC.

Hasmonean Dynasty: A line of Jewish kings ruling from 152 to 37 BC.

Hattusas: the capital of the Hittite homeland at modern Boghazköy in central Turkey.

Hazor: One of the largest Middle and Late Bronze Age cities in the Levant. Located to the north of Lake Kinnereth (= 'the Sea of Galilee').

Heb Sed: The jubilee festival of the reigning monarch during which he undergoes a ritual regicide followed by a miraculous rebirth. Thus rejuvenated, the king then undergoes a series of trials to demonstrate his fitness to rule. The first heb sed of the pharaoh usually coincides with his thirtieth year on the throne, to be followed by a repetition of the jubilee every three years.

Helck: (1915-1993).

Heliacal Rising: The appearance of a heavenly body above the horizon just before sunrise.

Heliopolis: 'City of the Sun' (Grk.) – the centre of sun-worship in Egypt (Egy. *Iunu*), north of modern Cairo.

Hellenistic Period: From the conquest of Alexander in 332 BC to the Roman occupation of Egypt in 30 BC.

Herodotus: Greek historian who visited Egypt in *c.* 445 BC.

Hieratic: The (non-monumental) cursive form of hieroglyphics used to write the Egyptian language on papyrus.

Hiram: Equivalent to the Phoenician name Ahiram.

House of Eternity: *hut neheh* (Egy.) – i.e. a royal tomb where the deceased monarch would rest for all time.

HPA: High Priest of Amun.

Hypostyle hall at Karnak: Columned hall representing the primeval swamp in the mythology of ancient Egypt. A hall filled with columns representing a papyrus marsh, separating the ground water from solid ground. The imagery is of reaching the mythological land upon which the creator-god performed his first acts of creation.

Induction: The installation of the young Apis bull calf as the living embodiment of the god Ptah.

INTERREGNUM: When the succession is interrupted and no king sits on the throne.

ISHBAAL: Hebrew for 'Man of Baal'.

ITJ-TAWY: 'Seizer of the Two Lands' near the modern village of Lisht.

JEBUSITE: Belonging to the Jebus – the independent enclave of Jerusalem before the capture of the city by David.

JEHOAHAZ: King of Israel, reigned 814-798 BC.

JEHU: King of Israel, reigned 841-814 BC.

JERICHO: One of the oldest cities in the world. Located to the west of the River Jordan at the southern end of the Jordan Valley.

JEROBOAM: Kingdom of Israel, reigned 931-910 BC.

JEZREEL VALLEY: Also known as the Plain of Esdraelon (especially its northern half), linking the Jordan valley to the Mediterranean coast at Akko.

KA: Usually interpreted as the 'spirit' of a person, as opposed to the Ba which is the 'soul'.

KADESH: Modern name – Tell Nebi Mend. Kadesh-on-the-Orontes in Syria, north of the Bekaa Valley. A large city strategically located on the Orontes river in Syria at the east end of the Homs/Tripoli gap.

KAHUN PAPYRI: A collection of papyri found by Petrie and now kept in the collections of the Berlin and Petrie Museums. They consist of documents from the pyramid town of Senuseret II which deal with temple and local administrative activities during the life of the settlement, extending down into the 13th Dynasty.

KAMAL: (1849-1923).

KAPES: Wife of Takelot I.

KARKAR: Location of the famous battle of 853 BC in the northern Orontes Valley.

KARNAK: The national shrine of the state god, Amun-re of Thebes, and the largest temple complex in Egypt.

KASED KHEIR: meaning 'sailing a true course' (Arab.).

KASHTA: Reigned OC – *c.* 760-747 BC.

KENYON: (1906-1978).

KHEPRI: The scarab beetle god who represents the rising sun.

KHIRBET: Arabic for 'ruin', equivalent to Hebrew *Horvat.*

KITCHEN: Professor of Egyptology at the University of Liverpool.

LAKE MOERIS: The name given by ancient writers to the inland sea today known as Birket Karun. The earlier Classical name may derive either from Egyptian *mer wer* 'great water' or from Nimaatre – the pre-nomen of Amenemhat III which was probably pronounced something like Nimuaria.

LATE BRONZE AGE: *c.* 1550-1150 BC.

LATE HELLADIC: A pottery period representing the Late Bronze Age in Greece and the Aegean.

LATE PERIOD: Dynasties 26 to 30, 664-343 BC.

LAYARD: (1817-1894).

LEPSIUS: (1810-1884).

LEVANT: An archaeological (non-political) term used to describe the land lying between the two great civilisations of Egypt and Mesopotamia. Today the area consists of the states of Syria, Lebanon, Jordan and Israel (and parts of NW Iraq and SE Turkey).

LIBYAN PERIOD: Normally considered to be Dynasties 22 to 24.

LIEBLEIN: (1827-1911).

LIMESTONE BURNING: Limestone was used to produced lime for the cement industry which serviced the city builders of the first millennium AD. Tanis, with its abundant supplies of neatly cut limestone blocks, lay at the mouth of the Tanitic branch of the Nile, close to the Mediterranean coast and the seagoing trade routes to the population centres of the Roman and Islamic worlds. The exploitation of Tanis as a 'quarry' was therefore long and exhaustive.

LIVINGSTONE: (1813-1873).

LOGOGRAM: From *logos* = 'word' (Grk.). An archaic Sumerian sign/character representing a single word or idea, often used in later Akkadian writing. When such logograms occur in a text scholars denote them by using capital letters – as with our example of SA.GAZ which most Amarna Letters use for Habiru.

MANETHO: A man of Sebennytus who became a High Priest at Heliopolis. He was commissioned by the early Ptolemies (3rd century BC) to write a history of Egypt. His original narrative no longer exists, but excerpts are given in Josephus: Contra Apionem, whilst redactions, in the form of king-lists, have been preserved in the works of the early Christian chronographers Africanus and Eusebius.

MASORETIC: The earliest surviving Hebrew version of the Old Testament narratives (excluding fragments found in the Kumran collection).

MASPERO: (1846-1916).

MASTABAS: From the Arabic word meaning 'bench'. A large mudbrick rectangle, often decorated with a niched façade, which forms the super-structure of a typical Early Dynastic/Old Kingdom tomb.

MASUDI: (*c.* 890-956).

MAX-MÜLLER: (1862-1919).

MENES: There are currently two candidates for the historical king remembered in this legendary founder of the 1st Dynasty: Narmer and Aha, with the latter now becoming the more popular choice amongst Egyptologists.

MERENPTAH: 19th Dynasty, reigned 1213-1203 BC.

MERETSEGER: The cobra goddess – 'She who loves silence' – protectress of the royal necropolis in Western Thebes.

MESOPOTAMIA: 'Between the two rivers' (Grk.) – i.e. the land watered by the Euphrates and Tigris rivers (modern Iraq, north-east Syria and eastern Turkey).

MESHWESH: A tribe originating from the Mediterranean coast of Libya.

METATHESIS: The accidental transposition of words or letters in words.

MIDDLE BRONZE AGE: From the second half of the 11th Dynasty to the beginning of the 18th Dynasty, *c.* 2000-1550 BC.

MIDDLE KINGDOM: Dynasties 11 (from Montuhotep II) & 12, 2007-1759 BC.

MIDIANITE: A person from the land of Midian (north-west Arabia near the Gulf of Aqaba).

MIDRASH: Extra scriptural dissertations and commentaries written by the rabbis of the Middle Ages to complement the study of the Tanaak.

MIGDOL: A large fortified tower. Also used to describe a tower-like temple commonly constructed in the Middle Bronze Age.

MITANNI: Also known as Naharin – the land between the two rivers of the Euphrates and Khabur in modern Syria/Iraq.

MONTET: (1885-1966).

MOTHER OF APIS: The cow which gave birth to the designated Apis bull. In the Late Period onwards, she was given an honoured burial in the Sakkara necropolis.

MOUNT HOREB: Usually identified with Gebel Musa ('Mountain of Moses') in Sinai, but it has also been identified with the volcanic mountain called Horeb in ancient Midian (NW Arabia).

MOUNT NEBU: East of the River Jordan near the north-east coast of the Dead Sea. In modern Jordan.

MUDIR: Arabic for 'boss' or 'leader'.

MUSEO GREGORIANO EGIZIO: 'The Egyptian Museum of Gregory'.

MUTBAAL: Canaanite for 'Man of Baal'.

NAVILLE: (1844-1926).

NEBUCHADNEZZAR II: 605-562 BC.

NECTANEBO I: Nakhtnebef (Egy.), 30th Dynasty, reigned 380-362 BC.

NECTANEBO II: Nakhthorheb (Egy.), 30th Dynasty, reigned 360-343 BC.

NEFERKHEPERURE-WAENRE: 'Perfect are the manifestations of Re – the sole one of Re'.

NEGEV: The extensive barren wasteland which lies between the plain of Philistia and the Wadi Arabah to the south of the Dead Sea.

NEHEMIAH: A contemporary of Ezra and governor of Judah following the return from the Babylonian exile. He served as governor between *circa* 444 and 420 BC.

NETJERHEKAIUNU: 'god and ruler of On' = Heliopolis (Grk.).

NEW KINGDOM: Dynasties 18 to 20. The conventional dating for the New Kingdom is 1539-1069 BC.

NEWTON: (1642-1727).

NINEVEH: One of the great royal cities of Assyria located on the River Tigris to the north of its confluence with the Greater Zab river.

NOMARCHS: From *nomos* and *arkhon* meaning 'ruler' or 'leader' of a nome (Grk.). The local governors or chieftains of the Egyptian nomes.

NOMES: From *nomos* (Grk.) meaning 'pasture' or 'region'. The districts or governorates of Egypt.

NUBIA: The region of the Nile Valley between Aswan and the Second Cataract.

NUDJMET: Wife of Herihor, the first 'priest-king' of the Theban 21st Dynasty.

OLD BABYLONIAN PERIOD: From Sumuabum to Samsuditana: OC – 1894 to 1595 BC.

OLD KINGDOM: Dynasties 3 to 6, *c.* 2589-2090 BC.

OMRI: 880-873 BC.

ONOMASTICA: From Greek *onomastikos.* The corpus of proper names in a language or subject.

OPHIR: Possibly the Indian sub-continent.

ORTHOGRAPHY: The spelling or writing of a word within the accepted usage of a language.

OSIRID: 'of Osiris' – mummiform statues (holding crook and flail across the chest) attached to pillars at the rear for support.

OSIRIS-APIS: The Egyptian god of the dead in the form of the sacred bull.

OSORKON I: 22nd Dynasty, reigned 924-889 BC.

OSORKON II: 22nd Dynasty, reigned 874-850 BC.

PARALLEL DYNASTIES: When there is more than one dynasty of kings ruling at the same time.

PARKER: (1906-1993).

PETRIE: (1853-1942).

PHILIP ARRHIDAEUS: 323-316 BC.

PINUDJEM II: 21st Dynasty, held office 990-969 BC.

PIRIFORM: Pear-shaped.

POST-EXILIC: After the return of the Israelites from their exile in Babylonia which began in 587 and ended in *c.* 539 BC.

POTIPHAR: Possibly Egy. Padipare.

PREDYNASTIC: The time before the unification of Egypt by King Menes and the beginning of the 1st Dynasty.

PRENOMINA: Plural of prenomen – the coronation name of the pharaoh, as opposed to the nomen which is assigned at birth.

PROSTHETIC: A linguistic term derived from Greek and Latin – *pros* = 'towards' and *tithenai* = 'to place', meaning 'to add'.

PSAMTEK I: Psammêtichus (Manetho), 26th Dynasty, reigned 664-610 BC.

PSUSENNES I: Pasbakhanniut (Egy.), reigned 1039-991 BC.

PTAH: State god of Memphis, represented as a human figure wearing a blue skull cap.

PTOLEMY SOTER I: 31st Dynasty, reigned 304-284 BC.

PTOLEMY (III) EUERGETES: Reigned 246-221 BC.

PTOLEMY XV: 44-30 BC.

PYLON: Greek for 'gate'. A pair of monumental towers which flank the entrance to an Egyptian temple.

PYRAMIDION: The capping stone at the apex of a pyramid.

QUINTUS CAERILLIUS: Born in AD 189.

RAMESSES II: Third king of the 19th Dynasty, reigned 1279-1213 BC.

RAMESSES III: OC – 1184-1153 BC.

RE: The great sun-god of Heliopolis, synonymous with Atum.

RE-HARAKHTE: 'the sun (Re) and the falcon (Horus) of the horizon'.

RECTO: The front or main side of a document/papyrus.

REDACTOR: The editor/compiler of the definitive Old Testament scrolls.

REHOBOAM: Kingdom of Judah, reigned 931-913 BC.

REIS: Arabic for 'chief' – in this case the pilot of a Nile steamer.

REISNER: (1867-1942).

REVERSE: The rear or second side of a tablet or document – to be read following-on from the obverse.

REVETMENT: A wall which supports an earthen bank and lines a ditch or trench at the bottom of a glacis fortification system.

ROMAN EMPIRE: From Augustus Caesar to Heraklios, 30 BC to AD 640.

ROSELLINI: (1800-1843).

SAKKARA: Located on the western desert ridge some 25 kilometres south of Cairo. The modern village name which the site has inherited probably derives from the ancient Egyptian local deity of the area, Sokar.

SALAH ED-DIN: (AD 1137-1193).

SARCOPHAGI: Plural of sarcophagus (Grk.) meaning 'flesh-eater' – the stone receptacle in which the mummified body of the deceased was interred (to be distinguished from the wooden coffin).

SCHIST: A grey-black stone of very fine grain used by the Egyptians usually in the production of statues; otherwise known as 'greywacke'.

SCHLIEMANN: (1822-1890).

SEBAKHIN: Peasant farmers who strip out ancient mudbrick buildings to use the material for soil enrichment.

SECOND INTERMEDIATE PERIOD: Dynasties 13 to 17. The era which falls between the Middle Kingdom and the New Kingdom. The conventional dating for the SIP is 1759-1539 BC.

SEKHEMKHET: 3rd Dynasty, reigned c. 2611-2603 BC.

SEPTUAGINT: The Old Testament translated into Greek in the third century BC.

SERABIT EL-KHADIM: The region of the turquoise mines in western Sinai where the Egyptians built a shrine temple to the goddess Hathor 'Mistress of Turquoise'.

SERANIM: 'Lords' (Heb.) – the rulers of the five principal cities of Philistia.

SERAPIS: Greco-Roman version of the Egyptian dual deity Usir-Hapu (Osiris-Apis).

SETI I: 19th Dynasty, reigned 1294-1279 BC.

SETI II: 19th Dynasty, reigned OC – 1200-1194 BC.

SETHE: (1869-1934).

SHALMANESER III: 859-824 BC.

SHARON: The swampy coastal plain of Canaan, north of Philistia and south of the Carmel mountain range.

SHASU: Beduin nomads from the Negev and northern Sinai.

SHECHEM: A small city located in the northern part of the central hill country at the modern town of Nablus.

SHEIKH ABD EL-GURNA: The main village on the west bank at Luxor.

SHEPHELAH: The hinterland of the southern coastal plain of Palestine. The low foothills between the coastal plain and the central hill country.

SHILOH: (1937-1988).

SHOFAR: A ram's-horn trumpet.

SHOSHENK I: 22nd Dynasty, reigned 945-924 BC.

SHOSHENK II: 22nd Dynasty, reigned 890-889 BC.

SHOSHENK III: 22nd Dynasty, reigned 825-773 BC.

SIAMUN: 21st Dynasty, reigned 978-959 BC.

SIRIUS: The Dog-star, represented in the Egyptian pantheon by the goddess Sopdet, herald of the new year.

SMENDES : Nesbanebdjed (Egy.), 21st Dynasty, reigned 1069-1043 BC.

SMITH, GRAFTON ELLIOT: (1871-1937).

SMITH, WILLIAM: (1907-1969).

SOLOMON: Reigned c. 971-931 BC.

SPEOS ARTEMIDOS: A rock-cut temple just south of Beni Hassan dedicated to the lion goddess Pakhet.

STELAE: Plural of stela (or stele), meaning 'standing stone' (Grk.) – used to denote an inscribed stone plaque. A stela acts as a boundary marker not just within the physical world but also, in this context, between the worlds of the living and the dead.

STIBADEION: A Greek word originally meaning 'circular mat'.

STRABO: (c 63 BC to after AD 21). Meaning 'squint-eyed' (Grk.). He visited Egypt in 24 BC. His work *Geographica* is divided into seventeen books of which Book XVII concerns Egypt and Africa.

STRATA: Plural of stratum – an archaeological level or occupation phase.

SYRO-PALESTINE: The area of modern Syria, northern Iraq, Lebanon, Israel, Palestine and western Jordan.

TAHARKA: 25th Dynasty, reigned 690-664 BC.

TAKELOT I: Takelôthis (Manetho), 22nd Dynasty, reigned 889-874 BC.

Takelot II: 22nd Dynasty, reigned 850-825 BC.

Tanaakh: The Hebrew Bible.

Tanis: Egy. *Djanet*, the biblical Zoan.

Tantamani: 25th Dynasty, reigned 664-656 BC.

Tell: An ancient ruin mound built up over the centuries by the constant destruction and rebuilding of mudbrick architecture.

Tell el-Yahudiya Ware: A type of pottery discovered by Petrie when excavating at Tell el-Yahudiya ('Mound of the Jew') in the eastern delta. Petrie named the pottery after the site where it was first unearthed.

Temenos: From *temnein* (Grk.) meaning 'to cut off' or 'separate' – a sacred enclosure or precinct.

Temple of Baal-Berith: 'Temple of the Lord of the Covenant', also known as 'Migdol Shechem'.

Temple of Relief: The toilets!

Terminus post quem: The date after which an event must have taken place but not necessarily the actual date of the event.

Tharbis: The legend of Moses' marriage to an Ethiopian princes also exists in the Talmudic literature.

Third Intermediate Period: Dynasties 21 to 25. The era which falls after the New Kingdom and before Late Period. The conventional dating of the TIP is 1069-664 BC.

Thutmose III: 18th Dynasty, reigned 1479-1425 BC.

Torr: (1857-1928).

Tumuli: Plural of tumulus – a funeral mound.

Tura: A region some 30 kms south of Cairo on the east bank of the Nile. The ancient quarries located here supplied the finest limestone for the monuments of Egypt. The stone from here is most famous for its use as the smooth, sparkling white outer casing which once adorned the pyramids of Giza.

Two Lands: Usually equated with Upper and Lower Egypt – the traditional boundary being at Memphis near Cairo; however it is also evocative of many domains, e.g. living/dead, heaven/earth, physical/spiritual etc.

United Monarchy: From the foundation of the Israelite kingdom under Saul, through the reigns of David and Solomon, to the schism and division of the state into the rival kingdoms of Judah and Israel, immediately following the death of Solomon.

Uraeus: The image of the cobra god Wadjet which was attached to the forehead of royal crowns and headdresses. Its mythological function was to protect the king by spitting flames at those who might try to harm the person of Pharaoh.

USERMAATRE-SETEPENRE RAMESSU-MERYAMUN: Powerful is the Divine Order of Re – Chosen of Re, Re is the one who bore him – Beloved of Amun.

USHABTI: A small figure of a household servant (made of clay, stone or wood) who magically comes to life in the netherworld in order to take care of the needs of the deceased. Small figurine, usually in human form, placed in the tomb so as to undertake menial tasks required by the deceased in the afterlife.

VERSO: The reverse or secondary side of a papyrus.

VIZIER: Arabic word equivalent to 'Prime Minister'– used by Egyptologists for Pharaoh's ring-bearer and the first official of the land.

WEKIL: Arabic for 'deputy'.

WEST SEMITIC: The principal language group of Syria and Palestine which includes Hebrew, Canaanite and Ugaritic.

WILBOUR. (1833-1896).

WINDOW OF APPEARANCES: In the Egyptian royal palaces and temples there is a window at which the pharaoh can 'appear' to receive the acclamation of his subjects – comparable to the balcony at Buckingham Palace where the British royal family always 'appear' on state occasions.

YADIN: (1917-1984).

YAHWEH. The Hebrew for Jehovah – the god of Moses and the Israelites.

ZAMBEELS: Baskets made out of old tyre rubber, used by the labour force to remove excavation debris to the waste dumps.

ZOAN: Tsoan (Heb.), Djanet (Egy.), Tjanni (Coptic).

ZOOMORPHIC: Animal shaped.

BIBLIOGRAPHY

A

Adam, S. – 1959: 'Report on the Excavations of the Department of Antiquities at Ezbet Rushdi' in *ASAE* 56, pp. 207-26.

Aharoni, Y. – 1972: 'The Stratification of Israelite Megiddo' in *JNES* 31, pp. 302-11.

Aharoni, Y. – 1979: *The Land of the Bible, 2nd ed.* (London).

Aharoni, Y. & **Amiran**, R. – 1958: 'A New Scheme for the Subdivision of the Iron Age in Palestine' in *IEJ* 8, pp. 171-84.

Aharoni, Y. & **Avi-Yonah**, M. (eds.) – 1977: *MacMillan Bible Atlas* (London).

Albright, W. F. – 1937: 'The Egyptian Correspondence of Abimilki, Prince of Tyre' in *JEA* 23, pp. 190-203.

Albright, W. F. – 1942: 'A Votive Stele Erected by Ben-Hadad I of Damascus to the God Melcarth' in *BASOR* 87, pp. 23-9.

Albright, W. F. – 1943: 'An Archaic Hebrew Proverb on an Amarna Letter from Central Palestine' in *BASOR* 89, pp. 29-32.

Albright, W. F. – 1943: 'Two Little Understood Amarna Letters from the Middle Jordan Valley' in *BASOR* 89, pp. 7-17.

Albright, W. F. – 1956: 'Further Light on Synchronisms Between Egypt and Asia in the Period 935-685 B.C.' in *BASOR* 141, pp. 23-7.

Albright, W. F. – 1964: 'The Eighteenth-Century Princes of Byblos and the Chronology of Middle Bronze' in *BASOR* 176, pp. 38-46.

Albright, W. F. – 1965: 'Further Light on the History of Middle-Bronze Byblos' in *BASOR* 179, pp. 38-43.

Albright, W. F. – 1966: 'Remarks on the Chronology of Early Bronze IV-Middle Bronze IIA in Phoenicia and Syria-Palestine' in *BASOR* 184, pp. 27-35.

Albright, W. F. – 1973: 'The Historical Framework of Palestinian Archaeology Between 2100 and 1600 B.C.' in *BASOR* 209, pp. 12-19.

Albright, W. F. – 1975: 'The Amarna Letters from Palestine' in *CAH*, vol. II:2A, pp. 98-116.

Albright, W. F. & **Mendenhall**, G. E. (transl.) – 1950: 'The Amarna Letters' in *ANET*, pp. 483-90.

Aldred, C. – 1991: *Akhenaten, King of Egypt* (London).

Aldred, C. – 1975: 'Egypt: The Amarna Period and the End of the Eighteenth Dynasty' in *CAH* II:2A, pp. 49-97.

Alliot, M. – 1935: *Fouilles de Tell Edfou (1933)* (Cairo).

Amiran, R. – 1969: *Ancient Pottery of the Holy Land* (Jerusalem).

Anati, E. – 1986: *The Mountain of God* (New York).

Arnold, D. & **Oppenheim**, A. – 1995: 'Reexcavating the Senwosret III Pyramid Complex at Dashur' in *KMT* 6:2, pp. 44-56.

Arnold, F. – 1992: 'New Evidence for the Length of the Reign of Senwosret III?' in *GM* 129, pp. 27-31.

Arnold, P. M. – 1990: *Gibeah: The Search for a Biblical City* (JSOT Supplement Series 79, Sheffield).

Aston, D. A. – 1989: 'Takeloth II - A King of the "Theban Twenty-third Dynasty"?' in *JEA* 75, pp. 139-53.

Avigad, N.– 1978: in Avi-Yonah, M. (ed.) *Encyclopedia of Archaeological Excavations in the Holy Land*, vol. IV (Oxford).

B

Badre, L. *et al.* – 1990: 'Tell Kazel, Syria: Excavations of the AUB Museum 1985-1987' in *Berytus* 38, pp. 17-22.

Baillie, M. G. L. – 1991: 'Dendrochronology and Thera: The Scientific Case' in *JACF* 4, pp. 15-28.

Bakie, J. A. – 1923: *A Century of Excavations in the Land of the Pharaohs* (London).

Baldwin, J. – 1988: *1 and 2 Samuel: An Introduction and Commentary* (Tyndale Old Testament Commentaries, Leicester).

Barkay, G – 1990: 'A Late Bronze Age Egyptian Temple in Jerusalem' in *Eretz-Israel* 21, pp. 94-106.

Barsanti, A – 1908: 'Stéle Inédite au Nom du Roi Radadouhotep Doudoumes' in *ASAE* 9, pp. 1-2.

Barta, W. – 1988: 'Das Kalendarium des Papyrus Ebers mit der Notizeines Sothisaufgangs' in *GM* 101, pp. 7-12.

Bartlett, J. – 1982: *Jericho* (Guildford).

von Beckerath, J. – 1958: 'Notes on the Viziers 'Ankhu and 'Iymeru in the 13th Egyptian Dynasty' in *JNES* 17, pp. 263-68.

von Beckerath, J. – 1966: 'The Nile Level Records at Karnak and their Importance for the History of the Libyan Period (Dynasties XXII and XXIII)' in *JARCE* 6, pp. 46-7.

von Beckerath, J. – 1990: 'Das Kalendarium des Papyrus Ebers und die Chronologie des Neuen Reiches. Gegenwartiger stand der Frage' in Abstracts of the Second International Coloquium on Absolute Chronology held at Schloss Haindorf, Langenlois, Austria from 12th to 15th August 1990 (*HML?*), pp. 4-11.

Bell, B. – 1975: 'Climate and the History of Egypt: The Middle Kingdom' in *AJA* 79, pp. 223-69.

Ben-Tor, A. (ed.) – 1992: *The Archaeology of Ancient Israel* (New Haven & London).

Bienkowski, P. – 1986: *Jericho in the Late Bronze Age* (Warminster).

Bierbrier, M. L. – 1975: *The Late New Kingdom in Egypt* (Warminster).

Bietak, M. – 1979: *Avaris and Piramesse: Archaeological Exploration of the Eastern Nile Delta* (London).

Bietak, M. – 1984: 'Problems of Middle Bronze Age Chronology: New Evidence from Egypt' in *AJA* 88, pp. 471-85.

Bietak, M. – 1989: 'The Middle Bronze Age of the Levant: A New Approach to Relative and Absolute Chronology' in *HML?*, part 3 (Gothenburg), pp. 78-123.

Bietak, M. – 1990: 'Zur Herkunft des Seth von Avaris' in *Ägypten und Levante* 1, pp. 9-16.

Bietak, M. – 1991: 'Egypt and Canaan During the Middle Bronze Age' in *BASOR* 281, pp. 27-72.

Bietak, M. – 1991: 'Der Friedhof in einem Palastgarten aus der Zeit des spaten mittleren Reiches und andere Forschung-sergebnisse aus dem ostlichen Nildelta (Tell el-Dab'a 1984-1987)' in *Ägypten und Levante* 2, pp. 47-109.

Bietak, M. – 1992: *Tell el-Dab'a*, vol. V (Vienna).

Bimson, J. J. – 1978: *Redating the Exodus and Conquest* (Sheffield).

Bimson, J. J. – 1978/79: 'A Chronology for the Middle Kingdom and Israel's Egyptian Bondage' in *SIS Review* III:3, pp. 64-9.

Bimson, J. J. – 1986: 'Shoshenq and Shishak: A Case of Mistaken Identity' in *SIS Review* 8, pp. 36-46.

Bimson, J. J. & **Livingston**, D. – 1987: 'Redating the Exodus' in *BAR* 13:5, pp. 40-53.

Bimson, J. J. – 1988: 'Exodus and Conquest - Myth or Reality? Can Archaeology Provide the Answer?' in *JACF* 2, pp. 27-40.

Biran, A. & **Naveh**, J. – 1993: 'An Aramaic Stele Fragment from Tel Dan' in *IEJ* 43, pp. 81-98.

Bonnet, C. – 1986: *Kerma: Territoire et Metropole* (Cairo).

Borchardt, L. – 1897: 'Ein Rechnungsbuch des königlichen Hofes aus dem alten Reiche' in *Aegyptiaca: Festschrift für G. Ebers* (Leipzig), pp. 8-15.

Borchardt, L. – 1935: *Die Mittel zur zeitlichen Festlegung von Punkten der ägyptischen Geschichte und ihre Anwendung* (Cairo).

Bordreuil, P. and **Teixidor**, J. – 1983: 'Nouvel Examen de l'Inscription de Bar-Hadad' in *Aula Orientalis* 1, pp. 271-6.

Bottero, J. – 1954: *Le Probleme des Habiru a la 4' Rencontre Assyriologique Internationale* (Paris), pp. xxxviii & 208.

Bourriau, J. – 1991: 'Relations Between Egypt and Kerma During the Middle and New Kingdoms' in W. V. Davies (ed.): *Egypt and Africa: Nubia from Prehistory to Islam* (London).

Breasted, J. H. – 1905: *A History of Egypt* (London).

Brissaud, P. 1987: 'Les Fouilles dans le Secteur de la Nécropole Royale (1984-1986)' in *Cahiers de Tanis*, vol. I (Paris), pp. 7-43.

Brugsch, H. F. K. – 1858: *Geographische Inschriften altägyptischer Denkmäler*, vol. II (Leipzig).

Brugsch, H. F. K. – 1884: *Thesaurus Inscriptionum Aegyptiacarum Altaegyptische Inschriften* (Leipzig).

Brugsch, H. F. K. – 1891: *Egypt Under the Pharaohs* (London).

Budge, E. A. W. – 1913: *Hieroglyphic Texts from Egyptian Stelae in the British Museum*, part IV (London).

C

Callaway, J. & **Weinstein**, J. – 1977: 'Radiocarbon Dating of Palestine in the EB Age' in *BASOR* 225, pp. 1-16

Caminos, R. – 1952: 'Gebel es-Silsilah No. 100' in *JEA* 38, pp. 46-61.

Caminos, R. – 1958: *The Chronicle of Prince Osorkon* (London).

Campbell, E. F. – 1964: *The Chronology of the Amarna Letters* (Baltimore).

Campbell, E. F. – 1965: 'Shechem in the Amarna Archive' in G. E. Wright (ed.): *Shechem* (London), pp. 191-2.

Ceram, C. W. (ed.) – 1966: *The World of Archaeology* (London).

Cerny, J. – 1945: 'Studies in the Chronology of the Twenty-First Dynasty' in *JEA* 32, pp. 24-30.

Champollion, J. F. – 1868: *Lettres écrites d'Égypte et de Nubie en 1828 et 1829*, 2nd ed. (Paris).

Chassinat, É. – 1899: 'Textes Provenant du Sérapéum de Memphis' in *RT* 21, pp. 56-73.

Clube, V & **Napier**, B. – 1982: *The Cosmic Serpent* (London).

Cohen, R. – 1983: 'The Mysterious MB I People' in *BAR* 9:4, pp. 16-29.

BIBLIOGRAPHY

Collins, J. J. – 1985: 'Artapanus' in J. M. Charlesworth (ed.): *The Old Testament Pseudepigrapha*, vol. II (London), pp. 889-903.

Corney, R. W. – 1962: 'Achish' in K. Crim *et al.* (eds.)*: Interpreters' Dictionary of the Bible*, vol. I (Nashville), p. 27.

Coughenour, R. A. – 1979: 'A Search for Mahanaim' in *BASOR* 273, pp. 57-66.

Courville, D. – 1971: *The Exodus Problem and its Ramifications* (Loma Linda).

Coutts, H. (ed.) – 1988: *Gold of the Pharaohs: Catalogue of the Exhibition of Treasures from Tanis* (Edinburgh).

Craigie, P. C. – 1983: 'The Tablets from Ugarit and their Importance for Biblical Studies' in *BAR* 9:5, pp. 62-73.

Cross, F. M. – 1972: 'The Stele Dedicated to Melcarth by Ben-Hadad of Damascus' in *BASOR* 205, pp. 36-42.

Curtis, A. – 1985: *Ugarit* (Cities of the Biblical World, Cambridge).

D

Daressy, G. – 1909: *Cercueils des Cachettes Royales* (Cairo).

Davies, G. I. – 1988: 'Solomonic Stables at Megiddo After All?' in *PEQ* 120 (July-Dec), pp. 130-41.

Davies, N. de G. – 1908: *The Rock Tombs of el-Amarna,* vols. V & VI (London).

Davies, N. de G. – 1934: 'A High Place at Thebes' in *Mélanges Maspero*, vol. I (Cairo), pp. 241-50.

Dirkzwager, A. – 1981: 'Pharaoh So and the Libyan Dynasty' in *Catastrophism and Ancient History* III:1, p. 23.

Dodson, A. M. – 1988: 'Enigmatic Cartouche' in *GM* 106, pp. 15-19.

Dodson, A. M. – 1992: *The Canopic Equipment of the Kings of Egypt* (London).

Dodson, A. M. – 1993: 'A New King Shoshenq Confirmed?' in *GM* 137, pp. 53-8.

Dorsey, D. A. – 1991: *The Roads and Highways of Ancient Israel* (Baltimore).

Doumas, C. G. – 1989: *Thera and the Aegean World III*, vols. I to III (London).

Doumas, D. & **Doumas** A. – 1992: *The Wall-paintings of Thera* (Athens).

Dunham, D. & **Janssen**, J. M. A. – 1960: *Semna Kumma* (Boston).

Dussaud, R. – 1925: 'Dedicace d'une statue d'Osorkon I par Eliba'al, roi de Byblos' in *Syria* 6, pp. 101-17.

Dussaud, R. – 1927: 'Nouveaux renseignements sur la Palastine et la Syrie vers 2000 avant notre ère' in *Syria* 8, pp. 216-33.

Dussaud, R. – 1937: Review of A. Jirku – *Die aegyptischen Listen Palaestinensischer und Syrischen Ortsnamen* (Leipzig) in *Syria* 18, pp. 394-5.

E

Edelman, D. – 1985: 'The "Ashurites" of Eshbaal's State' in *PEQ* 117 (July-December), pp. 85-91.

Edwards, A. – 1877: *A Thousand Miles Up the Nile* (London).

Eigner, D. – 1995: 'A Palace of the Early 13th Dynasty at Tell el Dab'a' in *Ägypten und Levante* 5 (forthcoming).

Eissfeldt, O. – 1975: 'The Hebrew Kingdom' in *CAH*, vol. II:2B, pp. 537-605.

Erman, A. & **Grapow**, H. – 1926: *Worterbuch der Aegyptische Sprache* I (Leipzig).

F

Fagan, B. M. – 1977: *The Rape of the Nile: Tomb Robbers, Tourists, and Archaeologists in Egypt* (London), pp. 271-87.

Fairbridge, R. W. – 1963: 'Nile Sedimentation above Wadi Halfa during the last 20,000 years' in *Kush* 11, pp. 104-7.

Feigin, S. – 1955: 'The Date List of the Babylonian King Samsuditana' in *JNES* 14, pp. 137-60.

Finkelstein, I. (ed.) – 1993: *Shiloh: The Archaeology of a Biblical Site* (Jerusalem).

Finkelstein, I & **Na'aman**, N (eds.) – 1994: *From Nomadism to Monarchy: Archaeological & Historical Aspects of Early Israel* (Jerusalem).

Flanagan, J. W. – 1983: 'Succession and Genealogy in the Davidic Dynasty' in H. B. Huffman *et. al.* (eds.): *The Quest for the Kingdom of God: Studies in Honor of George E. Mendenhall* (Winona Lake), pp. 35-55.

Fresnel, F. (transl.) –1838: Text of Abu el-Faradj: *Kitab-Alaghanity* in *JA* 6.

G

Gardiner, A. H. – 1914: 'New Literary Works from Ancient Egypt' in *JEA* 1, pp. 100-6.

Gardiner, A. H. – 1942: *Select Papyri in the Hieratic Character from the Collections of the British Museum*, vol. II (London), pls. XV-LXII.

Gardiner, A. H. – 1961: *Egypt of the Pharaohs* (London).

BIBLIOGRAPHY

Garstang, J. – 1930: 'Jericho. Sir Charles Marston's Expedition in 1931' in *PEFQS*, pp. 129-32.

Garstang, J. & **Garstang**, J. B. E. – 1940: *The Story of Jericho* (London).

Gauthier, H. – 1914: *Le livre des rois d'Égypte*, vols. I to III (Paris).

Gauthier, H. – 1915: *Le livre des rois d'Égypte*, vol. IV (Paris).

Gesenius, W. – 1921: *Hebräisches und Aramäisches Handwörterbuch über das Alte Testament* (Leipzig).

Gifford, E. H. (transl.) – 1903: *Eusebius Pamphilis: Evangelicae Preparationis*, book XV (London).

Ginzberg, L. – 1909: *Legends of the Jews* (Philadelphia).

Ginzberg, H. L. – 1950: 'The Tale of Aqhat' in *ANET*, pp. 149-55.

Goedicke, H. – 1994: 'Exodus: Myth or History?' in M. Rowland (ed.): *Exodus: Myth or History. The ISIS Seminar Meeting of 19th October 1993 Held at the Institute of Archaeology, London* (ISIS Occasional Publications, vol. II, Basingstoke), pp. 1-15.

Goetze, A. (transl.)– 1950: 'Hittite Treaty' in *ANET*, pp. 529-30.

Goetze, A. (transl.)– 1950: 'Hittite Historical Texts' in *ANET*, p. 319.

Gottwald, N. K. – 1979: *The Tribes of Yahweh* (London).

Grant, M. – 1984: *The History of Ancient Israel* (London).

Greenberg, M. – 1955: *The Hab/piru* (New Haven).

Griffith, F. Ll. – 1891: 'The Account Papyrus No. 18 of Boulaq' in *ZÄS* 29, pp. 102-15.

Griffith, F. Ll. – 1898: *Hieratic Papyri from Kahun and Gurob*, vol. II (London).

Griffith, F.. Ll. – 1909: *Catalogue of the Demotic Papyri in the Rylands Library at Manchester*, vol. III (London).

Gröndahl, F. – 1967: *Die Personennamen der Texte aus Ugarit* (Rome).

Gunn, B. – 1926: 'Two Misunderstood Serapeum Inscriptions' in *ASAE* 26, pp. 92-4.

Gutman, J. – 1963: *Ha Sifrut ha-Yehudit ha-Hellenistit*, vol. II (Jerusalem).

H

Haas, H. *et al.* – 1987: 'Radiocarbon Chronology and the Historical Calendar in Egypt' in O. Aurenche *et al.* (eds.): *Chronologies in the Near East, British Archaeological Report S379*, part 2, pp. 585-606.

Habachi, L. – 1954: 'Khatâ'na – Qantir: Importance' in *ASAE* 52, pp. 443-559.

Hamza, M. – 1930: 'Excavations of the Department of Antiquities at

Qantir (faqûs Distnet), (Season, May 21st-July 7th, 1928)' in *ASAE* 30, p. 31-68.

Hankey, V. – 1992: 'From Chronos to Chronology' in *JACF* 5, pp. 7-29.

Harris, Z. S. – 1978: *Development of the Canaanite Dialects* (Millwood).

Hawkins, J. D. – 1988: 'Kuzi-Teshub and the "Great Kings" of Karkamish' in *Anatolian Studies* 38, pp. 99-108.

Hayes, J. & **Miller**, M. – 1986: *A History of Ancient Israel and Judah* (Philadelphia).

Hayes, W. C. – 1955: *A Papyrus of the Late Middle Kingdom in the Brooklyn Museum* (Brooklyn).

Hedges, R. – 1981: An article reporting on the First Symposium on Carbon-14 and Archaeology, Groningen, 24-28 August, in *Nature* 29.10.81.

Helck, W. – 1961: *Materialen zur Wirtschaftgeschichte des Neuen Reichs*, vol. I (Wiesbaden).

Helck, W. – 1962: *Die Beziehungen Aegyptens zu Vorderasien im 3. und 2. Jahrtausend v. Chr.* (Wiesbaden).

Helck, W. – 1978: 'Ein indirekter Beleg für die Benutzung des leichten Streitwagens in Ägypten zu ende der 13. Dynastie' in *JNES* 37, pp. 337-40.

Helck, W. – 1983: 'Schwachstellen der Chronologie-Diskussion' in *GM* 67, pp. 43-9.

Helck, W. – 1990: Abstract for the *HML?* conference held at Schloss Haindorf, Langenlois, Austria in August 1990.

Helck, W. & **Otto**, E. (eds.) 1975: 'Apis' in *Lexicon der Ägyptologie*, vol. I, cols. 338-48.

Henzberg, H. – 1965: *Die Samuel Bucher* (Gottingen).

Herzog, C. & **Gichon**, M. – 1978: *Battles of the Bible* (London).

Hess, R. S. – 1993: *Amarna Personal Names* (Winona Lake).

Hoffman, M. – 1984: *Egypt Before The Pharaohs* (New York).

Hole, F. – 1987: 'Issues in Near Eastern Chronology' in O. Aurenche *et al.* (eds.): *Chronologies in the Near East, British Archaeological Report* S379, part 2, p. 562.

Hornung, E. – 1987: Discussion during the *HML?* conference held at the University of Gothenburg, Sweden in August 1987 (published in *HML?*, part 3).

Horowitz, W. & **Shaffer**, A. – 1992: 'A Fragment of a Letter from Hazor' in *IEJ* 42, pp. 165-6.

Hughes, J. – 1990: *Secrets of the Times: Myth and History in Biblical Chronology* (Sheffield).

I

Ibrahim, M. & **Rohl**, D. M. – 1988: 'Apis and the Serapeum' in *JACF* 2, pp. 6-26.

Ben Isaiah, Rabbi A. & **Sharfman**, Rabbi B. (transl.) – 1949: *The Pentateuch and Rashi's Commentary*, vol. I (Philadelphia).

Ishida, T. – 1977: *The Royal Dynasties in Ancient Israel* (New York).

J

James, P. – 1982/83: 'Forum' reply in *SIS Workshop* 5:3, pp. 11-12.

James, P. *et al.* – 1991: *Centuries of Darkness* (London).

Jean, C. F. – 1951: *Archives Royales de Mari*, vol. II (Paris).

Jones, A. – 1990: *Jones' Dictionary of Old Testament Proper Names* (first published in 1856) (Grand Rapids).

Jonsson, C. O. – 1987: 'The Foundations of the Assyro-Babylonian Chronology' in *C & C Review* 9, pp. 14-23.

K

Kammenhuber, A. – 1968: *Die Arier im Vorderen Orient* (Heidelberg).

Karouzou, S. – 1993: *National Museum: Illustrated Guide to the Museum* (Athens).

Kemp, B. J. – 1980: 'Egyptian Radiocarbon: A Reply to James Mellaart' in *Antiquity* 54, pp. 25-8.

Kemp, B. J. – 1984: *Amarna Reports* I (London), p. 185.

Kemp, B. J. – 1989: *Ancient Egypt: Anatomy of a Civilization* (London).

Kempinski, A. – 1974: 'Tell el-Ajjul – Beth-Aglayim or Sharuhen?' in *IEJ* 24, pp. 145-52.

Kempinski, A. – 1983: *Syrien und Palästina (Kanaan) in der letzten Phase der Mittelbronze IIB–Zeit (1650-1570 v. chr.)* (Wiesbaden).

Kempinski, A. – 1988: 'Jacob in History' in *BAR* 14:1, pp. 42-7.

Kenyon, K. M. in J. W. Crowfoot *et al.* – 1957(a): *The Objects from Samaria* (London).

Kenyon, K. M. – 1957(b): *Digging up Jericho* (London).

Kenyon, K. M. – 1960: *Archaeology in the Holy Land* (London).

Kenyon, K. M. – 1963: 'Excavations in Jerusalem, 1962' in *PEQ* 95, pp. 7-21.

Kenyon, K. M. – 1965: 'Excavations in Jerusalem, 1964' in *PEQ* 97, pp. 13-14.

Kitchen, K. A. – 1973: *Third Intermediate Period in Egypt* (Warminster).

Kitchen, K. A. – 1982: *Pharaoh Triumphant* (Warminster).

Kitchen, K. A. in P. Aström (ed.) – 1987: 'The Basics of Egyptian Chronology in Relation to the Bronze Age' in *HML?*, part 1 (Gothenburg), pp. 37-55.

Kitchen, K. A. – 1990: *The Egyptian Collection, Rio de Janeiro* (Warminster).

Kitchen, K. A. – 1991: Review of *Centuries of Darkness* in the *Times Literary Supplement* no. 4598 (17th May), p. 21.

Kitchen, K. A. – 1992: Discussion of the Exodus in D. N. Freedman (ed.): *Anchor Bible Dictionary*, vol. II (New York), pp. 702-7.

Kitchen, K. A. – 1993: 'Genesis 12 to 50 in the Near Eastern World' in R. S. Hess *et al.* (eds.): *He Swore an Oath: Biblical Themes from Genesis 12 to 50* (Cambridge), pp. 67-92.

Kline, D. L. – 1993: *Thomas Young: Forgotten Genius: An Annotated Narrative Biography* (Ohio).

Klostermann, D. A. – 1887: *Die Bucher Samuelis und der Konige* (Nordlingen).

Knudtzon, J. A. – 1915: *Die el-Amarna Tafeln* (Leipzig, 2nd ed., 1978).

Kuniholm, P. –1993: Appendix in G. Summers: *Tille Huyuk* 4, pp. 179-90.

L

Lacovara, P. – 1991: 'The Stone Vases at Kerma' in W. V. Davies (ed.): *Egypt and Africa: Nubia from Prehistory to Islam* (London), pp. 118-28.

Langdon, S. & **Fotheringham**, J. K. – 1928: *The Venus Tablets of Ammizaduga* (London).

Lasken, J. – 1991: 'Should the European Oak Dendrochronologies be Re-examined?' in *C & C Review* XIII, pp. 28-32.

Lasken, J. – 1992: 'The Radiocarbon Evidence From Thera: An Alternative Interpretation' in *JACF* 5, pp. 68-76.

Lauer, J.-P. – 1976: *Saqqara* (London).

Lauer, J.-P. & **Picard**, Ch. – 1955: *Les statues ptolemaiques du Sarapieion de Memphis* (Paris).

Leahy, A. (ed.) – 1990: 'Abydos in the Libyan Period' in *Libya and Egypt* c. *1300-750 BC* (London), pp. 155-200.

Leclant, J. & **Yoyotte**, J. – 1952: 'Notes d'Histoire et de Civilisation Éthiopienne' in *BIFAO* 51, pp. 1-39.

Legrain, G. – 1897: 'Deux steles trouvees a Karnak en fevrier 1897' in *ZÄS* 35, pp. 13-16.

BIBLIOGRAPHY

Legrain, G. – 1914: *Catalogue Général des Antiquités Égyptiennes du Musée du Caire: Statues et Statuettes*, vol. III (Cairo).

Lehmann, J. – 1977: *The Hittites* (London).

Lichtheim, M. – 1973: *Ancient Egyptian Literature*, vol. I (London).

Lichtheim, M. – 1980: *Ancient Egyptian Literature*, vol. III (London).

Lieblein, J. – 1914: *Recherches sur l'Histoire et la civilization de l'ancienne Egypte* (Leipzig).

Luckenbill, D. D. – 1926: *Ancient Records of Assyria and Babylon*, vol. I (Chicago).

Luckenbill, D. D. – 1927: *Ancient Records of Assyria and Babylonia*, vol. II (Chicago).

Luft, U. – 1986: 'Noch einmal zum Ebers-Kalender' in *GM* 92, pp. 69-77.

Luft, U. – 1992: 'Remarks of a Philologist on Egyptian Chronology' in *HML?* (*Ägypten und Levante* 3), pp. 109-14.

M

Macadam, M. F. L. – 1949: *The Temples of Kawa*, vol. I (London).

McCarter, P. K. – 1984: *II Samuel: A New Translation with Introduction Notes and Commentary* (Anchor Bible, New York).

McCarter, P. K. – 1986: 'The Historical David' in *Interpretation* 40:2, pp. 117-29.

McGovern, P. *et al.* – 1993: 'The Late Bronze Egyptian Garrison at Beth Shan: Glass and Faience Production and Importation in the Late New Kingdom' in *BASOR* 290/91, pp. 1-28.

Magnusson, M. – 1977: *The Archaeology of the Bible Lands* (London).

Malamat, A. – 1958: 'The Kingdom of David and Solomon in its Contact with Aram Naharaim' in *BA* 21:4, pp. 96-102.

Malek, J. – 1983: 'Who was the first to identify the Saqqara Serapeum?' in *Chronique d'Égypte* 58, pp. 69-72.

Malinine, M., **Posener**, G. & **Vercoutter**, J. – 1968: *Catalogue des Stèles du Sérapéum de Memphis* (Paris).

Manley, W. P. – 1988: 'Tomb 39 and the Sacred Land' in *JACF* 2, pp. 41-57.

Manley, W. P. – 1996: 'The King of Egypt and his Queen in the Early 18th Dynasty' in *Trahajos di Egiptologia* 1, forthcoming.

Mariette, A. – 1856: *Choix de Monuments* (Paris).

Mariette, A. – 1857: *Le Sérapéum de Memphis* (Paris).

Mariette, A. in Maspero (ed.) – 1882: *Le Sérapéum de Memphis* (Paris).

Mars, K. (ed.) – 1954: *Eusebius Werke Vol. III, Die Preparation Evangelica.*

Martin, G. T. – 1991: *The Hidden Tombs of Memphis* (London).

Maspero, G. – 1881: 'A hoard of royal mummies' in *Institut Égyptien Bulletin,* series 2, no. 2, reprinted in C. W. Ceram (ed.): *The World of Archaeology* (London, 1966), pp. 149-53.

Maspero, G. – 1889: *Les Momies Royales de Deir el-Bahari* (Cairo).

Maspero, G. – 1925: *The Struggle of the Nations,* 2nd ed. (London).

Mayrhofer, M. – 1966: *Die Indo-Arier im Alten Vorderasien* (Wiesbaden).

Mazar, B. – 1963: 'The Military Élite of King David' in *VT,* 13 (Leiden), pp. 310-20.

Mazar, A. – 1986: *The Early Biblical Period* (Jerusalem).

Mazar, A. – 1990: *Archaeology of the Land of the Bible: 10000-586 BCE* (New York).

Mellaart, J. – 1979: 'Egyptian and Near Eastern Chronology. A Dilemma?' in *Antiquity* 53, pp. 6-18.

Mellaart, J. – 1080: 'James Mellaart Replies to his Critics' in *Antiquity* 54, pp. 225-7.

Mendenhall, G. – 1973: *The Tenth Generation* (Baltimore).

Milik, J. T. & **Cross**, F. M. Jr. – 1954: 'Inscribed Javelin-heads from the Period of the Judges: A Recent Discovery in Palestine' in *BASOR* 134, pp. 5-15.

Miller, J. M. – 1974: 'Saul's Rise to Power' in *Catholic Biblical Quarterly* 36, pp. 160-4 & 173-4.

Miller, J. M. – 1975: 'Geba/Gibeah of Benjamin' in *VT* 25, pp. 145-66.

Mitchell, W. A. – 1990: 'Ancient Astronomical Observations and Near Eastern Chronology' in *JACF* 3, pp. 18-20.

Montet, P. – 1047: *Les constructions et le tombeau d'Osorkon II à Tanis* (Paris).

Montet, P. – 1951: *Les constructions et le tombeau de Psusennès I à Tanis* (Paris).

Montet, P. – 1960: *Les constructions et le tombeau de Chechanq III à Tanis* (Paris).

Montet, P. – 1968: *Lives of the Pharaohs* (Cleveland).

Moran, W. L. – 1987: *Les Lettres d'el-Amarna: Correspondance diplomatique du pharaon* (Paris).

Moran, W. L. – 1992: *The Amarna Letters* (Johns Hopkins, Baltimore).

Morkot, R. – 1991: Chapter 9 in P. James *et al.*: *Centuries of Darkness* (London).

Morkot, R.: *Economic and Cultural Exchange Between Kush and Egypt* *from the New Kingdom to the Meroitic Period,* PhD thesis (UCL).

Moscati, S. – 1973: *The World of the Phoenicians* (London).

Müller, W. M. in T. K Cheyne & J. Sutherland Black (eds.) – 1888: *Encyclopaedia Biblica,* vol. IV (London), col. 4486, n. 5.

Müller, P. M. & **Stephenson**, F. R. – 1975: 'The Acceleration of the Earth and Moon from Early Astronomical Observations' in G. D. Rosenberg & S. K. Runcorn (eds.): *Growth Rhythms and the History of the Earth's Rotation* (London), pp. 459-533.

Murnane, W. J. – 1977: *Ancient Egyptian Coregencies* (Chicago).

N

Na'aman, N. – 1986: 'Habiru and Hebrews: the Transfer of a Social Term to the Literary Sphere' in *JNES* 45:4, pp. 271-88.

Naville, E. – 1885: *The Store-City of Pithom and the Route of the Exodus* (London).

Naville, E. – 1887: *The Shrine of Saft el-Henneh and the Land of Goshen* (London).

Negev, A. (ed.) – 1986: *The Archaeological Encyclopedia of the Holy Land* (New York).

Newberry, P. E. – 1943: 'Co-regencies of Ammenemes III, IV and Sebeknofru' in *JEA* 29, pp. 74-5.

Newgrosh, B. – 1992: 'Living with Radiocarbon Dates: A Response to Mike Baillie' in *JACF* 5, pp. 59-67.

Newgrosh, B. *et al.* – 1994: 'The el-Amarna Letters and Israelite History' in *JACF* 6, pp. 33-64.

Newton, I. – 1728: *The Chronology of Ancient Kingdoms Amended* (London).

Nims, C. F. (ed.) – 1970: *Medinet Habu,* vol. VIII (Chicago).

Noth, M. – 1928: *Israelitische Personennamen* (Stuttgart).

Noth, M. – 1938: 'Die Wege der Pharaonenheere in Palästina und Syrien; IV. Die Schoschenkliste' in *ZDPV* 61, pp. 277-304.

Noth, M. – 1958: *The History of Israel* (London).

O

Odelain, O. & **Séguineau**, R. – 1981: *Dictionary of Proper Names and Places in the Bible* (London).

P

Pardee, D. & **Swerdlow** – 1993: 'Not the earliest solar eclipse' in *Nature* 363, p. 406.

Parker, R. A. – 1950: *The Calendars of Ancient Egypt* (Chicago).

Parker, R. A. – 1966: 'King Py, a Historical Problem' in *ZÄS*, pp. 111-14.

Parker, R. A. *et al.* – 1979: *Edifice of Taharqa* (London).

Petrie, W. M. F. – 1885: *Tanis* (London).

Petrie, W. M. F. – 1904: 'Notes on the XIXth and XXth Dynasties' in *PSBA* 26, pp. 36-41.

Petrie, W. M. F. – 1894: *A History of Egypt*, part 1 (London).

Petrie, W. M. F. – 1905: *A History of Egypt*, part 3 (London).

Petrie, W. M. F. – 1906: *Researches in Sinai* (London).

Pitard, W. T. – 1987: *Ancient Damascus* (Winoan Lake).

Pitard, W. T. – 1988: 'The Identity of Bir-Hadad of the Melqart Stela' in *BASOR* 272, pp. 3-21.

Poebel, A. – 1942: 'The Assyrian King List from Khorsabad' in *JNES* 1, pp. 247-102.

Poebel, A. – 1943: 'The Assyrian King List from Khorsabad – Concluded' in *JNES* 2, pp. 56-90.

Porter, B. & **Moss**, R. L. B. – 1981: *Topographical Bibliography of Ancient Egyptian Hieroglyphic Text, Reliefs, and Paintings, vol. III: Memphis*, part 2 (Oxford).

Porter, R. M. – 1994: 'Tree Rings from Tille Hoyuk' in *C & C Workshop* 1994:1, p. 20.

Posener, G. – 1939: 'Nouveaux Textes Hiératiques de Proscription' in R. Dussaud: *Mélanges Syriens offerts a M. René Dussaud*, vol. I, pp. 313-17.

Posener, G. – 1940: *Princes et Pays D'Asie et de Nubie* (Brussels).

Pritchard, J. B. –1969: *Ancient Near Eastern Texts Relating to the Old Testament* (Princeton).

Pritchard, J. B. (ed.) – 1974: *Solomon and Sheba* (London).

Q

Quibell, J. E. – 1898: *The Ramesseum* (London).

Quirke, S. – 1990: *The Administration of Egypt in the Late Middle Kingdom* (New Malden).

R

Rainey, A. – 1978: *El Amarna Tablets 257-379 – Supplement to J. A. Knudtzon: Die El Amarna Taffeln*, 2nd edn. revised (Neukirchen-Vluyn).

Rainey, A. – 1965: 'The Kingdom of Ugarit' in *BA* 28, pp. 102-28.

BIBLIOGRAPHY

Rammant-Peeters, A. – 1983: *Les Pyramidions Égyptiens du Nouvel Empire* (Leuven).

Ranke, H. – 1910: *Keilschriftliches Material zue altägyptischen Vokalisation* (Berlin).

Ranke, H. – 1935: *Die Ägyptische Personennamen*, vol. I (Glückstadt).

Ray, J. – 1991: 'The Name of the First: Thomas Young and the Decipherment of Egyptian Writing' in *JACF* 4, pp. 49-55.

Redford, D. B. – 1984: *Akhenaten: The Heretic King* (Princeton).

Reeves, C. N. – 1990: *Valley of the Kings* (London).

Reymond, E. A. E. – 1973: *Catalogue of Demotic Papyri in the Ashmolean Museum*, vol. I (Oxford).

Robins, G. – 1994: 'Women and Children in Peril: Pregnancy, Birth and Infant Mortality in Ancient Egypt' in *KMT* 5:4, pp. 24-35.

Rohl, D. M. & **James**, P. – 1983: 'An Alternative to the Velikovskian Chronology of Ancient Egypt: A Preview of Some Recent Work in the Field of Ancient History' in *SIS Workshop* 5:2, pp. 12-21.

Rohl, D. M. – 1985: 'Forum' in *SIS Workshop* 6:2, pp. 21-6.

Rohl, D. M. & **Newgrosh**, B. – 1988: 'The el-Amarna Letters and the New Chronology' in *C & C Review* 10, pp. 33-4.

Rohl, D. M. – 1989: 'Director's Report' in *JACF* 4, pp. 3-4.

Rohl, D. M. – 1990: 'The Early Third Intermediate Period: Some Chronological Considerations' in *JACF* 3, pp. 45-69.

Rohl, D. M. – 1992: 'A Test of Time: The New Chronology of Egypt and its Implications for Biblical Archaeology and History' in *JACF* 5, pp. 30-58.

Rohl, D. M. – 1992: 'Some Chronological Conundrums of the 21st Dynasty' in *Ägypten und Levante* 3, pp. 137-9.

Rohl, D. M. – 1992: 'The Length of Sojourn in Egypt' in *C & C Workshop* 1992:1, pp. 48-9.

Romer, J. – 1981: *Valley of the Kings* (London).

Rose, L. E. – 1994: 'The Astronomical Evidence for Dating the End of the Middle Kingdom of Ancient Egypt to the Early Second Millennium: A Reassessment' in *JNES* 53, pp. 237-61.

Ross, J. – 1967: 'Gezer in the Tell el-Amarna Letters' in *BA* 30, pp. 62-70.

Rowley, H. H. (ed.) – 1969: *New Atlas of the Bible* (London).

S

Sawyer, J. F. A. & **Stephenson**, F. R. – 1970: 'Literary and Astronomical Evidence for a Total Eclipse of the Sun Observed in

Ancient Ugarit on 3 May 1375 BC' in *BSOAS* 33, pp. 467-89.

Schaeffer, C. F. A. – 1948: *Stratigraphie comparée et chronologie de l'Asie occidentale (IIIe et IIe millénaires)* (Oxford).

Schley, D. G. – 1989: *Shiloh: A Biblical City in Tradition and History* (JSOT Supplement Series 63, Sheffield).

Seligman, C. G. – 1934: *Egypt and Negro Africa: A Study in Divine Kingship* (London).

Sethe, K. H. – 1904: 'Der Name Sesostris' in *ZÄS* 41, pp. 43-57.

Sethe, K. H. – 1926: *Die Ächtung feindlicher Fürsten, Völker und Dinge auf altägyptischen Tongefässcherben des Mittleren Rieches* (Berlin).

Shaw, I. M. – 1985: 'Egyptian Chronology and the Irish Oak Calibration' in *JNES* 44, pp. 295-304.

Shiloh, Y. – 1979: *The Proto-Aeolic Capital and Israelite Ashlar Masonry* (*Qedem* 11, Jerusalem).

Shiloh, Y. – 1981: 'The City of David Archaeological Project: The Third Season, 1980' in *BA* 44, pp. 161-70.

Singer, I. – 1985: 'The Beginning of Philistine Settlement in Canaan and the Northern Boundary of Philistia' in *Tel Aviv* 12:2, pp. 109-22.

Singer, I. – 1994: 'Egyptians, Canaanites, and Philistines in the Period of the Emergence of Israel' in Finkelstein & Na'aman (eds.), 1994, pp. 282-338.

Smith, G. A. – 1894: *The Historical Geography of the Holy Land* (London).

Smith, H. S. – 1972: 'Dates of the Obsequies of the Mother of Apis' in *Revue d'Égyptologie* 24, pp. 176-87.

Smith, W. S. – 1965: *The Art and Architecture of Ancient Egypt* (Baltimore).

von Soden, W. – 1966: *Akkadisches Handworterbuch* (Wiesbaden).

Soggin, J. A. – 1975: *Old Testament and Oriental Studies, Biblica et Orientalia* 29 (Rome).

Soggin, J. A. – 1984: *A History of Israel* (London).

Spalinger, A. – 1979: 'The military background of the campaign of Piye (Piankhy)' in *SAK* 7, pp. 273-301.

Stager, L. E. – 1982: 'The Archaeology of the East Slope of Jerusalem and the Terraces of the Kidron' in *JNES* 41, pp. 111-21.

Stager, L. E. – 1990: 'Shemer's Estate' in *BASOR* 277/8, pp. 93-107.

Stamm, J. J. – 1960: 'Der Name David' in *Supplement to VT* 7 (Leiden), pp. 175-81.

Steiner, M. L. – 1994: 'Redating the Terraces of Jerusalem' in *IEJ* 44, pp. 13-20.

BIBLIOGRAPHY

Stiebing, W. H. – 1989: *Out of the Desert?* (Buffalo).

Stock, H. – 1942: *Studien zur Geschichte und Archäologie der 13. bis 17. Dynastie Ägyptens, unter besonderer Berücksichtigung der Scarabäen dieser Zwischenzeit* (*ÄF* 12).

Strabo: *Histories*, book XVII.

Strong, J. – 1896: *The Exhaustive Concordance of the Bible* (New York).

T

Thiele, E. R.– 1983: *The Mysterious Numbers of the Hebrew Kings* (Grand Rapids).

Thomas, E. – 1979: 'The *k3y* of Queen Inhapi' in *JARCE* 16, pp. 85-92.

Thompson, T. L. – 1992: *Early History of the Israelite People From the Written and Archaeological Sources* (Leiden).

Torr, C. – 1896: *Memphis and Mycenae* (Cambridge) reprinted as ISIS Occasional Publication, vol. I (1988).

Tsevat, M. – 1954: 'The Canaanite God Salah' in *VT* 4, pp. 41-9.

Tsevat, M. – 1975: 'Ishbosheth and Congeners: The Names and their Study' in *HUCA* 46, pp. 71-87.

U

Ussishkin, D. – 1980: 'Was the "Solomonic" City Gate at Megiddo Built by King Solomon?' in *BASOR* 239, pp. 1-18.

Ussishkin, D. – 1990: 'Notes on Megiddo, Gezer, Ashdod, and Tel Batash in the Tenth to Ninth Centuries B.C.' in *BASOR* 277/278, pp. 71-91.

V

Valloggia, M. – 1974: 'Les Vizirs des XIe et XIIe Dynasties' in *BIFAO* 74, pp. 123-34.

de Vaux, C. (transl.) – 1898: *Masudi: L'Abrégé des merveilles* (Paris).

de Vaux, R. – 1940: Review of Publications on Ugarit in *Review Biblique* 49, pp. 248-58.

de Vaux, R. – 1978: *The Early History of Israel*, vol. II (London).

van der Veen, P. G. – 1989: *I Samuel and the Habiru-Problem* (Leuven); thesis submitted to the Evangelical Theological Faculty of Leuven in partial fulfilment of the requirements for the degree of Licentiate in Theology.

van der Veen, P. G. – 1990: 'The el-Amarna *Habiru* and the Early Monarchy in Israel' in *JACF* 3, pp. 72-8.

van der Veen, P. G. – 1991: Forum Debate in *C & C Review* 13, p. 49.

van der Veen, P. G. – 1993: 'The *Habiru* as the *Ibrim* of I Samuel and the Implications for the "New Chronology"' in *C & C Review* 15, p. 33.

Velikovsky, I. – 1952: *Ages in Chaos* (London).

Velikovsky, I. – 1960: *Oedipus and Akhnaton* (London).

Velikovsky, I. – 1977: *Peoples of the Sea* (London).

Velikovsky, I. – 1978: *Ramses II and His Time* (London).

Vercoutter, J. – 1958: 'Une Epitaphe Royale Inédite du Sérapéum' in *MDAIK* 16, pp. 340-1.

Vercoutter, J. – 1960: 'The Napatan Kings and Apis Worship' in *Kush* 8, pp. 62-76.

Vercoutter, J. – 1966: 'Semna South Fort and the Records of Nile Levels at Kumma' in *Kush* 14, pp. 125-64.

W

Waddell, W. G. (transl.) – 1940: *Manetho* (Loeb Classical Library, London).

Walker, C. B. F. – 1989: 'Eclipse seen at ancient Ugarit' in *Nature* 338, pp. 204-5.

Wallenfels, R. – 1983: 'Redating the Byblian Inscriptions' in *JANES* 15, pp. 79-118.

Ward, W. A. – 1984: in O. Tufnell: *Studies on Scarab Seals*, vol. II (Warminster).

Warren, P. & **Hankey**, V. – 1989: *Aegean Bronze Age Chronology* (Bristol).

Warren, P. – 1991: 'The Minoan Civilisation of Crete and the Volcano of Thera' in *JACF* 4, pp. 29-39.

Weigal, A. – 1911: 'Miscellaneous Notes' in *ASAE* 11, pp. 5-6.

Weinstein, J. – 1980: 'Palestinian Radiocarbon Dating: A Reply to James Mellaart' in *Antiquity* 54, pp. 21-4.

Weir, J. D. – 1982: 'The Venus Tablets: A Fresh Approach' in *JIIA* 13, pp. 23-49.

Whiston, W. (transl.) – 1960: *Josephus: Complete Works* (Glasgow).

Wightman, G. J. – 1985: 'Megiddo VIA-III: Associated Structures and Chronology' in *Levant* 17 , pp. 117-29.

Wilkinson, J. G. – 1828: *Materia Hieroglyphica* (Malta).

Wilson, E. – 1887: An article in *The Century Magazine*, May ed. (London).

Wilson, J. A. – 1950: 'The Hymn to the Aton' in *ANET*, pp. 369-71.

BIBLIOGRAPHY

Wilson, J. A. – 1969: 'An Egyptian Letter' in J. B. Pritchard (ed.): *ANET* (Princeton), p. 475.

Winkler, E. & **Wilfing**, H. – 1991: *Tell el-Dab'a VI: Anthropologische Untersuchungen an den Skelettresten der Kampagnen 1966-69, 1975-80, 1985* (Vienna).

Winlock, H. E. – 1931: 'The Tomb of Queen Inhapi: An Open Letter to the Editor' in *JEA* 17, pp. 107-10.

Wood, B. G. – 1990: 'Dating Jericho's Destruction: Bienkowski is Wrong on All Counts' in *BAR* 16:5, pp. 45-9 & 68-9.

Wright, G. E. – 1966: 'Fresh Evidence for the Philistine Story' in *BA* 29:3, pp. 70-86.

Y

Yadin, Y. – 1976: 'Hazor' in Avi-Yonah M. & Stern E. (eds): *Encyclopedia of Archaeological Excavations in the Holy Land*, vol. II (London), pp. 474-95.

Yadin, Y – 1977: 'Megiddo' in Avi-Yonah M. & Stern E. (eds): *Encyclopedia of Archaeological Excavations in the Holy Land*, vol. III (London), pp. 830-56.

Yamaguchi, D. K. – 1986: 'Interpretation of Cross Correlation Between Tree-Ring Series' in *Tree Ring Bulletin* 46, pp. 47-54.

Yoyotte, J. – 1961: 'Les principautés du Delta au temps de l'anarchie libyenne' in *Melanges Maspero* I:4 , pp. 121-79.

Yoyotte, J. – 1977: 'Osorkon, fils de Mehtyouskhe, un Pharaon Oublie' in *BSFE* 77/8, pp. 39-54.

Yurco, F. J. – 1986: 'Merenptah's Canaanite Campaign' in *JARCE* 23, pp. 189-215.

NOTES AND REFERENCES

Introduction

1   T. L. Thompson, 1992, p. 403-4.
2   E. R. Thiele, 1983, p. 33.
3   K. A. Kitchen, 1973.
4   The long shadow of the Greek Dark Age descends upon the Aegean, Crete and Cyprus, the Hittite empire of Anatolia disappears into a Neo-Hittite dark age of its own; the cities of Canaan suffer cultural impoverishment or abandonment; and Egypt loses its mighty empire which once stretched from northern Canaan right down to the Third Cataract of the Nile in the heartland of the African kingdom of Kush.
5   See for example, D. A. Aston, 1989, pp. 139-53 & P. James, 1991, pp. 220-59.
6   Throughout this book I will be quoting the orthodox dates as those determined by three publications. For Dynasties 21 to 26 I will be using dates provided in Kitchen's *TIPE*. For Dynasties 11 to 20 I will again be citing Kitchen's dates, this time using his low chronology as published in 'The Basics of Egyptian Chronology in Relation to the Bronze Age' in P. Astrom (ed.) *High, Middle or Low?* pt. 1 (Gothenburg, 1987), pp. 37-55. For Dynasties 1 to 10 I have decided to employ the dates given by John Baines and Jaromir Malek in *Atlas of Ancient Egypt* (Oxford, 1980), p. 36, as Kitchen has, so far, failed to publishe his chronology for this early period. As a result of this use of two chronologies (the low chronology of Kitchen and the standard chronology of Baines and Malek), there is a discrepancy of 60 years between the two for the dating of the start of the 11th Dynasty (= Year 1 of Inyotef I). In order to get an approximate chronology for Kitchen's Dynasties 1 to 10 the reader should subtract 60 years from the dates given in this book. I have chosen to include the extra 60 years in the duration allotted to the First Intermediate Period simply as a convenience which allows me to quote *actual* dates supplied in published works rather than interpolating dates which have not as yet been supplied.
7   See C. Schaeffer, 1948, pp. 534-7.
8   B. Bell, 1975, pp. 223-69.
9   Bietak suggests that the cult of Seth at Avaris was founded by King Nehesi or his father at the beginning of the 14th Dynasty; for a discussion of the Seth cult see M. Bietak, 1990, 11-16.
10 As transmitted 'verbatim' by Josephus (*Contra Apionem*, Book I, 14); for a translation see W. G. Waddell, 1940, pp. 77-91.
11 For the conflict between Sekenenre and Apophis see Papyrus Sallier I (BM 10185) with a translation in *ANET*, pp. 231-2.
12 Herodotus Book II, 102-10.
13 Diodorus Siculus Book I, 53-8.

14 E. R. Thiele, 1983, pp. 80-1.

15 Here I will continue to use the older form of the name rather than the more fashionable Piye. The issue as to whether Piankhy and Piye are the same Kushite pharaoh has not been confirmed to my satisfaction and the king who inscribed the great black stela recording his campaign against Tefnakht of Sais is called Piankhy in the text.

16 See Genesis 46:8-27. There are 70 direct members of Jacob's family (the Bible regards these as sons, daughters and their offspring) plus the wives of Jacob's sons whose number is not given. The LXX adds the five descendants of Ephraim bringing the total for Jacob's family to 75 – see Acts 7:14.

17 See A. Biran & J. Naveh, 1993, pp. 81-98.

18 The dating of the 'Solomonic' gates has been a contentious issue for some time now with a number of archaeologists arguing that the gates have a wide date range and that most are datable to the post-Solomonic era; see for example D. Ussishkin, 1990, pp. 71-91.

Chapter One

1 A. Mariette, 1882, p. 4; translation taken from J.-P. Lauer, 1976, pp. 21-2.

2 Another long-standing debate concerns the true location of the 1st Dynasty royal burial ground with the majority of scholars opting for the desert necropolis at Abydos but with others preferring Sakkara.

3 Strabo, Book XVII, i, 32.

4 J.-P. Lauer & Ch. Picard, 1955, pp. 108-18.

5 This account of Mariette's discovery is the standard version given by the author himself and later writers. However, for the sake of historical accuracy it should be noted that Járomír Malek [1983, pp. 69-72] has shown that the location of the Serapeum was already known to an English traveller to Egypt named A. C. Harris who visited Sakkara in 1847.

6 The stone sarcophagi were installed from Year 23 of Amasis onwards, those from Year 52 of Psamtek up to Amasis presumably being made of wood which has not survived. For a discussion of the date of the introduction of stone sarcophagi see B. Gunn, 1926, pp. 92-4.

7 *Mss Fonds français*, Nouv. acq., no. 22948, fo. 105:3.

8 A. Mariette, 1882, pp. 57 & 116.

9 Some stela from the Egyptian collection were given as gifts to European dignitaries by the viceroy of Egypt, Said Pasha. The majority of these monuments now reside in the national museums of Austria, Britain, Denmark, Germany and Russia.

10 For a brief report on the new excavations see M. Ibrahim & D. Rohl, 1988, pp. 12-14.

11 The evidence for the existence of this *Journal des Fouilles* and its subsequent fate comes from a footnote in an article by Émile Chassinat [1899, p. 56, n. 3] where he states: 'I have not been able to use Mariette's Excavation Journal and the inventory book he had compiled. These documents had been lent to M. Grébaut by the Administration of the [French] National Museum, fifteen years ago and more, and they have not yet been returned.'

12 M. Malinine *et al.*, 1968.

13 This re-assignment had to be done on the basis of style, content and the need to fill certain gaps in the burial sequence, as there was so little information available regarding the location of the finds.

14 For a discussion of the problems of dating the non-regnally dated stelae see the Preface to M. Malinine *et al.*, 1968, pp. vii-xv1.

15 The numbering system used here is that adopted in the new catalogue and is the last of a confusing series of numbers allocated to these stelae. Given the problem of referencing these inscriptions, it was felt best to adopt the new numbers, as the 1968 catalogue gives full referencing to all previous numbering systems.

16 J. Vercoutter, 1958, pp. 340-1.

17 All scholars are agreed that Psamtek I began his rule in 664/663 BC following the sacking of Thebes by the Assyrian army under Ashurbanipal. This date has been corroborated by cross-referencing of a network of data provided by the Greek historians and the records of the Neo-Babylonian period (as well as the Apis stelae themselves). For a summary of the evidence see C. O. Jonsson, 1987, pp. 14-23.

18 K. A. Kitchen, 1987, Table 5, p. 52.

19 For the attribution of the Year 4 stelae to Taharka see J. Vercoutter, 1960, pp. 67-71.

20 Personal communication from the current Serapeum excavator, Mohamed Ibrahim Aly, September 1991.

21 A single monument of Shoshenk I has been adduced as evidence of the existence of the cult of Apis in the early 22nd Dynasty. This monument is a limestone block from the 'Apis House' at Memphis, discovered in 1878 by Émil Brugsch (1878, pp. 37-43). It is generally described as an embalming table for the Apis and therefore connected with his burial cult. However, this does not itself connect Shoshenk I with the dating of any Apis burial, nor does it provide a link between the 21st Dynasty and the cult. Moreover, it has been demonstrated that this block was originally erected by the king as part of a building, reused in a pavement at some later date, and was never employed as an embalming table.

22 Mariette, 1882, pp. 152-3.

Chapter Two

1 G. Maspero, 1889, pp. 511-20.

2 For example, H. Brugsch, 1891, pp. 359-63; and G. Maspero himself, 1925, where he gives a popular account of the discovery.

3 For example, J. A. Bakie, 1923, pp. 157-61; E. Thomas, 1979, pp. 85-92; and especially J. Romer, 1981, pp. 127-52.

4 A. Edwards, 1877, p. 450.

5 As published in J. Bakie, 1923, pp. 158-9.

6 According to G. Daressy, 1909.

7 It might be argued that the Abd er-Rassuls were responsible for the four coffins being found near the entrance, the brothers having dragged them there to gain more light for their pillaging operations. However, this seems very improbable; as leading Valley of the Kings specialist Dr. Nicholas Reeves has pointed out [1990, p.186]: 'If one considers the weight of the coffins, and the space available to manoeuvre them – plus the fact that the Abd el-Rassuls are said to have visited the cache on only three occasions, and then merely for a few hours – it would appear unlikely that any radical alteration could have been affected in the basic sequence. The positions in which Brugsch encountered the coffins in 1881 are, I would suggest, essentially the positions they occupied in antiquity.'

Chapter Three

1   At the time of Montet's arrival in Egypt, Tanis was still believed to be the ancient city of Raamses – built by the Israelite slaves during their Bondage under Ramesses II. But there was also historical evidence which showed that the site of Pi-Ramesse (biblical Raamses) was at an earlier time the Hyksos capital of Avaris. The latter was built during the Second Intermediate Period (which immediately followed the Egyptian Middle Kingdom) by foreign invaders who came, according to Manetho, from Phoenicia. Montet figured that, as Byblos had been very closely tied to the 12th Dynasty pharaohs Senuseret III, Amenemhat III and Amenemhat IV, then his new excavations at Avaris (San el-Hagar) would open up the next chapter in his study of Phoenician relationships with the land of the pharaohs.

2   From a letter to Montet's wife who was then in France. The letters are currently in the possession of Madame Camille Montet-Beaucour. Translation taken from H. Coutts, 1988, p. 19.

3   See D. A. Aston, 1989, pp. 143-4.

4   See J. M. Ogden, 1991, pp. 6-14.

5   A. Lézine in P. Montet, 1947, p. 46.

6   See P. Montet, 1947, pp. 71-3 & pl. 22.

7   We know that Kapes was the mother of King Osorkon-sibast (II) from the genealogy recorded on the Pasenhor Stela (Stela 31) found by Mariette in the Lesser Vaults of the Serapeum. See M. Malinine *et al.*, 1968, pp. 30-1.

8   A. Lézine in P. Montet, 1947, p. 47, points 2 & 3.

9   P. Brissaud, 1987, pp. 22-5.

10 P. Montet, 1951, p. 84, fig. 31.

11 It was common practice in the Roman and Islamic periods to burn limestone to make lime for cement. Many of the ancient monuments of Egypt were built from limestone blocks which were therefore a ready source of raw material for the lime burners. The delta cities in Egypt suffered the worst of the 'quarrying' activities because they were nearest to the sea and hence transportation to the expanding cities of the Mediterranean world.

Chapter Four

1   It has been claimed by a number of researches that Thomas Young gave Champollion the vital clues to the decipherment of the hieroglyphs for which he did not receive a proper recognition; see for example J. Ray, 1991, pp. 49-54. For a fascinating insight into Thomas Young, the multidisciplinary scholar, see D. L. Kline, 1993.

2   E. Naville, 1885 & W. M. F. Petrie, 1885.

3   K. A. Kitchen, 1992, pp. 702-7.

4   According to Edwin Thiele's widely accepted chronology of the Hebrew monarchy; see E. Thiele, 1983.

5   K. A. Kitchen, 1987, p. 52.

6   To demonstrate this phenomenon I quote from Volume X of the 1904 edition of the *Chambers Encyclopaedia*, p. 781: 'Several of the emperors visited York (sic!), and here in 211 died Severus, and in 306 Constantius Chlorus. And from York (sic!) his son Constantine the Great, having been proclaimed by the soldiery, set forth to assume the purple.' Do we assume from this text that the Roman emperors mentioned above resided at a town known to them as York?

7 The Abbess Etheria mentions travelling through Ramesses during her pilgrimage through the lands of the Bible. The document containing her narrative was discovered in Arezzo by Gamurrini and is published in his work *I Mysteri e gl'Inni di San Ilario ed una Peregrinazione ai Luoghi Santi nel quarto Secolo*; see E. Naville, 1887, p. 19.

8 The term *dôr* is not easily definable; its context and usage seems to suggest something like 'era'. Albright has demonstrated that the Akkadian cognate *duru* represents a period of around 80 years. However, in most versions of the Bible, the term *dôr* has been loosely translated as 'generation'.

9 See M. Rowland (ed.), 1994, pp. 38-9.

10 J. J. Bimson, 1978, p. 324.

Chapter Five

1 Whilst preparing for publication the results of his expedition to Egypt in 1828-9 he collapsed in Paris with a severe stroke and died on the 4th of March 1832.

2 The Year 20 date of Shoshenk's Palestine campaign is not recorded on the Bubastite Portal itself; it derives from Stela 100, carved in the sandstone quarries of Gebel es-Silsila, where instructions are given by the king to erect a court and gateway at the temple of Karnak. There the date of the inscription is given as Year 21, 2nd month of Shemu (see R. Caminos, 1952, pp. 46-61). However, it should be noted that the grounds for dating the Palestinian campaign to the year before the ordering of the monument are not based on any concrete evidence; the campaign could quite easily have taken place earlier in the reign. Year 20 is therefore taken here as a convenient date for the purposes of calculation only.

3 J. F. Champollion, 1868, p. 81.

4 F. R. Thiele, 1983, pp. 80-1.

5 W. M. Müller, 1888, note 5.

6 Name-rings 26 and 27, to the right of number 29, spell out the names of Taanakh and Megiddo – both cities in the Jezreel valley – located nowhere near the mountain Kingdom of Judah; the location of ring 28 (Adar) is unknown; rings 30 to 33 ([Heb]el, Honim, Aruna and Borim), to the left of number 29, are in the Mount Carmel area, close by the city of Megiddo.

7 K. A. Kitchen, 1987, pp. 37-8: 'In Ancient Egypt, the earliest agreed fixed date is 664 BC, for the beginning of the reign of Psammetichus I, founder of the 26th Dynasty. Before this date, ending the 25th Dynasty, we have a clear 26-year reign of Taharqa during 690-664 BC, as a contemporary of the Assyrian kings Esarhaddon and Assurbanipal during 674-665 BC. Of his two predecessors in Egypt, the first – Shabako – had taken over that country not later than 712 BC on Assyrian evidence and not before 716 BC when Assyrian contacts were with Osorkon IV, (U)shilkanni, last king of the 22nd Dynasty.'

8 K. A. Kitchen, 1987, p. 38.

9 K. A. Kitchen, 1973, p. 72.

10 With the building of the High Dam, this inundation of Egypt has been halted and the excess water is now held in Lake Nasser, to be released gradually over the year rather than in one sudden rush. We will have to imagine the process as it was prior to the construction of the dam in order to understand the yearly agricultural cycle which pertained in the Egypt of old.

11 In astronomy there is no Year 0 between 1 BC and AD 1.

12 Reckoning from the Censorinus data, Sothis rose on the first day of the first month of Akhet in 2781 BC (two Great Sothic Years before AD 139). According

to Papyrus Ebers, Sothis rose in Year 9 of Amenhotep I on the ninth day of the third month (i.e. the month Ipet) of the Shemu season. We should not forget that this rising would have occurred on the same day in the civil calendar over four consecutive years of the king's reign. The number of days between Day 1, I Akhet and Day 9, III Shemu is 10 months times 30 days plus the first 9 days of Ipet = 309 days. The slippage of one day represents four years in the Great Sothic Year, thus a difference of 309 days represents 1236 years in the Sothic cycle (309 x 4) plus or minus 3 years (allowing for the possibility that the Day 9, III Shemu observation could have been made in any one of the four years in which Sothis rose heliacally on this day in the civil year). If the Sothic cycle began in 2781 BC, then Year 9 of Amenhotep I fell 1236+/-3 years later – in other words between 1548-1542 BC. In 1950 Parker opted for the lower figure of 1542, basing his calculations on the Papyrus Ebers observation of the heliacal rising taking place at Memphis. With Parker's date widely accepted, Amenhotep's first regnal year was then set at 1550 with the New Kingdom beginning in 1575 BC – coincident with the coronation of King Ahmose.

13 See E. Hornung, 1964, pp. 20-1.
14 Scholars usually assign Seti I a reign of about 15 years; see for example A. Gardiner, 1961, p. 249 and K. A. Kitchen, 1987, p. 52.
15 U. Luft, 1992, pp. 112-13; and 1986, p. 71.
16 U. Luft, 1992, p. 113.
17 J. von Beckerath, 1990, p. 5, where he states: 'The calendar on the *verso* of the Ebers Medical Papyrus ... is by now so disputed that we must ask ourselves whether we really possess a sure basis for the chronology of this period of Egyptian history which is, after all, of the greatest importance for fixing the sequence of historical events, also for the neighbouring countries.' (Translation by Birgit Liesching.)
18 W. Helck, 1990, p. 21, where he states: 'We therefore think it is safer to start from the regnal dates rather than from interpretations of real or supposed Sirius or New Moon dates.' (Translation by Birgit Liesching.)
19 E. Hornung, 1987, p. 35, where he states: '... all these data for the New Kingdom are valid without any computation of astronomical dates and are independent of any interpretation of the Ebers' datum. For the latter we still have disagreement about the point of observation and about the question if this notice in the Papyrus Ebers is really to be regarded as a fixed Sothic datum.'
20 U. Luft, 1986, p. 72.
21 W. Barta, 1988, pp. 7ff.
22 J. J. Janssen, personal communication 1989.
23 M. Bietak, 1987, p. 91.

Chapter Six

1 Good sets of statistics for average age at death are now beginning to appear from cemeteries of the Roman period in Egypt and from MBA sites such as Tell ed-Daba. One can conclude from these figures that if a person survived into adulthood then his/her life-expectancy would be around thirty years.
2 Both have the effect of increasing the average generation length because we would be left with an apparent span of two generations where, in reality, the brother or usurper would have been of the same generation as the previous ruler. So, for example, if 9 of the 88 kings in the Babylonian King List were of the same generation as their predecessors (i.e. *c.* 10%), then 1476 years would

have to be divided by 79 rather than 88 – an average generation length of 18.68 years.

3   K. A. Kitchen, 1973, p. 79; M. L. Bierbrier, 1975, p. xvi.

4   Clearly not all the holders of the office of Chief of Works will have been natural sons of the previous incumbent. It may have been the case that a son-in-law succeeded, or perhaps a brother. The term 'sa' in ancient Egyptian – translated 'son' – should perhaps be better understood as 'successor' or 'heir' and does not necessarily indicate any real, natural blood relationship. However, the average 18-year generation length would still apply, as the office of Chief of Works would reflect similar succession changes as dynasties of rulers. The genealogy of the Chiefs of Works is thus just as practical a tool for retrocalculations as any natural genealogy such as that of Ankhefenkhons.

5   It must also be remembered that these officials worked in quarries and supervised the construction of stone monuments – activities in which silicosis would have been highly prevalent.

6   R. Caminos, 1952, pp. 46-61.

7   OC – 1270 (early Ramesses II) minus OC – 925 (Stela 100 at Gebel es-Silsila, linked to the Chief of Works Haremsaf) = 345 years divided by 18 (average generation) = 19.16 generations; but the Wadi Hammamat list of architects only has nine officials between early Ramesses and late Shoshenk, therefore ten generations are omitted if the OC is correct.

8   OC – 925 (date of Stela 100 – Year 21 Shoshenk I) minus 495 (Year 26 Darius I) = 430 years divided by 18 (average generation) = 23.8 generations; but the Khnemibre genealogy only has 14 generations between Shoshenk I (Haremsaf A) and Darius I (Khnemibre), therefore up to ten generations are omitted if the OC is correct.

9   Kitchen, 1973, p. 189.

10 OC – 1203 (death of Merenptah) minus OC – 900 (mid reign of Osorkon I) = 303 years divided by 18 (average generation) = 16.83 generations; but the Nespaherenhat genealogy only has nine generations between Merenptah (Ipuy) and Osorkon (Nespaherenhat), therefore up to eight generations are omitted if the OC is correct.

Chapter Seven

1   Based on the verb *khef* 'to plunder' – see JEA 39, p. 7, fig. 2,9 – however the word *khefu* is often translated as 'seized' or 'made captive'.

2   See A. Jones, 1990, p. 196.

3   K. A. Kitchen, 1982, p. 67.

4   What adds to the interest is the fact that the scribes of the 7th-century Assyrian king, Ashurbanipal, using the same cuneiform script, also replaced the Egyptian 's' with the cuneiform 'sh' and on the other hand rendered 'sh' as 's', so that the kingdom of Kush appeared as Kûs(u)! For Kûs(u) and Susink(u), cf. the Rasam Cylinder of Ashurbanipal; a convenient translation is available in J. B. Pritchard, 1969, p. 294. The syllabary nature of the cuneiform script is such that a vowel is regularly written at the end of these words without any suggestion that one should be read.

5   See J. B. Pritchard, 1969, p. 294 & H. Ranke, 1910, p. 34.

6   Papyrus Leningrad 1116B dated to the 18th Dynasty. See A. Gardiner, 1914, pp. 100-6; or M. Lichtheim, 1973, pp. 139-45.

7   For a translation see J. B. Pritchard, 1969, p. 272.

8   C. F. Nims (ed.), 1970, pl. 636.

9   This is a doubtful translation. It may be possible that damage has eliminated

words from this phrase, but traces indicate that a bowl held by the first daughter takes up the space immediately below the surviving signs and so the phrase is actually complete as preserved.

10   Cf. for example, H. Ranke, 1935, pp. 297 & 320. For *Ssi* as an abbreviation of the name of a New Kingdom private individual named more fully Meryamun-Ramesses, cf. *ibid* number 11.

11   BM 10247. See facsimile in A. H. Gardiner, 1942, pls. XXXV-LXII; translation see J. B. Pritchard, 1969, pp. 475-9.

12   See L. Badre *et al.*, 1990, pp. 17-22.

13   K. H. Sethe, 1904, p. 55.

14   W. M. F. Petrie, 1906, pl. 156.

15   P. McGovern *et al.*, 1993, p. 18.

16   Vienna 209. Published for example in A. Rammant-Peeters, 1983, pp. 75-7, & pl. XXXII.

17   The Masoretes introduced pointing to indicate such things as vowels and the difference between 's' and 'sh' in their copies of the Hebrew scripture, but this did not happen until the 7th century AD, more than 600 years after the Dead Sea scrolls, the texts of which do not indicate the difference between *sin* and *shin*. By the time of the Masoretes more than 1500 years had therefore elapsed between the events surrounding the plundering of the Jerusalem temple and the written expression of the vocalisation of the name Shishak by the use of pointing.

18   This possibility was brought to my attention by Peter van der Veen, personal communication, April 1995.

19   First published as an abstract in SSEA Journal VIII:3 (1978), p. 70. The main discussion of his research appeared in F. J. Yurco, 1986, pp. 189-215.

20   Many of these points were raised by Professor Donald Redford in his critique of Yurco's findings, published in *IEJ* 36 (1986), pp. 188-200.

21   Hence the title 'Binder' or 'Reducer of Gezer' found in an inscription from Amada; see *RT* 18, p. 159.

22   I raised this point in a seminar discussion sponsored by ISIS at the Institute of Archaeology London in October 1993. Professor Kitchen responded by suggesting that the Israelites might have got hold of a couple of chariots for use in their Conquest campaign. I really do not think that this is a satisfactory explanation and goes against what the biblical texts actually state concerning Israelite military tactics in the Conquest and Judges period.

23   During the Conquest and Judges period it is clear from their military tactics that the Israelites have no access to chariot technology. When they confront the army of Hazor in the time of Deborah the Israelite forces choose swampy ground to fight in so as to prevent the successful deployment of the enemy chariots (see C. Herzog & M. Gichon, 1978, pp. 49 & 51-3). After defeating the chariot forces of Hazor and the northern confederacy at the Battle of Merom, Joshua orders the hamstringing of the enemy horses and the destruction of their chariots as the Israelites had no use for them (*ibid*, pp. 39-40).

Chapter Eight

1   O. Odelain & R. Séguineau, 1981, p. 357.

2   J. B. Pritchard, 1974, p. 35.

3   K. M. Kenyon, 1960, pp. 255-6.

4   Y. Shiloh, 1979, p. 84.

5   Unfortunately, the one site where we might expect easily to identify Solomonic architecture is Jerusalem and there it is quite impossible to access the Solomonic

levels of the Temple Mount – simply because the politics and religion of the site prevent any archaeological work.

6 In terms of the archaeological ages, superimposed upon the cultural remains of the ancient Near East, the time of Haremheb through to Ramesses II, is known as LB IIB. The earlier el-Amarna period is designated as LB IIA. The boundary between these two phases of the LBA is not clearly defined because the life-spans of certain diagnostic types of pottery vary from region to region. One area may continue to use a particular pot shape or decoration for a number of years after it has fallen out of use in other areas. With the typological boundary being so ill-defined, we might best regard the reign of Haremheb as transitional LB IIA to LB IIB.

7 A. Negev, 1986, p. 238.

8 The excavation techniques employed at Megiddo have led to considerable confusion in respect of the stratigraphy, so the best we can do is to say that the transition from stratum VIII to stratum VII-B falls some time during the reigns of Haremheb or Seti I.

9 A. Negev, 1986, p. 239.

10 Y. Yadin, 1977, p. 849.

11 Y. Yadin, 1977, p. 846.

12 This work of uncovering the stone glacis was continued by Yigael Shiloh in 1980; see Y. Shiloh, 1981, pp. 166-9.

13 See for example K. Kenyon, 1963, p. 14.

14 K. M. Kenyon, 1963, p. 13.

15 V. Hankey, 1992, p. 26; and P. Warren & V. Hankey, 1989, pp. 148-54 have the end of LH IIIA2 at 1330 BC (i.e. in the reign of Tutankhamun), however, LH IIIA2 pottery has recently been found by Geoffrey Martin in the tomb constructed for Haremheb at Sakkara (begun before he became pharaoh) in which the king's wife, Queen Mutnodjmet, was later buried in the 13th year of her husband's reign – at least 17 years after the death of Tutankhamun. This find suggests that some LH IIIA2 pottery may have survived for a considerable period beyond the reign of the boy-king. Even though, due to the find context, this evidence may be fairly inconclusive, we can at least say that late forms of LH IIIA2 were in use up to Year 9 of Haremheb as fragments of two transitional LH IIIA2/IIIB stirrup jars were recovered from the tomb of Maya at Sakkara in association with a docket dated to the 9th year of that king's reign – see V. Hankey, 1992, pp. 22-3.

16 K. M. Kenyon, 1963, p. 14; but see M. T. Steiner, 1994, pp. 13-20, for evidence that at least part of the terracing was constructed or repaired during the late LB IIB or early IA I.

17 See G. Barkay, 1990, pp. 94-106 (in Hebrew) and 1995 – to be published in English.

18 As suggested by W. P. Manley, personal communication December 1994.

19 A. Curtis, 1985, pp. 44-5. A number of scholars have suggested that 'Sharelli' may have been a daughter of Akhenaten and Nefertiti. Although this is possible, I find it rather difficult to accept given the semi-divine status of the Egyptian royal family at this time and the simple fact that most of Akhenaten's daughters were married to their father the pharaoh.

20 Unfortunately the hieroglyphic inscription which would have given details of the defeated cities has been destroyed or quarried away. However, Cyril Aldred did suggest that military preparations were under way at the end of Akhenaten's reign for a campaign against the city of Gezer – though I have to admit that I have been quite unable to confirm this unreferenced statement (C. Aldred, 1988, p. 283). Gezer, of course, was the city which Pharaoh

captured, burnt and then gave as a dowry for his daughter's marriage to Solomon [I Kings 9:16].

Chapter Nine

1   The New Chronology material represented in this chapter and the next is the result of research undertaken during the late 1980s and early 1990s by myself and two colleagues: Dr. Bernard Newgrosh and Peter van der Veen. A more detailed discussion and analysis of the Amarna Letters has been published in B. Newgrosh *et al.*, 1994, pp. 33-64. Earlier papers by the same authors include, D. M. Rohl & B. Newgrosh, 1988, pp. 23-42; P. G. van der Veen, 1989; *idem*, 1990, pp. 72-8.

2   The majority are now housed in the collections of the Vorderasiatisches Museum in Berlin (203 tablets), the British Museum (95 tablets) and the Cairo Museum (50 tablets).

3   Excluding EA 372 to EA 377 which are not letters but miscellaneous documents. See W. L. Moran, 1992, pp. xv-xvi.

4   It appears that Amenhotep III had resided at his son's new city for two or three years before his death and a number of letters may date from this time – explaining why some of the correspondence from the northern kings is addressed to 'Nimuaria' (their writing of Nebmaatre – the prenomen of Amenhotep III). We may conclude, therefore, that the Amarna archive dates from 1015 BC at the earliest.

5   The identification of Akhenaten with Oedipus was first suggested by Immanuel Velikovsky in his entertaining book *Oedipus and Akhnaton* (London, 1960).

6   For a detailed discussion of the political and social status of the Habiru see P. G. van der Veen, 1989.

7   Apart from the three scholars mentioned in the following references, I can also include W. Helck, 1971; N. Na'aman, 1986, p. 279-81; R. de Vaux, 1971.

8   M. Greenberg, 1955, pp. xiii & 99.

9   G. Mendenhall, 1973, pp. 135-6.

10 P. K. McCarter, 1986, p. 121.

11 Writing of Aram-Zobah, Malamat (1958, pp. 100-1) states: 'This political entity, whose strength is difficult to estimate from the fragmentary evidence found in the Bible, expanded during the reign of its king Hadadezer, a contemporary of David, over vast territories. … In the south it apparently reached the frontier of Ammon, as can be deduced from the intervention of Aramaean troops on the side of the Ammonites in their war with David [II Samuel 10:6ff]. In the northeast the kingdom of Zobah extended to the river Euphrates and even to territories beyond it [II Samuel 8:3, 10:16]. In the east it touched the Syrian desert and in the west it included Coelsyria. These boundaries roughly correspond to the expansion of the kingdom of Amurru which still flourished in the 13th century. We have no information on the political organisation in this area in the 12th century after Amurru was destroyed by the Sea Peoples, or in the 11th century during the period of Aramaean settlement until the period of consolidation of the Aramaean states on the eve of David's period.'

12 A. Malamat, 1958, p. 101.

13 P. Bordreuil & J. Teixidor, 1983, pp. 271-6; but see W. T. Pitard, 1988, pp. 3-21, for an alternative reading of the name and a different view of the historical context.

14 Moran, 1987, p. 382; see also R. S. Hess, 1993, pp. 102-3.

15 O. Odelain & R. Séguineau, 1981, p. 330.

16 J. T. Milik & F. M. Cross Jr., 1954, pp. 5-15.

17 B. Mazar, 1986, pp. 87-8: 'It is very likely that v.5 is speaking of mercenaries called *leba'im*, probably a military corps whose emblem was the lioness-goddess.'

18 Itamar Singer (1985, p. 116) argues that a large Amorite indigenous population lived in the coastal plain with their capital at Gezer. Y. Aharoni (1966, 2nd ed., 1979, p. 275) also sees the Israelites of Saul's time as natural allies of the Amorites settled in the region: 'The territory of Gath and mainly Ekron had evidently been expanded considerably at the expense of the neighbouring Shephelah settlements, Israelite and Amorite, who then banded together in opposition to the Philistines.'

19 Y. Aharoni, 1979, p. 175.

20 J. Hayes & M. Miller, 1986, pp. 140-1.

21 Y. Aharoni, 1979, pp. 174-5.

22 R. de Vaux, 1978, p. 801.

23 W. F. Albright, 1943, pp. 29-32.

24 W. F. Albright, 1943, p. 30.

25 W. F. Albright, 1943, pp. 7-8.

26 W. F. Albright, 1943, p. 11.

27 There is no reason to conclude from this passage that Labayu was the ruler of Shechem as has been so often stated. The 'land of Shechem' is simply one part of Labayu's kingdom. Père de Vaux writes: 'Labayu was not, however, given the title of king of Shechem and it is very doubtful whether he ever was. It would seem too that he did not live at Shechem; his authority was probably exercised from elsewhere by means of an agreement with the inhabitants. The latter took care of the internal administration of the city and recognised Labayu's authority as a kind of protectorate, giving him responsibility for defending and extending their territory (R. de Vaux, 1978, p. 801).

28 See P. G. van der Veen, 1989.

29 J. Baldwin, 1988, p. 104.

30 The Hebrew word *netsib* is often mistranslated. It means 'pillar' but you will see it translated as 'governor', 'garrison' etc. However, it appears to be an inanimate object. For instance, the term *netsib* is used for the 'pillar of salt' in the story of Lot's wife. I have not come across an instance where a *netsib* does anything – i.e. has human traits like moving or speaking. In all cases things are done to *netsib* – such as setting them up or overthrowing them. This includes King David setting up *netsib* in the lands which he conquered. This does not mean that he established governors in those regions, giving the impression of a formalised empire of the Israelites, but rather that he set up standing stones – an act which implies a more fluid hegemony over the conquered lands.

31 J. M. Miller, 1975, pp. 145-66.

32 Just as, for example, the biblical Bethel is located at the Canaanite town of Luz – the site of Bethel itself being the sanctuary located at Luz. See M. Noth, 1958, p. 148.

33 See *New Jerusalem Bible*, p. 367, note 10 c.

34 G. Mendenhall, 1973, p. 135.

35 The order of manoeuvres appears to have been confused as the retreat to the heights of Gilboa appears in I Samuel 28:4, before the mustering of Saul's forces at the Fountain of Jezreel in I Samuel 29:1. However, given that the battle reaches its climax on Mount Gilboa, scholars are in agreement that Saul must have repositioned his forces on the slopes of the mountain in order to take best advantage of the terrain.

36 Ishbaal ('man of Baal'), as the New Jerusalem Bible has it, is the correct rendition of the name of Saul's son. The Eshbaal (also 'man of Baal') of other versions is probably a copyist's error or amendment as the derogatory name given to this individual by the redactor is Ishbosheth ('man of shame'); see O. Odelain & R. Séguineau, 1981, pp. 122 & 172-3.

37 For the chronology of Ishbaal's reign see J. A. Soggin, 1975, 31-49.

38 I have chosen here to use the English translation of EA 366 made by Bernard Newgrosh from Moran's original French publication of the Amarna Letters. This is because Moran's later English edition of EA 366 is grammatically unacceptable.

Chapter Ten

1 J. A. Soggin, 1975, p. 35; P. K. McCarter, 1984, p. 89.

2 In B. Newgrosh *et al.*, 1994, pp. 51-2.

3 Two further examples are: (a) Atahmaya is the Akkadian vocalisation of the Egyptian name Ptahmose (W. L. Moran, 1992, p. 384), one of the commissioners of Pharaoh in the Amarna period. This name occurs in EA 265 but also in EA 303 where it is written Tahmashi. In the case of EA 265 we have another example of the (arbitrary) addition of the prosthetic aleph giving A-Tah-maya; and (b) Arshappa [EA 31] is, in the view of Frauke Gröndahl, the name of the Canaanite god Rashap followed by the genitive 'belonging to', giving us 'belonging to Rashap'. Here again we find the aleph prefix to produce the name A-Rashap-pa.

4 The home town of Ayab is given in the Letters as Ashtaroth in Bashan. It would not be exceptional for David to have a foreigner at the head of his armed forces. There are several non-Israelite warriors mentioned in II Samuel, including Uriah the Hittite [II Samuel 11]. It is interesting to note that in I Chronicles 2:54 Joab's home town is given as Ataroth!

5 Both Kammenhuber (personal communication to P. van der Veen) and Helck (1962, p. 371) have also suggested that Achish is a hypocoristicon, offering Akiteshub ('Teshub has given') as an example of this name formula.

6 M. Mayrhofer, 1966, p. 30.

7 Personal communication to P. van der Veen, January 1993.

8 As identified by Aharoni (1966, p. 285) and Ross (1967, p. 68, citing his paper in *IEJ* 16, 1966, p. 15).

9 G. E. Wright, 1966, p. 84.

10 Z. S. Harris, 1978, pp. 35 & 40.

11 W. Gesenius, 1921, pp. 669-75.

12 We have chosen to accept the original reading of Bi-en-e-ni-ma as given by Knudtzon (1915, p. 816) rather than Moran's Bi-en-e-li-ma (1987, p. 309). The syllable 'li' is interchangeable with 'ni' in Akkadian.

13 B. Mazar, 1986, p. 130, note 20.

14 K. A. Kitchen, 1990, p. 67.

15 M. Noth, 1928, p. 149.

16 See for example J. J. Stamm, 1960, pp. 175-81.

17 F. Gröndahl, 1967, p. 49.

18 P. K. McCarter, 1984, p. 250.

19 J. Lehmann, 1977, p. 225.

20 However, in this case the name has a feminine ending. This may simply imply that Gulatu is a family name, and I suppose that there is just a remote possibility that *the* Goliath was related in some way to this female Gulatu.

Chapter Eleven

1 For a dating to the reign of Nikmaddu II and therefore to early Akhenaten see J. F. A. Sawyer & F. R. Stephenson, 1970, p. 469.

2 Translation: W. L. Moran, 1992, p. 238.

3 The tablet has been dated to the reign of Nikmaddu II and the Amarna period by a number of scholars including Albright (1937, p. 203); de Vaux (1940, p. 255); and Rainey (1965, p. 109f).

4 The translation used here is that of Wayne Mitchell (1990, p. 19) which in turn is based on that of Sawyer and Stephenson with the added observation of C. B. Walker (see note 6).

5 There have been several different translations of this short text. One debate revolves around the meaning of the phrase *btt* with van Soldt tentatively suggesting the *tt* should be translated as 'six' and that the meaning should be 'the sixth hour' (*Nature* 338 (1989), p. 239). This is a very far-fetched working of the text. A far better translation is that of Sawyer and Stephenson who suggest that the phrase comes from the verb *ht*, 'to be ashamed' and that *btt* is the regular passive L-stem i.e. *batata*, 'was put to shame' (1970, p. 474). A new translation from Pardi gives: 'During the six days of (the rituals of) the new moon of (the month of) Hiyyaru, the sun set, her gatekeeper (being) Rashap. The men (?) shall seek out the prefect.' (*Nature* 363 (1993), p. 406) In my view this translation also suffers from incomprehensibility and should be disregarded. Of course the sun set – it sets every day – so why should this be significant enough to record and then to require the consultancy of a prefect? A translation of a text has to make sense if it is to be regarded as successful.

6 See C. B. F. Walker, 1989, p. 204 where he states: 'At first sight the text refers to an event occurring at sunset'.

7 W. G. E. Watson, personal communication, November 1994.

8 P. M. Muller & F. R. Stephenson, 1975, p. 462.

9 Based at Rutgers University, Piscataway, New Jersey.

10 Supplied by Professor P. J. Huber of the Massachusetts Institute of Technology, Cambridge, Massachusetts.

11 W. A. Mitchell, 1990, pp. 18-20.

12 W. P. Manley, 1996, forthcoming.

13 W. A. Mitchell, 1990, pp. 11-12; for a discussion of the source documents see S. Langdon & J. K. Fotheringham, 1928, pp. 1-4.

14 For references see S. Langdon & J. K. Fotheringham, 1928, p. 7, note 3.

15 J. D. Weir, 1982, pp. 23-49.

16 After eight years Venus repeats its cycle two and half days earlier in the solar year and four days earlier in the lunar month. This results in different cycles of periodicity. See J. D. Weir, 1982, p. 23.

17 See S. Feigin, 1955, p. 159.

18 See M. G. Dossin, 1939, p. 111.

19 The restoration of a simple offering formula is straightforward.

20 W. F. Albright, 1964, pp. 39-41.

Chapter Twelve

1 Artapanus gives Moses' age at Exodus as 89 years (Book 9, ch. 27:37).

2 Eusebius Pamphilis, Book 9, ch. 27:1-37. English translations used: (a) E. H. Gifford, 1903 and (b) J. J. Collins, 1985, pp. 889-903 – I would like to thank

Bob Porter for bringing this more recent translation and commentary to my attention.

3   Eusebius himself used a work by Alexander Polyhistor as his principal source, so the text of Artapanus has come down to us indirectly via at least three ancient writers if we include Clement of Alexandria.

4   *Stromata* 1.23.154, 2f.

5   J. J. Collins, 1985, pp. 890-1.

6   J. J. Collins, 1985, p. 891.

7   J. J. Collins, 1985, p. 898, note c, gives the MSS reading as 'Tessan' which he suggests should be understood as 'te San', i.e. Tanis.

8   See R. Cohen, 1983 & E. Anati, 1986.

9   Josephus: *Antiquities of the Jews*, Book I, ch. X.

10 Scholars who have concluded that Khenephrês represents Khaneferre include W. G. Waddell, 1940, p. 73, n. 3; and J. Gutman, 1963, p. 135.

11 J. H. Breasted, 1905, p. 212.

12 M. Alliot, 1935, p. 33.

13 Ptolemy, Book I, ch. iv, 5, 53.

14 See E. Naville, 1887, p. 15.

15 Gamurrini: *I Mysteri e gl'Inni di San Ilario ed una Peregrinazione ai Luoghi Santi nel quarto Secolo*; for a summary E. Naville, 1887, p. 19.

16 Taken from the recent edition of W. Whiston (transl.), 1960, Dissertation IV, p. 662.

17 W. Whiston, 1960, p. 662.

18 E. A. W. Budge, 1913, pl. 23.

19 For the alabaster vases see P. Lacovara, 1991, pp. 118-28.

20 See C. Bonnet, 1986, pp. 27-38.

21 Janine Bourriau, 1991, p. 130 has also argued that the statue may have been brought to Kush during the Ethiopian 25th Dynasty, but if this was the case one might have expected other statues of more illustrious ancestral kings to have been taken. It also seems strange that the statue of Sobekhotep was not therefore found in or near the 25th Dynasty Kushite capital of Napata which was much further south than the abandoned site of Kerma and its associated island of Argo.

22 A. Gardiner, 1961, p. 155.

23 E. Naville, 1887, pp. 21-3.

24 M. Hamza, 1930, p. 20.

25 L. Habachi, 1954, pp. 448-58.

26 L. Habachi, 1954, pp. 458-70.

27 S. Adam, 1959, pp. 207-26.

28 A fuller discussion of earlier work in the Kantir/Khatana region and a preliminary report on the excavations of the Austrian Institute of Egyptology can be found in M. Bietak, 1979.

29 For a detailed map of Avaris/Pi-Ramesse constructed from the drill-core survey of Josef Dorner see M. Bietak, 1991, p. 49.

30 In recent years it has been the practice to abandon the term MB IIC which marks the end of the Middle Bronze Age. Archaeologists have been unable to determine a clearly defined cultural or artefactual change between MB IIB and MB IIC. It is therefore better to refer to the period as one archaeological phase divided into 'early' and 'late' MB IIB with a gradual transition from one to the other.

31 M. Bietak, 1979, pp. 240-1.

32 For a brief summary in English see E. Winkler & H. Wilfing, 1991, p. 140.

33 M. Bietak, personal communication in 1994.

34 G. Robins, 1994, pp. 27-8.
35 L. Ginzberg, 1919, vol. II, pp. 155-7 & 163-4.

Chapter Thirteen

1 Published by W. C. Hayes, 1955.
2 W. C. Hayes, 1955, p. 92.
3 M. Bietak, 1979, p. 295.
4 M. Bietak, 1979, p. 295.
5 M. Bietak, 1979, p. 244.
6 M. Bietak, 1979, p. 241-2.
7 See for example W. G. Waddell (transl.), 1940, pp. 72-3, note 3.
8 I. Velikovsky, 1952.
9 E. H. Gifford (transl.), 1903, p. 466.
10 I. Velikovsky, 1952, pp. 32-4.
11 Bietak notes the discovery of equine molars in stratum E/2 at Tell ed-Daba
    (1979, p. 247); but clearer evidence for the use of horses in the early SIP
    comes from Tell el Kebir where Ali Hassan has found a tomb containing the
    skeleton of a horse which he has dated, from the associated finds, to the 13th
    Dynasty (see *Egyptian Archaeology* 4 (1994), p. 28); Kanawati has also uncovered
    a 12th Dynasty tomb at el Rakakna containing 'an object engraved with the
    head of a horse', see *KMT* 1:3 (1990), p. 5.
12 See N. de G. Davies, 1908, pl. 30.
13 A. Barsanti, 1908, pp. 1-2.
14 W. Helck, 1978, pp. 337-40.
15 To my knowledge Dr. Velikovsky was the first modern scholar to link the
    Arabian traditions of an Amalekite invasion of Egypt and the Levant with
    the Hyksos invasion of Egypt. He also linked that Amalekite incursion with
    the clash between Israelites and Amalekites in Sinai following the Exodus:
    see I. Velikovsky, 1952, pp. 63-66.
16 A. H. Gardiner, 1961, p. 165.
17 I. Velikovsky, 1952, pp. 69-70.
18 F. Fresnel (transl.), 1838, p. 207.
19 M. Bietak, 1979, p. 244.

Chapter Fourteen

1 D. A. Dorsey, 1991, p. 204.
2 J. Garstang, 1930, pp. 129-32; J. Garstang & J. B. E. Garstang, 1940, pp. 129-
   50.
3 K. M. Kenyon, 1957(b), pp. 259-60.
4 K. M. Kenyon, 1957(b), p. 230.
5 K. M. Kenyon, 1957(b), pp. 254-5.
6 It may be taking the connection between the Moabite prostitutes, the Israelite
   spies, and the Jericho bordello a little too far to suggest a link between the
   two plagues. However, it is true to say that, in the confined environment of a
   city such as Jericho, it is likely that any sexually transmitted disease would
   have spread like wildfire amongst the population. On the other hand the
   time interval between the Shittim story and the destruction of Jericho is perhaps
   too short for this type of disease to take hold to the point where people are
   dying, so either we are dealing with some other type of plague, such as cholera,

or the malaise was already rife throughout the entire region prior to the arrival of the Israelites.

7   P. Bienkowski, 1986, pp. 124 & 127.

8   J. J. Bimson, 1978; conveniently summarised in J. J. Bimson, 1988.

9   Personal communication from José Pérez-Accino, Spring 1995.

10 For a summary of recent work on the settlement patterns of Palestine, see I. Finkelstein & N. Na'aman, 1994, especially pp. 9-17.

11 A. Kempinski, 1983, pp. 150-65.

12 A. Kempinski, 1974, p. 147; and 1983, pp. 69-74.

13 W. A. Ward, 1984, pp. 162ff.

14 J. Bartlett, 1982, p. 93.

15 J. Bartlett, 1982, pp. 95-6.

16 A. Kempinski, 1983, pp. 69-74.

17 A. Kempinski, 1988, p. 47.

18 Bryant Wood (1990, p. 49) makes the following statement concerning what Garstang called the 'Middle Building' because its chronological position was between the MBA destruction and the later LBA village: 'Toward the end of the Late Bronze IIA period (second half of the 14th century BCE), a large palace or residency (Garstang's Middle Building), with its associated outbuildings, was built into the erosional layer on the east side of the tell. The Middle Building was occupied only for a generation or so and then abandoned.'

19 Y. Yadin, 1976, p. 482 where he states: 'Although only a small part of this structure was uncovered, it is clear from its size and location that it was either a palace or a citadel.'

20 W. Horowitz & A. Shaffer, 1992, p. 166.

21 Tablets from the Mari archive also give the ruler of Hazor's name as Ibni-Addad (see C. F. Jean, 1951, vol. II, 124). However, this archive dates to a period around 130 years earlier in the New Chronology. In Judges 4:2 the king of Hazor is also named Jabin. Thus we now know of at least three kings of Hazor named Jabin/Ibni. It would be reasonable to suggest therefore that Jabin is a dynastic name borne by the rulers of MBA Hazor just as Hadadezer was for Aram-Zobah or Ramesses was for the 20th Dynasty in Egypt.

22 H. Kjaer, 1930, pp. 87-174 & 1931, pp. 71-88.

23 See I. Finkelstein (ed.), 1993 & D. G. Schley, 1989.

24 Taken from I. Finkelstein, 1986, pp. 22-41.

25 K. M. Kenyon, 1960, p. 177.

Chapter Fifteen

1   See for example D. Redford, 1987, pp. 27-8.

2   This identification was first suggested by Immanuel Velikovsky in the 1950s; see I. Velikovsky, 1952, pp. 57-66.

3   Joseph became vizier of Egypt at the age of 30; there was then a period of 7 years of plenty; Jacob arrived in Egypt in the 2nd year of the 7-year famine according to Genesis 45:6; thus Joseph was 39 years old at the beginning of the Sojourn period $(30 + 7 + 2 = 39)$. Joseph married Asenath, daughter of Potiphera, after his elevation to high office, i.e. after his 30th year. Joseph's second son, Ephraim, was born before the beginning of the famine period [Genesis 41:50-52]; he was probably born when Joseph was about 34 years of age and was therefore himself about five years old at the start of the Sojourn.

4   I have demonstrated elsewhere that the other generations recorded in the

Bible are also compatible with a 215-year Sojourn; see D. M. Rohl, 1992, pp. 48-9.

5   The Royal Canon gives a year total for this king of 46+ years, the section of the papyrus containing the single-units having been damaged. However, the total cannot exceed 49 as only four ten-units are recorded. I have chosen 48 years as this best fits with the data offered in the various versions of Manetho.

6   Jean Vercoutter has proposed the construction of a dam across the Semna Gorge to explain the high Nile readings (see J. Vercoutter, 1966, pp. 126-64); however, this hypothesis fails to explain the high Nile level recorded at Askut north of, and therefore downstream from, the proposed dam.

7   The Year 3 and Year 5 inscriptions were located at the bottom of the cliff, having fallen from their original location. However, the Year 6 level has remained *in situ* at the 18.5-metre mark and I think it is not unreasonable to suggest that Years 3 and 4 will also have recorded unusually high Niles. The general pattern from Years 6 to 16 indicates a range in the height of the flood of between 16 and 18.5 metres and so I propose to include Years 3 and 4 within this range of inundation levels.

8   It is difficult to determine precisely where the line between 'very good flood' levels and 'disastrous flood' levels should be drawn because it depends on so many different factors, not least the location of the inundation record. Clearly an increase in levels at the point of a narrow gorge, such as at Semna, will not be the same increase as in the wide, almost flat Nile valley at Thebes or further downstream in the delta.

9   B. Bell, 1975, pp. 223-69.

10 W. S. Smith, 1965, p. 103.

11 P. Montet, 1968, p. 67.

12 B. Bell, 1975, p. 258.

13 A co-regency between these two pharaohs is rarely contemplated, however there is considerable evidence that a co-regency did occur. Felix Arnold (1992, p. 31) and others have suggested a co-regency of 'ten or more years' – I would argue for nearer twenty years. Recently, Dieter Arnold (1995, pp. 47-8) has produced evidence that Senuseret III celebrated his *Heb Sed* which in all likelihood occurred in his thirtieth year, yet it seems likely that Amenemhat III took over the running of the state soon after Senuseret's nineteenth year on the throne.

14 B. Bell, 1975, p. 260.

15 The name Moeris may derive from Nymaatre (the prenomen of Amenemhat), probably pronounced Nymuaria; however, it is more likely to originate from the Egyptian *Mer-wer* ('great water') which is attested in the name of a town on the shores of the Faiyum Lake.

16 For a discussion of the *khenret* see S. Quirke, 1990, pp. 136ff.

17 E. A. E. Reymond, 1973.

18 E. A. E. Reymond, 1973, pp. 110-11.

19 F. Ll. Griffith, 1909, p. 22, note 14.

20 K. A. Kitchen, 1993, pp. 80-4.

21 As yet, Kitchen has been unable to suggest a Middle Kingdom/SIP alternative to the TIP/Late Period name *Padipre* ('the Gift of Pre') for the biblical Potiphar. Padipre is not attested in the earlier period.

22 K. H. Sethe, 1926.

23 P. Montet, 1928, pp. 19-28.

24 See R. Dussaud, 1927, p. 231 and R. Dussaud, 1937, p. 395.

25 To date there are several published articles and preliminary reports on the archaeological excavations at Avaris/Tell ed-Daba, the most important of

which are: M. Bietak, 1979; M. Bietak, 1991, pp. 27-72; and M. Bietak, 1989, pp. 78-123. The final archaeological report on part of the stratum G settlement has been published in *Tell ed-Daba V* (Vienna, 1992) but the detailed report on the earliest Asiatic settlement (stratum H) has so far not appeared.

26 See M. Bietak, 1991, p. 28 where he comments on the excellent work of Josef Dorner who has completed a survey of the whole area which he based on an analysis of over 850 drill-core samples.

27 The settlement/foundation was known as 'The Estate of Amenemhat, true of voice, of the Mouth of the Two Ways' (*Hat-Amenemhat-maat-heru-Net-Rowarty*). The reference to the 'Mouth of the Two Ways' suggests the division of the Pelusiac branch of the river into two channels which occurs at this spot.

28 M. Bietak, 1991, p. 31.

29 E-M. Winkler & H. Wilfing, 1991.

30 D. Eigner, 1995 (forthcoming). I am grateful to Dietelm Eigner for providing me with an advance copy of his article on the F/1 palace compound.

31 To my knowledge there is evidence for two other non-royals having colossal statues made for them: (a) Djehutihotep, the 12th Dynasty nomarch, whose tomb at el-Bersha depicts the dragging of a colossus of the tomb owner from the quarries, and (b) Amenhotep son of Hapu who was later deified. In neither case is this a similar situation to our statue from Tell ed-Daba. Djehutihotep was one of the powerful independent nobles (who were soon to be eradicated by Senuseret III or Amenemhat III) and, as such, was a petty ruler in a position to order such a statue. Amenhotep, on the other hand, was commemorated long after his death and not during his own lifetime.

Appendix A

1 J. J. Bimson, 1986, updated in *JACF* 6 (1993), pp. 19-32.

2 D. M. Rohl, 1990, pp. 46-9; and 1992, pp. 134-6.

3 See W. F. Albright, 1947, p. 160; and R. Dussaud, 1925, pp. 101-17.

4 W. F. Albright, 1947, p. 153.

5 It is of course possible that Yehimilk was the father of both Abibaal and Elibaal, thus reversing the order to produce Yehimilk – Abibaal – Elibaal.

6 S. Moscati, 1973, p. 50.

7 The identification of Shipitbaal 'I' and Shipitbaal 'II' as one ruler was first proposed in A. Dirkzwager, 1981, p. 23.

8 D. D. Luckenbill, 1926, p. 276.

9 D. D. Luckenbill (transl.) in J. B. Pritchard, 1969, p. 282.

10 This was also suggested by Mazar, 1986, pp. 244-5.

11 R. Wallenfels, 1983, pp. 79-118.

12 As recorded on Nile Level Text no. 33, see K. A. Kitchen, TIPE, p. 154.

13 R. Caminos, 1958.

14 D. Rohl & P. James, 1983, p. 15-16.

15 D. Aston, 1989, pp. 143-4.

16 NLTs 6 & 7 dated to Usermaatre Osorkon (III); see K. A. Kitchen, 1973, pp. 88-94.

17 Heian Museum Archaeological Mission: *Preliminary Report, Second Season of the Excavations at the Site of Akoris, Egypt, 1982* (Kyoto, 1983).

18 D. A. Aston, 1989, pp. 139-53.

19 Cat. Caire 1040.

20 Translation taken from K. A. Kitchen, 1973, p. 317.

21 D. M. Rohl, 1985, p. 25, acknowledging that this prospect was brought to my attention by Peter van der Veen.

22 D. M. Rohl, 1990, pp. 66-7; this idea has subsequently been taken up by Aidan Dodson who adds a number of further arguments in support of the hypothesis, see A. Dodson, 1993, pp. 53-8.

23 P. Montet, 1960, pl. XLIX; one in Tanis magazine, no. 270, the other with the inscription in Zagazig Museum, SDR II.1235.

24 A. Dodson, 1992, pp. 78-97.

25 A. Dodson, personal communication, May 1987.

26 Hermitage 5630; see J. Yoyotte, 1961, pp. 142-3.

Appendix B

1 For the arguments that the mortuary cult of Merenptah did not last very long after his reign see W. Helck, 1961, p. 119. This makes it unlikely that Ipuy served in office long after the death of Merenptah.

2 M. Bierbrier agrees that the cartouches associated with the HPMs indicate the ruler in whose reign the official was inducted rather than his death or some other event. see M. Bierbrier, 1975, p. 48.

3 We cannot include the generation of Ashakhet himself because he was inducted into office during the very short (4-year) reign of Amenemnisu (as Bierbrier has argued, 1975, p. 48).

Appendix C

1 This appendix is based on a *JACF* paper written by B. Newgrosh in 1992; I am grateful to Dr. Newgrosh for his kind permission to republish the arguments here in an abbreviated form. See also J. Lasken, 1991, and 1992.

2 R. Hedges, 1981, p. 700.

3 J. Callaway & J. Weinstein, 1977, pp. 1-16.

4 J. Mellaart, 1979, pp. 6-18.

5 For the criticisms see J. Weinstein, 1980, pp. 21-4 and B. J. Kemp, 1980, pp. 25-8; for the withdrawal see J. Mellaart, 1980, pp. 225-7.

6 A. Mazar, 1990, p. 28.

7 F. Hole, 1987, p. 562.

8 H. Haas *et al.*, 1987, pp. 585-606.

9 B. Kemp, 1984, p. 185; I. M. Shaw, 1985, pp. 312-13.

10 See P. Warren, 1991.

11 See editorial note and photograph in J. F. Lasken, 1992, p. 75.

12 M. G. L. Baillie, 1991, pp. 26-7.

13 *New Scientist*, 16/06/1990, p. 30.

14 See J. Lasken, 1991 and B. Newgrosh, 1992.

15 J. Lasken, 1991, p. 30.

16 D. K. Yamaguchi, 1986, p. 48.

17 P. Kuniholm, 1993, pp. 179-90.

18 R. M. Porter, 1994, p. 20.

Appendix D

1 Usually given as 1872 BC, but see L. E. Rose, 1994, pp. 246-7.

2 L. E. Rose, 1994, p. 261.

3 See L. Habachi, 1974, pp. 207-14.

Appendix E

1   For example see W. F. Albright, 1956, pp. 23-7; K. A. Kitchen, 1973, p. 143.
2   For translations of the letters see W. L. Moran, 1992, pp. 37-41.
3   See for example A. Poebel, 1942, pp. 86-8.
4   For a translation and discussion see A. K. Grayson, vol. 1, 1972, pp. 137-8.
5   R. Borger, 1961, pp. 21 & 99 (in *EAK* 1).
6   A. Poebel, 1943, pp. 56-7.
7   For a summary of the Hittite/Assyrian correspondence see A. Hagenbuchner, 1989, pp. 158-68.
8   A. Hagenbuchner, 1989, p. 159, note 9.
9   The document – one of the Babylonian Chronicle texts – was published by Millard in 1964, pp. 14-35, and reads as follows: 'Shirikti-Shukamuna, brother of Nebuchadnezzar, ruled as king of Babylon for three months.'
10   D. D. Luckenbill, 1926, p. 21.
11   H. Coutts (ed.), 1988, p. 70.

Acknowledgements

1   First published in 1728 by Tonson, Osborn and Longman (London) but recently reprinted by Histories and Mysteries of Man Ltd (London, 1988).
2   J. Lieblein: *Recherches sur la chronologie égyptienne d'après les listes généalogiques* (Christiana, 1873); and *Recherches sur l'Histoire et la civilization de l'ancienne Égypte* (Leipzig, 1914).
3   The debate was sparked off by Petrie's article entitled 'The Egyptian Bases of Greek History' published in *JHS* XI (October 1890), pp. 271-7. This was followed by a review of Petrie's book *Illahun, Kahun and Gurob* (1889-90) by Torr (*Classical Review* VI (March 1892), pp. 127-31) which attacked Petrie's findings and the conclusions which he had claimed in the earlier article. The long debate between the two scholars then began in the pages of *The Academy* on May 14 1892 (pp. 476-7) and continued until November 12, 1992 (p. 442). The full text of that debate is reprinted in the second edition of Torr's *Memphis and Mycenae*, see note 5 below.
4   This second debate began in *Classical Review* X (1896), pp. 447-53, with a review of Torr's *Memphis and Mycenae*. It continued in *Classical Review* XI (1897), with a series of rebuttals published on pp. 74-82 (Torr), pp. 128-30 (Myres), and pp. 224-6 (Torr).
5   C. Torr: *Memphis and Mycenae* (ISIS Occasional Publication, vol. 1, Redhill, 1988).
6   I. Velikovsky: *Worlds in Collision,* 1950 (UK edition 1976); *Ages in Chaos,* 1952 (UK edition 1976).
7   Principally *Peoples of the Sea* (London, 1977) and *Ramses II and His Time* (London, 1978).
8   See *Ages in Chaos?* Proceedings of the Glasgow Conference in *SIS Review* VI:1-3 (Society for Interdisciplinary Studies, 1982).
9   K. A. Kitchen's reviews of *Centuries of Darkness* in the *Times Literary Supplement* no. 4598 (17th May, 1991), p. 21 & *TLS* no. 4603 (21st June, 1991), p. 13.
10   D. Rohl & P. James, 1983, pp. 12-21.

INDEX

A

Also available from Arrow Books

DAVID ROHL

LEGEND
THE GENESIS OF CIVILISATION

For centuries scholars and explorers have searched for Eden and its fabled Garden. Now, at last, the true location of the cradle of civilisation can be revealed. David Rohl peels back the layers of myth to expose the extraordinary truth which lies at the heart of the book of Genesis.

Legend overflows with amazing discoveries and brilliant archaeological detective work. Years of research have brought David Rohl within reach of solutions to many of the great mysteries surrounding our origins.

'The likeliest location of the Garden of Eden is by no means the only jaw-dropper in Rohl's new book... but then that's true to form... Rohl's real achievement is the way in which he's pieced the evidence together into a coherent, properly magnificent story, the first of all stories, for the first time.'

Sunday Times

'When it comes to exploring, David Rohl makes Indiana Jones look like an under-achiever... Rohl is Britain's highest profile Egyptologist.'

Express

The Official David Rohl Website is
www.Nunki.net

Ancient World Tours

Join David Rohl and other top experts on a journey back to ancient times

IN THE LAND OF THE PHARAOHS

Take a luxury Nile cruise through three thousand years of history. Discover the fabulous wonders of most ancient Thebes including an exploration of the Valley of the Kings. Experience the desolate majesty of Egypt's eastern mountains on an incredible desert safari in search of pharaonic origins. Follow in the footsteps of Alexander as he journeyed to the Oracle of Amun at Siwa Oasis in the Sahara. Investigate the mighty pyramids and tombs of Old and Middle Kingdom Egypt.

IN THE LAND OF LEGEND

Travel through the Zagros Mountains to the Garden of Eden and the Mountain of God. Visit the primeval Lands of Nod, Cush and Havilah. Stand before the awe-inspiring Tomb of Cyrus the Great. Walk in the footsteps of Alexander at mighty Persepolis. Climb to the summit of the red ziggurat at Choga Zambil.

IN THE LAND OF MILK AND HONEY

An opportunity to visit many of the sites in the Holy Land and Transjordan discussed in *A Test of Time*. Explore Bronze Age Jerusalem and the tomb of Pharaoh's Daughter. Wander through the ruins of Armageddon. Search for Joshua's Jericho and the palace of King Jabin at mighty Hazor. Pick a poppy on wind-swept Mount Gilboa 'where the hero's shield lies dishonoured'.

For further information and a colour brochure write to: Michael Ackroyd at AWT, PO Box 12950, London W6 8GY, UK. *AWT is an agent of Kuoni Travel Ltd.*

www.ancient.co.uk/awt